Second Edition
ESSENTIAL CASE LAW FOR POLICING AMERICA

by
JAMES R. PEVA
Associate Professor of Public and Environmental Affairs
Indiana University

RICHARD P. GOOD, Jr.
Executive Director
Indiana Prosecuting Attorneys Council

and

CHARLES N. BRAUN II
Staff Attorney
Indiana Law Enforcement Academy

Publishers
Graphics LTD
217 S. Belmont Ave., Suite F
Indianapolis, IN 46222

Copyright © 1989, 1992
by
Graphics LTD.
Indianapolis, Indiana

ISBN
1-878 760-06-8

Library of Congress Catalog Card Number: 92-72183

Printed in the
United States of America

Second Edition
1992

Reprinted
1994, 1995, 1998

DEDICATION
To the Peace Keepers

THE AUTHORS

JAMES R. PEVA, Associate Professor of Public and Environmental Affairs, Indiana University, Indianapolis, Indiana.

Born in 1928, Graduate of Indiana University, B.S., 1950; J.D., 1961. Distinguished service, Indiana State Police, 1950-1971 (retired with rank of Colonel). Memberships, past and present, include: Indiana State Bar; Indiana Criminal Law Study Commission; Indiana Law Enforcement Training Board, and Advisory Council; Board of Trustees, Indiana Criminal Justice Institute; Governor's Corrections Advisory Committee. Lecturer, Indiana Law Enforcement Academy.

RICHARD P. GOOD, Executive Director, Indiana Prosecuting Attorneys Council, Indianapolis, Indiana.

Born in 1932. Graduate of Indiana University, B.S., 1954, J.D., 1959. General practice of law, 1959-1975. Chief Deputy Prosecuting Attorney, 1964-1967, and Assistant City Attorney, 1969-1971, Kokomo, Indiana. Memberships, past and present, include: Indiana State Bar; House of Representatives, Indiana General Assembly; National District Attorneys Association; National Association of Prosecutor Coordinators; Criminal Law Study Commission; Indiana Criminal Justice Coordinating Council; Correctional Study Commission; Indiana Juvenile Justice Delinquency Advisory Board; Board of Trustees, Indiana Criminal Justice Institute; Governor's Corrections Advisory Committee. Adjunct Associate Professor of Public and Environmental Affairs, Indiana University; Lecturer, Indiana Law Enforcement Academy.

CHARLES N. BRAUN II, Staff Attorney, Indiana Law Enforcement Training Board and Academy, Plainfield, Indiana.

Born in 1952. Graduate of Indiana University, B.A., 1974, J.D., 1977. Has devoted legal career to providing counsel to agencies and employees of the criminal justice system. Formerly employed by U. S. Department of Justice, American Bar Association, and Attorney General of Indiana. Teacher, and frequent lecturer on police and correctional issues. Has extensive litigation experience; admitted to practice before Supreme Court of the United States; Lecturer, Indiana Law Enforcement Academy.

PREFACE

In simpler times long past, the American policeman patrolled his beat and kept the peace. When he found it necessary to arrest someone, usually for an act that he instinctively recognized as a crime, he took the alleged wrongdoer before a judge. It was the *judge* who advised the accused of his constitutional rights.

Then, during a decade of urban riots and assassinations, the Supreme Court of the United States began to change the nature of state and local law enforcement. A series of controversial decisions made names such as *Mapp*, *Escobedo*, and *Miranda* a part of police vocabulary. All law enforcement officers, whether local, county, or state, had to comply more strictly than ever before with the requirements of the federal Bill of Rights.

To assure admissability of evidence and to reduce the risk of civil liability of law enforcement officers, administrators must continue to upgrade police training programs; training must keep pace with the criminal law "revolution" which is still taking place. In a sense, that revolution is the subject of this book.

The purpose of this book is to provide basic instructional material for those charged with the training of the police recruit — police academy law instructors, prosecutors, police legal advisors, and others — to *close the communication gap* that tends to exist between the recruit (often only a high school graduate) and the professional lawyers in the system in which both play an important part.

In addressing this communication gap we hope to plant the seeds of the professional attitude which is required to meet the challenge of preserving the public safety while at the same time protecting individual rights.

The plan which we have adopted to set forth criminal procedure for police recruits is a modification of the law school case-study method. In Indiana this method of teaching law in a police academy setting has worked remarkably well since 1975.

PREFACE TO THE SECOND EDITION

The purpose of not using consecutive page numbers in the first edition was to enable yearly supplementation to the text thereby preventing it from ever becoming obsolete. The supplemental pages of 1990 and 1991 and the obsolete pages removed from the original 1989 edition are reflected in this second edition, which is current through the Supreme Court's 1990-91 term. Both the original and the second edition may be supplemented in the future by the same supplemental pages which are available from the publisher in the Fall of each year.

James R. Peva

Richard P. Good, Jr.

Charles N. Braun II

DISCLAIMER

The information and procedures contained herein are subject to constant change and should serve only as a foundation for further study of the current law and procedures in force in a particular jurisdiction. Forms contained herein are intended to be samples only and may require modification by a qualified legal advisor for specific cases. The authors hereby disclaim any and all responsibility or liability which may be asserted or claimed by any person arising from or claimed to have arisen from reliance upon the procedures, information, or forms contained herein.

To avoid conflicts of interest, or the appearance of any conflicts of interest, the authors receive no royalty or payment of any kind resulting from the sale or purchase of this publication for use within the State of Indiana.

TABLE OF CONTENTS

CHAPTER 1

INTRODUCTION AND FUNDAMENTALS

Section
1.1 Purposes and Use of Text
   (A) Introduction
   (B) Why Case Law For The Police?
   (C) Suggested Uses of Text
   (D) Supplementation
   (E) Don't Forget <u>State</u> Constitutional Law!
1.2 Sources and Forms of Laws
   (A) Using the Law Library
   (B) Reading and Briefing Legal Opinions
1.3 Constitutional Background
   (A) Origins of the Constitution
   (B) Independence Based on English Law
   (C) From One Extreme to the Other
   (D) Federalism — An Untried Idea
   (E) The Constitution and Criminal Justice
   (F) Federal Powers Restricted - The Bill of Rights
   (G) Slavery's Aftermath and Criminal Justice - The Fourteenth Amendment and Due Process of Law
1.4 Crimes and Civil Wrongs Distinguished

CHAPTER 2

REMEDIES FOR POLICE MISCONDUCT

Section
2.1 Introduction
2.2 Civil actions for money damages
   (A) Civil actions under federal law
   (B) Civil actions under state law
2.3 Criminal prosecution
2.4 Other judicial remedies
2.5 Administrative disciplinary actions
2.6 Exclusion of evidence; the Fourth Amendment exclusionary rule
   (A) At first, a federal rule of evidence
   (B) Later, a rule of constitutional dimension
   (C) Criticims and the good faith exception
2.7 Meeting the challenge

TABLE OF CONTENTS

CHAPTER 3

THE POLICE AND FIRST AMENDMENT RIGHTS

Section:
3.1 Introduction
3.2 Freedom of religion
3.3 Freedom of speech
3.4 Freedom of the press
3.5 Freedom of assembly and petition
3.6 Summary

CHAPTER 4

ARREST, SEARCH, AND SEIZURE

Section
4.1 Introduction
4.2 When an arrest takes place
4.3 The felony-midemeanor distinction
4.4 Probable cause
4.5 Issuance and execution of arrest and search warrants
4.6 Arrest, with or without a warrant
4.7 Use of force
4.8 Forced entry — knock and announce requirement
4.9 Territorial jurisdiction and fresh pursuit
4.10 Resistance to arrest
4.11 Infractions and ordinance violations
4.12 Citizen's arrest
4.13 Searches — Constitutional restrictions
4.14 Searches with warrant
    (A) Probable cause for warrant
        (1) Independent source
        (2) Reasonableness of request for warrant; civil liability of officer
    (B) Discovery of items not specified in warrant
    (C) Affidavit for warrant
    (D) Challenge to warrant affidavit
4.15 Warrantless searches
    (A) Search incident to arrest
        (1) Scope of search incident to arrest
        (2) Discovery of items not connected with arrest
        (3) Justification of search
        (4) Application of Robinson-Gustafson Rules
    (B) Automobile searches
        (1) Distinction between home and vehicle
        (2) Remote searches
        (3) Closed containers — the Chadwick rule
    (C) Exigent circumstances
        (1) Close pursuit and privacy
        (2) Evidence of intoxication — the fleeting opportunity to search
        (3) The murder scene exception

TABLE OF CONTENTS

Chapter 4 (continued)

- (D) Plain view and inventory
- (E) Stop and frisk and detentions on less than probable cause
  - (1) Stop and frisk
  - (2) Terry distinguished from search incident to arrest
  - (3) Terry rationale extended
  - (4) Proper use of stop and frisk authority
  - (5) Other detentions on less than probable cause
  - (6) The traffic roadblock
- (F) Consent searches
  - (1) Voluntariness requirement
  - (2) Miranda waiver not consent to search
  - (3) Scope of consent to search
- (G) Administrative inspections and searches based on less than traditional probable cause

4.16 Neutral magistrate; inadvertence; standing to object
  - (A) Neutral magistrate
  - (B) "Inadvertent" — totally unexpected, or lacking probable cause?
  - (C) Standing to object to a search
  - (D) Abandoned property and garbage

4.17 Wiretapping and Eavesdropping

4.18 Compelled evidence

4.19 Seizure and forfeiture or crime-related property

CHAPTER 5

CONFESSIONS AND ADMISSIONS; COMPULSORY SELF-INCRIMINATION; INTERROGATION; IMMUNITY

Section

5.1 Introduction
5.2 Voluntariness doctrine
5.3 Fourth amendment confession issues; fruit of the poisonous tree doctrine
5.4 Sixth amendment right to counsel in confessions
  - (A) Pre-charge questioning
  - (B) Post-charge questioning
5.5 Fifth amendment self-incrimination issues
  - (A) Highlights of Miranda
  - (B) Applicability of Miranda
  - (C) Volunteered Statements
  - (D) The Warnings
  - (E) The Waiver of Rights
  - (F) Exception to Miranda Rule — When warnings are not required
  - (G) Impeachment and Miranda
  - (H) Self-incrimination and Immunity

TABLE OF CONTENTS

CHAPTER 6

EYEWITNESS IDENTIFICATION AND LINEUPS

Section
6.1 Introduction
6.2 Highlights of *Wade-Gilbert*
6.3 The *Kirby* limitation on *Wade-Gilbert*
6.4 Suggestiveness
6.5 Use of photographs in identification procedures
6.6 Other developments concerning suspect identification

CHAPTER 7

RIGHTS OF THE CONFINED AND THE CONVICTED: JAIL AND PRISON PROCEDURES

Section
7.1 Introduction
7.2 Legal Duties of Arresting Officers to the Incarcerated Suspect
7.3 Legal Rights of the Confined and the Convicted
7.4 Jail and Prison Procedures

CHAPTER 8

JUVENILE OFFENDERS AND THE POLICE

Section
8.1 Introduction
8.2 The case law
8.3 Police handling of juvenile offenders

APPENDICES

A. The Constitution of the United States — Selected Provisions
B. Glossary
C. Table of Cases
D. Check Lists

INDEX

CHAPTER 1

INTRODUCTION AND FUNDAMENTALS

Section
1.1 Purposes and Use of Text
   (A) Introduction
   (B) Why Case Law For The Police?
   (C) Suggested Uses of Text
   (D) Supplementation
   (E) Don't Forget <u>State</u> Constitutional Law!
1.2 Sources and Forms of Laws
   (A) Using the Law Library
   (B) Reading and Briefing Legal Opinions
1.3 Constitutional Background
   (A) Origins of the Constitution
   (B) Independence Based on English Law
   (C) From One Extreme to the Other
   (D) Federalism — An Untried Idea
   (E) The Constitution and Criminal Justice
   (F) Federal Powers Restricted - The Bill of Rights
   (G) Slavery's Aftermath and Criminal Justice - The Fourteenth Amendment and Due Process of Law
1.4 Crimes and Civil Wrongs Distinguished

§ 1.1 PURPOSES AND USE OF TEXT

(A) Introduction

A fact which must be emphasized to each new class of police recruits—a fact which is easy for them to overlook (or to forget) — is that *the people who wrote the Bill of Rights feared the evil of an arbitrary government much more than they feared crime in the streets. And a uniformed police officer is the one symbol most readily identified with arbitrary government.* Once this lesson is firmly imbedded in the trainee's mind, the emphasis in exclusionary rule cases on "policing the police" makes more sense to him.

Police officers are like most other people. They seek shortcuts and tend to follow the line of least resistance. Most wish that lawyers, judges, and prosecutors would use "policeman's language" and concern themselves primarily with legal retribution against criminal wrongdoers. Many would prefer training academies to be staffed only with fellow officers who have shared their experiences and thus share their viewpoints about life and the criminal justice system.

But law enforcement — and the training required for it — cannot be made that easy in a nation which has celebrated the 200th anniversary of a written constitution dedicated to the rule of law and the preservation of liberty. It is the police officer who must learn the language of the courts, and not vice versa. The officer must understand the terms of the law that he is charged with enforcing.

It is not unusual for a uniformed officer to complete a twenty-year career still mystified by the "games that lawyers play." People tend to mistrust what they do not fully understand. Why is perfectly relevant physical evidence excluded at a suppression hearing? Why isn't the judge satisfied with the explanation that a car was stopped because the officer "had a hunch something was wrong?" Why did the judge rule that no consent to search was given even though the *Miranda* warnings were used? Why does the defendant's lawyer have to be notified before some lineups, but not before others? Why do lawyers and judges use such big words, and what do they mean? The answers to these questions, and many others, should be provided to a police officer at the beginning of his career. This text is designed to provide many of those answers in a manner that the authors hope will help to bridge the communication gap between law practitioners and law enforcement officers.

(B) Why case law for the police?

Our system of law has been developing for nine hundred years; it is carried forward from one generation to the next as case law — opinions of the courts which have been recorded and preserved since long before the United States was founded.

By reading case law the officer-trainee learns the real meaning of basic legal concepts. Terms such as "Probable Cause", "Exigent Circumstances", and "Good Faith" become more than mere vague phrases as the facts and events of case after case are studied. As a result, the policeman feels more at ease in the courtroom and experiences less resentment and frustration with pre-trial and trial procedures. He more fully understands the role of the prosecutor, the defense lawyer and the judge. Mistrust flowing from misunderstanding is less likely to occur, and the officer develops an improved ability to reason by analogy — to relate fact situations from cases he has studied to fact situations in his later work experiences. Finally, a policeman who has learned where to find new court rulings as they are published is more likely to keep himself current with laws governing how he should perform his job.

As police administration has moved slowly yet inexorably away from political patronage and toward merit service and professionalism, it has become increasingly evident that policemen *must* understand constitutional law as interpreted by the courts and as it relates to the function of police in the criminal justice system. They need to be convinced that the system expects them to act decisively, but reasonably, against people who commit criminal offenses; that the courts recognize a definite public interest in placing probative evidence before juries for the purpose of arriving at truthful decisions about guilt or innocence; and, perhaps more important to the trainee, that the courts will support an officer's taking reasonable steps to protect his own safety. In other words, the impression that some policemen have, that the courts tell them only what they *can't* do, is completely erroneous. The case law is replete with decisions upholding good, professional police work.

(C) Suggested uses of text

(1) IN BASIC POLICE TRAINING

Ideally, only a lawyer is qualified to teach law. In teaching policemen it is helpful for the instructor to be a lawyer with a background as a police legal advisor or as a prosecutor, although excellent law instructors obviously exist among the ranks of criminal defense attorneys as well. The one thing the instructor should keep in mind when teaching rookie policemen is that he is talking to laymen. He should not avoid legal terminology — quite the contrary — but he should be patient and remember that he must define unfamiliar words and phrases in language that a layman can understand. (A glossary of legal terms is printed in Appendix B of this text.)

In basic police training it is best to start at ground zero. Although some student officers may have had street experience, what they have learned on the job is often erroneous to some extent.

If the students have access to a law library, the material in this text may be supplemented by outside reading and briefing assignments. The next section in this chapter contains information on use of the law library and on reading and briefing legal opinions. If a library is not accessible, assignments can be made which utilize the edited cases which are included in this text.

(2) FOR IN-SERVICE POLICE TRAINING

Use of this text for in-service police training will vary depending on the basic training the officers have already received. Obviously, if a student has already been exposed to the case-study method of law instruction, the text may be useful to update his prior training.

If, in a particular class, some officers have undergone a case-study law course while others have not, the first period of instruction may be directed to those who are not familiar with case study, utilizing the appropriate parts of this chapter. Other officers may be excused during this orientation, after having been given an assignment for the second training session.

(3) AS A SUPPLEMENTAL TEXT FOR UNDERGRADATE CRIMINAL JUSTICE COURSES AT THE COLLEGE LEVEL

Many features of this book make it an excellent supplement to the principal texts in undergraduate criminal justice courses. It acquaints the student with the briefing of cases and the use of the law library. Its use is especially appropriate in introductory courses, but it also contains information which he will find useful in advanced ones.

(D) Supplementation

This text is easily adapted to loose-leaf format, with perforated and pre-punched pages. Beginning with Chapter 2, every chapter, section, and subsection begins on a right-hand page. This arrangement facilitates the insertion of state-specific and supplemental material under the proper headings without disturbing the continuity of the text. All such added material also begins on a right-hand page.

(E) Don't forget *state* constitutional law!

Most Americans think of their "constitutional rights" as being embodied in the Bill of Rights: the first ten amendments to our federal Constitution. What many of us overlook is that other important constitutional rights, which in some cases antedate those in the Bill of Rights, are set forth in the *state constitutions*. For more than half of our history as a nation these state constitutional rights were a citizen's main protection against arbitrary state government power. The Bill of Rights was drafted to protect the people against misuse of *federal*, not state power. It was only after the adoption of the Fourteenth Amendment that guarantees of the Bill of Rights were held to apply to the states, and thus to protect individual citizens against arbitrary state action. Many landmark cases of the Supreme Court of the United States which have found state laws and procedures unconstitutional were decided rather recently — in the 1950s, 1960s and 1970s. By these decisions, the Court created a uniform, nation-wide standard which represented the *minimum* protection to be provided to a criminal defendant. *But even greater protections might already have existed as a matter of state constitutional law.*

An interesting development is now taking place in American law. As the Supreme Court of the United States begins to modify or to reinterpret previous case holdings, sometimes with the result that a criminal defendant is viewed less favorably under the federal Bill of Rights and the Fourteenth Amendment, the protections afforded by *state* constitutions are being rediscovered. For example, when the decisions of *Illinois v. Gates*, 103 S.Ct. 2317 (1983), and *Massachusetts v. Sheppard*, 104 S.Ct. 3424 (1984), made it more permissible for police to use anonymous tips and easier for prosecutors to introduce evidence obtained in good faith but to escape the reach of the exclusionary rule if they had proceeded under a faulty warrant, many state courts adopted these federal rulings. Other states, however, were not so quick to fall in line with the newer federal interpretations. Some state courts continued to adhere to previous cases that are more favorable to defendants; others found *that their own state constitutions provided greater protections than did the federal Bill of Rights.*

One should always remember that no state can deny a defendant any protection provided by the Fourteenth Amendment, but all the states are free to grant *more* protection than is provided by it. In teaching case law to the police, the instructor should always determine whether the law of his state provides the accused with a greater measure of protection than is provided by federal law.

For an interesting discussion of the four distinct approaches the states use in resolving federal and state constitutional issues, see 20 Indiana Law Review, No. 3, 635 (1987).

§ 1.2 SOURCES AND FORMS OF LAWS

Common and statutory law. In ancient civilizations, the "law" was what the ruler declared it to be, and the source of all governmental power as we know it today (legislative, executive, and judicial), was vested in the king, prince, or tribal chief. Over the centuries a system evolved in England which is referred to as a constitutional monarchy. In that system the people began to limit the powers of the ruler. Old customs, unwritten but accepted standards, court opinions, and very early statutes (written laws) made up a body of law which came to be called the "common law" because it was common to the whole country. In the United States the English common law is the foundation for the legal system in every state except Louisiana. As the English Parliament (legislative branch) became more active, it began to enact statutes which in some cases changed or abolished the common law. In rare cases in England, criminal offenses defined by the common law can still be the basis of a criminal prosecution if the legislative branch has not abolished or changed the common law offenses. In the United States this is true in some states; in others all common law crimes have been abolished and replaced with statutes which clearly define each offense and provide a penalty for it. In these latter states, the common law is still used as an aid in interpreting the statutes.

The principle of stare decisis. Our courts must follow prior decisions as precedents except when there is a very good reason to depart from them. This important rule is called **stare decisis,** which means "let the decision stand". It provides a measure of certainty without which chaos would result in our legal system.

Other sources of criminal law. In addition to English common law and the case law of modern courts, other sources which define punishable offenses include federal and state constitutions, statutes enacted by Congress and the state legislatures, local ordinances, and rules and regulations of federal and state administrative agencies.

(A) Using the law library

Although the sheer number of volumes in a large law library is staggering, they can all be classified very simply. Morris L. Cohen in his *Legal Research in a Nutshell* (2d ed. 1971), divides them into three categories: (1) primary sources; (2) search books or finding-tools; and (3) secondary materials.

(1) PRIMARY SOURCES

Primary sources of the law include legislative enactments (statutes), court decisions (case law), executive decrees and orders, and administrative regulations and rulings. It is beyond the scope of this brief introduction to consider primary sources other than statutes and case law.

Federal Statutes

Statutes enacted by the Congress of the United States may be found in most law libraries in the West Publishing Company's *United States Code Annotated* (U.S.C.A.), a multi-volume set consisting of bound volumes and pocket-part supplements containing laws enacted after those printed in the bound volumes. All of the statutory law of the United States is published under titles, numbered from one to fifty, and the titles are subdivided into sections. The title(s) contained in each volume appears on the spine. The citation, 18 U.S.C.A. § 6002 is simply found by locating the volume containing that title and section, but the researcher must be sure to check the pocket supplement for recent amendments and annotations, if any, to that section.

If the researcher does not know the title and section number of the statute he is looking for, he may locate it by one of several methods. One involves the use of descriptive words or facts which logically relate to the subject of the statute. These words would be looked up in the five-volume *General Index* of U.S.C.A., which will refer the researcher to the correct title and sometimes to the very section he is attempting to find. If only the title is found in the *General Index*, the researcher should then proceed to the *Title Fact Word Index* located in the back of the volume containing that title; this index should lead him to the correct section.

Another method of finding a statute in U.S.C.A. is the *topic method*. The researcher scans the list of fifty titles printed in the front of any volume of U.S.C.A. Upon finding a title that should logically include the statute, he can proceed to the *Table of Contents* in the volume containing that title, which should lead him to the statute.

Many federal statutes acquire a "popular name" as a shorthand way of referring to them. The popular name may be descriptive or it may contain the author's name: e.g., "Federal Firearms Act"; "Hobbs Act". The last volume of the U.S.C.A. *General Index* contains a *Popular Name Table* which will lead the researcher to the correct title and section from the popular name only. For all expanded explanation of the use of U.S.C.A., see West's Law Finder.

State Statutes

The statutory law and constitutions of most states may be found in multi-volume sets which have features similar to those found in the *United States Code Annotated*, including helpful tables, indexes, and annotations. Annotations (notes of the compilers following the statutory law) often consist of very brief summaries of court decisions, as well as statutes, to law review commentaries, to attorney general opinions, and to other sources.

Case Law

Courts interpret criminal laws and apply them to the cases brought before them. Court decisions — and the written opinions which explain them — are as important to the understanding of the law as statutes and regulations. Opinions of appellate level courts — those to which trial court decisions are appealed — are published regularly in books called "reporters" and are cited by case name, volume number, abbreviated reporter title, page number and date.

Opinions of the Supreme Court of the United States are published in three different editions. The official edition is the *United States Reports* (abbreviated "U.S.") Two privately published sets are the *Supreme Court Reporter* (S. Ct.), published by West, and *Lawyer's Edition of the U.S. Supreme Court Reports* (L. Ed. or L. Ed. 2d), published by Lawyers Cooperative Publishing Company. The key number feature of the *Supreme Court Reporter* enables the researcher to cross reference specific issues of law to many other West publications, and to find other cases in point. *Lawyers Edition* includes summaries of lawyers' arguments and other helpful and informative features and is a companion publication to *American Law Reports* (A.L.R.), which publishes exhaustive annotations of important cases. In a complete citation to a decision of the Supreme Court, the official (U.S.) citation is given first, followed by the unofficial reports. In this text only the *Supreme Court Reporter* (S. Ct.) citation is given, except as part of a quoted portion of a decision. The first number is that of the volume containing the decision, and the second number (following the reporter abbreviation) is that of the page on which the decision begins. Example: *Kastigar v. United States*, 406 U.S. 472, 92 S.Ct. 1653, 32 L. Ed. 2d 212 (1972). The date following the citation (1972) indicates the year in which the decision was handed down. The

"2d" following the Lawyers Edition citation indicates that the *Kastigar* case is in the second series of Lawyers Edition, in volume 32, at 212. (Do not confuse this volume with volume 32 of the initial series, which was published many years earlier and contains much older cases.) While research features differ among the three difference editions, the text of the opinion is exactly the same in all three. If a researcher has a citation to a recent case (decided within the previous few months), he will probably find the case in a paperback booklet known as an *advance sheet*. These advance sheets are issued periodically during the term of court and the page numbers are the same as those that will be used in the later bound volume. Therefore, cases may be cited from the advance sheets just the same as from the bound volumes.

Loose-leaf services such as *U.S. Law Week* (U.S.L.W.) and *Criminal Law Reporter*, Crim. L. Rep. (CrL), published by the Bureau of National Affairs, publish Supreme Court decisions within hours after they are announced, thereby providing quicker access to these opinions than the Reporter advance sheets. These services are conveniently arranged and carefully indexed and they contain edited commentary on important decisions, both state and federal.

If the researcher does not have the volume and page number of a case he wishes to read, but has the name of the parties only — for example, *Miranda v. Arizona* — he may find the complete citation to the case in the *Table of Cases* in the *Supreme Court Digest*. This same feature may be found in other West digests.

Cases decided in the United States Court of Appeals are published in the *Federal Reporter* (F.), now in its second series (F.2d). This is also a West publication utilizing the key number system. Decisions of the United States District Courts are published in the *Federal Supplement* (F. Supp.), also a West key number publication.

West's *National Reporter System* publishes state appellate court cases in advance sheets shortly after they are decided, eventually replacing the advance sheets with bound volumes. Each of the fifty states is covered by one of seven regional reporters. For example, decisions of the supreme court and court of appeals of Indiana are reported, along with decisions from Illinois, Ohio, New York and Massachusetts, in the *North Eastern Reporter* (N.E.), now in its second series (N.E.2d).

(2) SEARCH BOOKS OR FINDING TOOLS

There are literally hundreds of ways to research a legal issue in a large law library. One method we have previously referred to is the West key number system. West has broken down the law into 420 broad headings which are then subdivided into subheadings, each with its own key number.

Digests

If the researcher has a case in point on a particular subject, he can find all of the other reported cases which discuss that identical point of law by searching the various West digests under the same key number. The *American Digest System* contains compilations of brief statements of law, similar to the headnotes found in all of the West reporters, both state and federal. Now issued as *Decennial Digests* (every ten years), the system enables the researcher, by use of cross-reference tables, to trace points of law through the use of the key number system, all the way back to the year 1658.

If the researcher is interested only in the court decisions of his own state or the Supreme Court of the United States, he can consult West digest for his state, or the *Supreme Court Digest*.

If the researcher has no case in point, and is starting from "scratch" to find case authority on a particular subject, the West digests are an excellent place to start; finding the right key number and thereby the cases in point is similar to the procedure for finding the statutory law when only the subject is known. The most satisfactory starting point is by the use of descriptive words. Each West digest has its own *Descriptive Word Index*. The words contained in these indexes are chosen because they describe (1) the parties to the action; (2) places and things; (3) basis of action or issue; (4) defenses; or (5) relief sought.

Annotations

Sometimes the case authority sought will involve the interpretation of statutory law. The researcher should not overlook the value of annotations contained in books of statutes, such as *United States Code Annotated*, *Burns Indiana Statutes Annotated*, and *West's Annotated Indiana Code*. This is often a logical starting point in finding case law authority. From a case cited in an annotation the researcher may find, in the West reporter containing that case, the appropriate key number(s); from there a perusal of the digests will reveal the cases in point.

Words and Phrases

If the researcher is concerned about judicial interpretation of the meaning of words, an excellent finding tool is the multi-volume set entitled *Words and Phrases*. In this set, arranged in alphabetical order, are thousands of words and phrases followed by short summaries similar to headnotes which summarize the judicial definitions and identify the cases in which the definitions appear. *National Reporter System* citations are used, which facilitate further research by means of the key number system. Again, the pocket supplements of these volumes should be checked for the most recent interpretations.

Encyclopedias

Another helpful finding tool in a law library is the law encyclopedia. *Corpus Juris Secundum* (C.J.S.), published by West, and *American Jurisprudence* (Am. Jur.), published by Lawyers Cooperative Publishing Company, are voluminous sets, containing thousands of case references from all jurisdictions, state and federal. They are well indexed, and serve as excellent case finding tools. West also publishes state-specific encyclopedias which can be used as finding tools for state and federal cases, state statutory law, Attorney General opinions and law review articles. All the encyclopedias are kept current with pocket supplements.

Citators

An amazing finding tool for advanced research is a set of books entitled *Shepard's Citations*. Through the use of *Shepard's*, the researcher may determine the history and current status of every reported decision in the American legal system, i.e., whether the decision has been explained, distinguished, followed, or overruled in another case, and whether it has been cited in periodicals or discussed in Attorney General opinions, or elsewhere. *Shepard's* performs similar functions for statutory law; it contains other features as well, the discussion of which is beyond the scope of these introductory remarks.

(3) SECONDARY MATERIALS

Secondary materials include periodicals, learned treatises, textbooks, commentaries, restatements of the law, and countless other publications which discuss and explain the law. Some of these secondary materials have their own finding tools, such as the *Index to Legal Periodicals*, which indexes, by author, subject, book reviews and cases, some 300 periodicals, including law reviews of all accredited law schools.

(4) CONCLUSION

This brief summary of legal bibliography will, it is hoped, encourage the beginning officer or criminal justice student to make full use of whatever resources are available to enrich his study of the law. Three excellent and inexpensive publications are recommended to students who are interested in more fully developing their legal research skills: (1) *Legal Research in a Nutshell* by Morris L. Cohen (West Publishing Company, 1971); paperback; (2) *West's Law Finder*, (West Publishing Company, St. Paul, Minn., 1967), paperback; and (3) *Legal Research, Writing and Analysis: Some Starting Points* by William P. Statsky, (2d edition, West Publishing Company, 1982), paperback. Computer-aided research is also available in some large law libraries.

(B) Reading and briefing legal opinions

The briefing of court opinions is a skill that can be acquired only by practice. Legal opinions are often confusing and complex, even to the lawyer who uses them as the tools of his trade. When an opinion is properly briefed, its various parts are put in logical order and a rule is extracted which is, more or less, what the case stands for and for which it may be cited as authority.

More often than not, a case stands for and may be cited for several rules of law. In studying a case which has been cited or briefed in this text, you should look for the particular rule which pertains to the topic under discussion at that point in the text; the case may contain other rules which are not relevant to this topic and which need not concern you for the moment.

As explained in subdivision 1.2(A), the citation of a case shows the year of the decision and the volume and page numbers of the reporter in which the case can be found. Thus, if you have access to a law library, you can read the full text of the case that is briefed, excerpted or cited in this text or another casebook; moreover, in the reporter the case is annotated with numbered headnotes to assist you in finding the particular rule under discussion.

You should not let the headnotes become a "crutch" to your study of law. In order to understand fully the implications of a court opinion and to grasp the full picture of the situation out of which a legal principle emerges, you must read the opinion in its entirety. Further, in order to brief a court opinion properly, you should read it at least twice: the first time to get an overall picture of the case, and the second time to break it down according to the briefing formula.

One standard method of briefing a court opinion is to rearrange the information contained therein into the following components: FACTS; ISSUE; DECISION; REASONS; RULE.

FACTS: This part contains, in summary form, all pertinent matters that occurred before the case came to the court which wrote the opinion you are briefing. Unfortunately, the facts do not always appear at the beginning of the case. They may be buried in the middle of the court's opinion, or may even be found in a concurring or dissenting opinion. One purpose for reading the opinion twice is to locate all of the information that belongs with each respective briefing component before starting to draft the brief. You may want to make light penciled notations in the margin of your casebook on the page or pages where the facts appear. Also included under FACTS, if the opinion reveals it, is the nature of the action involved; e.g., direct appeal of a criminal conviction; habeas corpus action by one held in custody; appeal from an adverse ruling on a motion to suppress evidence; appeal by the state; petition for certiorari, etc. To determine what should be included under the heading of FACTS in your brief, ask yourself the question, "What has happened prior to the time that the case got to this court?"; then proceed briefly to summarize the answer in chronological order, if possible.

ISSUE: The issue can usually be framed as a question. Just as a case may stand for several rules, it may deal with several issues; you should be concerned mainly with those issues in the case which relate to the primary subject matter of the chapter or section of this text or other casebook in which the case is located. The issue is the matter in controversy that the court is being asked to decide. It goes to the very heart of the dispute. It may concern a trial court ruling on admissibility of evidence; the constitutionality of a statute; the trial court's instruction to the jury; an alleged prejudicial comment by the prosecutor; or any of the hundreds of other issues which are alleged to have been erroneously handled by a lower court.

DECISION: This is the shortest part of the brief. It is a statement of how the reviewing court ruled on the issue or issues presented to it. If it agrees with the holding of the lower court from which the case was appealed (this may be the trial court or an intermediate appellate court, and either the defendant or the state may appeal), it will *affirm* the lower court holding. If the reviewing court disagrees with the lower court's holding, it will probably *reverse*, or *reverse and remand* (send back) the case to the lower court. The reviewing court may also *remand for further proceedings*, which means the lower court is required to do something further, not inconsistent with the appellate opinion. In your brief, you may simply note: "Reversed," or "Reversed and remanded," etc.

REASONS: This is usually the most extensive part of the brief. Under this heading you should summarize the justification given by the court for its decision. It may include citations to previous cases which the court views as binding precedent, or, in an issue of first impression before the court, may be decided on the basis of fundamental fairness or social consequences which the court believes necessary to achieve substantial justice. Most beginners make the mistake of copying, verbatim, large passages from the opinion of the court. This should be avoided because briefing a legal opinion is nothing more than a study technique. After you have read the opinion once for the purpose of separating it into its components, re-read it; then try to write the brief as nearly as possible in your own words. You may want to use the exact terminology of the court in certain parts of your brief, but this practice should be the exception, and not the rule. Trying to summarize the material in your own words is an important part of the learning process.

RULE: Arriving at a RULE of law is a process of distillation. Ask yourself, "If I had to state what this case stand for *in one sentence*, what would I say?" Everything except the primary principle must be discarded, leaving only a single statement which adequately but very briefly describes the majority holding, or that portion of it with which you are concerned. Sometimes you will not be able to state the rule adequately in one sentence, but try to do so. You may find that the author, after a discussion of the issues, will state the court's holding in words which you can easily adapt in stating the rule of the case. But more often than not you will have to summarize the rule of the case in your own words from the court's reasoning.

If you routinely follow these suggestions in reading and briefing legal opinions, you should develop the ability to reason by analogy: that is, to apply familiar principles or rules to unfamiliar fact situations. When you have acquired this skill, the study of law can be fascinating and enjoyable. But if you try to avoid the briefing process by looking for a "shortcut," you are likely to find the study of law to be an unendurable bore.

No two people, in briefing the same opinion, will produce exactly the same finished product. You should not be concerned about differences between your briefs and those of other students, as long as you recognize the primary issue in the case. If you can spot the issue, the rule will follow, because it is responsive to the issue. Unfamiliar terminology will be troublesome at first. Consult *Black's Law Dictionary* or an equivalent law dictionary, or the glossary of terms in the Appendix of this text. Again, repetition and diligent study is the key.

At this point it may be helpful to explain the terms used for the parties in a criminal proceeding. When a person is charged with a criminal offense, he is referred to as a "defendant" at the trial stage. If he is convicted and elects to appeal, he then becomes an "appellant," and the state (usually represented by the Attorney General at the appellate stage), becomes the "appellee." If the original defendant wins his appeal at the first appellate level (usually the Court of Appeals), the state may then petition to transfer the case to the State Supreme Court, in which case the state would become the "petitioner," and the original defendant would become the "respondent." The "petitioner-respondent" terminology is also applicable when the moving party petitions for a writ of habeas corpus, or for a writ of certiorari to the Supreme Court of the United States. A state criminal case may be appealed to a federal court if a "federal question" is involved — that is, if the *state* has allegedly taken an action which violates the appellant's rights, privileges, or immunities as a citizen of the *United States*.

You will, in time, develop your own briefing style. The use of abbreviations is encouraged. You may simply wish to refer to the original defendant as "D" in your brief, even though legalistically he is referred to by another title in various stages of the appellate or review process.

To conserve space in a casebook, the author often omits portions of an opinion which he feels are not of sufficient importance to include. The omission of material is usually noted by three asterisks *** or three dots . . . depending on the style followed by the author. If you wish to read the omitted material you may find the case in a law library under the citation given.

It is important to read dissenting and concurring opinions as well as majority opinions because they may contain information that will enable you to better understand the majority opinion. The rule of law, however, will always be based on the majority opinion, if there is one. When fewer than a majority of justices concur in the *reasoning* of an opinion, even though a majority concurs in the *result*, the opinion is known as a "plurality" opinion. It is often difficult to extract a single rule of law from a plurality opinion. Some casebooks include fragmentary materials such as a dissenting opinion without the majority opinion, or a portion of an opinion with no facts given. It is difficult to apply the briefing formula to such materials without looking up and briefing the case in a law library. If a law library is not available, do the best you can with the material that you have.

In any study of the criminal law as it has been interpreted and defined by the Supreme Court of the United States, it is interesting, and often instructive, to make note of the Justices who wrote the majority and dissenting opinions in a particular case and to bear in mind the political climate at the time of the decision.

§ 1.3 CONSTITUTIONAL BACKGROUND

The study of criminal law and procedure in the United States is, of necessity, a study of constitutional law. The Constitution of the United States is the fundamental organic law of our country; it is the foundation of our legal system. All laws of lesser standing, including the constitutions of the several states, the acts of Congress and of the state legislatures and the ordinances of counties, cities and towns, must be in harmony with the Constitution of the United States. It is a remarkable document, relatively short and for the most part framed in broad, general terminology. It contains the wisdom of centuries of human experience as refined and interpreted by notable English scholars such as John Locke and Sir William Blackstone. Within their own lifetimes the drafters of the Constitution experienced governmental extremes from tyranny on the one hand to anarchy on the other; in the Constitution they struck a compromise between these extremes.

(A) Origins of the Constitution

A combination of circumstances occurring within a relatively short span of time (1763 to 1789) had a profound effect on the nature of the Constitution of the United States.

In 1763 the Treaty of Paris ended the French and Indian War, in which the combined efforts of the English and the colonists against the French had secured English domination of America's midwestern region. France lost to England all lands east of the Mississippi River as well as Canada; Spain gave Florida to England in exchange for Cuba. The war had been an expensive undertaking for England, and because her economy was in no condition to absorb such costs it seemed only just that the colonists should share them. For this purpose various taxes were imposed on the colonists which they considered to be unjust and unreasonable.

This antagonism toward the English economic and political measures was in part the result of a new sense of security in the colonies, stimulated by the end of the French threat; the colonists were now feeling more independent of the mother country.

Between 1765 and 1769 there was published in England Blackstone's *Commentaries on the Laws of England*. By 1772 the *Commentaries* had been published in the colonies. Not only did this great work provide the embryonic legal system in the colonies with needed guidelines and precedents, but in the view of some historians its opening chapters became a "revolutionist's handbook." As had his predecessor, John Locke, Blackstone philosophized that somewhere there existed a state of perfect liberty, but that when men came together to form societies they had to surrender some individual liberty for the good of the whole. But even then certain absolute rights were retained, which he described as the rights of *personal security, personal liberty* and *private property*. In his view governments existed only to protect these basic rights. Locke had earlier based his "social contract" theory of government on the concept that governments existed only by the consent of the governed, and that if a government broke its trust with the people by interfering with their liberty, the people had the right to change the form of government. For fuller discussions of Blackstone's and Locke's influence see C. Gordon Post, *An Introduction to the Law* 64-68 (1963) and Angela Roddey Holder, *The Meaning of the Constitution* 1-3 (1972).

The quartering of English soldiers in the homes of the colonists against their will, the use of general warrants and writs of assistance to enforce unpopular regulations, the unreasonable and burdensome taxation and many other practices of the crown became intolerable to the colonists. Delegates from twelve of the colonies met in September, 1774 to petition the king for the right to life, liberty, property, trial by jury and peaceable assembly. This petition, drawn up by the first meeting of the Continental Congress, was ignored by King George III. In April, 1775 fighting broke out at Lextington and Concord.

(B) Independence based on English law

In June, 1776, a resolution was introduced in the Continental Congress which described in detail the most unpopular practices of the representatives of the crown. This resolution was adopted one month later as the Declaration of Independence. Its opening statements show the influence of the Magna Charta (1215), the English Petition of Right (1628) and Bill of Rights (1689), and the philosophy of Locke and Blackstone:

> We hold these truths to be self-evident, that all men are created equal, that they are endowed by their Creator with certain unalienable Rights, that among these are Life, Liberty and the pursuit of Happiness. That to secure these rights, Governments are instituted among Men, deriving their just powers from the consent of the governed, that whenever any Form of Government becomes destructive of these ends, it is the Right of the People to alter or to abolish it, and to institute new Government, laying its foundation on such principles and organizing its powers in such form, as to them shall seem most likely to effect their Safety and Happiness.

The uniqueness of the American Revolution is that, rather than being a military coup or seizure of governmental authority by sheer force of arms, it was based on historic and well-understood principles of the common law of the mother country from which the separation was made.

With the assistance of its new ally, France, American forces ended the armed conflict with the English when General Cornwallis surrendered his army at Yorktown, Virginia on October 19, 1781; in 1783 a peace treaty ended the Revolutionary War.

(C) From one extreme to the other

The United States of America first existed as a confederation of states under the Articles of Confederation, proposed in the Continental Congress in 1777 and ratified in 1781. Creating a perpetual Union, the Articles contained elements which were later incorporated into the Constitution, but they did not set forth a complete system of government. For example, there was no permanent executive and no national judiciary. Congress was the supreme governmental authority and a "Committee of the States" acted when Congress was in recess. The officer who presided over the Committee of the States was called the "President." This loose-knit confederation of sovereign states, which seems to have been an attempt to govern by the committee system, lacked essential central governmental powers such as the power to tax and the power to regulate interstate commerce.

That the drafters of the Articles designed a weak central government is understandable; the experience of living under a monarch was still fresh in their minds. It was soon apparent, however, that too little central control was no more workable than too much of it. Political and economic chaos — a condition approaching anarchy — resulted.

From May 25 to September 17, 1787 a constitutional convention at Philadelphia, chaired by General George Washington, worked at the task of amending the Articles of Confederation. What emerged from that convention was a proposal for an entirely new and untried form of government: a federal republic, under the yet-to-be ratified Constitution of the United States.

(D) Federalism—an untried idea

The Constitution created a government of two levels, federal and state. The states retained their identities as sovereign units of government but gave up some of their powers to the federal government, which was made up of representatives of the states. The federal government was to have only limited, or delegated powers and it consisted of three branches: the legislative, consisting of a House of Representatives and a Senate; the executive, or President; and the judiciary, or Supreme Court. The design was not created for efficiency, but rather to divide governmental authority so that too much power would not exist in any one person or unit; it was a hedge against tyranny.

All powers not expressly given to the federal government, or prohibited to the states by the Constitution, were reserved to the states. In this manner all governmental power that could be legitimately exercised was accounted for; in theory, at least, there was no overlapping of governmental authority.

In addition to creating the three branches of government and outlining the authority of each. The Constitution dealt with relations between states; the responsibility of the federal government to the states; the amendment of the Constitution; and the meeting of obligations contracted under the Articles of Confederation. It also established that it was the "supreme Law of the Land," and provided for the method of its ratification.

(E) The Constitution and criminal justice

Although most of the provisions of the Constitution which deal with criminal justice are in the Bill of Rights and the Fourteenth Amendment, a few very important provisions are in the first four articles.

Article I, Section 8 grants specific powers to Congress. These have been liberally interpreted by the Supreme Court, and far more activity is now subject to federal regulation than ever anticipated by the drafters of the Constitution. Under the "necessary and proper" clause of this section, Congress may create a federal criminal sanction whenever one is needed to exercise any of the powers expressly granted in the section. In this way a substantial body of federal criminal law has emerged, much of which overlaps the jurisdiction of the states.

The taxing power given to Congress by this section is used to regulate, by means of licensing requirements, activities such as the sale of firearms. *Sonzinsky v. United States,* 57 S. Ct. 554 (1937). The congressional power to regulate interstate commerce, also granted by this section, is the basis for controlling some apparently local commercial activities as well as interstate ones. In *Perez v. United States,* 91 S. Ct. 1357 (1971), a case involving loan-sharking, the Supreme Court held that any activity involving a channel or instrumentality of interstate commerce, or having an effect on it, is a proper subject for federal regulation. Other cases have held that the effect of the activity on interstate commerce need not be an actuality, but only a realistic possiblity, in order for the federal government to have jurisdiction. See *United States v. Staszcuk,* 517 F. 2d 53 (7th Cir. 1975). The Supreme Court has reasoned that since the Constitution gives Congress the full power to regulate interstate commerce, it will not question the manner in which Congress chooses to accomplish this task; as a result of this reasoning by the Court a substantial body of federal criminal law has emerged. It is not at all uncommon, therefore, for state criminal offenses to have a federal counterpart based on the power of Congress to regulate interstate commerce.

Article I, Section 8 also gives Congress the authority to create courts inferior to the Supreme Court, which is expressly created by Article III. These lower courts, because they were created by Congress, have only the jurisdiction which Congress grants to them. Federal courts are therefore referred to as courts of "limited" subject-matter jurisdiction, while state courts are called courts of "general" subject-matter jurisdiction. This is consistent with the Tenth Amendment to the Constitution, which says that powers not delegated to the federal government are reserved to the states or to the people.

Article I, Section 9 contains the only reference to an old English "writ". It provides that *habeas corpus* shall not be suspended unless the public safety requires it in cases of rebellion or invasion. Habeas corpus is the doctrine by which a person may challenge the lawfulness of his confinement (or other governmental restrictions on his liberty); it is such a basic right in a free society that the framers of the Constitution felt it must be specifically named and preserved. Section 9 also prohibits *bills of attainder* (legislative punishment of identifiable classes of persons) and *ex post facto* laws (the retroactive application of punishment).

Article II, Section 3, relating to the duties of the President, requires him to "take care that the Laws be faithfully executed." By this provision, federal law enforcement is made a function of the executive branch of government.

Article III, the judicial article, creates the Supreme Court and outlines its jurisdiction. It establishes the right to trial by jury in criminal cases and defines the crime of treason.

Article IV requires each state to recognize the laws and judicial decrees of every other state and, in general, entitles visitors to a state to be treated the same as residents. It also provides for extradition of fugitive criminals. In *Puerto Rico v. Branstad,* 107 S.Ct. (1987), the Supreme Court of the United States held that federal courts have the power to compel state governors to turn fugitives over to other states demanding their return. This decision overruled *Kentucky v. Dennison,* 65 U.S. (24 How.) 717 (1861), a case that had stood for 126 years. The *Branstad* case accurately reflects the shifts of governmental power - from state to federal levels - that has occurred during that period.

(F) Federal powers restricted—the Bill of Rights

Even before the Constitution replaced the Articles of Confederation upon the inauguration of George Washington as President on April 30, 1789, a movement was afoot to adopt amendments clearly limiting federal powers. There was little fear that the state governments would be oppressive, but the new federal government was a source of concern. It was argued that, without express restraints on the federal government, the individual rights so callously ignored by King George III might again be jeopardized despite the guarantees already provided by the Constitution. Twelve articles of amendment were prepared by the First Congress in September, 1789; ten of these, popularly called the "Bill of Rights," were ratified by the states and became effective in 1791. These amendments were originally intended as restrictions on federal power only, and had no applicability to the states.

It is important for police officers to remember that the greatest fear in the minds of the framers of the Bill of Rights was not crime in the streets, but the fear of oppressive government. A policeman in uniform is the one symbol most likely to be associated with oppressive government in the minds of citizens in a free society. This is one reason why a police officer often feels as if *he* were on trial when he testifies as a witness in a criminal case. A professional police officer must understand this fact and be prepared to meet it with a positive attitude.

THE BILL OF RIGHTS

AMENDMENT 1

Congress shall make no law respecting an establishment of religion, or prohibiting the free exercise thereof; or abridging the freedom of speech, or of the press; or the right of the people peaceably to assemble, and to petition the government for a redress of grievances.

AMENDMENT 2

A well regulated Militia, being necessary to the security of a free State, the right of the people to keep and bear Arms, shall not be infringed.

AMENDMENT 3

No Soldier shall, in time of peace be quartered in any house, without the consent of the Owner, nor in time of war, but in a manner to be prescribed by law.

AMENDMENT 4

The right of the people to be secure in their persons, houses, papers, and effects, against unreasonable searches and seizures, shall not be violated, and no Warrants shall issue, but upon probable cause, supported by Oath or affirmation, and particularly describing the place to be searched, and the persons or things to be seized.

AMENDMENT 5

No person shall be held to answer for a capital, or otherwise infamous crime, unless on a presentment or indictment of a Grand Jury, except in cases arising in the land or naval forces, or in the Militia, when in actual service in time of War or public danger; nor shall any person be subject for the same offense to be twice put in jeopardy of life or limb; nor shall be compelled in any criminal case to be a witness against himself; nor be deprived of life, liberty, or property, without due process of law; nor shall private property be taken for public use, without just compensation.

AMENDMENT 6

In all criminal prosecutions, the accused shall enjoy the right to a speedy and public trial, by an impartial jury of the State and district wherein the crime shall have been committed, which district shall have been previously ascertained by law, and to be informed of the nature and cause of the accusation; to be confronted with the witnesses against him; to have compulsory process for obtaining Witnesses in his favor, and to have the Assistance of Counsel for his defense.

AMENDMENT 7

In Suits at common law, where the value in controversy shall exceed twenty dollars, the right of trial by jury shall be preserved, and no fact tried by a jury, shall be otherwise reexamined in any Court of the United States, than according to the rules of the common law.

AMENDMENT 8

Excessive bail shall not be required, nor excessive fines imposed nor cruel and unusual punishments inflicted.

AMENDMENT 9

The enumeration in the Constitution, of certain rights, shall not be construed to deny or disparage others retained by the people.

AMENDMENT 10

The powers not delegated to the United States by the Constitution, nor prohibited by it to the States, are reserved to the States respectively, or to the people.

(G) Slavery's Aftermath and criminal justice — The Fourteenth Amendment and Due Process of Law

The issues of slavery and secession from the Union led to the Civil War, the darkest years of America's history. In its aftermath the Thirteenth Amendment outlawing slavery, was ratified in 1865. Closely following was the Fourteenth Amendment, ratified in 1868, which was intended to guarantee full rights of citizenship to emancipated slaves. Few could then foresee the important effect that this amendment would have on the American criminal justice system. Section 1 of the Fourteenth Amendment is as follows:

> All persons born or naturalized in the United States, and subject to the jurisdiction thereof, are citizens of the United States and of the State wherein they reside. No State shall make or enforce any law which shall abridge the privileges or immunities of citizens of the United States; nor shall any State deprive any person of life, liberty, or property, without due process of law; nor deny to any person within its jurisdiction the equal protection of the laws.

Unlike the Bill of Rights, the Fourteenth Amendment did not restrict the powers of the federal government; it restricted those of the states. In time it became the vehicle for a revolution in American criminal law and procedure which is still in progress today.

In interpreting the Fourteenth Amendment the Supreme Court was at first reluctant to impose on the states the standard of "due process of law"; instead, it imposed a standard of "fundamental fairness." But gradually, in one case at a time, the Court began to apply the Bill of Rights to the states as a matter of Fourteenth Amendment "due process of law." One of the clearest examples of the process is *Mapp v. Ohio,* 81 S. Ct. 1684 (1961), in which the Supreme Court ruled that not only did the Fourth Amendment guarantee against unreasonable searches and seizures apply to the states through the Fourteenth Amendment, but so did the exclusionary rule, a doctrine which many thought to be merely a federal rule of evidence (See Ch. 2).

The process of the constitutional interpretation continues as a never-ending parade of difficult issues is presented to the Supreme Court. Critics argue that the Court is preventing the states from experimenting in order to find better methods of handling criminal cases, but its defenders answer that uniformity and certainty in the protection of individual rights is worth that price.

§ 1.4 CRIMES AND CIVIL WRONGS DISTINGUISHED

As civilization progressed through the centuries, the exacting of vengeance by families in order to settle disputes or to reciprocate wrongs to its members (the "eye for an eye" concept) was replaced with retribution or punishment by the state, which was, in some respects, a sort of extended family. Breakers of the "King's peace" were subject to being punished by representatives of the Crown. Today in many jurisdictions formal written charges of criminal wrongdoing still end with the phrase, "and against the peace and dignity of the State of _____".

Individual rights cannot exist in a society without law, and it is the generally accepted view in Western society that the state, through its legal system, has the moral right to coerce obedience to its laws through the power to punish persons for criminal acts. See Louis A. Radelet, *The Police and the Community* (4th ed. 1986), 442-3. Thus, crime and punishment has evolved over time from a private to a public matter, and state-administered punishment is an accepted means of protecting individual rights.

A "crime" by modern definition, is an act which the law forbids, or a failure to perform an act which the law requires, under pain of punishment imposed by the state in a proceeding brought in the name of the state. The seven general principles of the criminal law, as described in J. Hall, *General Principles of Criminal Law* (2d ed., 1960), are as follows:

1. *Actus Res - The Act - Conduct.* Generally, conduct, to be criminal, must consist of something more than a mere bad state of mind. There must be some act that is voluntary or an omission when there is a duty to act.

2. *Mens Rea - Guilty Mind - Culpability.* An act does not make one guilty unless his mind is guilty. Most state criminal codes define criminal states of mind by such terms as "intentionally", "knowingly", and "recklessly." They also recognize defenses such as mistake of fact, insanity, duress, legal authority, abandonment, and entrapment, that rebut the allegation of guilty mind. If the defendent proves that he had no guilty mind, he has shown there was no crime, despite his conduct.

3. *Concurrence or Fusion of Mens Rea and Actus Res.* It is a basic requirement of Anglo-American criminal law that the physical conduct and the state of mind must concur. There is concurrence when the defendant's mental state actuates the physical conduct.

4. *Causation.* The defendant's conduct must be the "but-for" (actual cause) of the forbidden result; moreover, the forbidden result must be sufficiently similar to the result which the defendant intended that the defendant may fairly be held responsible for it. This casual connection is called "proximate cause", or "legal cause".

5. *Harm.* Only conduct harmful to others should be made criminal. In 1863 John Stuart Mill argued that the only purpose for which power can rightfully be exercised over any member of a civilized community against his will is to prevent him from harming others. The wisdom of using the criminal law for the promotion and protection of private morality, or to coerce a person into protecting his own safety, has long been a subject of debate.

6. *Punishment.* Punishment is the end result of the criminal law and, it is the major difference between a "tort" and a "crime".

7. *Legality.* There can be no crime or punishment unless established by pre-existing law.

Torts. Much of the conduct which is defined as criminal by statutory or case law, and for which the state may administer a punishment, is also subject to the civil, or tort, law. A tort is a private wrong or injury to a person which entitles the injured person to sue the wrongdoer in a civil action in court for money damages. If Smith hits Jones in the nose without justification or excuse he has, in many jurisdictions, committed the crime of "battery". Smith can be charged with this crime by the state, and, if convicted, he may be punished by the state. He may be fined or imprisoned. But Jones can also bring a private action against Smith, in his own name, for money damages for his injury, for his medical expenses, and for other appropriate relief. If Jones wins this lawsuit, the court can order Smith to compensate Jones for his injury and resulting losses by paying him a sum of money. This action is separate and distinct from the criminal prosecution for battery, which arose out of the same conduct.

On the other hand, a landlord cannot have a tenant arrested for nonpayment of rent, because failure to pay bills has not been made a crime by the state; it is a private matter between the parties to the contract. The landlord can only sue the tenant for the back payments and perhaps for other expenses arising from the tenant's "breach" of the terms of the lease agreement.

--**Notes**--

CHAPTER 2

REMEDIES FOR POLICE MISCONDUCT

Section
2.1 Introduction
2.2 Civil actions for money damages
    (A) Civil actions under federal law
    (B) Civil actions under state law
2.3 Criminal prosecution
2.4 Other judicial remedies
2.5 Administrative disciplinary actions
2.6 Exclusion of evidence; the Fourth Amendment exclusionary rule
    (A) At first, a federal rule of evidence
    (B) Later, a rule of contitutional dimension
    (C) Criticims and the good faith exception
2.7 Meeting the challenge

§ 2.1 INTRODUCTION

Law enforcement in America is subject to more public review than any other activity, bar none. Thousands of lawsuits are filed against law enforcement every year throughout this country. No other area receives more attention from the appellate court system than law enforcement cases and issues. But public review of law enforcement does not take place only within the legal system. There are many formal and informal ways by which the American people evaluate the actions of police officers in specific cases. An outline of typical ways in which members of the public seek to review and challenge law enforcement activity is presented below, but first this outline must be placed in perspective.

Police officers in the United States often feel that *they* themselves are on trial when they testify as witnesses for the state in a criminal case. Many officers become frustrated and resentful of the probing cross-examination of defense lawyers. They think to themselves, "who is being tried here — *me or the defendant?*". What these officers overlook - or forget - is that the single greatest fear of the drafters of the United States Constitution and Bill of Rights was the *fear of oppressive government*. It outweighed their fear of crimes committed by fellow-citizens. A uniformed police officer is the most visible reminder of possible oppression. The American legal system has therefore created remedies for governmental or police misconduct in order to permit effective law enforcement while at the same time protecting the citizen against governmental excesses.

The people living in the thirteen colonies at the time of the American Revolution by and large shared one common experience: governmental abuse and denial of individual liberty. The citizens who emigrated to North America came primarily from England, France, Spain and other western European nations. These countries' governments were, for the most part, highly centralized. Brutal, arrogant, and self-serving monarchies were prevalent. Monarchs would sometimes consume significant proportions of their country's gross national product for their own personal ends, the best example being the Sun King, Louis XIV of France, with his devotion to the creation of his palace at Versailles. Furthermore, justice, itself was in the hands of a few loyal "king's men". If anyone was caught violating the king's decrees, punishment was swift and cruel.

Against this common international experience, the founders of this country and drafters of its Constitution specifically set out to develop a new system of government whereby the rights of the individual would be paramount. The drafters were in part influenced by the famous French philosopher Jean Jacque Rousseau, who believed in the concept of the "noble savage". He taught that the corruption of mankind comes, not from human nature, but rather from the corruptions of government and society. If left alone, and not controlled by government, Rousseau believed that human beings would seek a peaceful and law abiding existence. While many of the founding fathers agreed in full or part with the natural law theories of Rousseau, they were also influenced by *Leviathan*, a pioneer treatise on political theory by English philosopher Thomas Hobbes. The term leviathan in the Bible denotes one of the primordial monsters destroyed by God in the creation of the world (Psalm 74:14; Isaiah 27:1). In this work Hobbes advocated a strong national form of government which would rescue man from his own weaknesses and inabilities — a principle very similar to that espoused in the book *The Prince* by Machiavelli, the Italian courier who is considered, by many to be the father of modern political science.

The founding fathers essentially believed the proper role for government was somewhere in between the recommendations of Rousseau (no or little government is best) on the one hand, and those of Hobbes and Machiavelli (a strong centralized government is the only way to create a peaceful and productive society), on the other. In addition, they had personally experienced the extremes of monarchy under King George III and anarchy under their own Articles of Confederation. When these facts are considered along with the overwhelming evidence that the founders were by and large powerfully influenced by the Judeo-Christian heritage, suddenly the reasons for the Constitution begin to be apparent.

A clear reading of the Declaration of Independence and the Constitution discloses a firm belief that the purpose of government is to *serve* the people, not to dominate, and that government should be reflective of majority rule, while at the same time protecting certain God-given rights which all the people possess.

Against this backdrop, police officers must realize that they are, to the American public, the most powerful representatives of the government. No one else has the ongoing legal authority to arrest or detain, or to cause criminal prosecutions to be filed against citizens. In addition, police comprise the only non-military group that has been given clear but limited authority to kill, in certain circumstances. Thus the police officer regularly deals with the two most cherished rights in the country: liberty and life itself. While they can be forgiven for their occasional bitterness with a system of public review that seems endless and sometimes unfair, police officers simply have to temper their feelings of frustration with the realization that in a society where life, liberty and the pursuit of happiness is valued above all else, it makes sense that the police should be the most critically reviewed group in America. Is there too much public review and criticism? Plausible arguments can be made to support either side of this question.

Public review of police conduct often begins immediately with observations by eye-witnesses to the initial police-citizen contact. Other forms of review of alleged police misconduct may include the following:

>observations by custodial staff and inmates at the jail to which the suspect is brought for booking and detention;
>
>review by the prosecutor, to determine if charges should be filed against a suspect;
>
>review of the circumstances by the the defense attorney;
>
>judicial review via an initial hearing before a judge, which begins the criminal justice process;
>
>media coverage, especially in reports by medical personnel in "newsworthy" cases, such as those involving the use of deadly force, if any of the parties were injured;
>
>inquiries by friends and family of the parties or by special interest organizations;

the process of full discovery in the course of preparing the criminal case for trial;

review by supervisory police officers or the department's internal affairs office;

the jury trial or bench trial (before a judge only), in which witnesses testify and exhibits are introduced;

review by state appellate courts following a conviction by the trial court;

a hearing before U.S. Supreme Court;

a petition for a writ of habeas corpus, filed in the federal district court nearest to an inmate's place of incarceration and appealed to the U.S. Circuit Court of Appeals and thence to the U.S. Supreme Court; these writs can also be filed in state courts and can be filed years after the original state court conviction;

state court civil lawsuits;

federal court civil lawsuits:

state post-conviction relief petitions; of counsel; and

federal and state criminal prosecution of police officers for crimes against citizens, including violation of their civil rights; in such situations the convicted police officers would have all of the review options listed above.

------------------------------------- **Notes** -------------------------------------

Sample Questions

In American criminal procedure, the meaning of the term "exclusionary rule" is:

A. a rule of law that excludes evidence because it is not relevant to the subject matter of the trial.
B. it is another name for the Fourth Amendment.
C. a rule of law that excludes evidence because it is not material, or not important enough for the court to bother with.
D. a rule of law that excludes evidence, regardless of its relevance or importance, if it is produced by police misconduct that violates the rights of the person objecting to its introduction.
E. all of the above.

The Fourth Amendment exclusionary rule:

A. is a judicially-created remedy with the purpose of "policing the police."
B. is clearly stated in the Fourth Amendment.
C. applies only against federal law enforcement officers.
D. applies only against state and local law enforcement officers.
E. when applied by the courts, always results in the defendant being set free.

Exclusionary rules of evidence:

A. exist only under the Fourth Amendment.
B. exist only under the Fifth Amendment.
C. in federal courts exist only under the Fourteenth Amendment.
D. exist only under the Sixth Amendment.
E. exist under the Fourth, Fifth, and Sixth Amendments, and in state cases are applied through the Fourteenth Amendment.

Exclusionary rules of evidence could be abolished by:

A. a state legislature.
B. the Congress of the United States.
C. the Supreme Court of the United States.
D. an amendment to the Constitution of the United States.
E. C and D above.

The "good faith" exception to the exclusionary rule:

A. has been proposed by members of the Supreme Court, but never adopted by the Court.
B. is based on the reasoning that if police officers proceed in good faith to obtain a necessary judicial warrant before conducting a search, it makes no sense to apply the rule (to police the police), if the alleged error was made by the judge who issued the warrant.
C. will validate any action of a police officer who honestly believes that he acted correctly.
D. was a concept that originated in a law enacted by Congress.
E. none of the above are correct.

§ 2.2 CIVIL ACTIONS FOR MONEY DAMAGES

(A) Civil actions under federal law

STANDARDS UPON WHICH LIABILITY MAY BE BASED

The concept of "liability" is not new. Early English common law developed a number of legal theories that recognized that individuals could be held either criminally or civilly liable if certain precepts were violated within a given set of circumstances. If a certain individual *owed a duty* to another to meet a specific standard of care, and *breached*, that duty, then liability might arise. This basic "tort" theory, was the foundation for most early American concepts of "liability".

The modern police officer, is required to apply numerous standards of care in various situations. When these "police standards" are violated, civil liability may result. But where do the police standards of today come from? In general, they are derived from the following sources:

    the U.S. Constitution, primarily the First, Second, Fourth, Fifth, Sixth, Eighth, and Fourteenth Amendments;
    state constitutions;
    federal, state and local statutes;
    federal, state and local case law;
    federal and state administrative rules and regulations; and
    police department standard operating procedures.

EXAMPLES OF CONDUCT WHICH MAY GIVE RISE TO CIVIL LIABILITY

From the long list of sources of standards cited above, one can see that there are numerous ways for a police officer to be found civilly liable - from violating federal civil rights statutes (42 U.S.C. §1983 et seq.) to violating a police department standard operating procedure. Of course civil liability depends upon the specific facts of each case; it arises most commonly in the following areas:

    false arrest and imprisonment;
    excessive use of force;
    illegal confessions and right-to-counsel violations;
    illegal searches and seizures;
    improper use of informants;
    departmental negligence in personnel practices such as hiring, training, supervision, retention, and disciplining of police officers;
    libel and slander;
    malicious prosecution;
    violating federal, state and local laws in conjunction with Fourteenth Amendment due process standards;
    race, sex, and age discrimination in conjunction with Fourteenth Amendment equal protection principles;
    First Amendment violations of freedom of speech, of religion, and of the press;
    prohibiting public access to departmental records which are not confidential;
    negligent operation of department vehicles;
    illegal handgun permit procdures; and
    illegal incarceration policies and practices.

SECTION 1983 CIVIL LIABILITY

Police officers often face civil actions in both federal and state courts under 42 U.S.C. §1983, formerly called the "Ku Klux Act:

> Every person who, under color of any statute, ordinance, regulation, custom, or usage, of any State or Territory, subjects, or causes to be subjected, any citizen of the United States or other persons within the jurisdiction thereof to the deprivation of any rights, privileges, or immunities secured by the Constitution and laws, shall be liable to the party injured in an action at law, suit in equity, or other proceeding for redress.

Thus a police officer is liable for his actions if: (1) he acts under color of *state* law (2) to deprive a person of rights, privileges, or immunities which are protected under *federal* law.

A leading case defining "color of state law" is *United States v. Classic*, 61 S. Ct. 1031 (1941). The laws of Louisiana mandated that citizens' votes be counted, but state officials refused to do so. The Supreme Court held that this refusal was actionable under the Civil Rights Act, in that the officials acted "under color of state law." The Court stated: "Misuse of power, possessed by virtue of state law and made possible only because the wrongdoer is clothed with the authority of state law, is action taken 'under color of state law.'" That view of the meaning of the term was reaffirmed in *Screws v. United States* 65 S. Ct. 1031 (1945) and in *Monroe v. Pape*, 81 S. Ct. 473 (1961).

In *Monroe v. Pape*, thirteen Chicago police officers allegedly broke into petitioners' home in the early morning, routed them from bed, made them stand naked in the living room and ransacked every room, emptying drawers and ripping mattress covers, all without a search or arrest warrant and without probable cause. Mr. Monroe was taken to the police station and held on "open charges." He was subsequently released without criminal charges being preferred against him. The police defendants argued that, because their conduct violated the law of Illinois, they were not "acting under color of state law." The Court rejected this argument, holding that they acted under the pretense of state law and were thus liable under the Civil Rights Act, even though they may not have had a specific intent to violate the civil rights of a person. The Court reasoned that a civil rights action is a tort action and should therefore be read against the background of tort liability, which makes a man responsible for the natural consequences of his actions.

Other examples of alleged conduct for which civil actions have been held to be properly brought under the Civil Rights Act include: unlawful threats to cause imprisonment or loss of employment *(Attreau v. Morris*, 357 F. 2d 871 (7th Cir. 1966)); holding injured persons incommunicado *(Hughes v. Noble*, 295 F. 2d 495 (5th Cir. 1961)); arresting a person three separate times without ever obtaining a warrant or filing charges against him *(Marland v. Heyse*, 315 F.2d 312 (10th Cir. 1963)); assault *(Byrd v. Brishke*, 466 F.2d 6 (7th Cir. 1972)); false arrest and detention *(Monroe v. Pape*, cited above); arrest of a person not named in a warrant *(Yates v. Village of Hoffman Estates*, 209 F. Supp. 757 (N.D. Ill. 1962)); unlawful search and seizure *(Monroe v. Pape*, cited above); *Fisher v. Volz*, 496 F.2d 333 (3rd Cir. 1974)); excessive force in effecting an arrest *(Williams v. Liberty*, 461 F.2 325 (7th Cir. 1972)); gross violation of privacy *(York v. Story*, 324 F.2 450 (9th Cir. 1963)); denial of proper medical treatment *(Robinson v. Jordan*, 494 F.2d 793 (5th Cir. 1974)); interference with First Amendment rights *(Lykken v. Vavreck*, 366 F. Supp. 585 (D. Minn. 1973)); denial to prisoner of religious materials solely because of his religious beliefs and denial of privileges enjoyed by other prisoners for the same reason *(Cooper v. Pate*, 84, S. Ct. 1733 (1964)) subjecting prisoners to cruel and unusual treatment *(Wright v. McMann*, 387

F.2d 519 (2nd Cir. 1967)); and denial of access to counsel *(Monroe v. Pape,* cited above).

A police officer is criminally liable under federal law if he *willfully* violates a citizen's civil rights under color of state law; 18 U.S.C. §242; *Screws v. United States,* cited above. The element of "willfulness" distinguishes the criminal violation from the civil violation.

"Conspiracy" to violate citizens' civil rights is another basis for police officers' civil liability. It is common for several police officers to be sued together in one lawsuit for conspiring to violate the civil rights of a citizen or group. This civil liability standard comes from 42 U.S.C. §1985, which states in pertinent part:

> If two or more persons in any State or Territory conspire or go in disguise on the highway or on the premises of another, for the purpose of depriving, either directly or indirectly, any person or class of persons of the equal protection of the laws, or of equal privileges and immunities under the laws; or for the purpose of preventing or hindering the constituted authorities of any State or Territory from giving or securing to all persons within such State or Territory the equal protection of the laws; or if two or more persons conspire to prevent by force, intimidation, or threat, any citizen who is lawfully entitled to vote, from giving his support or advocacy in a legal manner, toward or in favor of the election of any lawfully qualified person as an elector for President or Vice President, or as a Member of Congress of the United States; or to injure any citizen in person or property on account of such support or advocacy; in any case of conspiracy set forth in this section, if one or more persons engaged therein do, or cause to be done, any act in furtherance of the object of such conspiracy, whereby another is injured in his person or property, or deprived of having and exercising any right or privilege of a citizen of the United States, the party so injured or deprived may have an action for the recovery of damages occasioned by such injury or deprivation, against any one or more of the conspirators.

Subsection (1) of 42 U.S.C. §1985 deals with actions preventing an officer from performing duties and subsection (2) relates to obstructing justice, intimidating parties, witnesses or jurors.

Finally, every police officer should be aware of the most unique provision of the federal civil rights statute - 42 U.S.C. §1988, which was enacted in 1976. It provides that, if a plaintiff successfully sues a police officer for a civil rights violation, the plaintiff not only can recover nominal, actual and possibly punitive damages, but can also collect from the defendant police officer, if the court approves, the attorney fees that the citizen incurred as a result of having to hire an attorney in order to bring the civil liability lawsuit. As a result, judgments all across the United States contain attorney fees awards which are often larger in monetary value than the underlying damage award. This provision is also available to the police defendant - but the police officer must prove that the citizen's lawsuit was totally without merit. — *frivolous* — before he can collect attorney fees from the citizen plaintiff.

Two significant Supreme Court decisions on attorney fees include *Marek v. Chesny,* 105 S. Ct. 3012 (1985) (it was proper for a trial judge to deny attorney fees after the defendant's offer of settlement was refused by the plaintiff, an offer which was greater than the amount of damages awarded by a jury after a full trial) and *Blum v. Stenson,* 104 S.Ct. 1541, (1984)) (neither complexity nor novelty of the issues is usually an appropriate factor in determining whether to increase a basic fee award; usually the number of hours worked mutiplied by the hourly rate will establish a reasonable award of attorney fees).

The Supreme Court in *Pierson v. Ray,* 87 S. Ct. 1213 (1967) stated that police officers were entitled to the common-law defense of "good faith and probable cause." This meant that if the officer was acting in good faith and upon probable cause to arrest or search, then he would have a valid defense to a "1983 action."

For many years thereafter, police officers were very successful in civil liability lawsuits because of this good faith defense; the jury could rule in favor of the police officer even when there was a constitutional violation and even if the good faith on the part of the officer was totally "subjective" in nature. But in 1982 the Supreme Court dealt a blow to the subjective good faith defense in the landmark case which is briefed below.

CASE BRIEF

Harlow v. Fitzgerald, 102 S. Ct. 2727 (1982)

Justice Powell delivered the opinion of the Court

FACTS: Fitzgerald lost his job as management systems deputy to the Assistant Secretary of the Department of the Air Force, pursuant to an Air Force reorganization and reduction in force plan which eliminated his job. He then filed a federal civil suit for damages, alleging that the defendants, including Bryce N. Harlow and Alexander P. Butterfield, and President Richard M. Nixon, conspired to violate his constitutional rights under the First Amendment, as well as certain federal statutory rights in retaliation for his revealing to various Congressional committees that production of the C-5A transport plane had encountered unexpected technical difficulties and that cost-overruns could amount to two billion dollars.

The District of Columbia District Court denied the defendant's pretrial motion for summary judgment based on absolute immunity from damages. Their pretrial "collateral" appeal to the Court of Appeals for the District of Columbia, was also dismissed. The Supreme Court granted certiorari and decided two related cases: *Nixon v. Fitzgerald*, 102 S. Ct. 2690 (1982) and *Harlow v. Fitzgerald*. In *Nixon*, the Court held that the President enjoys absolute immunity from any damage liability for acts taken within the "outer perimeter" of his official responsibilities.

ISSUES: (1) Are presidential aides entitled to absolute immuity as the President is? (2) Are government officials, in performing discretionary functions, entitled to immunity from civil damages?

DECISION: No, to question one; yes, to question two — but only qualified immunity. Judgment of Court of Appeals vacated and case remanded to District Court for reconsideration.

REASONS: The Supreme Court has established absolute immunity from civil damages for only a select group of public servants acting within the scope of their duties: (1) presidential immunity *(Nixon v. Fitzgerald, supra)*; (2) legislators *(Eastland v. United States Servicemen's Fund*, 95 S. Ct. 1813 (1975) (3) judges *(Stump v. Sparkman*, 98 S. Ct. 1099 (1978); (4) prosecutors and executive officers engaged in adjudicative functions *(Butz v. Economou*, 98 S. Ct. 2894 (1978); and (5) aides of members of Congress when they perform acts for them which are related to their legislative functions *(Gavel v. United States*, 92 S. Ct. 2614 (1972)).

Absolute civil immunity from damages applies only to the above named government officials when they act within the scope of their official capacities and does not protect actions that would amount to criminal activity. Moreover, civil lawsuits seeking non-monetary relief in the form of injuctions or declaratory judgments are not necessarily barred. But absolute immunity from damages for the above types of government employees should be recognized, given their special functions and/or constitutional responsibilities.

The Court has consistently given all other executive officials (including presidential advisers like Harlow and Butterfield) some degree of immunity from civil damages in order to shield them from unnecessary threats of liability and interferences with their official responsibilities. But this is a *qualified* immunity, which is based upon the good faith defense.

Under the Constitution, the federal civil rights statutes, and common law, government officials are protected from civil liability as long as their conduct in question does not violate clearly established statutory or constitutional rights.

If a citizen can show that a government employee violated a clearly established statutory or constitutional right, liability will automaticaly be presumed in most cases. The subjective good faith of the defendant government official will not bar monetary recovery unless the official can clearly, concretely and objectively prove that he neither knew nor *should have known* of the relevant legal standards which applied to him and which he violated.

RULE: Most executive branch government employees enjoy a qualified good faith immunity from civil liability damages. But this immunity will be analyzed by a test that centers on the *objective* legal reasonableness of an official's actions. Ignorance of the law will be no excuse for violating citizens' constitutional rights. Any public official, including a police officer, is liable for monetary damages when he violates a clearly established constitutional or statutory right under circumstances in which the official knew or should have known of the relevant legal rights. If the plaintiff cannot meet this burden, the reviewing court can grant summary judgment before trial in favor of the government defendant. But lack of malicious intent (subjective good faith) on the part of the government employee will no longer act as a complete bar to civil liability where clearly established legal rights are violated.

A year following the *Harlow* decisison, a sharply divided Supreme Court handed down another decision which made substantial public official liability judgments even easier to obtain.

CASE BRIEF

Smith v. Wade, 103 S. Ct. 1625(1983)

Majority opinion: Brennan. Dissenting: Rehnquist, Burger, Powell, O'Connor.

FACTS: Plaintiff, Wade, an inmate in a Missouri reformatory for youthful first offenders, alleged that he was harassed, beaten, and sexually assaulted by fellow cellmates.

Wade had earlier voluntarily placed himself in protective custody; because of disciplinary violations he was eventually placed in administrative segregation. It was in the administrative segregation unit that the beating by fellow inmates occurred. A few weeks earlier, another inmate had been beaten to death in the same dormitory. Wade alleged that Smith, a guard on duty at the time of assault, had placed other inmates in his cell, one of whom had been involved in fighting, and that Smith knew that Wade was seeking protection from further inmate violence.

Wade filed a federal lawsuit against Smith and other correctional officials under 42 U.S.C. § 1983. He asserted that his Eighth Amendment rights had been violated because the defendants knew or should have known that an assault against him was likely to occur under the circumstances.

During trial, the district judge directed a verdict in favor of two defendants and instructed the jury that Wade could prove an Eighth Amendment violation only by showing "physical abuse of such base, inhumane and barbaric proportions as to shock the sensibilities"; that Wade could recover only if the defendants were guilty of gross negligence in the actions toward the plaintiff; and that the jury could award punitive damages if the conduct of one or more of the defendants was reckless or was in callous disregard of, or indifference to, the right or safety of others.

The jury returned verdicts in favor of two of the correctional officials but found Smith liable in the amount of $25,000.00 in actual damages as well as $5,000.00 in punitive damages. The court of appeals affirmed the verdict, and the Supreme Court granted certiorari.

ISSUE: Are punitive damages against a government official limited to conduct shown to be motivated by evil intent or can they also be assessed for conduct shown to be merely recklessly or callously indifferent to federally protected rights?

DECISION: Reckless or callous indifference is sufficient grounds. Affirmed.

REASONS: Under the Civil Rights Act of 1871, punitive damages are awardable by a judge (if it is a bench trial) or a jury (if it is a jury trial) in any proper case. At common law, at the time the civil rights act was adopted in 1871, and since that time, punitive damages have been available as relief against the wrongdoer and there is no need to depart from this tradition.

Since the Civil Rights Act of 1871 was intended to create a "species of tort liability" in favor of persons deprived of federally secured rights, the common law tort tradition with respect to damage awards (which allows punitive damages) must heavily influence the Court to permit them herein. And since the overall American tort tradition has been to allow punitive damages (also called exemplary damages, vindictive damages, or smart money) without a showing of actual ill will, spite, or *intent* to injure; this should also be the federal standard for civil rights cases.

> This common-law rule makes sense in terms of the purposes of punitive damages. Punitive damages are awarded in the jury's discretion "to punish (the defendant) for his outrageous conduct and to deter him and others like him from similar conduct in the future." Restatement (Second) of Torts §908 (1) (1979). The focus is on the character of the tortfeasor's conduct - whether it is of the sort that calls for deterrence and punishment over and above that provided by compensatory awards. If it is of such a character, then it is appropriate to allow a jury to assess punitive damages; and that assessment does not become less appropriate simply because the plaintiff in the case faces a more demanding standard of actionability. To put it differently, society has an interest in deterring and punishing *all* intentional or reckless invasions of the rights of others, even though it sometimes chooses not to impose any liability for lesser degrees of fault.

Furthermore, punitive damages must be an assessable damage award because without it, victims may not have any relief in those cases where their constitutional rights are maliciously violated but no compensable injuries are present.

RULE: Punitive damages can be awarded in federal and state court actions filed pursuant to 42 U.S.C. §1983 when government officials act with either evil motive/intent *or* when the officials' actions involve reckless or callous indifference to the federally protected rights of others.

DISSENTING: The awarding of punitive damages should be closely scrutinized and awarded in only the most egregious of cases. Indeed there is a strong legal tradition and argument which calls the awarding of punitive damages wrong - a monstrous heresy.

A basic principle of our legal system is that damages are awarded to *compensate* the victim for injuries *actually* suffered. Against this time-honored legal theory lies punitive damages: awards which exceed the most liberal of awards for actual injury incurred, for the purpose of punishing the defendant or deterring officials from violating the rights of others. Such awards are based upon "bounty" concepts; they encourage private litigation against public wrongdoers.

In light of legal history, and balancing the various interests, the proper standard for an award of punitive damages under federal civil rights laws is at least to require some degree of bad faith or improper motive on the part of the defendant. To allow punitive damages in those cases where the defendants are acting only with recklessness or indifference is simply too speculative, especially since there are no clear legal guidelines to control judges or juries in their punitive damage awards.

CASE BRIEF

Monell v. Department of Social Services of the City of N.Y., 98 S. Ct. 2018 (1978)

Majority opinion: Brennan. Dissenting: Burger, Rehnquist.

FACTS: Female employees of the Department of Social Services and the Board of Education of the City of New York filed a 42 U.S.C. § 1983 civil rights complaint against the Department, its commissioner, the board and its chancellor, and City and mayor of New York, challenging various policies which required that pregnant employees take unpaid leaves of absence before those leaves were required for medical reasons.

The District Court for the Southern District of New York and the Court of Appeals for the Second Circuit rejected the plaintiff's complaint. While both courts ruled that the women's constitutional rights had been violated, they denied back pay damage claims on the basis that local branches of government are not "persons" for purposes of monetary liability under the Civil Rights Act and, further, that when local governmental employees are sued as natural persons but in their official capacities as officers that they too enjoy the immunity which local governments possess. The Supreme Court granted certiorari.

ISSUES: (1) Are municipalities and other local government units "persons" for purposes of being sued under 42 U.S.C. §1983? (2) Are local government officials, sued in their official capacities, "persons" for purposes of 42 U.S.C. §1983? (3) Are local government units entitled to absolute immunity? (4) Should a municipal employer automatically be held liable for wrongs committed by its employee under the doctrine of respondeat superior?

DECISION: Issue (1) yes; issue (2) yes; issue (3), no; issue (4), no. Judgment of the court of appeals is reversed.

REASON: Presenting an exhaustive historical analysis of the concept of local government liability, the Court overruled its holding in *Monroe v. Pape*, 81 S.Ct. 473 (1961) that municipalities were not "persons" who could be sued under the federal Civil Rights Act.

RULE: Local governments are "persons" within the meaning of the Civil Rights Act. They can be sued directly for monetary damages or declaratory or injunctive relief, where the alleged unconstitutional action is by an officer or employee of the local government and is in furtherance of a governmental policy or custom. Even if the custom has not been written into law or received formal approval through the official decision making process, it can have the force of law, simply because it is permanently and regularly followed; therefore, if it violates federally-protected rights it can result in liability under the Civil Rights Act. The local government entity is not automatically liable, however, solely because the alleged unconstitutional act is committed by an employee, if the act is not in furtherance of governmental policy or custom.

In 1980 the Supreme Court issued an opinion which answered the only remaining question concerning municipal liability after *Monell* and which further exposed local government to civil rights liability. In *Owen v. City of Independence*, 100 S. Ct. 1398 (1980), the Court held that neither a municipality nor its employees are entitled to any kind of good faith defense when there is a substantial showing that the local government has overridden private rights secured by the Constitution. In this case, a former municipal police chief sued the city for wrongful discharge.

In another decision, the Supreme Court ruled that local branches of government cannot be held liable for punitive damages. *City of Newport v. Fact Concerts, Inc.*, 101 S. Ct. 2748 (1981).

These cases create a unique situation for local government. While *states by NAME*, *state* government agencies *by NAME*, and *state* employees acting in their official capacities usually cannot be sued for damages under the federal Civil Rights Act *(Alabama v. Pugh*, 98 S. Ct. 3057 (1978)), local government and it officials can be sued. Local government — the very level of government which can least afford civil liability is the most susceptible to it under federal law.

In the case of *City of Canton v. Harris*, 109 S.Ct. 1197 (1989) the Supreme Court of the United States held that if a local unit of government displays "deliberate indifference" to the constitutional rights of its inhabitants by failing to properly train its police officers, and that failure to train results in depriving a person of a constitutionally-protected right, the local governmental unit can be held liable in damages under the Federal Civil Rights Act sec. 1983. Consistent with the earlier *Monell* decision, however, the Court held that the failure to train must reflect a "deliberate" or "conscious" choice by the municipality, thereby constituting a "policy" of the municipality, and that civil liability would not result merely on the basis of the employer-employee relationship (respondeat superior).

Although this opinion would seem to create great potential for liability for those cities, towns and counties which follow the custom or "policy" of putting officers on the street to perform police duty without any pre-duty training at all, the opinion also states that the focus must be on the adequacy of training in relation to the tasks that the particular officers must perform. The opinion also notes that although a training program may be adequate, it may be negligently administered, or a well-trained officer may simply make a mistake. In neither case would liability automatically flow to the municipality under the Federal Civil Rights Act, unless the harm resulted from its custom or policy.

CIVIL LIABILITY OF PROSECUTORS

While public officials performing *executive* functions (such as police officers) have only *qualified* immunity from money damages, officials performing *legislative* or *judicial* functions have absolute immunity from money damages as long as the acts are performed within the scope of their original duties. Prosecuting attorneys perform a *judicial* function by preparing their cases for trial and by prosecuting defendants. But if a prosecutor does an act which is *outside* the scope of his judicial duties, he may have only *qualified* immunity from money damages (the same immunity that the police have).

In the case of *Burns v. Reed*, 111 S.Ct. 1934 (1991), the Supreme Court held that a prosecutor was entitled to only *qualified* immunity from damages for *giving legal advice to the police*. In that case, police asked a Chief Deputy Prosecutor whether they could lawfully interview a suspect in an attempted murder case while the suspect was under hypnosis, and they were advised that they could. The interview of the suspect (who was believed to have multiple personalities) was conducted while she was under hypnosis and the police interpreted her answers as a confession. At a probable cause hearing seeking a search warrant, the police, answering questions by the deputy prosecutor, indicated that the suspect had confessed but neither the deputy prosecutor nor the police told the judge that the "confession" was given under hypnosis or that the suspect had consistently denied the crime when not under hypnosis. A search warrant was issued, but before trial the suspect moved to suppress the statement taken under hypnosis and it was suppressed. As a result, the prosecutor dropped the criminal charges. The suspect brought a civil action under the Civil Rights Act seeking damages for violation of her 4th, 5th, and 14th Amendment rights and settlements were made with several parties, but not the deputy prosecutor, and the lawsuit against him went to trial.

The District Court granted the deputy prosecutor a directed verdict on the basis that he was absolutely immune from money damages and the U.S. Court of Appeals affirmed, holding that giving the police advice about the legality of investigative conduct was within the scope of a prosecutor's duty.

Because the U.S. Courts of Appeal were divided about the scope of a prosecutor's immunity, the Supreme Court of the United States granted certiorari. The Supreme Court held that the deputy prosecutor's participation in the probable cause hearing was clearly within the scope of his judicial duties and that he had absolute immunity from damages for that conduct. But it held that giving legal advice to the police was not so clearly a judicial function as to justify absolute immunity, and that qualified immunity only was appropriate.

"'As the qualified immunity defense has evolved, it provides ample support to all but the plainly incompetent or those who knowingly violate the law.'" . . . "Although the absence of absolute immunity for the act of giving legal advice may cause prosecutors to consider their advice more carefully," "[w]here an official could be expected to know that his conduct would violate statutory or constitutional rights, he *should* be made to hesitate.'" . . . "Indeed, it is incongruous to allow prosecutors to be absolutely immune from liability for giving advice to the police, but to allow police officers only qualified immunity for following the advice." . . . "Ironically, it would mean that the police, who do not ordinarily hold law degrees, would be required to know the clearly established law, but prosecutors would not."

It remains to be seen what effect the *Burns v. Reed* case will have on police — prosecutor relationships in the area of legal advice and training. Most police departments do not have legal advisers readily available to their officers, and in many cases the prosecutor has served this function. But the effect of the case should be tempered by the words of the opinion itself, i.e., "plainly incompetent"; "knowingly violate the law". Therefore it would seem that a prosecutor advising the police on the "clearly established law" would incur no civil liability under the qualified immunity standard.

-- **Notes** --

(B) Civil actions under state law

Police officers may be civilly liable under theories of common-law *tort* liability which is a legal term describing "a civil wrong, other than breach of contract, for which the court will provide a remedy in the form of an action for damages." *Prosser and Keeton on Torts* 2 (5th ed., 1984).

Torts can be divided into three basic categories: intentional wrongs; strict liability; and negligence. Civil liability also involves concepts of duty, breach of duty, proximate causation, and resulting damages.

Police officers face four principal kinds of common-law actions under state law: (1) assault and battery; (2) wrongful death; (3) false arrest; and (4) false imprisonment. They also have some exposure to actions for libel and slander, invasion of privacy, abuse of process, cruel and unusual punishment, and negligence resulting in injury to others (such as negligent vehicle operation and negligent administration of first aid).

In general, an officer may be held civilly liable for the damages that result from his use of excessive force in making or attempting an arrest. A police officer may use such force as may be reasonably necesary in the enforcement of the law and the preservation of order without civil liablity for such force; 6 Am. Jur. 2d *Assault and Battery* §125 (1963).

In the event the use of excessive force results in the death of another person, the officer may be liable for damages in a wrongful death action. An officer may not use deadly force in attempting to arrest a misdemeanant who is fleeing, but not resisting; *Durham v. State*, 159 N.E. 145 (Ind. 1927).

False arrest and false imprisonment are torts that are distinguishable only in the manner in which they arise. It is not necessary, to commit false imprisonment, either to intend to make an arrest or actually to make an arrest. However, a person who is falsely arrested is at the time falsely imprisoned; 32 Am. Jur. 2d *False Imprisonment* §2 (1963); *Heckart v. City of Yakima*, 708 P.2d 407 (Wash. App. 1985). False imprisonment consists of an unlawful restraint upon a person's freedom of movement or a deprivation of the liberty of another without his consent. False imprisonment may follow a lawful arrest where there is a detention without taking the arrested person before a magistrate within a reasonable period of time. *Matovina v. Hult*, 123 N.E. 2d 893 (Ind. App. 1955).

Special defenses to the various tort actions mentioned above, include the following: self-defense; comparative negligence; contributory negligence; assumption of risk; consent; lack of personal involvement; probable cause; good faith; the truth as a defense; and special immunities are sometimes available to police officers under state law. These defenses and immunities can vary greatly from state to state and it is recommended that the reader discover what immunities are available to the police officer in the state in which he is employed.

-------------------------------------- **Notes** --------------------------------------

Sample Questions

If, in performing his duties, a police officer injures or kills a person, damages property, or violates a person's rights, the law provides a number of "remedies" if the officer's actions were not privileged under the law. Included in these "remedies for police misconduct" are the possibilities of:

A. criminal prosecution of the officer.
B. civil actions against the officer for money damages, both under state and federal law, or a finding that the officer was in contempt of court.
C. administrative disciplinary action against the officer within the police department.
D. the exclusion of evidence, even though it is relevant and material, in the criminal case against the person whose rights were violated by the officer.
E. all of the above.

In a sense, a uniformed police officer exists in a "fishbowl", with members of the public constantly evaluating his actions. Sometimes police officers lose sight of the fact that behavior that might to them seem trivial, nevertheless can be regarded as serious by members of the pubic. Examples might include:

A. failure of the driver of a police vehicle to observe traffic regulations, except in an obvious emergency.
B. discourtesy.
C. profanity.
D. use of physical force when not obviously justified.
E. all of the above.

Law enforcement, by its very nature, sometimes requires police officers to use force or to restrain the liberty of persons, both of which can be potential "torts" (wrongs which can result in civil actions for money damages). The legal system attempts to balance the need for effective law enforcement against the rights of individuals not to be abused by government agents. The best way a police officer can live up to his job responsibilities and at the same time avoid the potential for civil liability is to:

A. avoid making arrests and all other situations in which the possibility of the use of force is apparent.
B. be thoroughly trained in his job responsibilities, including the extent of, and limitations on, his authority, and to take action only with probable cause, in good faith, and without malice.
C. seek a clerical or desk assignment.
D. put all his property in somebody else's name.
E. purchase liability insurance, forget his training, and simply do what comes naturally.

A city is considered to be a "person" for purposes of liability under the Federal Civil Rights Act.   T   F.

Most states have "Tort Claims Acts" which shield public employees from civil liability in damages if they perform their jobs wholly within the scope of governmental authority.   T   F.

§ 2.3 CRIMINAL PROSECUTION

As mentioned in Section 2.2 (A) above, 18 U.S.C. §242 provides that police officers can be criminally prosecuted for "willfully" violating a citizen's civil rights under "color of state law". Typically, such a prosecution is handled by the U.S. Attorney, in whose jurisdiction the crime was alleged to have occurred. At times the U.S. Department of Justice, through its Civil Rights Division, initiates a criminal prosecution against a local law enforcement officer. Depending upon state law, state prosecuting attorneys can seek similar actions.

Most importantly, police officers should never forget that their badge does not shield them from prosecution for violating traditional criminal law statutes under either federal or state law. Under the American system of justice, no person is above the law, from the "great and important" down to the bum on skid row.

While enforcing the law and pursuing the criminal element, especially when engaging in undercover operations, police officers should remind themselves that the law does not authorize governmental lawlessness. The legitimate end — arresting criminals — never justifies criminal behavior by police officers. For example, if a law enforcement officer kills a suspect by his excessive use of force, the officer could be charged with murder under criminal law. If a police officer is caught using drugs while acting undercover, drug possession charge could be filed against him.

These situations are very sensitive in nature, but one must remember that the prosecuting attorney has full authority to file criminal charges whenever there is probable cause to believe an individual (including a police officer, on or off duty) committed a criminal offense.

Finally, police officers are a tiny, numerical minority in our vast population. Without public support and a general respect for law and order, the police community cannot function effectively. If police officers are not consistent — if they violate the very laws that they arrest or stop citizens for violating, certainly the level of community support for the law enforcement effort will be reduced.

-------------------------------------- **Notes** --------------------------------------

Sample Questions

Liability in money damages under the Federal Civil Rights Act is based on the concept that:

A. a federal agent or employee (such as a police officer) has violated the rights of a person under state law.
B. a state or local government employee (such as a police officer) has violated the rights of a person protected by the Constitution of the United States.
C. a state or local government employee (such as a police officer) has violated the rights of a person protected by a state constitution.
D. a federal agent or employee (such as a police officer) has violated the rights of a person under the Constitution of the United States.
E. all of the above

A "tort" is:

A. a wrong committed by one individual against another not stemming from a contract relationship for which the law provides a remedy in money damages.
B. always punishable also by the state as a crime.
C. a broken contract.
D. in some cases also punishable by the state as a crime.
E. A and D above.

The process of public review of police conduct begins:

A. only after a civil lawsuit has been filed against an officer.
B. within the police department by the officers superiors.
C. when the prosecutor decides whether or not to file a charge based on the case made by the officer.
D. with the defense attorney representing the person arrested by the officer.
E. on the street, or wherever the initial police-citizen contact takes place.

An injunction is:

A. a declaration by a court which clarifies the legal rights and relationships between the parties to a lawsuit.
B. an order from a court directing that a person either do or refrain from doing a particular act.
C. an award of money damages.
D. an appeal of a criminal conviction.
E. where two highways meet.

A police officer is immune from criminal prosecution if the criminal act with which he is charged is performed while on duty.   T   F.

In a free society such as that of the United States, police officers could be very ineffective without public support, and public support is damaged when police officers disregard the very laws they are supposed to enforce.   T   F.

§ 2.4 OTHER JUDICIAL REMEDIES

In court proceedings, police officers must realize that they are perceived by judges as being "officers of the court." Under the Fourteenth Amendment due process standard, police officers and the prosecution team have a duty to disclose evidence favorable to the defendant. *Arizona v. Youngblood*, 109 S. Ct. 333 (1988).

Disclosure by the prosecution of evidence favorable to the defendant illustrates the central purpose of the American court system: to seek and find the truth. In both criminal and civil cases, the presiding judge is given great discretion (guided by court rules of procedure and evidence) in administering litigation. Police officers must obey court orders and help maintain the decorum of the court. If a police officer disobeys an order to appear at a court hearing, or disobeys a court order to initiate or to refrain from a certain practice, or if he commits perjury in a legal pleading or in testimony, the court may bring a civil or criminal action against him, as well as finding him direct or indirect contempt of court.

A citizen can also sue police departments and officers in civil actions commonly referred to as declaratory judgment or injunctive relief lawsuits.

Black's Law Dictionary (Revised 4th ed., 1968, p. 497) defines the term "declaratory judgment" as follows:

DECLARATORY JUDGMENT. One which simply declares the rights of the parties or expresses the opinion of the court on a question of law, without ordering anything to be done. Its distinctive characteristics are that no executory process follows as of course, nor is it necessary that an actual wrong, giving rise to action for damages, should have been done, or be immediately threatened (citations omitted).

Black's Law Dictionary (Revised 4th ed., 1968, p. 923) defines the term "injunction" as follows:

INJUNCTION. A prohibitive writ issued by a court of equity, at the suit of a party complainant, directed to a party defendant in the action, or to a party made a defendant for that purpose, forbidding the latter to do some act, or to permit his servants or agents to do some act, which he is threatening or attempting to commit, or restraining him in the continuance thereof, such act being unjust and inequitable, injurious to the plaintiff, and not such as can be adequately redressed by an action at law (citations omitted).

Injunctions can be temporary, preliminary, or final/permanent in nature. This legal process is resorted to when the plaintiff in a civil lawsuit, rather than seeking monetary damages for police misconduct, is actually seeking a court order to stop some form of ongoing police misconduct.

--------------------------------------- **Notes** ---------------------------------------

Sample Questions

The idea behind the award of money damages to a plaintiff who has won a civil damage lawsuit is:

A. purely and simply to punish the defendant.
B. to humiliate the defendant publicly.
C. to order the wrongdoer to pay a sum of money to the person injured or damaged by the defendant's act to compensate him for the injury or damage.
D. to enforce concepts of responsibility under the law.
E. both C and D are correct.

Standards by which police conduct is judged for the purpose of determining possible civil liability include:

A. federal and state constitutions and statutes.
B. federal and state case law.
C. police department regulations.
D. all of the above.
E. only A and C above.

The test used to determine whether a police officer is entitled to qualified immunity from money damages is:

A. a subjective test which considers primarily the state of mind of the defendant-officer.
B. the same test used to determine the immunity of judges.
C. the same test used to determine the immunity of legislators.
D. a test which considers the *objective* reasonableness of the officer's actions.
E. none of the above are true.

Federal law enforcement officers cannot be liable in damages under the Federal Civil Rights Act because it is directed at actions taken under color of *state* law, but they can be held liable under other remedies recognized by the law. T F.

A "tort" is a wrong committed by one individual against another which can result in a civil damage lawsuit. T F.

Some torts are also punishable as crimes. T F.

An example of a tort which can also be punishable as a crime is an unprivileged battery. T F.

If a police officer's negligence damages a citizen, he might be sued in state court for civil damages, but not liable under the Federal Civil Rights Act because the damage did not violate a federally-protected constitutional right. T F.

To determine the objective reasonableness of an officer's actions, the court will determine whether or not a clearly-established standard of conduct existed at the time the officer acted, and further, whether the officer reasonably should have been aware of the standard. T F.

§ 2.5 ADMINISTRATIVE DISCIPLINARY ACTIONS

Administrative remedies against police misconduct are often initiated because of a citizen's complaint against a particular police officer, but in the end the use of this remedy depends upon the law enforcement profession's enthusiasm for policing itself. The quality and quantity of the department's internal rules and regulations; the existence of an internal review system; the commitment of a department's leaders to taking disciplinary action against officers for police misconduct; and the rank and file's dedication to professional excellence — these are the factors that determine to what extent administrative disciplinary actions will be initiated.

It is important to note that administrative action is the one remedy for police misconduct that has a direct bearing on the officer's job status, and as such it has great importance for him. This remedy can be utilized even if others (such as civil lawsuits) are not resorted to; that is administrative action is totally independent of the other remedies for police misconduct discussed in this chapter.

------------------------------------- **Notes** -------------------------------------

Sample Questions

There is an old saying (that is generally true), that for every wrong, the law provides a "remedy".   (T)   F.

Lawsuits for damages, injunctive relief, contempt of court proceedings, administrative disciplinary action, and exclusionary rules of evidence all have one thing in common — they have been used by the law as remedies for police misconduct.   T   F.

If a county, city, or town police agency displays "deliberate indifference" to the training needs of its police officers — as a matter of policy — that county, city, or town can be sued under the Federal Civil Rights Act if that policy of lack of appropriate training causes the violation of a citizen's federally-protected rights, and the damages awarded can be collected from the public treasury.   T   F.

Placing a prisoner in a cell with other prisoners when there is a reason to believe he might be abused or injured by them is an example of police conduct that might result in civil liability if, in fact, the prisoner is abused or injured.   (T)   F.

Police officers, who carry out an *executive* function in enforcing the law, have only *qualified* immunity from money damages.   T   F.

The Federal Civil Rights Act provides a remedy in money damages for wrongful action taken under "color of" state law which violates a federally-protected right. Examples of action taken under "color of" state law would include:

A. a wrongful arrest not based on probable cause which resulted in loss of liberty to the person arrested.
B. use of deadly force by the police for the sole purpose of capturing a fleeing misdemeanant.
C. use of deadly force by one private citizen against another to settle a love-triangle dispute.
D. forced entry into a private home by the police without a warrant and without exigent circumstances orther lawful privilege.
E. A, B, and D above.

If a police officer is sued for damages under the federal Civil Rights Act:

A. the usual common-law defenses of good faith and probable cause will not be a valid defense.
B. good faith and probable cause will not even be relevant as a defense.
C. A and B above.
D. good faith and probable cause will usually be a valid defense.
E. the only valid defense is "acting under superior orders".

The Supreme Court of the United States has ruled, in effect, that action taken by local police under a local ordinance can still be considered as action taken under *state* law.   T   F.

Before the case of *Mapp v. Ohio* was decided, many of the states considered the Fourth Amendment exclusionary rule to be just a rule of evidence that was enforced in the federal courts.   T   F.

§ 2.6 EXCLUSION OF EVIDENCE — THE FOURTH AMENDMENT EXCLUSIONARY RULE

(A) At first, a federal rule of evidence

In *Weeks v. United States*, 34 S. Ct. 341 (1914) the Supreme Court held that in a *federal* prosecution, the Fourth Amendment barred the use of evidence which was the product of unreasonable search and seizure. Because the case grew out of a federal prosecution rather than that of a state and because the Supreme Court unquestionably could exercise its "supervisory" power or jurisdiction over lower federal proceedings, the *Weeks* rule was considered to be merely a federal rule of evidence which the states could follow or reject at their discretion.

CASE BRIEF
Weeks v. United States 34 S. Ct. 341 (1914)

Majority opinion: Day.

FACTS: D was indicted for, among other offenses, the federal crime of using the mails to transport documents used in a gambling enterprise. Police officers went to D's home without a warrant of any kind and, upon learning from a neighbor where the key was kept, entered and searched D's room; they seized various papers and articles which were later turned over to a United States marshal. Later the same day the officers returned with the marshal in search of additional evidence, which they also seized without a warrant. As was the customary procedure in 1914, D, prior to trial, made a timely application for the return to him of seized items. This application was denied by the court prior to and again at the beginning of the trial although D alleged violation of his Fourth Amendment right against unreasonable search and seizure. Some of the items seized were used in evidence against D. It was contended by the government that the Court relied on the correct rule of law under these circumstances—that the evidence, being competent, having come under the control of the court, it would not inquire into the manner in which it had been obtained. D was convicted and he appealed.

ISSUE: In a federal prosecution, is it proper for a court to admit into evidence items obtained by the government as a result of an unreasonable search and seizure?

DECISION: No; reversed.

REASONS: The history of the Fourth Amendment indicates that it is intended to further those safeguards developed in England as a result of abuses under the general warrant and in the American colonies under writs of assistance. A man's home is his castle, not to be invaded by any general authority to search and seize his goods and papers. Even in case of felony the sheriff must be furnished with a warrant and take great care lest he commit a trespass. These matters affect the very essence of constitutional liberty and security—the invasion of the indefeasible rights of personal security, personal liberty and private property where these rights have not been foreited by the conviction of some public offense.

The effect of the 4th Amendment is to put the courts of the United States and Federal officials, in the exercise of such power and authority, under limitations and restraints, as to the exercise of such power and authority, and to forever secure the people, their persons, houses, papers and effects, against all unreasonable searches and seizures under the guise of law. This protection reaches all alike, whether accused of crime or not, and the duty of giving to it force and effect is obligatory upon all entrusted under our Federal sytem with the enforcement of the laws. The tendency of those who execute the criminal laws of the country to obtain conviction by means of unlawful seizures and enforced confessions, the latter often obtained after subjecting accused persons to unwarranted practices destructive of rights secured by the Federal Constitution, should find no sanction in the judgments of the courts, which are charged at all times with the support of the Constitution, and to which people of all conditions have a right to appeal for the maintenance of such fundamental rights.

This is not a case involving the right of the government to search a person as an incident to arrest nor a case of challenged testimony offered at trial—this case involves the right of the court in a criminal case to retain as evidence items seized from D's house in his absence, and without his consent, by a United States marshal holding no warrant of arrest or search. If such items can be held and used as evidence, the protection of the Fourth Amendment is of no value and may as well be stricken from the Constitution.

Cases relied upon by the government in support of the rule that the court would not inquire into the manner in which competent evidence was obtained involved evidence incidentally seized during the execution of a legal warrant, or were otherwise inapplicable to this situation. There is prior case authority recognizing the right of the court to deal with papers and documents in the possession of the district attorney and other officers of the court.

We therefore reach the conclusion that the letters in question were taken from the house of the accused by an official of the United States, acting under color of his office, in direct violation of the constitutional rights of the defendant; that having made a seasonable application for their return, which was heard and passed upon by the court, there was involved in the order refusing the applicatlion a denial of the constitutional rights of the accused, and that the court should have restored these letters to the accused.

RULE: Evidence of a crime seized by federal officers in a manner that violates the accused's rights against unreasonable search and seizure under the Fourth Amendment should be returned to the accused upon timely motion therefor, and, such motion being denied, it is prejudicial error for the court to admit such evidence in a federal criminal trial.

-------------------------------------- **Notes** --------------------------------------

(B) Later, a rule of constitutional dimension

In 1949 the Supreme Court decided the case of *Wolf v. Colorado*, 69 S. Ct. 1359 (1949). At that time, only seventeen states had followed the federal example by adopting the exclusionary rule, while thirty states had rejected the suppression doctrine. In *Wolf* the Supreme Court stated that the *Weeks* ruling " * * * was not derived from the explicit requirements of the Fourth Amendment * * * "but was a matter of judicial implication. At that time the Court was not yet willing to extend the exclusionary rule to the states as a matter of Fourteenth Amendment due process, partly because so few of the states had adopted it voluntarily, and partly because those states which had rejected it had provided alternative civil remedies for victims of unreasonable searches and seizures.

CASE BRIEF
Mapp v. Ohio, 81 S. Ct. 1684 (1961)

Majority opinion: Clark. Dissenting: Harlan, Frankfurter, Whittaker.

FACTS: Police had information that a person they wanted to question was hiding in D's apartment, and also that D had a large quantity of policy paraphernalia there. They went to D's apartment and knocked on the door, demanding entrance. D, after calling her attorney, refused entrance to the police unless they had a warrant. The police left but came back later and forced entry to the apartment. D's attorney arrived but the police would not let him see D or enter the apartment. When D demanded to see a search warrant, one of the officers held up a piece of paper; D grabbed it and put it down the front of her dress. A struggle ensued and the police recovered the paper and handcuffed D because she was being " belligerent." An officer twisted D's hand and she yelled and pleaded with him because it hurt. The police then forcibly took D to the second floor, which they searched. They also searched the basement and the entire living quarters. In the course of this widespread search the police discovered some obscene material in a trunk, and D was arrested, tried, and convicted for possession of obscene material. No search warrant was produced at the trial. The Supreme Court of Ohio noted that "a reasonable argument" could be made for reversal of the conviction because of the methods employed to obtain the evidence, but it upheld D's conviction. The state argued that the evidence was admissible even if the search was unreasonable, citing *Wolf v Colorado*, 69 S. Ct. 1359 (1949). The primary issue at the trial level and on appeal to the state appellate court was the constitutionality of the obscenity ordinance under which the arrest was made. The Supreme Court of the United States was urged to review the claim of unreasonable search and seizure.

ISSUE: In a state prosecution for a state crime, is the federal exclusionary rule (which up to this time had been thought to be optional under state law) required to be followed?

DECISION: Yes; reversed.

REASONS: *Wolf v. Colorado* held that a state's approval of police incursions into privacy would run counter to the due process clause of the Fourteenth Amendment. But because of factual considerations in the Supreme Court was unwilling to apply the exclusionary rule against the states in 1949. In that year two-thirds of the states were opposed to the requirement of the exclusionary rule, but since that time one-half of the states passing on the question have adopted the rule on their own. The California supreme court adopted the exclusionary rule because other remedies for deterring police misconduct, such as civil damages and internal discipline, have failed. Also, since *Wolf, Elkins v. United States*, 80 S. Ct. 1437 (1960) discarded the "silver platter" doctrine, and other cases have relaxed the requirement of standing to challenge illegally seized evidence. Moreover, *Rea v. United States*, 76 S. Ct. 292 (1956) outlawed the state use of evidence illegally seized by federal agents. Therefore, the factual basis for the *Wolf* decision is no longer controlling.

Evidence seized in violation of the Fourth Amendment is also inadmissible in a state court. Allowing the states to use unlawfully seized evidence would encourage disobedience to the federal Constitution, which the states are bound to uphold. The ruling also avoids conflict in the federal system by eliminating the double standard, and it encourages federal-state cooperation. If the government is allowed to become a law-breaker in enforcing the law, it breeds contempt for the law and invites every man to become a law unto himself, thus inviting anarchy. The F.B.I. has operated efficiently under this rule for years and there is no reason why state and local police should not observe it also.

RULE: The Fourth Amendment guarantee against unreasonable searches and seizures applies directly in a federal prosecution and as a matter of Fourteenth Amendment due process of law in a state prosecution. In order to prevent a double standard of law enforcement and to prohibit unlawfulness in law enforcement, the exclusionary rule is applicable as a means to enforce the provisions of the Fourth Amendment both on a federal and a state level. Therefore, any evidence obtained as a product of an unreasonable search and seizure is inadmissible in either a federal or a state prosecution.

CONCURRING: The exclusionary doctrine is not a constitutional command of the Fourth Amendment, but instead a judicially created rule of evidence which Congress might repeal. But if the exclusionary rule is a means of enforcing the Fifth Amendment self-incrimination clause, the Fourth Amendment guarantee against unreasonable search and seizure is entitled to no less sanction. The "shocks the conscience" test of *Rochin v. California*, 72 S. Ct. 205 (1952) is too vague and indefinite.

DISSENTING: The central issue of this case was the constitutionality of the Ohio obscenity provision, not the search and seizure issue. Five members of the Court have "reached out" to overrule *Wolf v. Colorado* in variance with the rule that constitutional issues, will be avoided wherever possible. Here, the Court chose between two constitutional issues, one of which was formally presented and argued and one of which was not even argued. The least the Court could do would be to set the case down for reargument on the search and seizure issues. The means chosen by the Court to enforce the Fourth Amendment on the federal level are not absolutely necessary to maintain the "concept of ordered liberty" on the state level. There is not the slightest suggestion here that Ohio affirmatively approved the unreasonable search and seizure; it recognized that it was wrong. The real issue here is whether the state should be constitutionally free to use or not to use the exclusionary rule. Due process of law should allow a flexible course rather than a fixed and rigid one. A state criminal conviction comes to the Court as a finished product. The Court's task is not over-all supervision of state criminal procedure and rules of evidence, but rather to determine whether the prosecution was constitutionally fair. Also, the reasoning behind exclusion of statements under the Fifth Amendment (fairness and trustworthiness) does not necessarily apply to the exclusion of physical evidence under the Fourth Amendment.

--------------------------------------- **Notes** ---------------------------------------

(C) Criticisms and the good faith exception

Too often, the most bizarre and outrageous police conduct conceivable is the foundation upon which the Supreme Court of the United States bases major interpretations of the Constitution. This was the case in *Mapp v. Ohio*, briefed above. By 1961, as the Court observed in *Mapp*, more than one-half of the states passing on the exclusionary rule since *Wolf v. Colorado*, 69 S. Ct. 1359 (1949) had adopted the federal position and several significant decisions since *Wolf* had altered the legal climate. As a result of *Mapp* the Fourth Amendment guarantee against unreasonable searches and seizures came to be enforceable against the states by use of the same sanction which long before had been adopted in the federal system—the exclusionary rule—as a matter of Fourteenth amendment due process of law.

The exclusionary rule, that unlawfully seized evidence, though wholly relevant and material, is not admissible in a criminal trial, has not enjoyed unanimous support by legal commentators. Perhaps the most widely known critic of the rule was Chief Justice Warren Burger of the Supreme Court. In his dissent in *Bivens v. Six Unknown Named Agents*, 91 S. Ct. 1999 (1971) the Chief Justice suggested that the practice of suppressing unlawfully seized evidence be replaced with a statutory remedy to be enacted by Congress which would waive sovereign immunity and create a cause of action in damages for a person aggrieved by the action of government agents violating his Fourth Amendment rights. This remedy would be in lieu of the suppression of the evidence unlawfully seized. The tests for admissibility of evidence, however obtained by police, would be its relevance and materiality. The states could each enact similar statues replacing the rule.

Chief Justice Burger reasoned that the exclusionary rule has failed because it is not a realistic deterrent against police misconduct in the enforcement of the law. He urged that his proposed damages remedy would be a more direct deterrent and that it would not reward the criminal for the misconduct of the police. The full burden of the rule, he said, falls on the prosecutor, not on the police and society pays the price when countless guilty criminals are freed to continue their crimes because evidence against them is suppressed. Chief Justice Burger's suggestion that the exclusionary rule be abandoned entirely was never adopted by a majority of the Court.

Other disadvantages of the exclusionary rule are that it has no deterrent effect on police misconduct when the police aim is harrassment rather than criminal prosecution; that it allows dishonest authorities to appear to enforce the law, although in violation of the Fourth Amendment; and that, when evidence is suppressed, the public indignation is directed at the courts, rather than at the police.

One of the most valid criticisms of the exclusionary rule that continued to be expressed in the court opinions was that it applied with equal force to enforcement blunders made in good faith and those committed intentionally or recklessly. If the primary purpose of the rule was the deterrence of deliberate police misconduct, it made very little sense to apply it in situations in which police believed in good faith that they were performing their duties properly. In *Illinois v. Gates*, 103 S. Ct. 2317 (1983), briefed in sec. 4.14(A), the Supreme Court passed up an opportunity to rule on a "good faith exception" to the exclusionary rule because the point had not been properly raised in the state courts.

In the cases of *Massachusetts v. Sheppard*, 104 S. Ct. 3424 (1984) and *United States v. Leon*, 104 S. Ct. 3405 (1984), both of which are briefed below, the Court made it clear that a good faith exception to the exclusionary rule would be recognized as a matter of Fourth Amendment law when police officers proceeded *under the authority of a warrant* in the belief that they were authorized thereby to search or seize. Most (but not all) of the states have recognized this exception to the exclusionary rule under state law as well.

CASE BRIEF
United States v. Leon, 104 S. Ct. 3405 (1984)

Majority opinion: White, joined by Burger, C.J., Blackmun, Powell, Rehnquist and O'Connor. Concurring: Blackmun. Dissenting: Brennan, Marshall, and Stevens.

FACTS: City police, following information supplied by a confidential informant of unproven reliability, conducted an extensive investigation into alleged drug sales by the defendants. The investigation involved surveillance of three different residences and the activities and identities of persons observed there; examination of their previous criminal records; and a consent search of D's luggage at an airport, which revealed a small amount of marijuana. Based on the investigation, one of the officers, an experienced and well-trained narcotics investigator, prepared an affidavit for a warrant to search the three residences and the defendants' automobiles for an extensive list of drug-related items. The affidavit was reviewed by several deputy prosecutors; a state superior court judge issued a facially valid search warrant based on the affidavit. The searches produced large quantities of drugs and other incriminating evidence. The defendants were indicted by a federal grand jury and charged with conspiracy to possess and distribute drugs, as well as several other crimes.

The defendants filed motions to suppress the evidence seized pursuant to the warrant. The district court held a hearing and granted the motions except for evidence which some of the defendants lacked standing to challenge. At the government's request, the court made clear that the officer-affiant had acted in good faith; however, it rejected the suggestion that the exclusionary rule should not apply in cases where evidence is seized in good-faith reliance on a search warrant.

The government's motion for reconsideration was denied and a divided panel of the Court of Appeals for the Ninth Circuit affirmed, concluding that the affidavit did not establish probable cause because the informant's tip was fatally stale and because under *Aquilar v. Texas*, 84 S. Ct. 1509 (1964) and *Spinelli v. United States*, 89 S. Ct 584 (1969), it failed to establish the informant's reliability. The court of appeals also rejected the good-faith exception to the exclusionary rule. The government's petition for certiorari presented only the issue of the good faith exception; it did not challenge the lower court's determination of a lack of probable cause. Thus, although the Supreme Court might have disposed of this case under its ruling in *Illinois v. Gates*, 103 S. Ct. 2317 (1983) (probable cause under totality of circumstances replacing rigid *Aquilar-Spinelli* tests) it chose only to decide the issue squarely presented.

ISSUE: Should the Fourth Amendment exclusionary rule be modified to permit the use of evidence obtained by officers acting in reasonable reliance on a search warrant issued by a detached and neutral magistrate but ultimately found to be unsupported by probable cause?

DECISION: Yes; reversed.

REASONS: The Fourth Amendment has never been interpreted to forbid the introduction of illegally seized evidence in all proceedings or against all persons. The exclusionary rule cannot cure an invasion of a defendants' rights which has already occurred; it can only safeguard Fourth Amendment rights through its deterrent effect on the police. It is not in itself a constitutional right of the person whose rights have been violated. Whether the exclusionary sanction is appropriate in a particular case must be determined (as our past decisions make clear) by weighing societal costs against deterrent benefits. Indiscriminate application of the exclusionary rule may well generate disrespect for the law and the administration of justice. As with any remedial device, its application should be restricted to those cases where its objectives are best served.

We do not hesitate to apply the rule in cases where Fourth Amendment violations are substantial and deliberate (citing *Franks v. Delaware*, 98 S. Ct. 2674 (1978) and *Stone v. Powell*, 96 S. Ct. 3037 (1976)).(The Court then reviews past decisions in which a "balancing approach" has been used to determine whether the exclusion of evidence serves its primary deterrent purpose; the "standing" cases; the "dissipation of the primary taint" cases; and others in which the detrimental consequences of illegal police action has become so diluted that the deterrent effect of the exclusionary rule no longer justifies its costs.)

An important consideration is always an assessment of the flagancy of the police misconduct. Our decisions, as yet, have not recognized any form of good-faith exception to the Fourth Amendment exclusionary rule. But the balancing approach that has evolved during the years of experience with the exclusionary rule provides strong support for adoption of a good-faith exception.

Our past cases have expressed a strong preference for the use of warrants, where possible, and we have declared that in doubtful or marginal cases a search under a warrant may be upheld where one without it would fail (citing *United States v. Ventresca*, 85 S.Ct. 741 (1965) and *Aguilar v. Texas*). The preference for warrants is most appropriately aided by giving "great deference" to a magistrate's determination (citing *Spinelli*, *Gates*, and *Ventresca*). That deference is not without limits; inquiry can be made into the police — affiant's knowing or reckless falsity, and the magistrate must not merely serve as a "rubber stamp" for the police. A neutral and detached magistrate must always exercise his independent judgment, and the probable cause affidavit presented to him by the police must contain sufficient factual information, not merely bare conclusions. Reviewing courts may still disagree with the magistrate's analysis of the information in the affidavit or with the form of the warrant issued. But only in the case of deliberate or reckless falsity of the information presented by the police does the deterrent rationale of the exclusionary rule make sense. The exclusionary rule is designed to deter police misconduct—not to punish the police for the errors of judges or magistrates. There is no reason to believe that judges and magistrates are inclined to disobey the Fourth Amendment or that exclusion of evidence would have a deterrent effect on them. They are not members of the law enforcement "team", and as neutral judicial officers, they have no stake in the outcome of criminal cases. Their professional incentives to comply with the Fourth Amendment should not be affected by the adoption of a good-faith exception to the exclusionary rule.

If the exclusionary rule is to achieve its intended purpose, it should be applied only in cases where the police have engaged in willful, or at the very least, negligent, conduct that has deprived a defendant of some right. This usage of the rule should instill in officers a greater degree of care toward the rights of an accused. To exclude evidence when an officer has proceeded in an objectively reasonable, good-faith manner, perhaps because of a technical and not at all obvious mistake by the magistrate, will not further the purpose of the exclusionary rule in any respects.

We conclude that the marginal or nonexistent benefits of suppressing evidence obtained in objectively reasonable reliance on a subsequently invalidated search warrant cannot justify the cost of exclusion. But we do not suggest that exclusion will never be appropriate; it will continue to be proper in cases of false affidavits for cases where police—affiants show reckless disregard for the truth or where the warrant is obviously lacking in specificity or otherwise so obviously facially deficient that a reasonable officer could not presume it to be valid.

RULE: The Fourth Amendment exclusionary rule is a judicially-created deterrent against police misconduct; it is not a constitutional right of the accused whose rights may have been violated by the police. When searches are conducted under a search warrant issued by proper authority, suppression of evidence seized by a search warrant is appropriate only if the police were dishonest or reckless in preparing their affidavit or if they could not have objectively and reasonably believed in good faith in the existence of probable cause or the facial validity of the warrant.

CONCURRING: Police should realize that, because the application of the exclusionary rule is a judical determination, future abuse of the "good faith" exception to it may result in a returen to a broader application of the rule.

DISSENT: The majority opinion is based primarily on expediency. The Fourth Amendment restricts the actions of government generally, including the judiciary—not just the police. Admitting illegally seized evidence in a trial is just as wrong as seizing it in the first place. The exclusionary rule is more than a mere judicially-created deterrent. It is the only effective means of directly enforcing the Fourth Amendment; it is therefore a constitutional right of the accused. The government's case would not have been destroyed by rejecting the good faith exception; much of the evidence was admissible because of the defendants' lack of standing to challenge it. The majority gives no clear illustration of the great societal costs of the exclusionary rule. The good faith exception will lead to further abuses by the police, and it was not needed, especially in view of the relaxed standards of probable cause under *Illinois v. Gates*. The Court should not have reached out to decide the good faith issue, but rather should have remanded this case to the Court of Appeals for reconsideration in light of *Gates*.

CASE BRIEF
Massachusetts v. Sheppard, 104 S. Ct. 3424 (1984)

Majority opinion: White, joined by Burger, C.J., Blackmun, Powell, Rehnquist and O'Connor. Concurring in judgment: Stevens. Dissenting: Brennan and Marshall.

FACTS: The burned body of a female murder victim was discovered in a vacant lot. An autopsy revealed the victim was killed by multiple compound skull fractures caused by blows to the head. The police questioned D, one of the victim's boyfriends, and he offered the alibi that he had been at an all-night card game the night of the murder. To check out the alibi, police interviewed other persons who had been at the card game and learned that D had borrowed a car about 3:00 a.m. to give two men a ride home, and although the trip would normally take only fifteen minutes, D had not returned until nearly 5:00 a.m. Police then visited the owner of the borrowed car who consented to their inspection of the vehicle. They found bloodstains and hair in the trunk and on the rear bumper and strands of wire similar to wire found on and near the victim's body. The owner stated he had not noticed the bloodstains the last time he had used the car before lending it to D.

A detective drafted an affidavit for arrest and search warrants, setting forth the results of the investigation and stating the items to be searched for. He then showed the affidavit to the district attorney and his assistant, and to a sergeant, all of whom agreed it set forth probable cause for the arrest and search. Because it was Sunday and the courts were closed, police had difficulty finding proper warrant application forms; finally they used a form previously used in another police district for drug cases, realizing that changes in the form would be necessary. Some changes were made using a typewriter, but not all "controlled substances" references were deleted. The detective took the completed form to the home of a judge who had agreed to consider the warrant application. Upon examining the affidavit, the judge agreed to authorize the search. The detective then gave him the warrant form, pointing out that it was an altered form, designed for use in drug cases, and showing the judge the changes that he had made. The judge, unable to find a more suitable form, informed the detective that he would make the changes necessary to provide him with a proper search warrant. The judge then made some changes on the form and dated and signed it. But he failed to change the substantive part of the warrant, authorizing search for drugs only; nor did he alter the form so as to incorporate the affidavit. The judge then gave the affidavit and warrant to the detective, telling him that the warrant was sufficient in form and content to carry out the search as requested. The warrant was served, D's residence was searched, and several items of incriminating evidence were found. D was charged with murder.

At a pre-trial suppression hearing, the judge concluded that although the warrant was faulty in that it did not meet the particularity requirements of the Fourth Amendment, its evidence was admisible because the police had acted in good faith, reasonably believing the warrant to be valid. D was tried and convicted. On appeal, D argued that the evidence obtained under the defective warrant should have been suppressed. The Supreme Court of Massachusetts agreed, reversing D's conviction. The Supreme Court of the United States granted certiorari.

ISSUE: Having already decided that the exclusionary rule should not be applied when an officer acts in objectively reasonable reliance on a warrant later determined to be invalid, the sole issue here is whether the officers in this case had an objectively reasonable basis for their belief that the search they conducted was authorized by a valid warrant.

DECISION: Police acted in good faith under a warrant; reversed.

REASONS: The officers here did everything that could reasonably have been expected of them. The affidavit for the warrant was reviewd and approved by the prosecutor and his assistant. It was then presented to a neutral judge who concluded that it stated probable cause for a search of D's residence. The warrant form was then presented to the judge and the judge was told that certain changes in the form had been made and that other changes might be necessary. The officer observed the judge as he made further changes in the form and then received the warrant and affidavit back with the judge's assurance that it was valid. At this point, a reasonable officer would have concluded that the warrant authorized a search for the items specified.

We refuse to rule than an officer is required to disbelieve a judge who has advised him, by word and action, that the warrant he possesses authorizes him to conduct the search he has requested. In Massachusetts, as in most other jurisdictions, the determinations of a judge acting within his jurisdiction, even if erroneous, are valid and binding until set aside by a recognized procedure. If an officer is required to accept at face value a judge's conclusion that a warrant is bad, there is little reason why he should be expected to disregard assurances that the form is good—especially, as here, when he has alerted the judge to potential problem of form of the warrant.

In sum, the police conduct here was objectively reasonable and largely error-free. If there was an error, it was the judge, not the officer, who made the critical mistake. Since the exclusionary rule was adopted to deter unlawful *police* conduct, and not to punish them for the errors of magistrates and judges, there is no purpose to be served by suppressing the evidence seized in this case.

RULE: If the police seize evidence under a regularly issued search warrant in the objectively reasonable good-faith belief that the warrant legally authorized the seizure of those items, federal law does not require the suppression of the evidence because it is later determined that the issuing judge was mistaken as to the validity of the form of the warrant.

The Supreme Court's adoption of the good faith exception was not a complete surprise to court watchers. Earlier decisions had been based on the deterrent purpose of the rule and the inappropriateness of blindly applying it, to the benefit of the defendant, when its purpose of deterring police misconduct would not be served. The Court developed a "balancing test" in these cases.

In *Stone v. Powell*, 96 S. Ct. 3037 (1976), the Court identified the primary justification for the rule as being the deterrence of police practices that violate Fourth Amendment rights. It then proceeded to deny federal habeas corpus relief to a state prisoner who had already received full and fair litigation of his Fourth Amendment claim on the state level; the Court held that the additional deterent effect provided by federal review would be outweighed by the societal costs of such review. In *United States v. Calandra*, 94 S. Ct. 613 (1974), the Court refused to apply the rule to a grand jury proceeding where the questions put to a witness were based on evidence which was the product of an unreasonable search and seizure. In both of these cases the Supreme Court seemed to be balancing the potential deterrent effect of an extension of the rule against the cost to society in less efficient law enforcement. In his dissent in *Stone*, Justice White expressed a willingness to limit the rule to those cases in which an officer acted in bad faith.

The good faith exception to the exclusionary rule established by *United States v. Leon* and *Massachusetts v. Sheppard* was extended further in *Illinois v. Krull*, 107 S. Ct. 1160 (1987). The good faith exception was limited in *Leon* and *Sheppard* to cases in which an officer acted in the good faith reliance on a judicially-issued warrant apparently valid on its face. In *Krull* it was applied to actions taken under a state statute reasonably thought to be valid at the time but later determined to be unconstitutional. The statute in question authorized administrative police inspections (searches) of licensed dealers in automotive parts and scrap metal (junk yards); it was later declared to be unconstitutional, because it gave state officials too much discretion to decide whom, when, and how long to search. Under the statute, stolen vehicles were discovered by the police and used as a basis for making arrests. The vehicles were suppressed as evidence after the statute was found to be unconstitutional. A five-member majority of the Supreme Court held that the stolen vehicles should not have been suppressed as evidence, because the police acted in reasonable good-faith reliance on the statute which authorized their action, the Court once again stressed that the prime purpose of the exclusionary rule is to deter future unlawful police conduct and that this purpose would be not served by applying it where an officer acts in good faith reliance on the validity of a statute, any more then where he acts in good-faith reliance on the validity of a warrant. The Court noted that similar statutes authorizing warrantless administrative searches of closely-regulated business activities have been upheld as constitutional in the past and that in the present case, police reliance on the statue was "objectively reasonable".

Dissenting, Justice O'Connor, joined by Justice Brennan, Marshall and Stevens, argued that the majority opinion was not a logical extension of *Leon* and

Sheppard. The historical resentment against legislatively-authorized general searches by writs of assistance was, after all, the moving force behind the Fourth Amendment. Justice O'Connor was also critical of the application of the good faith exception in cases involving reliance on statutes, because it implies that at some point a reasonable officer should recognize that a statute is unconstitutional; it is "not apparent how much consitutional law the reasonable officer is expected to know."

In another case turning on the reasonable good faith of the police after securing a warrant, the Court ruled in *Maryland v. Garrison*, 107 S. Ct. 1013 (1987) that when, notwithstanding diligent and good-faith efforts to determine and describe specifically the place to be searched, the search warrant description of that place is nevertheless worded too broadly, a search by mistake of another nearby place, reasonably believed by police to be within the warrant description, will be lawful up to the point of discovery of the mistake, at which point the search should be discontinued.

------------------------------------- **Notes** -------------------------------------

Sample Questions

If a police officer takes enforcement action under a state law that is later declared to be unconstitutional:

A. if he is sued for damages after the law is declared unconstitutional he will be held liable in damages because the police are not entitled to take action under unconstitutional statutes.
B. if he acted in the good faith belief that the law was valid and he had no reason to believe otherwise, he will not incur civil liability for so acting.
C. he will probably not be held liable solely for acting under such a law because the courts do not expect police officers to be able to foresee the future course of constitutional law.
D. he will be subject to removal from office for such action.
E. B and C above.

People who are against the use of exclusionary rules as a means to police the conduct of the police have argued that:

A. the police are really not "penalized" by the use of such rules, and if anyone suffers from the consequences of the rules, it is probably the prosecuting attorney, who in most jurisdictions, has no direct control over the actions of the police.
B. it doesn't make much sense to reward one wrongdoer for the misconduct of another.
C. the exclusionary rules can be misused by corrupt police and prosecutors by allowing the appearance of vigorous law enforcement with the knowledge that evidence will be suppressed, thereby shifting the uninformed public blame to the courts, who must enforce the rules.
D. the exclusionary rules themselves will have little effect on police misconduct because the average policeman doesn't read appellate court opinions and therefore doesn't understand the reason why perfectly relevant and material evidence is excluded.
E. all of the above are true.

There are many reasons why the conduct of the police in the United States is subjected to such extensive review. Among these reasons are:

A. the people who wrote our constitution and Bill of Rights feared arbitrary government more than they feared crime by private individuals.
B. in a free society many people believe that if governmental police power is unchecked, the result will be a "police state".
C. in our society, while most people do support the police, at the same time there is a deep-seated fear of and resentment against governmental intervention in the private lives of citizens, and the uniformed police are the most visible symbol of the government.
D. the American people have a high regard for individual rights as opposed to governmental rights.
E. all of the above are true.

§ 2.7 MEETING THE CHALLENGE

American police officers do not perform their services involuntarily. They are not drafted into police service unwillingly, as civilians have been drafted into military service. On the contrary, there is keen competition for law enforcement positions. Many departments and agencies have the luxury of accepting only the "cream of the crop" of available applicants.

The United States Marines use as a recruiting slogan the assertion that they are looking for *"a few good men"*. This slogan could also apply to American law enforcement. As we have indicated in the preceding sections, the critical review process subjects officers to unbelievable scrutiny in which every word and action is examined and judged by extremely high standards of conduct. What an "ordinary" person would do in a given situation is not the standard by which a modern police officer is judged; our legal system expects him to be "extraordinary". Moreover a new standard is evolving in the case law — that of the "reasonably well-trained officer".

No person, attracted to the supposed glamour and adventure of a police career, and no one who is sincerely interested in law enforcement as an essential public service, should enter into that calling without the clearest understanding of the personal sacrifice, self-restraint, and high professional standard that will be required.

If that message is understood, and if police applicants strive to meet that professional challenge, we Americans should be very pleased. There is no higher or more honorable calling in a free society than that of becoming an honest and dedicated keeper of the peace. Without people willing to take risks, there would have been no Declaration of Independence; without the spirit of volunteerism and adventure, no Americans on the moon.

American police are often maligned, poorly compensated, and insufficiently appreciated by the public they serve. They are held to a standard of excellence disproportionate to their meager rewards. We should be thankful that, under these conditions, fine young men and women continue to step forward every day to meet this professional challenge.

-------------------------------------- **Notes** --------------------------------------

Sample Questions

A well-trained police officer with a professional attitude toward his job, and one who reasonably keeps up with changing developments in the law, and whose job performance reflects this, has little reason to worry about job-related civil liability in damages.   T   F.

Generally speaking, before one individual may be found by the courts to be "liable" in money damages to another individual:

A. the individual found to be liable must have breached some duty owed to the other individual by failing to follow a specific standard of care that flows from that duty.
B. a civil complaint will have to be filed with the court by the plaintiff.
C. the complaint filed by the plaintiff will have to state what the court recognizes as a legal "cause of action".
D. all of the above are true.
E. a complaint must be filed in Federal Court.

The Federal Civil Rights Act was enacted by Congress for the purpose of protecting rights secured by the Constitution of the United States from being violated by persons acting under color of *state* law.   T   F.

A police officer acts under "color of state law" within the meaning of the Federal Civil Rights Act when he misuses power possessed by virtue of state law and made possible only because he is clothed with the authority of state law; "state" includes political subdivisions of the state: and one power which has a great potential for misuse is the authority to arrest and use force.   T   F.

In our society, which stresses freedom, individual liberty, and the right of the people to "petition the government for a redress of grievances", the police holding a citizen "incommunicado", (refusing to let him contact a lawyer, friends, or family — even through he may be properly under arrest), is a situation which may incur civil liablility in damages for the police.   T   F.

In some civil cases against police officers it is possible for the losing defendant-policeman to be assessed the costs of the plaintiff's attorney fees, which in some cases may be greater than the damages awarded.   T   F.

CHAPTER 3

THE POLICE AND FIRST AMENDMENT RIGHTS

Section:
3.1 Introduction
3.2 Freedom of religion
3.3 Freedom of speech
3.4 Freedom of the press
3.5 Freedom of assembly and petition
3.6 Summary

§ 3.1 INTRODUCTION

Congress shall make no law respecting an establishment of religion, or prohibiting the free exercise thereof; or abridging the freedom of speech, or of the press; or the right of the people peaceably to assemble, and to petition the government for a redress of grievances. *Constitution of The United States, Amendment 1.*

The First Amendment has been considered a bulwark of freedoms for individuals since its ratification. Freedom of expression has been recognized as one of the preeminent rights of Western democratic theory, the touchstone of individual liberty. The great Justice Cardozo characterized it as ". . . the matrix, the indispensable condition of nearly every other form of freedom." *Palko v. Connecticut*, 58 S. Ct. 149 (1937). We, in law enforcement, always should remember what Justice Holmes observed, ". . . it is . . . not free thought for those who agree with us, but *freedom for the thought that we hate,*" which gives the theory of freedom of expression its most enduring value. *United States v. Schwimmer,* 49 S. Ct. 448 at 451 (1929). "Throughout human history, governments have sought to silence disagreeable persons. Their pamphleteering might stir political debate, their blasphemies religious revulsion, their pornographies sexual anarchy. The impulse to still these perils is worldwide; it has afflicted all governments at all times in all societies, including ours today." Lieberman, The Enduring Constitution, A Bicentennial Perspective (West, 1987) p. 216.

The First Amendment reserves to the people sovereignty in the important spheres protected by the First Amendment such as freedom of thought, conscience, expression, worship and affiliation. This is not only a remarkable philosophical doctrine but an even more remarkable political accomplishment.

-------------------------------------- **Notes** --------------------------------------

Sample Questions

The First Amendment covers the following subjects:

A. freedom from unreasonable searches and seizures.
B. privilege against compulsory self-incrimination.
C. right to counsel.
D. freedom of religion, speech, press, assembly and petition.
E. all of the above.

The First Amendment often causes public turmoil because:

A. it protects the rights of persons to speak out for unpopular causes.
B. it protects the rights of persons to criticize public officials, including the police.
C. it protects those who take political positions which to some people seem to be "anti-American."
D. not all persons have the same idea of what is immoral or shocking.
E. all of the above.

The First Amendment, as interpreted by the courts, protects against:

A. thought control dictated by the government.
B. religious preference dictated by the government.
C. censorship of the press.
D. holding prisoners in a totally "incommunicado" manner.
E. all of the above.

Under the First Amendment, with few exceptions, a person's freedom to *practice* his religious beliefs *can* be controlled by governmental actions, but only when:

A. the religious practice violates a criminal law and/or endangers someone else.
B. the Islamic religion is involved.
C. atheism is involved.
D. the religious practice violates a compelling state interest.
E. A and D above.

In the United States, the officially sanctioned religion of the people is the President's religious preference.   T   F.

The Constitution clearly defines what a religion is.   T   F.

Because the First Amendement states that, "*Congress* shall make no law respecting an establishment of religion, or prohibiting the free exercise thereof; . . . ," the states are unaffected.   T   F.

In a free society such as that of the United States, freedom of speech, (and all forms of Constitutionally-protected expression), are especially important because without these freedoms the people could not exchange the political and social ideas necessary to make important decisions in our representative form of government.   T   F.

One of the most difficult tasks for a police officer in the United States is that of enforcing laws which affect First Amendment values.   T   F.

§3.2 FREEDOM OF RELIGION

There are two clauses of the First Amendment dealing with the subject of religion. The first clause is referred to as the "establishment clause" which mandates that " Congress shall make no law respecting an establishment of religion . . ." and the second clause is referred to as the "free exercise clause" which mandates that Congress shall make no law "prohibiting the free exercise thereof . . ." There is a natural antagonism between a command not to establish religion and a command not to inhibit its practice. The opposing values require that the government act to achieve only secular goals and achieve them in a religiously neutral manner. This is easier said than done.

The "establishment clause" does not impact on criminal law; however the "free exercise clause" does. The first Supreme Court decision in this arena was *Reynolds v. United States* 98 U.S. 145 (1879), which upheld the application of a federal law prohibiting polygamy to a Mormon whose religion required him to engage in that practice. The Court in *Wisconsin v. Yoder* 92 S.Ct. 1526 (1972) employed a two part balancing test to hold that Wisconsin could not require members of the Amish Church to send their children to public schools after the eighth grade. The test balances the burden of the regulation on the free exercise of religion against the importance of the state's interest in the regulation and the degree to which it would be impaired by a religious exemption. The California Supreme Court applied this test in 1964 in *People v. Woody*, 394 P.2d 813 and held that a statute prohibiting the unauthorized use of peyote could not constitutionally be applied to a member of the North American Church, a native American Indian church. The court found that peyote constituted in itself an object of worship as well as a sacramental symbol and that its use was central to the worship of the church. This was balanced against the state's interest in enforcing this statute with the court finding that there was little evidence that either these persons would be seriously hurt or that this would lead to a wider distribution of the drug. Therefore the court found that the state's interest did not require the application of the law to this group. This defense has not been extended to possession of other drugs involving other "religions". *United States v. Kuch*, 288 F. Supp. 439 (1968); *Leary v. United States*, 383 F.2d 851 (1967). The general theory seems to be that the police power should and does predominate over one's right to freely practice his religious beliefs, where such practices involves conduct made criminal by law. This is especially true where the accused cannot demonstrate that the belief is sincere and not merely an attempt to subvert the drug laws.

In the case of *Employment Div., Dept. of Human Resources of Oregon v. Smith*, 110 S.Ct. 1595, (1990), the Supreme Court, while recognizing that states have the authority to decriminalize the sacramental use of peyote under state law, held that nothing in the Constitution of the United States requires this result. The five-member majority held that since the State of Oregon had included peyote in its list of controlled substances in an otherwise valid law prohibiting conduct that a state is free to regulate, nothing in the First Amendment bars criminal or administrative penalties against persons who violate this drug law, even as a part of religious worship.

Sample Questions

Criminal statutes which can be interpreted so as to punish free expression of ideas:

A. seldom are upheld by the courts as being constitutional.
B. are generally upheld by the courts if the expression is of an idea that is unpopular with the majority of people.
C. are generally upheld by the courts if the expression is of an idea that is popular with the majority of people.
D. seldom are upheld by the courts as being unconstitutional.
E. B and D above.

Criminal statutes which punish physical activity (conduct) are much more likely to be upheld as constitutional by the courts than those which punish speech or expressive acts.   T   F.

A criminal statute may be held to be unconstitutionally "overbroad" if:

A. in attempting to regulate certain activity, it makes criminal the use of constitutionally-protected speech.
B. it sweeps within its coverage activity that enjoys protection under the Constitution.
C. it is written in language so vague that the ordinary reasonable man could not understand what was required or prohibited.
D. all of the above.
E. A and B above.

If a criminal statute or ordinance is written in such vague terms that an ordinary person could not understand what is required or prohibited, the courts may hold it unconstitutional for violating the "fair notice" requirement which the Constitution is said to require.   T   F.

Freedom of speech under our Constitution has absolutely no limits, and anyone is free to say anything regardless of the circumstances under which the statement is made.   T   F.

Even in the United States, it has been said that a man has no constitutional right to shout "fire" in a crowded theater and thereby cause a panic.   T   F.

In the area of free expression, American law enforcement officers are often placed "between a rock and a hard place" in keeping the peace, because if they act too soon in silencing a speaker to prevent disorder they are criticized for violating First Amendment rights, but if they hesitate until disorder occurs, they are criticized for not acting soon enough.   T   F.

The tests prescribed in First Amendment cases by the courts, i.e., "clear and present danger", or "tendency to incite *imminent* lawless action", are very difficult for law enforcement officers to apply in practice.   T   F.

Flags have been recognized for decades as a primitive but effective way of communicating ideas.   T   F.

§3.3 FREEDOM OF SPEECH

Freedom of Expression

The First Amendment is the legal guardian of freedom of expression for the American people. Freedom of expression, in turn, allows us to have free elections, to encourage debate on all sides of political and social issues, to criticize public officers and employees, and within the legal framework provided, to even change the form and structure of our government. Unfortunately, police officers are often on the receiving end of public criticism because of the nature of their duties. Law enforcement in our free society demands professionalism because we expect our police to maintain law and order, keep the peace, and at the same time protect individual liberties, including freedom of speech.

The Overbreadth Doctrine
CASE BRIEF
City of Houston, Texas, v. Hill , 107 S.Ct. 2507 (1987)

Majority opinion: Brennan. Concurring: White, Marshall, Blackman, Stevens; Scalia and Powell concurring in part and dissenting in part. Dissenting: Rehnquist, joined by O'Connor.

FACTS: Upon shouting at police in an attempt to divert attention from his friend during a confrontation, D was arrested for "wilfully interrupting a city policeman by verbal challenge during an investigation," in violation of a municipal ordinance making it unlawful for any person "to assault, strike or in any manner oppose, molest, abuse or interrupt any policeman in the execution of his duty". After being acquitted he brought suit against the City of Houston challenging the constitutionality of the ordinance. The trial court upheld the ordinance as not overbroad on its face and the Court of Appeals reversed, finding the ordinance substantially overbroad since its literal wording punished and might deter a significant range of protected speech. The City of Houston appealed to the Supreme Court.

Issue: Whether the ordinance that makes it unlawful to interrupt a police officer in the performance of his duties is unconstitutionally overbroad under the First Amendment.

Decision: Yes, the ordinance was held to be overbroad and the Court of Appeals decision was affirmed.

Reasons: Since the ordinance language making it unlawful to "assault" or "strike" a police officer is expressly preempted by the State Penal Code, the enforceable portion of the ordinance prohibits verbal interruptions of police and thereby deals with speech rather than with core criminal conduct. The opinion stated: "The Houston ordinance is much more sweeping than the municipal ordinance struck down in [an earlier decision]. It is not limited to fighting words nor even obscene or opprobrious language, but prohibits speech that "in any manner . . . interrupt[s]" an officer. The Constitution does not allow such speech to be made a crime. The freedom of individuals verbally to oppose or challenge police action without thereby risking arrest is one of the principal characteristics by which we distinguish a free nation from a police state." The Houston ordinance criminalizes a substantial amount of constitutionally protected speech, and accords the police unconstitutional discretion in enforcement. ". . . the First Amendment recognizes, wisely we think, that a certain amount of expressive disorder not only is inevitable in a society committed to individual freedom, but must itself be protected if that freedom would survive."

Rule: A municipal ordinance that makes it unlawful to in any manner interrupt a police officer in the performance of his duty is substantially overbroad and therefore invalid on its face under the First Amendment, because it criminalizes constitutionally protected speech.

The Void-for-Vagueness Doctrine

Closely related to the overbreadth doctrine is the void-for-vagueness doctrine. The problem of vagueness in statutes regulating free speech is based on the same rationale as overbreadth. However, the vagueness doctrine applies to all criminal laws, not just those that regulate speech. The doctrine requires that special judicial strictness apply when reviewing laws that regulate fundamental constitutional rights to insure that such regulations are not vague. The populace must have notice as to precisely what activity is made criminal. An unclear law regulating speech might deter or chill persons from engaging in speech or like constitutional activity. The doctrine also requires that there be clear guidelines to govern law enforcement. Without such clear guidelines, law enforcement officers might enforce a vague statute on a selective basis and this discretion is most dangerous when the law regulates a fundamental right such as speech. In *Smith v. Goguen*, 94 S.Ct. 1242 (1974) D was convicted of violating a state flag-misuse statute for sewing a small United States flag to the seat of his pants. The statute made criminal conduct that publicly mutilates, tramples upon, defaces or treats contemptuously the flag of the United States. The Supreme Court held that the statutory language was void for vagueness and said that the void for vagueness doctrine "incorporates the notions of fair notice or warning . . . [I]t requires legislatures to set reasonably clear guidelines for law enforcement officials and triers of fact in order to prevent "arbitrary and discriminatory enforcement." Where a statute's literal scope, . . . is capable of reaching expressions sheltered by the First Amendment, the doctrine demands a greater degree of specificity than in other contexts." The standard "contemptuous treatment of the flag" was found to be so ambiguous that police, judges and juries were able to determine what actions were contemptuous on the basis of their personal preferences. This lack of ascertainable standards for defining "treats contemptuously" violated the due process clause.

Clear and Present Danger Test

In *Shenck v. United States*, 39 S.Ct. 247 (1919) D's conviction for conspiracy to violate the Espionage Act of 1917 was affirmed where the defendants had mailed leaflets to men eligible for the draft asserting that the draft violated the Thirteenth Amendment abolishing involuntary servitude. Justice Holmes, writing for the Court, upheld the convictions and the restraint on freedom of expression as necessary to prevent grave and immediate threats to national security. Under ordinary circumstances, Holmes believed the leaflets would have been constitutionally protected but: "[T]he character of every act depends upon the circumstances in which it is done . . . The most stringent protection of free speech would not protect a man in falsely shouting fire in a theater and causing a panic. It does not even protect a man from an injunction against uttering words that may have all the effect of force. . . . The question in every case is whether the words used are used in such circumstances and are of such a nature as to create a clear and present danger that they will bring about the substantive evils that Congress has a right to prevent. It is a question of proximity and degree." 39 S. Ct at 249.

CASE BRIEF

Brandenburg v. Ohio, 89 S.Ct. 1827 (1969)

Per Curiam, with Douglas concurring with opinion.

Facts: D was convicted under the Ohio Criminal Syndicalism statute for "advocating the duty, necessity or propriety of crime, sabotage, violence, or unlawful methods of terrorism as a means of accomplishing industrial or political reform," and for "voluntarily assembling with any society, group, or assembling with any society, group, or assemblage of persons formed to teach or advocate the doctrine of syndicalism." D challenged the constitutionality of the statute under the First and Fourteenth Amendments to the U.S. Constitution. D, a leader of the KKK, called a TV reporter and invited him to a KKK rally. The rally was filmed and later broadcast on local and national television. The state's case was based on the TV films and testimony that identified D as the person who communicated with the reporters and spoke at the rally. While most of the words uttered in the TV tape were incomprehensible, scattered phrases were derogatory of Negroes and Jews. D's speech referred to the large number of KKK members in Ohio and that the President, Congress and the Supreme Court continued to suppress the whites and that it was possible that there might have to be some "revengeance" taken.

Issue: Is the Ohio Criminal Syndicalism Statute Constitutional?

Decision: No Reversed.

Reasons: The Ohio statute was enacted in 1919, during a period when some 20 states and 2 territories enacted similar statutes. The California statute, very similar to Ohio's, was upheld in 1927 in *Whitney v. California* 47 S.Ct.641 (1927).

Since that time, however, the *Whitney* case has been thoroughly discredited by later decisions. These later decisions have fashioned the principle that the constitutional guarantees of free speech do not permit a State to forbid or proscribe advocacy of the use of force or of law violation except where such advocacy is directed to inciting or producing imminent lawless action and is likely to incite or produce such action. The mere abstract teaching of the moral propriety or even the moral necessity to a resort to force and violence, is not the same as preparing a group for violent action and steeling it to such action. A statute which fails to draw this distinction impermissibly intrudes upon the freedoms guaranteed by the First and Fourteenth Amendments. It sweeps within its condemnation speech which our constitution has immunized from government control. Measured by this test, Ohio's Criminal Syndicalism Act cannot be sustained. Neither the indictment nor the trial judge's instructions to the jury in any way refined the statute's bold definition of the crime in terms of mere advocacy as distinguished from incitement to iminent lawless action. We are therefore confronted with a statute which by its own words and as applied, purports to punish mere advocacy. The contrary teaching of *Whitney v. California* is overruled.

Rule of Case: The Constitutional guarantees of free speech and free press do not permit a State to forbid or proscribe advocacy of the use of force or of law violation except where such advocacy is directed in inciting or producing imminent lawless action and is likely to incite or produce such action.

In *Hess v. Indiana*, 94 S.Ct. 326 (1973), the Indiana Supreme Court upheld the conviction of the defendant of disorderly conduct where during an antiwar demonstration he shouted "we'll take the fucking street later" after the streets had just been cleared by the police. The United States Supreme Court reversed and in a per-curiam opinion said:

> At best . . . the statement could be as counsel for present moderation; at worst it amounted to nothing more than advocacy of illegal action at some indefinite future time. This is not sufficient to permit the state to punish Hess's speech. Under our decisions, the Constitutional guarantees of free speech and free press do not permit a state to forbid or proscribe advocacy of

the use of speech or of law violation except where such advocacy is directed to inciting or producing imminent lawless action and is likely to incite or produce such action.

The court concluded that since Hess's speech was not directed to any person or group of persons that he had not advocated action which would produce imminent disorder, his statements, therefore, did not violate the Indiana disorderly conduct statutes.

Fighting Words and Hostile Audiences.

In 1942 the United States Supreme Court in *Chaplinsky v. New Hampshire* 62 S.Ct. 766 (1942) unanimously upheld a statute which had previously been construed by the state court to ban "face to face words plainly likely to cause a breach of the peace by the addressee." Chaplinsky's conviction was based on his encounter with the City Marshal of Rochester whom he described as a "God damned racketeer and a damned fascist". The Court said that "fighting words-those which by their very utterance inflict injury or tend to incite an immediate breach of the peace" are not constitutionally protected because their "slight social value as a step to truth . . . is clearly outweighed by the social interest in order and morality."

CASE BRIEF
Cohen v. California, 91 S. Ct. 1780 (1971)

Justice Harlan, majority opinion. Blackmun, CJ Burger, Black, and White dissenting.

Facts: D was convicted in L.A. Municipal court for "offensive conduct" and sentenced to 30 days. He wore a jacket in the corridor outside the courtroom which bore the words "Fuck the Draft". D testified that this was his means of expressing his deep feeling to the public against the military draft. D did not engage in any act of violence or make any loud or unusual noise. In affirming his conviction the court of appeals held "offensive conduct" means behavior which has a tendency to provoke others to acts of violence or turn to disturb the peace. The court further reasoned that the wearing of the jacket might provoke violence against D himself.

Issue: Was the act of D a punishable criminal offense under the California "offensive conduct" statute?

Decision: No- Reversed.

Reasons: The case does *not* present an issue of offensive conduct for this was a communicative act or speech or *self-expression*. D's conviction rests squarely upon his exercise of the freedom of speech protected from arbitrary governmental interference by the constitution and can be justified, if at all, only as a valid regulation of the manner in which he exercised that freedom but not as a permissible prohibition on the substantive message it conveys. Several issues typically associated with "speech" cases are not present here-

(1) D was tried under state statute applicable throughout the entire state, therefore it could not be said to apply to courthouses only.

(2) This is not an *obscenity* case. "It could not plausibly be maintained that this vulgar allusion to the Selective Service System would conjure up such psychic (erotic) stimulation in anyone likely to be confronted with his crudely defaced jacket."

(3) This is not in a category of "fighting words" which states are free to regulate.

(4) Finally, it is argued that D's distasteful mode of expression was thrust on unwilling or unsuspected viewers and that the state could act to protect the

sensitive. This case does not involve an invasion of the privacy of the home and therefore to justify governmental interference with discourse solely to protect others from hearing it, is dependent upon a showing that substantial privacy interests are being invaded in an essentially intolerable manner. Any broader view would empower a majority to silence dissidents simply as a matter of personal predilections.

Here persons in the Court House were in a different posture than, for example, persons subjected to raucous emission of sound trucks blaring outside their residences. (Those offended could simply avert their eyes to avoid the "bombardment of their sensibilities.) The privacy interest here (in a courthouse) was nothing compared to that in one's own home- no record that any unwilling "listener" complained and the statute does not deal with the special plight of the "captive auditor" but indiscriminately sweeps within its prohibition all "offensive conduct" that disturbs any neighborhood or person.

Against this background the issue remaining is whether California can excise, as offensive conduct, one particular scurrilous epithet from public discourse, either on the theory of the court below, that its use is inherently likely to cause violent reaction or upon the theory of the state acting as guardians of public morality in removing this offensive word from the public vocabulary.

The lower court's rationale is untenable. There is no evidence that substantial numbers of citizens are standing ready to strike out physically at whoever may assault their sensibilities with those utterances, at least not enough to overcome freedom of expression. Most situations where the State has a justifiable interest in regulating speech generally fall within one or more of the various established exceptions such as obscenity, fighting words and invasions of privacy. The usual rule is that governmental bodies may not prescribe the form or content of individual expression. *"The constitutional right of expression is powerful medicine in a society as diverse and populous as ours."* "This is necessary for political and social change. Verbal tumult, discord, and even offensive utterance within established limits, are necessary side effects of the broader enduring values which the process of debate permits us to achieve."

The State has no right to cleanse public debate to the point where it is acceptable to the most squeamish of us. We cannot indulge the facile assumption that one can forbid particular words without running a substantial risk of suppressing ideas in the process. Governments might then seize upon the censorship of particular words as a convenient guise for banning the expression of unpopular views.

Rule: The expression of ideas, whether responsibly or foolishly, concerning public measures is so fundamental and basic a freeedom under the First Amendment that the State may not impose a criminal penalty for the public display, on a jacket, of the wearer's opinion of the military draft even though such writing contains a vulgarity which might shock the sensitive observer.

Regulation of Time, Place and Manner of Speech in Public Places.

In general, it may be said that the State may place reasonable time, place, or manner restrictions on speech that takes place in the public forum, but these regulations must be implemented without regard to the content of the speech. When the Court reviews time, place or manner restrictions, it is engaging in a two-step form of analysis. First, it seeks to determine whether the regulation is in fact an attempt to suppress content because of its message. A content-based restriction will be upheld only if the content fits within a category of speech unprotected by the First Amendment. Second, the court will determine whether the incidental restriction on speech is outweighed by the promotion of significant governmental interests.

Symbolic Speech
CASE BRIEF
United States v. O'Brien, 88 S. Ct. 1673 (1968)

Chief Justice Warren delivered opinion with Justice Douglas dissenting.

Facts: D publicly burned his draft card in the presence of a sizeable crowd to convey his antiwar and anti-draft beliefs. This was in violation of a federal statute making it a criminal offense to knowingly destroy or mutilate such certificates. D was convicted but claimed that statute unconstitutional as a restriction on freedom of speech, claiming that the act of burning the card was symbolic speech.

Issue: Is the law valid in this case?

Decision: Yes, conviction affirmed.

Reasons: The law on its face does not abridge free speech. We cannot accept the idea that a limitless variety of conduct can be labeled "speech" whenever a person engaging in the conduct intends thereby to express an idea. We have previously held that when speech and nonspeech elements are combined in same course of conduct, a sufficiently important governmental interest in regulating the nonspeech element can justify incidental limitations on First Amendment freedoms. The Court set out a four-part test for determining when a government interest sufficiently justifies the regulation of expressive conduct: "[A) government regulation is sufficiently justified [1] if it is within the constitutional power of the Government; [2] if it furthers an important or substantial governmental interest; [3] if the governmental interest is unrelated to the suppression of free expression; and [4] if the incidental restrictions on alleged First Amendment freedoms is no greater than is essential to the furtherance of that interest." There is no question about the power of Congress to raise and support armies and to make all laws necessary for that purpose. The requirement that the registration and classification cards not be mutilated or destroyed serves several purposes which include: quick determination of those registrants delinquent in Selective Service obligations; facilitation of quick induction in time of national crisis; facilitation of communication between registrants and local boards; reminders of notification of changes in status; deterrence for deceptive use of certificates. There was a legitimate and substantial interest in preventing the wanton and unrestrained destruction of draft cards. These regulations are limited to the *noncommunicative* aspect of D's conduct.

Rule: When speech and nonspeech elements are combined in the same course of conduct, a sufficiently important governmental interest in regulating the nonspeech element can justify incidental limitations on First Amendment freedoms. The power of Congress to raise and support armies is within Constitutional authority of Congress and therefore a smoothly administered selective service system is in furtherance of that power. Therefore, a person who claims that his public destruction of draft cards in violation of the Universal Military Training Act is not punishable because it was "symbolic speech" is nevertheless guilty of criminal conduct and subject to punishment because the regulation is directed at noncommunicative aspects of conduct and did not deprive him of other means of expression.

One year after *United States v. O'Brien* the Court upheld student protestors' right to wear armbands protesting the Vietnam War where the students were suspended for such conduct. The Court characterized the wearing of armbands as an action which involved "direct, primary First Amendment rights" entitling the students in comprehensive protection even though the school regulation forbade such conduct. The Court recognized that the wearing of armbands was "symbolic conduct" and that under the *O'Brien* test the regulation was not unrelated to the suppression of free expression since the regulation specifically prohibited the wearing of black armbands worn to exhibit opposition to this Nation's involvement in Vietnam. *Tinker v. Des Moines School District*, 89 S. Ct. 733 (1969).

CASE BRIEF

Spence v. Washington, 94 S.Ct. 2727 (1974)

Facts: D, a college student, hung an American flag out of his apartment window shortly after the invasion of Cambodia and the Kent State University shootings. The flag was displayed upside-down and superimposed on each side of the flag was a "peace symbol", fashioned with black tape. Three police officers observed the flag and entered the apartment house. They were met at the door by D, who said: "I suppose you are here about the flag. I didn't know there was anything wrong with it. I will take it down." D permitted the officers to enter his apartment, where they seized the flag, and arrested D, who cooperated fully. There was no altercation.

D was not charged under the Washington flag-desecration statute but rather under the "improper use" statute which prohibits the placing of any word, figure, mark, picture, design, drawing or advertisement of any nature on a flag of the United States, and it also prohibits the exposure to public view of any such flag. D was tried before a Justice Court and received 90 days confinement with 60 days suspended. D appealed and was granted a trial de novo in Superior Court, where he received a jury trial. The State based its case on the flag itself and the testimony of the three police officers. D testified in his own defense and said he put the peace symbol on his flag and displayed it as a protest against the invasion of Cambodia and the Kent State killings. He said his purpose was to associate the American flag with peace instead of war and violence.

"I felt there had been so much killing and that this was not what America stood for. I felt the flag stood for America and I wanted people to know that I thought America stood for peace."

D further testified that he fashioned the peace symbol from tape so it could be removed without damaging the flag. The trial court instructed the jury that the mere act of displaying the flag with the peace symbol attached, if proved beyond a reasonable doubt, was sufficient to convict. The jury returned a verdict of guilty and the court sentenced D to 10 days in jail, suspended, and a $75 fine. The Washington Court of Appeals reversed, holding the improper use statute overbroad and invalid on its face under the First and Fourteenth Amendments. The Supreme Court of Washington reversed, reinstating the conviction.

Issue: Was D's conviction valid under these circumstances?"

Decision: No, Reversed.

Reasons: First, this was a privately-owned flag, not the property of any government. We have no doubt that State or National Governments may constitutionally forbid anyone from mishandling a publicly-owned flag. Second, D displayed his flag on private property. He engaged in no trespass or disorderly conduct, nor can this case be analyzed in terms of reasonable time, place, or manner restraints on access to a public area. Third, the record shows no breach of the peace — it was not D's purpose to incite violence or even to stimulate a public demonstration — indeed there is no evidence that anyone except the three officers observed the flag. Fourth, the State concedes, as did the Washington Supreme Court, that D engaged in a form of communication. The undisputed facts are that D "wanted people to know that I thought America stood for peace". It is true that D did not choose to articulate his views through printed or spoken words — so we must determine whether his activity was sufficiently imbued with elements of communication to fall within the scope of the First and Fourteenth Amendments.

While we will not accept the view that a limitless variety of conduct can be labeled "speech" whenever a person is expressing an idea thereby, the nature of D's activity, combined with the factual context and environment in which it was undertaken, lead to the conclusion that he engaged in a form of protected expression.

Flags have been recognized for decades as a primitive but effective way of communicating ideas. On this record there can be little doubt that D communicated through the use of symbols.

The context in which a symbol is used for purposes of expression is important, for the context may give meaning to the symbol. Here, D's activity was roughly contemporaneous with two issues of intense public concern — the Cambodian incursion and the Kent State tragedy. While today D's activity might be interpreted a merely bizarre behavior of a student, its timeliness at the time the flag was so displayed got the point across.

We are confronted then with a case of prosecution for the expression of an idea through activity which took place on private property, where the State was not exercising supervisory powers unrelated to expression.

We are met at the outset with the puzzling manner in which the case was presented to us. The Washington Supreme Court rejected any reliance on a breach-of-the peace rationale, basing its result primarily on the ground that "the nation and state both have a recognizable interest in preserving the flag as a symbol of the nation. . .". Yet counsel for the State declined to support this rationale in argument, pursuing instead the breach of the peace theory. We believe the Washington Supreme Court correctly rejected this notion.

We are also unable to affirm the judgment on the ground of protecting the sensibilities of passersby. It is firmly settled that under our Constitution the public expression of ideas may not be prohibited merely because the ideas are themselves offensive to some of their hearers. Nor were the ideas imposed on a captive audience — nor could D be punished for failing to show proper respect for our national emblem.

We need not decide in this case whether or not Washington's interest in preserving the national flag as an unalloyed symbol of our country is valid. We assume *arguendo* that it is. *The statute is nonetheless unconstitutional as applied to D's activity.* There was no risk that D's act would mislead viewers into assuming that the Government endorsed his viewpoint — to the contrary he was plainly and peacefully protesting the fact that it did not. D was not charged under the desecration statute, nor did he permanently disfigure the flag or destroy it. He displayed it as a flag of his country to convey an idea. His message was direct, likely to be understood, and within the contours of the First Amendment, given the protected character of his expression and in light of the fact that no interest the State may have in preserving the physical integrity of a privately owned flag was significantly impaired on these facts, the conviction must be invalidated.

Concurring Opinion: (Douglas) — views D's act as symbolic speech — and while some might be so intemperate as to disrupt the peace because of the display, if absolute assurance of tranquility is required, we may as well forget about free speech. Under such a requirement the only "free" speech would consist of platitudes — that kind of speech does not need constitutional protection.

Rule: The public display of an upside-down American flag with a peace symbol temporarily attached thereto, at a time contemporaneous with non-peaceful issues of intense public concern, when such flag is privately-owned and displayed on private property — is an act which sufficiently expresses a viewpoint protected by the First and Fourteenth Amendments as to be beyond the reach of a criminal statute punishing improper use of the American flag.

Dissent: The States should have the power to enact statutes dealing with the improper use of the flag, the symbol of nationhood and unity and D here is seeking license to use the flag however he pleases so long as the use can be tied to a concept of speech. The statute here does not sufficiently chill freedoms of expression so as to violate the First and Fourteenth Amendments.

Note: In one of the most controversial free speech cases ever decided, a case which resulted in a proposed Constitutional Amendment by President Bush, the Supreme Court held, in *Texas v. Johnson.*, 109 S. Ct. 2533 (1989), that a conviction under the Texas flag desecration statute must be overturned. In this case the defendant burned an American flag while participating in a political demonstration during the Republican National Convention in Dallas. The Court held that under the circumstances, the defendant's burning of the flag was expressive conduct protected by the First Amendment.

EMAs a legislative reaction to *Texas v. Johnson*, which involved a state flag desecration statute, the Federal Flag Protection Act was enacted by the United States Congress in 1989. That statute stated:

> Whoever knowingly mutilates, defaces, physically defiles, burns, maintains on the floor or ground, or tramples upon any flag of the United States shall be fined under this title or imprisoned for not more than one year, or both.

In the cases of *United States v. Eichman* (and others), 110 S.Ct 2404 (1990), the same five-member majority which had decided *Johnson*, ruled that the Federal Flag Protection Act was an unconstitutional content-based restriction on freedom of expression, and therefore in violation of the First Amendment. In 1990, a proposed constitutional amendment to authorize the Congress and the states to prohibit the physical desecration of the flag failed to receive sufficient votes in either house of Congress to move forward in the amendment process.

Sample Questions

The courts may hold that a statute is unconstitutional "on its face", or, in the alternative, "as applied" to a particular fact situation.   T   F.

Under our constitution the practice of "prior restraint" on freedoms of expression is hardly ever approved by the courts.   T   F.

The word "press" used in the First Amendment is now understood to include radio, television, and other forms of media.   T   F.

When a trial court imposes a "gag order" on witnesses before they testify in court, the press is usually upset.   T   F.

If the press obtains *confidential* information in a lawful manner and prints it accurately, it has been held that criminal punishment imposed for such publication is unconstitutional.   T   F.

If a newspaper reporter is subpoenaed as a witness in court or before a grand jury and claims that he has a *consitutional* privilege to refuse to divulge evidence of crime and the sources thereof under the First Amendment:

A. the court will uphold this constitutional privilege.
B. the court will rule that the reporter has no constitutionally-based privilege not to testify and is in the same position under the Constitution as any other witness.
C. despite ruling as in B above, the reporter may be allowed to decline to testify if there is a *statutorily-based* privilege in existence in a particular state.
D. if no privilege exists for the reporter to refuse to testify either under the Constitution or a statute and he still refuses to testify, he may be held in contempt of court.
E. B, C, and D are all correct.

Even though obscenity and pornography in and of themselves have no protection under the First Amendment, the private possession of such material in the privacy of one's home has been ruled to be beyond the reach of the criminal law because if it were otherwise, the first step might be taken toward governmental "thought control."   T   F.

In the area of pornography, one of the primary problems for law enforcment is the difficulty in applying the court's legal definition of such material in practice.   T   F.

First Amendment restrictions on governmental power, (obviously directed at the *"Congress"):*

A. have no restrictive effect on the states and their political subdivisions.
B. also restrict states and their political subdivisions as a part of Fourteenth Amendment "Due Process of Law."
C. control unreasonable searches and seizures made by the police.
D. cover matters of religion only.
E. do not mention the "press".

§3.4 FREEDOM OF THE PRESS

In 1769 Sir William Blackstone stated, "The liberty of the press is indeed essential to the nature of a free state: but this consists in laying no *previous* restraints upon publications, and not in freedom from censure for criminal matter when published." 4 Bl. Comm. 151 (1769). In The *Federalist*, No. 84, Hamilton, in arguing against the need for a Bill of Rights for the newly-drafted, Constitution of the United States, made the point that a restriction on the national government against limiting freedom of the press would be interpreted by some people as an indication that the government *had* such a power, when obviously, it did not. Nevertheless, a Bill of Rights was adopted which included the restriction that "Congress shall make no law . . . abridging the freedom of speech or of the press . . .".

While the power of the press has always been great in our society, the development of the electronic media (radio and television), has broadened the meaning of the term "press" far beyond the printed word alone. And although First Amendment restrictions on governmental power to curb expression were aimed at Congress, these same restrictions now apply against state governments through the Fourteenth Amendment. *Gitlow v. New York*, 45 S. Ct. 625 (1925). The seed of freedom of the press mentioned by Blackstone was further nourished in the American legal system under the First Amendment and today the American media enjoys a position of power and influence which is unequaled anyplace in the world, including England.

The case law involving freedom of the press is voluminous. Many cases deal with the concept of *prior restraint* (a governmental silencing of a speaker or writer *before* he expresses a thought). These procedures are sometimes referred to as "gag" orders, and the Supreme Court has ruled that an extremely heavy burden must be met in order to justify such a curb on expression. *Nebraska Press Association v. Stuart*, 96 S. Ct. 2791 (1976). In the case of *Landmark Communications, Inc. v. Virginia*, 98 S. Ct. 1535 (1978), the Court held that although it is proper to maintain confidentiality of ongoing investigations of judicial misconduct, that a statute imposing criminal penalties for publishing an accurate report of such proceedings when the information came to the press by lawful means, was unconstitutional. But in *Zurcher v. Stanford Daily*, 98 S. Ct. 1970 (1978), the Court ruled that the First Amendment by itself does not prohibit the search of a newspaper office under a proper search warrant issued after a finding of probable cause. The power of the American media was amply demonstrated following the *Zurcher* case when Congress enacted a statute requiring that a *subpoena*, rather than a search warrant must ordinarily be obtained when evidence is in the possession of the media. 42 U.S.C. sec. 2000aa to 2000aa-12 (Supp. 1980). Although the Supreme Court has ruled that a newspaperman has no First Amendment-based privilege from revealing evidence of crime and sources to a grand jury, *Branzburg v. Hayes*, 92 S. Ct. 2646 (1972), such a privilege does exist in some states by virtue of statutory law. (Ind. Code 34-3-5-1, for example.)

Both members of the public and of the press have a First Amendment right to attend criminal trials and ordinarily trials cannot be closed in the absence of findings which outweigh the presumption of openness. *Richmond Newspapers, Inc. v. Virginia*, 100 S. Ct. 2814 (1980); *Globe Newspaper Company v. Superior Court*, 103 S. Ct. 2613 (1982).

One of the most troublesome areas for law enforcement under the general concept of freedom of the press involves obscenity and pornography. The Supreme Court has held that obscene materials are not protected by the First Amendment because they are not essential to the dissemination of political and social ideas, which is what the First Amendment is all about. *Roth v. United*

States, 77 S. Ct. 1304 (1957). The difficulty lies in the definition of obscenity which has emerged from the case law. In *Miller v. California*, 93 S. Ct. 2607 (1973) the Supreme formulated the following test for obscenity:

> (a) whether 'the average person, applying contemporary community standards' would find that the work, taken as a whole, appeals to the prurient interest, (b) whether the work depicts or describes, in a patently offensive way, sexual conduct specifically defined by the applicable state law, and (c) whether the work, taken as a whole, lacks serious literary, artistic, political, or scientific value.

By way of further illustration, the Court set forth the following description of sexual conduct which would fall within the previous test: "(a) Patently offensive representations or descriptions of ultimate sexual acts, normal or perverted, actual or simulated. "(b) Patently offensive representations or descriptions of masturbation, excretory functions, and lewd exhibition of the genitals." Under such a definition, as quoted above, it is obvious that police officers should not initiate enforcement action without a clear understanding of the enforcement policies and procedures which have met the constitutional tests of the Courts within their particular jurisdictions. When the additional element of privacy of the home is involved, the Supreme Court held, in *Stanley v. Georgia*, 89 S. Ct. 1243 (1969), that while the states retain broad powers to regulate the public display or dissemination of obscene material, the First and Fourteenth Amendments prohibit making mere private possession of such material in one's home a crime.

One of the primary functions of the press in the United States is to act as a watchdog on the government and the public treasury. The police, the most highly visible representative of the government, get their full share of attention from the press. In many ways, a police officer exists in sort of a fishbowl, with every word and action subject to the public scrutiny of the press. In a free society, the concept of a secret police is abhorrent to our way of thinking. And yet, many types of investigations cannot be undertaken with full public knowledge without destroying sources of information, encouraging suspects to flee the jurisdiction, or in other ways hampering the gathering of evidence. If the police are to be effective, therefore, a reasonable level of confidentiality of information must be maintained. Thus, in a free and open society there exists an inherent conflict between the professions of policing and reporting, with regard to the respective mission of each. This fact requires professionalism from both so they may each work harmoniously to fulfill their constitutionally recognized functions of keeping the public informed and insuring the domestic tranquility.

-------------------------------------- **Notes** --------------------------------------

In the case of *Osborne v. Ohio*, 110 S.Ct. 1691 (1990), the issue before the Court was the constitutionality of a statute which provided a criminal penalty for the possession or viewing of *child pornography*. The Court reviewed its earlier holding in *Stanley v. Georgia*, 89 S.Ct. 1243 (1969), which had long been interpreted to limit the power of the state to punish the possession and viewing of pornographic material in the privacy of one's own home. In upholding the Ohio law against child pornography in this case, even though the possession was in the D's home the Court looked to the *purpose* of the statutes involved in each case. The purpose of the Georgia law in the *Stanley* case, the Court indicated, was related to the concern that pornography/obscenity would "poison the minds of its viewers". Reasoning that this purpose was dangerously close to an attempt by the government to control a person's private thoughts, the Court, in *Stanley*, held the Georgia law to be a violation of the First Amendment. (It should also be noted that *Stanley* involved *adult*, and not *child* pornography). The clear purpose of the Ohio law in *Osborne*, the Court found, was to safeguard the physical and psychological well-being of minors, which is a "compelling" interest. The Court stated:

> "The legislative judgment, as well as the judgment found in relevant literature, is that the use of children as subjects of pornographic materials is harmful to the physiological, emotional, and mental health of the child."

***

> ". . . the materials produced by child pornographers permanently record the victim's abuse. The pornography's continued existence causes the child victims continuing harm by haunting the children in years to come.***The State's ban on possession and viewing encourages the possessors of these materials to destroy them. Second, encouraging the destruction of these materials is also desirable because evidence suggests that pedophiles use child pornography to seduce other children into sexual activity."

Finding that the gravity of the state interest, (protection of children), clearly outweighed the slight First Amendment right to possess and view such material, the Court upheld the constitutionality of the statute, although the defendant's conviction was reversed because of faulty jury instructions by the trial judge.

The *Osborne* case did not overrule *Stanley v. Georgia*, it distinguished the two cases, holding, in effect, that while governmental thought control violates the First Amendment, that the Amendment will tolerate some invasion to accommodate a purpose as important as the protection of children.

Sample Questions

In the case of *Stanley v. Georgia,* 89 S.Ct. 1243 (1969), the Supreme Court of the United States ruled, in effect, that although a state could regulate the public display or distribution of obscene material, it could not make the mere private possession or viewing of such material a crime if done in the privacy of the home. Later, in *Osborne v. Ohio,* 110 S.Ct. 1691 (1990), the Court upheld a state law which criminalized the possesion of *child pornography* even in the privacy of the home. How can the apparent inconsistency between these two cases be explained?

A. the Court simply overruled *Stanley v. Georgia.*
B. the Court found that the purpose in the *Stanley* case had been dangerously close to "thought control", an unconstitutional exercise of state power under the First Amendment.
C. the Court found that the purpose in the *Osborne* case had been the safeguarding of the physical and psychological well-being of children, a valid exercise of state power.
D. it cannot be explained, the two cases are simply in conflict with each other.
E. B and C above.

The sacramental use of peyote, or other controlled substances, in religious worship services;

A. is absolutely protected from criminal prosecution by the First Amendment.
B. while it may be decriminalized by an individual state, if that is the will of the legislative branch, nothing in the First Amendment bars either criminal or administrative penalties for such use of controlled substances.
C. cannot be made non-criminal by a state law.
D. can be made a criminal offense by state law.
E. B and D above.

The burning of the American Flag, as a form of political protest:

A. has been brought within First Amendment protection by a majority of the Supreme Court of the United States.
B. is a major criminal offense, uniformly punished in all states.
C. is unlawful under a federal statute, but lawful under state law.
D. is lawful under a federal statute, but unlawful under state law.
E. is unlawful both under federal and state law.

It is not "disorderly conduct" under the laws of most states merely to express an unpopular or social idea in public.   T   F

An arrest made under a law that makes it an offense to "in any manner interfere with a police officer in the performance of his duties" may be unconstitutionally overbroad if the "interference" is only vocal, and not physical, in character.   T   F.

Often, the turning point between upholding a statute as constitutional, or overturning it as unconstitutional, will be the court's determination of whether the activity regulated was *conduct* or *expression*.   T   F.

§3.5 FREEDOM OF ASSEMBLY AND PETITION

The First Amendment allows a peaceful gathering of persons for any lawful purpose. The Supreme Court had early recognized that it could not be made a crime to participate in a peaceful assembly. Thus, participation in a Communist Party political meeting was held in *DeJonge v. Oregon*. 57 S. Ct. 255 (1937) not to be a crime unless violence is advocated, and under the broad category of civil rights, assembly for marches, demonstrations, and picketing have been protected as lawful assemblages. *Hague v. CIO,*, 59 S. Ct. 954 (1939).

Perhaps the best illustration of the constitutional right of freedom to petition the government for a redress of grievances is the nearly unrestrained flow of cases filed in federal courts by state prisoners who have been convicted of serious crimes and who are serving time in state institutions. In 1941 it was established by the ruling in *Ex Parte Hull*, 61 S. Ct.640 (1941), that states could not interfere with the right of state prisoners to apply to the federal courts for a writ of habeas corpus. Since that time, the concept that a convicted felon had become a "slave of the state" who had lost all of his constitutional rights by being convicted through due process of law, has vanished, along with the so-called "hands-off" doctrine, which was a refusal of the courts to hear lawsuits brought by prisoners against their keepers. In the case of *Cooper v. Pate*, 84 S. Ct. 1733 (1964) the Supreme Court of the United States expressly held that a state prison inmate could sue his keepers under the federal Civil Rights Act, and since that time a virtual flood of lawsuits has been filed in federal courts by state inmates. Obviously, if convicted persons have the right of meaningful access to the courts, every other person may also petition the government, both state and federal, for appropriate legal or equitable relief. For a discussion of remedies against police misconduct, see Chapter 2.

--------------------------------------- **Notes** ---------------------------------------

Sample Questions

In America the Constitution often protects the right of one citizen to express an idea that another citizen not only disagrees with, but despises with all his being. If the citizen who disagrees with the statement is a police officer, there may be a temptation for him to misuse the authority of his office to silence or retaliate against the speaker. This is one reason why professional conduct is required in American law enforcement.   T   F.

One of the dangers of allowing untrained police officers to enforce the law is that they may erroneously believe thay have the authority to take enforecment action against citizens simply because they disagree with them.   (T)   F.

A statute which makes it a crime to "engage in foolish conduct in a public place", might be held by the courts to be unconstitutional on the ground of:
A. vagueness.
B. overbreadth
C. allowing too much discretion to be exercised by the police in the enforcement of the statute.
D. giving inadequate notice to the citizen of the conduct prohibited.
E. all of the above.

An acceptable definition of "fighting words" might be:
A. words expressing the political views of an unpopular minority group.
B. speech containing vulgarities.
C. words expressing ideas of either white or black racial supremacy.
D. words which carry no significant social or political message and which by their very utterance inflict injury or tend to incite an immediate breach of the peace by the person to whom they are directed in a face-to-face encounter.
E. none of the above.

The term "prior restraint," used in a First Amendment sense, refers to the limitation of expression before the expression is written or spoken, and is condemned by the First Amendment.   T   F.

A state statute outlawing and punishing "blasphemy" would be upheld as constitutional by most courts.   T   F.

The states have no right to regulate the public display or dissemination of obscene material.   T   (F.)

Both the police and the press have legitimate functions in a free society, but with regard to certain types of information and sources of information, a conflict is inherent between the two.   T   F.

In situations involving First Amendment issues, (religion, speech, press, assembly, and petition), but which do not threaten imminent violence and which do not involve criminal conduct, it is probably best for the police to follow a policy of tolerance and restraint, even when one side or the other demands law enforcement action.   T   F.

§3.6 SUMMARY

To sum it all up, the freedoms recognized in the First Amendment are jealously guarded by the courts because they all have to do with the lifeblood of a free society, which is freedom of expression, (written, verbal, pictorial, and sometimes symbolic). Without the free exchange of political and social ideas between citizens, no meaningful change could ever be accomplished in government or governmental structure by peaceable means. Because the First Amendment provides the vehicle for political and social change, the government should not be allowed to silence people before they speak, and with very few exceptions ("fighting words", danger of inciting *imminent* lawlessness, obscenity per se, etc.,) the *content* of expression, is protected by law and should not be subject to criminal punishment. Certain rules of thumb emerge which should be remembered by every police officer: (1) It is much easier for the government to regulate *conduct* (physical activity) than it is to regulate expression; (2) The *content* of expression, written or verbal, foolish or wise, critical or praiseworthy, can seldom be the basis for law enforcement action; (3) Police officers will often find themselves in "no-win" situations which involve First Amendment issues, because they will be severely criticized *regardless* of whether they take action or not; and (4) In First Amendment situations which do not threaten imminent violence or criminal conduct, tolerance and restraint are the best guidelines for the police. Questionable cases not involving exigent circumstances should usually be referred to the prosecuting authority or a superior officer before action is taken.

-------------------------------------- **Notes** --------------------------------------

Sample Questions

Kinds of speech that the courts have ruled are *not* deserving of constitutional protection include:

A. religious expression.
B. political expression.
C. obscenity for the sake of obscenity alone, when it is not a part of a political or social expression.
D. fighting words.
E. C and D above,

The basic reason for freedoms of expression under the Constitution of the United States is to provide the necessary means for political or social change, if that is the will of the people.   T   F.

The following acts have been held to be protected expression under the First Amendment:

A. public burning of a draft card.
B. public burning of the American flag during a political demonstration.
C. an obscene reference to the selective service system worn as a part of a three-word message on an acticle of clothing.
D. burning down a public building as a part of a political protest.
E. B and C above.

In a labor dispute, picketing, within reasonable limits, involves First Amendment issues.   T   F.

In many First Amendment cases, the courts are involved with the difficult task of drawing a line between protected forms of expression, and conduct which is subject to the regulation of the law. Examples of expression which are not protected by the First Amendment include:

A. the burning of a draft card, claimed as "symbolic speech".
B. obscenity for the sake of obscenity alone.
C. fighting words.
D. libel and slander
E. all of the above.

In cases in which the "free exercise" of religion comes into conflict with the criminal law, the courts will:

A. always decide the case in favor of the prosecution.
B. always decide the case in favor of the defendant.
C. refuse the take jurisdiction of the case because the First Amendment's requirement of separation of church and state strips the judicial branch of the government of any power to decide issues involving religious rights.
D. balance the burden of the criminal regulation on the free exercise of religion against the importance of the state's interest in enforcing the regulation and the degree to which it would be impaired by a religious exemption.
E. defer the matter to the legislative branch of government.

CHAPTER 4

ARREST, SEARCH, AND SEIZURE

Section
4.1 Introduction
4.2 When an arrest takes place
4.3 The felony-midemeanor distinction
4.4 Probable cause
4.5 Issuance and execution of arrest and search warrants
4.6 Arrest, with or without a warrant
4.7 Use of force
4.8 Forced entry — knock and announce requirement
4.9 Territorial jurisdiction and fresh pursuit
4.10 Resistance to arrest
4.11 Infractions and ordinance violations
4.12 Citizen's arrest
4.13 Searches — Constitutional restrictions
4.14 Searches with warrant
    (A) Probable cause for warrant
        (1) Independent source
        (2) Reasonableness of request for warrant; civil liability of officer
    (B) Discovery of items not specified in warrant
    (C) Affidavit for warrant
    (D) Challenge to warrant affidavit
4.15 Warrantless searches
    (A) Search incident to arrest
        (1) Scope of search incident to arrest
        (2) Discovery of items not connected with arrest
        (3) Justification of search
        (4) Application of Robinson-Gustafson Rules
    (B) Automobile searches
        (1) Distinction between home and vehicle
        (2) Remote searches
        (3) Closed containers — the Chadwick rule
    (C) Exigent circumstances
        (1) Close pursuit and privacy
        (2) Evidence of intoxication — the fleeting opportunity to search
        (3) The murder scene exception
    (D) Plain view and inventory
    (E) Stop and frisk and detentions on less than probable cause
        (1) Stop and frisk
        (2) Terry distinguished from search incident to arrest
        (3) Terry rationale extended
        (4) Proper use of stop and frisk authority
        (5) Other detentions on less than probable cause
        (6) The traffic roadblock
    (F) Consent searches
        (1) Voluntariness requirement
        (2) Miranda waiver not consent to search
        (3) Scope of consent to search
    (G) Administrative inspections and searches based on less than traditional probable cause
4.16 Neutral magistrate; inadvertence; standing to object
    (A) Neutral magistrate

(B) "Inadvertent" — totally unexpected, or lacking probable cause?
   (C) Standing to object to a search
   (D) Abandoned property and garbage
4.17 Wiretapping and Eavesdropping
4.18 Compelled evidence
4.19 Seizure and forfeiture or crime-related property

§ 4.1 INTRODUCTION

The right of the people to be secure in their persons, houses, papers, and effects, against unreasonable searches and seizures, shall not be violated, and no warrants shall issue, but upon probable cause, supported by oath or affirmation, and particularly describing the place to be searched, and the persons or things to be seized. *Constitution of the United States, Amendment 4.*

William Blackstone defined an arrest as "the apprehending or restraining of one's person, in order to be forthcoming to answer an alleged or suspected crime". 4 Bl. Comm. 286 (1769).

In *Terry v. Ohio*, 88 S. Ct. 1868 (1968) the Supreme Court of the United States described an arrest as the "initial stage" of a criminal prosecution. Other characterizations of arrest include the following:

An arrest is the taking, seizing, or detaining the person of another either by touching, or by any act which indicates an intention to take him into custody and subject the person to the actual control and will of the person making the arrest. 6A C.J.S. Arrest § 2.

In criminal procedure an arrest is the taking of a person into custody in order that he may be held to answer for, or be prevented from committing, a criminal offense. 6A C.J.S. Arrest § 4.

In order to constitute an arrest there must be an intent to arrest, under a real or pretended authority, accompanied by a seizure or detention of the person which is so understood by the person arrested. 6A C.J.S. Arrest § 43.

The cases cited in 6A C.J.S. Arrest indicate that no formal or particular words need to be used in the making of an arrest and that the fact of arrest may be shown by surrounding facts and circumstances; however, any words which are used are relevant to the determination of whether or not an arrest took place. As to whether the arrested person should have known that he was under arrest, the test is what a reasonable man, innocent of any crime, would have thought if he had been in the same position.

Cases cited in 5 Am Jur 2d Arrest, §1, characterize arrest as follows:

An arrest is the taking, seizing, or detaining of the person of another, by touching or putting hands on him; or by any act that indicates an intention to take him into custody and that subjects him to the actual control and will of the person making the arrest; or by the consent of the person to be arrested.

To effect an arrest, there must be actual or constructive seizure or detention of the person arrested, or his voluntary submission to custody, and the restraint must be under real or pretended legal authority. There can be no arrest where there is no restraint or where the person sought to be arrested is not conscious of any restraint.

Even a brief official detention, such as where police officers stop a moving vehicle, may be sufficient to constitute an arrest, according to some authorities. But when one is merely approached by a police officer and questioned about his identity and actions, there is only an accosting, not an arrest.

The mere fact that an officer makes a statement to an accused that he is under arrest is not sufficient to complete the arrest. But if an officer having authority to make an arrest lays his hand upon the person of the suspect, however slightly, with the intention of taking him into custody, it is an arrest, even though the officer may not succeed in stopping or holding the suspect even for an instant. If the person arrested understands that he is in the power of the one arresting and submits in consequence, it is not necessary that there be an application of actual force, a manual touching of the body, or a physical restraint that may be visible to the eye.

The act relied upon as constituting an arrest must have been performed with the intent to effect an arrest and must have been so understood by the party arrested. In all cases in which there is no manual touching or seizure, or any resistance, the intentions of the parties are important. There must have been the intent on the part of one of them to arrest the other and the intent on the part of the other to submit, under the belief and impression that submission was necessary. However, no formal declaration of arrest is required. 5 AM Jur 2d Arrest, § 1.

In *Commonwealth v. Holmes*, 183 N.E.2d 279 (Mass. 1962), the court, in reviewing the fact situation before it, stated:

The facts fall within the rule that"[t]o constitute an arrest there must be either a physical seizure of the person by the arresting officer, or a submission to his authority and control."

The court concluded in *Holmes* that an arrest had taken place, despite the fact that the word "arrest" was never used by the officer.

------------------------------------- **Notes** -------------------------------------

Sample Questions

When there is probable cause to arrest the occupants of an automobile for a felony and there is also probable cause to believe the automobile contains items subject to seizure:

A. a warrant must be secured to search the automobile.
B. the search of the automobile need not be made as an incident to the arrests and it may be searched later and at a different place without a warrant.
C. the search of the automobile must be made at the same time and at the same place that the arrests take place.
D. the "Carroll rule" has nothing to do with this situation.
E. A and D above.

The use of deadly force by the police solely to arrest a fleeing felon when all other means of arrest have failed is constitutional only when:

A. the arresting officer has probable cause to believe that the fleeing felon has committed a crime involving the infliction of or threat of serious physical harm, or that the fleeing felon poses a threat of serious physical harm to others if not immediately arrested.
B. any felony, regardless of its nature, has been committed, and the person to be arrested has disregarded a police order to halt.
C. the arresting officer knows or has reason to believe that the fleeing felon has previously been convicted of another unrelated felony.
D. the arresting officer knows as a matter of fact that the fleeing felon is over the age of eighteen.
E. all of the above are true.

If, several hours after the arrest of a person, law enforcement officers have in their possession luggage or other personal property which they have seized which is not immediately associated with the person arrested nor immediately associated with a suspected automobile under the "Carroll" rule, and the luggage or property is under the exclusive control of the police and there is no danger that the person arrested might gain access to the property to seize a weapon or destroy evidence, and there is no other "exigent" circumstance with reference to the seized property:

A. Such property may nevertheless be searched without a warrant as an incident to the arrest.
B. Such property, being in "plain view" may be opened and searched without a search warrant.
C. Such property may be opened and searched, but only if it is located in an automobile.
D. Any search of such property is no longer an incident to the arrest or booking procedure and therefore a search warrant should be obtained in order to lawfully search it.
E. Such property may not be searched under any circumstances. With or without a search warrant.

§ 4.2 WHEN AN ARREST TAKES PLACE

An arrest is a "seizure" of a person under the Fourth Amendment and, as such, it must be reasonable. *Tennessee v. Garner*, 105 S. Ct. 1694 (1985). "A person has been 'seized' within the meaning of the Fourth Amendment only if, in view of all circumstances surrounding the incident, a reasonable person would believe that he was not free to leave." *United States v. Mendenhall*, 100 S. Ct. 1870, 1877 (1980).

The custody or control, the assumption of which is involved in an arrest ordinarily imports an actual restraint or detention of the person arrested, or a significant restraint of his freedom of movement, and an arrest is complete where coexistent intention and power to arrest are made known to the subject of the arrest and are followed by submission. 6A C.J.S. Arrest § 43b.

From the above it seems clear that an arrest is complete when, after actions or words, or both, by an officer indicating an intent to arrest, a person either submits to the authority of the officer or is forcibly restrained by the officer.

In *Bey v. State*, 355 So.2d 850 (Fla. App. 1978), the court summarized what seem to be the generally accepted elements of an arrest:

    (a) a purpose or intention to effect an arrest under real or pretended authority;

    (b) an actual or constructive seizure or detention of one by another having present power to control the person arrested;

    (c) a communication by the person making the arrest to the person whose arrest is sought, of an intention or purpose then and there to effect an arrest; and

    (d) an understanding by the person whose arrest is sought that it is the intention of the arresting officer then and there to arrest and detain him.

When the above elements are present as shown by the facts and circumstances, an arrest has taken place.

The *Mendenhall* test was used by the Supreme Court in the case of *Michigan v. Chesternut*, 108 S. Ct. 1975 (1988), to determine whether a "seizure" under the Fourth Amendment had taken place as a result of "investigatory pursuit" by the police. In that case, police officers on routine patrol in a marked police cruiser saw a car stop and a man get out and approach D, who was standing alone on a corner. When D saw the police car nearing the corner, he turned and began to run. The officers in the cruiser followed D around the corner to see where he was going. The police car quickly caught up with D and drove alongside him for some distance. As the police drove along beside D, he discarded a number of packets from his right-hand pocket. One of the officers got out of the police car and picked up and examined the packets, which contained pills. As the officer was examining the packets, D stopped running. Based on his experience as a paramedic, the officer suspected that the pills contained codeine. D was arrested for the possession of narcotics and taken to the police station. In an ensuing search, more pills, a packet of heroin, and a hypodermic needle were found on the D's person.

The issue in this case is, under these circumstances, when did an arrest (seizure) take place? If the investigatory pursuit of D by the police constituted a seizure under the Fourth Amendment, a second issue arises, and that is whether or not the mere flight of a person upon seeing a marked police car amounts to reasonable suspicion justifying the seizure.

In *Chesternut*, the Michigan Courts ruled that any investigatory pursuit amounted to a seizure under *Terry v. Ohio*; that D's flight, by itself, was insufficient justification to authorize the seizure, and therefore in violation of the Fourth Amendment — rendering the discarded packets inadmissible as the product of improper police conduct. The Supreme Court granted certiorari to the State of Michigan and reversed the state court holdings.

The Supreme Court held that the *mere following of D by the police after he began to run from them did not constitute a seizure*, and it was therefore unnecessary to decide whether flight alone is sufficient to justify a seizure. Citing the *Mendenhall*, *Terry*, *Delgado* and *Royer* cases, the Court stated:

> The test provides that the police can be said to have seized an individual "only if, in view of all of the circumstances surrounding the incident, a reasonable person would have believed that he was not free to leave."

* * *

Applying the Court's test to the facts of this case, we conclude that respondent was not seized by the police before he discarded the packets containing the controlled substance.

* * *

. . . the police conduct involved here would not have communicated to the reasonable person an attempt to capture or otherwise intrude upon respondent's freedom of movement. The record does not reflect that the police activated a siren or flashers; or that they commanded respondent to halt, or displayed any weapons; or that they operated the car in an aggressive manner to block respondent's course or otherwise control the direction or speed of his movement. * * * While the very presence of a police car driving parallel to a running pedestrian could be somewhat intimidating, this kind of police presence does not, standing alone, constitute a seizure.

* * *

Without more, the police conduct here — a brief acceleration to catch up with respondent, followed by a short drive alongside him — was not "so intimidating" that respondent could reasonably have believed that he was not free to disregard the police presence and go about his business.

-- **Notes** --

CASE BRIEF

California v. Hodari D, 111 S.Ct. 1547 (1991)

Majority: Scalia, joined by Rehnquist, White, Blackmun, O'Connor, Kennedy, and Souter. Dissenting: Stevens, Marshall.

FACTS: Police, wearing street clothes with "Police" embossed on front and back of jackets, were patrolling a high-crime area in an unmarked car. Rounding a corner, they came upon 4 or 5 youths huddled around a car parked at the curb. Seeing the officers, the youths scattered and ran. D and one other youth ran through an alley and the others ran in another direction and the car sped off. The officers were suspicious and gave chase, one on foot, who circled the block, and came upon D, who was looking back as he ran. D did not see the officer until he was almost upon him, whereupon he tossed away a small rock. The officer tackled D and handcuffed him and then radioed for assistance. D had $130 in cash and a pager on his person. The rock he had discarded was crack cocaine.

D moved to suppress evidence relating to the cocaine. The trial court denied the motion, but the Court of Appeals reversed, holding that D had been "seized" when he saw the officer running toward him; that this seizure was unreasonable; and that evidence of the cocaine had to be suppressed as the fruit of an illegal seizure. The state supreme court denied the state's application for review and the Supreme Court of the United States granted certiorari.

ISSUE: Does a show of authority by police with intention to seize a person, which falls short of an actual touching of the person or his submission to the officer's authority, amount to a 4th Amendment seizure?

DECISION: No; there was no seizure in this case until D was tackled by the officer, and his discarding of the crack cocaine before he was touched by the officer was therefore not the product of an illegal seizure, and it was admissible in evidence against him. Reversed and Remanded.

REASONS: The 4th Amendment's proection against unreasonable seizures includes seizures of persons, but generally a seizure does not occur until there has been a "taking of possession", or bringing within physical control. But the case law is clear that an arrest takes place when there is a grasping or touching of a person by an officer who has lawful authority to arrest, with that purpose in mind, even though the grasping or touching does not succeed in stopping or holding the person. [But such a person who has been touched or grasped by an officer for purpose of arrest who breaks away does not remain under arrest until he is again brought under control by physical force or until he submits to the authority of the officer.]

In this case D had not been touched by the officer at the time he discarded the cocaine, and he had not previously submitted to the officer's authority before he was tackled. There had been a show of authority by the officer but this does not constitute an arrest unless the person yields or submits. The test used in *United States v. Mendenhall*, 100 S.Ct. 1870, (1980), ("A person has been 'seized' within the meaining of the Fourth Amendment only if, in view of all the circumstances surrounding the incident, a reasonable person would have believed that he was not free to leave.") is not inconsistent with the above, because it states only a necessary condition of a seizure, not the total definition of a seizure, and it creates an objective test for a "show of authority". In *Michigan v. Chesternut*, 108 S.Ct. 1975 (1988), the Court decided that a police car's slow following of a person as he ran along a sidewalk did not amount to an objective "show of authority", but it did not address the issue presented in this case.

In *Brower v. Inyo County*, 109 S.Ct. 1378 (1989), where the police with flashing lights chased a fleeing motorist for 20 miles (certainly a "show of authority"), the

Court did not even consider whether a seizure occurred before the fatal crash into the police roadblock because the "show of authority" did not produce the stop. The Court also discusses *Hester v. United States*, 44 S.Ct. 445 (1924), (police seizure of discarded jugs, jars, and bottles by "moonshiners" while they were being pursued by police), which it holds is consistent with the results of this case.

RULE: A mere show of authority by police with intention to arrest does not constitute an arrest unless there is a touching of the person by the officer or unless the person yields or submits to the show of authority. Therefore, evidence of criminal activity discarded by a person after a police show of authority has taken place but before a touching or submission occurs is admissible because it is not the product of an unlawful seizure.

DISSENTING: In light of cases such as *Katz v. United States*, 88 S.Ct. 507 (1967) and *Terry v. Ohio*, 88 S.Ct. 1868 (1968), which have broadened the common law interpretation of what a "seizure" is, the dissenters believe the majority holding is unduly narrow, and they feel that the facts in this case should be controlled by common law protection against *attempted* unlawful arrest.

-- **Notes** --

§ 4.3 THE FELONY-MISDEMEANOR DISTINCTION

A felony is a crime carrying a relatively severe punishment; a misdemeanor is a crime punishable to a lesser degree than a felony. In 1769, William Blackstone defined a felony as:

> ... an offense which occasions a total forfeiture of either lands, or goods, or both, at the common law; and to which capital or other punishment may be superadded, according to the degree of guilt. 4 Bl. Comm. 95.

The severity of criminal punishments has diminished considerably since Blackstone's time and several states have discontinued the use of the death penalty entirely. Although definitions vary from state to state, a felony in many states is a crime punishable by death or imprisonment for a minimum of one year; a misdemeanor in most states is punishable by less than a year in prison. (See table below.) In most states the need for an arrest warrant is affected by whether the arresting officer is dealing with a felony or a misdemeanor. (See § 4.6 herein.)

Table 5. Felony definitions of the States and the District of Columbia: From U.S. Department of Justice, *Bulletin of the Bureau of Justice Statistics*, August, 1987, p. 5b.

Alabama. Felony. An ofense for which a sentence to a term of imprisonment in excess of 1 year is authorized by this title.

Alaska. (Statutory law does not define the term felony.)

Arizona. (Statutory law does not define the term felony.)

Arkansas. An offense is a felony if: it is so designated by this Code; or it is so designated by a statute not a part of this Code.

California. A felony is a crime which is punishable with death or by imprisonment in the State prison.

Colorado. The term felony, wherever it may occur in this constitution, or the laws of the State, shall be construed to mean any criminal offense punishable by death or imprisonment in the penitentiary, and none other.

Connecticut. An offense for which a person may be sentenced to a term of imprisonment in excess of 1 year is a felony.

Delaware. (Statutory law does not define the term felony.)

Florida. The term "felony" shall mean any criminal offense that is punishable under laws of this State, or that would be punishable if committed in this State, by death or imprisonment in a State penitentiary.

Georgia. "Felony" means a crime punishable by death, by imprisonment for life, or by imprisonment for more than 12 months.

Hawaii. A crime is a felony if it is so designated in this Code or if persons convicted thereof may be sentenced to imprisonment for a term in excess of 1 year.

Idaho. A felony is a crime which is punishable with death or by imprisonment in the State prison.

Illinois. "Felony" means an offense for which a sentence to death or to a term of imprisonment in a penitentiary for 1 year or more is provided.

Indiana. "Felony conviction" means a conviction, in any jurisdiction at any time, with respect to which the convicted person might have been imprisoned for more than 1 year; but it does not include a conviction with respect to which the person has been pardoned, or a conviction of a Class A misdemeanor or under Section 7(b) of this chapter.

Iowa. A public offense is a felony of a particular class when the statute defining the crime declares it to be a felony.

Kansas. A felony is a crime punishable by death or by imprisonment in any State penal institution.

Kentucky. Offenses punishable by death or confinement in the penitentiary, whether or not a fine or other penalty may also be assessed, are felonies.

Louisiana. "Felony" is any crime for which an offender may be sentenced to death or imprisonment at hard labor.

Maine. (Statutory law does not use the term felony.)

Maryland. (Statutory law does not use the term felony.)

Massachusetts. A crime punishable by death or imprisonment in the State prison is a felony.

Michigan. The term "felony" when used in this act, shall be construed to mean an offense for which the offender, on conviction may be punished by death, or by imprisonment in State prison.

Minnesota. "Felony" means a crime for which a sentence of imprisonment for more than 1 year may be imposed.

Mississippi. The term "felony," when used in any statute, shall mean any violation of law punished with death or confinement in the penitentiary.

Missouri. A crime is a "felony" if it is so designated or if persons convicted thereof may be sentenced to death or imprisonment for a term which is in access of 1 year.

Montana. "Felony" means an offense in which the sentence imposed upon conviction is death or imprisonment in the State prison for any term exceeding 1 year.

Nebraska. (Statutory law does not use the term felony.)

Nevada. Every crime which may be punished by death or by imprisonment in the State prison is a felony.

New Hampshire. A felony is murder or a crime so designated by statute within or outside this Code or a crime defined by statute outside of this Code where the maximum penalty provided is imprisonment in excess of 1 year; provided, however, that a crime defined by statute outside of this Code is a felony when committed by a corporation or an unincorporated association if the maximum fine therein provided is more than $200.

New Jersey. (Statutory law does not use the term felony.)

New Mexico. A Crime is a felony if it is so designated by law or if upon conviction thereof a sentence of death or of imprisonment for a term of 1 year or more is authorized.

New York. "Felony" means an offense for which a sentence to a term of imprisonment in excess of 1 year may be imposed.

North Carolina. A felony is a crime which: was a felony at common law; is or may be punishable by death; is or may be punishable by imprisonment in the State's prison; or is denominated as a felony by statute.

North Dakota. (Statutory law does not use the term felony.)

Ohio. Regardless of the penalty which may be imposed, any offense specifically classified as a felony is a felony, and any offense specifically classified as a misdemeanor is a misdemeanor. Any offense not specifically classified is a felony if imprisonment for more than 1 year may be imposed as a penalty.

Oklahoma. A felony is a crime which is, or may be, punishable with death, or by imprisonment in the State penitentiary.

Oregon. Except as provided in ORS 161.585 and 161.705, a crime is a felony if it is so designated in any statute of this State or if a person convicted under a statute of this State may be sentenced to a maximum term of imprisonment of more than 1 year.

Pennsylvania. (Statutory law does not use the term felony.)

Rhode Island. Unless otherwise provided, any criminal offense which at any given time may be punished by imprisonment for a term of more than 1 year, or by a fine of more than $1,000 is hereby declared to be a felony.

South Carolina. The crimes referred to in the following sections . . . (specific statutory sections cited) and all other criminal offenses punishable under the laws of this state which were felonies under the common law are hereby classified as and declared to be felonies (parens added).

South Dakota. A felony is a crime which is or may be punishable by imprisonment in the State penitentiary.

Tennessee. All violations of law punished by imprisonment in the penitentiary or by the infliction of the death penalty are, and shall be denominated, felonies.

Texas. "Felony" means an offense so designated by law or punishable by death or confinement in a penitentiary.

Utah. (Statutory law does not use the term felony.)

Vermont. Any other provision of law notwithstanding any offense whose maximum term of imprisonment is more than 2 years, for life or which may be punished by death is a felony.

Virginia. Such offenses as are punishable with death or confinement in the penitentiary are felonies.

Washington. (Statutory law does not use the term felony.)

West Virginia. Such offenses as are punishable by confinement in the penitentiary are felonies.

Wisconsin. A crime punishable by imprisonment in the Wisconsin State prisons is a felony.

Wyoming. Crimes which may be punished by death or by imprisonment for more than 1 year are felonies.

Source: Annotated code of each State, 1986.

From Bureau of Justice Statistics, U.S. Department of Justice Bulletin. "State Felony Courts and Felony Laws" August, 1987.

§ 4.4 PROBABLE CAUSE

In discussing probable cause as the standard for arrest, the Supreme Court of the United States said, in *Gerstein v. Pugh*, 95 S. Ct. 854 (1975):

> Both the standards and procedures for arrest and detention have been derived from the Fourth Amendment and its common-law antecedents. * * * The standard for arrest is probable cause, defined in terms of facts and circumstances "sufficient to warrant a prudent man in believing that the [suspect] had committed or was committing an offense." * * * This standard, like those for searches and seizures, represents a necessary accommodation between the individual's right to liberty and the State's duty to control crime.

These long-prevailing standards seek to safeguard citizens from rash and unreasonable interferences with privacy and from unfounded charges of crime. They also seek to give fair leeway for enforcing the law in the community's protection. Because many situations which confront officers in the course of executing their duties are more or less ambiguous, room must be allowed for some mistakes on their part. But the mistakes must be those of reasonable men, acting on facts leading sensibly to their conclusions of probability. The rule of probable cause is a practical, non-technical conception affording the best compromise that has been found for accommodating those often opposing interests. Requiring more would unduly hamper law enforcement. To allow less would be to leave law-abiding citizens at the mercy of the officers' whim or caprice.

To implement the Fourth Amendment's protection against unfounded invasions of liberty and privacy, the Court has required that the existence of probable cause be decided by a neutral and detached magistrate whenever possible. The classic statement of this principle appears in *Johnson v. United States*, * * * 68 S. Ct. 367, 369 (1948):

> The point of the Fourth Amendment, which often is not grasped by zealous officers, is not that it denies law enforcement the support of the usual inferences which reasonable men draw from evidence. Its protection consists in requiring that those inferences be drawn by a neutral and detached magistrate instead of being judged by the officer engaged in the often competitive enterprise of ferreting out crime.

CASE BRIEF

Draper v. United States, 79 S. Ct. 329 (1959)

Majority opinion: Whittaker. Dissenting: Douglas.

FACTS: H, a reliable paid informant, told a federal narcotics agent that a certain person had recently moved to Denver and was peddling drugs. Four days later H told the agent that the person had gone to Chicago and would return to Denver by train on the eighth or ninth of that month with three ounces of heroin. H gave the agent a detailed description of him including the kind of clothing he wore, that he carried a tan zipper bag, and that he habitually "walked real fast." Agents conducted surveillance of the train station on the days mentioned by H and, on the ninth, a person, D, exactly matching the description given by H got off the train from Chicago. The agents stopped D and arrested and searched him. They found heroin in his coat pocket and a syringe in the zipper bag. There was statutory authority for the agents to make an arrest without a warrant if they had "reasonable grounds" to believe that a person was violating or had violated drug laws. D moved to suppress the evidence, claiming the arrest was not made with probable cause and therefore the search incidental thereto was unlawful. The motion to suppress was denied and the evidence was admitted at trial. D was convicted.

ISSUE: Was the arrest made with probable cause?

DECISION: Yes; conviction affirmed.

REASONS: D's claim that hearsay from H could not be used as part of probable cause is erroneous. The distinction between admissible evidence (which is required to establish guilt at trial) and hearsay (which can be used to establish probable cause for arrest) was made in an earlier case; *Brinegar v. United States*, 69 S. Ct. 1302 (1949). D's further claim that, even if admissible, the information did not establish probable cause, is also incorrect. H had always supplied reliable information; the agents had a duty to pursue his tip. When the agents personally verified the tip by observation at the train station, there was probable cause to believe the unverified part of the information (that D had drugs in his possession) was also true. The test for probable cause is what a man of reasonable caution would believe under the same circumstances; it deals in probabilities — factual and practical considerations of everyday life on which reasonable and prudent men, not legal technicians, act. Under these facts there was probable cause for arrest; because the arrest was lawful, although without a warrant, the search incident thereto was valid.

RULE: An arrest made upon verification of the details of a tip from a known and reliable informant will be made with probable cause if (1) the informant's predictions unfold precisely as foretold and (2) what the officers observe is consistent with the probability that a crime is being committed.

DISSENTING: Dissenting opinion omitted.

CASE BRIEF

Beck v. Ohio, 87 S. Ct. 223 (1964)

Majority Opinion: Stewart

FACTS: Police observed D driving his car. Recognizing him as someone previously arrested for gambling violations, they pulled him over and arrested him. After searching D's car and finding no incriminating evidence, they took him to the police station, where an envelope of gambling slips was found hidden in his sock. The police had no arrest or search warrant. D filed a motion to suppress the gambling slips as evidence on the basis of unreasonable search and seizure, but they were admitted and D was convicted. The conviction was affirmed by the Ohio Court of Appeals and Ohio Supreme Court.

ISSUE: Did the police have probable cause for D's arrest?

DECISION: No; reversed.

REASONS: The record is very limited with reference to the probable cause of D's arrest. To uphold this arrest as being valid under the Constitution would mean that anyone with a prior arrest record whom the police could recognize and identify as having an arrest record could be arrested at will. Probable cause for a warrantless arrest must meet the same standard required by a judge for the issuing of a warrant. When the constitutionality of an arrest is challenged, a court must determine whether the facts and circumstances known to the police at the moment the warrantless arrest is made would justify a man of reasonable caution believing that an offense has been committed by the person arrested. Here, the officer testified only that he had "information", and had "heard reports" about D, but the content or source of the information and reports was undisclosed in the record of the trial. Nor does the record contain any indication that the officer saw D make a "stop" to further the suspected gambling activity, or that the officers saw, heard, smelled or otherwise perceived anything else to give them a ground for believing that D had, or was then, acting unlawfully. If these officers were in fact acting in good faith on information supplied by an informer, it was the responsibility of the prosecution to show with more specificity than appears in this record what the informer said and why the officers believed the information. Good faith on the part of the arresting officers is not enough to establish the probable cause required by the Fourth Amendment. Without probable cause, the arrest and search incident thereto were invalid and the conviction of D must be reversed.

RULE: An arrest made without a warrant must meet the same test of probable cause at the moment the arrest is made as would be needed to secure a warrant from a judge, and when the constitutionality of such an arrest is challenged, there must be a showing of adequate probable cause in the trial record.

CASE BRIEF

Gerstein v. Pugh, 95 S. Ct. 854 (1975)

Majority opinion: Powell. Concurring in part: Stewart, joined by Douglas, Brennan and Marshall.

FACTS: D1 and D2 were arrested and charged with several offenses under a prosecutor's information and without a prior preliminary hearing or leave of court. Under Florida law a defendant could not get a judicial determination of probable cause in less than thirty days. D1 was denied bail because he was charged with an offense carrying a potential life sentence; D2 was unable to post bail. D1 and D2 sued in federal district court, claiming the right to judicial determination of probable cause. The district court granted the relief sought, holding that the Fourth and Fourteenth Amendments give all persons arrested and charged by information the right to a judicial hearing on the question of probable cause. Before the district court issued its findings he Florida Supreme Court amended procedural rules to require that every arrested person must be taken before a judicial officer within 24 hours. In a supplemental opinion the district court held the amended rules did not correct the constitutional error because the judicial officer was not required to rule on probable cause. In the judicial determination of probable cause, the district court also held that the hearing must be adversary in character. The court of appeals affirmed these holdings.

ISSUES: (1) Is a person arrested and held for trial on an information entitled to a judicial determination of probable cause for detention; (2) if so, is an adversary hearing required by the Constitution at this stage?

DECISION: (1) Yes; (2) no. Affirmed in part, reversed in part.

REASONS: Standards and procedures for arrest and detention are derived from the Fourth Amendment and the common law. The accepted standard for arrest is "probable cause," defined in terms of facts and circumstances sufficient to warrant a prudent man believing that the suspect has committed or is committing an offense. The existence of probable cause must be decided, wherever possible, by a neutral and detached magistrate instead of by law enforcement officers engaged in the often competitive enterprise of ferreting out crime.

Ideally, the determination of probable cause should be made by the magistrate prior to the arrest, but this would place an intolerable burden on law enforcement.

Once a warrantless arrest has been made there is no reason to delay or dispense with the magistrate's neutral judgment on probable cause. There is no longer danger that the in-custody suspect will flee the jurisdiction or commit further crimes. The suspect's job, sources of income, and family relationships may all be seriously jeopardized by continued custody without a hearing. The Fourth Amendment requires a judicial determination of probable cause as a prerequisite to extended restraint on liberty following an arrest as a protection against unfounded interference with liberty.

Although the prosecutor's screening and decision to prosecute offers some measure of protection against unfounded detention, they do not, standing alone, meet the requirements of the Fourth Amendment. A prosecutor's responsibility to law enforcement is inconsistent with the constitutional role of a neutral and detached magistrate to determine probable cause.

This does not imply that an accused is entitled to review of the decision to prosecute. A judicial hearing is not a prerequisite to prosecution by information, nor is illegal arrest or detention cause to void a subsequent conviction. Although a suspect who is presently detained may challenge the probable cause for that confinement, a conviction will not be vacated because there was detention pending trial without a determination of probable cause. Some states utilize adversary hearings to determine whether the evidence justifies going to trial under an information or presenting the case to a grand jury. These adversary safeguards are not essential for a probable cause determination under the Fourth Amendment when the only issue is detention pending trial. That issue can be determined reliably by the magistrate from hearsay and written testimony. The "reasonable doubt" or "preponderance" standards are not involved. The standard is the same as that for arrest — to determine if the evidence supports a reasonable belief in guilt.

Because of its limited function and nonadversary character, the probable cause determination is not a critical stage in a criminal proceeding that requires appointed counsel.

RULE: The Fourth and Fourteenth Amendments require a judicial determination of probable cause either before or promptly after arrest as a condition to extended restraint on liberty, but this proceeding need not be adversary in nature.

------------------------------------- **Notes** -------------------------------------

"PROMPT" PROBABLE CAUSE HEARING DEFINED

In the case of an arrest made without a previously-issued arrest warrant, the Constitution requires that a "prompt" *judicial* determination of probable cause be made after the arrest. *Gerstein v. Pugh*, 95 S.Ct. 854 (1975). The meaning of the word "prompt" as used in this context was clarified in the case of *Riverside County, Calif. v. McLaughlin*, 111 S.Ct. 1661 (1991). The probable cause hearing need not be conducted immediately after the booking process, the Court held, but may be delayed for combination with other pre-trial appearances before the judge. Unless the D can show it is unreasonable delay, a probable cause hearing held within 48 hours from the time of arrest, including weekends, is presumptively reasonable. Delays exceeding 48 hours from the time of arrest are presumptively unreasonable and shift the burden to the state to show justification by emergency or other extraordinary circumstances. The Court stated:

"The fact that in a particular case it may take longer than 48 hours to consolidate pretrial proceedings does not qualify as an extraordinary circumstance. Nor, for that matter, do intervening weekends. A jurisdiction that chooses to offer combined proceedings must do so as soon as is reasonably feasible, but in no event later than 48 hours after arrest."

[This holding may have great potential for creating civil liability in cases of arrests made late on Fridays or on 3-day holiday weekends when there is a shortage of judge availability and/or a lack of other proper release procedures].

--------------------------------- **Notes** ---------------------------------

Sample Questions

Prosecuting attorneys, whose duties generally fall within the judicial area, are absolutely immune from money damages in lawsuits filed against them for:

A. any act committed during their term of office.
B. acts committed as private citizens.
C. acts committed within the scope of their judicial duties.
D. legal advice given to the police.
E. all acts committed, whether as public office holders or as private citizens.

The Federal Civil Rights Act creates a right to sue:

A. any federal officeholder.
B. any state officeholder.
C. a federal officeholder who has violated the plaintiff's rights under a State Constitution under color of federal law.
D. persons who commit acts of simple negligence.
E. a person who is alleged to have violated federally-protected rights under color of state law.

In fifty words or less define the meaning of "under color of state law", as those words are used in connection with the Federal Civil Rights Act.

In fifty words or less indicate the difference between "absolute" immunity and "qualified" immunity from money damages.

A prosecutor's participation in a probable cause hearing, in which he directs questions to the state's witnesses, including police officers, in the presence of a judge, but through avoiding certain questions he withholds pertinent information from the judge which results in an alleged violation of federally-protected rights of a criminal defendant:

A. will result in the prosecution being absolutely liable in money damages if the violation of rights is proved.
B. will result in no liability to the prosecutor because his participation in a probable cause hearing is clearly a judicial function.
C. will result in the prosecutor being held to the standard of qualified immunity.
D. raises no question of civil liability because prosecutors are simply not liable in money damages for any conduct, within or without the scope of their duties.
E. None of the above.

The reason justifying money damage lawsuits against governmental employees, including police officers, is that while government must be allowed to perform its functions, including law enforcement, a citizen should not be without a legal remedy if injured by an act of a police officer that is unreasonable and not authorized by the scope of his duties. In other words, a balance must be maintained between effective government and unjustifiable injury to citizens by governmental agents. T F.

A theory of the law regarding the liability of police officers is that as long as a police officer acts within the scope of his authorized duties, he is acting for the government, and cannot be held liable for a valid governmental act, but if his action falls outside the scope of his authorized duties, (such as the use of excessive and unreasonable force), he is acting as an individual, and may be held liable in money damages. T F.

§ 4.5 ISSUANCE AND EXECUTION OF ARREST AND SEARCH WARRANTS

". . . no warrants shall issue, but upon cause, supported by oath or affirmation, and particularly describing the place to be searched, and the persons or things to be seized." Constitution of the United States, Amendment 4.

Only a neutral and detached judicial officer may issue a warrant. *Coolidge v. New Hampshire*, 91 S. Ct. 2022 (1971). The common law required that the application for a warrant be made in person before a judicial officer in order that the applicant could be examined under oath and the judicial officer could be satisfied that a crime had in fact been committed. 4 Bl. Comm. 287. Today, the laws of some states, as well as the federal Rules of criminal Procedure, authorize applications for warrants to be made over the telephone; but putting the sworn application for a warrant in writing preserves the record and provides notice to the subject of the warrant.

In some states, courts are willing to issue "anticipatory" warrants (see *Illinois v. Gates*, 103 S. Ct. 2317 (1983), at §4.15(A) herein), but in others, the warrant statutes are interpreted too narrowly to permit this practice.

The persons or things to be seized under a warrant must be described in the warrant "particularly," but just how specifically depends to some extent on the facts and circumstances of each case. For example, if the true name of an individual to be arrested is unknown, he should be described with "reasonable certainty." Indiana Code, IC 35-33-2-2. See also *Maryland v. Garrison*, 107 S. Ct. 1013 (1987), with reference to the description of the place to be searched.

"The right of the people to be secure in their persons, houses, papers, and effects, against unreasonable searches and seizures, shall not be violated . . ." U.S. Const. Amendt. 4.

A search may be unreasonable even though it is conducted under a properly issued warrant. Obviously, if the object described in the warrant measures two by three by four feet, it could not be found in a medicine cabinet or desk drawer. The officer would be authorized to search only those areas where an item of that size could reasonably be found, and only those houses or other structures particularly described in the warrant.

Some states have restrictions on the nighttime execution of warrants; in other states warrants can be served at any time.

The requirement that an officer serving a warrant knock first and announce his authority and purpose is discussed in §4.8 herein.

Because a search warrant is issued upon probable cause to believe that certain items are then located — or will be located — at a described place, the warrant can become "stale" if too much time elapses between issuance and execution; the items could be moved to another place. Each state has established time limits for the execution of search warrants by statute or by case law.

Arrest warrants, on the other hand, are issued on probable cause to believe that an individual has committed a crime in the past. This allegation (be it fact or not) will not change with the passage of time. Arrest warrants, therefore, are generally not subject to the "staleness" theory, but, again, each state has its own rules concerning how long an arrest warrant may be considered to be a valid continuing order of the issuing court.

If a search warrant specifically names a person to be searched, that person can be searched under the authority of the warrant. But if the warrant is for the search of a *place*, can a person found in that place be searched under the warrant? This was the issue in *Ybarra v. Illinois*, 100 S. Ct. 338 (1979). The Court held that unless there was suspicion that such persons might be armed and dangerous within the meaning of *Terry v. Ohio*, 88 S. Ct. 1868 (1968), they could not be frisked for weapons.

In *Michigan v. Summers*, 101 S. Ct. 2587 (1981) The Supreme Court held that in the execution of a search warrant there is a limited authority for the police to detain persons who are occupants of the premises to be searched, while the search is being conducted. In *Summers* the police encountered D leaving his residence by the front steps as they prepared to enter. They detained him on the premises while they conducted the search. Noting that both arrest and search warrants require prior determination of probable cause by a neutral and detached magistrate, and that legitimate purposes are served by detaining occupants during the search of a house, the Court stated:

> If the evidence that a citizen's residence is harboring contraband is sufficient to persuade a judicial officer that an invasion of the citizen's privacy is justified, it is constitutionally reasonable to require the citizen to remain while officers of the law execute a valid warrant to search his home. Thus, for Fourth Amendment purposes, we hold that a warrant to search for contraband founded on probable cause implicitly carries with it the limited authority to detain the occupants of the premises while a proper search is conducted.

------------------------------------- **Notes** -------------------------------------

§ 4.6 ARREST, WITH OR WITHOUT A WARRANT

As was mentioned in §4.3 herein, in many states the arrest authority of a police officer is affected by whether he is dealing with a felony or a misdemeanor. The Supreme Court of the United States stated, in *Carroll v. United States*, 45 S. Ct. 280, 286 (1925):

> The usual rule is that a police officer may arrest without warrant one believed by the officer upon reasonable cause to have been guilty of a felony, and that he may only arrest without a warrant one guilty of a misdemeanor if committed in his presence.

* * *

The rule is sometimes expressed as follows:

> In cases of misdemeanor, a peace officer like a private person has at common law no power of arresting without a warrant except when a breach of the peace has been committed in his presence or there is reasonable ground for supposing that a breach of peace is about to be committed or renewed in his presence. * * *

> The reason for arrest for misdemeanor without warrant at common law was promptly to suppress breaches of the peace . . . while the reason for arrest without warrant on a reliable report of a felony was because the public safety and the due apprehension of criminals charged with heinous offenses required that such arrests should be made at once without warrant.

In most states the arrest authority of police officers is specified in statutory law. The basic common law rule as stated in *Carroll* is reflected in many state statutes, but some states have enlarged these powers in specific situations in response to the demands of modern law enforcement.

Arrest authority, with or without a warrant, may also be affected by whether the arrest takes place in a public or a private place.

CASE BRIEF

United States v. Watson, 96 S. Ct. 820 (1976)

Majority opinion: White. Concurring: Stewart, Powell. Dissenting: Marshall, joined by Brennan.

FACTS: K, an informant, told a postal inspector that D had stolen a credit card and had asked K to help him use the card to their mutual advantage. K had previously given reliable information to postal authorities. Later that day K delivered the card to the inspector. On learning that D had agreed to furnish additional stolen cards, the authorities urged K to meet with D. K met D at a restaurant. K had been instructed that if D had additional stolen cards, he was to give a designated signal. The signal was given, the officers closed in and D was arrested. D was moved from the restaurant to the street, where he was given the *Miranda* warnings. A search of D's person revealed no additional credit cards. An inspector then asked D if he could look inside D's car, which was nearby. D said, "Go ahead," and repeated these words when the inspector cautioned him, "If I find anything it's going to go against you." Using keys furnished by D, the inspector entered the car and under the floor mat found two credit cards in the names of other persons. These cards were the basis of an indictment against D.

Before trial D moved to suppress the cards, claiming that the arrest was without probable cause and that his consent to search his car was invalid and ineffective because he was not told he could without consent. The motion was denied and D was convicted. The U.S. Court of Appeals, Ninth Circuit, reversed, ruling that the admission into evidence of the stolen credit cards violated the Fourth Amendment because (1) even though K was a known and reliable informant and there was probable cause to arrest D, the arrest was unconstitutional because the inspector had failed to secure an arrest warrant although he had time to do so, and (2) based on a totality of the circumstances D's consent to search his car was coerced.

ISSUES: (1) Is a warrantless arrest made on good probable cause unconstitutional for failure to secure an arrest warrant when there was opportunity to do so? and (2) Was D's consent to search valid?

DECISION: (1) No; (2) Yes. Court of appeals decision reversed and conviction upheld.

REASONS: Federal law expressly empowers the postal service to authorize postal inspector to make an arrest without warrant is they have reasonable grounds to believe that the person to be arrested has committed or is committing a felony. The postal service board of governors has exercised that power by regulation, authorizing warrantless arrests. There was probable cause (same as reasonable grounds) in this case. The effect of the court of appeals decision was to invalidate the statute and the regulation as to all situations where exigent circumstances are lacking. The statute represents a judgment by Congress that it is not unreasonable under the Fourth Amendment for postal inspectors to make arrests without a warrant if they have probable cause to do so. Many other federal enforcement officers have been granted the same authority. There is a strong presumption of constitutionality of an act of Congress, especially when it turns on what is "reasonable." Moreover, there is nothing in the Court's prior cases indicating that under the Fourth Amendment a warrant is required to make a valid arrest for a felony — indeed, the relevant prior decisions are to the contrary.

The usual rule is that a police officer may arrest without warrant one believed by the officer upon reasonable cause to have been guilty of a felony. The necessary inquiry, therefore, was not whether there was a warrant or whether there was time to get one but whether there was probable cause for the arrest.

The Court has never invalidated an arrest supported by probable cause solely because the officer failed to secure a warrant. The cases construing the Fourth Amendment reflect the ancient common-law rule that a peace officer was permitted to arrest without a warrant for a misdemeanor or felony committed in his presence as well as for a felony not committed in his presence if there was reasonable grounds for making the arrest.

The Court will not interpret the Constitution as requiring that warrants for felony arrests must be obtained where possible, absent exigent circumstances. Police may prefer to obtain warrants in such cases, and their judgments about probable cause may be more readily accepted where backed by a warrant, but they are not required to obtain warrants, constitutionally, when making a felony arrest in a public place, based on probable cause.

In this case, therefore, D's consent to the search of his car was not the product of an illegal arrest. In the totality of circumstances D's consent was "essentially free and unconstrained." There was no overt threat or force against D proved or even claimed. There were no promises or subtle forms of coercion. He had been arrested and was in custody. Custody *alone* has never been enough, in itself, to demonstrate a coerced confession or consent to search. As in the case of *Schneckloth v. Bustamonte*, 93 S. Ct. 2041 (1973), the absence of proof that D knew he could withhold his consent, though a factor in the overall judgment, is not to be given controlling significance. D had been given his *Miranda* warnings and was further cautioned that the results of the car search could be used against him. He persisted in his consent nevertheless.

RULE: The validity of a warrantless arrest in a public place for the commission of a felony does not turn on the officer's opportunity to obtain an arrest warrant. Such an arrest will be valid, if based on probable cause (or reasonable grounds), regardless of whether there was an opportunity to secure an arrest warrant. Custody, in and of itself, is not enough to invalidate consent to search an automobile, if the totality of the circumstances shows no threat, promise or other coercion, and if the person in custody has been given *Miranda* warnings and notice of possible consequences of the search.

DISSENTING: The majority need not have decided case on the basis it did because the arrest of D (upon signal from the informant) fell within the exigent circumstances exception and was proper. The same warrant rules for searches should also apply to arrests. The burden should be on the government to show that a suspect in custody knew he need not give consent.

CASE BRIEF

Payton v. New York, 100 S. Ct. 1371 (1980)

Majority opinion: Stevens. Concurring: Blackmun. Dissenting: White, Burger, Rehnquist.

FACTS: After an intensive investigation police had probable cause to believe that D1 had murdered a gas station manager. At 7:30 a.m. six officers went to D1's apartment to arrest him without warrant. There were lights on in the apartment and music was playing, but there was no response to a knock on the door. After summoning emergency assistance the officers forced entry into the apartment, but no one was there. A 30-caliber shell casing found in plain view was seized. D1 later surrendered and was indicted for murder. At his trial D1 moved to suppress all evidence taken from his apartment. (The prosecutor stipulated that the search of the entire apartment was illegal and that all evidence found there except the shell casing should be suppressed.) The trial judge held that the warrantless and forcible entry was authorized by New York statutes and that the evidence found in plain view was properly seized. He also ruled that exigent circumstances justified the officers' failure to announce their purpose as required by statute. The trial judge had no occasion to decide whether the circumstances justified the failure to obtain a warrant of arrest because he concluded the warrantless entry was authorized by statute regardless of the circumstances. D1 was convicted and his conviction was affirmed by the New York Court of Appeals.

D2 was arrested for the commission of two armed robberies. He had been identified by the victims; officers went to his home without a warrant and knocked on the door. When D2's young son opened the door, the police saw D2 sitting in bed, covered with a sheet. The police entered and place D2 under arrest. Before allowing him to dress they opened a chest of drawers two feet from the bed in search of weapons and found drugs and related paraphernalia. D2 was later indicted on drug charges. At a suppression hearing the trial judge held that the warrantless entry to arrest was authorized by New York statute and that the search was reasonable under *Chimel v. California*, 89 S. Ct. 2034 (1969). D2 was tried and convicted and the New York Court of Appeals affirmed. The court of appeals recognized that the question of whether and under what circumstances the police may enter a suspect's home to make a warrantless arrest had not been settled by that court or the Supreme Court of the United States; it justified its ruling on the "substantial differences" between an intrusion for the purpose of search and an intrusion for the purpose of making a felony arrest. The court noted the "apparent historical acceptance" of warrantless entries to make felony arrests, both in common law and in the practice of many states.

Three justices dissented, arguing that the Constitution requires a warrant to enter a home to arrest or seize a person, just as it does to enter a home to search for and seize an object, unless there are exigent circumstances. This dissent ran counter to the statutory authority to make a warrantless entry for a felony arrest that had existed in New York for almost 100 years.

ISSUE: Does the Constitution permit the warrantless entry into the private home of an arrestee to make a routine felony arrest when there are no exigent circumstances and where there was ample time to obtain an arrest warrant?

DECISION: No; reversed and remanded.

REASONS: Abuses under the authority of "general warrants" led to the adoption of the Fourth Amendment. Its first clause protects the right to be free from unreasonable searches and seizures, and the second requires that warrants be particular and supported by probable cause. Unreasonable searches and seizures conducted without any warrant at all are condemned by the first clause of the Amendment. Since the arrest of a person is a seizure, a warrantless arrest is required to be reasonable. The amendment applies equally to seizures of persons and of property. The Court unanimously held only a few years ago that "physical entry of the home is the chief evil against which the wording of the Fourth Amendment is directed"; *United States v. United States District Court*, 92 S. Ct. 2125 (1972). The warrant procedure minimizes the danger of needless intrusions of that sort.

While it is a basic principle of Fourth Amendment law that searches and seizures inside a home without a warrant are presumptively unreasonable, it is also well settled that objects such as weapons or contraband found in a *public place* may be seized by the police without a warrant. Plain view seizures involve no invasion of privacy and are presumptively reasonable provided there is probable cause to associate the property with criminal activity. These distinctions have equal force when the seizure of a person is involved. An entry to arrest and an entry to search for and seize property both raise the issue of the sanctity of the home and justify the same level of constitutional protection.

Any differences in the intrusiveness between entries to search and entries to arrest are merely ones of degree rather than kind; they both breach the entrance to an individual's home.

At the very core of the Fourth Amendment stands the right of a man to retreat into his own home and there be free of unreasonable governmental intrusion. In terms that apply equally to seizures of property and to seizures of persons, the Fourth Amendment has drawn a firm line at the entrance of the house. Absent exigent circumstances, that threshold may not reasonably be crossed without a warrant.

United States v. Watson [briefed above] approved warrantless felony arrests in a *public place;* there is little common-law authority for warrantless entries into a home for a felony arrest. Leading commentators on the common law were divided on the question, and the issue was not definitely settled by the common law at the time the Fourth Amendment was adopted.

A survey of the states indicates that only New York and Florida have expressly upheld warrantless entries to arrest in the face of federal constitutional challenge. There is no evidence that effective law enforcement has suffered in those states that have forbidden warrantless entries of homes to arrest.

The state suggests that only a search warrant based on probable cause to believe the suspect is at home at a given time can adequately protect the privacy interests at stake — and, since this requirement would be manifestly impractical, that there need be no warrant of any kind. This argument is unpersuasive. While it is true that an arrest warrant requirement may afford less protection than a search warrant requirement, it still places the magistrate's determination between the zealous officer and the citizen, and if the magistrate is persuaded that probable cause exists for a felony arrest warrant, it is constitutionally reasonable to require the citizen to open his doors to officers of the law. Thus, for Fourth Amendment purposes, an arrest warrant founded on probable cause implicitly carries with it the limited authority to enter a dwelling in which the suspect lives when there is reason to believe the suspect is within.

RULE: In the absence of exigent circumstances, the warrantless and nonconsensual entry of a private residence by the police, for the purpose of effecting a routine felony arrest of a resident therein, violates the Fourth and Fourteenth Amendments, and any evidence seized as a product of such warrantless entry or arrest is inadmissible.

DISSENTING: The majority opinion creates a rule which is too inflexible. It was the abuses that had taken place under the color of warrants, and not under the inherent power of a constable to make warrantless arrests, that led to the drafting of the Fourth Amendment. The scarcity of case law on the subject of warrantless entries to make routine felony arrests is due to the wide acceptance of the practice under the common law. This common-law view has been adopted in many states by statute. The privacy of the home is already protected against unreasonable warrantless entries by four restrictions on home arrests; (1) the requirement that the offense be a felony; (2) the knock and announce requirement; (3) the daytime arrest requirement; and (4) the stringent probable cause requirement. The majority opinion will also hamper effective law enforcement and create uncertainty as to what constitutes "exigent circumstances."

CASE BRIEF

Steagald v. United States, 101 S. Ct. 1642 (1981)

Majority opinion: Marshall. Concurring: Burger. Dissenting: Rehnquist, White.

FACT: Drug enforcement authorities received a tip from a confidential informant that R.L., the subject of a six-month-old arrest warrant, was at a specified telephone number. Cross-checking the phone number and the address, agents went to the address (not R.L.'s home) to search for R.L. The officers saw two men standing outside the house to be searched. One of these men was D. The officers approached with guns drawn, frisked the men and determined that neither was R.L. A woman answered the door and told the officers she was alone in the house. She was told to place her hands against the wall and she was guarded while officers searched the house for R.L. He was not found, but an officer observed in plain view what he believed to be cocaine. An officer was sent to obtain a search warrant; meanwhile additional incriminating evidence was discovered. Later, in a search conducted pursuant to the search warrant, 43 pounds of cocaine was discovered and seized. D was arrested and indicted on federal drug charges.

Before trial D moved to suppress all items seized because the agents had failed to obtain a search warrant before entering the house. The government responded that no search warrant had been necessary because the arrest warrant for R.L., coupled with reasonable belief that he was present in the house, was sufficient to justify the entry and search. The district court agreed and denied the suppression motion. D was convicted and the conviction was upheld on appeal. The Supreme Court granted certiorari.

ISSUE: Is a valid arrest warrant — as opposed to a search warrant — sufficient authority to enter the home of a third party to search for the person named in the arrest warrant when there is reasonable belief that the wanted person is there, but when there is no consent and no exigent circumstances?

DECISION: No; reversed.

REASONS: Here there was no consent to search and there were no exigent circumstances such as fresh pursuit. The Fourth Amendment has drawn a firm line at the entrance to a residence. Without exigent circumstances or consent, the threshold may not reasonably be crossed without a warrant. Here, the agents had a warrant for the arrest of R.L., but the appellant is not R.L. He is a person not named in the warrant who was convicted on the basis of evidence found during a search of his residence for R.L.

The purpose of a warrant is to allow a neutral judicial officer to assess whether police have probable cause to arrest or search. The interests protected by an arrest warrant requirement and a search warrant requirement differ. An arrest warrant protects an individual from unreasonable seizure, while a search warrant protects against unjustified intrusion by the police on privacy. The warrant authorized the officers to arrest R.L. But the agents sought to do more than to arrest R.L. in his home or in a public place; they relied on the same warrant to enter the home of a third person in the belief that R.L. was there. Regardless of how reasonable this belief might have been, it was never subjected to the detached scrutiny of a judicial officer. Thus, while the warrant protected R.L. from an unreasonable seizure, it did nothing to protect D's privacy interests. D's only protection from an unreasonable entry into his home was the agents' personal determination of probable cause. In the absence of exigent circumstances an officer's own determination of probable cause is not reliable enough to justify entering a person's home to make an arrest or to search for objects. The same rule holds when the search of a home is for a person rather than an object. A contrary conclusion, that police could act alone and in the absence or exigent circumstances, would create a significant potential for abuse, such as searching for an arrestee named in an arrest warrant in the homes of all his friends and acquaintances. Nor will existing remedies such as motions to suppress evidence and damage actions serve to safeguard Fourth Amendment rights. The Fourth Amendment is designed to prevent, not simply to redress, unlawful police action.

The common law seems to have justified forcible entry into a third party's house only in a fresh pursuit situation. The common-law authorities upon which the government relies were concerned mainly with the question of whether the subject of an arrest warrant could claim sanctuary from arrest by hiding in the home of a third party. But the issue here is not whether the subject of an arrest warrant can object to the absence of a search warrant when he is apprehended in another's home, but rather whether the residents of that home can complain of the search. The common-law authorities therefore are of limited use in this case; if anything, they undercut the government's position by reference to the home as the "castle" of its residents.

The Fourth Amendment was designed to protect against the evils of general warrants, which typically specified only an offense and left to the discretion of the officers the persons to be arrested and places to be searched, and *writs of assistance*, which specified only the object of the search. The objectionable feature of both was that they provided no judicial check on the discretion of executing officials before an intrusion into any home. An arrest warrant, to the extent that it is used as authority to enter the homes of third parties, suffers from the same infirmity.

The search warrant requirement will not significantly impede law enforcement efforts. An arrest warrant alone is sufficient to enter a suspect's residence. If probable cause exists, no warrant is necessary to apprehend a felony suspect in a public place. Moreover, the exigent circumstances doctrine limits the situations in which a search warrant would be needed.

If police know the location of the felon when they obtain an arrest warrant, the additional burden of obtaining a search warrant is small. In contrast, the right protected — that of presumptively innocent people to be secure in their homes from unjustified forcible intrusions by the government — is weighty.

RULE: An arrest warrant empowers police to enter residence of the person to be arrested. To arrest the subject of a warrant in the residence of a third person, a search warrant, in addition to the arrest warrant, should be obtained in order to protect the rights of the third person, unless consent is obtained or exigent circumstances, such as fresh pursuit, exist. Without the search warrant, evidence found in the third person's home during the arrest may not be admissible in a prosecution against the third person.

DISSENTING: The majority opinion is not supported by past decisions or the common law. Reasonableness is still the ultimate standard. The imposition of the search warrant requirement will frustrate interests of the government in the arrest of highly mobile felons. The invasion of property of the third party is not as significant as is made out in the majority opinion; no general search is authorized by the arrest warrant, only a search of areas where the fugitive might hide. There need be no invasion at all if the wanted felon surrenders at the door or if the harboring individual points out his hiding place.

The *Steagald* case creates potential for confusion concerning the validity of arresting, with a warrant, a person in the home of a third person when no search warrant is obtained to enter and search for the wanted person. It should be remembered, however, that the validity of the arrest of R.L. was *not* an issue in *Steagald* because R.L. was not present in the home of D. The issue was the admissibility of incriminating evidence against the third person-householder (Steagald) whose home had been entered for the purpose of arresting R.L. under the authority of an arrest warrant. The cases on standing to object to the violation of rights of others would seem to shed light on this situation. One of the leading cases on standing is *Rakas v. Illinois*, 99 S. Ct. 42 (1978), which holds that Fourth Amendment rights are personal and that a person cannot have evidence which incriminates him suppressed merely because it was seized in violation of somebody else's rights. Although most cases on standing involve the question of admissibility of physical evidence, *Steagald* implies that a similar issue might arise concerning the validity of an arrest.

In *United States v. Buckner*, 717 F.2d 297 (6th Cir. 1983) the United States Court of Appeals, Sixth Circuit, upheld the validity of the warrantless arrest of D, a suspected bank robber, on probable cause, even though the arrest was made in the home of D's mother without a search warrant for her home having been obtained. The Court discussed both *Payton* and *Steagald*, but ruled that in light of the *Rakas* case and others, D could not show that he had a legitimate expectation of privacy in his mother's home; therefore, both D's arrest and the seizure of evidence found there were valid. Unlike *Steagald* there was no issue concerning admissibility of evidence against the third party homeowner. The court stated:

> "In summary, we conclude that the defendant did not have a legitimate expectation of privacy in the premises which were searched and therefore could not challenge the search. Since the police had probable cause to arrest the defendant for bank robbery, both the arrest and the search were valid *as to him*" (our emphasis).

The *Buckner* holding was further supported by the fact that police had verified the existence of a previously-issued but unexecuted warrant for D on a previous, unrelated crime; thus the *existence* of an arrest warrant (not necessarily the physical possession of it), plus reason to believe D was on the premises, justified police entry of a private home to effect an arrest. The holding of *Buckner* is further supported by the observation of the Court that it would be illogical to afford a defendant any greater protection in the home of a third party than he would be entitled to in his own home.

The United States Court of Appeals for the Ninth Circuit agreed with the *Buckner* holding in *United States v. Underwood*, 717 F.2d 482, (9th Cir. 1983):

> A person has no greater right of privacy in another's home than in his own. If an arrest warrant and reason to believe the person named in the warrant is present are sufficient to protect that person's fourth amendment privacy rights in his own home, they necesarily suffice to protect the privacy rights in the home of another. *U.S. v. Clifford*, 664 F.2d 1090, 1093 (8th Cir. 1981).

An exigent circumstance that will justify the warrantless entry by the police into a private dwelling for the purpose of making a felony arrest is the existence of "fresh" or "hot" pursuit; *Warden v. Hayden*, 87 S. Ct. 1642 (1967). A unique application of this doctrine occurred in *United States v. Santana*, (briefed below.

CASE BRIEF
United States v. Santana, 96 S. Ct. 2406 (1976)

Majority opinion: Rehnquist. Concurring: White, Stevens, Stewart. Dissenting: Marshall, Brennan.

FACTS: G, an undercover narcotics officer, arranged a heroin "buy" with M, from whom he had purchased narcotics previously, and M said they should "go down to D1's for the dope." G notified his superiors of the impending buy, recorded the serial numbers of the buy money and met M at a prearranged location. M got into G's car and directed him to D1's residence. M took the marked money and went inside, stopping briefly to speak to D2, who was seated on the front steps.

M came out of the house a short time later, got into G's car, and on request, gave G several glassine envelopes containing a brownish-white powder. G stopped his car, displayed his badge, and arrested M. He told M that the police were going back to D1's and asked M where the money was. M said D1 had the money. At this point other officers came up to the car. G showed them the envelopes and told them D1 had the money. G then took M to the police station.

The other officers drove back to D1's residence where they saw D1 standing in the doorway of the house with a paper bag in her hand. The pulled up to within fifteen feet of D1 and got out of their van, shouting "Police!" and displaying identification. As the officers approached, D1 retreated into the vestibule of the house. The officers followed D1 through the open door, catching her in the vestibule. As she tried to pull away, two bundles of glazed paper packets containing a white powder fell to the floor. D2 tried to make off with the dropped envelopes and was forcibly restrained. When D1 was told to empty her pockets, she produced some of the marked money used by M. The white powder was later determined to be heroin.

Indictments were filed against M, D1 and D2 in U.S. District Court, charging distribution of heroin and possession with intent to distribute. M pleaded guilty; D1 and D2 moved to suppress the heroin and money as evidence on the basis of unlawful seizure. The district court granted the motion, holding that although there was strong probable cause, the facts required a warrant of arrest to make a lawful arrest of D1 and a search warrant to recover the bait money. The district court further held that the "fresh pursuit" doctrine applied only to a chase on and about public streets. The court of appeals affirmed and the government sought review.

ISSUE: Were the warrantless arrests of D1 and D2 lawful?

DECISION: Yes, the arrests were lawful; reversed.

REASONS: It was held in *United States v. Watson*, 96 S. Ct. 820 (1976) that a warrantless arrest of a person in a public place on probable cause alone did not violate the Fourth Amendment. In the present case D1 was standing directly in the open doorway when the officers got out of their van. One step forward would have put her outside and one step backward would have put her in the vestibule of her home. Under the common law of property the threshold of one's dwelling is private, as well as the yard surrounding the house, but under cases interpreting the Fourth Admendment, D1 was in a public place. She was not in a place where she could expect privacy. She was not merely visible to the public, but was as exposed to public view, speech, hearing and touch as if she had been standing completely outside her house.

When the police, who had probable cause to arrest D1, sought to arrest her, they were merely intending to perform in a manner already approved in *Watson*. Moreover, D1's act of retreating into her house could not thwart an otherwise proper arrest. This case, involving a true "hot pursuit," is governed by the decision in *Warden v. Hayden*, 87 S. Ct. 1642 (1967) where the police, having probable cause to believe that an armed robber had entered a house a few minutes before, had the right to search for weapons. In the present case the need to act quickly was even greater, while the intrusion was less. The fact that the pursuit in this case ended almost as soon as it began did not make it any less a "hot pursuit" justifying the warrantless entry. There was also a realistic expectation that once D1 saw the police she would destroy the evidence. Once she had been arrested, the search incidential thereto was justified.

RULE: When a warrantless arrest for a felony based on adequate probable cause is set in motion in a public place, the suspect may not defeat the arrest by retreating into a private place. The police, being in hot pursuit, may enter such private place without a warrant to effect the arrest and conduct a search incidential thereto.

CONCURRING: (1) Longstanding statutory or judicial rules in the majority of jurisdictions in the United States concur with the Court's opinion, at least where entry by force was not required. (2) Having probable cause, the police were justified in deciding not to seek a warrant for D1's arrest, and even if not justified, the decision was harmless. It would have been proper to keep D1's house under surveillance while a warrant was being sought, and since she ventured into plain view a warrantless arrest would have been justified before the warrant could have been procured.

DISSENTING: Absent exigent circumstances police may not arrest a suspect without a warrant, and the arguable exigent circumstances here (the chance that word of M's arrest a block and a half from D1's house would get back to D1 in a matter of seconds) were a product of police conduct which may have been deliberately planned to defeat the warrant requirement.

--------------------------------------- **Notes** ---------------------------------------

Sample Questions

The Supreme Court of the United States has ruled that during the routine stationhouse "booking" of a person who is under custodial arrest, the police can, without a search warrant:

A. search the person of the arrestee as well as any container in his possession, whether open or closed.
B. only conduct a "frisk" of the arrestee's person.
C. only search the person arrested, but not containers in his possession.
D. only search the person arrested and containers in his possession which they have probable cause to believe contain items subject to seizure.
E. search the person arrested, but not any articles or containers in his possession unless written consent to search is obtained.

If there is probable cause to believe that a certain automobile contains items subject to seizure, and the automobile is stopped by the police on the street or highway under the authority of the "Carroll" automobile exception to the warrant requirement:

A. the car can only be searched as an incident to the arrest of the driver or passengers.
B. the car cannot be searched but may be detained until a search warrant is obtained.
C. every part of the car and its contents, including closed containers, may be searched without a warrant if the location or container searched could logically conceal the items searched for.
D. only the driver and occupants may be searched.
E. only the driver may be searched.

The temporary detention of a person by the police, short of actual arrest:

A. is always unlawful.
B. is always lawful.
C. must pass the "reasonableness" test of the 4th Amendment.
D. may lawfully occur during a "stop and frisk" situation.
E. C and D above.

The rules concerning searches of automobiles and the rules concerning searches of dwelling house are different because:

A. there is a greater privacy interest in a dwelling house than in an automobile.
B. the ancient English adage that "a man's home is his castle" is still generally true under American law when it concerns governmental intrusions into dwelling houses, but this concept is not as strong with reference to automobiles.
C. the justifications that may exist for automobile searches which are based on the mobility of the vehicle do not apply to fixed dwelling houses.
D. all of the above are true.
E. dwelling houses existed when the Fourth Amendment was written, but automobiles did not.

§ 4.7 USE OF FORCE

While an officer or private person may use such force as is necessary to make an arrest, he cannot use force or violence disproportionate to the nature and extent of the resistance offered. 6A C.J.S. Arrest §49a.

Reasonable force is authorized to secure and detain the offender, overcome his resistance, prevent his escape, recapture him if he escapes, and protect the arresting officer from bodily harm. But unnecessary force is never justified; the only force permitted is that which an ordinarily, prudent and intelligent person would use if he had the knowledge and if he were in the same situation as the arresting officer.

If an officer is assaulted, he is not bound to retreat, but may stand his ground and may even kill the attacker if that is necessary to save his own life or to protect himself against great bodily harm. This is true even when the assault grows out of an attempted arrest for a misdemeanor. (This is nothing more than the application of the doctrine of self-defense to an arrest situation). If what begins as a peaceful arrest for either misdemeanor or felony suddenly changes into a situation in which force applied by the arrestee imperils the life of the arresting officer, he may defend himself with like force, but again, with no more force than is necessary.

Tennessee v. Garner, briefed below, has established the standards for the use of deadly force by a police officer in apprehending a fleeing felon situation; it seems to apply the Fourth Amendment standard of reasonableness for searches and seizures to all arrests, regardless of the degree of force used.

In making an arrest for a misdemeanor an officer or private person is generally not authorized to use such force as will injure or imperil the life of the misdemeanant. 6A C.J.S. Arrest §49c.

In a misdemeanor arrest there is no right to use firearms, to endanger human life, to shed blood, to shoot or kill an offender in order to prevent his escape, even though he can't be otherwise overtaken, unless such force is necessary to the self-defense of the officer. The basis for this rule is that the security of persons and property is ordinarily not endangered by a misdemeanant at large.

CASE BRIEF
Tennessee v. Garner, 105 S. Ct. 1694 (1985)

Majority opinion: White. **Concurring:** Brennan, Marshall, Blackmun, Powell, and Stevens. **Dissenting:** O'Connor, Burger, and Rehnquist.

FACTS: Memphis police were dispatched to investigate a possible residence burglary at 10:45 p.m. Upon arrival at the scene, a neighbor woman standing on her porch told them she had heard breaking glass next door and thought someone had broken in. While one officer radioed the dispatcher, the other went to the rear of the house. He heard a door slam and saw someone run across the back yard and stop at a 6-foot-high chain link fence. With the aid of a flashlight, he could see the face and hands of the suspect, who appeared to be a teen-age male of slight build. No weapon was observed. The officer called out, "Police, halt" as he approached the suspect, but the latter started to climb the fence. The officer, convinced that he would be unable to capture the suspect if he made it over the fence, shot him. The wound was fatal. Ten dollars and a purse taken from the burglarized house were found on the suspect's body.

The officer's actions were seemingly authorized by the Tennessee statute which provided that ". . . if, after notice of the intention to arrest the defendant, he either flee or forcibly resist, the officer may use all the necessary means to effect the arrest." The police department policy was slightly more restrictive than the statute, but it, too, allowed the use of deadly force to apprehend a fleeing burglar. Neither the firearms review board nor the grand jury took any action against the officer because the shooting appeared to be proper use of police authority.

The dead suspect's father then filed a civil rights lawsuit in federal district court seeking damages against the officer involved, the police department and its director, the mayor, and the city of Memphis. After a trial before the district court judge, without a jury, the court found for the defendants, dismissing the claims against the mayor and the director for lack of evidence. It concluded that the police officer's action was authorized by the Tennessee deadly force statute, which, it held, was constitutional.

The U.S. Circuit Court of Appeals, Sixth Circuit affirmed with regard to the officer (holding him immune from damages because of his good faith reliance on the statute), but it remanded the case for reconsideration of possible liability of the city. On remand, the district court held that the city was not liable. The court of appeals then reversed the district court's ruling, holding that the killing of a fleeing felon is a "seizure" under the Fourth Amendment and must therefore meet the test of "reasonableness": officers cannot use deadly force to apprehend a fleeing suspect without probable cause to believe that he has committed a felony and poses a threat to the safety of the officer or to the community if allowed to escape. The state of Tennessee appealed to defend its statute and the city petitioned for certiorari.

ISSUES: (1) Is the Tennessee deadly force statute constitutional? (2) Were the rights of the deceased burglar violated?

DECISION: (1) The statute is unconstitutional in so far as it purports to allow the use of deadly force to capture *any* fleeing felon; (2) The deceased's Fourth and Fourteenth Amendment rights were violated, because he was the victim of an unreasonable seizure. Court of appeals judgment affirmed, case remanded for consideration of liability of city and the police department.

REASONS: An arrest is a "seizure" in the Fourth Amendment sense, and is therefore subject to the reasonableness requirement. To determine reasonableness this Court has in many past cases balanced the extent of the intrusion on Fourth Amendment interests against the importance of governmental interests alleged to justify the intrusion. Reasonableness depends on not only when a seizure is made, but also how it is carried out. (The Court then gives examples of past cases in which the "balancing test" has been applied to determine Fourth Amendment reasonableness.)

The intrusiveness of a seizure accomplished by deadly force is unmatched. It also frustrates the interests of the suspect, and of society, in judicial determination of guilt and punishment. The government interest, of course, is that of effective law enforcement. It is urged by the Tennessee authorities that the meaningful threat of the use of deadly force in fleeing felon situations is important to effective law enforcement. But we are not convinced that use of deadly force is a sufficiently productive means to accomplish law enforcement effectiveness to justify the killing of nonviolent suspects. The available evidence does not support the Tennessee position. In fact, most police departments have internal regulations forbidding the use of deadly force against nonviolent suspects.

The use of deadly force to prevent the escape of all felony suspects, whatever the circumstances, is constitutionally unreasonable. It is not better that all felony suspects die than that they escape. Where the suspect poses no immediate threat to the officer or to others, the harm resulting from failing to apprehend him does not justify the use of deadly force to do so. The Tennessee statute is unconstitutional insofar as it authorizes the use of deadly force against unarmed, nondangerous fleeing felons. But when the officer has probable cause to believe that the suspect poses a threat of serious physical harm, either to the officer or to others, the Constitution does not prohibit deadly force to prevent escape. Thus, if the suspect threatens the officer with a weapon or there is probable cause to believe that he has committed a crime involving the infliction of serious physical harm, deadly force may be used if necessary to prevent escape, and if, where feasible, some warning has been given.

Although the Tennessee statute is based on the common law rule, many changes have taken place which make the common law no longer binding: (1) Common law principles that existed at the time of the Fourth Amendment's adoption are not simply frozen into constitutional law. (2) The common law rule arose at a time when virtually all felonies were punishable by death, and at a time when most felonies were dangerous offenses. Today, few offenses are, or can be, punishable by death; we have many non-dangerous offenses which are felonies; and some misdemeanors involve conduct which is more dangerous than many felonies. (3) The common law rule also developed at a time when weapons were less refined and deadly force could be inflicted almost solely in a hand-to-hand struggle during which, necessarily, the safety of the arresting officer was at risk. (4) Finally, the common law rule prohibits the use of deadly force to apprehend a fleeing *misdemeanant* because it considers such force disproportionately severe. This fact lends support to today's holding.

(The Court then summarizes the law in the various states concerning the use of deadly force and concludes that while there is no overwhelming trend away from the common law rule, the long-term trend over time is away from the concept that deadly force may be used to apprehend any fleeing felon.) The Court finds more impressive than the state statutory and case law, and internal policies of police departments, only 7.5% of which explicitly permit the use of deadly force against any fleeing felon, and 86.8% of which explicitly do not.

The evidence does not indicate that crime has worsened or that lawsuits against officers have increased in those police jurisdictions which have adopted a policy restricting the use of deadly force, and the decision-making process under the restricted policy is no more difficult than the decision an officer makes as to use of deadly force based on the traditional felony/misdemeanor distinction.

In this case, the officer who killed the fleeing burglary suspect had no articulable basis to believe the suspect was armed — he never attempted to justify his actions on any basis other than to prevent an escape. The fact that the victim was a fleeing suspected burglar, in and of itself, did not justify the use of deadly force. The officer did not have probable cause to believe that the fleeing suspect (whom he correctly believed to be unarmed) posed any physical danger to himself or others. Although an armed burglar would present a different situation, the fact that an unarmed suspect has broken into a dwelling at night does not automatically mean he is physically dangerous. Available statistics demonstrate that burglaries only rarely involve physical violence.

Judgment of court of appeals is affirmed and case is remanded to determine if the city of Memphis and its police department are liable.

RULE: The arrest of a fleeing felon is a seizure in the Fourth Amendment sense. As such, it must be reasonable. Reasonableness is determined by balancing the extent of intrusion on Fourth Amendment rights against the public interest served by that intrusion. The use of deadly force to accomplish an arrest in any and all fleeing felon situations is not essential to maintain effective law enforcement, and is therefore unconstitutional. Deadly force may be used by police only when a lesser degree of force would not accomplish the arrest *and* when the arresting officer has probable cause to believe that the fleeing suspect poses a threat of serious physical harm to the officer or others, or that he has committed a felony involving the infliction or threatened infliction of serious physical harm.

DISSENTING: The majority has relied on judicial hindsight rather than constitutional law to create an unnecessarily broad constitutional rule. Without question, the fact that the slain burglar was an unarmed 15-year-old youth is a tragic consequence of the officer's action, but this cannot justify the holding. A night-time house burglary is an extremely serious offense which statistics show is often connected to other serious felonies such as rape and robbery. Even if we were to agree with the majority's application of the Fourth Amendment test of reasonableness, a proper balancing of interests indicates that a last resort of the use of deadly force to arrest a fleeing night-time house burglar is not unreasonable. It is true that the suspect's interest in his right to life is great, but he need not have risked that interest had he obeyed the police command to halt.

In *Dodd v. City of Norwich*, 827 F.2d 1 (2nd Cir. 1987), the court noted that under *Garner* the use of force by the police had become a Fourth Amendment issue based on the concept of reasonableness. The *Dodd* case involved a damage action against the city under the Civil Rights Act, 42 U.S.C. §1983. A police officer, following the department policy of handcuffing an apprehended suspect with one hand while keeping his service weapon trained on the suspect at the same time, was involved in a scuffle with the suspect. In a struggle for the weapon the suspect was fatally shot. The court drew a distinction between this case and the situation in *Garner*. In *Garner* the deadly force was deliberately used by the officer in order to effect the seizure of the fleeing burglar. In *Dodd*, the officer had already effected the seizure and the deadly force was accidental. The court stated:

> It makes little sense to apply a standard of reasonableness to an accident. If such a standard were applied, it could result in a Fourth Amendment violation based on simple negligence. The Fourth Amendment, however, only protects individuals against "unreasonable" seizure, not seizures conducted in a "negligent" manner. The Supreme Court has not yet extended liability under the Fourth Amendment to include negligence claims.

In *Lester v. City of Chicago*, 830 F.2d 706 (7th Cir. 1987), the Court also held that deliberate force used in order to accomplish an arrest has, since *Garner*, clearly become a Fourth Amendment issue. The court said:

> . . . we hold that Fourth Amendment standards govern all excessive force in arrest claims. Under the Fourth Amendment, a police officer's use of force in arresting a suspect violates the Constitution if, judging from the totality of the circumstances at the time of the arrest, the officer used greater force than was reasonably necessary to make the arrest.

The significance of these case holdings is that police use of force, deadly or non-deadly, is governed by the Fourth Amendment standard of reasonableness if the force is deliberately used in enforcing the law; but this Fourth Amendment standard may not apply to civil rights lawsuits growing out of the accidental application of force after an arrest or "seizure" has already been made.

CASE BRIEF
Graham v. Connor, 109 S. Ct. 1865 (1989)

Majority opinion: Rehnquist. Concurring: White, Stevens, O'Connor, Scalia, and Kennedy. Concurring in part and concurring in the judgment: Blackmun, joined by Brennan and Marshall.

FACTS: Petitioner (P), feeling a diabetic reaction coming on, asked a friend to drive him to a store to purchase orange juice. On arriving at the store P saw there were several people ahead of him in the checkout line and he ran out of the store and asked to be driven to another friend's house. A policeman who had observed P running into and out of the store was suspicious of P's behavior, and followed, and made an investigative stop of the car. When told that P was suffering from "sugar reaction," the officer ordered P and his driver to wait until he found out what had happened at the store. When the officer went to his car to call for backup assistance, P got out of the car, ran around it twice, sat down on the curb and passed out briefly. Other officers arrived, rolled P over and handcuffed his hands behind his back, ignoring P's requests to get him some sugar. Another officer stated: "I've seen a lot of people with sugar diabetes that never acted like this. Ain't nothing wrong with the M.F. but drunk. Lock the S.B. up." P was then lifted up, carried to his friend's car and placed face down on the hood. P, regaining consciousness, asked officers to check his wallet for diabetic I.D., but he was told to "shut up," and shoved face down on the car hood. Officers then grabbed P and threw him head first into the police car. When a friend brought P some orange juice to the car, the officers refused to let him have it. When word was received that P had done nothing wrong at the store, P was driven home and released. P, alleging he received a broken foot, cuts on his wrists, bruised forehead, and injured shoulder, (plus a persistent ringing in his right ear), filed a civil damage lawsuit under sec. 1983, the Federal Civil Rights Act, claiming the police used excessive force. In granting a motion for a directed verdict in favor of the defendant police officers, the District Court found the force used was "appropriate under the circumstances" and that the force "was not applied maliciously or sadistically for the very purpose of causing harm." A divided panel of the Court of Appeals affirmed, but a dissenting judge argued that the wrong standard had been used by the trial court in determining whether the force used was excessive. The Supreme Court granted certiorari.

ISSUE: What is the correct standard for a Court to use in a federal civil rights lawsuit to determine whether the police have used excessive force?

DECISION: Reversed. The Fourth Amendment "objective reasonableness" standard should have been used. District Court judgment vacated, case remanded for reconsideration. (*Note:* this decision does *not* determine whether or not excessive force was used; it only holds that the trial court used the wrong standard in arriving at its decision.)

REASONS: Three constitutional standards have been used by the courts in the past in excessive force cases: (1) substantive due process (depriving a person of "liberty" — or freedom from governmental force without due process of law); (2) Eighth Amendment "cruel and unusual punishment"; and (3) Fourth Amendment "unreasonable seizure." Since the case of *Johnson v. Glick*, 481 F.2d 1028 (2d Cir.—), cert. denied, 414 U.S. 1033 (1973), most lower federal courts have used the Due Process analysis which involves a four-part test (including the subjective state of mind of the officer). We reject the position that all excessive force claims brought as civil rights cases are governed by the Due Process standard. The Civil Rights Act is not a source of substantive rights, it merely provides a means of protecting rights conferred by the Constitution. The Fourth Amendment and the Eighth Amendment are the two primary sources of constitutional protection against physically abusive governmental conduct. *Tennessee v. Garner*, 105 S. Ct. 1694 (1985) rejected the Due Process approach and applied the Fourth Amendment unreasonable seizure approach in an arrest situation. There we held that the "reasonableness" of a particular seizure depends not only on *when* it is made, but also *how* it is carried out. Today we hold that all claims that law enforcement officers have used excessive force, deadly or not, in the course of an arrest, investigatory stop, or other "seizure" of a free citizen, are questions under the Fourth Amendment "reasonableness" standard rather than under the generalized notion of "substantive due process." The Fourth Amendment requires the balancing of the nature and quality of the intrusion on the individual's Fourth Amendment interests against the countervailing governmental interests at stake. We have long recognized that the right to make an arrest or investigative stop carries with it the right to use some degree of physical coercion or threat to effect it. Careful attention must be given to the facts and circumstances of each case, including the severity of the crime, whether the suspect poses an immediate threat to the safety of the officer or others, and whether he is actively resisting arrest or fleeing. The question is whether the totality of circumstances justifies a particular sort of seizure. The presence or absence of evil intentions on the officer's part have no part in the analysis. It is an objective test. An officer's evil intentions will not make a Fourth Amendment violation out of an objectively reasonable use of force; nor will an officer's good intentions make an objectively unreasonable use of force constitutional. The test is not based on the 20/20 vision of hindsight, but rather on the perspective of a reasonable officer on the scene. The Fourth Amendment is not violated by an arrest based on probable cause, even though the wrong person is arrested. *Hill v. California*, 91 S. Ct. 1106 (1971), nor by the mistaken execution of a valid search warrant on the wrong premises, *Maryland v. Garrison*, 107 S. Ct. 1013 (1987). With regard to excessive force, the same standard of reasonableness at the moment applies: "Not every push or shove, even if it may later seem unnecessary in the peace of a judge's chambers" violates the Fourth Amendment. *Johnson v. Glick*. But what is reasonable must allow for the fact that police officers are often forced to make split-second judgments in tense, uncertain, and rapidly-evolving circumstances. (The Court then discusses how malicious and sadistic states of mind might be very relevant in deciding *Eighth Amendment* cases of cruel and unusual punishment which arise after a person has been tried and convicted, but notes that the *Fourth Amendment* inquiry is one of "objective reasonableness" under the circumstances, and does not concern the presence or absence of evil intent).

RULE: In a civil rights lawsuit against the police for the alleged use of excessive force in making an arrest, investigative stop, or other "seizure" of a person who has not yet been tried and convicted, the correct standard for the court to apply is that of "reasonableness" under the Fourth Amendment "seizure" clause. This standard is objective and balances the rights of the complaining citizen against the rights of the government, considering the totality of all of the circumstances as would be viewed by a reasonable officer on the scene, taking into consideration that police often must make split-second judgments, in tense, uncertain, and rapidly-evolving circumstances. Because the standard is an objective one, the presence or absence of evil intent by the officer has no bearing on whether a particular seizure is reasonable under the Fourth Amendment.

CONCURRING OPINION: Agrees the Fourth Amendment standard is the *primary* test to be applied in pre-arrest excessive force cases and that this case should be sent back for reconsideration under that standard, but feels that the question of "unreasonable seizure" versus "substantive due process" standard as the proper standard to be used in *all* pre-arrest excessive force cases was not properly presented and should have been left for another day.

CASE BRIEF

Brower v. Inyo County, 109 S. Ct. 1378 (1989)

Majority opinion: Scalia, joined by Rehnquist, C.J., White, O'Connor, and Kennedy. Concurring in judgment: Stevens, Brennan, Marshall, and Blackmun.

FACTS: Section 1983 Civil Rights lawsuit. B, while driving a stolen car and fleeing from pursuing police for 20 miles, eventually crashed into a police roadblock and was killed. Complaint alleges that in order to stop B, police placed a tractor-trailer rig across both lanes of a 2-lane highway behind a curve, leaving the rig unilluminated and positioning a police car with headlights on between B's oncoming car and the roadblock, so as to "blind" B. The District Court granted defendant's motion to dismiss the complaint. The Court of Appeals affirmed the dismissal on the basis that no Fourth Amendment "seizure" had occurred, (hence, no federal rights claim involved to support a sec. 1983 lawsuit). The Supreme Court of the United States granted certiorari.

ISSUE: When police set up a roadblock for the purpose of stopping a fleeing motorist and he crashes into the roadblock, has a "seizure" occurred in a Fourth Amendment sense?

DECISION: Yes, reversed and remanded.

REASONS: In *Tennessee v. Garner*, 105 S. Ct. 1694 (1985), the Court held that a police fatal shooting of a fleeing burglary suspect constituted a Fourth Amendment seizure. The roadblock accomplished the same purpose in this case as the bullet did in *Garner*. If a motorist being chased by the police unexpectedly loses control of his car and crashes (without a roadblock being involved), no seizure occurs. The very word "seizure" implies willfulness, — it cannot be applied to an unknowing act. If a parked and unoccupied police car slips its brake and pins a person against a wall, it is likely that a "tort" has occurred, but not a violation of the Fourth Amendment. A Fourth Amendment seizure occurs when there is a governmental termination of freedom *through means intentionally applied*. If, in a police chase, a police cruiser pulled alongside a fleeing car and sideswiped it, producing a crash, this would be a Fourth Amendment seizure. (The Court then discussed a similar case in which a pursued moonshiner dropped jugs of illegal whisky during a chase. The Court ruled that the revenue agent's examination of the contents of the abandoned jugs was not a seizure because dropping the jugs was the act of the D, although the result would have been different had the agent commanded, "Stop and give us those bottles, in the name of the law!" Then the taking possession of the jugs would have been not merely the result of government action, but the result of the *very means* (the verbal command) that the government used, and it would have been a Fourth Amendment seizure.)

A roadblock, (contrasted to a pursuing police car with flashing lights or to a policeman in the road signaling a car to stop), is not just a show of authority to induce a voluntary stop, but is designed to produce a stop by physical impact if voluntary compliance does not occur. The police may sincerely hope that the fleeing motorist does stop voluntarily without striking the roadblock, but that is not the point. Nor is it pertinent to the issue here whether the roadblock was set up in a highly visible place at the end of a long straightway (giving the fleeing motorist every opportunity to stop), or whether it is set up just around a bend in the road. A Fourth Amendment seizure has occurred when a person is in fact stopped by the very instrumentality set in motion (for example, a bullet), or put in place (for example, a roadblock), by the police, in order to achieve that result.

(By this opinion, the Court only decides the very narrow issue of whether a Fourth Amendment seizure occurred under these facts. It does not decide the issue of liability under the Civil Rights Act, which would require a determination by the District Court as to whether the seizure was "unreasonable" under the Fourth Amendment after hearing evidence on the claim that the roadblock was set up just around a bend in the road and that the fleeing car thief was blinded by headlights of a parked police car).

RULE: A Fourth Amendment seizure occurs when a person fleeing the police is in fact stopped by the very means set in motion or put in place by the police to accomplish the stop, whether it is a bullet, a roadblock, or some other means.

CONCURRING: The four concurring Justices agree with the result of the case — that a Fourth Amendment seizure did occur — but disagree on the necessity of the majority opinion to discuss the intent factor.

--------------------------------------- **Notes** ---------------------------------------

§ 4.8 FORCED ENTRY — KNOCK AND ANNOUNCE REQUIREMENT

Although the Supreme Court of the United States has not held that the Fourth Amendment requires an officer to knock and announce his authority and purpose before forcing entry to execute a warrant, it is clear that this preliminary action is preferred by the common law. In *Miller v. United States*, 78 S. Ct. 1190 (1950), in discussing the background of a federal statute requiring such a procedure in Washington, D.C., the Court noted:

> From the earliest days, the common law drastically limited the authority of law officers to break the door of a house to effect an arrest. Such action invades the precious interest of privacy summed up in the ancient adage that a man's house is his castle. As early as the 13th Yearbook of Edward IV (1461-1483), at folio 9, there is a recorded holding that it was unlawful for a sheriff to break the door of a man's house to arrest him in a civil suit in debt or trespass, for the arrest was then only for the private interest of a party. Remarks attributed to William Pitt, Earl of Chatham, on the occasion of debate in Parliament on the searches incident to the enforcement of an excise on cider, eloquently expressed the principle:
>
>> "The poorest man may in his cottage bid defiance to all the forces of the Crown. It may be frail; its roof may shake; the wind may blow through it; the storm may enter; the rain may enter; but the King of England cannot enter — all his force dares not cross the threshold of the ruined tenement!"
>
> But the common law recognized some authority in law officers to break the door of a dwelling to arrest for felony. The common law authorities differ, however, as to the circumstances in which this was the case. . .
>
> Whatever the circumstances under which breaking a door to arrest for felony might be lawful, however, the breaking was unlawful where the officer failed to first state his authority and purpose for demanding admission. The requirement was pronounced in 1603 in Semayne's Case . . .
>
>> "In all cases where the King is a party, the sheriff (if the doors not be open) may break the party's house, either to arrest him, or to do other execution of the King's process, if otherwise he cannot enter. *But before he breaks it, he ought to signify the cause of his coming, and to make request to open doors.* . .

Each state has developed its own requirements concerning knock and announce and the breaking of doors either by statute, case law, or both.

-------------------------------------- **Notes** --------------------------------------

Sample Questions

Probable cause for an arrest or search warrant:
A. cannot include hearsay.
B. cannot include personal observations by someone other than the person seeking the warrant.
C. cannot include any type of evidence that would be inadmissible at a trial.
D. all of the above are true.
E.) can include hearsay

Any item found in "plain view" by a police officer can be seized without a warrant for use as evidence.   T   F.

Smith, the next-door neighbor of Jones, enters Jones' garage while Jones is away from home for the purpose of borrowing a rake. While in the garage, he observes several brick-sized packages wrapped in duct tape. On a bench near the packages is the residue of a leaf-like material which Smith suspects is marijuana. Smith collects some of this material in an envelope and delivers it to the police station where tests reveal that it is, in fact, marijuana. On the basis of these tests, plus Smith's statement describing what he saw, and Jones' prior record as a drug dealer, the police obtain a search warrant and enter the garage and seize a large quantity of marijuana and bring criminal charges against Jones. Is the seized evidence admissible?
A. no, because the entry of the garage by Smith was without consent.
B. yes, because the evidence was produced by a "private search" without any prompting from the police, and the Fourth Amendment does not apply in such a case.
C. yes, but only on the theory of "exigent circumstances".
D. no, because when Smith took the envelope to the police station, he became an "agent" of the government.
E. no, because the action of Smith was an unreasonable search and seizure which is prohibited by the Fourth Amendment.

Notwithstanding the differences in the rules concerning searches of automobiles and the rules concerning searches of dwelling houses:
A. there are still many situations in which the search of an automobile would not be proper without a search warrant.
B. both dwelling houses and automobiles are protected by the right of privacy, but to different degrees.
C. there are no situations in which an automobile may be searched without a warrant.
D. there are no situations in which a dwelling house may be searched without a warrant.
E. Both A and B above are true.

Although the Fourth Amendment seems to prefer that all searches and seizures be made only after a warrant has been obtained, the Supreme Court of the United States has recognized that this would be an impractical standard in modern law enforcement, and it therefore recognizes certain "exceptions" to the warrant requirement.   T)   F.

One exception to the warrant requirement is based on the existence of probable cause, coupled with "exigent circumstances".   T)   F.

§ 4.9 TERRITORIAL JURISDICTION AND FRESH PURSUIT

Generally, a lawful arrest may be made anywhere, even on private property. 6A C.J.S. Arrest §52.

An offense against the law of one state does not authorize an arrest therefor in another state except where and as authorized by the laws of the latter state, and a peace officer acting in his official capacity can make an arrest only within the state from which his authority is derived. 6A C.J.S. Arrest §53a.

In the absence of statutory permission, a peace officer when making an arrest within the state, has authority to make an arrest only within the confines of the geographical unit of which he is an officer. 6A C.J.S. Arrest §53b.

The general principles stated above were developed during a time when the automobile and other means of rapid transportation were unknown. Many states have adopted the Uniform Act on Fresh Pursuit, granting arrest powers to out-of-state police officers who pursue fleeing suspects into their jurisdiction. Other states have broadened the territorial jurisdiction in which county and local officers may exercise arrest powers within their respective states, or have enacted "interlocal cooperation" statutes which may have an effect on arrest powers.

The statutory and case law of each state must be examined in order to determine the area within which arrest may be made by the various types of peace officers.

Under the common-law doctrine of fresh pursuit, an officer may, with or without a warrant, pursue a suspected felon into another jurisdiction and arrest him there. Similar powers are sometimes conferred by statute. The common-law doctrine, however, applies only to cases of felony; and this limitation is sometimes created by statute. According to one view, even an officer in hot pursuit of one who has committed an offense in his presence must halt at the jurisdictional boundaries if the offense was only a misdemeanor. According to another view, the arrest may be treated as part of one continuous transaction which, having been begun within the jurisdiction, can be completed anywhere within the state.

Where fresh-pursuit arrest in another jurisdiction is permissible, the pursuit must be immediate and continuous, but the continuity is not broken by the mere fact that the officer may temporarily lose sight of the fugitive. 5 Am Jur 2d Arrest §51.

In *Warden v. Hayden*, 87 S. Ct. 1642 (1967), the concept of fresh pursuit (sometimes called "hot" or "close" pursuit), was recognized by the Supreme Court:

> We agree with the Court of Appeals that neither the entry without warrant to search for the robber, nor the search for him without warrant was invalid. Under the circumstances of this case, "the exigencies of the situation made that course imperative." *McDonald v. United States*, 69 S. Ct. 191, 193 (1948). The police were informed that an armed robbery had taken place, and that the suspect had entered 2111 Cocoa Lane less than five minutes before they reached it. They acted reasonably when they entered the house, and began to search for a man of the description they had been given and for weapons which he had used in the robbery or might use against them. The Fourth Amendment does not require police officers to delay in the course of an investigation if to do so would gravely endanger their lives or the lives of others. Speed here was essential, and only a thorough search of the house for persons and weapons could have insured that Hayden was the only man present and that the police had control of all weapons which could be used against them or to effect an escape.

In the above case, (see brief, §4.15(C)(1) herein), the Court treated fresh pursuit as an exigent circumstance excusing the warrant requirement to enter a residence for the purpose of arresting a fleeing felon. In a later case, *Payton v. New York*, 100 S. Ct. 1371 (1980) (briefed at §4.6 herein), there was no fresh pursuit or any other exigency, and the Court ruled that a warrant was required to enter the suspect's residence to arrest him for a felony. See also *United States v. Santana*, 96 S. Ct. 2406 (1976), (briefed at sec. 4.6 herein).

Just as the threshold of a private residence is a barrier to certain law enforcement activities, so may be the jurisdictional boundaries of towns, cities, townships, counties, and states. Here, too, fresh pursuit may affect the permissibility of arrest. As stated in *Commonwealth v. Grise*, Mass. Sup. Jud. Ct. (1986); 39 CrL 2450:

> While a police officer may execute an arrest warrant anywhere in the state, his power at common law to make a warrantless arrest is limited to the boundaries of the government unit by which he was appointed, *unless the officer is acting in fresh and continued pursuit of a suspected felon who has committed an offense in the officer's presence and within his territorial jurisdiction.* (emphasis added).

In some states, the fresh pursuit authority of police has been expanded to include misdemeanor pursuits as well as felonies. See the *Grise* case and also *State v. Blake*, 468 N.E.2d 548 (Ind. App. 1984).

Officers should check their own state statutes to determine: (a) whether they have state-wide police powers; and (b) their states extradition procedures, in the event that crossing a state line is necessary. Officers should also check adjoining states' laws concerning arrest powers of foreign officers entering in fresh pursuit. It must be remembered that the arrest powers of any individual depend on the law that governs the territory where the arrest is made, and if an officer chases a suspect into another state, the law that controls is the law of the state which is entered, not the law of the state where the chase started. Finally, each officer should be familiar with his own department's regulations dealing with fresh pursuit.

------------------------------------- **Notes** -------------------------------------

§ 4.10 RESISTANCE TO ARREST

Under common law a person had a right forcibly to resist an unlawful arrest. The newer rule, adopted by some states, is that, unless excessive or unnecessary force is used by the arresting officer, a person may not use force to resist arrest by one who he knows or has good reason to believe is a police officer engaged in performing his duties, regardless of whether the arrest is lawful under the circumstances. The trend away from the common law rule follows the reasoning that the legality of an arrest is better resolved within the judicial process by detached judges than by the use of self-help. Today there are many statutory safeguards to citizens' rights under these circumstances. See 68 Mass. Law Review, 200, December, 1983, in which J. E. Miles discusses *Commonwealth v. Moreira*, 447 N.E.2d 1224 (Mass. 1983). The purpose of the newer rule is to promote the peaceful settlement of disputes. See also 18 Suffolk U. L. Rev. 107 - 113, Spring, 1984, in which J. C. Engel also discusses the *Moreira* case.

In many states it is a misdemeanor to resist a law enforcement officer lawfully engaged in the performance of his duties, and in some circumstances the resistance may amount to a felony. See Indiana Code, IC 35-44-3-3. Resistance may not be a crime, if the person resisting arrest has no reason to believe he is dealing with a police officer. For legal reasons, and for the officer's own safety, it is essential that the latter clearly identify himself as a police officer.

-------------------------------------- **Notes** --------------------------------------

Sample Questions

If the police have probable cause to believe that the occupants of an automobile have just committed an armed robbery within the past few minutes, and they stop the car and order the occupants to get out, and place them under arrest:
A. they must have a warrant in order to search the car.
B. the search of the car must be made at the same time and place that the arrests are made.
C. this is not a "Carroll rule" situation.
D. the search of the automobile need not be made as an incident to the arrests, because there is also probable cause to believe the car may contain items taken in the robbery, and it may be seached later and at a different place, without a warrant being obtained.
E. B and C above are both correct.

The law of the use of deadly force by the police as a means to capture a fleeing felon:
A. is controlled by the Fourth Amendment as a "seizure", and therefore must be reasonable under the circumstances.
B. is never justified.
C. developed in the English common law at a time when most felony offenses were punishable by the death penalty.
D. authorizes the use of deadly force to capture a fleeing felon in every case where all other means would fail to accomplish the capture.
E. Both A and C are true.

The Supreme Court of the United States has ruled that the arrest of a fleeing felony suspect is a "seizure" under the Fourth Amendment, and therefore must be reasonable under the circumstances.   T   F.

The use of force by a police officer to arrest a fleeing felony suspect is never reasonable under the Fourth Amendment.   T   F.

Probable cause is a greater standard of proof than proof beyond a reasonable doubt.   T   F.

A stop and frisk procedure is a search for criminal evidence   T   F.

An officer who is actively involved in a criminal investigation cannot issue a valid search warrant in that same case even though he possesses judicial powers under state law because he is not a "neutral and detached magistrate".   T   F.

Even though a police officer has a search warrant, a search conducted under a warrant can be challenged as being unreasonable.   T   F.

Drugs discovered in a damaged package in the hands of a private commercial carrier result in the calling of drug enforcement agents who conduct a field screening test on powder leaked from the package. The tests are valid without a warrant.   T   F.

The Supreme Court of the United States has clearly indicated that the use of "profiles" by the police as an aid in the determination of probable cause is unconstitutional.   T   F.

§ 4.11 INFRACTIONS AND ORDINANCE VIOLATIONS

Generally, infractions and local ordinance violations are not considered to be crimes. In *People v. Battle*, 123 Cal. Rptr. 636 (Cal. App. 1975), the court held that an infraction is not a criminal offense. In that case a defendant who had previously plead *nolo contendere* to an infraction charging failure to maintain his brakes in good condition, and who had been fined $50.00, was later charged with manslaughter because of three traffic fatalities resulting from the same violation. To the appellant's double jeopardy argument, the court answered that an infraction under California law was not a criminal offense, and therefore the concept of double jeopardy did not apply. The court found some inconsistencies in the California statutes, but it based its finding that an infraction is not a criminal offense partly on the fact that the legislature had deprived persons committing infractions of the right to a jury trial and the right to counsel at public expense — rights which are clearly guaranteed to persons charged with criminal offenses.

In *Meredith v. Whillock*, 158 S.W. 1061 (Mo. App. 1913), the court stated:

> Since the case of *Kansas City v. Clark*, 68 Mo. loc. cit. 589, was decided, it has been uniformly held in this state (Missouri) that the violation of a city ordinance is not a crime. The proceeding is only a civil suit and has the incidents and attributes merely of a quasi criminal character . . . The law is well established that a prosecution from a violation of a city ordinance is a civil action . . .
>
> It is also settled law that an acquittal or conviction under a city ordinance is no bar to a prosecution for the same offense by the state, and vice versa a conviction or acquittal under a state law is no bar to a prosecution for the same offense by a city.

Municipal ordinances, though penal, are not criminal statutes.

In *State v. Jamieson*, 300 N.W. 809 (Minn. 1941), the court stated:

> It is well established under our decisions that violations of an ordinance need not be proved beyond a reasonable doubt . . . In *State v. Robitshek*, 61 N.W. 1023, it was said: "It has repeatedly been decided by this court, as it has elsewhere, that municipal ordinances are not criminal statutes; that violations thereof are not crimes, nor are such violations governed by the rules of the criminal law, save in certain specified exceptional particulars.
>
> So also in *City of Red Wing v. Nibbe*, 199 N.W. 918, it was held: "It has long been settled that the violation of a city ordinance is not a criminal offense against the state, but only against the municipality enacting the ordinance, and that the provisions for enforcing such ordinances and for prosecuting violations thereof need not conform to the provisions for prosecuting violations of the state laws."

In Indiana, infractions and ordinance violations are treated as civil offenses, punishable by fine (civil penalty) only, and custodial arrests for such violations are not authorized, and violators may be detained only for the time necessary to execute a summons, or notice to appear. See Indiana Code, IC 34-4-32-3 and IC 34-4-32-4.

The statutory and case law of each state should be examined to determine precisely the status of, and the procedure for the enforcement of infractions and ordinance violations.

Because penalties for ordinance violations and infractions generally do not involve a loss of liberty, but only a fine or other monetary penalty, many of these classes of offenses go unchallenged in the courts, and, over time, become obsolete and perhaps unconstitutional. But an officer is entitled to take enforcement action under a city ordinance unless the ordinance is so "grossly and flagrantly unconstitutional" that any reasonable person would recognize it as invalid. This principle was announced by the Supreme Court in *Michigan v. DeFillippo*, 99 S. Ct. 2627 (1979). In that case, a Detroit police officer took a person into custody under a city ordinance which was later declared to be unconstitutional by the state court of appeals. Drugs seized incident to the arrest, which were declared inadmissible because they were seized pursuant to an arrest made under an unconstitutional ordinance, were later declared to be admissible by the Supreme Court, which stated:

> On this record there was abundant probable cause to satisfy the constitutional prerequisite for an arrest. At that time, of course, there was no controlling precedent that this ordinance was or was not constitutional, and hence the conduct observed violated a presumptively valid ordinance. A prudent officer, in the course of determining whether respondent had committed an offense under all the circumstances shown by this record, should not have been required to anticipate that a court would later hold the ordinance unconstitutional.
>
> Police are charged to enforce laws until and unless they are declared unconstitutional. The enactment of a law forecloses speculation by enforcement officers concerning its constitutionality — with the possible exception of a law so grossly and flagrantly unconstitutional that any person of reasonable prudence would be bound to see its flaws. Society would be ill-served if its police officers took it upon themselves to determine which laws are and which are not constitutionally entitled to enforcement.

--------------------------------------- **Notes** ---------------------------------------

§ 4.12 CITIZEN'S ARREST

The concept of citizen's arrest was recognized in the English common law. In 1769, William Blackstone wrote:

> Any private person (and *a fortiori* a peace officer) that is present when any felony is committed, is bound by the law to arrest the felon; on pain of fine and imprisonment, if he escapes through the negligence of the standers by. And they may justify breaking open doors upon following such felon: and if *they kill him*, provided he cannot be otherwise taken, it is justifiable; though if *they are killed* in endeavouring to make such arrest, it is murder. Upon probable suspicion also a private person may arrest the felon, or other person so suspected, but he cannot justify breaking open doors to do it; and if either party kills the other in the attempt, it is manslaughter, and no more. It is no more, because there is no malicious design to kill: but it amounts to so much, because it would be of most pernicious consequences, if, under pretence of suspecting felony, any private person might break open a house, or kill another; and also because such arrest upon suspicion is barely *permitted* by the law, and not *enjoined*, as in the case of those who are present when a felony is committed. 4 Bl. Comm. 289.

It appears that in Blackstone's time, citizen's arrest was not only permitted, it was a duty of those citizens in whose presence a felony was committed. Much has changed since those times. No organized governmental police force existed then, and deadly force in the capture of a fleeing felon has been greatly restricted in modern times. Citizen's arrest powers still are recognized, but are seldom used.

A private person may, ordinarily, arrest without a warrant one who is committing, or is attempting to commit, a felony in his presence. 6A C.J.S. Arrest §13.

Generally, a private person may lawfully arrest one without a warrant for a felony not committed in his presence if a felony has actually been committed, and the private person has probable cause to believe that the person arrested committed the felony. 6A C.J.S. Arrest §14.

Ordinarily, a private person may arrest without a warrant one committing a misdemeanor or a breach of the peace in his presence. 6A C.J.S. Arrest §15.

As is true of most general rules developed in the common law, rules concerning citizens arrest are subject to statutory change in each state. In many states a citizen is held to a stricter standard of arrest than a police officer; he may find himself civilly liable for making an arrest where no felony has in fact been committed, even though his mistaken action was a reasonable one. Again, unless modified by statute, where the citizen's arrest is for a misdemeanor committed in his presence, the offense must be a breach of peace and the citizen must act immediately, since his arrest powers derive from the common law theory that it was a citizen's duty to restore the peace. If he fails to act until after the breach of peace has subsided, his authority no longer exists and the arrest is invalid. (See cases cited in the 6A C.J.S. Arrest sections quoted above.)

-------------------------------------- **Notes** --------------------------------------

Sample Questions

In many jurisdictions the powers of arrest that a police officer may exercise are affected by whether he is taking action for a felony or a misdemeanor.   T   F.

A felony is generally a less serious offense than a misdemeanor.   T   F.

Police observe what they believe to be a drug transaction taking place on the sidewalk. When one of the participants spots the police car, he turns and runs and the police follow along in their car, driving alongside him for some distance, during which time the suspect discards several objects from his possession by dropping them on the sidewalk. One of the officers gets out of the car and picks up one of the dropped objects, which is a packet of illegal drugs. How would the Supreme Court of the United States rule on the admissibility of the drugs in evidence if they were later used in a criminal prosecution?

A. they would rule that following the individual in a police car while he was running on the sidewalk amounted to a "seizure", and therefore the admissibility of the drugs depend on whether the mere flight of a person upon seeing the police was reasonable suspicion justifying the seizure.
B. they would rule that the action of running away upon seeing the police is always probable cause for arrest, and therefore, the drugs are admissible.
C. they would rule that because the police activated no flashing lights or siren and gave no command to halt and did not attempt to head the person off or block his path, that no "seizure" occurred. (Therefore, drugs would be admissible as "abandoned property", because abandonment was not caused by improper police conduct.)
D. they would rule that an arrest took place at the moment the first packet of drugs was picked up.
E. they would rule that no "seizure" occurred, but that the police have no authority to pick up objects discarded by anyone.

The term "felony" is defined exactly the same in each of the fifty states.   T   F.

An acceptable definition of "probable cause" would be:

A. enough evidence upon which to convict an accused in a criminal trial.
B. when there is more evidence to show that a certain fact exists than evidence to show that it does not exist.
C. clear and convincing evidence.
D. facts and circumstances sufficient to warrant a prudent man in believing that a suspect had committed or was committing an offense.
E. proof beyond a shadow of a doubt.

An arrest made without a warrant must meet the same test of probable cause at the moment the arrest is made as would be needed to secure a warrant from a judge.   T   F.

If there is to be extended restraint on the liberty of a person arrested without a warrant, the Constitution of the United States requries that there be a reasonably prompt:

A. judicial determination of probable cause.
B. lineup.
C. confession.
D. photographic array.
E. conviction.

§ 4.13 SEARCHES—CONSTITUTIONAL RESTRICTIONS

The Fourth Amendment to the Constitution of the United States prohibits "unreasonable searches and seizures" of persons and their possessions.

The development of the law making the Fourth Amendment binding upon the states and the adoption of the "exclusionary rule", which is designed to deter police misconduct by barring evidence seized through unlawful governmental action, are covered in Chapter Two.

In analyzing a search and seizure problem, one must determine, first, whether the Fourth Amendment is applicable and, second, if it is, whether there has been compliance therewith. Following are two outlines. The first lists instances in which the amendment does not apply; the second lists categories of searches which are in compliance with the amendment.

Searches and Seizures to which Fourth Amendment Is Inapplicable

1. Inapplicability as to property or place.
   a. It does not apply outside the jurisdiction of the United States. *Brulay v. United States*, 383 F.2d 345 (9th Cir. 1967); *Stonehill v. United States*, 405 F.2d 738 (9th Cir. 1968).
   b. It does not apply to abandoned property or to abandoned (though once protected) places. *Abel v. United States*, 80 S. Ct. 683 (1960); *California v. Greenwood*, 108 S. Ct. 1625 (1988)
   c. It does not apply to those things exposed to public view. *Katz v. United States*, 88 S. Ct. 507 (1967); *Maryland v. Macon*, 105 S. Ct. 2778 (1985).
   d. It does not apply to "open fields." *Hester v. United States*, 44 S. Ct. 445 (1924); *Air Pollution Variance Board v. Western Alfalfa Corp.*, 94 S. Ct. 2114 (1974); *United States v. Dunn*, 107 S. Ct. 1134 (1987); *Oliver v. United States* and *Maine v. Thornton*, 104 S. Ct. 1735 (1984); *California v. Ciraolo*, 106 S. Ct. 1809 (1986); *Dow Chemical Co. v. United States*, 106 S. Ct. 1819 (1986).
2. Inapplicability as to searchers.—It applies *only* to governmental agents— not to private persons. *Burdeau v. McDowell*, 41 S. Ct. 574 (1921); *United States v. Jacobsen*, 104 S. Ct. 1652 (1984).
3. Inapplicability as to the victim.—It applies only to a victim who has standing, because the rights are personal. *Brown v. United States*, 93 S. Ct. 1565 (1973); *Rakas v. Illinois*, 99 S. Ct. 421 (1978).
4. Inapplicability because of waiver of Fourth Amendment rights.—See *Schneckloth v. Bustamonte*, 93 S. Ct. 2041 (1973).

In *Maryland v. Macon*, 105 S. Ct. 2778 (1985), the action of a plain-clothes police officer in entering a bookstore and purchasing an allegedly obscene publication on display for sale to potential customers did not constitute an unreasonable search or seizure under the Fourth Amendment. After the magazine was examined by other officers and the conclusion was made that it was obscene, police returned to the bookstore, retrieved the marked money with which the purchase was made, and arrested the seller without a warrant.

The concept of "curtilage" originated in the English common law; it extended to the area immediately surrounding the dwelling house the same protection, under the law, that was accorded to the dwelling itself. Under the Constitution of the United States the curtilage is protected against governmental invasion by the Fourth Amendment. But these protections do not extend to "open fields". *Hester v. United States*, 44 S. Ct. 445, (1924); *Oliver v. United States*, 104 S. Ct. 1735, (1984).

In the case of the *United States v. Dunn*, 107 S. Ct. 1134, (1987); the Supreme Court of the United States was faced with the issue of whether an area was within the protection of the curtilage concept or whether it was an open field. Federal drug agents traced quantities of chemicals and equipment through use of a court-approved "beeper" to defendant's 198-acre ranch. Suspecting a drug manufacturing enterprise, the agents took aerial photographs and later made several warrantless entries onto the property to confirm their suspicions and to develop probable cause for a search warrant which was later issued by a U. S. Magistrate. During their warrantless entries onto the ranch, which was completely enclosed by a fence, the agents had to cross several interior fences to reach a clearing in which was located a dwelling house (one-half mile from the road), and two barns. They approached one of the barns from which a strong chemical odor was coming and they could hear the loud noise of what sounded like a pump motor running inside. They did not enter the barn, but directed a flashlight beam inside, through a netting which was suspended from the ceiling to the top of a waist-high locked gate; they observed what they believed to be an unlawful drug laboratory. The critical issue before the Court was whether the observation was made from within the curtilage of the dwelling or in open fields.

In resolving this issue, the Court indicated that at least 4 factors should be considered: (1) *How close is the area to the home?* In this case, the barn in question was 50 yards from the fence surrounding the house, and 60 yards from the house itself. This substantial distance supports no inference in and of itself that the barn should be considered within the curtilage. (2) *Is the area included within an enclosure surrounding the home?* The barn did not lie within the fenced area surrounding the house. As noted in *Oliver*, "for most homes, the boundaries of the curtilage will be clearly marked; and the conception defining the curtilage—as the area around the home to which the activity of home life extends—is a familiar one easily understood from our daily experience." Here, the fenced area immediately adjacent to the house, and the barn, (the front portion of which was enclosed by a separate fence), stand out as distinctly separate areas. (3) *Was the area being used for the intimate activities of the home?* In this case the agents had objective data, coupled with their observations, indicating that the barn was not being used for intimate activities of the home, i.e., the aerial photograph showing the truck used to transport the chemicals and equipment backed up as if unloading; the strong odor of chemicals coming from the barn; the sound of a "pump motor" which was very loud in the barn. (4) *Had the resident taken steps to protect the area from observation by people passing by?* The interior fences on D's ranch were posts with multiple strands of barbed wire, typical of those used to corral livestock and not to prevent observation.

Applying these four factors to the facts, the Court concluded that the criminal activity observed by police was outside the curtilage of the dwelling house; therefore, the warrantless observation did not violate the Fourth Amendment, and it could be used in establishing probable cause for the search warrant which was obtained and later served.

The Court also stated, "The term 'open fields' may include any unoccupied or undeveloped area outside of the curtilage. An open field need be neither 'open' nor a 'field' as those terms are used in common speech."

The Court also indicated that there is no constitutional difference between police observations conducted in a public place and those conducted in open fields, and it held that to use a flashlight to illuminate the interior of the barn, without physically entering the barn, did not violate the Fourth Amendment.

The "open fields" doctrine was strengthened and clarified in *Oliver v. United States* and *Maine v. Thornton*, 104 S. Ct. 1735 (1984). Both cases involved warrantless, nonconsensual entry by police investigating reports of marijuana patches growing on private property not visible from any public access point. The areas in question were remote from the owners' residences. The Court determined that they were "open fields," even though they were fenced, posted or surrounded by dense woods; therefore the owners had no reasonable expectation of privacy in them, and entering them or observing them from aircraft was not a violation of the Fourth Amendment.

In *California v. Ciraolo*, 106 S. Ct. 1809 (1986) the Supreme Court of the United States upheld a police overflight procedure. Santa Clara police, acting on an anonymous tip, conducted a warrantless aerial observation at 1000 feet from public, navigable airspace and made naked-eye observations of marijuana plants 8 to 10 feet in height growing inside the defendant's *doubled fenced backyard*. The observations and an aerial photograph taken by the officers were used to establish probable cause to obtain a search warrant and 73 marijuana plants were seized. In upholding the seizure, the Court stated:

> That the area is within the curtilage does not itself bar all police observation. The Fourth Amendment protection of the home has never been extended to require law enforcement officers to shield their eyes when passing by a home on public thoroughfares. Nor does the mere fact that an individual has taken measures to restrict some views of his activities preclude an officer's observations from a public vantage point where he has a right to be and which renders the activities clearly visible.

In a case decided the same day as *Ciraolo*, the Supreme Court of the United States upheld aerial surveillance and photography of a chemical plant for the purpose of discovering violations of Environmental Protection Agency regulations. In *Dow Chemical Co. v. United States*, 106 S. Ct. 1819 (1986) the Court held that open spaces between buildings of an industrial complex were similar to "open fields" for purposes of aerial observation, and it refused to accept the defendant's theory that the spaces constituted an "industrial curtilage."

In case of *Florida v. Riley*, 109 S. Ct. 693 (1989), the Supreme Court, relying on the previous case of *California v. Ciralo*, 106 S. Ct. 1809 (1986), upheld a police helicopter overflight at a height of 400 feet as a proper means to observe a marijuana crop in a partially covered greenhouse in the defendant's back yard. Four of the Justices relied heavily on the fact that helicopter flying altitudes are not regulated as closely as those of fixed-wing aircraft, and that any member of the public could have lawfully made the same observation as the police did in this case. Therefore, the observation by the police did not violate any law or regulation, and it was proper to use the observation as probable cause to secure a search warrant. The fifth member of the plurality (O'Connor), agreed with the result of the case, but would not have stressed the compliance with the FAA regulations, but concluded that the police observation did not violate an expectation of privacy "that society is prepared to recognize as reasonable."

It should be noted that, in these overflight cases, the observations were made from a height that was within permissible navigable airspace. In *Ciraolo* and *Dow*, aerial photographs were also taken. In *Dow* the Supreme Court discussed the modern technology which allows magnification of photographs that could reveal details not visible to the naked eye. The Court stated that surveillance of private property by highly sophisticated equipment not generally available to the public, such as satellite technology, might be constitutionally impermissible without a search warrant, but it concludes that "The mere fact that human vision is enhanced somewhat, at least to the degree here, does not give rise to constitutional problems."

In *United States v. Jacobsen*, 104 S. Ct. 1652 (1984) private freight carrier employees opened a damaged carton to inspect its contents pursuant to company policy. Upon finding bags of white powder inside, they notified a Drug Enforcement Administration agent, who removed the powder from the carton, tested a very small quantity of it and found it to be cocaine. The Supreme Court held that the agent's removal and visual inspection of the powder was not a "search" under the Fourth Amendment because it did not exceed the scope of the carrier employees' search and provided no additional information. The warrantless field test, because it was limited to the detection of a contraband substance and destroyed only a trace amount of material, compromised no legitimate privacy interests.

Searches and Seizures in Compliance with Fourth Amendment

1. Pursuant to a valid search warrant.
    a. Warrant based on personal observation by officer.
    b. Warrant based on hearsay information from reliable informant: Test of *Aguilar v. Texas*, 84 S. Ct. 1509 (1964) and *Spinelli v. United States*, 89 S. Ct. 584 (1969).
    c. Warrant based on hearsay tip—anonymous but corroborated: *Illinois v. Gates*, 103 S. Ct. 2317 (1983).
2. Exceptions to the warrant requirement.
    a. Search incident to a lawful arrest: *Chimel v. California*, 89 S. Ct. 2034 (1969); "arms-reach" or "immediate physical control" test.
    b. The automobile exception: *Carroll v. United States*, 45 S. Ct. 280 (1925); "independent probable cause" test. Also consider "police inventory": *South Dakota v. Opperman*, 96 S. Ct. 3092 (1976).
    c. Exigent circumstances: *Warden v. Hayden*, 87 S. Ct. 1642 (1967); "hot pursuit" test and other emergency situations.
    d. The "plain view" doctrine: *Harris v. United States*, 88 S. Ct. 992 (1968); "officer in a place where he has a lawful right to be."
    e. Stop and frisk: *Terry v. Ohio*, 88 S. Ct. 1868 (1968); "pat-down type search."
    f. Consent search: *Schneckloth v. Bustamonte*, 93 S. Ct. 2041 (1973); "knowing and intelligent waiver."

-------------------------------------- **Notes** --------------------------------------

§ 4.14 SEARCHES WITH WARRANT

(A) Probable cause for warrant

In *Aguilar v. Texas*, 84 S. Ct. 1509 (1964) the Supreme Court of the United States stressed that a probable cause affidavit presented to a judge by a police officer (affiant) as the basis for issuance of a search warrant must state the facts and underlying circumstances constituting the probable cause. In other words, a mere conclusory statement such as "Affiant has received reliable information from a credible person and believes that...," is insufficient because it provides no factual basis on which the judge may make an independent assessment of probable cause. The court reasoned that a judge cannot always be expected to accept the officer's judgment, even though the officer is under oath, because the officer, deeply involved in the investigative process and prompted by an overriding sense of duty to solve a crime, may not be as objective as he should be.

The Court indicated in *Draper v. United States*, 79 S. Ct. 329 (1959) (briefed above, § 4.4) that hearsay evidence (what somebody else told the affiant-officer) can be considered as a part of probable cause in issuing a warrant. This point was again made in *Aguilar* and later in *United States v. Ventresca*, 85 S. Ct. 741 (1965). In *Ventresca* the Court emphasized that courts should not apply to probable cause affidavits standards so technical as to discourage the police from seeking warrants before conducting searches. Review of an affidavit should be made in a common-sense, realistic and non-technical manner. These points were again made in *Spinelli v. United States* and *Dawson v. State*, both briefed below in this section.

Despite these guidelines for common-sense review of probable cause, many courts adhered so rigidly to the "two-pronged" tests of *Aguilar* and *Spinelli* (*how* did the informant get his information and *why* should he be believed) that *anonymous* tips to the police, even if verified by observation, became nearly useless. This result was reached in a pretrial suppression hearing in *Illinois v. Gates*, 103 S. Ct. 2317 (1983) (briefed below in this section), in which the trial court ruled that a search warrant based on an anonymous letter accurately predicting a drug transaction which was verified by police surveillance was not supported by the *Aguilar-Spinelli* test, and therefore not supported by probable cause. In reversing the Illinois court, the Supreme Court of the United States seems to have replaced the rigid, two-pronged test for probable cause based on information from unnamed informants with a "totality of the circumstances" test, thus recognizing the value of the anonymous tip, if carefully corroborated by intelligent police investigation.

The lessons of *Aguilar* and *Spinelli* should not be discarded, however; the police should always strive to furnish the judge with the best probable cause that they can gather to justify the issuance of a warrant. If possible, the answers to "what, who, how, and why" should be supplied by informing the judge, under oath, *what* the incriminating facts are; *who* determined the facts (the officer by his personal observation, or a named or unnamed informant); if determined by a known informant, *how* he came by the information; and, if the informant is unnamed, *why* the affiant believes he is a credible source.

If an anonymous tip is used as the basis for a probable cause affidavit, the tip should be verified in the greatest detail possible by careful investigation and observation, so that the judge will have a basis for finding probable cause from the totality of the circumstances presented to him.

CASE BRIEF

Spinelli v. United States, 89 S. Ct. 584 (1969)

Majority opinion: Harlan. Concurring: White. Dissenting: Black, Fortas, Stewart.

FACTS: D was convicted of interstate travel with intent to conduct unlawful gambling. He challenged the constitutionality of the warrant which uncovered the evidence by which he was convicted. The affidavit for the warrant contained four major allegations: (1) The FBI kept track of D's movements for five days during August, 1965 and on four occasions D was seen crossing the bridge from Illinois to Missouri and on four of five days was seen parking his car in an apartment house parking lot in St. Louis between 3:30 and 4:45 p.m. On one occasion D was followed and was seen to enter a particular apartment in the building. (2) An FBI check with the telephone company revealed that the apartment had two telephones with specified numbers. (3) D was known to the affiant and to federal law enforcement agents and local law enforcement agents as a bookmaker, an associate of bookmakers, a gambler, and an associate of gamblers. (4) The Federal Bureau of Investigation was informed by a confidential, reliable informant that D was operating a handbook, accepting wagers and disseminating wagering information by means of telephones with the same numbers as those specified in (2).

ISSUE: Is the affidavit for the search warrant constitutionally sufficient?

DECISION: No; reversed.

REASONS: Without the information in item (4), probable cause could not be established. The conduct described in items (1) and (2) is innocent in and of itself. Item (3) is a bald assertion of suspicion only and not entitled to any weight in appraising the magistrate's decision. Where an informant's tip is a necessary element in finding probable cause, its proper weight must be determined by a more precise analysis. Measuring the informant's report in this case against the standard in *Aguilar v. Texas*, 84 S. Ct. 1509 (1964), without regard to the other three items, it is insufficient. The affiant offered no reason in support of his claim that his informant was reliable. There is no information on the underlying facts and circumstances from which the informant concluded that D was running a bookmaking operation. If the informant came by his information indirectly, he did not explain why his source was reliable. How the informant received his information is not explained. It is not alleged that the informant saw or personally observed D at work. It is not alleged that the informant ever placed a bet with D.

It is essential that the magistrate know that he is relying on something more substantial than a rumor overheard in a bar or an accusation based on D's general reputation. For example, in *Draper v. United States*, 79 S. Ct. 329 (1959), the particularity of the description given would lead a magistrate to believe he was receiving information obtained in a reliable manner, such as personal observation. Here, the doubts raised as to the informant's story are not cured by the FBI investigation, which merely shows that the phones could have been used as stated. The tip needed more support than bald assertions of suspicion and observation of seemingly innocent conduct.

RULE: When an affidavit for a search warrant contains information from a known—but unnamed—reliable informant, and when that information is essential to the finding of probable cause, there must appear in the affidavit: (1) statements explaining why the informant is considered reliable; and (2) the underlying facts and circumstances showing how the informant came by his information.

CONCURRING: An unsupported assertion or belief of an officer does not satisfy the requirement of probable cause. But the *Draper* case is not necessarily good precedent for the holding in this case because *Draper* was primarily concerned with the reliability of the informant.

DISSENTING: The Court is expanding *Aguilar* beyond reason and nearly requiring a trial before a warrant is issued.

CASE BRIEF
Dawson v. State, 276 A.2d 680 (Md. App. 1971)

FACTS: D1 and D2, husband and wife, were convicted of unlawfully maintaining premises for purposes of selling lottery tickets. On appeal they contended that the search warrant for their home had been issued and executed without adequate probable cause. The affidavit for the warrant consisted of nine paragraphs. The first stated the investigative experience of the affiant-detective and his conclusion that gambling was taking place at the suspected premises. The second paragraph dealt with hearsay evidence. It stated that the affiant had interviewed a confidential informer who in the past had given reliable information relating to gambling, which had resulted in arrests and convictions; that the informer was personally known to the affiant; that the informer had told the affiant that there were gambling activities taking place at the address in question; and that the informer had called and placed horse bets with D1. Paragraphs 3 through 9 stated the results of investigations and surveillance by affiant himself, and alleged the following:

(1) Three years before the current observations D1 had been convicted of gambling violations;
(2) Over a portion of two weeks D1 had not been observed to have any legitimate employment;
(3) D1 had two separate phone lines in his residence;
(4) One of D1's unlisted numbers had been picked up in the course of a gambling raid at another place;
(5) On each day of surveillance, D1 had purchased an "Armstrong Scratch Sheet" (information on horses running at various tracks that day);
(6) On each morning, D1 had left his home between 9:02 and 10:20 and had returned between 11:20 a.m. and 12:06 p.m.;
(7) On each day of surveillance D1 had remained in his home, once he had returned, until after 6:00 p.m.;
(8) On each day of surveillance, D1 had stopped at liquor stores, restaurants, etc. for a few minutes only, and except for the "scratch sheet," had made no purchases;
(9) On one of the days of observation, D1 had been seen in close association during all the day's activities with W.A., who was known by affiant to have been arrested in 1966 along with D1 for gambling violations.

ISSUE: Was sufficient probable cause alleged in the affidavit to justify the issuance of a search warrant?

DECISION: Yes; affirmed.

REASONS: A warrant for search or arrest may be issued on the basis of two broad categories of probable cause information:

(1) Direct observations by affiant;
(2) Hearsay information furnished by someone else and recited by the affiant in the affidavit.

Probable cause may be based on either type of information or a combination of both. Both of the broad categories are evaluated by the same general standard of measurement. The magistrate must make two distinct determinations. He must:

(1) Evaluate the truthfulness of the source of the information;
(2) Evaluate the adequacy of the factual premises furnished by that source to support the validity of the source's conclusion.

In (1) he is judging the integrity of a person; in (2) he is judging the logic of a proposition.

The affiant-observer's oath affirms the honesty of his statement; but where the source is an informant, the magistrate must have some other reason to be persuaded of the credibility of the source of the information. The naming of a source may go a long way toward establishing credibility; but where the informer is unnamed, the magistrate must be furnished sufficient background information to judge for himself the credibility of the unnamed source and/or the reliability of that source's information. To conclude that trustworthiness is probably present, the magistrate must be convinced either that (1) the source himself, as a person, is inherently honest and credible, or (2) that the information was furnished by that source under circumstances which guaranteed trustworthiness. A bare assertion by the affiant that the informant is credible is conclusory and unacceptable; the affidavit must contain allegations of facts supporting this assertion.

Once the magistrate has decided the information is trustworthy, he must evaluate this information to see what probabilities emerge.

After evaluating both the trustworthiness of the source of information and the weight and worth of the information, the magistrate may reach one of four conclusions:
  (1) The information based on direct observation is adequate by itself to establish probable cause;
  (2) The hearsay information is adequate by itself to establish probable cause;
  (3) Neither the direct observations nor the hearsay, standing alone, is sufficient, but together they establish probable cause;
  (4) The sum total of both kinds of information does not establish probable cause.

The most logical procedure in evaluating a warrant application is to look first at the hearsay information. If the affiant has furnished enough underlying facts to persuade the magistrate (1) that the informant is credible or his information otherwise reliable, and (2) that informant's conclusion was validly arrived at, then probable cause is established.

If the hearsay portion fails to pass either test, it is not rendered totally valueless but may need support. The magistrate may then look to the direct observations recounted by the affiant. These may serve a dual function:
  (1) They may bear directly on the question of probable cause;
  (2) They may corroborate the hearsay information.

If some significant details of the informer's story are shown to be true, the magistrate is encouraged to believe that all of the story is probably true. Then the magistrate must ask: is the tip, even when certain parts of it have been corroborated by independent sources, as trustworthy as a tip which would pass, without independent corroboration, the tests of *Aguilar v. Texas*, 84 S. Ct. 1509 (1964)?

In looking at the second paragraph of the probable cause affidavit here (where the affiant relates informant's tip), it is clear that the informant is not merely passing on idle rumor; he has personally placed phone bets. His knowledge is firsthand and his facts support his conclusion.

Here the assertion of credibility/reliability contains a statement that this informant's information in the past has led to convictions for gambling activities. This assertion goes further than *Spinelli v. United States*, 89 S. Ct. 584 (1969) where the source was simply described as a "confidential reliable informant," with no recitation of any prior successes.

Whether or not the magistrate is satisfied with credibility/reliability allegations in the affidavit, he may then look to the direct observations sworn to by the affiant to see if they verify the informant's story.

The direct observations strongly suggest a middle-echelon executive in the gambling business, dealing in both horses and numbers, since both activities are geared to the same hourly schedule and look to the same sporting events.

While any one observation alleged, standing alone, may be innocent enough, the overall pattern portrays a great deal; the whole may, indeed, be greater than the sum of its parts.

Each level of the gambling enterprise pyramid has its own telltale pattern of activity. Not to realize this would be to condemn law enforcement to the futility of reeling in only the "little fish."

The bare assertion that the defendant in *Spinelli* was "known" to the FBI as a gambler is far weaker than the sworn recitation here that D1 had a previous criminal record of gambling convictions.

The magistrate is not required to weigh each of the direct observations in a vacuum; in weighing the relative probabilities the reasonable mind cannot ignore the number and privacy of D1's telephones; the times when D1 was near those phones; his criminal history; and his apparent lack of legitimate employment. The brevity and frequency of the stops made by D1 and the methodical regularity of the daily activities are classic characteristics of the pick-up man in a gambling operation. This conclusion is further bolstered by his close association on one day with a previously convicted gambler, a fact which lends interpretive color to otherwise ambiguous activity.

In review, the magistrate must ask "What is revealed by the whole pattern of activity?" Here, the various strands of observation, insubstantial unto themselves, together weave a strong web of probable guilt.

RULE: A search or arrest warrant may be based on direct observations of the affiant, on hearsay information furnished to the affiant by an informant (named or unnamed), or on both. To establish probable cause the affidavit must allege sufficient underlying facts for the magistrate independently to evaluate (1) the truthfulness of the source of the information; and (2) the logic of the factual proposition. Once the magistrate is satisfied that the information is trustworthy, he must evaluate it to see what probabilities emerge. He should evaluate the hearsay portion first and determine if it is independently sufficient to establish probable cause. If not, he should determine if it is supported by the direct observations. Bare conclusive statements by the affiant or informant, standing alone, are not sufficient to establish probable cause. Although direct observations, considered separately, may be inconclusive, the magistrate is not bound to consider them in a vacuum; if together they form a pattern which is consistent with the hearsay and leads to the same conclusion, probable cause may be established for the issuance of a warrant for search or arrest.

CASE BRIEF

Illinois v. Gates, 103 S. Ct. 2317 (1983)

**Majority opinion: Rehnquist. Concurring: White.
Dissenting: Brennan, Marshall, Stevens.**

FACTS: The Bloomingdale, Illinois police received an anonymous handwritten letter which named a local couple, D and his wife, as drug dealers. The letter indicated the area of the city in which the couple lived and stated that most of their buys were made in Florida. It further indicated the method of operation: D's wife would drive the family car to Florida and leave it to be loaded with drugs; D would fly down to Florida later and drive the car back; D's wife would fly back home after leaving the car. It also stated that D's wife was next leaving for Florida on May 3; that D would fly down a few days later to drive the car back with over $100,000 worth of drugs; that the couple had over $100,000 worth of drugs in their basement; and that they brag that they never have to work, but make their entire living on drug pushers.

Police decided to follow up the tip. D's address was determined, and it was learned that D had made reservations for a flight to Florida on May 5. Police arranged with the D.E.A. for surveillance of the flight. D.E.A. agents later reported to police that D had boarded the flight and that agents in Florida had observed him to arrive in West Palm Beach and take a taxi to a nearby motel, where he went to a room registered in his wife's name. They also reported that the next morning D and an unidentified woman left the motel in a car bearing Illinois license plates registered to D, and drove northbound on an interstate on the route to Illinois. Agents also advised police that estimated driving time from West Palm Beach to Bloomingdale was 22-24 hours.

Based on this information, police submitted an affidavit and a copy of the anonymous letter to the circuit judge, who issued a search warrant for D's residence and automobile. Early the next day, D and his wife returned to their home in the car which had left West Palm Beach 22 hours earlier. The police were waiting with the search warrant and recovered 350 pounds of marijuana from the car and a quantity of marijuana, weapons and other contraband from the residence. D and his wife were indicted on drug charges.

Prior to D's trial the court ordered suppression of all items seized on the basis that the affidavit and letter did not show sufficient probable cause. This ruling was affirmed by the Illinois Appellate Court and by the Supreme Court of Illinois.

ISSUES: (1) Should the exclusionary rule be modified to allow the admissibility of evidence when the police have acted in good faith, although there may have been a judicial error in the determination of probable cause for a search warrant? (2) Was there probable cause for the issuance of a search warrant in this case?

DECISION: (1) Not decided; (2) yes; reversed.

REASONS: (1) Although the Court specifically requested the parties to address the question of a "good faith" exception to the Fourth Amendment exclusionary rule, it declined to decide this issue, holding that the question was not properly presented to and decided by the Illinois courts. (2) Standing alone, the anonymous letter did not furnish probable cause to issue a search warrant. It provided virtually nothing from which one might conclude that its author was honest or his information reliable and it gave no indication of the basis for the writer's prediction of D's criminal activity.

In applying the "two-pronged test" of *Spinelli v. United States*, 89 S. Ct. 584 (1969), the Illinois court apparently thought that the veracity or reliability of the informant and the soundness of his knowledge must be independently established. To be sure, these elements are highly relevant in determining probable cause when dealing with an unknown informant, but they are not necessarily separate and independent requirements to be rigidly exacted in every case; they are closely intertwined issues that may usefully illuminate the commonsense, practical question of probable cause.

The determination of probable cause should consider the totality of the circumstances presented; it should not depend on rigid, technical rules to be applied in every case. Probable cause is a practical, nontechnical conception. It deals with probabilities: factual and practical considerations of everyday life on which reasonable and prudent men, not legal technicians, act.

Informants' tips may vary greatly in their value and reliability. One simple rule will not cover every situation. The "two-pronged test" is better understood as relevant considerations in the totality of circumstances that has traditionally guided the determination of probable cause. A weakness in one may be compensated for, in determining the overall reliability of the tip, by a strong showing as to the other, or by some other indicator of reliability. For example, when dealing with a particular informant who has been consistently reliable in the past, a failure by him to set forth in detail the basis of his knowledge in one instance should not be an absolute bar to a finding of probable cause. Likwise when an unquestionably honest citizen reports criminal activity under pain of penalty for false reporting.

Strict adherence to the "two-pronged test" of probable cause has encouraged an excessively technical examination of informants' tips with undue attention being placed on isolated issues that really can't be divorced from other facts also presented to the magistrate.

Past cases have recognized that finely tuned trial standards of proof such as "beyond a reasonable doubt" or "preponderance," have no place in the magistrate's determination of probable cause. It is clear that "only the probability, and not a prima facie showing, of criminal activity is the standard of probable cause" (citing *Spinelli*). Affidavits for search and arrest warrants are normally drafted by nonlawyers and sometimes these warrants are issued by persons who are neither lawyers nor judges on the basis of nontechnical commonsense judgments applying a standard less demanding than those used in formal legal proceedings.

After-the-fact scrutiny by courts of the sufficiency of an affidavit should not be a "de novo" review; a magistrate's determination of probable cause should be paid great deference by reviewing courts. A negative attitude by reviewing courts is inconsistent with the Fourth Amendment's strong preference for searches by warrant and might contribute to an increase in warrantless searches by police relying on consent or some other exception to the warrant clause. The traditional standard for review of an issuing magistrate's probable cause determination has been that the Fourth Amendment requires no more than that the magistrate had a "substantial basis for ... concluding" that a search would uncover evidence of wrongdoing; *Jones v. United States*, 80 S. Ct. 725 (1960). Reaffirmation of this standard better serves the purpose of encouraging recourse to the warrant procedure and is more consistent with traditional deference to the probable cause determinations of magistrates than is the "two-pronged test."

The direction taken by many decisions following *Spinelli* seriously impedes the task of law enforcement by making anonymous tips to police of very little value. Anonymous tips seldom could survive a rigorous application of either of the *Spinelli* prongs. Yet such tips, particularly when supplemented by independent police investigation, frequently contribute to the solution of otherwise "perfect crimes." While a conscientious standard for crediting such tips is required by the Fourth Amendment, a standard that leaves virtually no place for anonymous citizen informants is not. For all these reasons, it is wiser to abandon the "two-pronged test" established by *Spinelli* and *Aguilar v. Texas*, 84 S. Ct. 1509 (1964). In its place we reaffirm the totality of the circumstances that traditionally has informed probable cause determinations; *Jones v. United States*, 80 S. Ct. 755 (1960); *United States v. Ventresca*, 85 S. Ct. 741 (1965); *Brinegar v. United States*, 69 S. Ct. 1302 (1949).

The issuing magistrate must simply make a practical, common-sense decision based on all the circumstances set forth in the affidavit before him (including "veracity" and "basis of knowledge" when applicable), and the duty of the reviewing court is simply to ensure that the magistrate had a "substantial basis" for concluding that probable cause existed.

Mere conclusory statements will not establish probable cause; sufficient information must be presented to allow the magistrate to determine probable cause. His action cannot be a mere ratification of the bare, unsupported conclusions of others.

Past decisions have often stressed the importance of corroboration of the details of an informant's tip by independent police work. The showing of probable cause in the present case was fully as compelling as that in *Draper v. United*

States, 79 S. Ct. 329 (1959). Even standing alone, the facts obtained through the independent police investigation and that of the D.E.A. at least suggested that D and his wife were involved in drug trafficking. Florida is a well-known source of illegal drugs as well as a popular vacation site. D's flight to Palm Beach and his brief overnight stay in a motel and apparent immediate return north in the family car, conveniently awaiting him, is as suggestive of a prearranged drug run as it is of a vacation trip. In addition, the magistrate could rely on the anonymous letter, corroborated in major part by police efforts, as in *Draper*. It is true that *Draper* involved a known, reliable informant, and while this distinction may have been important at the time the anonymous letter was received, it became far less significant after the independent investigative work occurred. The amount of detail in the letter also suggested the author obtained the information directly from D or from someone he trusted, and the police corroboration of the predicted activity provided the magistrate with a substantial basis for concluding that probable cause to search D's home and car existed.

RULE: Probable cause deals in probabilities as determined by the practical, commonsense reasoning of reasonable and prudent men, not legal technicians, and the determination of probable cause for the issuance of a warrant is not to be restricted by the rigid, two-pronged formula of *Spinelli* in every case. Rather, probable cause is a fluid concept depending on the totality of all the circumstances presented to the magistrate in the affidavit. Reviewing courts should give great deference to a magistrate's determination of probable cause so as not to discourage use of the warrant procedure by police, and as long as there is a substantial basis for the finding, which must, of course, be more than bare, conclusory statements, the probable cause determination should be upheld. Probable cause can be supported by independent and substantial corroboration of a detailed anonymous tip to police, even though it would fail the rigid two-pronged test of *Spinelli*.

In *New York v. P.J. Video, Inc.*, 106 S. Ct. 1610 (1986), the Supreme Court of the United States, with reference to probable cause for a search warrant, stated:

> The task of the issuing magistrate is simply to make a practical, commonsense decision whether, given all the circumstances set forth in the affidavit before him ... there is a fair probability that contraband or evidence of a crime will be found in a particular place. And the duty of a reviewing court is simply to ensure that the magistrate has a 'substantial basis for ... concluding' ... that probable cause existed.

Despite the difficulty that the Supreme Court has had in formulating a workable and enforceable definition of obscenity because of the First Amendment protections of freedom of expression, the Court held in *P.J. Video, Inc.*, that application for a warrant to seize allegedly obscene materials requires no higher standard than the practical common-sense standard which applies to other than First Amendment cases.

--------------------------------------- **Notes** ---------------------------------------

4.14(A)(1) INDEPENDENT SOURCE

If a police officer makes an unauthorized, non-consensual entry into a private place and as a result observes evidence of crime, can he obtain a search warrant based on the unlawful observation and then make a lawful seizure of the evidence with the search warrant? The answer is obviously that he cannot, because the probable cause is tainted (secured unlawfully). For the law to allow the officer to proceed in this maner would violate the rule that judges call "fruit of the poisonous tree"; it would undermine the purpose of the exclusionary rule, which is to deter the police from breaking the law in order to enforce the law. But if an officer first developed probable cause to search a private place and then made an unauthorized entry, observed incriminating evidence, and secured a search warrant, using only the probable cause that he had developed earlier, would the later, unauthorized entry and observation "spoil" the probable cause developed lawfully? This situation was before the Supreme Court in *Murray v. United States*, 108 S. Ct. 2529 (1988). Justice Scalia, writing for a 4 to 3 majority (Justices Brennan and Kennedy not participating), held that application of the "independent source" doctrine rendered the evidence seized by the warrant admissible *if the facts showed that the search warrant would have been secured even if the unauthorized entry and observation had not been made.*

In *Murray*, federal drug agents, while conducting surveillance as a result of information received from informants, observed the defendants, who were driving a truck and a camper, drive into a warehouse. About 20 minutes later they drove their vehicles out of the warehouse, and inside through its open door, the agents saw a tractor-trailer with a long container on it and two persons. The defendants later turned the vehicles over to other drivers who were followed and arrested and the vehicles lawfully seized. Both the truck and the camper contained marijuana.

Several of the agents then returned to the warehouse and made a forced, warrantless entry. The warehouse was unoccupied, but the agents observed in plain view several burlap-wrapped bales, later found to contain marijuana. Leaving the bales undisturbed, they kept the warehouse under surveillance. They obtained a search warrant, without revealing the prior entry of the warehouse, or the observation of the bales; they related only probable cause elements derived prior to the entry. With the warrant the agents reentered the warehouse and seized 270 bales of marijuana and notebooks containing customer records. The defendants filed motions to suppress the evidence found in the warehouse on the theory that the search warrant was invalid because the agents did not inform the judge of the prior warrantless entry, and the warrant was thus "tainted" by that entry. Both the trial court and the court of appeals ruled against the defendants (the court of appeals assuming, for purposes of its decision, that the first entry into the warehouse *was unlawful*).

In the Supreme Court opinion, Justice Scalia, citing *Silverthorne Lumber Co. v. United States*, 40 S. Ct. 182 (1920), observed that the "independent source" doctrine developed at about the same time as the exclusionary rule. It asserted that evidence obtained independently of unlawful police activity should be admissible despite the police misconduct, and was applied in *Segura v. United States*, 104 S. Ct. 3380 (1984). In that case the Court held that unlawful entry by police on private premises did not require the suppression of evidence subsequently discovered at the same place when a search warrant was obtained on the basis of probable cause wholly unconnected with the initial entry. Justice Scalia also noted that the "inevitable discovery" doctrine of *Nix v. Williams*, 104 S. Ct. 2501 (1984) is based on, and assumes the validity of, the "independent source" doctrine.

The law enforcement implications of the *Murray* holding are discussed in the opinion. The defendants argued that such a holding would encourage police, to routinely enter without a warrant in order to verify that what they expect to find is there; if it is not, they will have spared themselves the time and trouble of obtaining a search warrant. Justice Scalia disagrees with this analysis, pointing out that it would be foolish for an officer already possessing probable cause, to risk suppression of evidence and an additional burden of probable cause by entering unlawfully before obtaining the warrant. *If the decision to obtain a search warrant* is found to stem from the unlawful verification rather than wholly from the previously untainted probable cause, the independent source doctrine does not apply and the evidence is suppressible. To emphasize this point, the lower court judgments in the *Murray* case (favoring admissibility of the bales of marijuana as evidence) were vacated, and the case was remanded (sent back), for a trial court determination of whether the decision to obtain a search warrant of the warehouse was wholly and independently made on the basis of probable cause that existed before the unlawful entry, or was "tainted" by the observations made as a result of the unlawful entry.

Law enforcement officers should view the *Murray* case, not as providing a technique to verify probable cause already lawfully developed, but as a warning that such a pre-warrant unlawful entry can *destroy* a case made after hours of surveillance and proper police investigation.

--------------------------------------- **Notes** ---------------------------------------

4.14(A)(2) REASONABLENESS OF REQUEST FOR WARRANT; [CIVIL LIABILITY OF OFFICER]

Probable cause might be referred to as the *foundation* of law enforcement authority. A constitutional concept, the existence of probable cause has traditionally determined the validity of arrests, searches, and seizures, as well as civil liability of law enforcement officers. The very strict rules concerning probable cause for a warrant have been relaxed somewhat by *Illinois v. Gates* 103 S. Ct. 2317 (1983) concerning the development of probable cause by the investigative corroboration of anonymous tips, and the cases of *United States v. Leon* 104 S. Ct. 3405 (1984) and *Massachusetts v. Sheppard* 104 S. Ct. 3424 (1984) concerning the exclusionary rule of evidence when an officer proceeds under a warrant with an objective good-faith belief that probable cause exists. Accompanying these criminal cases has been a series of cases concerning the qualified immunity of law enforcement officers from civil damages (Chapter 2). These cases, like the good-faith exception to the exclusionary rule, also turn on the existence of an objectively reasonable belief in the existence of probable cause. Emerging from all of these cases is a new legal standard—that of the "reasonably well-trained officer".

With increased training and education comes increased responsibility. While the good-faith exception to the exclusionary rule benefits the public to some degree by making it more certain that those guilty of crime will be convicted, and while it may encourage the police to seek judicial warrants instead of arresting and searching without prior approval of neutral and detached judges, such a relaxation of the exclusionary rule has its price. In *Malley v. Briggs* 106 S. Ct. 1092 (1986), the Supreme Court of the United States held that the fact that a police officer acts under the authority of a warrant does not *automatically* relieve him from the potential of civil liability and money damages when a judge "rubber stamps" a warrant application that is wholly deficient in probable cause.

In legal theory, there is a level at which all policemen, prosecutors and judges would agree that probable cause for arrest or search *does* exist. Again in theory, there is a middle ground, where reasonably well-trained officers might *disagree* as to whether or not probable cause exists. In the middle ground, the good-faith exception to the exclusionary rule will apply, and most motions to suppress evidence seized by a warrant will be denied; moreover, civil liability for unconstitutional arrests made with a warrant is less likely to be found. There is also a third and lower theoretical level, which falls below the standard of "objective reasonableness." At this level, no reasonably well-trained officer would believe that probable cause for a warrant exists. At this level, motions to suppress evidence—even though seized under a warrant—will be granted; the evidence will be excluded because it falls below the objective reasonableness standard that is a part of *Leon-Sheppard* good faith exception to the exclusionary rule. Also at this lowest level, under *Malley v. Briggs*, a police officer can be held civilly liable for damages for an arrest made under a warrant that he obtained by presenting to a judge information which no reasonably well-trained officer would believe amounted to probable cause. The Court stated, in *Malley v. Briggs:*

> It is true that in an ideal system an unreasonable request for a warrant would be harmless, because no judge would approve it. But ours is not an ideal system, and it is possible that a magistrate, working under docket pressures, will fail to perform as a magistrate should. We find it reasonable to require the officer applying for the warrant to minimize this danger by exercising reasonable professional judgment.

How can a police officer protect himself from civil liability—and also guard against motions to suppress evidence? Obviously, he should proceed under the authority of a warrant whenever practicable. In preparing warrant applications or affidavits he should get a "second opinion" whenever possible. He should seek the opinion of the prosecutor or his deputies, or a police legal advisor if available, or the opinions of other trained and experienced officers as to the existence of probable cause, before presenting the warrant application to the judge.

-------------------------------------- **Notes** --------------------------------------

(B) Discovery of Items Not Specified In Warrant

In executing a search warrant, if items not specified in the warrant are observed in places where the specified items might logically be, and these unspecified items are immediately recognized as contraband or as items otherwise subject to seizure, may they be seized without obtaining an additional warrant? This situation would seem to be controlled by the "plain view" doctrine (see § 4.15(D)), and the items not specified in the warrant would be subject to warrantless seizure:

(1) the search warrant would serve as a *prior valid intrusion on privacy;*

(2) the discovery of the unspecified items was *inadvertent* (in the sense of either being unexpected or insufficient probable cause to have included them in the warrant);

(3) when inadvertently discovered there was *probable cause to believe* the unspecified items were evidence of criminal activity. See *Texas v. Brown*, 103 S. Ct. 1535 (1983); *Arizona v. Hicks*, 107 S. Ct. 1149 (1987).

In discussing the "plain view" doctrine in *Texas v. Brown*, the Court stated:

> The *Coolidge* [v. New Hampshire, 91 S. Ct. 2022 (1971)] plurality observed: " it is important to keep in mind that, in the vast majority of cases, *any* evidence seized by the police will be in plain view, at least at the moment of seizure," simply as "the normal concomitant of any search, legal or illegal." Id., at 465, 91 S. Ct., at 2037. The question whether property in plain view of the police may be seized therefore must turn on the legality of the intrusion that enables them to perceive and physically seize the property in question. The Coolidge plurality, while following this approach to "plain view," characterized it as an independent exception to the warrant requirement. At least from an analytical perspective, this description may be somewhat inaccurate. We recognized in *Payton v. New York*, * * * 100 S. Ct. 1371, 1380, * * * (1980), the well-settled rule that "objects such as weapons or contraband found in a public place may be seized by the police without a warrant. The seizure of property in plain view involves no invasion of privacy and is presumptively reasonable, assuming that there is probable cause to associate the property with criminal activity." A different situation is presented, however, when the property in open view is "'situated on private premises to which access is not otherwise available for the seizing officer.'" Ibid. quoting *G.M. Leasing Corp. v. United States*, * * * 97 S. Ct. 619, 629, * * * (1977). As these cases indicate, "plain view" provides grounds for seizure of an item when the officer's access to an object has some prior justification under the Fourth Amendment.[4] "Plain view" is perhaps better understood, therefore, not as an independent "exception" to the Warrant Clause, but simply as an extension of whatever the prior justification for an officer's "access to an object" may be.

In footnote 4 to the above, the Court stated:

> Thus, police may perceive an object while executing a search warrant, or they may come across an item while acting pursuant to some exception to the Warrant Clause...".

------------------------------------- **Notes** -------------------------------------

Sample Questions

Courts have found that an arrest has taken place in situations where the word "arrest" was never used by the officer.   T   F.

One element of a criminal arrest is "custody".   T   F.

Police surveillance from fixed-wing aircraft has been held proper by the Supreme Court of the United States, but police surveillance from helicopters can never be constitutional.   T   F.

If a police roadblock is set up in such a manner as to create a high probability that a fleeing motorist will crash into the roadblock and be stopped, (such as placing an obstruction across the highway just around a "blind" curve at night without illuminating the obstruction), and the fleeing motorist crashes into the roadblock and is killed:

A. the courts are likely to rule that this is a "seizure" under the Fourth Amendment and therefore subject to the Fourth Amendment "reasonableness" requirement.
B. this clearly would not be a "seizure" because the motorist ran into the obstruction of his own free will.
C. the motorist should not be fleeing the police, so there can be no possibility of police civil liability.
D. the situation may be controlled by the rule in *Tennessee v. Garner.*
E. A and D above.

To constitute an arrest there must be either a physical seizure of the person by the arresting officer, or a submission to his authority and control by the person arrested.   T   F.

Differences between search and arrest warrants include:

A. a court is more likely to find a search warrant has become "stale" than it is to find an arrest warrant has become "stale".
B. search warrants are issued by "courts", while arrests warrants are issued by "magistrates".
C. only a search warrant requires a prior judicial determination of probable cause before it is issued.
D. the "knock and announce" requirement applies only to arrest warrants.
E. none of the above was true.

A search conducted under a properly-issued search warrant can still be unreasonable if places are searched where the items authorized to be seized could not possibly be located because of the size of the items described.   T   F.

It is a violation of the Constitution of the United States for a police officer to make a warrantless arrest for a felony in a public place on probable cause alone if the officer had the opportunity to obtain an arrest warrant but did not do so.   T   F.

In a routine felony arrest situation, if the police have a warrant of arrest for D, and reason to believe he is in his residence, the Constitution of the United States requires that the police obtain a search warrant, in addition to the arrest warrant before they attempt to serve the arrest warrant.   T   F.

CASE BRIEF

Horton v. California, 110 S.Ct. 2301 (1990)

Majority opinion: Stevens, J., joined by Rehnquist, C.J., White, Blackmun, O'Connor, Scalia, and Kennedy, JJ. Dissenting: Brennan, J., joined by Marshall, J.

FACTS: Victim was accosted by two masked robbers armed with a machine gun and a "stun gun" when he returned home. Victim was submitted to electrical shock, bound, handcuffed, and robbed of jewelry and cash. Leads developed from D's distinctive sounding voice, from witnesses who saw robbers leave, and from other evidence resulted in investigating officer's preparation of affidavit for search warrant which referred to police reports describing the weapons and the proceeds of the robbery. The search warrant issued for D's residence by the judge, however, authorized only a search for the proceeds, including three specifically described rings. The search was made, with the warrant, but the stolen cash and jewelry were not found, but the weapons were discovered in plain view and they were seized. The officer who made the search testified that while searching for the rings, he was also interested in finding other evidence that would link D to the crime. (Therefore it is clear the weapons were not discovered "inadvertently", in the sense of being totally unexpected). D's motion to suppress the evidence was denied and he was tried, convicted, and sentenced to prison and the state courts affirmed his conviction. The Supreme Court granted certiorari.

ISSUE: If, during execution of a search warrant which authorizes specified items to be seized, other items connected with the crime, but not specified in the search warrant are observed in plain view, are these unspecified items subject to warrantless seizure, even though their discovery by the officer conducting the search is not "inadvertent", but on the other hand, expected?

DECISION: Yes, under these circumstances items not specified in the search warrant which are obviously connected to the crime are subject to seizure. Affirmed.

REASONS: "Inadvertence" is a characteristic of many plain view seizures, but it is not a necessary condition. A *search* affects *privacy* interests, while a *seizure* affects an individual's *control* over person or property. If an article is already in plain view, neither its observation nor its seizure involves an invasion of *privacy* but its seizure would obviously invade possessory interests. So if "plain view" justifies an exception to the warrant requirement, the exception involves *seizures* rather than *searches*. (The Court then discusses the "inadvertent discovery" concept as it was developed in *Coolidge v. New Hampshire*, 91 S.Ct. 2022 (1971), noting that only a plurality of four Justices agreed on the requirement of inadvertent discovery in plain view seizures).

It is an essential condition to any lawful warrantless seizure of evidence that the officer did not violate the Fourth Amendment in getting to the place where he could observe the evidence in plain view. Two additional conditions also exist: (1) not only must the item be in plain view, but its incriminating character must be immediately apparent (citing *Arizona v. Hicks*, 107 S.Ct. 1149 (1987)), and (2) not only must the officer be lawfully located in a place from which the item can be plainly seen, but he must have lawful right of access to the object itself.

(The Court then discusses Justice Stewart's reasoning in the *Coolidge* opinion, which based the inadvertence requirement on the "particularity" requirement of the Fourth Amendment — that is, that if the police already know a seizable item is located in the place to be searched when they obtain a search warrant for something else, they should identify this item in the warrant also, and should not be allowed to make a warrantless seizure of it as an incident to the seizure under the warrant — even though it is in plain view). The Court says it finds two flaws in this reasoning:

(1) Evenhanded law enforcement is best achieved by applying objective standards of conduct — not standards that are based on the subjective state of mind of the officer. The mere fact that an officer might expect to find other incriminating evidence in the course of a search under a warrant naming specified items should not invalidate seizure of the expected items if the search is confined in area and duration by the terms of the search warrant — or by another valid exception to the warrant requirement. If an officer has probable cause to believe an item will be found, we see no reason why he would omit it from his warrant application, but if he has probable cause as to item 1, but only suspicion as to item 2, whether or not it amounts to probable cause, we fail to see why that suspicion should keep item 2 from being seized if it is found during a lawful search for item 1.

(2) The position that the inadvertence requirement is necessary to prevent converting specific warrants into general warrants is not persuasive because that interest is already protected by the particularity requirement of the Fourth Amendment and by the requirement that a warrantless search be limited by the exigent circumstanes justifying it. Both of these factors limit the area and duration of the search, and if satisfied, the officer has a lawful right of access and no additional Fourth Amendment interests are furthered by requiring that discovery of evidence be inadvertent. "If the scope of the search exceeds that permitted by the terms of a validly issued warrant or the character of the relevant exception from the warrant requirement, the subsequent seizure is unconstitutional without more."

In this case, the area or duration of the search was not enlarged in the slightest by the fact that the weapons were not specified in the warrant. If the rings and other named items had been found at the outset of the search, or if D had produced them immediately, no search for the weapons could have taken place. General searches and general warrants are prohibited because they violate constitutionally-protected privacy interest. Here, privacy interests were protected by the search warrant for the robbery proceeds. The weapons were discovered in plain view during a lawful search for the proceeds. The search was authorized by the warrant and the seizure of the weapons was authorized by the "plain view" doctrine because it was immediately apparent to the officer that they were incriminating evidence.

RULE: Plain view seizures of evidence are lawful if: (1) the officer is lawfully located in a place from which the object can be plainly seen, i.e., a public place, or a private place by virtue of a warrant or other prior valid intrusion on privacy; (2) the incriminating character of the object is immediately apparent; and (3) the officer has a lawful right of access to the object itself. If these criteria are met, the object may be seized whether or not it is described in a search warrant, and whether or not its discovery is expected or inadvertent.

DISSENT: If an officer with probable cause to believe an item is located in a certain place fails to include it in his application for a search warrant, his conduct is *per se* unreasonable. The majority opinion has eliminated a rule designed to protect possessory interests on the ground that it fails to protect privacy interests. The opinion will encourage the police to conduct pretextual searches and to circumvent constitutional requirements. An overwhelming number of states and federal jurisdictions have already adopted the inadvertence requirement.

(C) Affidavit For Warrant

In the past, state statutes authorizing search warrants were very restrictive concerning the items which could be seized. Generally, "mere evidence", not amounting to contraband or the fruits or instrumentalities of crime, could not be seized pursuant to a warrant. When the Supreme Court of the United States identified privacy, rather than property, as being the right primarily protected by the Fourth Amendment, the reasoning concerning "mere evidence" began to change. In *Warden v. Hayden*, 87 S. Ct. 1642 (1967), the Court reasoned that, since the Fourth Amendment protects privacy rather than property, it is no more of an intrusion of privacy for the police to search for mere evidence than for fruits, instrumentalities, or contraband, so long as the other requirements of the amendment are met.

More recent cases have turned not so much on what may be seized under a warrant as on the magistrate's determination of probable cause by common-sense, non-technical standards which encourage, rather than discourage, the seeking of warrants.

With the holding in *Illinois v. Gates*, 103 S. Ct. 2317 (1983), the Supreme Court reaffirmed that the judicial determination of probable cause for the issuance of a warrant is not to be governed by fixed and rigid technical formulas, but, rather, by the "totality of circumstances" made known to the judge in the affidavit, or sworn application for the warrant. In *Massachusetts v. Upton*, 104 S. Ct. 2085 (1984), the Court discussed the sufficiency of an affidavit for a search warrant prepared by a police officer as a result of a phone call he received from an unidentified woman. The officer had participated just three hours earlier in search under warrant of a motel room, in which some, but not all, items belonging to victims of recent burglaries had been recovered. The anonymous caller revealed that she was aware of the motel search and told the officer that there was "a motor home full of stolen stuff" parked behind #5 Jefferson Ave., which was the home of D and his mother. She said the stolen items included jewelry, silver, and gold—the same kinds of items sought but not recovered in the motel search. At the conclusion of the anonymous call, the officer went to D's home and verified that a motor home was parked there. Then, while other officers watched the premises, the officer prepared an application for a search warrant, which included the following statement:

> She further stated that George Upton was going to move the motor home any time now because of the fact that Ricky Kelleher's motel room was raided and that George [Upton] had purchased these stolen items from Ricky Kelleher. This unidentified female stated that she had seen the stolen items but refused to identify herself because "he'll kill me," referring to George Upton. I then told this unidentified female that I knew who she was, giving her the name of Lynn Alberico, who I had met on May 16, 1980, at George Upton's repair shop off Summer St. in Yarmouthport. She was identified to me by George Upton as being his girlfriend, Lynn Alberico. The unidentified female admitted that she was the girl that I had named, stating that she was surprised that I knew who she was. She then told me that she'd broken up with George Upton and wanted to burn him. She also told me that she wouldn't give me her address or phone number but that she would contact me in the future, if need be.

The officer also attached the police reports on the two prior burglaries, along with lists of the stolen property. A magistrate issued a search warrant, and a subsequent search of the motor home produced the items taken in the burglaries. D was tried and convicted on multiple counts, including receiving stolen property. The Massachusetts Supreme Court reversed, holding, in effect, that the *Gates* decision had not altered the *Aguilar-Spinelli* "two-pronged test" for probable cause to the extent that the informant's tip could be held to be sufficiently corroborated to meet that test. The corroboration was that the motor home was where the informant said it was; she knew of the motel raid three hours earlier; and she knew the name of George Upton and his girlfriend. But, the court reasoned, each of these items of corroborative evidence related either to nonsuspicious conduct or to an event that took place in public.

The Supreme Court of the United States granted certiorari to the State of Massachusetts and reversed and remanded, holding that the "totality of circumstances" test for probable cause had replaced the "two pronged test", and that the affidavit was sufficient to establish probable cause. The Court stated:

> Examined in light of *Gates*, Lieutenant Beland's affidavit provides a substantial basis for the issuance of the warrant. No single piece of evidence in it is conclusive. But the pieces fit neatly together and, so viewed, support the Magistrate's determination that there was "a fair probability that contraband or evidence of a crime" would be found in Upton's motor home. * * * The informant claimed to have seen the stolen goods and gave a description of them which tallied with the items taken in recent burglaries. She knew of the raid on the motel room—which produced evidence connected to those burglaries—and that the room had been reserved by Kelleher. She explained the connection between Kelleher's motel room and the stolen goods in Upton's motor home. And she provided a motive both for her attempt at anonymity—fear of Upton's retaliation—and for furnishing the information—her recent breakup with Upton and her desire "to burn him."
>
> * * *
>
> In concluding that there was probable cause for the issuance of this warrant, the Magistrate can hardly be accused of approving a mere "hunch" or a bare recital of legal conclusions. The informant's story and the surrounding facts possessed an internal coherence that gave weight to the whole. Accordingly, we conclude that the information contained in Lieutenant Beland's affidavit provided a sufficient basis for the "practical common-sense decision" of the Magistrate. "Although in a particular case it may not be easy to determine when an affidavit demonstrates the existence of probable cause, the resolution of doubtful or marginal cases in this area should be largely determined by the preference to be accorded to warrants." *United States v. Ventresca*, supra, at 109, 85 S. Ct., at 746.

CASE BRIEF

Maryland v. Garrison, 107 S. Ct. 1013 (1987)

Majority opinion: Stevens, joined by Rehnquist, White, Powell, O'Conner and Scalia. Dissenting: Blackmun, joined by Brennan and Marshall

FACTS: Police, after a reasonable investigation including verification of information from a reliable informant, exterior examination of the 3-story building involved, and an inquiry of a utility company serving it, concluded that there was only one apartment on the 3rd floor and that it was occupied by M, whose apartment they had probable cause to search. Police obtained a warrant to search the person of M and "the premises known as 2036 Park Avenue third floor apartment." When six officers served the warrant they encountered M in front of the building and they used his key to gain entrance to the 3rd floor hallway. D was standing in the hallway. There were two open doors in the hallway and they could see into the interior of both M's apartment and another apartment, later determined to be that of D. Still proceeding under the belief that M was the only permanent resident, the police entered the apartment on the right and found heroin, cash, and drug paraphernalia. Only then did they realize that there were two separate apartments on the third floor and that they had entered D's apartment rather than M's. Upon realizing their mistake they discontinued the search, but they seized the evidence. The trial court denied D's motion to suppress and he was tried and convicted. The Special Court of Appeals affirmed the conviction but the Court of Appeals of Maryland reversed and remanded for a new trial. The Supreme Court of the United States granted the state's petition for certiorari.

ISSUES: 1). Was the warrant valid?

2). Was the warrant executed in a reasonable manner?

DECISION: Reversed (having the effect of reinstating the conviction).

REASONS: The "particularity" requirement of the Fourth Amendment was written to prevent general searches. Specific areas and specific things must be described in a search warrant. Thus, the scope of a lawful search is defined by the object of the search and the places in which there is probable cause to believe it may be found. Using hindsight, we now know that the description of the place in this case was broader than it should have been because it was based on the mistaken belief that there was only one apartment of the third floor of the building (and that it was M's apartment). the question, then, is whether this mistake of fact invalidated the warrant. Plainly, if the officers knew, or should have known, that there were two separate dwellings on the third floor, they would have been obligated to exclude D's apartment from the search under the warrant; but we must judge the constitutionality of their conduct on the information available to them when they acted. *Just as the discovery of contraband cannot validate a warrant which was invalid when issued, it is equally clear that discovery of facts demonstrating that a warrant was unnecessarily broad does not retroactively invalidate a warrant based on probable cause and therefore valid when issued.* Based on the facts of this case, we conclude that the warrant was valid when issued.

The question of whether the execution of the warrant violated D's constitutional rights is less clear. The legality of the police entry into the third floor common hallway is not in question. They had a warrant for the premises and were accompanied by M, whose key they used. But if the police had known, or should have known that there were two third floor apartments *before* they entered D's living quarters, they would have been obligated to limit their search to M's apartment only. When they did realize that two separate apartments existed, they properly discontinued further search of D's apartment.

> While the purposes justifying a police search strictly limit the permissible extent of the search, the Court has also recognized the need to allow some latitude for honest mistakes that are made by officers in the dangerous and difficult process of making arrests and executing search warrants.

In *Hill v. California*, 91 S. Ct. 1106 (1971), a case involving an arrest without a warrant, we upheld police action based on a reasonable mistake. (The police had probable cause to arrest Hill but arrested Miller instead based on the reasonable but mistaken belief that Miller was Hill). That same rationale applies in this case where there was a reasonable failure by the police to realize that a valid warrant described the premises to be searched too broadly. Here, prior to their discovery of the fact that two apartments were located on the third floor rather than only one, the execution of the warrant reasonably included the entire third floor. For that reason the officers properly responded to the command of the warrant even if the warrant is interpreted as authorizing a search limited to M's apartment alone rather than the entire third floor.

RULE: When, despite diligent and good faith efforts to determine and describe specifically the place to be searched the search warrant description of that place is nevertheless worded too broadly, a search by mistake of another nearby place, reasonably believed by police to be within the warrant description, will be lawful up to the point of discovery of the mistake, at which point the search should be discontinued.

DISSENT: A reasonable interpretation of the search warrant description would limit it to M's apartment only. Therefore the search of D's apartment was a warrantless search without exigent circumstances and therefore unreasonable. The officers' mistakes, both in obtaining and executing the warrant, were unreasonable, and they should have realized before discovering any incriminating evidence, that there were two apartments on the third floor.

-- **Notes** --

(D) Challenge to warrant affidavit

If a probable cause affidavit for a search or arrest warrant meets all of the criteria set forth in the cases discussed in § 4.14(A) above, so that it appears, on its face, to be legally sufficient, can a search and seizure conducted under the resulting warrant nevertheless be challenged on other grounds? Can the truthfulness of the warrant affidavit be challenged after the warrant has been issued and served? These are the issues of *Franks v. Delaware*, decided by the Supreme Court of the United States in 1978 and briefed below.

CASE BRIEF
Franks v. Delaware, 98 S. Ct. 2674 (1978)
Majority opinion: Blackmun. Dissenting: Rehnquist, Burger.

FACTS: B, a rape victim, gave a detailed description of her attacker to police. On the same day, D was taken into custody for an assault on another victim which had occurred six days earlier. While in custody D inadvertently mentioned B's name to a youth officer, who passed this information on to a detective working on the rape case of B. Because of this tip, D became a suspect in the rape of B; the detective and another officer, after conducting an investigation, submitted the following affidavit to a Justice of the Peace in support of a warrant to search D's apartment:

IN THE MATTER OF: Jerome Franks, B/M, DOB: 10/9/54 and 222 S. Governors Ave., Apt. #3, Dover, Delaware. A two room apartment located on the South side, second floor, of a white block building on the west side of S. Governors Avenue, Between Loockerman Street and North Street, in the City of Dover. The ground floor of this building houses Wayman's Barber Shop.

STATE OF DELAWARE)
                         : ss:
COUNTY OF KENT)

Be it remembered that on this 9th day of March A.D. 1976 before me John Green, personally appeared Det. Ronald R. Brooks and Det. Larry Gray of the Dover Police Department who being by me duly sworn depose and say:

that they have reason to believe and do believe that in the 222 S. Governors Avenue, Apartment #3, Dover Delaware. * * * the occupant of which is Jerome Franks there has been and/or there is now located and/or concealed certain property in said house * * * in particular, a white knit thermal undershirt; a brown ¾ length leather jacket with a tie-belt; a pair of black mens pants; a dark colored knit hat; a long thin bladed knife or other instruments or items relating to the crime.

Articles, or things were, are, or will be possessed and/or used in violation of Title 11, Sub-Chapter D, Section 763, Delaware Code in that (see attached probable cause page).

Wherefore, affiants pray that a search warrant may be issued authorizing a search for the aforesaid 222 S. Governors Avenue, Apartment #3, Dover, Delaware. * * *

/s/ Det. Ronald R. Brooks
    affiant

/s/ Det Larry D. Gray
    affiant

SWORN to (or affirmed) and subscribed before me this 9th day of March A.D. 1976.

/s/ John (illegible) Green
    Judge Ct 7

The facts tending to establish probable cause for the issuance of this search warrant are:

1. On Saturday, 2/28/76, Brenda L. B. ___, W/F/15, reported to the Dover Police Department that she had been kidnapped and raped.
2. An investigation of this complaint was conducted by Det. Boyce Failing of the Dover Police Department.
3. Investigation of the aforementioned complaint revealed that Brenda B. ___, while under the influence of drugs, was taken to 222 S. Governors Avenue, Apartment #3, Dover, Delaware.
4. Investigation of the aforementioned complaint revealed that 222 S. Governors Avenue, Apartment #3, Dover, Delaware, is the residence of Jerome Franks, B/M DOB: 10/9/54.
5. Investigation of the aforementioned complaint revealed that on Saturday, 2/29/76, Jerome Franks did have sexual contact with Brenda B. ___ without her consent.
6. On Thursday, 3/4/76 at the Dover Police Department, Brenda B. ___ revealed to Det. Boyce Failing that Jerome Franks was the person who committed the Sexual Assault against her.
7. On Friday, 3/5/76, Jerome Franks was placed under arrest by Cpl. Robert McClements of the Dover Police Department, and charged with Sexual Misconduct.
8. On 3/5/76 at a Family Court in Dover, Delaware, Jerome Franks did, after being arrested on the charge of Sexual Misconduct, make a statement to Cpl. Robert McClements, that he thought the charge was concerning Cynthia Bailey not Brenda B. ___.
9. On Friday, 3/5/76, Cynthia C. Bailey, W/F/21 of 132 North Street, Dover, Delaware, did report to Dover Police Department that she had been raped at her residence during the night.
10. Investigation conducted by your affiant on Friday, 3/5/76, revealed the perpetrator of the crime to be an unknown black male, approximately 5'7", 150 lbs., dark complexion, wearing a white thermal undershirt, black pants with a belt having a silver or gold buckle, a brown leather ¾ length coat with a tie belt in the front, and a dark knit cap pulled around the eyes.
11. Your affiant can state, that during the commission of this crime, Cynthia Bailey was forced at knife point and with the threat of death to engage in sexual intercourse with the perpetrator of the crime.
12. Your affiant can state that entry was gained to the residence of Cynthia Bailey through a window located on the east side of the residence.
13. Your affiant can state that the residence of Jerome Franks is within a very short distance and direct sight of the residence of Cynthia Bailey.
14. Your affiant can state that the description given by Cynthia Bailey of the unknown black male does coincide with the description of Jerome Franks.
15. On Tuesday, 3/9/76, your affiant contacted Mr. James Williams and Mr. Wesley Lucas of the Delaware Youth Center where Jerome Franks is employed and did have personal conversation with both of these people.
16. On Tuesday, 3/9/76, Mr. James Williams revealed to your affiant that the normal dress of Jerome Franks does consist of a white knit thermal

undershirt and a brown leather jacket.
17. On Tuesday, 3/9/76, Mr. Wesley Lucas revealed to your affiant that in addition to the thermal undershirt and jacket, Jerome Franks often wears a dark green knit hat.
18. Your affiant can state that a check of official records reveals that in 1971 Jerome Franks was arrested for the crime of rape and subsequently convicted with Assault with Intent to Rape.

On the basis of the above-quoted affidavit a search warrant was issued and D's apartment was searched. The search resulted in the seizure of a white thermal undershirt, a knit hat, dark pants, a leather jacket and a single-blade knife. All of these items were ultimately introduced in evidence at D's trial.

D's attorney filed a pretrial motion to suppress these items from evidence on the basis that the affidavit did not state probable cause and that the search violated the Fourth and Fourteenth Amendments. At the hearing on the motion D's lawyer also orally attacked the truthfulness of the affidavit (concerning statements made in paragraphs 15, 16, and 17), and requested to call witnesses whose testimony would prove that Williams and Lucas were never personally interviewed by the detectives who prepared the search warrant affidavit—and although Williams and Lucas might have talked to another police officer, the information given by them was "somewhat different" than that recited in the affidavit. D's attorney also charged that the misstatements were made in "bad faith" and not inadvertently. He also offered to call witnesses to establish that D's statement to the youth officer (in which he mentioned B's name) had been obtained in violation of the *Miranda* requirements and therefore the entire search warrant was a product of an illegally obtained confession. The state objected to D's "going behind the warrant affidavit in any way" and argued that the court must decide D's motion "on the four corners" of the affidavit. The trial court ruled for the state, the motion to suppress was denied and D was tried and convicted of rape, kidnapping and burglary. The Supreme Court of Delaware affirmed the convictions.

ISSUE: Do the Fourth and Fourteenth Amendments and exclusionary rule ever require that a defendant be permitted to challenge the truthfulness of a warrant affidavit after the warrant has been issued and executed?

DECISION: Yes; reversed and remanded.

REASONS: The probable cause requirement of the Fourth Amendment requires a "truthful" showing of probable cause—not in the sense that every fact recited in the affidavit must necessarily be correct—but in the sense that the information put forth must be believed or appropriately accepted by the affiant as true. It would be an unthinkable imposition upon the authority of the issuing magistrate if a warrant affidavit, revealed after the fact to contain a deliberate or reckless false statement, were to stand beyond impeachment.

(The Court then examines—and repudiates—six arguments by the state for retaining the position that a warrant affidavit not be subject to challenge for untruthfulness.)

First, the state argues that the exclusionary rule, which is not a personal constitutional right of a defendant, but rather a judicially created remedy as a deterrent to police misconduct, should not be further extended because it is already too much of a burden on society. The Court answers that despite the nonextension of the exclusionary rule to civil or grand jury proceedings, the Court has not hesitated to apply the rule in any case where a Fourth Amendment violation has been substantial and deliberate (citing *Brewer v. Williams*, 97 S. Ct. 1232 (1977).

Second, the state argues that citizens' privacy interests are already sufficiently protected by the existing penalties for perjury including criminal prosecution, departmental discipline, contempt of court and civil actions. The Court notes that in *Mapp v. Ohio*, 81 S. Ct. 1684 (1961) it had already rejected the adequacy of these alternatives to the extension of the exclusionary rule to the states. It is not likely that a prosecuting attorney will prosecute himself or his associates for enforcement-encouraged violations of the search and seizure clause.

Third, the state contends the magistrate is already equipped to conduct a vigorous inquiry into the accuracy of the probable cause affidavit. But, the Court points out, the pre-search proceeding is necessarily one-sided and hasty because of the desire to act before the evidence disappears. It will not always suffice to discourage lawless or reckless conduct.

Fourth, the state says that to question the magistrate's inquiry into the veracity of probable cause would unwisely diminish the solemnity and moment of the magistrate's proceeding. The Court states that it is the ex parte (one-sided) nature of the initial hearing, rather than the magistrate's capacity, that is the reason for the review. A magistrate's determination is already subject to review before trial as to *sufficiency* without any undue interference with the dignity of his function. The rule of exclusion is extended by this holding only in the areas of deliberate misstatement and reckless disregard for the truth. This leaves a broad area where the magistrate is the sole protector of citizen's Fourth Amendment rights.

Fifth, the state urges that permitting a post-search evidentiary hearing on issues of truthfulness would confuse the pressing issue of guilt or innocence with the collateral question of official misconduct in drafting the affidavit. If such hearings became routine, they could be misused by the defendant as a means of discovery and forcing the identity of informants. In answer to this charge the Court notes that the hearing on the challenge to the truthfulness of the warrant affidavit would not be in the presence of the jury. Any review of probable cause already involves an issue extraneous to guilt. If sensible threshold showings are required and sensible requirements for suppression are maintained there need not be any additional great burden on judicial personnel. Many claims will wash out at an early stage. The requirement of a substantial preliminary showing will prevent the misuse of a veracity hearing for discovery or obstruction. The question of using the hearing to reveal the identity of informants need not be decided here because in this case we are dealing only with the affiant's representation of his own activities.

Finally, it is argued by the state that because a probable cause affidavit may properly be based on hearsay, tips, or fleeting observations, its accuracy is in large part beyond the control of the affiant, which makes a post-search veracity challenge inappropriate. The Court answers by stating that a flat ban on impeachment of veracity could make the probable cause requirement meaningless. Such a rule would ban a reexamination even in cases of deliberate falsification by the police-affiant.

There will still be presumption of validity with respect to the warrant affidavit. To justify an evidentiary hearing the challenger's attack must not simply be conclusory and it must be supported by more than mere desire to cross-examine. Allegations of negligence or innocent mistake are insufficient. There must be charges of deliberate falsehood or reckless disregard for the truth and there must be an offer of proof. The portion of the warrant affidavit that is claimed to be false must be specified and supporting reasons should be alleged. Affidavits of sworn or otherwise reliable witnesses should be furnished, or their absence satisfactorily explained.

If these requirements are met and the challenged portions of the affidavit are set aside and there still remains in the remainder of the affidavit sufficient content to support a finding of probable cause, no hearing is required. But if the remaining content is insufficient, the defendant is entitled, under the Fourth Amendment, to his hearing. Whether or not he prevails is another issue.

RULE: When a proper offer of proof is made by a defendant along with charges that an affidavit supporting a search warrant contained deliberate falsehoods or reckless disregard for the truth by a governmental affiant, the Fourth and Fourteenth Amendments and the exclusionary rule require that the defendant be given a hearing on such charges, and such a hearing may be proper after the warrant has been issued and served and evidence seized thereby.

DISSENTING: The issuing magistrate's examination was adequate; the majority opinion merely provides another avenue of re-litigation of issues already resolved and has nothing to do with the innocence or guilt of the defendant as determined at trial.

-- **Notes** --

Sample Questions

Only a neutral and detached judicial officer may issue a warrant of arrest or search.   T   F.

The "particularity" requirement for warrants is found in the Fifth Amendment.   T   F.

Deadly force is always justified as a last resort in order to caputre a fleeing felon.   T   F.

In a routine felony arrest situation, if the police have a warrant of arrest for D, but reason to believe D is temporarily staying in the home of A:
A. no additional warrant of any kind need be obtained.
B. if the arrest warrant for D will have to be served in the home of A, the police, if they have the opportunity, should obtain a search warrant for the home of A.
C. the reason for the additional search warrant in this situation is to protect the rights of A, because if the warrant for D is served in A's home, any evidence found in plain view during the service of the arrest warrant for D may otherwise be inadmissible against A.
D. B and C above.

The Supreme Court of the United States has ruled that when a warrantless arrest for a felony based on adequate probable cause is set in motion in a public place, the suspect may not defeat the arrest by retreating into a private place.   T   F.

The amount of force that may be used by the police in any arrest situation is governed by the reasonableness standard of the Fourth Amendment.   T   F.

The amount of non-deadly force which may be used by the police in any arrest situation is only that amount which is absolutely necesary under the circumstances, in order to accomplish the arrest.   T   F.

If a police officer is sued under the Federal Civil Rights Act for the use of excessive force, the courts will use an objective standard to determine if, under all the circumstances, the force used was reasonable. This may require the "balancing" of the rights of the complaining citizen against the right of the government to enforce the law.   T   F.

The courts may consider a police roadblock a "seizure" under some circumstances, but not under other circumstances.   T   F.

The "knock and announce" requirement developed in the English common law, but may differ from one state to another in the United States.   T   F.

When a police officer in fresh pursuit of a fleeing felon chases the fleeing felon into an adjoining state, the authority to arrest depends on the law of the state in which the arrest is consummated.   T   F.

Whether or not a city police officer has arrest authority outside the corporate jurisdiction of his city may vary from state to state and depends on the law of the state in which the city is located.   T   F.

§ 4.15 WARRANTLESS SEARCHES

(A) Search incident to arrest

(1) SCOPE OF SEARCH INCIDENT TO ARREST

Perhaps in no other field of the law of search and seizure have so many different standards of reasonableness been applied as in search incident to arrest. Admitting its failure to define adequately the scope of a search incident to arrest, the Supreme Court of the United States in *Chimel v. California* (briefed below) attempted to adopt a standard which will provide more definite guidelines for law enforcement. Out of *Chimel* came the rule that incident to an arrest the person of the arrestee might be searched, as well as the area under his immediate control (the "arms-length" rule).

CASE BRIEF

Chimel v. California, 89 S. Ct. 2034 (1969)

Majority opinion: Stewart. Dissenting: White, Black.

FACTS: Police served a warrant for the arrest of D for the burglary of a coin shop. After being admitted by D's wife, they waited several minutes until D arrived, after which they arrested him and asked him for permission to "look around" his house. D objected but the police advised him they would conduct a search anyway on the basis that it was incidental to the arrest. They proceeded to look through the entire three-bedroom house, including the attic, garage, and a workshop, accompanied by D's wife. They looked into drawers, having D's wife move items from side to side so they could view the contents; the search lasted from 45 minutes to one hour. Numerous items were seized and some of the items were admitted in evidence at D's trial over his objections. D was convicted; the California appellate courts upheld the search as valid.

ISSUE: Was this a permissible search incidental to a valid arrest?

DECISION: No; reversed.

REASONS: The Court admits that its past decisions on this issue have not been consistent, and it looks to the history of these decisions.

In *Weeks v. United States*, 34 S. Ct. 341 (1914), the search of the person of accused incident to arrest was approved. In *Carroll v. United States*, 45 S. Ct. 280 (1925), the subject matter of such a search was extended to whatever is found upon his person or *in his control*. In *Agnello v. United States*, 46 S. Ct. 5 (1925), the Court approved a "contemporaneous search of the person lawfully arrested and the place where the arrest is made for fruits, instrumentalities, weapons, and means of escape." This was repeated in *Marron v. United States*, 48 S. Ct. 74 (1927), in which the "right to contemporaneously search the place where the arrest was made" was approved. In *GoBart Importing Co. v. United States*, 51 S. Ct. 153 (1931) and *United States v. Lefkowitz*, 52 S. Ct. 420 (1932), however, the search of the place of arrest accompanying a lawful arrest was held to be invalid because there had been time and opportunity to obtain a search warrant. In *Harris v. United States*, 67 S. Ct. 1098 (1947), the search of an apartment incident to an arrest made therein was approved, but in *Trupiano v. United States*, 68 S. Ct. 1229 (1948), a search incident to an arrest was disapproved because of opportunity to obtain a search warrant. In *United States v. Rabinowitz*, 70 S. Ct. 430 (1950), a search of the place of arrest incidental thereto was approved, even though there had been opportunity to obtain a search warrant.

When a valid arrest is made, it is reasonable for the officer to search the person arrested for weapons or means of escape and it is also reasonable for the officer to search for and to seize evidence on the arrestee's person to prevent concealment or destruction. Also, the area into which an arrestee might reach to grab a weapon or to destroy evidence may also be searched, i.e., the area within his *immediate* control.

There is no justification, incidental to the arrest, for routinely searching rooms other than the one in which the arrest is made, or desk drawers or other small spaces in the room in which the arrest occurs. Such searches, in the absence of well-recognized exceptions, can be made only under a search warrant; the Fourth Amendment requires no less. No consideration relevant to the Fourth Amendment suggests any point of rational limitation once the search is allowed to go beyond the area from which the person arrested might obtain weapons or evidentiary items.

One unfortunate result of holdings such as those in *Rabinowitz* and *Harris* is that, when officials lack probable cause for obtaining a search warrant, they will arrange to serve an arrest warrant in the suspect's home in order to conduct a search incidental to the arrest.

RULE: The scope of a search made incidental to a lawful arrest includes the person of the arrestee and the area into which he could reach to obtain a weapon or to destroy evidence; i.e., the area under his immediate control.

DISSENTING: The arrest itself may trigger exigent circumstances justifying a broader search than approved in the majority opinion, if, in fact, probable cause exists for such a broader search.

CASE BRIEF

New York v. Belton, 101 S. Ct. 2860 (1981)

Majority opinion: Stewart. Concurring: Rehnquist, Stevens. Dissenting: Brennan, Marshall, White.

FACTS: A state trooper stopped D for speeding. There were four men in the car, including D. None of the four could produce a vehicle registration nor were any related to the owner. The policeman smelled burnt marijuana and saw on the floor of the car an envelope marked "Supergold" that he associated with marijuana. He directed the men to get out of the car and placed them under arrest for unlawful possession of marijuana. The trooper frisked each of the men and made them stand out of reach of each other. He then picked up the envelope marked "Supergold" and found that it contained marijuana. The officer then gave the arrestees the *Miranda* warnings and searched each of them; then he searched the passenger compartment of the car. He found D's black leather jacket on the back seat, and when he unzipped one of the pockets, he discovered cocaine. Placing the jacket in the police car, the trooper then drove the four arrestees to the police station. D was indicted for possession of a controlled substance. He moved for the suppression of the cocaine seized from the jacket pocket, but his motion was denied. D pleaded guilty to a lesser included offense, but preserved his objection that the cocaine had been seized in violation of the Fourth and Fourteenth Amendments. The appellate division upheld the legality of the search but the court of appeals reversed, holding that a warrantless search of a zippered pocket of an inaccessible jacket may not be upheld as a search incident to a lawful arrest where there is no longer any danger that the arrestee or a confederate might gain access to the article.

ISSUE: When the driver and passengers of an automobile are removed therefrom and placed under arrest, do the Fourth and Fourteenth Amendments allow a search of the passenger compartment of the automobile and closed containers therein, as an incident to the custodial arrests?

DECISION: Yes; reversed.

REASONS: Although the first principle of Fourth Amendment jurisprudence is that police may not conduct a search unless they first convince a neutral magistrate that there is probable cause to do so, this Court has recognized that the "exigencies of the situation" may make exemption from the warrant requirement "imperative." In *Chimel v. California*, 89 S. Ct. 2034 (1969) a lawful custodial arrest was held to justify the contemporaneous warrantless search of the person arrested as well as the immediately surrounding area. These searches have long been considered valid for purposes of securing weapons and preventing concealment or destruction of evidence.

But in *Chimel* as well as in *Terry v. Ohio*, 88 S. Ct. 1868 (1968), the Court ruled that the scope of a search must be strictly tied to and justified by the circumstances which rendered its initiation permissible; therefore, the scope of a search incident to arrest is limited to the person and to the immediate area. Although this principle may be stated clearly enough, courts have discovered it difficult to apply in specific cases.

The protection of the Fourth and Fourteenth Amendments can only be realized if the police are acting under a set of rules which, in most instances, makes it possible to reach a correct determination beforehand as to whether an invasion of privacy is justified in the interest of law enforcement. A single, familiar standard is needed to guide police officers, not a highly sophisticated set of rules which may be literally impossible of application by the officer in the field.

The ruling in *United States v. Robinson*, 94 S. Ct. 467 (1973) justifies the search of the person incident to a custodial arrest based on probable cause. This is a straightforward rule, easily applied and predictably enforced.

But no straightforward rule has emerged with regard to the scope of a search of the interior of an automobile incident to a lawful custodial arrest of its occupants. While the law is in this shape a person cannot know the scope of his protection nor can a policeman know the scope of his authority.

Chimel set the standard of the "area within the *immediate control*" of the arrestee. Articles inside the relatively narrow compass of the passenger compartment of an automobile are in fact generally within the "area into which an arrestee might reach in order to grab a weapon or evidentiary item." When a policeman has made a lawful custodial arrest of the occupant of any automobile, he may, as an incident of that arrest, search the passenger compartment of that automobile. It also follows that he may search the contents of any container, open or closed, that he may find in the passenger compartment, for if the passenger compartment is within the reach of the arrestee, so also will containers be within his reach, (citing *United States v. Robinson*, 94 S. Ct. 467 (1973) and *Draper v. United States*, 79 S. Ct. 329 (1959). The justification for the container search is not that the arrestee has no privacy interest in the container, but that the lawful custodial arrest justifies the infringement of any privacy interest the arrestee may have.

The Court of Appeals relied on *United States v. Chadwick*, 97 S. Ct. 2476 (1977) and *Arkansas v. Sanders*, 99 S. Ct. 2586 (1979) in concluding that the search and seizure was invalid. But neither of those cases involved an arguably valid search incident to a lawful custodial arrest.

It is not questioned that D was the subject of a lawful custodial arrest for possession of marijuana. The search of D's jacket followed immediately upon that arrest. The jacket was located inside the passenger compartment of the car in which D had been a passenger just before this arrest. The jacket was thus within the area we have concluded was "within the arrestee's immediate control" under *Chimel*.

RULE: When a lawful custodial arrest based on probable cause is made of the driver and/or passengers of an automobile, the passenger compartment of the automobile is considered, for purposes of search incident to arrest, to be within the immediate control of the arrestee(s), even after driver and/or passengers have been removed therefrom; it and any containers found therein, whether open or closed, may be searched as an incident to the arrest.

NOTE: Foonote 4 of the majority opinion gives further clarification: " 'Container' here denotes any object capable of holding another object. It thus includes closed or open glove compartments, consoles or other receptacles located anywhere within the passenger compartment, as well as luggage, boxes, bags, clothing, and the like. Our holding encompasses only the interior of the passenger compartment of an automobile and does not encompass the trunk."

-------------------------------------- **Notes** --------------------------------------

(2) DISCOVERY OF ITEMS NOT CONNECTED WITH ARREST

If, in conducting a search incident to a custodial arrest based on probable cause to believe a person has committed a particular crime, evidence of another, totally unrelated crime is discovered, is it subject to warrantless seizure and is it admissible in a prosecution for the unrelated crime? The answer to both questions would seem to be yes, when discovery of the items is inadvertent and when there is probable cause to believe they are connected with criminal activity. See the discussion in 4.14(B). See also § 4.15(D), Plain View and Inventory.

--------------------------------------- **Notes** ---------------------------------------

Sample Questions

It is a good idea for police officers who work near state boundaries to be familiar with the fresh pursuit and extradition laws of the adjoining state(s), as well as those of their own state.   T   F.

Whether or not resisting arrest is prosecutable as a criminal offense may depend on whether the person resisting knew he was dealing with a police officer.   T   F.

Generally, infractions and ordinance violations are not considered to be criminal offenses.   T   F.

The concept of citizen's arrest was unknown to the English common law.   T   F.

Property that a person abandons, or throws away, is usually not protected from governmental seizure by the Fourth Amendment.   T   F.

Constitutionally, the term "open fields" may include a forest or woods for purposes of warrantless aerial observation by the police.   T   F.

The Fourth Amendment guarantee against unreasonable searches and seizures applies only against governmental action. It does not apply against private persons in their private capacities.   T   F.

There are certain situations/places/people to which the Fourth Amendment has no application; among these are;
A. complainants who lack "standing" to object.
B. searches made with valid consent.
C. places outside the jurisdiction of the United States.
D. federal law enforcement officers.
E. A, B, and C above.

The term "curtilage":
A. originated under the English common law and referred to the area immediately surrounding the dwelling house.
B. may be difficult to define precisely with reference to every search situation.
C. inferred protection from governmental seach to the same extent as the dwelling house.
D. means a strip of hardened skin at the base of the fingernail.
E. A, B, and C above.

Tests used by the courts to determine whether an area is within the "curtilage" include:
A. how close is the area to the home?
B. is the area included within an enclosure surrounding the home?
C. was the area being used for the intimate activities of the home?
D. had the residents taken steps to protect the area from observation by people passing by?
E. all of the above.

All searches made by the police must be under the authority of a warrant unless they come within one of the clearly-established exceptions to the warrant requirement.   T   F.

(3) JUSTIFICATION OF SEARCH

Because of the complex and varied nature of fact situations controlled by the Fourth Amendment, which is couched in such generalities as "unreasonable" and "probable cause," it falls to the courts to lend more definite meaning to these terms. Considering the thousands of cases tried in the United States and the many appellate court reviews of these cases, it is little wonder that a confused mass of interpretations emerges. But the saving grace of our legal system is that one court—the Supreme Court of the United States—can speak with finality in interpreting the generalities of our Constitution. So many of the provisions of the Bill of Rights have now become binding on the states as a matter of Fourteenth Amendment due process that little room remains for differing procedures from state to state in the area of search and seizure; a state may, however, adopt provisions more favorable to the defendant than those of the Bill of Rights, under its own state constitution.

Prior to *United States v. Robinson* and *Gustafson v. Florida* (both briefed below) a line of reasoning had been developing in both federal and state appellate courts that the right of a police officer to search a person incident to a lawful arrest depended, in some measure, either on whether the officer believed he was in danger or on the nature of the crime for which the arrest was made. If the particular offense (such as speeding or running a stop sign) was one not normally expected to involve instrumentalities, fruits, evidence or contraband, it was reasoned that no search was justified unless a protective frisk was also in order. While not illogical, this rule left the search decision to a case by case determination by the arresting officer. In an apparent attempt to provide more certain guidelines for the police, the Court held in *Robinson* and *Gustafson* that a lawful custodial arrest based on probable cause is the determining factor justifying the incidental search.

CASE BRIEF

United States v. Robinson, 94 S. Ct. 467 (1973)

Majority opinion: Rehnquist. Concurring: Powell. Dissenting: Marshall, joined by Douglas and Brennan.

FACTS: A D.C. police officer observed D driving a car and stopped him because he recognized him as one whose operator's permit had been revoked. In D.C. this is an offense carrying a mandatory minimum jail term, a mandatory minimum fine, or both. When D got out of his car, the officer advised him he was under arrest for driving while his permit was revoked and for obtaining a permit by misrepresentation. The Court of Appeals and D both conceded that the officer had probable cause for arrest and that he effected a "full custody" arrest. In accordance with police department procedures the officer then began to search D. He did not conduct a "spread eagle" search, but instead "patted down" D and felt an object in D's left breast coat pocket which he removed; it was a crumpled-up cigarette package which contained something that didn't feel like cigarettes. The officer then opened the package, which contained fourteen capsules of white powder which the officer suspected and later examination revealed was heroin. The officer then continued the search. The heroin seized was later admitted into evidence and D was convicted of heroin possession in federal district (trial) court. D appealed to the Court of Appeals for D.C., which first remanded the case to the district court for an evidentiary hearing on the scope of the search incidental to the arrest. The district court found against D and he again appealed. The court of appeals "en banc" reversed the conviction on the basis that the search violated the Fourth and Fourteenth Amendments.

ISSUE: Was the search in this case, made incidental to a valid traffic arrest, so excessive in its scope as to be unreasonable under the Fourth and Fourteenth Amendments?

DECISION: No; search was valid; court of appeals decision reversed.

REASONS: It is well settled that a search incident to a lawful arrest is an exception to the warrant requirement of the Fourth Amendment. Historically this exception applies to the person of the arrestee and the area within his control. The validity of the search of the person has been regarded as settled since its first enunciation, but the search of the area has been subject to differing interpretations as to extent. Virtually all search and seizure law has been developed since *Weeks v. United States*, 34 S. Ct. 341 (1914) established the exclusionary rule of evidence. All through the line of cases relating to the permissible area of search incident to lawful arrest, there has been expressed no doubt as to the unqualified authority to search the arrestee's person. This authority has been based on the reasonableness of a search of the person for weapons, means of escape and evidence to prevent its concealment or destruction. All of the cases since *Weeks* concerning the search of the arrestee's person as an incident to arrest speak not simply in terms of an exception to the warrant requirement, but in terms of affirmative authority to search.

The court of appeals in this case felt that the limited *Terry* "frisk" (based on an investigative stop on less than probable cause to arrest) should apply under the facts of this case, justifying only a search for weapons. But *Terry v. Ohio*, 88 S. Ct. 1868 (1968) recognized a distinction in purpose, character and extent between a search incident to arrest and limited search for weapons. Therefore, *Terry* affords no basis to carry over to a probable cause arrest situation.

Peters v. New York, 88 S. Ct. 1889 (1968) also affords no basis for limiting a search of the person of an arrestee following a probable cause arrest.

Since virtually all of the Court's statements on the existence of unqualified authority to search a person incident to an arrest are dicta, it is not foreclosed by stare decisis to inquire into history to determine if the qualifications imposed by the court of appeals were intended by framers of the Fourth Amendment, or recognized in cases prior to *Weeks*. Early English and American state cases tend to support broad authority to search the arrestee incident to arrest.

The court of appeals in effect determined that the only justification for a full search incident to lawful arrest was the possibility of discovering evidence or fruits of crime. In concluded that, because of its nature, the crime for which the arrest was made could produce no further evidence or fruits and that any protective search must be limited by the conditions of a *Terry* search for weapons.

The justification for searching incident to a lawful arrest rests as much on the need to disarm the suspect as it does on the need to preserve evidence for later use at trial. The standards traditionally governing a search incident to lawful arrest are not, therefore, commuted to the stricter *Terry* standards by the absence of probable fruits or further evidence of the particular crime for which the arrest is made.

The increased danger to the arresting officer posed by the extended exposure of an in-custody arrest—as opposed to the fleeting exposure of the *Terry* situation—is adequate reason for treating all custodial arrests alike for purposes of search justification.

The court of appeals decision would require a case-by-case adjudication, whereas a police officer must make a quick, ad hoc decision whether to search. The Fourth Amendment does not require this decision to be broken down in each instance into an analysis of every step in the search. The authority to search does not depend on what a court may later decide was the probability in a particular arrest situation that weapons or evidence would in fact be found upon the person of the arrestee.

The search and seizure here, as an incident to a probable cause arrest, were permissible under Fourth Amendment law. Having come upon the crumpled pack of cigarettes in the course of a lawful search, the officer was entitled to inspect it; when the inspection revealed heroin he was entitled to seize it as "fruits, instrumentalities or contraband probative of criminal conduct."

RULE: A custodial arrest based on probable cause is a reasonable intrusion under the Fourth Amendment; that intrusion being lawful, a search incident to the arrest requires no additional justification. It is the fact of the lawful arrest which establishes the authority to search; in the case of a lawful custodial arrest, a full search of the person is not only an exception to the warrant requirement of the Fourth Amendment, but is also a "reasonable" search under that amendment.

DISSENTING: The majority has departed from the case-by-case adjudication of "reasonableness" of search; the Fourth Amendment requires that inferences drawn by police be subject to scrutiny by a neutral and detached magistrate; the majority opinion is inconsistent with this principle. There are exceptions recognized by law (moving vehicle, exigent circumstances and search incident to lawful arrest), but these do *not* preclude further judicial inquiry. The majority places undue emphasis on a police department order authorizing a full search; runs counter to a long line of federal and state cases which qualify the right to search a person fully according to the offense for which he was arrested. A search for weapons is needed for the safety of the officer but it should not be extended further in a simple traffic arrest. The majority rule will lead to police abuse and "pretext arrest." The matter of search here divides into three distinct phases: (1) patdown of the arrestee; (2) removal of an unknown object; and (3) opening the cigarette package. Even the removal of the object exceeded authority unless there was reason to believe it was a weapon. The *Terry* rationale should apply; here the search went beyond "person" to include "effects:" opening the package once it was under the officer's control exceeded the protective purpose of the search. The search was an unauthorized intrusion into the privacy of an individual's "papers and effects." It went far beyond what was necessary to protect the arresting officer from harm and to ensure that the arrestee would not escape. The evidence should have been surpressed.

SUMMARY OF DISSENTING OPINION: When a probable cause arrest is made for an offense not involving fruits, instrumentalities or further evidence of the offense, a search must be limited to that which is necessary to protect the officer and prevent escape.

CASE BRIEF

Gustafson v. Florida, 94 S. Ct. 488 (1973)

Majority opinion: Rehnquist. Concurring: Stewart, Powell. Dissenting: Marshall, joined by Douglas and Brennan.

FACTS: At approximately 2:00 a.m. a police officer observed D's car driving back and forth across the center line of the street. Two occupants of the car looked back and apparently saw the squad car; the car then proceeded across the highway and behind a grocery store and headed south on another street. At that point the officer turned on his flashing light and stopped the car. He asked D, the driver, for his driving license and D informed the officer that he had left it in his college dormitory. D was then arrested for failing to have his license in his possession. (Probable cause for the arrest was stipulated by both parties below.) The officer then took D into custody to transport him to the stationhouse for further inquiry; contemporaneously with the arrest he conducted a full "pat down" of D's person. The officer placed his hand into the left coat pocket of D and removed a long chain and a Benson and Hedges cigarette box. The officer opened the box and discovered what he believed were marijuana cigarettes. D was charged, tried, and convicted for unlawful possession of marijuana. The District Court of Appeals of Florida reversed D's conviction on the basis that the search was unreasonable under the Fourth and Fourteenth Amendments. The Supreme Court of Florida, in turn, reversed that decision. D sought certiorari, which was granted by the Supreme Court of the United States and the case was set for argument with *United States v. Robinson*, 94 S. Ct. 467 (1973). D urges that there could be no evidentiary purpose for the search (traffic arrest) and, therefore, only a weapons-type search as in *Terry v. Ohio*, 88 S. Ct. 1868 (1968) was authorized. D says that his case differs from *Robinson* in that the police had no previous encounters with him and that the offense for which he was arrested carried no mandatory minimum sentence as in *Robinson* and, further, that unlike *Robinson* there were no police regulations which required the officer to take D into custody; nor were there police department policies requiring full-scale body searches upon an arrest in the field. D also says that, like *Robinson*, the officer expressed no fear of his well-being.

ISSUE: Was a full-scale body pat-down following an arrest for a minor traffic violation carrying no mandatory minimum jail term a "reasonable" search under the Fourth and Fourteenth Amendments?

DECISION: Yes; opinion of Supreme Court of Florida affirmed.

REASONS: The limitations placed by *Terry v. Ohio*, 88 S. Ct. 1868 (1968) on protective searches conducted in an investigatory stop situation based on *less than* probable cause are *not* to be carried over to searches of the arrestee made incident to lawful custodial arrests (quoting from *Robinson*). Neither *Chimel v. California*, 89 S. Ct. 2034 (1969) nor *Peters v. New York*, 88 S. Ct. 1889 (1968) purported to limit the traditional authority of an arresting officer to conduct a full search of the person of an arrestee incident to a lawful custodial arrest. Although the officer here was not required by police regulations to take D into custody, and there was no department policy establishing conditions under which a full body search should be conducted, these differences from the *Robinson* facts are not determinative of the constitutional issue. It is sufficient that the officer had probable cause to arrest D and that he lawfully effectuated the arrest and placed the petitioner in custody. The lawfulness (reasonableness) of a body search in such a situation does not depend on what a court may later decide was the probability in a particular arrest situation that weapons or evidence would in fact be found on the person of the suspect. It is the fact of custodial arrest which gives rise to the authority to search, and it is of no moment that the officer did not indicate any subjective fear of D or did not himself suspect that D was armed. Having in the course of this lawful search come upon a box of cigarettes, the officer was entitled to open and inspect it and when he discovered what appeared to be marijuana cigarettes, he was entitled to seize them as "fruits, instrumentalities or contraband probative of criminal conduct."

RULE: It is the fact of a custodial arrest, made on probable cause, that establishes the authority for the arresting officer to conduct, contemporaneously with the arrest, a full body search of the arrestee, and the lawfulness of such a search is not dependent on (1) a mandatory jail term for the offense; (2) the fear or suspicion of the officer that the arrestee may be armed and dangerous; (3) the existence or nonexistence of police department regulations or policy requiring a full body search incident to arrest; or (4) the nature of the offense as related to the probability of the presence of further evidence, fruits, instrumentalities or contraband related to the offense. Items probative of criminal conduct found on the arrestee's person during such a search are subject to seizure by the arresting officer.

CONCURRING (Stewart): D here *might* have made a persuasive claim that a "custodial arrest" for this minor traffic arrest violated his Fourth and Fourteenth Amendment rights, but no such claim was made; instead, D fully conceded the constitutional validity of his custodial arrest and therefore is bound by the *Robinson* rule.

CONCURRING (Powell): The thrust of opinions is that the Fourth Amendment safeguards the right of people to be secure in their persons, houses, papers, and effects against unreasonable searches and seizures and to have legitimate expectations of privacy. An individual lawfully subjected to a custodial arrest retains no significant Fourth Amendment interest in the privacy of his person. The *custodial arrest* is the significant intrusion of state power into the privacy of one's person. No reason then exists to frustrate law enforcement by requiring some independent justification for a search incident to a lawful arrest.

DISSENTING: As was stated in *Robinson* dissent, any search beyond the *Terry* type is unreasonable in this type of situation. The cigarette package should not have been opened. The record does not show a suspicion of intoxication upon which a more extensive search might have been justified.

In *United States v. Hill*, 730 F.2d 1163 (8th Cir. 1984), after serving a search warrant for marijuana growing on a farm, officers accompanied D, who had been arrested, into his bedroom for the purpose of obtaining personal items to take with him on his trip to jail. Upon entering the bedroom, an officer saw a suitcase about ten feet away and asked D if it belonged to him. D said that it did, but made no move toward the suitcase nor did he indicate that he wanted to open it or take it with him. The officer immediately walked over the the suitcase and opened it and found further incriminating evidence, which was seized and used against D in his trial. On review, the Court of Appeals held that under these facts no exigent circumstance, or any other exception to the Fourth Amendment warrant requirement justified the officer's opening and search of the suitcase. (One might speculate that if *D* had indicated he wanted to use or open the suitcase or take it with him, an inspection of the contents to protect the officer's safety might well have been proper, and the evidence discovered admissible.)

------------------------------------- **Notes** -------------------------------------

Sample Questions

Exceptions to the warrant requirement include searches:
A. which are incident to a lawful arrest, or which come under the circumstances justifying "stop and frisk".
B. made pursuant to the "automobile exception" established by the *Carroll* case.
C. made pursuant to "exigent circumstances".
D. with probable cause under the "plain view" doctrine.
E. all of the above.

Search warrants are never issued by the courts if they are based on information from unnamed informants.　　T　　F.

Hearsay evidence cannot be used as a part of probable cause to obtain a search warrant.
　　T　　F.

The probable cause used to obtain a search warrant must be entirely made up of direct observations of, and facts within the personal knowledge of the affiant.　　T　　F.

Information passed on to the police by unknown persons is entirely useless because the police are required to know the reputation of the source of the information for truth and veracity before they can attempt to verify the information.　　T　　F.

The probable cause determination is basically a practical, common sense decision, but courts will not find a probable cause from conclusive statements only, and a warrant application should contain enough facts and circumstances from which the neutral and detached judge can make an independent decision as to the existence of probable cause.　　T　　F.

Because the exclusionary rule exists to "police the police", the "independent source" doctrine may allow the admission of evidence despite police misconduct if the evidence is not the product of the police misconduct, but the product of an independent source.　　T　　F.

Service of a warrant issued by a judge in a "rubber stamp" routine, when the warrant is so totally lacking in probable cause that all reasonably well trained officers would agree that no probable cause exists, may result in civil liability to the police despite the warrant.　　T　　F.

If a police officer, in serving a search warrant and while looking in places where the items described in the search warrant could logically be found, discovers other evidence not described in the warrant, or contraband:
A. it must be ignored and cannot be seized because it is not described in the warrant.
B. the evidence may be seized, but only after obtaining a second search warrant which describes it with particularity.
C. the evidence may be seized, but an additional warrant must be otained to seize the contraband.
D. the contraband may be seized, but an additional warrant must be obtained to seize the evidence not described in the original warrant.
E. both the evidence and/or contraband so found may be seized without obtaining an additional search warrant.

(4) APPLICATION OF ROBINSON-GUSTAFSON RULES

Perhaps the most significant statement in the *Robinson-Gustafson* cases is this statement in the holding of *United States v. Robinson*, 94 S. Ct. 467 (1973):

> A custodial arrest of a suspect based on probable cause is a reasonable intrusion under the Fourth Amendment; that intrusion being lawful, a search incident to the arrest requires no additional justification.

While seemingly a straightforward rule, the statement gives rise to at least two other important considerations: (1) What is a "custodial" arrest; and (2) What are the limits on the scope and nature of the search?

The elements of a custodial arrest are discussed in § 4.1 and § 4.2. Probable cause is discussed in § 4.4. Obviously, under *Robinson-Gustafson* a warrantless search incident to an arrest is not justified unless there is probable cause for the arrest and unless there is an intention to take the arrested person into custody. These requirements rule out the "Terry stop" cases (§ 4.15(E)), which are temporary detentions based on less than probable cause, and the usual traffic stops, which, though based on probable cause, are coupled with an intention to *release* upon citation or summons. What makes this subject difficult to discuss is the fact that both the *Terry* and the *traffic* situations may, under certain circumstances, blossom into full-blown custodial arrests. At the outset, however, a protective stop and frisk must be limited to just that—protection of the officer and others in the immediate area—and is not to be a subterfuge for a search for evidence. And one can imagine the justifiable public outrage that would result if all minor traffic offenders were subjected to a complete search of the person incident to the issuance of a traffic citation or summons.

A search "incident to" an arrest must, of course, be made close in point of time and place to the arrest which serves as its justification. Generally, the search will be made after or at the time of the arrest, although some searches made before the arrest have been held proper if independent probable cause for the arrest existed at the time of the search and the search was related to the safety of the officer. But the law will not allow an arrest to go unchallenged if its sole justification is evidence of crime discovered as the result of an unprivileged search, nor will it allow the use of evidence discovered incident to an arrest made without probable cause. See *Beck v. Ohio*, 85 S. Ct. 223 (1964) (briefed at § 4.4).

When the *Robinson* and *Gustafson* cases are considered in light of the rulings of *Chimel v. California* and *New York v. Belton* (briefed at § 4.15(A)(1)), it could logically be assumed that the scope of a search incident to an arrest would include the person of the arrested party and the area under his immediate control, the personal effects carried by him, and, in the case of automobile drivers and passengers, the interior of the passenger compartment and closed containers located therein. Some state courts have agreed with this broad authority, while some have limited the scope of a search incident to arrest under state constitutions and law.

All searches must be reasonable under the circumstances. Strip searches and body cavity inspections have been successfully challenged as unreasonable when made incident to arrests for minor violations. *Mary Beth G. v. City of Chicago*, 723 F.2d 1263 (7th Cir. 1983).

--------------------------------------- **Notes** ---------------------------------------

Sample Questions

When a lawful custodial arrest based on probable cause has been made of the driver, and/or passengers of a motor vehicle, and they have been removed from the vehicle and secured by handcuffing or otherwise:

A. the vehicle cannot be searched as an incident to the arrest(s).
B. the passenger compartment of the vehicle can be searched, but closed containers found therein cannot be searched.
C. only the trunk or equivalent area of the vehicle can be searched.
D. the vehicle must be secured and searched later under a valid search warrant.
E. both the passenger compartment of the vehicle and containers located therein, whether open or closed, may be searched without a warrant, as an incident to the arrest(s).

When the Supreme Court of the United States decided that the Fourth Amendment primarily protected *privacy,* as opposed to *property* rights, some of the changes in search and seizure theory which resulted included:

A. "mere evidence" seizures were no longer banned if there was a prior valid intrusion on privacy.
B. a different analysis had to be used in cases involving a parent consenting to the search of a child's room
C. wiretapping and eavesdropping standards had to comply with federal constitutional and statutory standards.
D. physical trespass was no longer the controlling consideration in "bugging" cases.
E. all of the above.

If the description of a place to be searched in a search warrant application is the result of a diligent and good faith investigation, but despite reasonable care results in a search warrant that describes the place too broadly and the police reasonably search the wrong place:

A. the search may nevertheless be ruled lawful—up to the point of the discovery of the mistake — and evidence seized in wrong place up to that point may be held to be admissible.
B. any evidence seized as a result of too broad a description in the warrant of the place to be searched will be inadmissible.
C. the word "reasonable" in its constitutional sense, does not allow for any mistakes.
D. civil liability will automatically result from such an erroneous search.
E. B and C above.

Once a search warrant has been obtained from a court and a search conducted under the warrant which results in the seizure of items described in the warrant:

A. there can be no challenge by the defendant to the validity or truthfulness of the warrant affidavit.
B. all items seized are automatically admissible at trial.
C. the issuing judge's examination of the warrant application and his issuance of the warrant is conclusive as to the truth of the matters stated therein.
D. on a proper offer of proof by the defendant, he is entitled to a hearing challenging content of the warrant affidavit as to deliberate falsehoods or reckless disregard for the truth.
E. A and C above.

(B) Automobile searches

(1) DISTINCTION BETWEEN HOME AND VEHICLE

Ours is a mobile society. Motor vehicles are involved in a high percentage of crime, and are themselves subject to a large body of statutory regulation which accounts for countless citizen-police contacts. The law early recognized a distinction between the search of a house and the search of an automobile. Aside from the age-old "a man's home is his castle" viewpoint, another obvious difference is involved. Houses are permanent structures. They do not speed down the highway with the capability to quickly leave one governmental jurisdiction and enter another. The very mobility of an automobile can, in the right setting, create what is recognized in the law of search and seizure as an "exigent circumstance," justifying an exception to the warrant requirement. The leading case on automobile searches is *Carroll v. United States*, which is briefed below.

When there is probable cause (to the same extent that would be reqired by a judge for the issuance of a search warrant) to believe that a motor vehicle contains items subject to seizure; when the vehicle is not in the custody or control of the police; when there is only a "fleeting opportunity" to search the vehicle; and when no warrant can be obtained in time to conduct the search, a warrantless search may be made under the *Carroll* rule. A *Carroll* search is not dependent on a prior arrest; an innocent carrier, such as a commercial bus, may be the target of such a search even if nobody aboard the bus has guilty knowledge of the contraband being carried.

When the driver and/or occupants of a motor vehicle are felony suspects and there is also independent justification to search the vehicle under the *Carroll* rule, the circumstances of *Chambers v. Maroney*, 90 S. Ct. 1975 (1970) are present. This case is briefed below in § 4.15(B)(2).

CASE BRIEF

Carroll v. United States, 45 S. Ct. 280 (1925)

Majority opinion: Taft. Concurring: McKenna, joined by Sutherland.

FACTS: Federal prohibition agents, posing as buyers for illegal whiskey, attempted to set up a buy with Ds and another man, all of whom were known bootleggers. Although Ds appeared in person and promised delivery of the whiskey for $130 a case, the transaction never came about, probably because Ds were suspicious of the deal. The officers did observe Ds, the automobile they were driving, and its registration number. It was the duty of the agents to patrol the road between Detroit and Grand Rapids looking for violations of the Prohibition Act. The agents later observed Ds going eastward from Grand Rapids in the same automobile; they followed them but lost them. Two months later Ds were again observed in the same car, coming from the direction of Detroit to Grand Rapids. This time the agents turned and followed Ds to a point east of Grand Rapids where they stopped them and searched the car. Concealed behind the upholstery of the seats the agents found 68 bottles of whiskey and gin. Ds attempted to bribe the arresting officers but were unsuccessful. The officers had not anticipated meeting Ds, but they believed Ds were carrying liquor; hence the search, seizure, and arrest. Ds were indicted, tried, and convicted for violations of the National Prohibition Act. They appealed, alleging that the search of their car violated the Fourth Amendment guarantee against unreasonable searches and seizures and that the use of liquor as evidence in their trial was not proper.

ISSUE: Was the search of Ds' car lawful?
DECISION: Yes; affirmed.
REASONS: The Fourth Amendment does not forbid search, but only unrea-

sonable search. The National Prohibition Act contains penal provisions applicable against officers who search private dwellings or "any other building or property" without a warrant, "maliciously and without probable cause." The act allows the searching of an automobile or other vehicle without a warrant if the search is not malicious or without probable cause. The case law on searches and seizures shows that the National Prohibition Act is consistent with the Fourth Amendment. In *Boyd v. United States*, 6 S. Ct. 524 (1886), *Weeks v. United States*, 34 S. Ct. 341 (1914), *Silverthorne Lumber Co. v. United States*, 40 S. Ct. 182 (1920), *Gouled v. United States*, 41 S. Ct. 261 (1921) and *Amos v. United States*, 41 S. Ct. 266 (1921), where the Court has addressed a variety of violations of the Fourth Amendment, the settled rule since *Weeks* is that illegally seized evidence is inadmissible. But no previous case has dealt with a warrantless seizure of contraband goods in the course of transportation.

> [T]he guaranty of freedom from unreasonable searches and seizures by the Fourth Amendment has been construed, practically since the beginning of the government, as recognizing a necessary difference between a search of a store, dwelling house, or other structure in respect of which a proper official warrant readily may be obtained and a search of a ship, motor boat, wagon, or automobile for contraband goods, where it is not practicable to secure a warrant, because the vehicle can be quickly moved out of the locality or jurisdiction in which the warrant must be sought.

If contraband goods concealed and illegally transported in an automobile or other vehicle may be searched for without a warrant, under what circumstances may such a search be made? It would certainly be unreasonable for prohibition agents to stop and search every vehicle on the highway on the chance of finding liquor. Unlike those subject to border seaches justified by national self protection, travelers in the interior of the country are entitled to the uninterrupted use of the highways without governmental search unless an official who is authorized to search has probable cause to believe that their vehicles contain contraband or illegal merchandise. It follows that if such a warrantless search and seizure is made, but for some reason no conviction follows, the officer may escape costs or a suit for damages by showing that he had reasonable or probable cause for the seizure.

> The measure of legality of such a seizure is, therefore, that the seizing officer shall have reasonable or probable cause for believing that the automobile which he stops and seizes has contraband liquor therein which is being illegally transported.
>
> We here find the line of distinction between legal and illegal seizures of liquor in transport in vehicles. It is certainly a reasonable distinction. It gives the owner of an automobile or other vehicle seized under section 26, in absence of probable cause, a right to have restored to him the automobile, it protects him under the Weeks and Amos Cases from use of the liqor as evidence against him, and it subjects the officer making the seizure to damages. On the other hand, in a case showing probable cause, the government and its officials are given the opportunity which they should have, to make the investigation necessary to trace reasonably suspected contraband goods and seize them.
>
> Such a rule fulfills the guaranty of the Fourth Amendment. In cases where the securing of a warrant is reasonably practicable, it must be used and when properly supported by affidavit and issued after judicial approval protects the seizing officer against a suit for damages. In cases where seizure is impossible except without warrant, the seizing officer acts unlawfully and at his peril unless he can show the court probable cause.

Was there probable cause in this case? The court was bound to take notice of public facts and geographical positions. Grand Rapids is about 152 miles from Detroit and its neighborhood along the Detroit River, which is the international boundary, and is one of the most active centers for the introduction of illegal liquor into the United States for distribution into the interior. The agents knew Ds, their automobile, and their reputation as bootleggers. They had previously sighted them proceeding from Grand Rapids to Detroit but lost them. On the day of the seizure the agents met Ds coming from the direction of the great source of supply of illegal liquor. The officers, when they saw them, believed that they were carrying liquor, and it is clear that they had reasonable cause for thinking so. That the officers were not looking for Ds at this particular time is immaterial. When they saw them, the officers were entitled to use their reasoning faculties upon all the facts of which they had previous knowledge in respect to the defendants.

The phrase "probable cause" has been frequently defined, and among these definitions are:

> If the facts and circumstances before the officer are such as to warrant a man of prudence and caution in believing that the offense has been committed, it is sufficient.

* * *

> If a constable or other peace officer arrests a person without a warrant, he is not bound to show in his jurisdiction a felony actually committed, to render the arrest lawful; but if he suspects one on his own knowledge of facts, or on facts communicated to him by others, and thereupon he has reasonable ground to believe that the accused has been guilty of felony, the arrest is not unlawful.

* * *

The substance of all the definitions is a reasonable ground for belief of guilt.

Good faith alone is not enough to constitute probable cause. That faith must be grounded on facts within knowledge of the officer which in the judgment of the court would make his faith reasonable.

RULE: For the purposes of search and seizure under the Fourth Amendment, the law recognizes a distinction between fixed structures and movable vehicles, such as automobiles, which can easily be moved from the jurisdiction before a search warrant can be obtained. If an officer has probable cause to believe that a vehicle he encounters contains items subject to seizure, and the circumstances are such that he has no opportunity to obtain a warrant, he is privileged to stop such a vehicle and search it without a warrant and items seized are admissible in evidence because under those circumstances the search is reasonable.

In *California v. Carney*, 105 S. Ct. 2066 (1985), the Supreme Court was faced with the issue of whether or not the *Carroll* rule applied to motor homes. D.E.A. agents had received uncorroborated information that a certain motor home was being used as a place to exchange marijuana for sex. A surveillance was set up and agents saw D approach a youth in downtown San Diego. D and the youth returned to the motor home which was located in a parking lot, entered it, and closed all the window shades. After an hour and fifteen minutes, the youth left the motor home. He was stopped by the agents and told them he had been given marijuana by D in return for sexual contacts. At the request of the agents, the youth returned to the motor home and knocked on the door; D stepped out.

The agents identified themselves; without a warrant or D's consent, they entered the motor home and found, in plain view, marijuana, plastic bags and a scale for weighing drugs. D was arrested and the motor home was impounded. A later search revealed additional marijuana in the cupboards and refrigerator. D's conviction was reversed by the Supreme Court of California, which held that the expectations of privacy in a motor home are more similar to a dwelling than to an automobile; that the *Carroll* rule did not apply; and that the warrantless search was unconstitutional. The Supreme Court of the United States granted certiorari and reversed, reinstating D's conviction. The Court discussed the case law since *Carroll* (1925), and noted that the *Carroll* warrant exception was originally based on the existence of probable cause coupled with a fleeting opportunity to search because of the mobility of vehicles. Later cases have also recognized that there is a reduced expectation of privacy in vehicles which use the public highways. This reduced expectation of privacy is evident in the many safety, equipment, registration and licensing regulations which apply to motor vehicles. Both the mobility factor and the regulatory factor apply to motor homes, and in this case the location of the motor home in a parking lot justified the conclusion that it was being used as a vehicle, and not as a residence. Therefore, the *Carroll* exception to the search warrant applied; the warrantless search of the motor home was proper in view of the abundant probable cause that existed and the ease of quick mobility of the motor home.

In *United States v. Hamilton*, 792 F.2d 837 (9th Cir. 1986), another motor home search situation was presented. Agents knew that this vehicle had been parked in a private residential driveway since the previous night. It was connected to the residence with an electrical extension cord. The agents had probable cause to believe the motor home contained evidence connected with an armed robbery. A warrantless search of the motor home uncovered evidence used to convict D of the armed robbery. In its opinion, the Court of Appeals stated:

> We find that the search of the motor home falls within the scope of the vehicle exception. The mobility of the motor home is amply demonstrated by the fact that it was moved the night before the search was conducted. Although the registration had lapsed, the motor home was licensed with the State of California. Because it was located in a residential driveway, it had easy access to a public road. The fact that the motor home was attached to 'utilities' in the broad sense is not very significant. A connection to electrical utilities by means of an extension cord is hardly the kind of 'pipe and drain' connection that would render the motor home more permanent and less mobile as was contemplated by the court in *Carney*.

It thus appears that a self-propelled motor home, unless actually being used as a residence, has much in common with an automobile for purposes of the *Carroll* exception to the search warrant requirement. But police officers should always remember that the law requires that a warrant be obtained unless the situation clearly falls within an established exception.

--------------------------------------- **Notes** ---------------------------------------

(2) REMOTE SEARCHES

In *Preston v. United States*, 84 S. Ct. 881 (1964), police received a tip that two men had been sitting in a car from 10:00 p.m. until 3:00 a.m., acting suspiciously. The police questioned the suspects but got less than satisfactory answers. The two were arrested for vagrancy and their car was towed to a garage. After the suspects were booked the police went to the garage and searched the car without a warrant. In the car the police found loaded revolvers, stocking masks, caps, rope, pillow slips, illegal license plates and other items, all of which were seized and later introduced as evidence in a trial for conspiracy to rob a federally insured bank. The defendants' objections to the admission of the evidence seized from the car were overruled and they were convicted. The Supreme Court held that, while the police unquestionably have a right to conduct a search incidental to an arrest for the purpose of discovering weapons and means of escape and evidence of crime, the search must be contemporaneous with the arrest. Here, the search of the car was remote in time and place from the arrest and therefore was improper in the absence of a warrant. The convictions were reversed and the case remanded.

Out of *Preston* grew the generally understood rule that if a car is to be searched as an incident to the arrest of its occupants, it must be searched at the time and place of the arrest. As later clarified in *Chambers v. Maroney* (briefed below), this rule applies only to automobile searches made incident to the arrest of the occupants. When an automobile search can also be justified under *Carroll v. United States*, 45 S. Ct. 280 (1925), the rule does not necessarily apply. Note that the issues of *scope* of the search and *inventory of contents* did not arise in *Preston*.

CASE BRIEF

Chambers v. Maroney, 90 S. Ct. 1975 (1970)

Majority opinion: White. Concurring: Stewart. Concurring in part and dissenting in part: Harlan

FACTS: Two armed men robbed a gas station. Witnesses noted a blue compact station wagon in the area before the robbery and saw it speed away from the vicinity at about the same time that the robbery took place. Witnesses also reported that one of the men in the suspect car was wearing a green sweater. The station attendant told the police that one of the men who robbed him was wearing a green sweater, and the other, a trench coat. A description of the car and the two robbers was broadcast over the police radio and within an hour a car answering the description and carrying four men was stopped about two miles from the crime scene. D was in the car; he was wearing a green sweater. There was also a trench coat in the car. All four men were arrested and taken to the police station and their station wagon was driven to the police station and there searched without a warrant. The police found two .38 caliber revolvers, the attendant's glove full of small change and cards from the victim of a previous robbery. D was convicted and did not appeal. Later, D petitioned for habeas corpus, which was denied.

ISSUE: Were the items of evidence seized during the warrantless search of the station wagon admissible?

DECISION: Yes; affirmed.

REASONS: There was adequate probable cause for the arrests, but the search of the station wagon, being remote in time and place from the place of arrest, cannot be sustained as being incidental to arrest. The fact situation here is distinguishable from that in *Preston v. United States*, 84 S. Ct. 881 (1964). In *Preston* the arrest was for vagrancy; any search of the car in that case would have been justified only as incidental to arrest, and the search should have been contemporaneous with the arrest, which it was not. Here the arrest was for armed robbery; weapons and fruits of the crime could logically be expected to be in the vehicle. (The Court then distinguishes between searches of mobile vehicles and searches of fixed places of residence, citing *Carroll v. United States*, 45 S. Ct. 280 (1925)). The justification for the search of an automobile on probable cause is wholly different from the justification for a search incidental to arrest. Searches with a warrant are constitutionally preferable to searches on probable cause without a warrant. What are the practical effects of allowing the remote search of the automobile in this case? Arguably, only the immobilization of the car should be permitted until a warrant could be obtained to search it. But in this case, probable cause to search the car under the *Carroll* rule existed even before the arrests were made. This probable cause still existed after the car had been removed to the police station. If the Fourth Amendment allows the immobilization of the car until a warrant can be obtained, there is no greater intrusion, where probable cause exists under the *Carroll* rule, in approving the warrantless search at the police station. Under these facts the warrantless search of the station wagon was reasonable and the evidence seized, admissible.

RULE: Where probable cause for the search of an automobile exists under the *Carroll* rule and there is also probable cause for the arrest of the driver and/or occupants of the same vehicle, the search of the vehicle need not be justified as incidental to the arrest and the search may be conducted, without a warrant, either at the time and place of the arrest or later and at a different place.

DISSENTING: This opinion is seriously at odds with the principle that departures from the warrant procedure must strictly conform to the exigency presented. Under the facts, the police had adequate time to secure a warrant because the car was under their control. Even under other facts, the preferable course of action would be to seize the car temporarily for as long as necessary to obtain a warrant to search it, or to obtain consent to search. There are no essential differences between the facts here and those in *Preston*, which states the best rule.

In *Michigan v. Thomas*, 102 S. Ct. 3079 (1982) and *Florida v. Meyers*, 104 S. Ct. 1852 (1984) the Supreme Court emphasized that, under the rule of *Chambers v. Maroney*, 90 S. Ct. 1975 (1970), police need no warrant to search an arrested person's vehicle, even after it has been impounded. If they have probable cause for search and arrest, their authority to make a warrantless search or inventory does not vanish simply because the vehicle has been immobilized and is fully under police control.

In *United States v. Johns*, 105 S. Ct. 881 (1985), as a result of an ongoing drug smuggling investigation, two pickup trucks were followed by ground and air surveillance to a remote private airstrip about 50 miles from the Mexican border. While the trucks were still under surveillance, a small aircraft landed and one of the trucks approached it. After a short time, the aircraft departed and a second small aircraft landed and departed. Two agents then drove closer to the trucks, parked, and approached on foot; in doing so, they were able to smell the strong odor of marijuana. The trucks contained packages wrapped in dark green plastic and secured with tape, a common method of packaging smuggled marijuana. Five D's were arrested at the scene. The two aircraft were followed by Customs Office surveillance aircraft and the pilots were arrested upon landing. The pickup trucks were not searched at the airstrip but were taken back to D.E.A. headquarters where the packages were removed and placed in a warehouse. Three days later, without a warrant, agents opened some of the packages and took samples which proved to be marijuana. D's were indicted but the district court suppressed the marijuana, and the Court of Appeals held that the warrantless search three days after seizure of the packages was not authorized. The Supreme Court granted certiorari, and reversed the Court of Appeals, holding that the search was proper and the marijuana should have been admissible in evidence. It ruled that under these circumstances the officers who seized the pickup trucks had probable cause to believe that not only the package, but also the trucks, contained contraband. (The trucks were obviously a part of a well-planned and coordinated smuggling operation). Therefore, since probable cause justified the seizure of the trucks, it justified a search of every part of the vehicle and its contents, including the plastic-wrapped packages (citing *United States v. Ross*, 102 S. Ct. 2157 (1982)). There is no requirement that the warrantless search of a vehicle occur contemporaneously with its lawful seizure (citing among other cases, *Chambers v. Maroney*, 90 S. Ct. 1975 (1970)), because the justification for conducting such a warrantless search does not vanish once the vehicle has been immobilized (citing *Michigan v. Thomas*, 102 S. Ct. 3079 (1982)).

In further explanation of its holding, the Court indicated that a *Carroll-Ross* search does not have to take place immediately upon the seizure of the vehicle, and if the search taken place (as it did here) several days later, no warrant is necessary to open containers or packages which were in the vehicle at the time of its seizure. (It should be kept in mind, however, that prompt searching may be dictated by some "*Carroll* rule" situations, such as the stopping and searching of a commercial passenger bus when there may be probable cause to believe it is transporting contraband without the knowledge of the driver.)

-------------------------------------- **Notes** --------------------------------------

Sample Questions

If a person is arrested without a warrant for a robbery within a short time after the commission of the crime and he is searched without a warrant incident to the robbery arrest, only items pertaining to the robbery may be seized as a result of the search and any other item of evidence of a different crime must be disregarded.   T   F.

The *Chimel* case limited the scope of a search made incident to an arrest to the room in which the arrest was made.   T   F.

The *Chimel* case limited the scope of a search made incident to an arrest to the person of the arrestee and the area into which he could reach to obtain a weapon or to destroy evidence; i.e., the area under his immediate control.   (T)   F.

If a full custodial arrest is made based on proable cause, but without a warrant, no search of the individual arrested is valid in those cases (such as traffic offenses), in which no further evidence of the crime could logically be found on his person.   T   F.

A custodial arrest based on probable cause is a reasonable instrusion under the Fourth Amendment, and that intrusion being lawful, a search incident to the arrest requires no additional justification.   (T)   F.

The constitutionality of a search of the person made incident to a custodial arrest based on probable cause:

A. depends on whether or not a "jailable" offense is involved.
B. depends on the fear of the officer for his safety.
C. depends on the existence of police department regulations requiring the search.
D. depends on the nature of the offense.
(E) none of the above.

A search of a person incident to his custodial arrest made on probable cause should be made immediately after the arrest, and, if practicable, at the place of the arrest.   T   F.

If a search of a person arrested is made at the time and place that he is arrested, this prohibits a later, more complete search at the "booking" procedure.   T   F.

A search incident to a custodial arrest based on a probable cause may be lawfully made only if a justification for it exists under the case of *Terry v. Ohio*.   T   F.

The legal rules governing searches of vehicles and the rules governing searches of homes are identical because both are controlled by the Fourth Amendment.   T   F.

Probable cause is the same as proof beyond a reasonable doubt.   T   F.

One way to resolve the confusion caused by the *Chadwick* (search of closed containers) case, is to remember that in that case, the probable cause, from the beginning, was centered in the *container,* as opposed to a vehicle transporting the container, and at the time the container was opened, it had been reduced to the complete control of the government for a substantial period of time.   T   F.

The use of a drug-sniffing dog constitutes a search.   T   F.

(3) CLOSED CONTAINERS—THE CHADWICK RULE

In *United States v. Chadwick*, 97 S. Ct. 2476 (1977), railroad officials in San Diego notified federal agents when they observed defendants load a footlocker onto a train bound for Boston. Their suspicions were aroused because the footlocker seemed unusually heavy for its size and it was leaking talcum powder, a substance often used to disguise the odor of marijuana. One of the defendants also matched a profile used to spot drug traffickers. The federal agents relayed this information to their counterparts in Boston, along with detailed descriptions of defendants the footlocker.

When the train arrived at Boston two days later, narcotics agents were waiting. They identified the two defendants from the description and kept them under surveillance. When the footlocker was removed from a baggage cart the defendants put it on the floor and sat on it. The agents released a trained dog near the footlocker, and without alerting the defendants, the dog signaled the presence of marijuana. Defendant Chadwick then joined the other two defendants and the footlocker was moved and placed in the trunk of his waiting car. While the trunk lid was still open and before the car was started, the agents arrested all three defendants and seized the car and footlocker. This action was taken without a warrant, but was based on probable cause to believe that a felony was being committed. The defendants, Chadwick's car and the footlocker were all taken to the federal building in Boston, where the double-locked footlocker was opened with keys seized from one of the defendants. It was full of marijuana. The defendants were indicted but moved to suppress the marijuana, which had been discovered without a search warrant and without defendants' consent to search. The district court granted the pretrial motion to suppress and the court of appeals affirmed. The government's petition for certiorari to the Supreme Court was granted. Held:

> In this case, important Fourth Amendment privacy interests were at stake. By placing personal effects inside a double-locked footlocker, respondents manifested an expectation that the contents would remain free from public examination. No less than one who locks the doors of his home against intruders, one who safeguards his personal possessions in this manner is due the protection of the Fourth Amendment Warrant Clause. There being no exigency, it was unreasonable for the government to conduct this search without the safeguards a judicial warrant provides.

In reaching its conclusion, the Supreme Court made the following observations: (1) judicial warrants have often been required outside the four walls of the home; (2) the fact that the footlocker was locked mainifested a privacy interest against public examination; (3) many factors that diminish privacy interests in automobiles did not apply to the footlocker in this case (the government did not try to justify the seizure and search under the *Carroll* rule, because the vehicle was clearly under governmental control); (4) once the footlocker had been seized and removed to the federal building, there was no danger that its contents would be removed before a warrant could be obtained; and (5) the search could not be justified as incident to arrest, because it was remote in time and place from the arrest and there was no danger of defendants seizing it to obtain weapons or to destroy evidence.

How does this case square with *Chambers v. Maroney*, 90 S. Ct. 1975 (1970), in which there was probable cause to believe that the occupants of an automobile had recently committed a felony (robbery), and that the automobile contained fruits, evidence and instrumentalities of that crime? In *Chambers* the Court indicated that the automobile could be searched either at the time and place of the arrest or later, at a different place, without a warrant. But *Chambers* involved a true *Carroll* situation at the time of the apprehension, and the subject of the search was the passenger compartment of an automobile—a mobile vehicle—as opposed to a double-locked, nonmobile footlocker designed for and use as a depository of personal property. In any event, the *Chadwick* case illustrates for police the wisdom of the often-repeated admonition: *if there is an opportunity to obtain a warrant, get one.*

In *Arkansas v. Sanders*, 99 S. Ct. 2586 (1979), the Supreme Court held that the warrantless search of a suitcase (which, as in *Chadwick*, the police had allowed to be placed in an automobile although they had probable cause to seize it previously) could not be justified under the *Carroll* rule, even though the car had been driven away after the suitcase was placed therein. The Court noted that as a general rule there is no greater need for warrantless searches of luggage taken from automobiles than for warrantless searches of containers taken from other places. Once in the control of the police no exception to the warrant requirement any longer exists, if the original probable cause was directed toward the *container* as opposed to the vehicle.

CASE BRIEF

United States v. Ross, 102 S. Ct. 2157 (1982)

Opinion: Stevens. Concurring: Blackmun, Powell. Dissenting: White; Marshall, joined by Brennan.

FACTS: Washington, D.C. police received information from a known and reliable informant that D was selling narcotics out of the trunk of his car parked at a stated address. The informant indicated that he had just observed D complete a sale and that D had told him that additional drugs were in the trunk. The informant also gave a detailed description of D and of his car. Police drove to the address and found the car parked there. They checked the registration plate and determined the owner's name. A further computer check revealed that the owner fit the description and used an alias, "Bandit," as stated by the informant.

A short time later police observed D driving the car; they stopped it and told D to get out of the car. While they searched D, one of the officers observed a bullet on the front seat. They searched the car and found a pistol in the glove compartment. D was then arrested and handcuffed. The police used D's keys to open the trunk where they found a brown paper bag. Inside the bag were glassine bags of white powder. Police replaced the bag, closed the trunk, and drove the car to headquarters where they searched the car thoroughly without obtaining a warrant. A zippered red leather pouch was discovered in the trunk in addition to the paper bag. In the pouch was $3,200 in cash. A lab test of the white powder showed that it was heroin.

D was charged with possession of heroin with intent to distribute. Prior to trial D moved to suppress the heroin and the cash as evidence. After a hearing the district court denied the motion to suppress and D was tried and convicted.

A three-judge panel of the court of appeals reversed the conviction. While the panel found the stop and the search to be reasonable under *Carroll v. United States*, 45 S. Ct. 280 (1925) and *Chambers v. Maroney*, 90 S. Ct. 1975 (1970), they considered separately the warrantless search of the paper bag and the leather pouch. Applying the test of "reasonable expectation of privacy" the panel held the search of the paper bag was proper but the search of the leather pouch was not.

The case was then reheard by the court of appeals en banc, which ruled that the warrantless searches of both closed opaque containers (the paper bag and the zippered pouch) were improper. In reaching this result, the majority of the en banc court of appeals was influenced by *Arkansas v. Sanders*, 99 S. Ct. 2586

(1979) and *Robbins v. California*, 101 S. Ct. 2841 (1981). The Supreme Court granted certiorari to determine if *Robbins* should be reconsidered.

ISSUE: When police have probable cause to believe that a mobile vehicle contains contraband under the *Carroll* rule, may they open closed, opaque containers found in that vehicle in a warrantless search for the contraband?

DECISION: Yes; reversed.

REASONS: Contemporaneously with the adoption of the Fourth Amendment, Congress passed legislation recognizing a difference as to the necessity for a search warrant between goods subject to forfeiture, when concealed in a dwelling house or in a movable vessel. But warrantless searches of movable vessels or vehicles can only be made when, based on objective facts that could justify the issuance of a warrant by a court, there is probable cause to believe that the vessel or vehicle contains contraband.

In both *United States v. Chadwick*, 97 S. Ct. 2476 (1977) and *Arkansas v. Sanders* (cited above) the closed, opaque containers were allowed to be placed in an automobile, and later were seized by police and searched without a warrant. In both cases it was held that the mere placing of a container in a vehicle does not render the *Carroll* rule applicable. The police had probable cause to seize the containers *before* they were placed in the vehicles, but no independent probable cause to search the *vehicles* themselves.

Chadwick and *Sanders* were not "automobile exception" cases, as was *Carroll*, in which the probable cause is directed at the entire vehicle; rather, they were "container" cases, in which the probable cause was directed at the containers.

Robbins was a plurality opinion decided on the basis of "reasonable expectation of privacy"; it seemingly followed *Chadwick* and *Sanders;* but the question of the scope of the automobile exception to the warrant requirement, although mentioned in a concurring opinion, was not pressed by the parties. The present case, however, squarely presents the question. Here, the police had probable cause to search D's entire vehicle.

In *Carroll v. United States*, 45 S. Ct. 280 (1925) the whiskey seized was not in plain view in D's car; it was discovered by removing part of the upholstery of the rumble seat. Such a search could have been authorized by a magistrate (if one had been available), so the scope of the warrantless search was constitutionally permissible.

In *Chambers v. Maroney*, cited above, the weapons and stolen property were found concealed in a compartment under the dashboard. In its application of *Carroll* the Court has previously sustained warrantless searches of containers found during a lawful automobile search. Prior to the rulings in *Chadwick* and *Sanders*, courts routinely held that containers and packages found during a legitimate warrantless search of an automobile could also be searched without a warrant. As noted in *Henry v. United States*, 80 S. Ct. 168 (1959), the decision in *Carroll* "merely relaxed the requirements for a warrant on grounds of impracticability." It did not broaden—or limit—the scope of a lawful search based on probable cause.

When a legitimate search is being made and when its purpose and its limits have been precisely defined, nice distinctions between closets, drawers, and containers, in the case of a home, or between glove compartments, upholstered seats, trunks, and wrapped packages in the case of a vehicle, must give way to the interest in the prompt and efficient completion of the task at hand.

A constitutional distinction between "worthy" and "unworthy" containers would be improper. The scope of a warrantless search of an automobile is not defined by the nature of the container in which the contraband is secreted; rather, it is defined by the object of the search and the places in which there is probable cause to believe that it may be found.

As far as this decision is inconsistent with *Robbins* and some of *Sanders*, the doctrine of *stare decisis* does not prevent this action. The Court rejects some of the reasoning in *Sanders* while adhering to its holding in that case, but it rejects the precise holding in *Robbins* because there was no Court opinion supporting a single rationale for its judgment and the reasoning in the present case was not presented in that case.

RULE: The scope of a warrantless search under the *Carroll* exception to the warrant requirement is no broader and no narrower than a judge could legitimately authorize by warrant. If independent probable cause justifies the search of a vehicle lawfully stopped, it justifies the search of every part of the vehicle and its contents (including closed containers) that logically could conceal the object of the search.

DISSENTING: Although the Court purports to rely on the mobility of an automobile and the impracticability of obtaining a warrant, it never explains why these concerns permit the warrantless search of a container which can easily be seized and immobilized while a search warrant is obtained.

A closed container, as opposed to the car itself, does not reflect diminished privacy interests. The majority's rule makes a policeman's determination of probable cause the functional equivalent of the determination of a neutral and detached judge.

The difficulty of immobilizing a vehicle while a search warrant is obtained was a practical consideration in *Carroll* (where the contraband was hidden in the rumble seat upholstery); but this consideration does not apply to movable closed containers and packages which may be seized and removed from the automobile. The majority ignores the clear distinction that *Chadwick* established between movable containers and automobiles. This holding will likely result in abuses of privacy by police.

The *Chadwick* "container" case has caused confusion in the automobile search cases. It must be remembered that in *Chadwick* the probable cause, from the beginning, was centered in the *container* (footlocker), and not in the entirety of any vehicle. Apparently, when the probable cause is less specific as to location, and is simply a probability that contraband is contained "someplace within the vehicle," all parts of the vehicle in which the contraband could be located including containers, may be searched without a warrant, under the *Carroll-Ross* exception to the warrant requirement.

It seems that the Supreme Court of the United States has been trying to provide the police with readily applicable guidelines in search and seizure cases at least since *Chimel v. California*, but the endless variety of fact situations giving rise to theses cases has defied all attempts to eliminate confusion, even in the courts. In discussing the holding in *United States v. Johns*, 105 S. Ct. 881 (1985), the Court of Appeals said, in *United States v. Mazzone*, 782 F.2d 757 (7th Cir. 1986):

> The rule we distill from these cases, from *Johns*, and from the need to provide police with (if possible) simple and readily applicable guidelines to lawful searches of vehicles, is that if there is some reason to believe that a full search may turn up more than is just in the sealed container, the police can make the full search and as part of it open and search the container itself. The rule was flunked in *Chadwick* and *Sanders* but is passed in this case as in all the other pertinent cases since *Ross* that we have found.

CHADWICK RULE ABANDONED

In a further attempt to furnish law enforcement with a consistent guideline concerning automobile searches involving closed containers, the Supreme Court, in *California v. Acevedo*, 111 S.Ct. 1982 (1991), acknowledged that its past decisions had created confusion, and stated:

> "Until today, this Court has drawn a curious line between the search of an automobile that coincidentally turns up a container and the search of a container that coincidentally turns up in an automobile. The protections of the Fourth Amendment must not turn on such coincidences. We therefore interpret *Carroll* as providing one rule to govern all automobile searches. The police may search an automobile and the containers within it where they have probable cause to believe contraband or evidence is contained."

It therefore appears that as a result of the holding in *Acevedo*, (briefed below), that police may open and search closed containers found in automobiles, without a warrant, when the probable cause is centered in either the automobile generally, or in the container, (provided the container could hold the contraband or evidence that is the subject of the probable cause). But if the probable cause is centered only in the container, this alone will not justify a complete search of the rest of the automobile.

CASE BRIEF

California v. Acevedo, 111 S.Ct. 1982 (1991)

Majority opinion: Blackmun, joined by Rehnquist, O'Connor, Kennedy, and Souter. Concurring in judgment: Scalia. Dissenting: White, Stevens, Marshall.

FACTS: Through a cooperative drug investigation involving federal agents and local police it was determined that a package of marijuana had been picked up at Federal Express and taken to an apartment. Later officers observed the person who had picked up the package leave the apartment and discard the paper and box that had contained the marijuana into a trash bin. At this point one of the officers left the surveillance site to secure a search warrant. 20 minutes later a man left the apartment carrying a knapsack which appeared to be half full. Officers stopped this person and found 1 1/2 pounds of marijuana. Shortly thereafter D arrived and entered the apartment. 10 minutes later D left carrying a brown paper bag that looked full. Officers noticed that the bag was the size of one wrapped marijuana package earlier described to them by the federal agent. D walked to a car in the parking lot and placed the bag in the trunk and started to drive away. Fearing they were about to lose the evidence, officers in a marked police car stopped D, opened the car's trunk and the bag, which contained marijuana. D was charged with possession of drugs for sale; he moved to suppress the evidence but motion was denied; D pleaded guilty but appealed the denial of his motion to suppress. The Calif. Court of Appeal held that the evidence should have been suppressed because the probable cause was centered in the *paper bag* and not in the *automobile*. Therefore, it ruled, the case was controlled by *United States v. Chadwick*, 97 S.Ct. 2476 (1977), and not by *United States v. Ross*, 102 S.Ct. 2157 (1982), with the result being that while the officers had the privilege to *seize* the paper bag, they could not *open* it without first obtaining a search warrant. The Calif. Supreme Court denied the state's petition for review and the Supreme Court of the United States granted certiorari.

ISSUE: Does the Fourth Amendment prohibit the warrantless opening of containers found in vehicles by police when the probable cause is centered in the container rather than the vehicle generally, while at the same time permitting the warrantless opening of containers found in vehicles when the probable cause is centered in the vehicle generally?

DECISION: No, Reversed and remanded; the warrantless opening of a container is permitted in either case.

REASONS: The Congress of the United States, at the same period of time in which the Fourth Amendment was adopted, distinguished between the need for a warrant to search dwellings and the need for a warrant to search movable vessels. Much later, this Court, in *Carroll v. United States*, 45 S.Ct. 280 (1925), established an exception to the warrant requirement in cases in which police had probable cause to believe a moving vehicle contained evidence of a crime, there was no opportunity to get a warrant, and only a fleeting opportunity to search. In *Chambers v. Maroney*, 90 S.Ct. 1975 (1970), the Court ruled that if police have probable cause to justify a warrantless seizure of an automobile on a public roadway under the *Carroll* rule, they may either search it immediately or later.

The cases of *United States v. Chadwick*, 97 S.Ct. 2476 (1977), and *Arkansas v. Sanders*, 99 S.Ct. 2586 (1979), were both concerned with the privacy interest in personal luggage and the Court refused to extend the *Carroll* rule to luggage in transit, even though it was located in an automobile. [This resulted in the situation that although instances might arise in which probable cause would justify the *seizure* of luggage being transported in an automobile, a warrant was necessary before the luggage could be *opened*].

In 1982, the case of *United States v. Ross*, 102 S.Ct. 2157 again addressed the subject of containers (including luggage), found in automobiles. The rule that emerged from the *Ross* case was that if the probable cause was centered in the automobile generally (as opposed to being centered in the container), all parts of the automobile which could contain the contraband or evidence (including closed containers), could be searched, and opened, under the authority of the *Carroll* case.

> "The scope of a warrantless search based on probable cause is no narrower — and no broader — than the scope of a search authorized by a warrant supported by probable cause." . . . "Thus, if probable cause justifies the search of a lawfully stopped vehicle, it justifies the search of every part of the vehicle and its contents that may conceal the object of the search."

[At this point in the development of the case law it seemed that *Ross* covered the situation when the probable cause was centered in the automobile generally, but that when the probable cause was centered in the container found in the automobile, as in *Sanders*, a warrant was required to search the container.]

These conflicting rules confused the police and provided very little extra privacy protection for the individual. For example, they may have tempted police to make unnecessarily intrusive searches of entire vehicles in order to justify warrantless opening of containers in which their probable cause was really centered. Also, under the rule of *New York v. Belton*, 101 S.Ct. 2860 (1981), police are authorized to open closed containers found in the driver and passenger compartments of automobiles as an incident to the arrest and search of drivers and/or passengers. These seemingly conflicting rules have impeded effective law enforcement and they have been criticized by the academic community. The Court has a responsibility to provide clear guidelines for the police in the area of search and seizure and the case law discussed above has failed to do this.

[At this point in its opinion, several arguments of the dissenting Justices are discussed and rejected.]

Although *stare decisis* (following past case law) is important, the Court has overruled a prior case on the comparatively rare occasion when it has caused confusion or when it has led to abnormal results. The *Sanders* case was partially undermined by the *Ross* holding, but the two different container search rules that resulted have been confusing. One clear-cut rule to govern automobile searches and eliminate the *Sanders* warrant requirement to open closed containers is much better.

RULE: If the police have probable cause to believe that a mobile vehicle, not under their control, contains items subject to seizure and there is no opportunity to obtain a search warrant, they may stop the vehicle and conduct a warrantless search of the parts of it or the containers within it that they have probable cause to believe may contain said items.

CONCURRING: Justice Scalia concurs in the result of the case but discusses whether or not "reasonableness," rather than the existence of a warrant, should govern searches and seizures in view of the growing number of exceptions to so-called "general rule" that a warrant is always required in the absence of a "few specifically established and well-delineated exceptions".

DISSENTING: Dissenting opinion omitted.

For a case involving the scope of a consent search of an automobile and the containers therein, see *Florida v. Jimeno*, 111 S.Ct. 1801 (1991), briefed on page 4.15(F)(3)-1.

-- **Notes** --

Sample Questions

A show of authority by police, with intention to make an arrest:
A. will not amount to an arrest unless there is a touching of the person who the police intend to arrest, or until that person yields to the authority of the police.
B. will not amount to an arrest unless a chase is involved.
C. is a seizure under the Fourth Amendment.
D. is an arrest under the Fourth Amendment.
E. amounts to an arrest if the person to be arrested so understands it, even though he is never touched by the police and does not yield to their authority.

Two police officers on routine patrol see a car being driven by a young man who looks like he might be under the legal age to hold a driver's license, but they observe no improper driving or other cause to stop the car. Nevertheless, the police decide to stop the car to check the driver's license. When the officer turns on the red light and siren, the driver pulls to the side of the road, but tosses a small paper bag with a twisted top out the driver's window. After the car is stopped, one of the officers retrieves the bag, opens it, and discovers illegal drugs. Will the drugs be admissible in a drug prosecution? Why or why not? If you were the prosecutor, what case law precedent would you use to justify the retrieval and opening of the bag? What type of argument can you expect from the defense to justify the suppression of the bag and its contents?

Does your state recognize the power of a citizen to make an arrest? If so, what are the circumstances under which a citizen's arrest may be made, and how does civil liability for false arrest differ from that of a police officer?

In the case of *Riverside County, Calif., v. McLaughlin,* 111 S.Ct. 1661 (1991), the Supreme Court of the United States defined what they meant by the words "prompt judicial determination of probable cause" after a warrantless arrest. The Court held:
A. the probable cause hearing must be held immediately after the booking process.
B. unless the defendant can show unreasonable delay, a probable cause hearing held within 48 hours of arrest, excluding weekends, is presumptively reasonable.
C. unless the defendant can show unreasonable delay, a probable cause hearing held within 24 hours of arrest, including weekends, is presumptively reasonable.
D. unless the defendant can show unreasonable delay, a probable cause hearing held within 48 hours of arrest, including weekends, is presumptively reasonable.
E. both C and D are correct.

The police have probable cause to believe that a certain unoccupied automobile, parked at a parking meter with 30 minutes left unexpired, contains illegal drugs in a brown leather briefcase located in the trunk. How should the police proceed to lawfully seize the drugs so they will be admissible in a criminal prosecution?

(C) Exigent circumstances

(1) CLOSE PURSUIT AND PRIVACY

If the law required blind adherence to the warrant requirement many crimes would go undetected, unprosecuted and unpunished, and the law might fail in its duty to protect the public safety. As the law grows within its constitutional framework, certain exceptions to the general rules are recognized because of necessity; modifications in the general rules themselves are made because of changes by the Supreme Court in its interpretation of what the Constitution actually means.

Just as the mobility and widespread use of the automobile have created a widely recognized exigent-circumstances exception to the warrant requirement, so have other recurring situations not involving the automobile. In each situation in which the warrant requirement is excused, however, the following circumstances are present: (1) there is probable cause for a search; (2) because of exigent circumstances there is a need for immediate action by the police; and (3) there is no opportunity to obtain a warrant from a neutral and detached judge.

In the development of the law of search and seizure, the older view was that the right of the government to seize items from individuals depended upon a superior property interest vested in the government. Clearly this superior governmental property interest was present in stolen property (fruits of the crime of theft); in instrumentalities of a crime (misuse resulting in forfeiture of property rights); and in contraband (items in which no property or possessory rights may be claimed). On the other hand, "mere evidence" (such as clothing worn during the commission of a crime, or a person's private papers) were historically not the proper subject of a governmental seizure because the government had no superior property or possessory interest in these items. This line of judicial reasoning created what became known as the "mere evidence rule"; *Gouled v. United States*, 41 S. Ct. 261 (1921). The rule was also probably based in part on the historic prohibitions against general searches, which were among the English abuses of individual rights during the American Colonial period.

In *Warden v. Hayden*, briefed below, the Supreme Court of the United States changed the general rule and abandoned the older property-interest concept of seizure. It held that what the Fourth Amendment *really* protects is the right of privacy. This being so, once a privileged intrusion on privacy has been made it is no more of a violation of the privacy right for the police to seize mere evidence of a crime than to seize fruits, instrumentalities or contraband. The *Hayden* case also clarifies the rule that it is reasonable for the police to make a warrantless entry into a private residence for the purpose of arresting a fleeing felon whom they are following in close pursuit, when they possess adequate probable cause for the felony arrest. Close or "fresh" pursuit apparently is the exigent circumstance which, coupled with probable cause and lack of opportunity to obtain a warrant, excuses the warrant requirement.

Hayden also approves the search of the entire house (to ensure that other armed and dangerous persons are not present and to secure weapons which may be used against the police), and the seizure of items of "mere evidence" found while searching for such persons and weapons.

CASE BRIEF

Warden v. Hayden, 87 S. Ct. 1642 (1967)

Majority opinion: Brennan. Concurring: Fortas, joined by Warren. Dissenting: Douglas.

FACTS: D held up the business office of a taxicab company and ran from the scene with the loot. Cab drivers in the vicinity, attracted by shouts of "holdup," followed D as he ran down the street and entered a house. One driver notified the company dispatcher by radio of D's description and the address of the house he had entered. This information was relayed immediately to the police who proceeded to the address within minutes and knocked at the door. The police told D's wife they had information that a robber had just entered the house; they asked to conduct a search and she offered no objection. The police spread out through the first and second floors and the cellar simultaneously. D was found in a bedroom pretending to be asleep and he was placed under arrest. No other man was found to be in the house. Meanwhile an officer attracted by the sound of running water in the bathroom, discovered a pistol and a shotgun in the flush tank; another found a jacket and trousers that matched the description of the robber's clothing; a pistol ammunition clip and a cap were found under D's bed. Shotgun ammunition was also found in D's bedroom. All of these items of evidence were introduced against D at his trial. The court, without a jury, found D guilty of armed robbery. After unsuccessful appeals on the state level, D sought and was denied habeas corpus in federal district court. This denial was reversed by the United States Court of Appeals, Fourth Circuit on the basis that D was correct in asserting that the items of clothing seized were improperly admitted because they were "mere evidence" and not instrumentalities, fruits of a crime, weapons or contraband.

ISSUE: Was the evidence seized during the search of a house without a warrant for a fleeing felon admissible?

DECISION: Yes; Court of Appeals decision reversed.

REASONS: Neither the entry without a warrant nor the search for the fleeing felon was invalid; the exigencies of the situation made such a course imperative. The Fourth Amendment does not require police officers to delay the course of an investigation if to do so would gravely endanger their lives or the lives of others. Speed here was essential, and only by a thorough search of the house could police assure themselves that D was the only man present and that they had control of all weapons that might be used against them. The scope of the search must be as broad as may reasonably be necessary to prevent resistance or escape. There is a reasonable inference that the officer who found the clothing was searching for weapons. (The Court rejects its prior holdings that the seizure of "mere evidence"—as opposed to instrumentalities, fruits, or contraband—was improper. The Court then traces the history of the "property concept" of the Fourth Amendment and says that it has abandoned the concept that in order to seize an item the government must have a superior property interest.)

The Fourth Amendment protects *privacy*, and privacy is disturbed no more by a search directed to mere evidence than by one directed to fruits, instrumentalities or contraband. A search may be unreasonable even though the government has a superior property interest. The legitimate interest of the government is in solving crime. Fourth Amendment rights can secure the same protection of privacy whether the search is for more evidence or for fruits, contraband, or instrumentalities. But of course there must be probable cause to believe that the mere evidence will aid in an apprehension or conviction. Here, the clothing seized matched to description given by the cab driver witness.

RULE: The Fourth Amendment protects privacy rather than property. It is no more of an intrusion on privacy for the police to search for mere evidence of a crime than to search for fruits, instrumentalities or contraband, as long as the requirements of probable cause and particularity are observed. In exigent circumstances (such as fresh pursuit) police can enter a private home without a warrant to search for a fleeing armed felon that they have probable cause to believe is therein, and in conducting the search (prior to or simultaneously with finding the fugitive) they may search for and seize weapons, fruits of crime, instrumentalities, contraband and mere evidence, if connected with the crime.

Concurring and dissenting opinions omitted.

(2) EVIDENCE OF INTOXICATION—THE FLEETING OPPORTUNITY TO SEARCH

Evidence of alcohol intoxication is important in many criminal cases. While it may mitigate a specific intent crime to a lesser offense, intoxication is usually encountered by the police as an element of criminal offense such as driving while intoxicated. Because alcohol, the evidence, is dissipated by body chemistry, there is only a fleeting opportunity to determine the extent of intoxication. This is recognized as an exigent circumstance which, coupled with probable cause, justifies a warrantless search and seizure. The leading case involving blood-alcohol seizures is *Schmerber v. California*, briefed below.

CASE BRIEF

Schmerber v. California, 86 S. Ct. 1826 (1966)

Opinion: Brennan. Concurring: Harlan, joined by Stewart. Dissenting: Warren, Black, Douglas, Fortas.

FACTS: D was involved in an automobile accident. Police observed him at the scene of the accident and again at a hospital where he was taken for the treatment of injuries. He displayed all the usual symptoms of being under the influence of intoxicating liquor. After arresting him for driving while under the influence and warning him of his *Miranda* rights, police requested a physician at the hospital to withdraw a blood sample from D for alcohol analysis. The sample was taken over the objection of D and his attorney. A report of the analysis was admitted in evidence against D at his trial and he was convicted of the offense of driving while under the influence of intoxicating liquor. The California courts affirmed D's conviction. D contends that in taking the blood sample despite his refusal, the state of California violated certain rights secured to him by the Constitution of the United States.

ISSUE: Were any constitutional rights of D violated by the taking of the involuntary blood sample under these circumstances?

DECISION: No; affirmed.

REASONS: In *Breithaupt v. Abram*, 77 S. Ct. 408 (1957) police had a blood sample drawn in similar circumstances from an unconscious accident victim. In that case and the present one the blood samples were taken "by a physician in a simple, medically acceptable manner in a hospital environment." In *Breithaupt* the Court had ruled that this simple procedure did not offend the "sense of justice" as had the procedure used in *Rochin v. California*, 72 S. Ct. 205 (1952), which involved recovery of drug evidence by stomach pumping after an invalid warrantless invasion of D's home by a "no-knock" entry.

The Privilege Against Compulsory Self-Incrimination Claim

The Fifth Amendment privilege against compulsory self-incrimination is concerned only with evidence of a testimonial or communicative nature. The blood sample, which falls in the general category of physical, or nontestimonial evidence, was not affected by the Fifth Amendment privilege.

The Right to Counsel Claim

Because no "critical stage of criminal proceeding" was involved, D cannot assert the right to counsel simply because his lawyer erroneously advised him that he could assert it. His claim is limited to the failure of the police to respect his wish, reinforced by counsel's advice, to be inviolate.

The Unreasonable Search and Seizure Claim

The officers clearly had probable cause to believe that D was under the influence of intoxicating liquor. In blood-alcohol cases there also exists the exigent circumstance that the body is using up and destroying the evidence (the alcohol). In view of this fact there is not time enough to seek out a magistrate in order to comply with the search warrant requirement. The search and seizure here could also be deemed incident to D's arrest. Under the facts of this case the blood extraction was a reasonable one. Blood tests are commonplace today. There was no issue of undue fear and no concern for health or religious scruples; D had already refused to take a breathalyzer test. Finally, the facts show the test was administered in a reasonable manner by a physician in a hospital environment.

RULE: When police have probable cause to believe that a person is under the influence of intoxicating liquor and that he has committed an offense in which evidence of his intoxication is admissible, it is not a violation of due process of law, right to counsel, or the guarantees against self-incrimination or unreasonable searches and seizures to have a blood sample taken by a physician in a proper medical environment to determine the extent of blood alcohol. The suspect's refusal to submit to a blood test or a breath test on advice of his counsel does not make the tests improper, and if an arrest has been made the blood sample is also proper as a search incident to arrest.

Concurring and dissenting opinions omitted.

In *Winston v. Lee*, 105 S. Ct. 1611 (1985), D was wounded in the chest when the victim he was attempting to rob shot him. D was apprehended eight blocks away a short time later, and he was identified by the victim (also wounded) in the hospital emergency room. The state of Virginia attempted to get a court order directing surgery on D to recover the bullet fired from the victim's gun, as evidence. Although approved in the Virginia courts, the surgery was enjoined (prevented) by the U.S. district court. The U.S. court of appeals affirmed, and the Supreme Court of the United States granted certiorari. The Supreme Court held that the State of Virginia had ample probable cause, but that the seriousness of the intrusion into D's body (general anesthetic required and extensive surgical probing, risk of infection, etc.), must be balanced against the State's need for the evidence. The Court found that there was no compelling need for the bullet as additional evidence, and ruled that the surgical procedure, in light of these facts, would be unreasonable under the Fourth Amendment.

------------------------------------- **Notes** -------------------------------------

(3) THE MURDER SCENE EXCEPTION

Although exigent circumstances excuse the warrant requirement in many situations, at some time the exigency ends and the warrant requirement reasserts itself. This point is illustrated in the case of *Mincey v. Arizona*, briefed below.

CASE BRIEF

Mincey v. Arizona, 98 S. Ct. 2408 (1978)

Majority opinion: Stewart. Concurring: Marshall, joined by Brennan. Dissenting (in part) Rehnquist.

FACTS: After arranging a heroin "buy" with D earlier in the day, H, an undercover narcotics officer, returned to D's apartment accompanied by nine other plainclothes officers and a deputy county attorney. Upon H's entering the apartment a gun battle occurred which resulted in the serious wounding of D and the ultimate death of H. Several other persons were in the apartment, at least two of whom were also wounded. Emergency assistance was immediately requested; pursuant to a departmental directive, the narcotics officers made no further investigation (because they had been involved in the incident), but merely guarded the premises and the suspects. Within ten minutes homicide detectives arrived and took charge of the investigation. The search of the apartment lasted four days, during which time the entire apartment was photographed, diagrammed, and closely examined. Every item in the apartment was closely examined and inventoried and hundreds of objects were seized. No search warrant was ever obtained.

D's pretrial motion to suppress was denied. Much of the evidence introduced against D at trial (he was convicted of murder, assault, and three counts of narcotics offenses) was the product of the four-day search of his apartment. On appeal the Supreme Court of Arizona reaffirmed previous decisions in which it had held, in effect, that the warrant requirement is subject to a "murder scene" exception:

> We hold a reasonable, warrantless search of the scene of a homicide—or of a serious personal injury with likelihood of death where there is reason to suspect foul play—does not violate the Fourth Amendment to the United States Constitution where the law enforcement officers were legally on the premises in the first instance....For the search to be reasonable, the purpose must be limited to determining the circumstances of death and the scope must not exceed that purpose. The search must also begin within a reasonable period following the time when the officials first learn of the murder (or potential murder).

The Supreme Court of Arizona reversed the murder and assault convictions on state-law grounds, but it affirmed the narcotics convictions.

ISSUE: Was the warrantless search of D's apartment under the circumstances of this case constitutionally permissible?

DECISION: No; reversed as to narcotics convictions (the state court's murder and assault reversals on state law grounds were not reviewable by the Supreme Court of the United States).

REASONS: The Fourth Amendment prohibits all unreasonable searches and seizures. Searches conducted outside the judicial process, without prior approval of a judge, are unreasonable *unless* they fall within the few specifically established and well-delineated exceptions. The Supreme Court of Arizona did not hold that this search fell within any of these established exceptions, but instead recognized an additional exception. The exceptions to the warrant requirement which might have applied in this case include (1) search incident to lawful arrest, as in *Chimel v. California*, 89 S. Ct. 2034 (1969); (2) exigent circumstances, as in *Warden v. Hayden*, 87 S. Ct. 1642 (1967); (3) the plain view doctrine, as in *Coolidge v. New Hampshire*, 91 S. Ct. 2022 (1971); and (4) consent to search, as in *Schneckloth v. Bustamonte*, 93 S. Ct. 2041 (1973).

First, the state says that the search did not violate any constitutionally protected right of privacy because D forfeited any reasonable expectation of privacy in his apartment by shooting the police officer. A similar waiver argument was recently rejected in *Michigan v. Tyler*, 98 S. Ct. 1942 (1978). Such reasoning would impermissibly convict the suspect even before the evidence against him was gathered. On the other hand, the state argues that since D's privacy had already been invaded by the police entry for the purpose of arresting him, the additional intrusion caused by the search was constitutionally irrelevant. But this claim cannot stand in light of the extensive nature of the search. The very argument that D had a lessened right of privacy in his entire house because of the entry to arrest him was rejected in *Chimel v. California*, cited above.

Secondly, the state claims that the search was a justifiable response to an emergency situation demanding immediate action. The police have a right to respond to emergency situations. The need to protect or preserve life or avoid serious injury is justification for what otherwise would be illegal; and the police may seize evidence in plain view after such an emergency entry. But a warrantless search must be "strictly circumscribed by the exigencies which justify its initiation." This extensive, four-day search was not justified by any emergency threatening life or limb. Everybody in the apartment had been located before the homicide officers arrived and began their search.

Third, the state points to the vital public interest in prompt investigation of the extemely serious crime of murder. But the public interest is comparable in the investigation of other serious felonies, and no consideration relevant to the Fourth Amendment suggests that there would be any point of rational limitation of such a doctrine.

The mere fact that law enforcement may be made more efficient cannot by itself justify disregard of the Fourth Amendment. Criminal investigation would certainly be simplified if warrants were unnecessary, but the Fourth Amendment reflects the view of those who wrote the Bill of Rights in order that the privacy of a person's home and property would not be totally sacrificed in the name of simplified criminal law enforcement. For this reason warrants are normally required to search a person's home or his person unless the exigencies of the situation make the needs of law enforcement so compelling that the warrantless search is objectively reasonable under the Fourth Amendment.

Except for the fact that the offense was a homicide, there were no exigent circumstances in this case. There was no indication that evidence would be lost, destroyed or removed during the time required to obtain a search warrant. In fact, the police guard of the scene minimized this possibility. There is no suggestion that a search warrant could not easily have been obtained. The seriousness of the crime itself does not create exigent circumstances of the kind that under the Fourth Amendment justify a warrantless search.

Finally, the state argues that the "murder scene exception" is constitutionally permissible because it is narrowly confined under prior decisions of the Arizona supreme court. But these "guidelines" allow little protection, as is evidenced by the extensive search here found proper by the Arizona court. These "guidelines" confer unbridled discretion upon the investigator to interpret such terms as "reasonable search."

The point of the Fourth Amendment which often is not grasped by zealous officers, is not that it denies law enforcement the support of the usual inferences which reasonable men draw from evidence. Its protection consists in requiring that those inferences be drawn by a neutral and detached magistrate instead of being judged by the officer engaged in the often competitive enterprise of ferreting out crime.

The "murder scene exception" created by Arizona supreme court is inconsistent with the Fourth and Fourteenth Amendments. The extensive and warrantless search of D's apartment was not constitutionally permissible simply because a homicide had recently occurred.

RULE: When the police are called to the scene of a reported homicide in a dwelling, a warrantless entry is privileged because of the exigency of the situation involving the possibility of preserving or protecting human life. A prompt warrantless search of the dwelling for other victims or for the assailant is also privileged. Evidence of crime found in plain view during this prompt search is subject to seizure. But once the crime scene is secured and the exigent circumstances are past, no further detailed and exhaustive search of the area may be made unless a search warrant is first obtained. The mere fact that the crime being investigated is homicide does not constitute a further exception to the warrant requirement of the Fourth Amendment.

Concurring and dissenting opinions omitted.

------------------------------------- **Notes** -------------------------------------

Sample Questions

If too much time unnecessarily elapses, what began as a proper and lawful temporary detention of a person or his property based on reasonable suspicion, can ripen into an unlawful detention or arrest because full probable cause is lacking.   T   F.

If the police stop a motor vehicle under the authority of the *Carroll* rule exception to the warrant requirement and conduct a search of the vehicle:
A. only the passenger compartment of the vehicle may be searched.
B. any part of the vehicle may be searched, including closed containers, which logically could conceal the item or items that the police have probable cause to believe is in the vehicle.
C. only the trunk may be searched.
D. any part of the vehicle may be searched, but if evidence or contraband is found, it may not be seized until a warrant is obtained.
E. the vehicle can only be searched with the consent of the driver.

If the police make a valid entry of a private home under "exigent circumstances", and they discover items in plain view that they have probable cause to believe are subject to seizure:
A. they may seize the items, but only if they had probable cause to believe they were present before the entry was made.
B. they may seize the items, but only if they are "inadvertently" discovered and no warrant could have been previously obtained because of a prior lack of probable cause.
C. they may seize the items only if they have a logical connection to the purpose for which the exigent circumstances entry was made.
D. they may not seize the items without first obtaining a proper search warrant.
E. they may not seize the items with or without a search warrant.

In the case of an arrest for drunken driving, the suspected presence of alcohol in the blood of the driver presents an "exigent circumstance" because the body chemistry is causing the evidence to disappear and there is only a limited time in which the evidence may be seized.   T   F.

Under the "privacy" concept of search and seizure, the only items which are subject to seizure by the police are weapons, instrumentalities of crime, fruits of criminal activity and contraband.   T   F.

The taking of a blood sample by a physician or other qualified person for use as evidence in a drunk driving case at the request of the police violates Fourteenth Amendment Due Process of Law if done without a search warrant or without the consent of the person from whom the sample is taken.   T   F.

The Fifth Amendment privilege against compulsory self-incrimination:
A. concerns only evidence of a testimonial or communicative nature.
B. is violated by the taking of involuntary blood samples.
C. is violated by causing a suspect in a lineup to speak for the purpose of demonstrating the sound of his voice.
D. is violated when a person is subpoenaed before a grand jury for the purpose of giving a handwriting sample.
E. does not apply to the states through the Fourteenth Amendment.

(D) Plain view and inventory

A general rule is that when a police officer is in a place he has a right to be, doing something he has a right to do, and he observes in plain view items he may lawfully seize, i.e., instrumentalities, fruits or evidence of crime or contraband, he may seize them without a warrant. In these cases there has been no search; it would be unreasonable to force the officer to ignore what he saw from a position in which he had every right to be. The law could require the item to be guarded until a warrant was obtained for its seizure, but this requirement would be entirely inconsistent with the rule that a warrantless arrest may be made for a crime committed in an officer's presence and with the rule that evidence of an unrelated crime may be seized when discovered in a place that the officer is privileged to search by a prior lawful intrusion. The courts are very sensitive, however, to situations in which plain view seizures may be subterfuges for otherwise impermissible searches. The seizure of "abandoned" evidence falls generally into this category of questionable seizures.

In *Texas v. Brown*, 103 S. Ct. 1535 (1983), the Supreme Court, in a plurality opinion, addressed the subject of plain view seizure. It held that, before a plain view seizure is justified: (1) there must be a prior valid intrusion on privacy (or the officer must properly be in a position from which he can view the area in question); (2) the incriminating evidence must be discovered "inadvertently"; and (3) the officer must have probable cause to believe that the item seized is evidence of criminal activity. In this case police officers were conducting a valid traffic check consistent with the guidelines of *Delaware v. Prouse*, 99 S. Ct. 1391 (1979). Brown's car was stopped shortly before midnight and the officer asked Brown, who was alone in the car, for his driver's license. As he shined his flashlight into the car's interior the officer saw Brown remove his right hand from his pants pocket and drop a green party balloon which was knotted about one-half inch from the tip onto the seat beside him. Brown then leaned over across the passenger seat and opened the glove compartment. Alerted by his knowledge that drugs are often packaged in balloons, the officer shifted his position to get a better view of the interior of the glove compartment and observed that it contained small plastic vials, a quantity of loose white powder and an open bag of party balloons. After rummaging briefly through the glove compartment, Brown told the officer that he had no driver's license with him. The officer then told Brown to get out of the car and stand at the rear, which he did. Picking the green balloon up from the car seat, the officer noticed that it seemed to contain a powdery substance in the tied-off portion. Brown was then arrested and his car was inventoried at the scene and a quantity of green leafy substance and milk sugar discovered. Lab tests proved the powder in the balloon to be heroin. Held: the traffic stop was a valid prior intrusion on privacy; the officer could properly view the car's interior, and the use of a flashlight did not constitute a "search"; the officer's previous experience that party balloons are sometimes used as containers for illegal drugs and his lawful view of the suspicious contents of the glove compartment gove him probable cause to believe that criminal activity was present; finally, there was no indication that the traffic stop was a pretext or subterfuge and therefore the discovery was "inadvertent" and the plain view seizure was lawful and proper.

CASE BRIEF
Arizona v. Hicks, 107 S. Ct. 1149 (1987)

Majority opinion: Scalia, joined by Brennan, White, Marshall, Blackmun and Stevens. Dissenting: Powell, Rehnquist and O'Connor.

FACTS: A bullet was fired through the floor of D's apartment, injuring a man in the apartment below. The police arrived and made a proper warrantless entry (justified by exigent circumstances) of D's apartment to search for the shooter, other victims, and weapons. Three weapons were found, including a sawed-off rifle, as well as a stocking-cap mask. One of the officers noticed some expensive stereo equipment that seemed "out of place" in the poorly-furnished apartment and he moved some of the equipment so he could read and record the serial numbers, suspecting it might be stolen. A call to police headquarters confirmed that some of the items had been taken in an armed robbery, and they were seized. Later a warrant was obtained and executed seizing other equipment taken in the same robbery. D was indicted for the robbery but the trial court granted his motion to suppress the evidence seized. The court of appeals affirmed the original entry holding that the obtaining of the serial numbers was an additional search unrelated to the exigent circumstances which justified the original entry, and was therefore in violation of the Fourth Amendment. Both the trial court and the court of appeals rejected the state's argument that the warrantless seizures were justified under the "plain view" doctrine of *Coolidge v. New Hampshire*, 91 S. Ct. 2022 (1971). The Arizona supreme court denied review and the Supreme Court of the United States granted the State's petition for certiorari.

ISSUE: When a police officer who is in a private dwelling by virtue of a valid warrantless entry observes an item in plain view that he suspects, without probable cause, is contraband or evidence of a crime, may he move it to reveal an identifying feature? Stated differently, does a warrantless search and seizure under the plain view doctrine require probable cause to believe the item seized is criminal evidence or contraband at the time it is first observed?

DECISION: Probable cause is required; Affirmed.

REASONS: The mere recording of the serial numbers was not a "seizure" because it did not interfere with D's possessory interests, but the moving of the equipment in order to observe the serial numbers was a "search" separate and apart from a search for the shooter, victims, or weapons. Merely observing something in plain view is not a search, but taking action unrelated to the objective of the authorized intrusion—even by moving an object a few inches, as occurred here—constitutes a search. The remaining question is whether it was a reasonable search under the Fourth Amendment.

The fact that the stereo equipment had nothing to do with the valid purpose of the exigent circumstances entry (to search for the shooter, victims and weapons) does not in itself make the officer's actions unreasonable. That lack of relationship always exists when a seizure must be validated under the plain view theory, because if the seizure is made for the purpose which justified the entry (in this case, shooter, victim, and weapons), it is not necessary to justify it under plain view.

It is well established, moreover, that under certain circumstances the police may seize evidence in plain view without a warrant: where the initial intrusion that brings the police within plain view of the evidence is supported (as in this case) by a recognized exception to the warrant requirement. It would be absurd to say that an item could be seized and taken from the premises but that it couldn't be moved for a closer examination. Therefore, the search here would be valid *if* the plain view doctrine justified the seizure. There is no doubt that, if the officer had probable cause to believe the stereo equipment was stolen when he first observed it, he could have moved it to reveal the serial numbers. But the state has admitted he had a suspicion not amounting to probable cause.

We hold that probable cause is required in order to justify a warrantless seizure under the plain view doctrine. The theory of the plain view doctrine extends to *non-public* places, such as a home (where warrantless searches and seizures are presumptively unreasonable), the longstanding authority to make warrantless seizures in *public places* of objects such as weapons and contraband. The practical justification for extending the plain view doctrine to non-public places is to spare the police inconvenience and the risk—to themselves and to the evidence—of leaving the scene to obtain a warrant when they have already made a valid intrusion of privacy for another purpose. But excusing the need for a warrant is entirely a different thing than permitting a lesser standard of cause for a search without a warrant than would be needed to obtain a warrant. There are situations in which seizures have been justified on less than probable cause—such as certain cases dealing with vehicles suspected of transporting aliens and temporary seizures of luggage at airports for "drug sniffing" dog examination, but no such special circumstances existed in this case.

The probable cause requirement applies to both searches and seizures. Therefore, probable cause must exist in a plain view situation before the officer is justified to search (in this case to move the equipment to inspect its serial numbers) or to seize evidence (in this case to remove it from the premises). To adopt a lesser standard for searches than is required for seizures would be to permit general exploratory searches from one object to another until something incriminating at last emerges.

We are unwilling to create a new category of "cursory inspection" as opposed to a "full-blown searches", for probable cause purposes. A "cursory inspection" (merely looking at what is already exposed to view without disturbing it) is not a search in the first place and does not even require reasonable suspicion. As to the question of what the officer *should have done* in this case—if he *had* probable cause at the time he observed the equipment—he did precisely what he should have done—but if he did *not* have probable cause then he should have followed up his suspicions by means other than a search. There is nothing new in the realization that the Constitution sometimes insulates the criminality of a few in order to protect the privacy of us all.

RULE: When a police officer is lawfully on private premises (with a warrant or circumstances excusing the need for one) and he inadvertently observes in plain view something which might be evidence or contraband unrelated to the initial purpose of his entry, he is not authorized to pick it up or move it to reveal hidden identifying features unless he has probable cause to believe it is seizable evidence or contraband. While the mere observation of something under such circumstances is not a search, the moving of it is a search and requires probable cause.

DISSENT: There should be a distinction between a minimally intrusive "cursory examination" which should be allowable on reasonable suspicion less than probable cause, and a "full-blown" search, which should require probable cause. While general searches must be guarded against, the majority's position that "a search is a search", and always requires probable cause, disregards a large number of cases recognizing the reasonable suspicion justification for cursory examinations; such a position deals a damaging blow to effective law enforcement. In any event, the facts of this case indicate that probable cause to believe the stereo equipment was stolen existed at the time it was moved to reveal the serial numbers.

Closely akin to the "plain view" doctrine is the police procedure of "inventory of contents" of an impounded vehicle. This is a proper procedure because it safeguards the interests of the property owner, helping to ensure that the valuables in the car will be returned to their rightful owner when the car is released; it also discourages false claims against the police for loss of property. This procedure must be routinely followed in every case of vehicle impoundment, however, lest it take on the appearance of subterfuge for an impermissible search. Strictly speaking, an inventory is not a search, because the purpose is not to discover incriminating evidence. But if such evidence is discovered during the course of the inventory, it may be seized and used as the basis of a criminal prosecution because it is not the product of unlawful police activity.

As previously indicated, some order is emerging in the law governing searches of closed containers. Closed containers found in an automobile stopped and searched pursuant to the rule in *Carroll v. United States*, 45 S. Ct. 280 (1925) can be searched without a warrant; see *United States v. Ross*, 102 S. Ct. 2157 (1982). Closed containers found in the passenger compartment of a motor vehicle stopped to arrest the driver or a passenger thereof may be searched as an incident to arrest, without a warrant; see *New York v. Belton*, 101 S. Ct. 2860 (1981). The inventory of closed containers found in the possession of a person under custodial arrest, as an incident to the "booking" procedure prior to incarceration, has been addressed in *Illinois v. Lafayette*, 103 S. Ct. 2605 (1983), briefed below in this subsection. In *Colorado v. Bertine*, 107 S. Ct. 738 (1987), the same reasoning was applied to the inspection of closed containers found in a motor vehicle pursuant to a routine inventory of contents.

TEXT OF CASE

Harris v. United States, 88 S. Ct. 992 (1968)

Majority opinion: Per curiam. Concurring: Douglas.

PER CURIAM.

Petitioner was charged with robbery under the District of Columbia Code. D.C. Code Ann. § 22-2901. At his trial in the United States District Court for the District of Columbia, petitioner moved to suppress an automobile registration card belonging to the robbery victim, which the Government sought to introduce in evidence. The trial court after hearing, ruled that the card was admissible. Petitioner was convicted of the crime charged and sentenced to imprisonment for a period of two to seven years. On appeal, a panel of the United States Court of Appeals for the District of Columbia Circuit reversed, holding that the card had been obtained by means of an unlawful search. The Government's petition for rehearing *en banc* was, however, granted, and the full Court of Appeals affirmed petitioner's conviction, with two judges dissenting. We granted certiorari to consider the problem presented under the Fourth Amendment. 386 U.S. 1003, 87 S. Ct. 1353, 19 L.Ed.2d 432 (1967). We affirm.

Petitioner's automobile had been seen leaving the site of the robbery. The car was traced and petitioner was arrested as he was entering it near his home. After a cursory search of the car, the arresting officer took petitioner to a police station. The police decided to impound the car as evidence, and a crane was called to tow it to the precinct. It reached the precinct about an hour and a quarter after petitioner. At this moment, the windows of the car were open and the door unlocked. It had begun to rain.

A regulation of the Metropolitan Police Department requires the officer who takes an impounded vehicle in charge to search the vehicle thoroughly, to remove all valuables from it, and to attach to the vehicle a property tag listing certain information about the circumstances of the impounding. Pursuant to this regulation, and without a warrant, the arresting officer proceeded to the lot to which petitioner's car had been towed, in order to search the vehicle, to place a property tag on it, to roll up the windows, and to lock the doors. The officer entered on the driver's side, searched the car, and tied a property tag on the steering wheel. Stepping out of the car, he rolled up an open window on one of the back doors. Proceeding to the front door on the passenger side, the officer opened the door in order to secure the window and door. He then saw the registration card, which lay face up on the metal stripping over which the door closes. The officer returned to the precinct, brought petitioner to the car, and confronted petitioner with the registration card. Petitioner disclaimed all knowlege of the card. The officer then seized the card and brought it into the precinct. Returning to the car, he searched the trunk, rolled up the windows, and locked the doors. The sole question for our consideration is whether the officer discovered the registration card by means of an illegal search. We hold that he did not. The admissibility of evidence found as a result of a search under the police regulation is not presented by this case. The precise and detailed findings of the District Court, accepted by the Court of Appeals, were to the effect that the discovery of the card was not the result of a search of the car, but of a measure taken to protect the car while it was in police custody. Nothing in the Fourth Amendment requires the police to obtain a warrant in these narrow circumstances.

Once the door had lawfully been opened, the registration card, with the name of the robbery victim on it, was plainly visible. It has long been settled that objects falling in the plain view of an officer who has a right to be in the position to have that view are subject to seizure and may be introduced in evidence. Ker v. State of California, 374 U.S. 23, 42-43, 83 S. Ct. 1623, 1634, 1635, 10 L.Ed.2d 726 (1963); United States v. Lee, 274 U.S. 559, 47 S. Ct. 746, 71 L.Ed. 1202 (1927); Hester v. United States, 265 U.S. 57, 44 S. Ct. 445, 68 L.Ed. 898 (1924)

Affirmed.

Mr. Justice MARSHALL took no part in the consideration or decision of this case.

Mr. Justice DOUGLAS, concurring.

Though Preston v. United States, 376 U.S. 364, 84 S. Ct. 881, 11 L.Ed.2d 777, is not mentioned in the Court's opinion, I assume it has survived because in the present case (1) the car was lawfully in police custody, and the police were responsible for protecting the car; (2) while engaged in the performance of their duty to protect the car, and not engaged in an inventory or other search of the car, they came across incriminating evidence.

CASE BRIEF

South Dakota v. Opperman, 96 S. Ct. 3092 (1976)

Majority opinion: Burger. Concurring: Powell. Dissenting: Marshall, joined by Brennan and Stewart.

FACTS: D's car was impounded by police after being ticketed twice for having been parked overtime in a restricted parking zone. At the city impound lot a police officer observed a watch on the car's dashboard and other items of personal property on the back seat and back floor. At the officer's direction the car was unlocked, and using a standard inventory form pursuant to standard police procedures the officer inventoried the contents of the car, including the contents of the glove compartment, which was unlocked. In the glove compartment there was a plastic bag of marijuana. All items of personal property, including the contraband, were taken to the police property room for safekeeping. D was subsequently arrested for possession of marijuana. He moved to suppress the evidence but this was denied and D was convicted. On appeal, the Supreme Court of South Dakota reversed, concluding that the evidence had been obtained in violation of the Fourth and Fourteenth Amendments.

ISSUE: Is a routine police inventory of contents of a lawfully impounded car in violation of the Fourth and Fourteenth Amendments?

DECISION: No; reversed.

REASONS: Although automobiles are "effects," and thus within the protection of the Fourth Amendment, they are clearly distinguishable from homes and offices. Warrantless examinations of automobiles have been upheld in circumstances where a search of a home or office would be improper. The primary reasons for the distinction are (1) the mobility of the automobile; and (2) a lesser expectation of privacy in an automobile than in one's home or office. Local police, in ensuring the public safety, are brought into frequent contact with automobiles, mostly for non-investigatory purposes such as registration and equipment inspection. The expectation of privacy is further diminished by the obviously public nature of automobile travel.

In the interest of public safety, and in carrying out their "care-taking" functions, police often take automobiles into custody. Examples are removal of wrecked vehicles from the highways and enforcement of parking regulations. The authority of the police to seize and remove from the streets vehicles impeding traffic or threatening public safety and convenience is beyond challenge.

When vehicles are impounded the police usually follow an inventory of contents procedure for three reasons: (1) to protect the owner's property while in police custody; (2) to protect the police against claims or disputes over lost or stolen property; and (3) to protect the police from potential danger.

Applying the Fourth Amendment standard of "reasonableness" the state courts have overwhelmingly concluded that, even if an inventory is characterized as a "search," the intrusion is constitutionally permissible. Likewise, the majority of federal courts of appeals have held the inventory to be a valid police procedure. The courts have recognized that standard inventories often include an examination of the glove compartment, which is a customary place for documents of ownership and registration as well as for the temporary storage of valuables.

In applying the reasonableness standard adopted by the framers of the Constitution, the Court has consistently sustained police intrusions into automobiles impounded or otherwise in lawful police custody where the process is aimed at securing or protecting the car and its contents.

Holdings in *Cooper v. California*, 87 S. Ct. 788 (1967); *Harris v. United States*, 88 S. Ct. 992 (1968); and *Cady v. Dombrowski*, 93 S. Ct. 2523 (1973), although not involving the precise situation presented here, point the way to the correct resolution of this case. The police here were indisputably engaged in a caretaking search of a lawfully impounded automobile. The owner was not present to make arrangements for the safekeeping of his belongings. The inventory was prompted by the presence in plain view of valuables in the car. There is no suggestion that the standard procedure, essentially like that followed by police throughout the country, was a pretext concealing an investigatory police motive. The conduct was not unreasonable under the Fourth Amendment. The marijuana inadvertently found, therefore, was admissible in evidence.

RULE: A standard police procedure to inventory the contents of lawfully impounded automobiles is, under the Fourth Amendment, a reasonable intrusion to safeguard the owner's property, to ensure the safety of the police and to protect against claims of lost or stolen property; evidence of crime found during such a standard inventory may be seized by the police and is admissible in a criminal case.

DISSENT: The majority has "watered down" the right ot privacy; an inventory is an unreasonable search without probable cause, exigent circumstances, consent of owner, or search warrant.

CASE BRIEF

Illinois v. Lafayette, 103 S. Ct. 2605 (1983)

Majority opinion: Burger. Concurring: Marshall, Brennan.

FACTS: Police, responding to a disturbance call from a local theater, arrested D for disturbing the peace, handcuffed him, and took him to a police station. D was carrying a purse-type shoulder bag. At the station the handcuffs were removed and D was taken to the booking room where he was ordered to empty his pockets and place the contents on the counter. D took a package of cigarettes from his shoulder bag and placed the bag on the counter. The arresting officer then removed the contents of the bag and found drugs inside a cigarette package. D was charged with a drug violation. At a pretrial suppression hearing the state argued that the search of the shoulder bag was an inventory, valid under *South Dakota v. Opperman*, 96 S. Ct. 3092 (1976). The officer testified that it was standard operating procedure to inventory everything in the possession of an arrested person as a part of the booking procedure. He testified that he was not seeking, and did not expect to find drugs or weapons, and that the shoulder bag was small enough that it could have been placed and sealed in another container for safekeeping, or it could have been put in a locker, unopened. After the suppression hearing, but before any ruling by the court, the state submitted a brief, arguing for the first time that the search was valid as a delayed search incident to the arrest. The trial court ordered the drugs suppressed.

On appeal, the appellate court affirmed, holding that the search was neither a valid search incident to arrest nor a valid inventory procedure. It distinguished *South Dakota v. Opperman* on the basis that there is greater privacy interest in a shoulder bag than in an automobile and that the state's legitimate interests could have been met in a less intrusive manner. The state supreme court denied discretionary review, and the Supreme Court of the United States granted certiorari.

ISSUE: Is it a reasonable (and constitutional) procedure for police to search the personal effects of a person under lawful custodial arrest as a part of a routine administrative procedure at a police stationhouse incident to booking and jailing a suspect?

DECISION: Yes; reversed.

REASONS: The justification for an inventory search such as that which occurred here does not rest on probable cause; hence, the absence of a warrant is immaterial to the reasonableness of the search. An inventory search is a well-defined exception to the warrant requirement (citing *South Dakota v. Opperman*). The Illinois courts relied on *United States v. Chadwick*, 97 S. Ct. 2476 (1977) and *Arkansas v. Sanders*, 99 S. Ct. 2586 (1979), but *Chadwick* held that probable cause is irrelevant in inventory searches.

The inventory search is an incidental administrative step following arrest and preceding incarceration; to determine its reasonableness, its intrusion on the arrestee's Fourth Amendment interests are balanced against its promotion of legitimate governmental interests (citing *Delaware v. Prouse*), 99 S. Ct. 1391 (1979).

Immediately upon arrest, an officer may lawfully search the person of an arrestee, and the area within his immediate control; citing *United States v. Robinson*, 94 S. Ct. 467 (1973) and *Chimel v. California*, 89 S. Ct. 2034 (1969). *Robinson* held that a search incident to a lawful custodial arrest based on probable cause needs no justification in addition to the lawful intrusion of the arrest itself, and that it is an exception to the warrant requirement and also "reasonable." These "incident to arrest" searches are based on the need to disarm and discover evidence, and to prevent escape.

If a person is taken to a police station after arrest, the custody of the arrest status is continued, but the factors justifying a search of the person and personal effects are somewhat different from those at the time and place of arrest. The governmental interests underlying a stationhouse search of the person and his possessions may in some circumstances be even greater than those supporting a search immediately after arrest; and consequently, the scope of the stationhouse search may vary from that made at time of arrest. Police conduct that would be impractical or unreasonable—or embarrassingly intrusive—on the street can more readily—and privately—be performed at the station. The interests supporting a search incident to arrest would hardly justify a "strip search" on the street—although the practical necessities of jail administration may require such a search in rare cases. It may be jail policy to take an arrestee's clothing from him and keep it in official custody substituting jail clothing (citing *United States v. Edwards*, 94 S. Ct. 1234 (1974)).

It is entirely proper and reasonable for police at the stationhouse to remove and inventory personal property found on, or in the possession of, an arrested person who is to be jailed. A whole range of governmental interests supports this procedure—prevention of theft by police or false claims to that effect; prevention of careless handling of the arrestee's property; prevention of injury to the arrestee or others with belts, knives, drugs or other items carried either openly or concealed. It is immaterial whether the police actually fear any particular package or container; the need to protect against such risks arises independent of subjective concerns. Finally, an inspection of the arrestee's personal possessions may aid in verifying his identity. In short, every consideration of orderly police administration, benefitting both police and the public, justifies the examination of D's shoulder bag.

Today's holding finds support in prior cases (citing *South Dakota v. Opperman*). The Illinois courts held that the inventory search in this case was unreasonable because the governmental and private interests could have been protected in a "less intrusive manner" (such as sealing the unopened bag in a plastic bag, box, or locker). The real question, however, is whether the Fourth Amendment *requires* such steps.

The reasonableness of any particular governmental activity does not necessarily turn on the existence of "less intrusive" alternatives (citing *Cady v. Dombrowski*, 93 S. Ct. 2523 (1973)). The fact that "less intrusive" means existed to accomplish a proper purpose does not, by itself, render a search unreasonable. We are not in a position to second-guess police departments as to what practical administrative methods will best deter theft, false claims, and security. We hold it is not "unreasonable" for police, as a part of a routine procedure incident to incarcerating an arrestee, to search any container or article in his possession, in accordance with established inventory procedures.

RULE: It is reasonable and constitutional for police to conduct a routine inventory search of all items and containers on, or in possession of, an arrested person as an incident to his incarceration. Such a search does not depend on the existence of probable cause, but is a valid adminstrative procedure serving the governmental and private interests of jail security and of preventing theft or false claims thereof.

CASE BRIEF

Colorado v. Bertine, 107 S. Ct. 738 (1987)

Majority opinion: Rehnquist. Concurring: White, Blackmun, Powell, Stevens, O'Connor and Scalia. Dissenting: Marshall and Brennan.

FACTS: D was arrested for D.W.I. and taken into custody. Before a tow truck arrived to take D's vehicle to an impoundment lot, police, following a routine department procedure, inventoried its contents. Controlled substances (drugs) were discovered in the vehicle in closed containers, along with large amounts of cash. D was charged with D.W.I. and with unlawful possession of drugs with intent to sell. Before trial, D moved to suppress the drugs as evidence on the theory that his Fourth Amendment rights had been violated. The trial court ruled that the arrest for D.W.I. was based on probable cause; the vehicle impoundment and inventory procedures were standard procedures for a proper purpose and did not violate D's rights; but it suppressed the evidence as having been seized in violation of the *Colorado state constitution*. The supreme court of Colorado, on appeal by the state, affirmed the trial court's suppression of the evidence, but based its rulings on the *Constitution of the United States*, holding, in effect, that *United States v. Chadwick* was controlling authority. The Supreme Court of the United States granted certiorari.

ISSUE: If evidence of criminal activity is discovered by the police in closed containers located in a vehicle during a routine "inventory of contents" of the vehicle prior to its being impounded, is the evidence admissible?

DECISION: Yes; judgment of supreme court of Colorado reversed.

REASONS: The inventory of contents procedure folowed here was a standard practice—a routine followed by the police in every case in which a vehicle is impounded. The purposes of such inventories are to protect the owner's property and to protect the police from subsequent claims of lost or stolen property and from dangerous instrumentalities. Inventories of the property contained in vehicles impounded by the police are administrative caretaking functions. They are not searches for evidence and are, therefore, not governed by the standards of probable cause or the warrant requirement of the Fourth Amendment. The cases of *South Dakota v. Opperman* and *Illinois v. Lafayette* indicated that inventory procedures such as the one in this case are well-defined exceptions to the warrant requirement. The cases of *United States v. Chadwick* and *Arkansas v. Sanders*, on the other hand, both concerned searches related to criminal conduct, and were, therefore, controlled by the probable cause standard and the warrant requirement.

The purposes served by inventory procedures are legitimate governmental interests. In the present case, as in *Opperman* and *Lafayette*, there was no showing that the police, who were following standardized procedures, acted in bad faith or for the sole purpose of investigation.

The Court rejects D's argument that a "less intrusive means" might have been followed than the opening of closed containers, or that they could have decided to park and lock the vehicle in a public place.

> Even if less intrusive means existed of protecting some particular types of property, it would be unreasonable to expect police officers in the everyday course of business to make fine and subtle distinctions in deciding which containers or items might be searched and which must be sealed as a unit.
>
> A single familiar standard is essential to guide police officers who have only limited time and expertise to reflect on and balance the social and individual interests involved in the specific circumstances they confront. (citing *Illinois v. Lafayette; New York v. Belton*).

The discretion exercised by the police in this case, relating to the feasibility and appropriateness of parking and locking a vehicle rather than impounding it, was guided by standardized criteria on the basis of something other than suspicion of evidence of criminal activity (for example, the risk of damage or vandalism, or the arrestee's intoxicated condition, which would have made his approval to park and lock the vehicle questionable).

RULE: When police follow a reasonable standardized and routine procedure which guides their decision to impound a vehicle and inventory its contents, to protect the property located therein and to protect them from claims of theft or negligent loss of property or from the presence of dangerous instrumentalities, their inadvertent discovery of evidence of crime in the vehicle or in closed containers therein does not violate the Fourth Amendment and evidence so found is admissible.

DISSENTING: Disagrees that facts show a "standardized" procedure in this case—feels that inventory was the result of unbridled police discretion of a kind disapproved in *Delaware v. Prouse*. Of the three justifications stated for the inventory, the availability of secure impoundment facilities eliminated the "protection against claims" justification, and no sane individual would inspect for booby traps by opening a closed container. Therefore the only plausible justification for inventory was to protect the owner's property. Here, D was arrested for a traffic offense and could have made arrangement for the temporary safekeeping of his property because it was unlikely he would remain in custody for more than a few hours. The governmental interests here were weaker than in *Opperman* but the intrusion on privacy was greater. *Lafayette* was a station-house case with different interests involved.

--------------------------------------- **Notes** ---------------------------------------

CASE BRIEF

Florida v. Wells, 110 S.CT. 1632 (1990)

Majority opinion: Rehnquist, C.J., joined by White, O'Connor, Scalia, and Kennedy, JJ. Concurring in judgment only; Brennan, Marshall, Blackmun, and Stevens, JJ.

FACTS: A state trooper stopped D for speeding, and, after detecting odor of alcoholic beverages on his breath, arrested D for DWI and took him to station for breathalyzer test. D was informed his car would be impounded and he gave permission for police to open the trunk. At the impoundment facility, an inventory of the contents of the car disclosed 2 marijuana cigarette butts, and a locked suitcase in the trunk. Under the trooper's direction, the suitcase was forcibly opened and a garbage bag of marijuana was found. D was charged with drug offense and he moved to suppress marijuana as having been seized in violation of Fourth Amendment. Motion was denied by trial court and D pleaded *nolo contendere*, but reserved right to appeal denial of his motion to suppress. The state District Court of Appeal held that the marijuana should have been suppressed, and the state Supreme Court affirmed, (on the basis that the police department involved in this case had *no policy* requiring the opening of closed containers during an impounded automobile inventory). The state Supreme Court further indicated that it interpreted *Colorado v. Bertine*, 107 S. Ct. 738 (1987) to require a policy that either *all* containers would be opened during such an inventory, or that *none* be opened, and that *no discretion* could be left to the police. The Supreme Court of the United States granted certiorari.

ISSUES: (1) Should a police department have a policy governing the opening of closed containers during impounded automobile inventories; and (2) If so, can the policy leave any discretion to the police officers involved?

DECISION: (1) There must be a department policy; (2) The policy need not be of the "all or nothing" type. Affirmed, (on basis that here, *no policy* existed).

REASONS: The *Bertine* opinion indicated that nothing in *South Dakota v. Opperman*, 96 S.Ct. 3092 (1976), or in *Illinois v. Lafayette*, 103 S.Ct. 2605 (1983) prohibits exercise of police discretion so long as discretion is exercised according to standard criteria and on the basis of something other than suspicion of evidence of criminal activity. (In other words, so long as the guidelines the police must follow in conducting inventories do not allow them to circumvent constitutional requirements regarding searches for evidence of crime.) An inventory must not become a ruse (or a subterfuge) for a general search to discover incriminating evidence. The policy should be so worded so as to produce an *inventory*. (our emphasis). But the policy need not be totally mechanical (all or nothing).

While an "all or nothing" policy would be constitutionally permissible, it is not constitutionally required. Purposes of inventories of the contents of impounded vehicles include: to protect the owner's property while in police custody; to insure against claims of lost, stolen, or vandalized property; and to guard the police from danger. With these purposes in mind, a policy allowing the opening of closed containers whose contents cannot be determined from examining the containers' exteriors would be constitutionally permissible. But in cases where no policy exists at all, leaving the total, unbridled discretion to the officer, evidence found by opening closed containers during an inventory must be suppressed.

RULE: Police departments must have policy regulating the inventory of contents of impounded vehicles and the policy should reflect the purposes of the inventory, which include protection of the owner's property while in police custody, insuring against claims of lost, stolen or vandalized property, and protection of the police from danger. The policy may allow discretion with regard to the opening of closed containers so long as the discretion is related to the purposes of a legitimate inventory and does not allow the inventory to become a subterfuge for a generalized search for evidence of crime.

CONCURRING; Concurring opinions agree with the *result* of the case — upholding the suppression of the evidence because of the lack of any policy controlling the opening of closed containers — but disagreed with the majority's attempt to define how much discretion could be allowed under such a policy.

------------------------------------ **Notes** ------------------------------------

(E) Stop and frisk and detentions on less than probable cause

(1) STOP AND FRISK

In the landmark case of *Terry v. Ohio* (briefed following), the Supreme Court held that in certain narrow circumstances police intrusion into a citizen's privacy may be justified and constitutionally reasonable even though probable cause for arrest is not present. In the heart of the opinion Mr. Chief Justice Warren stated:

> We merely hold today that where a police officer observes unusual conduct which leads him reasonably to conclude in light of his experience that criminal activity may be afoot and that the persons with whom he is dealing may be armed and presently dangerous; where in the course of investigating this behavior he identifies himself as a policeman and mades reasonable inquiries; and where nothing in the initial stages of the encounter serves to dispel his reasonable fear for his own or other's safety, he is entitled for the protection of himself and others in the area to conduct a carefully limited search of the outer clothing of such persons in an attempt to discover weapons which might be used to assault him. Such a search is a reasonable search under the Fourth Amendment, and any weapons seized may properly be introduced in evidence against the persons from whom they were taken.

CASE BRIEF
Terry v. Ohio, 88 S. Ct. 1868 (1968)

Majority opinion: Warren. Concurring: Black, White. Dissenting: Douglas.

FACTS: A police officer with thirty-nine years of experience observed with suspicion the activities of three men who seemed to be "casing" a store. When all three finally converged on the store entrance, the officer, suspecting a robbery was about to take place, identified himself and asked their names. When he got only a "mumbled" reply, he grabbed one subject, spun him around and placed him between himself and the other two, patted him down and discovered a pistol. He then ordered the three men into the store, where he conducted a "wall" search and found a pistol on one of the other men. All three were then taken to the police station and two were charged with carrying concealed weapons. D attempted to have the evidence suppressed, but the court held that the officer had a right to conduct the pat-down search for his own protection; the pistols were admitted in evidence against the defendants, who were convicted. D's conviction was affirmed by the Ohio courts.

ISSUE: Was a limited search for weapons constitutionally permissible under these circumstances?

DECISION: Yes; affirmed.

REASONS: The Fourth Amendment is applicable to these facts because the stop was a seizure, the pat-down was a search and both were more than petty indignities. The scope of a permissible search must be strictly tied to and justified by the circumstances which render its initiation permissible. The fact situation here could not be subject to the warrant requirement. To justify his conduct however, the officer must be acting on more than a "hunch." He must be able to point to specific and articulable facts which, taken together with rational inferences from those facts, warrant the intrusion. The test is: would the facts available to the officer at the moment of the seizure or the search "warrant a man of reasonable caution in the belief that the action taken was appropriate?" The governmental interest here is in effective crime prevention and detection. Under the facts here it would have been poor police work for the officer to have failed to investigate further. Once the right to stop and interrogate arises it would be unreasonable to require an officer to take unnecessary risks in the performance of his duties. If an officer is justified in believing that a subject may be armed and presently dangerous to himself or others it is reasonable that he be allowed to conduct a "carefully limited search" of the outer clothing of the suspect for the purpose of discovering weapons that may be used against him. This is not to be a general exploratory search for instrumentalities, fruits and evidence of crime, but a "self-protective" search. It does not follow that because an officer may lawfully arrest a person only when he is appraised of facts sufficient to warrant a belief that the person has committed or is committing a crime, the officer is equally unjustified, absent that kind of evidence, in making any intrusion short of an arrest. A perfectly reasonable apprehension of danger may arise long before the officer is possessed of adequate information to make an arrest on probable cause to believe a crime has been or is being committed. The original belief (even though short of probable cause) must be reasonable and there must be nothing to dispel this belief (such as answers to questions which rationally explain the suspicious activity) prior to the search. Blanket Fourth Amendment limitations are not hereby developed—these will have to be developed in the concrete factual circumstances of individual cases. As the action of the officer here was consistent with reasonableness, the evidence seized (the pistols) was admissible.

RULE: Where a police officer observes unusual conduct leading him reasonably to conclude in light of his experience that criminal activity may be afoot and that the person with whom he is dealing may be armed and presently dangerous; where in the course of investigating this conduct he identifies himself as a policeman and makes reasonable inquiries; and where nothing in the initial stages of the encounter serves to dispel his reasonable fear for his own or others' safety, he is entitled for the protection of himself and others in the area to conduct a carefully limited search of the outer clothing of such person in an attempt to discover weapons which may be used to assault him. Such a search is reasonable under the Fourth Amendment and weapons thereby seized are admissible in evidence.

CONCURRING: There is no need to ask questions; the answer may be a bullet. The right to frisk sprang from the right to force an encounter with D in order to prevent or investigate a crime.

Nothing in the Constitution prohibits a policeman from asking questions of persons on the street, but of course they need not answer. Brief restraint to ask pertinent questions is not prohibited.

DISSENTING: Excusing the age-old requirement of probable cause to justify the stop gives the police greater power than the magistrate and is a long step down the totalitarian path. Action such as this should be accomplished only by constitutional amendment.

CASE BRIEF

Sibron v. New York and Peters v. New York, 88 S. Ct. 1889 (1968)

Majority opinion: Warren. Concurring: Douglas. Dissenting in part: Black.

FACTS: *(Sibron):* A police officer observed D1 for eight hours continually, during which time D1 was in conversation with six or eight persons that the officer knew were drug addicts. He did not overhear any of the conversations or see anything pass between D1 and the addicts. Late in the evening D1 entered a restaurant where he spoke with three other known addicts and then sat down and ordered pie and coffee. As D1 was eating the officer approached him and told him to come outside. Once outside, the officer said to D1, "You know what I am after." In his complaint the officer said that D1 thrust his hand into his pocket, pulled out a tinfoil envelope and attempted to throw it on the ground, and that the officer seized it; but at the hearing on the motion to suppress the officer said that when D1 thrust his hand into his pocket, he (the officer) put his hand into the same pocket before D1 could withdraw the contents. The officer never seriously suggested that he was in fear of bodily harm or that his search of D1 was to discover weapons. The New York "stop and frisk" statute was never mentioned in the trial court. The trial judge ruled that the officer had probable cause for arrest and that the search was incidental thereto. D1 was convicted for narcotics possession and the New York courts upheld the conviction, the court of appeals indicating that the search was justified under the stop and frisk statute.

FACTS *(Peters)*: A police officer was at home in his apartment when he heard a noise at his door. He looked through the peephole in his door and saw two men tiptoeing out of an alcove and toward the stairway. The officer called the police station, dressed quickly and grabbed his service revolver. Returning to the peephole the officer observed the men still acting suspiciously, tip-toeing away from the alcove. The officer had lived in the same apartment building for twelve years and he didn't recognize either of the two men. When the officer opened his door and slammed it, with his revolver in his hand, the two men took off, running down the stairway. He chased them and caught D2 by the collar between the fourth and fifth floors. D2 explained that he had been visiting a girl friend but he declined to name her because, he said, she was married. The officer patted D2 down and felt a hard object in his pocket. (The officer testified at a hearing that it didn't feel like a gun but could have been a knife.) He removed the object from D2's pocket; it was an opaque envelope containing burglar's tools. D2 was tried and convicted. The New York courts upheld the conviction on the basis that the officer proceeded properly under the New York stop and frisk statute.

ISSUES: D1 and D2 claim that the New York stop and frisk statute is unconstitutional. The Supreme Court declines to decide that issue and says instead that the primary issue is the constitutionality of the officers' actions under the Fourth and Fourteenth Amendments.

DECISION: D1's conviction reversed; D2's conviction affirmed.

REASONS *(Sibron)*: Nothing resembling probable cause existed to arrest and search D1 until *after* the drugs were seized. A search incident to arrest may not precede the arrest and serve as part of its justification. Mere conversation by D1 with known addicts, in itself, does not constitute probable cause for arrest. It is clear from the officer's testimony that he was after a narcotics violator. He never did articulate any grounds for fear of his safety, which might have provided the only grounds for a "frisk" under the rule of *Terry v. Ohio*, 88 S. Ct. 1868 (1968). As a *Terry* situation simply did not exist here, and because there was no probable cause for arrest which might have justified an incidental search, the seizure and the accompanying search were unreasonable under the Fourth and Fourteenth Amendments, and the evidence should have been suppressed.

REASONS: *(Peters)*: The search in this case was justified as incident to a lawful arrest based on probable cause. A search incident to a lawful arrest is necessary for seizing weapons and other things which might be used to assault the officer or effect an escape, as well as for preventing the destruction of evidence of the crime.

RULE: In the absence of a *Terry*-type situation, a seizure and a search must be based on probable cause. A search incident to an arrest may not precede the arrest and serve as a part of its justification.

CONCURRING AND DISSENTING OPINIONS: It is not proper for the Supreme Court to overturn the lower state court's findings that the officer thrust his hand into D1's pocket as a matter of self-defense. If this was the purpose of the search, the drugs should be admissible.

The Court should not have ignored the New York stop and frisk statute but should have indicated the extent to which it was constitutional. In D2's case there was no probable cause for arrest; who wouldn't run if an armed man suddenly came out a door and slammed it loudly? It was a *Terry* situation justifying a "stop" for reasonable inquiry and a "frisk"; the hard object that reasonably felt like a weapon, but turned out to be burglary tools, should have been admissible on that basis.

In *United States v. Hensley*, 105 S. Ct. 675, (1985) the Supreme Court unanimously extended the rule of *Terry v. Ohio*, 88 S. Ct. 1868 (1968) to permit brief, warrantless stops, not only of persons reasonably suspected to be presently engaged in criminal activity, but also of those being sought for past crimes. From a "wanted" flier circulated by a neighboring police department, officers recognized the car of a suspect in an armed robbery which had occured a week earlier. They stopped him briefly for questioning and discovered firearms in the car. The Court of Appeals overturned the suspect's conviction on federal firearms charges, holding that, without probable cause or a warrant, the investigatory stop for a completed felony was improper. In reinstating the conviction the Supreme Court said that it had never established an "inflexible rule" prohibiting brief, warrantless detentions to investigate past crimes and that "if police have a reasonable suspicion, grounded in specific and articulable facts, that a person they encounter was involved in or is wanted in connection with a completed felony, then a Terry stop may be made to investigate that suspicion."

-------------------------------------- **Notes** --------------------------------------

(2) *TERRY* DISTINGUISHED FROM SEARCH INCIDENT TO ARREST

In *Sibron v. New York*, briefed above, the Supreme Court was careful to point out that the frisk permitted in *Terry v. Ohio*, 88 S. Ct. 1868 (1968) was justified upon a basis entirely different from a search for instrumentalities, fruits, evidence or contraband made incidental to an arrest. The *Terry* frisk is grounded only on considerations of the officer's safety and the safety of those in the immediate area, while the search of the person incident to a valid, probable cause arrest is justified by the need to seize weapons and other things which might be used to assault an officer or effect an escape, as well as by the need to prevent the destruction of evidence of the crime; *Preston v. United States*, 84 S. Ct. 881 (1964). The later cases of *United States v. Robinson*, 94 S. Ct. 467 (1973) and *Gustafson v. Florida*, 94 S. Ct. 488 (1973) (both briefed in § 4.15(A)(3) above), further refined the distinction between a search for evidence incidental to a custodial arrest and a *Terry* stop and frisk situation. These cases put an end to a line of reasoning which had been developing in the lower courts that the nature of the offense governed the extent of the search in a probable cause custodial arrest situation. In *Robinson* the Court stated:

> The former [search incident to arrest], although justified in part by the acknowledged necessity to protect the arresting officer from assault with a concealed weapon is also justified on other grounds, and can therefore involve a relatively extensive exploration of the person. A search for weapons in the absence of probable cause to arrest, however, must, like any other search, be strictly circumscribed by the exigencies which justify its initiation. Thus it must be limited to that which is necessary for the discovery of weapons which might be used to harm the officer or others nearby, and may realistically be characterized as something less than a "full" search even though it remains a serious intrusion.
>
> * * * An arrest is a wholly different type of intrusion upon the individual freedom from a limited search for weapons, and the interests each is designed to serve are likewise quite different. An arrest is the initial stage of a criminal prosecution. It is intended to vindicate society's interest in having its laws obeyed, and it is inevitably accompanied by future interference with the individual's freedom of movement, whether or not trial and conviction ultimately follows. The protective search for weapons, on the other hand, constitutes a brief though far from inconsiderable, intrusion upon the sanctity of the person.

-------------------------------------- **Notes** --------------------------------------

Sample Questions

A vehicle traveling on a public highway may be stopped and searched by the police without a warrant:
A. at any time, because of its mobility.
B. only in the daytime, but not at night.
C. only if the police have probable cause to believe that it contains items subject to seizure and the circumstances are such that there is no opportunity for the police to obtain a warrant.
D. because there is an "implied consent" to search a vehicle that is a condition of using the public highways.
E. only if the driver of the vehicle is a fugitive from justice.

When the motorist is stopped and temporarily detained as a suspect in a drunk driving case, this is a "critical stage" of a criminal proceeding requiring the immediate notification of counsel.   T   F.

When police receive a call to come to the scene of an apparent criminal homicide in a private dwelling:
A. the initial entry into the dwelling is privileged because of the exigency of the situation.
B. a prompt "protective sweep", or warrantless search to discover if other victims, or the assailant, may be present in the dwelling is also privileged.
C. once the crime scene is secured and the exigent circumstances are past, a search warrant should be obtained to conduct any further exhaustive searches of the dwelling.
D. because of the possibility that murder may have been committed, the Constitution of the United States recognizes what is know as a "murder scene exception" to any further requirement for a search warrant.
E. A, B, and C above.

Under the "plain view doctrine":
A. there is really no *search* if it is apparent that the item in plain view is subject to seizure.
B. there must have been a prior valid intrusion on privacy, or the officer must be in a place he has a right to be, and the officer must have probable cause to believe the item is subject to seizure before it can be seized.
C. in a plurality opinion, the Supreme Court of the United States held that such seizures are justified only if evidence is inadvertently discovered.
D. a flashlight may be used to illuminate a place when it is dark.
E. all of the above.

When a police officer is lawfully on private premises with a warrant or circumstances excusing the need for a warrant and he inadvertently sees in plain view something which might be evidence or contraband, which is unrelated to the initial purpose of his entry, he is not authorized to pick it up or move it to reveal hidden identifying features (such as serial numbers) unless he has probable cause to believe it is evidence of criminal activity, or contraband.   T   F.

The case of *Terry v. Ohio* gave rise to a whole series of later cases based on the concept that proper temporary detentions by the police could be justified on less than traditional probable cause for arrest.   T   F.

Under the case of *Terry v. Ohio,* the Supreme Court of the United States held that a *stop was* a seizure, and a *frisk was* a search, but under the circumstances of that case, they were *reasonable* under the Fourth Amendment.   T   F.

(3) *TERRY* RATIONALE EXTENDED

In *Adams v. Williams*, 92 S. Ct. 1921 (1972), the Supreme Court extended one step further the rationale of *Terry v. Ohio*, 88 S. Ct. 1868 (1968). In *Terry* and *Sibron* the fact situations dealt with conduct witnessed by the officer; the fact situation in *Adams* was somewhat different. In that case an informant, known by the officer, told him that an individual who was sitting in a nearby vehicle had narcotics in his possession and a gun in his waistband. The officer had no reason to disbelieve the informant; under Connecticut law it is an offense to give a false report of a crime. After radioing for assistance the officer approached the car of the suspect and tapped on the window, asking the occupant to open the door. Instead of opening the door the occupant, Williams, rolled down the window. Immediately, the officer reached into the car and removed a loaded revolver from Williams' waistband. The weapon was not visible to the officer from outside the car but he found it exactly where the informant had said it would be. An arrest was then made for the weapon violation and, incidental to that arrest, a search of Williams' person produced heroin. In upholding the officer's action as justifiable and proper, the Supreme Court noted that the informant was known to the officer and had given reliable information in the past. Also, as it has consistently done in these cases, the Court gave specific recognition to a law enforcement officer's right to take whatever reasonable action is necessary to protect his own and others' safety. This concept is carried even further in *Pennsylvania v. Mimms*, 98 S. Ct. 330 (1977), briefed below in this subsection. In *Mimms* the Court ruled that a police officer may, as an incident to a lawful traffic stop of a motorist for the purpose of issuing a traffic ticket, ask that the motorist get out of his car. (The stop was made because officers noticed an expired license plate.) In concluding that having the motorist get out of his car was reasonable police action under the Fourth and Fourteenth Amendments, the Court balanced the safety of the officer against the mere inconvenience to the motorist. These cases seem to be saying that while a non-articulable "gut" reaction will never justify the initial intrusion on privacy (the stop), an articulable observation indicating danger will justify the "frisk" once a valid stop has been made. Note that in *Delaware v. Prouse*, 99 S. Ct. 1391 (1979), the Supreme Court held that a traffic stop may not be made for the sole purpose of checking the motorist's driving license or registration. There must be an articulable reason for the initial stop; it cannot be made at the unbridled discretion of police officers.

CASE BRIEF
Pennsylvania v. Mimms, 98 S. Ct. 330 (1977)

Majority opinion: Per curiam. Dissenting: Marshall, Stevens, Brennan.

FACTS: Police officers on routine traffic patrol observed D driving an automobile with an expired license plate. They stopped D for the purpose of issuing a traffic summons. One of the officers approached D's car and asked him to step out of the car and show his driving license and registration certificate. When D got out of his car the officer noticed a bulge under his sport coat. Fearing that the bulge might be a weapon, the officer frisked D and discovered a loaded .38 caliber revolver. The other occupant of D's car was also frisked and he, too, was armed with a revolver. D was arrested, indicted, tried, and convicted of the offense of carrying a firearm without a license. D's motion to suppress the revolver as evidence was denied by the trial court.

The Supreme Court of Pennsylvania reversed D's conviction, holding that the revolver should have been suppressed because it was seized contrary to D's Fourth and Fourteenth Amendment rights. The court held that although the initial stop was lawful, the order for D to get out of his car was unreasonable because the officers could not point to "objective observable facts to support a suspicion that criminal activity was afoot or that the occupants of the vehicle posed a threat to police safety." Since this "unconstitutional intrusion" led directly to the observation of the bulge and the subsequent frisk, the revolver, according to the Supreme Court of Pennsylvania, was the fruit of an unconstitutional search and it should have been suppressed.

ISSUE: Following a routine traffic stop of a motorist for the purpose of issuing a traffic summons, is it reasonable under the Fourth and Fourteenth Amendments for the police officer to ask the violator to step out of his car in the absence of suspicion of criminal activity or conditions posing a threat to police safety?

DECISION: Yes, this is reasonable police conduct; reversed and remanded.

REASONS: The touchstone of an anlysis under the Fourth Amendment is always the "reasonableness in all the circumstances of the particular governmental invasion of a citizen's personal security" (citing *Terry v. Ohio*, 88 S. Ct. 1868 (1968)). Reasonableness depends on a balance between the public interest and the individual's right to personal security, free from arbitrary interference by law officers.

Here there is no question about the reasonableness of the initial stop of the car, because the officers observed expired license plates. So the only question deals with the order to get out of the car. This inquiry must focus not on the intrusion resulting from stopping the car or the later "frisk" but upon the incremental intrusion resulting from the order to get out of the car once it was lawfully stopped.

This was a precautionary measure to afford a degree of protection to the officer and it is justified on that ground. When a driver is out of the car, the possibility of his making unobserved movements is reduced and it is less likely that the officer will be the victim of a surprise assault.

Certainly it would be unreasonable to require that police officers take unnecessary risks in the performance of their duties. A 1963 study of police officer shootings indicates that approximately 30% of them occurred when an officer approached a suspect seated in an automobile. Not all of these assaults occurred when officers where issuing traffic tickets; nevertheless, stops for traffic violations do not necessarily involve less danger to officers than do other types of confrontations. Indeed, it appears that a significant percentage of police murders involve traffic stops.

Also to be considered is the exposure of the officer to danger from passing traffic while standing in the roadway on the driver's side. The officer may prudently prefer to ask the driver to step out of the vehicle and onto the shoulder of the road where inquiry may be pursued with less danger to both.

Against the interest in the personal safety of the police officer is balanced the intrusion into the driver's personal liberty occasioned not by the initial stop of the vehicle—which was admittedly justified—but by the order to get out of the car. This additional intrusion is minimal.

The initial stop being lawful, and the additionl intrusion of asking the driver to get out of his car being reasonable, the propriety of the frisk upon observing the bulge under the jacket was controlled by the *Terry* case, and was also justified. Under these circumstances any man of reasonable caution would likely have conducted the "pat-down" search for weapons.

RULE: A police officer may, as an incident to a lawful traffic stop of a motorist for the purpose of issuing a traffic ticket, ask that the motorist get out of his car. This action is reasonable under the Fourth and Fourteenth Amendments when the safety of the officer is balanced against the mere inconvenience to the motorist. Should the officer discover suspicious circumstances after the motorist gets out of his car, leading him reasonably to the fear for his safety, he may "frisk" the motorist, and if a weapon is discovered it will be admissible in evidence.

DISSENTING: The majority opinion (6-3) is an unreasonable extension of the *Terry* holding. The case should not have been decided without full argument and briefing, especially in view of the "mootness" of the issue (D had already served his sentence). This blanket rule might lead to more, rather than fewer, assaults on police officers.

The *Terry* "frisk" rationale was extended to the passenger compartment of an automobile in *Michigan v. Long*, 103 S. Ct. 3469 (1983). Police noticed defendant's erratic driving, which terminated when his car nosed into a ditch. They approched the rear of the car, where defendant was standing. He appeared to be under the influence of something, and only after repeated requests did he produce his driving license. When his automobile registration was also requested, defendant walked toward the open door of his car. The police followed and observed a large hunting knife on the floor of the car. Defendant was then stopped and frisked for weapons but none were found on his person. One officer then shined his flashlight into the car's interior and noticed something protruding from under the armrest in the front seat. Lifting the armrest, the officer discovered an open pouch containing what appeared to be marijuana. Defendant was then arrested for possession of marijuana. Upholding the "frisk" of the passenger compartment of the car under these circumstances, the Supreme Court balanced the safety of the officers against the limited intrusion on defendant's privacy. The Court noted that at the time the officers spotted the hunting knife, the defendant was not yet under arrest; had he been permitted to enter the car to obtain his vehicle registration, he would have had access to any weapons hidden therein.

In *United States v. Place*, 103 S. Ct. 2637 (1983), the Supreme Court extended the "stop" rationale of *Terry* to include luggage moving though a public airport when there is reasonable suspicion (short of probable cause) to believe that it contains illegal drugs. Justice O'Connor framed the issue presented to the court and the court's holding as follows:

> This case presents the issue whether the Fourth Amendment prohibits law enforcement authorities from temporarily detaining personal luggage for exposure to a trained narcotics detection dog on the basis of reasonable suspicion that the luggage contains narcotics. Given the enforcement problems associated with the detection of narcotics trafficking and the minimal intrusion that a properly limited detention would entail, we conclude that the Fourth Amendment does not prohibit such a detention.

In this case, agents at the Miami airport were aroused by the suspicious behavior of defendant; they talked to him, but decided not the seize his luggage because his plane was departing momentarily. After defendant departed for New York the agents discovered that the addresses on his luggage tags were fictitious. Their suspicions had been further aroused when defendant had told them he had recognized them as police before the conversation. This information was relayed to DEA agents in New York who approached defendant after his arrival and after he had claimed his luggage and called a limousine. His behavior was again suspicious; he told the agents that he had "spotted" them when he got off the plane and that the police in Miami had already searched his luggage at the airport. The agents responded that their information was to the contrary. The agents then requested defendant's identification, and he gave them a driver's license and his airline ticket receipt. They did not arrest him but informed him that they were going to take his luggage to a federal judge to obtain a search warrant and that he could go along if he wanted to. Defendant declined to accompany the agents but did obtain their phone number.

The agents then took the luggage to another airport where a trained narcotics dog reacted positively after sniffing one of the bags. The "sniff test" occurred approximately ninety minutes after the seizure of the luggage. Because it was late on Friday afternoon, the agents retained the luggage until Monday morning when, with a search warrant, they opened the suspect bag and found cocaine. Defendant was convicted but the court of appeals reversed, holding that while the *Terry* "stop" rationale justified the warrantless seizure of the luggage on less than probable cause, the period for which the luggage was retained exceeded the permissible limits of a *Terry* investigative stop. The Supreme Court agreed, ruling that, because of the ninety-minute delay, the privileged stop had ripened into a seizure without probable cause, in violation of the Fourth Amendment, and that the evidence should have been suppressed.

Although defendant's conviction was reversed, this case is very instructive in several important areas. First, while the "frisk" rationale of *Terry* continues to be limited to the issue of the personal safety of the officer and others in the immediate area, the "stop" rationale (which is actually investigative detention short of arrest, based on suspicion short of probable cause) can be justified in many instances by the exigencies of the situation. Second, the stop must be kept to the minimum possible under the circumstances; in this case, the agents should have arranged to have a narcotics-trained dog waiting at the airport at which defendant landed. Third, the use of a trained drug-sniffing dog *is not a search requiring probable cause* under the Fourth Amendment; it is only an investigative technique. It does not require luggage to be opened or its contents exposed to public view, and it can be accomplished quickly. Fourth, even though, as in this case, evidence is seized by virtue of a search warrant, if the probable cause (in this case, defendant's actions, the discrepancies in the address tags, defendant's statements, all supported by the positive "alert" of the drug-sniffing dog) was the product of an unreasonably intrusive *Terry* "stop," the evidence can still be suppressed. In other words, just as mere suspicion can ripen into probable cause, so probable cause can deteriorate into useless information if it was not obtained in a reasonable manner.

In *United States v. Sharpe*, 105 S. Ct. 1568 (1985), a federal drug agent in an ummarked car was following a pickup truck with a camper shell attached, traveling on a coastal road which was under surveillance for drug trafficking. The pickup appeared to be heavily loaded, its contents were obscured by a quilted material covering the camper shell windows. The truck was accompanied by a Pontiac automobile. The agent's suspicion caused him to ask the highway patrol to make an investigative stop of the vehicles. When the marked state highway patrol car caught up with the procession, the pickup and the Pontiac turned off the main highway onto a campground road. The agent and trooper followed, and eventually the road looped back to the highway, where the agent asked the trooper to signal both vehicles to stop. Only the Pontiac pulled to the side of the road, the pickup continued, followed by the trooper. The agent asked for identification from the driver of the Pontiac and was handed a Georgia driving license (later determined to have been issued to someone else). The agent was unable to contact the trooper by radio. Meanwhile, the trooper had stopped the pickup and was out of his patrol car questioning its driver. When told he would have to wait until a DEA agent arrived, the pickup driver became nervous, said he wanted to leave, and asked the trooper to return his driver's license. The trooper told him he was not free to leave at that time. After securing the assistance of local police to stay with the Pontiac and its occupants, the DEA agent arrived at the pickup truck about 15 minutes after it had been stopped. D, the pickup driver, refused to give the agent permission to search the truck. After observing by standing on the rear bumper that the truck was loaded to capacity, and after detecting the odor of marijuana, the agent, without permission, took the keys from the ignition and opened the pickup's camper shell. It contained a large number of burlap-wrapped bales, similar to bales of marijuana the agent had encountered in other investigations. The defendants were arrested, tried and convicted in federal district court, but the convictions were reversed by the U.S. court of appeals on the ground that the 15 to 20-minute detention of the pickup truck and its driver until the DEA agent arrived had transformed an initially proper investigative detention into an improper arrest without probable cause. The Supreme Court granted certiorari and reversed (reinstating the conviction). The Court's analysis was twofold: (1) whether the officer's action was justified in the beginning (whether there were articulable facts which justified the initial stop); and (2) whether it was reasonably related in scope (length of the stop) to the circumstances which justified the stop in the first place. The court found that the record abundantly supported the initial investigative stop, and that defendant by not pulling over when first ordered to do so by the trooper himself transformed what could have been a delay of only a few minutes into a longer period of time. The Court held that the agent was not responsible for any *unnecessarily* prolonged detention; that, during the detention, he proceeded by the means which under the circumstances, were most likely to quickly confirm or dispel his suspicion. Therefore, even though D was detained for 15 to 20 minutes after an investigative stop based on less than probable cause, the delay was not unnecessary under these facts, and therefore, not an unreasonable seizure under the Fourth Amendment.

This case clearly indicates that no set time limit can apply to all temporary detentions short of arrest, and that a reasonable time must be determined from the particular facts of each case.

When police make a lawful entry into a private residence to serve an arrest warrant, and they conduct a "protective sweep" to safeguard themselves against possible attack by others who might be present in the house, must they have a warrant, or probable cause to believe that others who are dangerous are present before the protective sweep is lawful? In *Maryland v. Buie*, 110 S.Ct. 1093 (1990), the Supreme Court held that neither an additional warrant, or probable cause is necessary, and that the lesser standard of "reasonable belief based on specific and articulable facts" is enough. In so holding, the Court resorted to the same "balancing test" to determine reasonableness that it had used in *Terry v. Ohio*, 88 S.Ct. 1868, and *Michigan v. Long*, 103 S.Ct. 3469 (1983), two other cases in which the safety of the police was held to outweigh the intrusion on Fourth Amendment interests. (Officers should remember that like all other "exceptions" to usual Fourth Amendment requirements, a protective sweep should be limited to its intended protective purpose and the courts are very sensitive to claims of subterfuge for an otherwise improper search for evidence, but if conducted properly and with explainable reasonable belief, evidence found in plain view will be subject to seizure and will be admissible).

Sample Questions

An inventory of the contents of an impounded automobile:
A. is purely and simply a search for incriminating evidence.
B. is a proper police administrative procedure to protect against theft or false claims of theft.
C. should be a standard practice and the information should be noted on a standard form in every case in which a vehicle is impounded.
D. if done only occasionally may cause courts to be suspicious that it is a subterfuge to avoid obtaining a search warrant.
E. B, C, and D.

If evidence of criminal activity or contraband is discovered in the course of a regular, standard, inventory of contents of an impounded automobile:
A. it maybe seized and used as evidence in a criminal prosecution.
B. it may not be seized unless it pertains to the cause of the vehicle's impoundment.
C. it may not be seized unless a search warrant is obtained.
D. it may be seized and destroyed but it may not be used as evidence.
E. it must be returned to the owner of the vehicle despite the fact that it is evidence of crime or contraband.

The routine inventory of personal items of an arrestee during the booking procedure:
A. depends for its validity on the existence of probable cause to believe the personal items contain evidence or contraband.
B. is proper as a police administrative procedure for similar reasons justifying inventories of impounded vehicles.
C. may also be related to jail security.
D. does not depend on probable cause to believe the personal items may contain evidence or contraband.
E. B, C, and D above.

When the contents of an impounded vehicle are routinely inventoried, closed containers may be opened.   T   F.

Under the case of *Terry v. Ohio,* the Supreme Court of the United States held that a "stop" was not a "seizure", and a "frisk" was not a search.   T   F.

Police officers should think of the "stop and frisk" authority identified by *Terry v. Ohio* as purely a protective measure — a quick check for weapons — in circumstances when a reasonable officer would believe that criminal activity is afoot — and not as a search for evidence of crime.   T   F.

If a stop and frisk procedure reveals a hard object which feels like it might be a weapon, it can be removed for the protection of the officer, but if it turns out to be a metal container of illegal drugs:
A. it can be seized for possible use in a drug prosecution.
B. it must be returned to the owner.
C. if the officer reasonably believed he was seizing a weapon, the evidence may be admissible in a drug prosecution.
D. the evidence will not be admissible in any sort of prosecution.
E. A and C above.

(4) PROPER USE OF STOP AND FRISK AUTHORITY

Among civil libertarians, both before and after the decision in *Terry v. Ohio*, there was concern that the police would use this seemingly enlarged power to harass citizens—particularly minority groups. This concern was shared by Chief Justice Warren, who authored the opinion; *Terry v. Ohio*, 88 S. Ct. 1868, 1867 (1968). It was also shared by the chief proponent of stop and frisk, the not-for-profit educational organization known as Americans for Effective Law Enforcement, Inc., which published an editorial soon after the *Terry* decision; see 59 Journal of Criminal Law, Criminology & Police Science, No. 3, 333 (1968). In 1970 as an aid to law enforcement with cautionary overtones, the United States Department of Justice prepared a *Manual on the Law of Search and Seizure* containing a section entitled "Legal Guidelines: Stop and Frisk," which is reproduced below.

LEGAL GUIDELINES: STOP AND FRISK

[Excerpted from *Manual on the Law of Search and Seizure*. Chicago: National District Attorneys Association, 1974]

"The Legal Rules and Definitions"

[Quotations (B) through (E) are from *Terry v. Ohio*]

(A) "The Right of the People to be secure *in their persons*, houses, papers, and effects, against *unreasonable* searches and seizures shall not be violated..." (Fourth Amendment to the United States Constitution.)

(B) "What the Constitution forbids is *not* all searches and seizures, but *unreasonable* searches and seizures."

(C) "Ever since its inception, the *rule excluding evidence* seized in violation of the Fourth Amendment has been recognized as a principal mode of discouraging lawless *police* conduct."

(D) "...whenever a police officer accosts an individual and restrains his freedom to walk away, he has 'seized' that person."

(E) "...a careful exploration of the outer surfaces of a person's clothing all over his or her body in an attempt to find weapons is a 'search.'"

"We do not retreat from our holding that the police must, *whenever practicable*, obtain advance judicial approval of searches and seizures..."

The Tests

Seizure (Stop) - "would the facts available to the officer *at the moment of the seizure or the search* 'warrant a man of *reasonable caution* in the belief' that the action taken was appropriate?" [*Terry v. Ohio*, supra]

Search (Frisk) - "whether a reasonably prudent man in the circumstances would be warranted in the belief that his safety or that of others was in danger." [*Terry v. Ohio*, supra]

The Test Results

If your stop and frisk leads to the arrest and trial of the person stopped, your on-the-street actions may become critical. If you passed the Constitutional tests, the evidence you may have gathered will be admitted. However, if you failed the test, such evidence will be excluded regardless of the apparent guilt of the defendant. Therefore, you bear a heavy responsibility to the public to conduct yourself in a manner consistent with the rules as interpreted by the courts.

The following guidelines are designed to help you pass the test in the stop and frisk situation. Remember your contact with the public ranges from voluntary conversations to deadly confrontations. These Guidelines are directed *at only one level of police contact* with the public. They do not apply when you merely talk to a person so long as he knows he is free to go. They also do not apply when you are stopping an individual in order to make an arrest. *They apply only in situations where you do detain an individual but do not have probable cause to arrest him.* These Guidelines are not to be read technically, rather, read them with the common sense that must guide all "on the beat" action. Do not attempt to correct an illegal stop or frisk by retrospectivley trying to to fit them. Follow them initially before and during the stop and save yourself embarrassment later.

A. Guidelines for a Reasonable Stop.

1. You do *not* need probable cause to make a stop.
2. You do *not* have to rely only upon the visible activity of a person. You may consider the area, the time of day, the knowledge you may have of the person, hearsay information or any other facts you may have. *If all the circumstances indicate that you have reasonable grounds to suspect the individual has committed, is committing, or is about to commit a crime, stop him.* If you do not have such grounds, continue your surveillance until you do, or drop the matter as the circumstances warrant.
3. The Court is not interested in your gut reaction, they will want to know the *specific* facts and your inferences therefrom. Take note of them as soon as circumstances permit, while they're fresh in your mind. If you can't verbalize them, you probably didn't have grounds for a legal stop anyway even if your "hunch" was right. (In short, ask yourself why did I believe I could stop and/or frisk him.)
4. Before you make a stop, ask yourself this question: Can I get additional information to develop probable cause without endangering the public or losing the suspect? If the answer is yes, don't stop him; seek out the additional information.
5. Before you make a stop, announce your identity *and* your purpose for the stop unless the purpose of the stop is obvious.
6. Valid grounds for a stop do not license unreasonable police conduct. *Every phase of your investigation must be reasonable*. Therefore, do not detain an individual beyond the time absolutely necessary to clear up the situation. One way or another. (Normally, this should be a matter of minutes.) The sooner you excuse the person, the better, *if* there is no reason to detain him further. (i.e., If there is no probable cause for arrest.)
7. You may move the person a *short distance* to carry out your questioning, or to take other appropriate action. (i.e., You could require him to go to the car or nearest telephone, while you called to check a registration; you could not require him to go to the stationhouse.) But do not require any unnecessary movement or inconvenience.
8. You may use force to detain a rebellious person, but not deadly force, or force likely to cause serious injury unless necessary for your own protection. (i.e., You may handcuff him, lock him in a room, etc., but you may not shoot or seriously injure him.)
9. You may consider a refusal to answer a question as an element adding to probable cause only if the question posed is one which an innocent person would normally respond to.
10. You may consider an attempt to escape, as well as facts you learn during your investigation to determine whether you have probable cause for an arrest.
11. If, as a result of your questioning or as a result of your frisk, you decide to arrest, advise the person of his Constitutional rights before any further questioning.

B. Guidelines for a "Reasonable Frisk".

1. *There is only one valid ground for a pat down.* Do you think that your safety or the safety of those around you may be in danger? If the answer is no, don't search the person (unless and until you make an arrest at which time you may act to preserve evidence as well as protect yourself). If the answer is yes, then you may subject the person to a thorough pat down, but only over *exterior* clothing. (You may go inside a heavy overcoat if necessary for an effective pat down, but not inside the clothes normally worn inside a building, such as a jacket or sweater.)
2. A valid stop does not, standing alone, justify a frisk. You must perceive danger to yourself or others either because of the events leading to the stop, or the events which occur during the stop.
3. If you feel anything which could reasonably be a weapon, you may take it from him; if not, stop your frisk at once. (The Court may allow evidence other than weapons, but *only if* such evidence was taken with the reasonable belief that it was a weapon.)
4. Unless your stop meets the test of reasonableness, the frisk is no good even if you passed the test as to the frisk itself. (i.e., If you had no grounds to stop him, the fact that you have reason to believe he is armed during the stop won't help. Evidence so obtained (even if it is a weapon) will be excluded by the Court.)
5. Do not take any item from the individual other than the items you believed to be a weapon upon your pat down. In other words, if you feel a soft object which may be heroin, leave it alone.
6. Be sure to take note of the reasons you believed the item (weapon or not) was a weapon. The fact that you were right does not validate the search if your action was not, *in the first instance*, reasonable. (The same concept applies to why nonweapons are not excluded. The issue is the reasonableness of the search itself which centers around the belief that the person had a weapon.)
7. If your stop and/or frisk is valid, you may use any information you obtain to show probable cause and make an arrest. If you have probable cause, a search incident to an arrest is in order and the above guidelines become irrelevant. Follow arrest procedure.

Policy Considerations

1. Never stop an individual unless *you* feel there is no reasonable alternative to prevent a crime, *or learn of its existence*, or to prevent the person's escape from detection.
2. Cause as little disturbance as possible, especially in areas where public relations are bad (i.e., minority ghettos).
3. If possible, be polite and non-offensive. Remember, the person stopped has not been found guilty of a crime; nor do you have probable cause to arrest him. An innocent person will be less disturbed by your courteous stop and a criminal will be no less cooperative because of it.
4. Follow the Guidelines *when you act*, don't try to justify your actions after the fact. Review the following chart frequently.

Good luck.

Degree of Police Contact	Evidence Necessary to Justify the Police Action	The Degree of Force that May be Used	Warnings Necessary Prior to Questioning	Search that May Accompany the Police Action
1. The "Voluntary Conversation".	None.	None.	None.	None.
2. The "Stop".	Reasonable suspicion based on objective circumstances, that the person stopped has committed, is committing, or is about to commit a crime.	Reasonable force not likely to cause death or serious bodily injury.	If you decide to arrest, the warnings in the arrest situation become necessary.	A "pat down" for weapons when, and only when, the officer has reason to conclude that the suspect may be armed and dangerous.
3. The "Arrest".	Probable cause to believe that the suspect is guilty of a *specific* crime.	All force reasonably necessary to effect the arrest, including deadly force in cases involving serious felonies [subject to the ruling in *Tennessee v. Garner*, 105 S. Ct. 1694 (1985)].	Suspect has a right to remain silent; anything he says may be used against him; he has the right to the presence of an attorney; and if he cannot afford an attorney, one will be provided for him at government expense.	A full search, designed to protect the officer *and* to prevent the destruction of evidence of a crime.

------------------------------------ **Notes** ------------------------------------

(5) OTHER DETENTIONS ON LESS THAN PROBABLE CAUSE

While the holding in *Terry v. Ohio*, 88 S. Ct. 1868 (1968) created a minor sensation in criminal justice circles, there is evidence that the investigative stop aspect was known to the common law. In discussing the requirement of the Uniform Vehicle Code that a motorist must exhibit his driving license and registration on demand of a police officer, the Criminal Court, City of New York, Kings County, stated:

> This statutory provision of the Vehicle and Traffic Law is but declaratory of a long-established and recognized common law right of police officers on crime prevention patrol duty to briefly stop and inquire of citizens and/or criminals to ascertain that only legal activity is being carried on. The performance of such crime prevention patrol duty is one of the very reasons that metropolitan police forces were brought into being in the mid nineteenth century. This established a common law right of police crime prevention patrol duty has not been outlawed, as defense counsel insists.

People v. Russo, 239 N.Y.S.2d 374, 377 (1963).

Opinions which surrounded the old common law view of a police officer's authority to stop motorists on a mere "hunch" or "gut feeling" have since been modified by later holdings, such as *Delaware v. Prouse*, 99 S. Ct. 1391 (1979) (arbitrary stop of vehicle solely to check license and registration not permissible) and *Terry v. Ohio*, 88 S. Ct. 1868 (1968) (specific and articulable facts necessary to justify stop when there is not probable cause for arrest).

In *Lawrence v. United States*, 795 F.2d 1017 39 CrL 2212, (D.C. Ct. App. 1986 unpublished opinion), a police officer on patrol noticed two individuals late at night behaving suspiciously outside a liquor store. One entered and then left the liquor store without making a purchase and then both men walked by the store twice. One was wearing army fatigue pants. The officer called the dispatcher for a description of two suspects in a robbery occurring earlier that evening, and learned that they also were wearing army fatigue pants. The officer then turned on his vehicle's emergency lights and sounded his horn. The two men immediately reacted, fleeing in opposite directions. Both were chased down, detained by police, and frisked for weapons. D was found to have a loaded revolver in his jacket pocket. He was tried and convicted of weapons offenses. On appeal, the D.C. court of appeals held that under these facts the flight from authority—particularly the "splitting up" and running in different directions—implies a consciousness of guilt which could be considered, along with all of the other circumstances, justification for investigative detention and frisk for weapons. The court noted that "splitting up" is a common tactic used by criminals to frustrate police.

What appeared to be "unusual conduct" to a highly-trained county narcotics officer with 18 months experience in the airport unit was held, in *Florida v. Rodriguez*, 105 S. Ct. 308 (1984), to justify investigative detention, questioning, and eventually a consent to search of luggage, which produced three bags of cocaine. When the three defendants left the airport ticket counter and took an escalator, one of them looked back and apparently realized they were being followed by two plain-clothes detectives. The three conversed in low tones, glancing nervously at the officers, and one of them said, "Let's get out of here" when they left the escalator. One of the defendants appeared to be running in place—as if he wanted to flee, but couldn't; he looked at one of the officers and uttered a vulgarity. The officers identified themselves and asked if they could talk to the defendants. When one was asked to display some I.D. and an airline ticket, he said he had neither, but a second defendant handed the officer a cash ticket with three names on it. In ensuing conversation two of the defendants at first gave the same last name, but one later changed his story and gave his correct name. At that point, the officers identified themselves as narcotics officers and asked consent to search the defendants' luggage. One said he didn't have a key, but when told by another that he should give consent to search, the first defendant handed the officer the key. The search revealed the drugs. One of the officers testified that until the cocaine was found, the three men were free to leave. He also testified that he did not advise any defendant that he could refuse consent to search the luggage. The Supreme Court in reversing the Florida court of appeals' ruling which upheld suppression of evidence, said that the initial contact, in which the officers simply asked the defendants to pause and talk with them, was the sort of "consensual encounter" that is not prohibited by the Fourth Amendment. Without deciding whether a "seizure" actually took place after the initial verbal contact, but before the search, the court held that such a seizure (investigative detention) was (or would have been) justified by "articulable suspicion."

CASE BRIEF
United States v. Sokolow, 109 S. Ct. 1581 (1989)

Majority Opinion: Rehnquist. Concurring: White, Blackmun, Stevens, O'Connor, Scalia, and Kennedy. Dissenting: Marshall, joined by Brennan.

FACTS: DEA agents stopped D and companion at Honolulu Airport upon his return from a round-trip to Miami. When they stopped him they knew:
(1) D had paid $2,100 for 2 round trip tickets from a large roll of $20 bills;
(2) D was using a name that did not match name under which his phone number was listed;
(3) D's destination had been Miami, a city known to be a source of illegal drugs;
(4) D had stayed in Miami for only 48 hours, though the round-trip flight takes 20 hours;
(5) D had appeared nervous during trip;
(6) D had not checked any of his luggage.

When the agents stopped D, he was in process of getting a cab. When asked to see his airline ticket and identification, D said he had neither; and his name was "Sokolow," but he was traveling under his mother's maiden name, "Kray." Agents took D to DEA airport office where luggage was examined by a drug-sniffing dog. When dog alerted to presence of drugs, D was arrested, advised of rights, but made no statement. Later search with a warrant revealed presence of illegal drugs. D's conviction was reversed by U.S. Court of Appeals on the basis that the agents did not have reasonable suspicion to justify the stop of D at the airport. The government appealed and the Supreme Court granted certiorari.

ISSUE: Was the information known to the agents at the time of the stop sufficient to justify a detention based on less than probable cause?

DECISION: Yes, detention was proper, Reversed.

REASONS: Test used by Court of Appeals in this case (dividing the facts into 2 categories of "ongoing criminal behavior," and "probabilistic" evidence), was not in keeping with our decision in *Terry v. Ohio*, 88 S. Ct. 1868 (1968), holding that police can stop and briefly detain persons for investigative purposes if they have reasonable suspicion supported by articulable facts that criminal activity "may be afoot" even if they lack probable cause for arrest. The concept of reasonable suspicion, like probable cause, is not "readily, or even usefully, reduced to a neat set of legal rules." (citing *Illinois v. Gates*, 103 S. Ct. 2317 (1983).

"Paying $2,100 in cash for two airplane tickets is out of the ordinary, and it is even more out of the ordinary to pay that sum from a roll of $20 bills containing nearly twice that amount of cash. Most business travelers, we feel confident, purchase airline tickets by credit card or check so as to have a record for tax or business purposes, and few vacationers carry with them thousands of dollars in $20 bills. We also think the agents had a reasonable ground to believe that respondent was traveling under an alias; the evidence was by no means conclusive, but it was sufficient to warrant consideration. While a trip from Honolulu to Miami, standing alone, is not a cause for any sort of suspicion, here there was more; surely few residents of Honolulu travel from that city for 20 hours to spend 48 hours in Miami during the month of July.

"Any one of these factors is not by itself proof of any illegal conduct and is quite consistent with innocent travel. But we think taken together they amount to reasonable suspicion." (Citing many cases).

The mere fact that the factors involved here also were consistent with one of the DEA's "drug courier profiles" does not affect our analysis. Courts sitting to determine the existence of reasonable suspicion (like probable cause), must require police to articulate the factors leading to that conclusion. We hold that the agents had a reasonable basis to suspect that D was transporting illegal drugs on the facts involved in this case.

RULE: A temporary investigative stop by police based on reasonable suspicion not amounting to probable cause for arrest is permissible under the Fourth Amendment. Reasonable suspicion, like probable cause, must be based on articulate facts. Even though these facts, considered individually, might be entirely consistent with innocent behavior, when considered collectively, they can amount to reasonable suspicion of criminal activity which will justify an investigative stop, or detention. Once such a stop is properly made, additional factors may be developed within a reasonable time, that will constitute probable cause for arrest.

(Dissenting Opinion omitted).

Similar reasoning to that used in *Illinois v. Gates*, 103 S.Ct. 2317 (1983) (See brief at Section 4.4.14(A)), was used by the Supreme Court in *Alabama v. White*, 110 S.Ct. 2412, (1190) to uphold an investigative detention in that case. Police received an anonymous telephone tip that D (not identified by name) would leave a particular apartment at a particular time in a specifically-described vehicle, and that she would proceed to a named motel and would be carrying cocaine. Police verified the tip by surveillance and by following D in the described car for four miles, the most direct route to the named motel, and stopped her car just short of the motel. While indicating that the anonymous tip, standing alone, would not have justified the stop, the Court held that the corroboration of surveillance and following to the identified destination was sufficient to support an investigative detention. Police advised D why she was stopped and she consented to a vehicle search and gave them the combination to a locked attache case in which marijuana was discovered. During a booking inventory, cocaine was discovered in D's purse.

Sample Questions

If a police officer makes a routine stop of an automobile for a traffic violation, he can, for his own safety, request that the motorist get out of his car.   T   F.

If a policeman stops an individual temporarily because he has a "gut" feeling that the person is involved in criminal activity, but he cannot give the court an "articulable" reason for the stop, any evidence of crime so discovered might be ruled inadmissible.   T   F.

"Articulable" reasons for a stop may include the area where the stop was made, the time of day, the actions of the individual, the officer's prior knowledge of the individual, hearsay about a planned crime, or any or all of these.   T   F.

The scope of the search involved in *Terry v. Ohio,* which was found by the Supreme Court of the United States not to violate the Constitution was:

A. a full body search.
B. a carefully limited exploration of the outer surfaces of the suspect's clothing all over his or her body in an attempt to find evidence of crime.
C. a carefully limited exploration of the outer surfaces of the suspect's clothing all over his or her body in an attempt to find weapons.
D. a strip search.
E. no search at all was involved in the *Terry* case.

Before a *Terry* stop is authorized, there must be reasonable grounds to suspect that a person has committed, is committing or is about to commit a crime.   T   F.

If, after a *Terry* stop is made, there is no reason to believe that the officer's or anybody else's safety may be in danger, no "frisk" should be made —unless, of course probable cause is developed for a custodial arrest in which case a full search would be authorized.   T   F.

Many civil libertarians feel that the stop and frisk authority recognized in the *Terry* case could be used by unscrupulous police to harass minorities.   T   F.

A momentary stop of a person on the street by a police officer only for the purpose of conversation is a "seizure" under the Fourth Amendment.   T   F.

The use of "drug courier profiles" by police as an aid in spotting drug violators has been specifically disapproved by the Supreme Court of the United States.   T   F.

In enforcing the driver license and motor vehicle registration laws the police may:

A. arbitrarily single out vehicles and stop them for the sole purpose of driver license inspection and registration checking.
B. stop a vehicle for an "articulable reason", and once the vehicle is stopped, ask to check license and registration.
C. set up traffic roadblocks on any part of a public highway at any time, and at the total discretion of the traffic patrolmen involved.
D. use deadly force to stop motor vehicles.
E. none of the above.

In the case of *Delaware v. Prouse,* (involving restrictions on stopping automobiles for the sole purpose of checking driver licenses and registrations), the Supreme Court expressed concern over the exercise of "standardless and unconstrained discretion" by police officers on patrol.   T   F.

(6) THE TRAFFIC ROADBLOCK

In 1979 the Supreme Court, in *Delaware v. Prouse*, 99 S. Ct. 1391 (1979), held that a police officer with traffic enforcement authority cannot arbitrarily single out an automobile and stop it for the sole purpose of determining whether the driver is properly licensed and whether the car is properly registered. In balancing the value of random spot checks of automobiles as a highway safety measure against the Fourth Amendment intrusion involved, the Court held that privacy interests must prevail. Noting that the usual method of enforcing traffic and vehicle safety regulations is by acting upon "observed violations," the Court concluded that random stops are of only marginal utility, and therefore not "reasonable" in a constitutional sense. The Court stated:

> The marginal contribution to roadway safety possibly resulting from a system of spot checks cannot justify subjecting every occupant of every vehicle on the roads to a seizure—limited in magnitude compared to other intrusions but nonetheless constitutionally cognizable—at the unbridled discretion of law-enforcement officials. To insist upon neither an appropriate factual basis for suspicion directed at a particular automobile nor upon some other substantial and objective standard or rule to govern the exercise of discretion "would invite intrusions upon constitutionally guaranteed rights based on nothing more substantial than inarticulate hunches..." *Terry v. Ohio*, [88 S. Ct. 1868 (1968)] *supra*, at 22 [1880]. By hypothesis, stopping apparently safe drivers is necessary only because of the danger presented by some drivers is not observable at the time of the stop. When there is not probable cause to believe that a driver is violating any one of the multitude of applicable traffic and equipment regulations—nor other articulable basis amounting to reasonable suspicion that the driver is unlicensed or his vehicle unregistered—we cannot conceive of any legitimate basis upon which a patrolman could decide that stopping a particular driver for a spot check would be more productive than stopping any other driver. This kind of standardless and unconstrained discretion is the evil the Court has discerned when in previous cases it has insisted that the discretion of the official in the field be circumscribed, at least to some extent.* * *
>
> An individual operating or travelling in an automobile does not lose all reasonable expectation of privacy simply because the automobile and its use are subject to government regulation. Automobile travel is a basic, pervasive, and often necessary mode of transportation to and from one's home, workplace, and leisure activities. Many people spend more hours each day travelling in cars than walking on the streets. Undoubtedly, many find a greater sense of security and privacy in travelling in an automobile than they do in exposing themselves by pedestrian or other modes of travel. Were the individual subject to unfettered governmental intrusion every time he entered an automobile, the security guaranteed by the Fourth Amendment would be seriously circumscribed. As *Terry v. Ohio, supra*, recognized, people are not shorn of all Fourth Amendment protection when they step from their homes onto the public sidewalks. Nor are they shorn of those interests when they step from the sidewalks into their automobiles. See *Adams v. Williams*, 407 U.S. 143, 146 [92 S. Ct. 1921, 1923] (1972).
>
> Accordingly, we hold that except in those situations in which there is at least articulable and reasonable suspicion that a motorist is unlicensed or that an automobile is not registered, or that either the vehicle or an occupant is otherwise subject to seizure for violation of law, stopping an automobile and detaining the driver in order to check his driver's license and the registration of the automobile are unreasonable under the Fourth Amendment. This holding does not preclude the State of Delaware or other States from develop-

ing methods for spot checks that involve less intrusion or that do not involve the unconstrained exercise of discretion. Questioning of all oncoming traffic at roadblock-type stops is one possible alternative. We hold only that persons in automobiles on public roadways may not for that reason alone have their travel and privacy interfered with at the unbridled discretion of police officers. The judgment below is affirmed.

-- **Notes** --

CASE BRIEF

Michigan State Police, Petitioners, v. Sitz, 110 S.Ct. 2481 (1990)

Majority opinion: Rehnquist, C.J., joined by White, O'Connor, Scalia, and Kenndy, JJ. Concurring in judgment: Blackmun, J. Dissenting: Brennan, Marshall, Stevens, JJ.

FACTS: Michigan State Police established sobriety checkpoint pilot program under guidelines of an advisory committee which recommended procedures on checkpoint operation, site selection, and publicity. Guidelines called for checkpoints to be at selected sites on state roads; all vehicles passing through were to be stopped and drivers briefly examined for signs of intoxication; if signs of intoxication were detected, motorists were to be directed to a point out of traffic flow where driver's license and vehicle registration would be checked and further sobriety tests conducted, if warranted; all other drivers to be allowed to proceed on their way. One checkpoint was conducted in cooperation with a sheriff's department. In one hour and fifteen minutes, 126 vehicles passed through, the average delay for each, about 25 seconds. Two drivers were detained for field testing, one of whom was arrested for DWI, in addition to a third driver who drove through without stopping, who was also arrested for DWI.

On the day before this checkpoint was held, plaintiffs, licensed drivers in Michigan, filed a lawsuit seeking declaratory judgment and injunction against being subjected to the checkpoint procedure. At pretrial stage, state police agreed to suspend further checkpoints pending outcome of the lawsuit. The trial court, which heard testimony on the "effectiveness" of sobriety checkpoints, held in favor of the plaintiffs, ruling that the procedure violated the Michigan Constitution and the Fourth Amendment. The Michigan Court of Appeals affirmed, but only on the basis of the Fourth Amendment. The Supreme Court of the United States granted certiorari.

ISSUE: Do police sobriety checkpoints, such as were involved in this case, which allow the initial stopping of motorists without individualized suspicion, violate the Fourth Amendment?

DECISION: No, case reversed and remanded.

REASONS: The "balancing test" used by the trial court to determine reasonableness in this case relied heavily on findings that sobriety checkpoints are generally ineffective in combatting DWI, and that the intrusion on individual liberties is substantial. The state Court of Appeals agreed. A checkpoint stop is a "seizure" because it is a "governmental termination of freedom of movement *through means intentionally applied*". The issue therefore, is the reasonableness of such a seizure. Here, we deal only with the *initial stop* of motorists passing through the checkpoint and the associated brief questioning and observation — we are *not* presented with issues concerning more extensive detention or investigation, which may require individualized suspicion.

No one can dispute the magnitude of the drunken driving problem or the states' interest in eradicating it, (citing statistics and previous recognition by the Court of the problem). On the other hand, the "objective" intrusion on individual motorists stopped briefly at sobriety checkpoints is slight, (citing previous approval of similar checkpoint procedures to detect illegal aliens in *United States v. Martinez-Fuerte*, 96 S.Ct. 3074 (1976)). While holding that the guidelines involved here did minimize discretion of officers at the checkpoints, the state courts found that the "subjective" intrusion was substantial because checkpoints can generate fear and surprise in motorists. But they misread our cases on "subjective instrusion" — the fear and surprise to be considered is not that of one who has been drinking, but the fear and surprise engendered in the law-abiding motorist by the nature of the stop. In *Martinez-Fuerte* we found the subjective fear generated by a checkpoint-type stop to be appreciably less than that generated by a roving-patrol stop. Checkpoints here are selected by guidelines, officers are in uniform, and every approaching motorist is stopped — constitutionally the same as in *Martinez-Fuerte*.

(As to the "effectiveness" of checkpoints, the Court indicates that nothing in the language of its previous cases was meant to transfer from politically accountable officials to the courts the decision of which among reasonable alternative law enforcement techniques is to be selected to combat a serious public safety problem).

Delaware v. Prouse, 99 S.Ct. 1391 (1979) disapproved random police stops involving standardless and unconstrained discretion for the purpose of apprehending unlicensed drivers and unsafe vehicles. (Not to be confused with stops made for an "articulable" — or explainable reason.) Here, the state's interest in combatting DWI, and the extent to which sobriety checkpoints can be said to advance that interest — (higher % of apprehensions than in the alien checkpoints), and the degree of intrusion on individual rights, weighs in favor of the checkpoints and they do not violate the Fourth Amendment.

RULE: Sobriety checkpoints established by guidelines which control their operation, site selection, and publicity, and which allow the initial brief stop of all motorists without individualized suspicion of DWI do not violate the Fourth Amendment.

DISSENTING: Effectiveness overvalued; citizen's rights undervalued; comparison with alien checkpoints inappropriate.

------------------------------------Notes------------------------------------

(F) Consent searches

(1) VOLUNTARINESS REQUIREMENT

The Supreme Court of the United States, in *Schneckloth v. Bustamonte* (briefed below), indicated that the Constitution of the United States does not require a police officer to advise a person *not in custody* of his Fourth Amendment rights prior to obtaining the person's consent to search. But this consent must be freely and voluntarily given; it must not be tainted by duress, fraud, intimidation or simple submission to the supremacy of the law, as represented by the police. Despite the holding in *Bustamonte* the surest way for the police to establish free and voluntary consent to search is through the use of a simple form which serves to advise the individual of his right to withhold consent to search and to insist on the authority of a search warrant. The use of such a form establishes not only consent, but *waiver* of a constitutional right of which the person has been advised, which is *more* than the Constitution of the United States requires.

FORM FOR CONSENT TO SEARCH
(Person Not in Custody)

_____
(date)

_____
(location)

I, _____, having been informed of my Fourth Amendment constitutional right not to have a search made of the premises (vehicle) herinafter mentioned without a search warrant and of my right to refuse to consent to such a search, hereby authorize:

_____, and _____

_____
(titles of officers)
to conduct a complete search of my premises located at _____

_____

These (officers) are authorized by me to take from my premises (vehicle) any letters, papers, materials or other property which they may desire.

This written permission is being given by me to the above named persons voluntarily and without threats or promises of any kind.

Witnesses: _____ (Signed) _____

_____

CASE BRIEF

Schneckloth v. Bustamonte, 93 S. Ct. 2041 (1973)

Majority opinion: Stewart. Concurring: Blackmun, Burger, Powell, Rehnquist; Dissenting: Douglas, Brennan, Marshall.

FACTS: D was a front seat passenger in an automobile stopped by the police at 2:40 a.m. for inadequate lights. There were five other persons in the car. When the driver could not produce a driver's license, the officer asked if any of the others could show identification. Only one of the passengers, A, produced a license, and he stated that the car belonged to his brother. After the six men had stepped from the car at the officer's request and after two other policemen had arrived, the officer asked A if he could search the car, and A replied, "Sure, go ahead." No one had been threatened with arrest and the attitude was very congenial. A actually helped in the search of the car by opening the trunk and the glove compartment. The police found three stolen checks under the left rear seat.

The trial judge denied a motion to suppress the checks as evidence and D was convicted. The California court of appeals affirmed the conviction, using as the test for voluntary consent to search the "totality of the circumstances." D sought habeas corpus in a federal district court, but it was denied. On appeal from this denial the U.S. Court of Appeals, Ninth Circuit reasoned that consent to search was a waiver of D's Fourth and Fourteenth Amendment rights and therefore the prosecution was obliged to show not only that the consent had been uncoerced, but also that consent had been given with an understanding that it could be freely and effectively withheld. Consent could not be found, the court held, solely from an absence of coercion and a verbal expression of assent. Because the district court had not determined that A had known that his consent could have been withheld and that he could have refused the vehicle search, the court of appeals vacated the order denying habeas corpus and remanded the case for further proceedings.

ISSUE: What must the prosecution prove to demonstrate that consent to search was voluntarily given? Must it prove D knew he had a right to refuse or is this just one factor in the totality of all the circumstances in the factual determination of voluntariness?

DECISION: Knowledge of right to refuse need not be proved; reversed.

REASONS: The Constitution requires the sacrifice of neither security nor liberty. While due process does not require the police to forego all questioning, neither does it give them the right to use any means to extract what they can from a suspect. The ultimate test is voluntariness: is the confession the product of essentially free and unconstrained choice? If so, it may be used against him. But if his will has been overborne and his capacity for self-determination critically impaired, then the use of his confession offends due process.

In determining whether D's will was overborne the court will assess the totality of all the surrounding circumstances—both the characteristics of the accused and the details of the interrogation. Factors which have been considered include the youth of the accused; his lack of education; low intelligence; lack of advice of constitutional rights; length of detention; repeated and prolonged questioning; and the use of physical punishment such as deprivation of food or sleep. Few if any cases turn on the presence or absence of a single controlling criterion, but instead reflect a careful scrutiny of all the surrounding circumstances. In none of the (non-custodial) confession cases was it held that the due process clause required the prosecution to prove that D knew he had a right to refuse the questions that were put to him.

In many situations in law enforcement, consent searches play an important role. As well as turning up evidence of crime when there had been no prior probable cause for arrest, such searches may also convince the police that no further investigation or inconvenience to suspects is justified.

Consent must involve no coercion by explicit or implicit means, or by implied threat or covert force. Therefore consent searches must be subjected to careful scrutiny, but there is no reason to depart from the traditional definition of "voluntariness."

To require the prosecution to prove D's knowledge of his right to refuse a consent search would be to impose a nearly impossible burden. The requirement of advice of rights before a consent search has been almost universally repudiated by both federal and state courts because these searches normally are used as a standard investigatory technique by the police in non-custodial situations. These are a far cry from the structured atmosphere of a trial where, assisted by counsel if he chooses, a defendant is informed of his trial rights. Consent search situations are also far removed from the custodial interrogation situation of *Miranda v. Arizona*, 86 S. Ct. 1602 (1966). The Court in *Miranda* expressly stated that its decision was not intended to hamper the traditional function of police officers in investigating crime. Neither prior cases nor the traditional definition of "voluntariness" requires proof of knowledge of a right to refuse as the *sine qua non* of an effective consent to search.

As to the argument that consent to search is actually a *waiver of rights*, the requirement of "knowing" and "intelligent" *waiver* normally involves a right constitutionally guaranteed to protect a fair trial and the reliability of the truth-determining process, such as right to counsel at trial or upon a guilty plea; right to confrontation; to a jury trial; to a speedy trial; and the right against double jeopardy. These rights are far different from those protected by the Fourth Amendment, which protects the security of one's privacy against arbitrary intrusion by the police, and which deals with physical evidence, which is not subject to unreliability or coercion.

> Nor can it even be said that a search, as opposed to an eventual trial, is somehow "unfair" if a person consents to a search. While the Fourth and Fourteenth Amendments limit the circumstances under which the police can conduct a search, there is nothing constitutionally suspect in a person's voluntarily allowing a search. The actual conduct of the search may be precisely the same as if the police had obtained a warrant. And, unlike those constitutional guarantees that protect a defendant at trial, it cannot be said every reasonable presumption ought to be indulged against voluntary relinquishment.

Citizens should be encouraged to aid in the apprehension of criminals; the community has a real interest in encouraging consent, for the resulting search may yield necessary evidence for the solution and prosecution of crime—evidence that may ensure that a wholly innocent person is not wrongly charged. A "waiver" approach to consent searches would also be inconsistent with prior decisions that have approved "third party consents" (room mate, spouse, etc.).

The *Miranda* rationale does not carry over to the consent search situation because in *Miranda* (in-custody interrogation) there were involved inherently compelling pressures not present in the usual consent search situation. In this case there was no evidence of any coercive police conduct either from the nature of the police questioning or the environment in which it took place. Nor does the failure to require the government to establish knowledge as a prerequisite to a valid consent relegate the Fourth Amendment to the special province of the "sophisticated, v. knowledgeable and the privileged." The traditional definition of voluntariness has always taken into account evidence of minimum schooling, low intelligence and lack of effective warnings.

RULE: "Our decision today is a narrow one. We hold only that when the subject of a search is not in custody and the State attempts to justify a search on the basis of his consent, the Fourth and Fourteenth Amendments require that it demonstrate that the consent was in fact voluntarily given, and not the result of duress or coercion, express or implied. Voluntariness is a question of fact to be determined from all the circumstances, and while the subject's knowledge of a right to refuse is a factor to be taken into account, the prosecution is not required to demonstrate such knowledge as a prerequisite to establishing voluntary consent."

DISSENTING: "Consent" should be taken to mean "knowing choice." Experience under *Miranda* shows that in the area of in-custody interrogations the warning requirement has not disrupted effective law enforcement, and a warning requirement in consent search situations would not be an impossible burden. The majority opinion will allow the police to continue to capitalize on the ignorance of citizens so as to accomplish by subterfuge what they could not achieve by relying only on the knowing relinquishment of constitutional rights."

The Fourth Amendment prohibits *unreasonable* searches and seizures, but it does not require that agents of the government be *factually* correct in every case, so long as their actions are *reasonable*. This principle has been previously recognized in *Maryland v. Garrison*, 107 S.Ct. 1013 (1987) [brief at sec. 4.14(C)] (wrong apartment entered because of factually incorrect description in search warrant due to reasonable mistake); and in *Hill v. California*, 91 S.Ct. 1106 (1971) (search incident to arrest OK although wrong person arrested because of reasonable mistake). In *Illinois v. Rodriguez*, 1105 S.Ct. 2793, (1990), police, with the reasonable belief that they were accompanying F, a victim of a severe beating, to her apartment and that she had the authority to consent to a warrantless entry made after she unlocked the door with her key, discovered drugs and drug paraphernalia in plain view. The evidence was seized and D, who lived in the apartment was arrested and charged with possession of controlled substances with intent to deliver. In fact, F did not live in the apartment at the time of the consensual entry, but had vacated it several weeks earlier and had moved some of her possessions out; she did not pay rent, nor was her name on the lease; she was not allowed to invite others there on her own; nor did she have access to the apartment when D was away. The trial court granted D's motion to suppress the evidence, concluding that F was merely an "infrequent visitor" without common authority over the apartment and had no authority to consent to the police entry. The court further rejected the prosecution's position that there was no Fourth Amendment violation if the police *reasonably believed* F had authority to consent at the time of the entry. The state appellate court affirmed and the state supreme court denied appeal. The Supreme Court of the United States reversed the state appellate court, holding that the reasonableness of the police entry must be judged not by whether the police were actually correct, but by an objective standard of, "would the facts available to the officer at the moment . . warrant a man of reasonable caution in the belief that the consenting party had authority over the premises?"

CONSENT SEARCHES — "WORKING THE BUSES"

A police technique which has emerged as a part of the "war on drugs" is "working the buses". Uniformed and armed police officers board buses at regular stops, explain to the seated passengers that they are looking for unlawful drugs and that anyone may refuse consent to search. Then, without any probable cause to arrest or even reasonable suspicion concerning any particular passenger, they proceed to ask permission to examine tickets and identification, and in some cases, consent to search luggage.

In one Florida case, a passenger gave permission for police to search his luggage, and cocaine was found and the passenger was prosecuted for drug trafficking. The trial court denied the D's motion to suppress the evidence and the D pleaded guilty but reserved the right to appeal, however the trial court made no finding as to whether a seizure had occurred. On appeal, the Florida District Court of Appeal affirmed the trial court's decision, but certified the case to the Florida Supreme Court which reversed D's conviction, holding that when uniformed police board buses as they did in this case, and question passengers without any explainable suspicion, and thereby obtain consent to search luggage, an "impermissible seizure" occurs. The State of Florida petitioned for review, which was granted by the Supreme Court of the United States in *Florida v. Bostick*, 111 S.Ct. 2382 (1991).

The Supreme Court of the United States disagreed with the Supreme Court of Florida (which had held that an impermissible seizure occurred because a "reasonable bus passenger" would not have felt "free to leave" under these circumstances because there is no place to go on a bus, and the bus was about to depart). The U.S. Supreme Court reasoned that this sense of confinement was not caused by the police, but by the decision to travel by bus, and that the issue, properly stated, was whether a reasonable innocent bus passenger, under all the circumstances and in light of the conduct of the police, *would have felt free to decline the officer's requests, or otherwise terminate the encounter.*

In its discussion of the case, the Court noted that a seizure does not occur just because a police officer approaches an individual and asks a few questions; mere police questioning, by itself, does not constitute a seizure. [It should be remembered that while police have the right to question persons not in custody, those persons have an equal right not to answer.] The Court also noted that it has consistently held that neither refusal by a citizen to answer police questions or to give voluntary consent to a warrantless search, by itself, amounts to minimal objective justification for a detention or a seizure.

The U.S. Supreme Court also emphasized that the state courts had found that the police had not threatened D and that they had advised him that he need not consent to a search of his luggage.

The Court quoted from *Terry v. Ohio*, 88 S.Ct. 1868 (1968):

> "Obviously, not all personal intercourse between policemen and citizens involves 'seizures' of persons. Only when the officer, by means of physical force or show of authority, has in some way restrained the liberty of a citizen may we conclude that a 'seizure' has occurred."

Had this encounter taken place *before* D boarded the bus, or in the lobby of the bus station, the Court observed, it would not have been considered a seizure. Only the fact that it took place *on a bus* seemed to influence the Florida Supreme Court, rather than viewing the encounter from the totality of all the circumstances involved, including the conduct of the police. The Court stated:

> "As we have explained, no seizure occurs when police ask questions of an individual, ask to examine the individual's identification, and request consent

to search his or her luggage — so long as the officers do not convey a message that compliance with their requests is required. Here, the facts recited by the Florida Supreme Court indicate that the officers did not point guns at Bostick or otherwise threaten him and that they specifically advised Bostick that he could refuse consent.

Because of the lack of findings as to seizure by the trial court in the case, the case was remanded back to the state courts to evaluate the seizure question under the correct legal standard.

[Perhaps crucial to the holding in this case, in addition to the minimal show of authority and lack of any threats by police, is the fact that they *warned D that he did not have to consent to a search of his luggage*. This would seem to remove the case from the category of a "consent search", and make it a *waiver of 4th Amendment rights case,* as discussed in *Schneckloth v. Bustamonte,* 93 S.Ct. 2041 (1973). It is also interesting that the Court in discussing the "reasonable person" test, (the objective test to determine if a seizure occurred), stated, ". . . the 'reasonable person' test presupposes an *innocent* person." (citing *Florida v. Royer,* 103 S.Ct. 1319 (1983)). ". . . the potential intrusiveness of the officer's conduct must be judged from the viewpoint of an innocent person in [his] position . . ."].

-- **Notes** --

(2) MIRANDA WAIVER NOT CONSENT TO SEARCH

It should be remembered that the *Miranda* waiver form concerns the Fifth Amendment right to remain silent and the Sixth Amendment right to counsel; it will not serve as a consent to search form, which concerns Fourth Amendment rights.

However, obtaining the valid consent of a person in *custody* to search a vehicle or other place may involve a *Miranda* waiver as well as consent to search. If a suspect who is in custody has not waived his right to remain silent and to have counsel present before being questioned by the police, it is doubtful that he can give a valid consent to search. Under these circumstances a waiver of *Miranda* rights may be required before consent to search is obtained, and any form used to document such consent should indicate that this necessary step was taken. See *Sims v. State*, 413 N.E.2d 556 (Ind. 1980).

FORM FOR CONSENT TO SEARCH
(person in custody)

_____
(date)

_____
(location)

I, _____, having been advised of my right to remain silent; that anything I say may be used against me; that I have the right to talk to a lawyer before talking to the police and to have a lawyer present while answering police questions; and that if I cannot afford to hire a lawyer to represent me that a lawyer will be provided to me at government expense; and having understood and waived these rights and having agreed to talk to the police without a lawyer being present now consent and grant permission to

_____ and _____ of the

_____ police department to conduct a complete search of my premises located at _____

_____ or my vehicle _____

_____.
(description of vehicle)

These officers are authorized by me to take from my premises (or vehicle) any letters, papers, materials or other property. This written waiver and consent is being given by me to the above-named police officers voluntarily and without threats or promises of any kind.

_____
(Signature of person consenting)

_____
(Witness)

Sample Questions

The approach that the Supreme Court of the United States has taken in the consent cases and in the waiver cases seems to indicate that they are more concerned about the "unfairness potential" of evidence which may be coerced (confessions and admissions), than about evidence that can be examined and analyzed by both parties (physical evidence), and this is consistent with the fact that the Fifth Amendment right against compulsory self-incrimination applies only to testimonial or communicative acts and not to physical evidence.   T   F.

Administrative inspections, such as building inspections for compliance with fire and safety codes are totally unaffected by the requirements to the Fourth Amendment.   T   F.

The difference between "consent" (as in consent search), and "waiver" (as in waiver of *Miranda* rights), is:

A. consent is determined by the test for voluntariness (absence of duress or coercion under all of the circumstances) — an act of free and unconstrained choice.
B. waiver is the intentional giving up of a *known* right or privilege, and requires a showing that the individual *knew what he was giving up.*
C. waiver normally involves a right constitutionally guaranteed to protect a fair trial and the reliability of the truth-determining process.
D. all of the above are true.
E. none of the above are true: there is no significant difference between consent and waiver.

Administrative inspections are governed by the Fourth Amendment but a different level of probable cause may be involved.   T   F.

If an occupant objects to a routine, non-emergency entry of his residence for a health or safety inspection, it may be necessary for the inspector to obtain a suitably restricted search warrant to make the entry and inspection.   T   F.

If a suspect is in the custody of the police and the police want to secure from him a consent to search his home or automobile:

A. The *Miranda* warning and waiver procedure may be necessary preliminary to obtaining valid consent, becasue if he has not waived his right of silence and right to counsel the validity of this consent to search would be questionable.
B. a written consent form should be used in most cases to document the consent to search.
C. they need no consent because the suspect is in custody.
D. they should go ahead and conduct the searched and if they find incriminating evidence, secure a search warrant after the fact.
E. A and B above.

Although school children are protected by the Fourth Amendement against unreasonable searches and seizures, the standard that is applied to the seach of a student by a teacher is usually not as strict as that applied against law enforcement officers because a balance must be struck between the student's legitimate expectation of privacy and the school's equally legitimate need to maintain an environment in which learning can take place.   T   F.

(3) SCOPE OF CONSENT TO SEARCH

CASE BRIEF

Florida v. Jimeno, 111 S.Ct. 1801 (1991)

Majority opinion: Rehnquist, joined by White, Blackmun, O'Connor, Scalia, Kennedy, and Souter. Dissenting: Marshall, Stevens.

FACTS: A police officer who had overheard D arranging what appeared to be a drug transaction over a public telephone, followed D's car and stopped him for the infraction of making a right turn at a red light without stopping. The officer advised D that he was being stopped for committing the traffic infraction but that he had reason to believe D was carrying drugs in his car. The officer asked D for permission to search the car, explaining that he did not have to consent to the search. D said he had nothing to hide, and gave permission to search the car. After two passengers got out of D's car, the officer saw a folded brown bag on the floorboard; he picked it up and opened it and found cocaine inside. D was charged with possession of drugs with intent to distribute and before trial D moved to suppress the evidence. The theory of his motion to suppress was that his consent to search the car did not extend to the folded paper bag on the floor.

The motion to suppress was granted by the trial court which found that D's mere consent to search the car did not include specific consent to open the bag. The Florida District Court of Appeal affirmed, as did the Supreme Court of Florida. The Supreme Court of the United States granted certiorari.

ISSUE: Can general consent to search a vehicle extend to closed containers found inside the vehicle?

DECISION: Yes, Reversed.

REASONS: The touchstone of the Fourth Amendment is reasonableness. It is reasonable for the police to conduct a search once they have been given consent to do so. The standard for measuring the scope of a suspect's consent is "objective reasonableness", or what would the typical reasonable person have understood by the exchange between the officer and the suspect? — Is it reasonable for an officer to consider a suspect's general consent to search his car to include consent to search a paper bag on the car's floor? We think that it is.

Here, after being informed by the officer that he was suspected of carrying drugs in his car, D gave his consent without placing any explicit limitations on the scope of the search. A reasonable person may be expected to know that drugs are generally carried in some form of container rather than being strewn across a trunk or floor of a car. The consent therefore, extended beyond the surfaces of the car's interior to the paper bag lying on the floor.

[The court then distinguishes the facts of this case from the facts of the case relied upon by the Supreme Court of Florida, and it indicates that a person consenting to a police search *may* specifically limit the scope of that search.].

There is a public interest in encouraging consent, as the resulting search may yield evidence for the solution and prosecution of crime and may insure that a wholly innocent person is not charged with a crime. (citing *Schneckloth v. Bustamonte*, 93 S.Ct. 2041 (1973)).

RULE: When a person, having been advised of what police are looking for — and that he does not have to consent to a warrantless search — nevertheless gives general consent for the police to conduct a warrantless search of his automobile, it is objectively reasonable for the police to open and look into containers that may contain the evidence or contraband they are looking for.

DISSENTING: Dissenting opinion omitted.

Sample Questions

If the police have probable cause to believe that a mobile vehicle, not under their control, contains items subject to seizure, and there is no opportunity to obtain a search warrant:

A. they may stop the vehicle, but must detain it until a search warrant can be obtained before they can lawfully search it.
B. they may not lawfully stop the vehicle.
C. they may stop the vehicle, but may search only the passenger compartment, excluding closed containers and the trunk.
D. they may stop the vehicle and conduct a warrantless search of any part of it, or any container in it, open or closed, that could contain the items which are the subject of the search.
E. they may stop the vehicle, but must obtain consent to search the vehicle from the driver before search will be lawful.

A part of the test that the Supreme Court has developed to determine whether a "seizure" has taken place is whether a reasonable person, under the circumstances, would have felt "free to leave", or, as in the *Bostick* case, "free to decline the officer's requests [for a consent search], or otherwise terminate the encounter". What sort of "reasonable person" does the Court have in mind?

A. a reasonable guilty person who has something to hide.
B. a reasonable innocent person.
C. a reasonable person with prior experience with the police.
D. a reasonable person with no prior experience with the police.
E. the Court has not elaborated on what it meant by a "reasonable person".

If, before conducting a warrantless consent search, the officer advises the person that he does not have to consent to the search, is a court more or less likely to find the consent valid?

A. more likely, if there are no other indications of coercion.
B. less likely.
C. the court could treat the consent as a *waiver of rights,* as in a *Miranda* situation.
D. A and C are both correct.
E. the advice should not even be considered by the court in determining voluntariness of consent.

A uniformed police officer approaches people seated in a bus station lobby, at random, with no reasonable suspicion or probable cause to believe any of them are law violators, and asks to check identification, bus tickets, and to search luggage, after explaining to each person that consent need not be granted. The first six people approached consent to the identification and bus ticket inspection and also allow the officer to search their luggage, with no evidence of criminality being found. The seventh person approached, a male in his early twenties, refuses to speak to the officer, gets up from his seat, picks up his luggage, and walks away. Does the officer have either reasonable suspicion or probable cause to take any further action? Explain your answer.

(G) Administrative inspections and searches based on less than traditional probable cause

The Supreme Court of the United States has recognized that certain searches or inspections may lawfully be carried out without warrant and/or without meeting the traditional probable cause standard generally required by the Fourth Amendment in criminal cases. Situations to which these exceptions apply include those in which there are "special needs" which make warrant and probable cause requirements impracticable and those in which there is a reduced expectation of privacy. Examples include work-related searches of desks and offices of government employees *(O'Connor v. Ortega*, 107 S. Ct. 1492 (1987)); searches of student property by school officials *(New Jersey v. T.L.O.*, 105 S. Ct. 733 (1985)); searches by government investigators in certain circumstances pursuant to a regulatory scheme meeting reasonable legislative or administrative standards *(Camara v. Municipal Court*, 97 S. Ct. 1727 (1967)); *See v. City of Seattle*, 87 S. Ct. 1737 (1967)); *(New York v. Burger*, 107 S. Ct. 2636 (1987)); *Donovan v. Dewey*, 101 S. Ct. 2534 (1981)); *(United States v. Biswell*, 92 S. Ct. 1593 (1972)).

In *Camara v. Municipal Court of San Francisco*, 87 S. Ct. 1727, the Court held that, if an occupant objects to entry for a routine, non-emergency inspection of his apartment to inspect for compliance with health and safety codes, the Constitution requires that a search warrant be obtained before entry is made. The occupant is not criminally liable for refusing warrantless entry. But the Court also held that the facts and circumstances supporting the issuance of such a warrant need not meet traditional criminal probable cause criteria, but could be based on reasonable legislative or administrative regulations (for example a health and safety code provision requiring the periodic inspection, along with statements that the time for the inspection has arrived and that the inspector has been refused entry). If the legislative and administrative regulations reflect a valid public interest, the Court held, there would be probable cause to issue a suitably restricted search warrant for this non-criminal purpose. Moreover, in an emergency situation involving the public health and safety, the Court noted that even a warrantless entry and inspection might be reasonable.

In a companion case, *See v. City of Seattle*, 87 S. Ct. 1737 (1967), the Supreme Court held that the same general principles apply to administrative inspections of commercial buildings.

In *New Jersey v. T.L.O.*, 105 S. Ct. 733 (1985), the Supreme Court held that while the Fourth Amendment's application to the states through the Fourteenth Amendment provides protection against unreasonable searches of school children by teachers, the standard of reasonableness is not as strict in a school setting as it is in a typical criminal investigation involving the police. A balance in school search cases must be struck between the students' legitimate expectation of privacy and the school's equally legitimate need to maintain an environment in which learning can take place. Teachers are not required to obtain search warrants to search students under their supervision, nor is the strict criminal law standard of probable cause required. A search is justified if there are reasonable grounds for believing that it will turn up evidence of a student's violation of either a law or the rules of the school. If the scope of the search is reasonably related to its objectives, and is not excessively intrusive in light of the age and sex of the student and the nature of the suspected violation, it is reasonable under the Fourth and Fourteenth Amendments. In this case, T.L.O., a 14-year-old high school freshman, was caught smoking in a school lavatory by a teacher. This was a violation of school rules. When taken to the principal's office,

T.L.O. denied that she had been smoking, or that she smoked at all. The assistant vice principal demanded to see her purse, and in searching it found cigarettes and rolling papers commonly associated with marijuana use. This prompted a more thorough search, which revealed marijuana, a pipe, plastic bags, money, and other evidence implicating T.L.O. in marijuana dealing. The Supreme Court found that no Fourth Amendment rights were violated under these facts.

In the case of *Griffin v. Wisconsin*, 107 S. Ct. 3164 (1987), the Supreme Court took note of the relationship between a probationer and his probation officer and the special needs involved in administering a successful probation system. Probation is an alternative to incarceration after a person has been adjudged guilty of a criminal act. It is a liberty conditioned on the probationer's following restrictions which are designed both to rehabilitate the probationer and to protect the community. The supervision of the probationer by his probation officer is a special need resulting in an encroachment on privacy that would not be constitutional if applied to the public at large.

In this case, a police officer told a probation supervisor that he had information that there were, or might be, guns in a probationer's (Griffin's) apartment. Two probation officers, accompanied by three plainclothes policemen, went to the apartment. Griffin answered the door; the officers identified themselves and told him they were going to search his home. The two probation officers then conducted a warrantless search and found a handgun. The police officers did not participate in the search. Griffin was tried and convicted of a weapons offense. He unsuccessfully appealed on the basis that the warrantless search violated the Fourth and Fourteenth Amendments. On appeal the Supreme Court held that the warrantless search was reasonable, considering the special needs of a successful probation system. Probationers are not entitled to the absolute liberty enjoyed by other persons. To hold that a search warrant based on probable cause is required by a probation officer in a situation such as this would frustrate quick response to evidence of probation violations, and it would require a judge, rather than the probation officer, to decide how closely each probationer needed to be supervised. Although a probation officer is not an impartial magistrate, neither is he a police officer, who normally conducts searches against ordinary citizens. His duties are a unique combination of individualized counseling, supervision, and, when the need arises, investigation and enforcement. Although the unauthenticated tip in this case would not constitute probable cause in the ordinary criminal case, it is sufficient or reasonable grounds upon which a probation officer could conduct a warrantless search of a probationer's home. The supervisory arrangement in probation must have a deterrent effect which could not exist if the traditional probable cause and warrant requirements were applied.

Although a probationer's home, like everyone else's, is protected against "unreasonable" searches and seizures, the search conducted in this case, under valid state probation regulations, and considering the special needs of a successful probation system, was reasonable under the Fourth Amendment.

In *New York v. Burger*, 107 S. Ct. 2636 (1987), a New York statute which authorized warrantless inspections by police of automobile junkyards was upheld by the Supreme Court. The Court noted that the dismantling of junked automobiles and the selling of parts, while it has no "ancient" common law history, is really a business related to second-hand shops and general junkyards, which have been closely regulated for years. Such a business enterprise has a reduced expectation of privacy. A carefully-worded law which requires automobile junkyards to be licensed; to meet certain registration requirements; to pay a fee; to keep records of purchases and sales of vehicles and parts; to prominently display a registration number; and to submit to reasonable periodic administrative inspections, can be legally enforced by loss of license and criminal penalties.

The statute was found to be constitutional under the Fourth and Fourteenth Amendments because it met the following criteria: (1) the state had a substantial interest in regulating the junkyard industry (in its reduction of motor vehicle thefts); (2) it could be reasonably expected to serve that interest (junkyards and vehicle dismantlers provide a major market for stolen vehicles and parts); (3) in its inspection procedure, it provided a constitutionally adequate substitute for a warrant (here, the statute informs the junkyard operator that inspections will be made on a regular basis, notifies him what he must do to comply, tells him who will conduct the inspections, and limits the time, place, and scope to regular business hours, to vehicle-dismantling and related activities, and to records, vehicles, and parts which are on the premises).

The court, rejecting the defendant's position that the inspection statute was a subterfuge, allowing police to circumvent the warrant requirement, held that it is proper for a state to attack a criminal problem by an administrative regulation as well as through the criminal law.

Does a governmental employee have a reasonable expectation of privacy in his office, desk, and file cabinets at his place of work? If so, what is the appropriate standard for a search *by his employer*, when it is for a noninvestigatory, work-related reason, or is an investigatory search for evidence of suspected improper job performance? These were the issues before the Supreme Court in *O'Connor v. Ortega*, 107 S. Ct. 1492 (1987). In a plurality opinion (only four justices agreeing with the reasoning, but a majority of five agreeing that the court of appeals holding should be reversed), the Court held that a search by governmental employers or supervisors of the private property of their employees at the work place is subject to limits under the Fourth Amendment. But only those expectations of privacy that society is prepared to consider reasonable are protected. People do not lose Fourth Amendment rights merely because they work for the government, but the nature and condition of public employment may make *some* employees' expectations of privacy unreasonable when the intrusion or search is by a supervisor rather than a police officer. An employee's expectation of privacy must be viewed in light of the conditions of his public employment. Generally, public offices are not totally private enclaves. In many cases they are continually entered by fellow employees and other visitors — even the general public — for work-related business. Because of the nature of the governmental function being served, some offices may be so open that *no* expectation of privacy is reasonable. (In this case, the complainant, Dr. Ortega, was a physician and psychiatrist at a state hospital, and evidence in the record supported a finding that he had a reasonable expectation of privacy in his desk and file cabinets).

As to the Fourth Amendment standard governing employer searches of employees' work places for noninvestigatory work-related intrusions or for investigatory searches for evidence of work-related misconduct, the Court concluded that the traditional probable cause standard used in criminal cases is *not* required. Important governmental services to the public would be more difficult to deliver if public employers had to meet the full probable cause or warrant standards to conduct such searches of their employees' workplaces. There are "special needs, beyond the normal needs of law enforcement" involved in the operations of government offices, that make the criminal probable cause standard inapplicable to work-related searches for non-criminal investigations. In balancing the public employees' reasonable expectation of privacy (which in many cases will be a *reduced* expectation of privacy), against the government employers' duty to provide supervision, control, and efficiency in governmental services, the standard required is one of reasonableness under all the circumstances of each case; that is, "reasonable suspicion," rather than traditional probable cause.

The search will be permissible in its scope when "the measures adopted are reasonably related to the objective of the search and not excessively intrusive in light of . . . the nature of the [misconduct]."

-------------------------------------- **Notes** --------------------------------------

§ 4.16 NEUTRAL MAGISTRATE; INADVERTENCE; STANDING TO OBJECT; ABANDONED PROPERTY

(A) Neutral magistrate

CASE BRIEF

Coolidge v. New Hampshire, 91 S.Ct. 2022 (1971)

Majority opinion: Stewart. Concurring in part: Black, Burger, Harlan, White. Dissenting in part: Black, Burger, White.

FACTS: A fourteen-year-old girl left her home in response to a man's call for a baby-sitter and disappeared until a week later when, after a thaw, her murdered body was found in a snow drift by the side of the road. D's car had been seen the night the victim disappeared near the place where the body was found. D became a suspect; after police had acquired other evidence of his guilt, including a lie-detector test result and four guns from D's wife in his absence (he had previously only admitted owning three guns), they obtained a warrant to search his car for evidence that the victim had been in the car. D was cooperative in the investigation and never gave any indication that he would flee the jurisdiction. In accordance with New Hampshire law the search warrant was signed and issued by the attorney general, who, although he was coordinating the investigation, also possessed the powers of a justice of the peace. After D's arrest in his home, his car was seized from the driveway where it had been parked for several days; it was taken to the police station and subjected to a thorough search, including vacuum sweepings for trace evidence. D's pre-trial motions to suppress the physical evidence, based on several grounds discussed below, were denied; he was convicted and sentenced to life in prison.

ISSUES: Can the seizure and search of D's car and the introduction of the evidence thereby produced be legally justified on the basis of:
 (a) a search conducted pursuant to a valid search warrant?
 (b) a search incident to a valid arrest?
 (c) a search under the rule of *Carroll v. United States*, 45 S.Ct. 280 (1925)?
 (d) the seizure of an instrumentality of the crime found in "plain view"?

DECISION: No; reversed and remanded.

REASONS: (a) Although the procedure complied with New Hampshire law, the attorney general was not a "neutral and detached magistrate" under the Fourth and Fourteenth Amendments of the Constitution of the United States, because he was actively engaged in the investigation of the crime. Therefore the search warrant was constitutionally invalid and the evidence seized thereunder inadmissible unless the seizure can be justified under one of the exceptions to the warrant requirement.

 (b) Even before *Chimel v. California*, 89 S.Ct. 2034 (1969) and under *United States v. Rabinowitz*, 70 S.Ct. 430 (1950) a search incident to arrest was limited to the immediate vicinity of the arrest. Here, an arrest of D inside his house does not justify a search of the car outside in the driveway as an incident thereto.

 (c) The application of the *Carroll* rule to these facts extends it far beyond its original rationale, which is that the warrant requirement is dropped when it is not practicable to secure a warrant because the vehicle can be quickly moved or because of "exigent circumstances." Here the police knew for some time of the probable role of the car in the crime. D was aware that he was a suspect, but was cooperative and gave no indication whatever that he intended to flee. The car was regularly parked in the driveway and so the opportunity to search was not "fleeting." The objects the police wanted to search the car for were neither stolen nor contraband nor dangerous. Since the *Carroll* situation was nonexistent, the later search at the police station cannot be justified under the rule of *Chambers v. Maroney*, 90 S.Ct. 1975 (1970).

(d) *Warden v. Hayden*, 87 S. Ct. 1642 (1967) removed the distinction between searching for an instrumentality and "mere evidence." Even assuming that the police had probable cause for seizure and search, the "plain view" doctrine is inapplicable. The problem with the plain view doctrine is to identify circumstances in which it has legal significance rather than merely being the normal concomitant of *any* search. Examples of "plain view" applicability are: when the police inadvertently come across evidence while in hot pursuit (*Warden v. Hayden*); when an object comes into view during a search incident to an arrest, which search is appropriately limited in scope (*Chimel*); or when a police officer, doing something he has a right to do in a place he has a right to be, inadvertently discovers an incriminating object (inventory of contents cases). In all of these instances the officer has prior justification for the intrusion in the course of which he *inadvertently* discovers evidence in plain view.

The plain view doctrine may not be used to extend a general exploratory search. The rationale of the plain view exception is evident by the two distinct constitutional protections served by the warrant requirement: (1) the magistrate's scrutiny, which is intended to eliminate searches not based on probable cause (the premise being that any intrusion via search is an evil, so none is justified without prior determination of necessity); and (2) the limitation of those searches deemed necessary as much as possible to the things particularly described in the warrant.

The plain view doctrine is not in conflict with the first protection, above, because in each case the intrusion is justified by a warrant or by an exception, such as hot pursuit, etc. Given the initial intrusion, the seizure of an object in plain view is also consistent with the second protection, since it does not convert the search into a general or exploratory one. As against minor peril to Fourth Amendment protections, there is a major gain to effective law enforcement. When an otherwise lawful search is in progress and police come upon a piece of evidence inadvertently it would be a needless inconvenience — and sometimes dangerous — to the evidence or to the police themselves to require them to ignore it until they have obtained a warrant particularly describing it.

Plain view alone is never enough to justify warrantless seizure of evidence. No amount of probable cause can justify warrantless seaches and seizures without exigent circumstances.

The discovery of evidence in plain view must be inadvertent. Where the discovery is anticipated, the requirement of a warrant imposes no inconvenience in the absence of exigent circumstances. If the initial intrusion is bottomed on a warant which fails to mention a particular object although the police know of its location and intend to seize it, there is a violation of the Fourth Amendment "particularity" requirement.

Here, the plain view exception cannot apply. There was plenty of opportunity to obtain a valid warrant. The police knew the car's description and location. There was no "inadvertent" discovery of the car. The case did not involve contraband, stolen goods, or objects dangerous in themselves.

RULES: One actively engaged in criminal investigation, though he possesses judicial powers, cannot be a "neutral and detached magistrate" for the purpose of issuing a warrant.

A vehicle parked in a driveway cannot be seized and searched incident to an arrest of a person inside the adjoining house.

The *Carroll* rule cannot be applied to a situation involving an automobile which has been parked in a driveway for several days when there is no indication of flight, no exigent circumstances and no mere "fleeting" opportunity to search.

An automobile parked on private property cannot be seized under the plain view doctrine (even though it may have been an instrumentality of a crime) because the plain view doctrine requires a prior valid intrusion justified by a warrant or exigent circumstances and inadvertent discovery of the item to be seized.

-- **Notes** --

Sample Questions

While there seems to be a reduced expectation of privacy while traveling in an automobile, (as opposed to the privacy expectation while in one's home), still a driver or passenger in an automobile on the public highways does not lose all reasonable expectation of privacy. T F.

Constitutionally, the use of force by the police in an arrest situation is governed by:
A. Fifth Amendment due process of law.
B. Eighth Amendment cruel and unusual punishment.
C. Fourth Amendment concepts of seizure.
D. compulsory self-incrimination.
E. Fourth Amendment concepts of search.

Cases in which the Supreme Court of the United States has found "special needs" which generally make unnecessary the traditional strict probable cause standards for search that are required in criminal cases include:
A. the relationship between a probationer and his probation officer.
B. cases involving the inspection of "closely-regulated" businesses such as automobile junkyards.
C. teachers or school administrators and public school children.
D. some searches of public employees' workplaces by their supervisors where the nature and conditions of the employment does not create an expectation of privacy that society is prepared to consider reasonable.
E. all of the above.

Only a "neutral and detached" judge can issue warrants. T F.

Fourth Amendment rights are personal and cannot be asserted vicariously and only those persons whose personal and legitimate expectation of privacy is violated have "standing" to object to the lawfulness of a search. T F.

The degree of proof necessary to establish guilt in a criminal case is:
A. proof beyond a reasonable doubt.
B. proof by clear and convincing evidence.
C. a preponderance of the evidence.
D. proof beyond a shadow of a doubt.
E. more likely than not.

If a defendant is tried for a crime but is acquitted of the charge and found not guilty, double jeopardy prohibits a civil forfeiture proceeding against the crime-related property which was seized pursuant to the criminal charge if the forfeiture is for remedial rather than punitive purposes. T F.

The people who drafted the Bill of Rights as the first formal amendment to the Constitution of the United States had one primary fear foremost in mind; it was the fear of:
A. crime in the streets.
B. an oppressive federal government.
C. oppressive state governments.
D. white collar crime.
E. criticism of governmental officers and programs.

(B) "Inadvertent" — Totally unexpected, or lacking probable cause?

The controversy in the lower courts over the precise meaning of the "inadvertent discovery" requirement of the plurality in the case of *Coolidge v. New Hampshire*, 91 S.Ct. 2022 (1971) has apparently been rendered a moot question by the case of *Horton v. California*, 110 S.Ct. 2301 (1990) — see Section 4.14(b). As the Court indicated in *Horton*, although inadvertent discovery is a characteristic in many plain view seizures, it is not a condition necessary to make the seizure lawful under the Constitution of the United States.

Since the *Coolidge* decision was handed down in 1971, however, an overwhelming number of the states have adopted some form of inadvertent discovery requirement (see dissenting opinion in the *Horton* case). This area may very well be another in which some state courts will require inadvertent discovery in plain view seizures as a matter of *state* constitutional law, depending on whether or not the state adopts the *Horton* holding wholly, partially, or rejects it as a matter of state law.

--- **Notes** ---

Sample Questions

The authority of a police officer to conduct a search of the person and the area under his immediate control as an incident to a valid custodial arrest based on probable cause:

A. is based on the theory that the officer should have the opportunity to immediately seize weapons, means of escape, and evidence which might otherwise be destroyed.
B. is based on the "open fields" exception to the warrant requirement.
C. is based on the theory of implied consent.
D. also includes the passenger compartment of an automobile as an incident to the arrest of the driver and/or passengers, even though they have been removed from the car.
E. A and D above.

Consent to search must be voluntarily given in order to be effective. The test that the courts use to determine if consent was voluntary is:

A. whether the consent was given in writing.
B. whether the suspect was given his *Miranda* warnings.
C. whether the police had probable cause to get a search warrant.
D. whether the consent was the product of a free and unrestrained choice, considering the totality of all the circumstances, or whether it was the product of overbearing official conduct.
E. whether the suspect was expressly warned that he need not submit to the search.

With reference to a judge's decision as to whether or not a police officer has probable cause for the issuance of a warrant based on an informant's tip, the Supreme Court of the United States has ruled that:

A. probable cause must be determined on the basis of rigid and technical rules which must be applied in every case.
B. the identity of the informant must be revealed to the judge in every case.
C. the source of the informant's information must be stated in every application for a warrant.
D. probable cause is a fluid concept depending on the totality of all the circumstances presented to the judge in the probable cause affidavit.
E. probable cause cannot be supported by independent and substantial corroboration of a detailed tip to the police by an unknown informant.

The Supreme Court of the United States has held that a trained drug-sniffing dog cannot be used to detect drugs in suspected luggage temporarily detained at a public airport because such a procedure would constitute a "search" and can only be justified after the issuance of a search warrant.   T   F.

A Trained drug-sniffing dog can be used to determine the presence of drugs in luggage which is only temporarily detained under the "stop" authority of the *Terry* case, but detention of the luggage beyond a reasonable time under *Terry* can make the entire procedure unlawful.   T   F.

Since the case of *Tennessee v. Garner,* the privileged use of deadly force by the police has become almost totally *defensive* in character, i.e., self defense of the officer or a third person, or in defense of an immediate threat to the public safety unless an arrest is promptly made.   T   F.

(C) Standing to object to a search

Just as the Fourth Amendment is inapplicable to certain places and to certain trespassers, so too is it sometimes inapplicable to particular defendants. A defendant must have "standing" to object to a search. Standing is the passkey to the forum of a suppression hearing. The essential attribute of the standing determination is that it is a decision whether to decide the legality of a search.

"Fourth Amendment rights are personal rights which * * * may not be vicariously asserted. A person who is aggrieved by an illegal search of a third person's premises or property has not had any of his Fourth Amendment rights infringed." *Alderman v. United States*, 89 S.Ct. 961 (1969).

A person who claims ownership of the seized property or who had possession of the seized items does have standing. *Simmons v. United States*, 88 S.Ct. 967 (1968), *Dalton v. State*, 105 N.E.2d 509 (Ind. 1952). Thus a defendant charged with a possessory offense was caught in the horns of a dilemma: to obtain standing to object to the search, he had to claim ownership or possession of the illegal contraband, admitting guilt, or else forego his objection.

To remedy this dilemma the courts developed the doctrine of automatic standing for any person charged with a possessory offense. *Jones v. United States*, 80 S.Ct. 725 (1960); *State v. Porter*, 324 N.E.2d 857 (Ind. App. 1975).

The *Jones* case, supra, also developed the concept of derivative standing and coined the phrase, "legitimately on premises" to describe that concept. In 1978, the Supreme Court limited the concept of derivative standing by requiring a person to have a "legitimate expectation of privacy in the premises" in order to have standing in a third person's premises. See *Rakas v. Illinois*, briefed below in this section.

The following persons have been held to have sufficient interest to establish standing: (1) an owner or lesee of property, *Jones*, supra; (2) a resident of the searched premises, *Bumper v. North Carolina*, 88 S.Ct. 1788 (1968); (3) a guest, *Leeper v. United States*, 446 F.2d 281 (10th Cir. 1971); (4) a person given permission to use the searched premises, *Idol v. State*, 119 N.E.2d 428 (Ind. 1954); (5) an occupant or guest in a hotel room, *Stoner v. California*, 84 S.Ct. 889 (1964); (6) a person whose office is searched, *Mancusi v. DeForte*, 88 S.Ct. 2120 (1968). The "guest" standing cases may now be limited by *Rakas v. Illinois*, briefed below, to a legitimate expectation of privacy.

A corporation has standing to challenge an illegal search and seizure of its property, *Silverthorne Lumber Co. v. United States*, 40 S.Ct. 182 (1920). An officer, stockholder, or employee of a corporation does not himself have standing to challenge a search or seizure of the corporation's property, *Lagow v. United States*, 159 F.2d 245 (2d Cir. 1946). However, there may be a legitimate expectation of privacy in a small closely held corporation by the officer or stockholder in the corporate property; see *Henzel v. United States*, 296 F.2d 650 (5th Cir. 1961).

CASE BRIEF

Rakas v. Illinois, 99 S. Ct. 421 (1978)

Majority opinion: Rehnquist. Concurring: Burger, Powell. Dissenting: White, Brennan, Marshall, Stevens.

FACTS: D's were convicted of armed robbery and their convictions were affirmed on appeal. Police received a radio dispatch reporting a robbery and describing the getaway car. Shortly thereafter an officer spotted a car he thought might be involved; after following it for some distance and after the arrival of assistance, he stopped the vehicle. The four occupants were ordered out of the car and the interior of the car was searched. A box of rifle shells was found in the locked glove compartment and a sawed-off rifle was found under the front passenger seat. After the discovery of this evidence D's were placed under arrest. D's were passengers in the car, which was owned by the driver; they moved to suppress the rifle and shells from evidence on Fourth and Fourteenth Amendment grounds. D's conceded they did not own the automobile nor the evidence seized. The prosecutor challenged D's standing to object to the lawfulness of the search. The trial court agreed and denied the motion to suppress. (In view of this holding, the court did not determine whether there was probable cause for the search and seizure.)

ISSUE: Can passengers in an automobile in which they are riding with the driver/owner's permission object to the admissibility of evidence seized from the automobile by the police when they have no possessory or ownership rights in the vehicle or the evidence seized?

DECISION: No; convictions affirmed. Passengers have insufficient expectation of privacy to invoke the exclusionary rule.

REASONS: D's urge the court to adopt a rule that any criminal defendant at whom a search is directed has standing to challenge the legality of the search and the admissibility of evidence thereby seized. In the alternative, D's urge the Court to find that they had standing to object to the search under the rule of *Jones v. United States*, 80 S.Ct. 725 (1960), which was based on the individual being "legitimately on the premises" at the time of the search. The *Jones* rule of standing focuses on whether the person seeking to challenge the search was *himself* the victim of the search or seizure. The adoption of the "target" theory advanced by D's would, in effect, permit D to assert that a violation of Fourth Amendment rights of a third party entitled him to suppress any evidence seized.

The Court declines to extend the rule of "standing." Fourth Amendment rights are *personal* rights which, like some other constitutional rights, may not be asserted vicariously. A person aggrieved by an illegal search and seizure only through introduction of damaging evidence secured by a search of a *third person's* premises or property, has not had his *own* Fourth Amendment rights infringed.

Because the exclusionary rule is an attempt to enforce the Fourth Amendment, it is proper to permit *only* D's who have had their own Fourth Amendment rights violated to benefit from the rule. There is no reason to think that these persons will not move to suppress, or take advantage of civil remedies for damages if their rights are violated.

The Court expressly rejects the concept that anyone who may have been the victim of a search and seizure may move to exclude evidence seized.

The "target" theory would entail substantial administrative difficulties, involving an extension of the exclusionary rule. Each time that rule is applied, it exacts a substantial social cost. Relevant and reliable evidence is kept from the trier of fact and the search for truth at trial is deflected.

In re-examining the *Jones* case, the Court can think of no decided cases that would have come out differently had it concluded — as it now does — that the type of standing requirement discussed in *Jones* is more properly classified under substantive Fourth Amendment doctrine.

The issue of standing involves two inquiries: (1) whether the proponent of a particular legal right has alleged "injury in fact"; and (2) whether the proponent is asserting his own legal rights and interests rather than basing his claim for relief upon the rights of third parties.

The question is whether the challenged search or seizure violated the Fourth

Amendment rights of a criminal defendant who seeks to exclude the evidence thereby obtained. That inquiry in turn requires a determination of whether the disputed search and seizure has infringed an interest of the defendant which the Fourth Amendment was designed to protect.

Here, D's attempt to compare their situation to the one in *Jones*. In that case, D was present at the time of the search of an apartment which was owned by a friend. He had permission to use the apartment and had a key. He also had a few articles of clothing there and had slept there "maybe a night." At the time of the search D was the only person present; he had complete dominion and control of the apartment to the exclusion of all others except the lessee. Under these circumstances the Court ruled that while one wrongfully on the premises could not move to suppress evidence as a result of a search, "anyone legitimately on premises where a search occurs may challenge its legality."

The Court does not question the conclusion in *Jones* that D there suffered a violation of his *personal* Fourth Amendment rights. Nonetheless, the phrase "legitimately on premises" used in that case creates too broad a gauge for measurement of Fourth Amendment rights.

Jones on its facts merely stands for the unremarkable proposition that a person can have a legally sufficient interest in a place other than his own home so that the Fourth Amendment protects him from unreasonable governmental intrusion into that place. The *Katz* case is an example, using the test, not of property rights, but rather "legitimate expectation of privacy"; *Katz v. United States*, 88 S. Ct. 507 (1967). Viewed in this manner *Jones* can best be explained by the fact that D had a legitimate expectation of privacy in the premises he was using and therefore was protected by the Fourth Amendment, although his interest might not have been a recognized property interest at common law.

The "legitimately on premises" test is not nearly so clear a guideline as the dissenters indicate. The phrase has, at most, superficial clarity. Legitimate presence on the premises is not irrelevant to one's expectation of privay, but it cannot be deemed controlling.

Judged by the foregoing analysis, D's claims must fail. They had neither a property nor a possessory interest in the car or property seized from it. The fact that D's were in the car with the permission of its owner is not determinative of whether they had a legitimate expectation of privacy in the particular areas of the automobile searched. While cars are not to be treated identically with houses or apartments for Fourth Amendment purposes, D's claims would fail in an analogous situation in a dwelling place since they made no showing that they had any legitimate expectation of privacy in the glove compartment or area under the seat of the car in which they were merely passengers. Like the car's trunk, these are areas in which a passenger in his character as a passenger simply would not normally have a legitimate expectation of privacy.

Therefore the state courts were correct in concluding that it was unnecessary to decide whether the search of the car might have violated the Fourth and Fourteenth Amendment rights of *someone else*. Since it did not violate the rights of D's, the convictions are affirmed.

RULE: Fourth Amendment rights are personal and cannot be asserted vicariously. The right of a person to challenge the lawfulness of a search and seizure, and the consequent admissibility of evidence seized, depends not on derivative standing to assert the challenge but rather on whether or not the person's *personal and legitimate expectation of privacy* in the place searched was violated by governmental intrusion. Under this rule, mere passengers of an automobile may not object to incriminating evidence seized therefrom when they have no possessory or property interest in the automobile or the evidence seized.

DISSENTING: While the majority gives lip-service to the privacy interests protected by the Fourth Amendment, they decide the case on principles of property law. In previous decisions of the Court searches have been overturned although the petitioner was not the owner of the automobile. The *Jones* rule would be much easier of application than the rule of the majority. In the *Katz* case there was no ownership or possessory interest, but only legitimate presence. This decision invites police to engage in patently unreasonable searches every time an automobile contains more than one occupant.

In *Rakas v. Illinois*, 99 S. Ct. 421 (1978) (briefed above), the Supreme Court held that only those with personal and legitimate expectations of privacy in the place searched could object to the search. The Court again recognized such privacy interests in *United States v. Karo*, 104 S.Ct. 3296 (1984). In this case agents had installed a sound-monitoring device (beeper) in a can of ether with the consent of its supplier, who had told the agents it was to be purchased for illegal drug processing. The beeper was then monitored to determine the can's location. The Supreme Court held that, when the can was moved to a private residence, the continued monitoring of the beeper violated the Fourth Amendment rights of those persons having legitimate privacy interests in the residence; as to those persons, information concerning the beeper signals should not have been used to show probable cause in obtaining a search warrant.

-------------------------------------- **Notes** --------------------------------------

CASE BRIEF

Minnesota v. Olson, 110 S.Ct. 1684 (1990)

Majority opinion: White, J., joined by Brennan, Marshall, Stevens, O'Connor, Scalia, and Kennedy, JJ. Separate concurring opinions by Stevens and Kennedy, JJ. Dissenting: Rehnquist, CJ., and Blackmun.

FACTS: Robbery-murder case in which gunman, weapon and robbery loot were quickly apprehended/recovered, but driver of getaway car escaped. Car title and letter found in getaway car contained name and address of D and police verified D's address. Next morning (Sunday), a woman, who identified herself, called police and stated D had driven getaway car in robbery-murder and was planning to leave town by bus. Later, same woman called back, giving her address and phone number and told police D had told two other women he was the driver in the crime and she gave police the names and address of the two women. Police were sent to the address, a duplex, but the women were not at home. Police spoke to H, (the mother/grandmother of the two women), who lived in the lower unit of the duplex, and she confirmed that D had been staying upstairs and she agreed to call police when he returned. Police put out a "probable cause arrest bulletin" for D and instructed officers to stay away from the duplex. That afternoon, at about 2:45 p.m., H called police and said D had returned. Police went to the duplex and surrounded it and called the upstairs duplex by phone and told the woman who answered that D should come out. The officer making the call heard a male voice say, "tell them I left", (which the woman did). At 3:00 p.m., police entered the house, without permission and with guns drawn, found D hiding in a closet, and arrested him. Less than an hour later, D made an incriminating statement at the police station. The trial court denied D's motion to suppress his statement, and D was tried and convicted of murder, robbery, and assault. On appeal, the state Supreme Court reversed, holding that D had a sufficient privacy interest in the duplex where he was arrested to challenge the warrantless entry, and that the arrest was illegal in the absence of exigent circumstances, and that the statement therefore should have been suppressed. D's conviction was reversed and the case was remanded for a new trial. The state petitioned for certiorari, which was granted by the Supreme Court of the United States. (NOTE: Because of the way the issues were argued in the lower courts, the sole issue before the Supreme Court in this case is the privacy interest of an overnight guest staying in someone's else's home, and the admissibility of D's statement is not at issue, because the state had never argued that if the arrest was illegal the statement could nevertheless be admissible.)

ISSUE: Does an overnight guest staying in someone else's home have a sufficient privacy interest in his host's home to object to a warrantless police entry to arrest him when there are no exigent circumstances justifying such warrantless entry?

DECISION: Yes. State Supreme Court decision affirmed.

REASONS: *Payton v. New York*, 100 S.Ct. 1371 (1980), held that without exigent circumstances, a suspect should not be arrested in his own home without a warrant even though the arrest was supported by probable cause. The purpose of *Payton* was not to protect the person, but to protect his home from entry without a *judge's* finding of probable cause. *Katz v. United States*, 88 S.Ct. 507 (1967), held that a person can claim protection of the Fourth Amendment if he has a "legitimate expectation of privacy in the invaded place." *Rakas v. Illinois*, 99 S.Ct. 421 (1978) held that an expectation of privacy is legitimate if it is "one that society is prepared to recognize as reasonable." (Here, the Court considers, but rejects a 12 point formula that the state proposed as a test to determine if a dwelling is a "home", with the statement that, "We need go no further than to conclude, as we do, that Olson's status as an overnight guest is alone enough to show that he had an expectation of privacy in the home that society is prepared to recognize as reasonable.")

Although the "legitimately on the premises" test of *Jones v. United States*, 80 S.Ct. 725 (1960) was rejected in *Rakas* as being too broad, still the *Rakas* case reaffirmed the holding in *Jones* that a person *can* have a legally sufficient interest in a place other than his own so that the Fourth Amendment protects him from unreasonable governmental invasion.

An overnight guest need not be given a key to his host's home, or be left alone in charge of it, to have a sufficient privacy interest entitling him to Fourth Amendment protection. Everyday expectations associated with the social custom of staying in another's home — for example, that the guest or his possessions will not be disturbed by anyone except the host or those the host allows inside — are legitimate expectations of privacy that society recognizes as reasonable. We will all be hosts and guests during our lifetimes, and we seek shelter in the homes of others precisely because they provide privacy.

> "The point is that hosts will more likely than not respect the privacy interest of their guests, who are entitled to a legitimate expectation of privacy despite the fact that they have no legal interest in the premises and do not have the legal authority to determine who may or may not enter the household."

D's expectation of privacy in this case was based on understandings that are recognized and permitted by society, and it was therefore legitimate, and entitled to the protection of the Fourth Amendment.

The Court then concludes that the state Supreme Court's determination that there were no "exigent circumstances" in this case which would have justified a warrantless entry was correct — (there was no hot pursuit of a fleeing felon — no imminent destruction of evidence — no need to prevent a suspect's escape — or risk of danger to the police or other persons inside or outside the dwelling). The Court does not disagree with the state Supreme Court's position that in the absence of hot pursuit there must be at least probable cause to believe that one or more of the other factors justifying a warrantless entry was present, and that in assessing the risk of danger, the gravity of the crime and likelihood of an armed suspect should be considered. Although a grave crime was involved here, D was known not to be the murderer, but the getaway driver, and the weapon had been recovered; there was no reason to believe the women in the house were in danger; and the house was surrounded by police.

RULE: An overnight guest in the home of another with his consent has a legitimate expectation of privacy which society recognizes as reasonable, and before the host's home is entered by police without exigent circumstances being present for the purpose of arrresting the guest, a warrant of arrest should be obtained.

Note: Although the issue was *not* involved in this case, *Steagald v. United States*, 101 S.Ct. 1642 (1981) would indicate that before any evidence could be seized in plain view upon entry of the host home and used against the host, a search warrant should also be obtained.

(D) Abandoned Property and Garbage

Can a person claim a legitimate or reasonable expectation of privacy that the Constitution will protect in something that he has abandoned or thrown away? The answer is apparently that he cannot, and that items thrown away can be seized by the police and used as evidence — provided, of course, that they are connected to criminal activity. There is some case authority, however, that if activity of the police is the cause of the abandonment, it must be lawful police activity or the abandonment will be considered "fruit of the poisonous tree," and the evidence inadmissible. See *State v. Smithers*, 269 N.E.2d 874 (Ind. 1971).

A comparison could be made in the usual abandoned property case with the reasoning used in eavesdropping cases, i.e., neither the person who throws away an object nor the person who carries on a loud conversation with another person which can be easily overheard is exhibiting a "reasonable expectation of privacy" in the object or the conversation.

In the case of *California v. Greenwood*, 108 S.Ct. 1625 (1988), the Supreme Court of the United States for the first time considered the issue of criminal evidence discovered by the police in garbage set out by the defendant for collection. In that case, the police had received information that D was dealing in drugs. They also had received information from D's neighbors concerning heavy vehicular traffic late at night in front of D's home — and that the cars remained at the house for only a short time. Police surveillance verified this activity, and a vehicle was followed from D's house to another suspected illegal drug location.

With this information, the police arranged for the garbage collector to pick up the opaque plastic garbage bags that D left at the curb for pickup and to turn them over to the police without mixing them with trash left out by neighbors. A police examination of the contents revealed items indicating narcotics use and, upon this basis, a search warrant for D's house was obtained. In the search, cocaine and hashish were found, and D was arrested and later posted bail. After his release on bail, police continued to receive complaints about suspected drug activity at D's house. The garbage was again inspected through the same arrangement, and a second search warrant was obtained and served. Drugs were again found in the search, and D was arrested for the second time.

The California trial court dismissed the charges against D on the authority of the case of *People v. Krivda*, 486 P.2d 1262 (Cal. 1971), which had held that warrantless trash searches violated the Fourth Amendment. The California Court of Appeals affirmed the dismissal, and the California Supreme Court denied review. The State of California petitioned for certiorari, which was granted by the Supreme Court of the United States.

The Supreme Court held that D's right against unreasonable search and seizure as protected by the Fourth Amendment would be violated only if D had a "subjective expectation of privacy" in his garbage that *society* accepts as "objectively reasonable." (D's argument was that he had set the garbage out in *opaque* bags, which the garbage man was expected to pick up, mingle with the trash of other people and deposit at the dump. The garbage was only to be temporarily on the street, and there was little chance it would be inspected by anyone.) The Supreme Court observed that:

> It is common knowledge that plastic garbage bags left on or at the side of a public street are readily accessible to animals, children, scavengers, snoops, and other members of the public. Moreover, respondents placed their refuse at the curb for the express purpose of conveying it to a third party, the trash collector, who might himself have sorted through respondent's trash or permitted others, such as the police, to do so. Accordingly, having deposited their garbage "in an area particularly suited for public inspection and, in a manner of speaking, public consumption, for the express purpose of having

strangers take it" (citing *United States v. Reicherter*, 647 F.2d 397 (3d Cir. 1981)), respondents could have had no reasonable expectation of privacy in the inculpatory items that they discarded.

The Court then proceeded to compare similar cases turning on reasonable expectation of privacy involving the use of pen registers to record phone numbers dialed, surveillance by police from airplanes from permissible altitudes, and it cited numerous lower federal court opinions and state court opinions holding that there is no reasonable expectation of privacy in garbage left for collection outside the curtilage of a home.

It is important to remember that in this case, a single-family dwelling was involved. Multiple-family dwellings or apartment houses would involve difficult proof problems not involved in this case. Also, the Court discussed the somewhat complicated issues resulting from California's adoption, since the *Krivda* case, of a state constitutional amendment prohibiting exclusion of evidence by state law that is admissible under the Constitution of the United States.

--------------------------------------- **Notes** ---------------------------------------

§ 4.17 WIRETAPPING AND EAVESDROPPING

"Wiretapping" occurs when, without lawful authority, the police or their agents, by electronic means, tap into a conversation being transmitted by wire for the purpose of overhearing the conversation without the knowledge or consent of the parties to it. "Eavesdropping" is a broader term; it includes the unauthorized interception of face-to-face conversations (which would not otherwise be overheard) by the secret use of an electronic device (usually referred to as a "bug") when no party to the conversation is aware of the monitoring. For the constitutional rights to be violated, the parties to the conversations must have a reasonable expectation of privacy, and must be conversing in a manner consistent with that expectation.

In early cases involving electronic eavesdropping, the Supreme Court held that, unless a physical trespass occurred, there was no unreasonable search or seizure within the meaning of the Fourth Amendment. At that time the Fourth Amendment was interpreted to protect *property* interests. See *Olmstead v. United States*, 48 S. Ct. 564 (1928). In 1934 Congress specifically prohibited unauthorized wiretapping in the Federal Communications Act. In the *Nardone* cases, 58 S. Ct. 275 (1937) and 60 S. Ct. 266 (1939), the exclusionary rule was extended to wiretap evidence, gathered in violation of the Communications Act and offered in federal courts. The Supreme Court continued to follow the "property interest" theory of Fourth Amendment protection in the *Goldman v. United States*, 62 S. Ct. 993 (1942) (bugging); *On Lee v. United States*, 72 S. Ct. 967 (1952 ("wired" government informer); and *Silverman v. United States*, 81 S. Ct. 679 (1961) (physical penetration of wall by a "spike mike").

In *Wong Sun v. United States*, 83 S. Ct. 407 (1963), the Court held that verbal evidence — as well as tangible, or real evidence — could be the fruit of official illegality under the Fourth Amendment and therefore subject to the exclusionary rule.

In *Katz v. United States*, briefed below, the Supreme Court abandoned the concept that the Fourth Amendment protects property interests and instead held that it protects reasonable expectations of *privacy*. The identification of privacy as a federally-protected right, at least in certain situations, has given rise to case law in many areas of interest to law enforcement officers.

CASE BRIEF
Katz v. United States, 88 S. Ct. 507 (1967)

Majority opinion: Stewart. Concurring: Douglas, Brennan, Harlan, White. Dissenting: Black.

FACTS: D was convicted of transmitting gambling information by telephone in violation of federal law. The government introduced at trial, over D's objection, evidence of D's end of phone calls, made from a public phone booth, which had been overheard by F.B.I. agents by means of a listening and recording device attached to the outside of the booth. D claimed the gathering of evidence in this manner violated his rights under the Fourth Amendment. D was convicted and his conviction was upheld by the Court of Appeals on the basis that there was no physical entry into the area of the booth occupied by D. The Supreme Court granted certiorari.

ISSUE: Was the evidence of D's conversations seized in accordance with constitutional standards?

DECISION: No; reversed.

REASONS: The Fourth Amendment protects persons, not areas, and it cannot be reduced to a general constitutional right to privacy. What a person knowingly exposes to the public, even in his own home or office, is not subject to

Fourth Amendment protection. But what he seeks to preserve as private, even in an area accessible to the public, may be constitutionally protected. What D intended to exclude here was the "uninvited ear." Just as in a business office, a friend's apartment, or a taxicab, a person in a phone booth, although it is designed for public use, may rely on Fourth Amendment protection. Lack of physical penetration into the phone booth makes no difference, because the concept that property interests control the right of the government to search and seize has been discredited — now, privacy interests control. We depart from the narrow view of the *Olmstead* case. The governmental action here violated the privacy upon which D justifiably relied, and this constituted an unreasonable search and seizure. Although this was a narrowly circumscribed surveillance for a brief period and for a specific purpose — the kind which a duly authorized magistrate could have authorized with appropriate safeguards (citing *Osborn v. United States*, 87 S. CT. 429 (1966), here there was no neutral and detached magistrate who intervened, as constitutionally required under the facts of this case.

RULE: When a person uses any place, public or private, for conversational purposes with the reasonable expectation of privacy and in a manner which is consistent with that expectation, he is protected against unreasonable governmental search and seizure by the Fourth Amendment; no governmental eavesdropping may occur without the intervention and approval of a neutral and detached magistrate.

CONCURRING: The concurring opinions discuss the application of the principle of this case to national security cases, and electronic, as well as physical intrusions.

DISSENTING: The Fourth Amendment is talking about tangible things. The framers were aware of eavesdropping and simply didn't intend to cover it. To support the majority view, the Fourth Amendment has to be rewritten; for years the common law right of the government to seize was based on a superior property interest; the Court has invented a privacy right to suit its own ends.

Many states have laws prohibiting wiretapping, and some of them apply the exclusionary rule to enforce the prohibition. The issue before the Court in *Berger v. New York*, 87 S. Ct. 1873 (1967), was the constitutionality of New York's statute, which prohibited wiretapping except with prior court approval. In holding the New York statute to be unconstitutional, the Court found the "particularity" requirements of the Fourth Amendment lacking. The *Berger* opinion served as a "blueprint" for a constitutional wiretapping statute which was enacted by Congress a year later as a part of the Omnibus Crime Control and Safe Streets Act of 1968. (18 U.S.C.A. §2510 et seq.) This federal statute established a very detailed procedure for the interception of wire or oral communications. A judicially approved wiretap or eavesdrop order is, in essence, a search warrant, but because of the nature of the thing to be seized (a conversation) and the dangers to a free society inherent in governmental "spying" on citizens, great care is taken to provide safeguards over and above ordinary search warrant procedures.

The states are authorized to enact their own legislation controlling electronic eavesdropping and wiretapping, but they must in all particulars conform to the federal standards, except, of course, that the state statutes may specify which officers may apply for, and which state courts may grant, the eavesdrop/wiretap orders.

No state or local police officer may lawfully engage in eavesdropping or wiretapping except as authorized by the laws of his state, which, in turn, must be in conformity with the federal wiretap legislation. Violations are punishable as federal offenses and may carry civil damage sanctions as well. Not all states have adopted such legislation, and some states have adopted legislation which restricts law enforcement eavesdropping more than does the federal legislation.

Unless a state has more restrictive standards, state and local officers may conduct investigations following the "one party to the conversation is aware" rule without violating suspects' rights. This rule was announced in *United States v. White*, briefed below. It would apply to situations in which one party to a telephone conversation permits a police officer to listen on an extension phone, even though the other party is unaware it is being monitored, and those in which the officer himself is a party to a conversation while secretly "wired" to transmit or record the conversation. In the latter cases, however, officers should keep in mind that direct approaches to and conversations with criminal suspects who have already been formally accused of crime by indictment or information and who are represented by counsel may be in violation of the Sixth Amendment rights discussed in Chapter 5.

CASE BRIEF

United States v. White, 91 S. Ct. 1122 (1971)

Majority opinion: White, joined by Burger, Stewart, Blackmun. Concurring: Black. Concurring in result: Brennan. Dissenting: Douglas.

FACTS: This was a drug case. D was convicted as a second offender. "J", a false friend of D, was a government informer who had wired himself with a radio transmitter, allowing federal drug agents to overhear conversations between himself and D. These took place at J's home, D's home, at a restaurant, and in J's car. J could not be produced at D's trial and the agents who overheard the conversations were allowed to testify. The court of appeals reversed D's conviction, basing its decision on *Katz v. United States*, 88 S. Ct. 507 (1967) and petition for certiorari was granted.

ISSUE: Was the Fourth Amendment violated by the law enforcement techniques used in this case?

DECISION: No, reversed. Conviction upheld.

REASONS: The *Katz* ruling did not involve a party to the conversation who was a government informer, nor did the Court in *Katz* rule that there is a justifiable and constitutionally protected expectation that a person with whom a D has a conversation will not later reveal the conversation to the police. (Also, the *Katz* case is inapplicable because the events here occurred before the *Katz* ruling.)

There is no constitutional difference between a false friend who immediately reports a conversation to a police after it takes place, and one who simultaneously broadcasts it to a police listener or simultaneously records it for later use.

Nor should we be too ready to erect constitutional barriers to relevant and probative evidence which is also accurate and reliable. An electronic recording of a conversation is more accurate than the memory of a police informer.

In *Hoffa v. United States*, 87 S. Ct. 408 (1966) the Court held that, a defendant's trust in an apparent colleague is not protected by the Fourth Amendment. In *Lewis v. United States*, 87 S. Ct. 424 (1966), no warrant was required when an undercover agent made a drug buy at defendant's home, and in *Lopez v. United States*, 83 S. Ct. 1381 (1963), the secret recording of words in such a case was approved. Conceding that *Hoffa*, *Lewis*, and *Lopez* remain unaffected by the *Katz* holding, the court of appeals nevertheless held that *Katz* and the Fourth Amendment required a different result if the agent records and/or transmits his conversation with defendant as happened in this case. This was error.

The disappearance of the informer at trial, while it may raise evidentiary problems when the testimony of other agents is proffered (as well as questions of prosecutorial misconduct), does not appear critical to deciding whether prior events invaded D's Fourth Amendment rights.

RULE: If one party to a conversation is aware that the conversation is being secretly monitored by agents of law enforcement, there is no expectation of privacy so great on the part of the other party as to be protected by the Fourth Amendment; this is true whether the party who is aware is secretly transmitting or recording the conversation electronically, or later divulges the content of the conversation to the police from memory.

The many technological advances which have occurred in the communications industry since the passage of the Omnibus Crime Control and Safe Streets Act of 1968, have made it necessary for Congress to amend the portion of it dealing with wiretapping and eavesdropping. This amendment, effective in 1987, was responsive to the development of cellular and cordless telephones, paging devices, electronic mail, computer to computer data transmission, video teleconferencing, and other electronic innovations.

Police use of "pen registers" (devices which the telephone company may install to record only the numbers dialed from a particular phone), are affected by the 1987 amendment. Despite the rulings of the Supreme Court in *United States v. New York Telephone Co.*, 98 S. Ct. 364 (1977), and *Smith v. Maryland*, 99 S. Ct. 2577 (1979), to the effect that warrantless use of pen registers by police violates neither the Fourth Amendment nor the federal wiretapping statute, the 1987 amendment to that law prohibits their use for law enforcement purposes without a court order.

Again, the legality of wiretapping or eavesdropping activities of the state and local police in each state must be determined by reference to that state's law.

------------------------------------- **Notes** -------------------------------------

§ 4.18 COMPELLED EVIDENCE

CASE BRIEF

United States v. Dionisio, 93 S. Ct. 764 (1973)

Majority opinion: Stewart. Concurring in part: Brennan. Dissenting: Brennan (in part), Douglas, Marshall.

FACTS: A special federal grand jury, investigating possible violations of federal gambling statutes, received in evidence voice recordings obtained through judicially authorized wiretapping. It subpoenaed approximately twenty persons, including D, and sought to obtain voice exemplars for comparison with the recorded conversations. Each witness was advised that he was a potential defendant and was asked to examine a transcript of a recorded conversation and read it into a tape recorder microphone. Witnesses were also advised that their attorneys could be present when they read the transcripts. D and other witnesses refused to give voice exemplars, asserting their Fourth and Fifth Amendment rights. The government filed a petition in United States district court to compel D to furnish a voice examplar. The district court ruled in favor of the government, but D still refused. The district court ruled that he was in contempt of court and ordered him into custody until he complied or until the end of the grand jury session.

The United States Court of Appeals for the Seventh Circuit reversed, holding that while there was no Fifth Amendment violation (self-incrimination), there was a violation of the Fourth Amendment. It viewed the use of grand jury subpoena powers as in lieu of probable cause for the seizure of the voice exemplars; that is, it applied the Fourth Amendment to the grand jury process and ruled that the subpoena power could not be used to "short-cut" the warrant requirement. It held that, under the Fourth Amendment, law enforcement officials may not compel the production of physical evidence without a showing of reasonableness of the seizure, drawing an analogy to the situation in *Davis v. Mississippi*, 89 S.Ct. 1394 (1969), which involved a wholesale roundup of suspects for fingerprinting without probable cause.

ISSUE: Can a grand jury, through its subpoena power, compel the production of voice exemplars from potential defendants to compare with recorded conversations of unknown persons, previously obtained through judicially authorized wiretapping?

DECISION: Yes; reversed and remanded.

REASONS: The court of appeals was correct with respect to the Fifth Amendment. The self-incrimination clause is limited to testimonial or communicative acts, i.e., the content of what is said or written as opposed to the sound of the voice or the characteristics of handwriting.

The court of appeals held that a preliminary showing of reasonableness was required by the Fourth Amendment before a grand jury witness could be forced to furnish a voice exemplar and that here the proposed seizures of voice exemplars were unreasonable because of the large number of witness-suspects, which caused the situation to have the character of a general, or exploratory, search.

Any Fourth Amendment violation in the present setting must rest on a lawless governmental intrusion upon the privacy of persons, rather than on interference with property relationships or private papers. Wherever a person may harbor a reasonable expectation of privacy, he is entitled to be free from unreasonable governmental intrusion.

As the Court made clear in *Schmerber v. California*, 86 S.Ct. 1826 (1966), the obtaining of physical evidence from a person involves a potential violation of the Fourth Amendment at two different levels: (1) the seizure of the person, and (2) the subsequent search for and seizure of the evidence.

In *Schmerber* the initial seizure of the person was justified by a lawful arrest, and the subsequent seizure of the blood sample was reasonable in light of exigent circumstances.

In *Terry v. Ohio*, 88 S.Ct. 1868 (1968) neither the initial seizure of the person nor the pat-down search for weapons — under those circumstances — was held to have violated the Fourth Amendment.

But a subpoena to appear before a grand jury is not a seizure in the Fourth Amendment sense, even though it may be inconvenient or burdensome. Every person has an obligation to appear before a grand jury and give evidence when subpoenaed to do so (short of constitutional conflicts such as self-incrimination).

The compulsion under a grand jury subpoena is not as harsh or abrupt as a criminal arrest or even a *Terry*-type stop. The grand jury subpoena to testify is simply not the kind of governmental intrusion on privacy against which the Fourth Amendment affords protection once the Fifth Amendment is satisfied.

The Fourth Amendment does protect against a grand jury subpoena duces tecum which is too sweeping in its terms to be regarded as reasonable.

In *Katz v. United States*, 88 S. Ct. 507 (1967), the Fourth Amendment was held to provide no protection for what a person knowingly exposes to the public even in his own home or office. Except for the rare recluse, most persons expose the sound of their voice to the public every day. Therefore, the sound of the voice is immeasurably further removed from Fourth Amendment protection than the blood extracted in the *Schmerber* case, and the giving of a voice exemplar is not a humiliating experience, as a *Terry* pat-down search might be.

Since neither the grand jury summons nor its directive to make a voice recording infringed on any interest protected by the Fourth Amendment, there was no justification for requiring the grand jury to satisfy even the minimal requirement of reasonableness imposed by the court of appeals.

No grand jury witness is entitled to set limits on the investigation the grand jury may conduct. Any holding that would saddle a grand jury with mini-trials and preliminary showings would impede its function and frustrate the public's interest in the fair and expeditious administration of the criminal laws.

RULE: A grand jury order to provide voice exemplars of witnesses for comparison purposes with tapes of judicially authorized wiretapping evidence does not violate the Fifth Amendment protection against compulsory self-incrimination, because that protection is concerned with testimonial or communicative acts (as opposed to the sound or physical characteristics of the voice). It also does not violate the Fourth Amendment guarantee against unreasonable searches and seizures, because every citizen has a duty to give evidence before the grand jury upon proper subpoena. The sound or physical characteristics of one's voice are exposed to the public every day; therefore, requiring a voice exemplar does not violate a reasonable expectation of privacy.

--------------------------------------- **Notes** ---------------------------------------

§ 4.19 SEIZURE AND FORFEITURE OF CRIME-RELATED PROPERTY

In a rare unanimous holding, the Supreme Court of the United States, in the case of *United States v. One Assortment of 89 Firearms*, 104 S. Ct. 1099 (1984), approved the use of an important alternative weapon against criminal activity. In order to understand this case, it is necessary to recognize the difference in the burden of proof required to establish a criminal violation (proof beyond a reasonable doubt), and the lesser standard of proof required in civil cases (preponderance of the evidence). It is also necessary to recognize that the dismissal of a criminal charge — a finding of not guilty — *is not proof that a defendant is innocent* — it is merely an indication that the government failed to prove its case "beyond a reasonable doubt."

In the case of *89 Firearms*, the defendant was charged with the federal offense of dealing in firearms without a license. At his trial he relied on the defense of entrapment and he was found not guilty by the trial jury. Following the acquittal on the criminal charges the government, pursuant to its authority under federal law, filed a civil action for forfeiture of the firearms which had been seized in the criminal case. (This type of lawsuit is called an *in rem* action, which is brought for the purpose of establishing rights in a *thing*. Criminal cases, on the other hand, are actions *in personam*, to establish rights against an individual *person*.) The defendant claimed in the forfeiture trial that the controversy had already been settled by the outcome of the criminal case and that the government was stopped from its forfeiture lawsuit by its previous unsuccessful criminal prosecution. The trial court ruled against the defendant, holding that the forfeiture proceeding was "remedial" in nature and therefore a civil action, it ordered the weapons to be forfeited. On appeal, the United States court of appeals reversed, holding that the forfeiture proceeding was *punitive* in nature, and therefore barred by the constitutional right against double jeopardy. In its opinion the court of appeals also relied on the 1886 case of *Coffey v. United States*, 116 U.S. 436, and held that the forfeiture was also prohibited by "collateral estoppel" (it was based on the same facts as the previous criminal action). The Supreme Court of the United States granted certiorari, reversed, and upheld the forfeiture.

The Supreme Court discussed the *Coffey* case and subsequent decisions which have cast doubt on its holding. The Court stated:

> The time has come to clarify that neither collateral estoppel nor double jeopardy bars a civil, remedial forfeiture proceeding initiated following an acquittal on related criminal charges. To the extent that *Coffey v. United States* suggests otherwise, it is hereby disapproved.

Concerning the collateral estoppel issue, the Court observed that the difference in the relative burdens of proof in criminal and civil actions made this defense inapplicable. (The fact that the government failed to establish its criminal case beyond a reasonable doubt does not indicate that it could not prove its civil case by a preponderance of the evidence.)

As to the double jeopardy defense, the Court held that unless the forfeiture proceeding was *intended as punishment* (so as to be essentially criminal in character), the Double Jeopardy Clause of the Constitution does not apply. The Court then proceeded to interpret the federal firearms statute and determined that the forfeiture proceeding was intended to be remedial in nature rather than an additional penalty. It reviewed the purposes of federal gun control legislation and noted that Congress was concerned with the widespread traffic in firearms and their availability to persons whose possession of them was "contrary to the public interest." The Court further stated:

> Keeping potentially dangerous weapons out of the hands of unlicensed dealers is a goal plainly more remedial than punitive. Accordingly, we hold that

Congress viewed sec. 924(d) forfeiture as a remedial civil sanction rather than a criminal punishment.

This case is an important one for effective law enforcement because it indicates that the federal government — and the states as well, under properly worded laws — can use both criminal prosecutions and civil forfeiture procedures against certain criminal activity and thereby take the "profit" out of crime without violating defendants' constitutional rights.

Similar *in rem* forfeiture proceedings are used to combat organized crime, illegal traffic in drugs, continuing criminal enterprises, and other criminal violations involving proceeds of crime or other crime-related property. Items involved in such proceedings have included money, motor vehicles, buildings, and real estate.

------------------------------------- **Notes** -------------------------------------

CHAPTER 5

CONFESSIONS AND ADMISSIONS; COMPULSORY SELF-INCRIMINATION; INTERROGATION; IMMUNITY

Section

5.1 Introduction
5.2 Voluntariness doctrine
5.3 Fourth amendment confession issues; fruit of the poisonous tree doctrine
5.4 Sixth amendment right to counsel in confessions
  (A) Pre-charge questioning
  (B) Post-charge questioning
5.5 Fifth amendment self-incrimination issues
  (A) Highlights of Miranda
  (B) Applicability of Miranda
  (C) Volunteered Statements
  (D) The Warnings
  (E) The Waiver of Rights
  (F) Exception to Miranda Rule — When warnings are not required
  (G) Impeachment and Miranda
  (H) Self-incrimination and Immunity

§ 5.1 INTRODUCTION

No person shall * * * be compelled in any criminal case to be a witness against himself * * * *United States Constitution, Amendment 5.*

Even though it seems apparent from the study of its opinions that the Supreme Court of the United States is inherently suspicious of criminal convictions which are based primarily on admissions or confessions, this type of evidence is one of the most powerful weapons employed in the prosecution of crimes. Nothing else has more influence on the fact finder than an apparent admission of guilt by the party charged.

A "confession" is the admission of guilt by a defendant of *all* the necessary elements of the crime charged, while an "admission" merely admits some fact which tends to connect the defendant with the alleged offense. *Worthington v. State*, 409 N.E.2d 1261 (Ind. App. 1980).

There are at least four constitutional provisions that impact upon confessions and admissions: the voluntariness doctrine of the Fourteenth Amendment; the "fruit of the poisonous tree" doctrine of the Fourth Amendment; the right to counsel guaranteed by the Sixth Amendment; and the self-incrimination doctrine of the Fifth Amendment.

Perhaps no other case decided by the Supreme Court had such a far-reaching effect on the criminal justice system or stirred such emotional protest as *Miranda v. Arizona*, 86 S. Ct. 1602 (1966). Critics proclaimed that the Court had assumed a legislative role denied to it by the Constitution, was "handcuffing the police", and was "soft on crime". Congress reacted swiftly and enacted the 1968 Omnibus Crime Control and Safe Streets Act, which contained a section which seemed to be an attempt to overrule the *Miranda* decision on admissibility of confessions. (18 U.S.C.A. §3501). At least in part due to the furor created by the *Miranda* decision, Congress appropriated millions of dollars for law enforcement assistance, including sophisticated equipment, education and training.

It seems that *Miranda*, a decision intended to guarantee for criminal suspects the Fifth Amendment right against self-incrimination and the Sixth Amendment right to counsel, coincidentally hastened the *professionalization* of American law enforcement.

-------------------------------------- **Notes** --------------------------------------

§ 5.2 VOLUNTARINESS DOCTRINE

Under the early common law, confessions were admissible at trial without any restrictions whatsoever, so that even an incriminating statement obtained by torture was not excluded. Morgan, *The Privilege Against Self-Incrimination*, 34 Minn. L. Rev. 1 (1949). The first "exclusionary rule" was stated in the early English case of *The King v. Warickshall*, 168 Eng. Rep. 234, L. Leach Cases 263 (K.B. 1783), wherein it was stated:

> A free and voluntary confession is deserving of the highest credit, because it is presumed to flow from the strongest sense of guilt, and therefore it is admitted as proof of the crime to which it refers; but a confession forced from the mind by the flattery of hope, or by the torture of fear, comes in so questionable a shape when it is to be considered as the evidence of guilt, that no credit ought to be given to it; and therefore it is rejected.

The *Warickshall* rule, as followed in England and the United States, was designed to protect an accused from an erroneous conviction based upon a false confession. The rule is now discussed in terms of "voluntariness" with the test for this being "whether the confession is the product of an essentially free and unconstrained choice by its maker". *Schneckloth v. Bustamonte*, 93 S. Ct. 2041 (1973). Due Process requires that a confession must be the product of the defendant's free and rational choice. *Watts v. Indiana*, 69 S. Ct. 1347 (1949).

There are two categories of factors that courts take into consideration in determining the voluntariness and admissibility of a confession as part of the "totality of the circumstances": the condition of the defendant and the nature of the interrogation.

Age, sobriety, intellectual and educational background, and mental condition are examples of condition of the defendant. Length of interrogation, physical abuse, psychological influences, threats of violence and promises made to suspect are examples of nature of the interrogation factors.

If an interrogation is accompanied by physical violence, a virtual *per se* rule of involuntariness applies. *Brown v. Mississippi*, 56 S. Ct. 461 (1936). Psychological stress such as telling a suspect that her children would be deprived of welfare and taken from her was sufficient to establish that the confession was coerced and not admissible in *Lynumn v. Illinois*, 83 S. Ct. 917 (1963). "There is torture of mind as well as body; the will is as much affected by fear as by force." *Watts v. Indiana*, 69 S. Ct. 1347 (1949).

Because the right against compulsory self-incrimination is protected under the Fifth Amendment to the Constitution of the United States (which in turn applies to the states as a matter of Fourteenth Amendment due process of law), a state court's determination of voluntariness may be overturned by a reviewing federal court. This is what happened in *Woods v. Clusen*, 794 F.2d 293 (7th Cir. 1986). While local police were investigating the beating deaths of two persons, the defendant was observed watching from a distance. He thus became a prime suspect, but no probable cause was developed to arrest him for the murders. Later, police received information that he had, several months earlier, attempted to sell a stolen chain saw to a local resident. The police decided to arrest the defendant, who was 16½ years of age, for the chain saw theft, in order to question him about the murders.

At 7:30 a.m. the police drove to the trailer home where the defendant lived with his grandparents. They received consent to enter the home, went to the defendant's bedroom, and awakened and arrested him. He was handcuffed and driven to police headquarters. En route, he was advised of his *Miranda* rights and he stated that he did not want to consult an attorney. He did not respond when asked if he would like to answer questions or make a statement. After processing by a juvenile intake worker, he was fingerprinted, photographed, and asked to remove his clothes and put on jail overalls; however, was not issued shoes or socks and was left barefoot.

The defendant was then taken to an interrogation room and seated at a table. Photographs of the murder scene were displayed close to the table. Two officers asked him if he was willing to talk to them. He did not respond. The officers questioned the defendant about the murders for 15 to 20 minutes, during which time they used deceptive and intimidating tactics. They falsely told him they had enough evidence to convict him whether he talked or not. Except for stating, "I never went in the woods the next day" in response to a question as to why he was in the woods the day after the murders, he remained unresponsive, although in a clearly emotional state of mind.

The original interrogating officers were then replaced by two fresh investigators. Again, deceptive tactics were used, including a false indication that the defendant's fingerprints had been found on one victim's wallet. After 20 to 30 minutes of continuous interrogation, he began to cry. At this point, one of the officers put his hand on his shoulder in a fatherly manner, the defendant orally confessed to the murders. Later he pled guilty to murder, after unsuccessfully moving to suppress the oral confession.

The Wisconsin supreme court upheld the conviction; the defendant petitioned for habeas corpus in United States District Court on the theory that the interrogation tactics of the Wisconsin police had violated his federally-protected rights against compulsory self-incrimination. The district court agreed that his rights had been violated and the State of Wisconsin appealed. The United States Court of Appeals for the Seventh Circuit affirmed the district court's ruling, holding that the totality of circumstances indicated an "overreaching" of police conduct. In arriving at this conclusion, the court noted that the defendant was a juvenile, 16½ years of age, with no prior criminal record or serious previous contact with the criminal justice system. He was awakened by police officers surrounding his bed, handcuffed, and arrested, ostensibly for a theft. At the police station he was stripped of his clothes and given jail clothing but left barefoot. After fingerprinting and photographing he was subjected to murder scene photographs and was interrogated by two teams of police officers, even though he had not agreed to answer questions or to give a statement. The interrogating officers used intentional misrepresentations during their questioning session. They continued their relentless questioning despite the defendant's emotional reaction, and when he began to cry one officer further took advantage of his emotional immaturity by making a gesture of concern of doubtful sincerity. The court noted that, while no one aspect of police conduct would by itself amount to compulsory self-incrimination, in the totality of circumstances the defendant's confession was made less than voluntarily.

In *Barrera v. Young*, 794 F.2d 1264 (7th Cir. 1986) two defendants accused each other for the crimes of armed robbery and murder. One defendant asked to be given a polygraph examination. The polygraph examiner read him his *Miranda* rights on each of three occasions and both the defendant and his lawyer signed written waivers. Three tests were necessary, because the first two times the defendant was so anxious that the tests did not produce reliable results. Before the tests, which were conducted with the defendant's lawyer just outside the examining room, it was agreed that either he or his lawyer could stop the questioning at any time. Before the polygraph machine was turned on for the third test, the examiner, in his pre-test interview, advised the defendant that his co-defendant's polygraph results indicated that the defendant was lying. The examiner also appealed to the defendant's religious sensibilities. The defendant broke down and confessed to the examiner before the polygraph was turned on. The federal circuit court of appeals held that, when a suspect is psychologically prepared for interrogation, with his lawyer only seconds away, a 45-minute monologue by the examiner, which included appeals to religion and reminders that the state's evidence was strong, did not make the defendant's confession involuntary.

Although the Supreme Court, in *Miranda v. Arizona, supra*, was highly critical of police trickery and deception, as a general rule courts have not deemed such conduct sufficient of itself to make a confession involuntary. In *Frazier v. Cupp*, 89 S. Ct. 1420 (1969), police falsely stated to the defendant that his cousin had confessed and implicated him. The Court held that this misrepresentation, while relevant to the issue of voluntariness, was insufficient to make the otherwise voluntary confession inadmissible. Thus, misrepresenting the strength of the case against a suspect may be permissible deception. However, the courts are much less likely to tolerate misrepresentations of law, such as falsely asserting that a confession could not be used against the defendant at trial. *Commonwealth v. Dustin*, 368 N.E.2d 1388 (Mass. 1977). The most common form of deception involves confronting the suspect with nonexistent evidence implicating him in the crime under investigation. This technique has enjoyed widespread acceptance.

In summary, confessions are admissible as evidence when they are voluntarily given and are not the result of threats, promises, violence, or other improper influences or inducements. However, the state bears the burden of proving voluntariness. *Boyd v. State*, 430 N.E.2d 1146 (Ind. 1982).

A procedure for determining voluntariness was set forth in *Jackson v. Denno*, 84 S. Ct. 1774 (1964). The Court held that, under the Fourteenth Amendment, a defendant is entitled to an *in camera* determination of the voluntariness of his confession before it is presented to the jury. The jury may then hear evidence on the voluntariness of the confession which might affect its weight and credibility. *Craig v. State*, 370 N.E.2d 880 (Ind. 1977).

-- **Notes** --

Sample Questions

Before the case of *Miranda v. Arizona* was decided, the primary test the Courts used to determine if a confession was admissible was whether or not it was:
A. truthful.
B. credible.
C. self-incriminating.
D. voluntary.
E. complete.

The constitutional provision upon which the *Miranda* case is based is:
A. the Sixth Amendment right to counsel provision.
B. the Fifth Amendment privilege against compulsory self-incrimination.
C. the Fourth Amendment privilege against unreasonable searches and seizures.
D. the Eighth Amendment protection against cruel and unusual punishment.
E. the Fifth Amendment Due Process Clause.

If a confession is the product of unlawful police conduct, it may be held inadmissable under the "fruit of the poisonous tree" doctrine of the Fourth Amendment.   T.   F.

If a confession is obtained by the police from a suspect after he has asked to see a lawyer but who has been denied access to a lawyer by the wrongful action of the police, it may be held to be inadmissible under the Sixth Amendment.   T.   F.

Although the *Miranda* case was once a very important decision in American criminal procedure, it is of little effect now because it has been overruled by the Supreme Court.   T.   F.

In the determination of whether or not a confession was voluntary, the courts may consider the age, intellect, and mental condition of a defendant.   T.   F.

Physical torture will render a confession inadmissible, but psychological coercion will not.   T.   F.

Whether or not a confession was voluntary is determined by the courts by considering:
A. the totality of all the circumstances.
B. only the physical condition of the suspect.
C. only the mental condition of the suspect.
D. only the age of the suspect.
E. the recommendation of the jury as to whether it believes the confession to have been voluntary or involuntary.

The admissibility of a confession, and the weight and credibility it will be given are two separate and distinct questions decided by two different entities in a jury trial.   T.   F.

After the *Miranda* case was decided, the test for admissibility of a confession no longer involved the voluntariness test.   T.   F.

§5.3 FOURTH AMENDMENT CONFESSION ISSUES; FRUIT OF THE POISONOUS TREE DOCTRINE

If a defendant makes incriminating statements after being subjected to an illegal seizure, the statements may be suppressed as the "fruit of the poisonous tree". But in *Wong Sun v. United States*, 83 S. Ct. 407 (1962), the defendant made a voluntary statement several days after he had been arraigned and released on his own recognizance. This intervening time period so attenuated the taint of the illegal seizure that the statement was admissible.

The supreme court of Indiana addressed the "fruit of the poisonous tree" question in *Hendricks v. State*, 371 N.E.2d 1312 (1978) and held that, in order for a subsequent confession to be admissible, there must be a break in the chain of events sufficient to insulate the statement from the improper influence which went before. The court then stated:

> The totality of the circumstances should be reviewed in determining the admissibility of a subsequent statement, but the U.S. Supreme Court has suggested three primary factors for scrutiny: (1) the temporal proximity of the illegality and the confession; (2) the presence of intervening circumstances; and (3) the flagrancy of the official misconduct [citing *Brown v. Illinois*, briefed below].

CASE BRIEF

Brown v. Illinois, 95 S. Ct. 2254 (1975)

Majority opinion: Blackmun. Concurring: White; Powell (in part), joined by Rehnquist.

FACTS: D was arrested without probable cause and without a warrant after which he was given, in full, the warnings prescribed by *Miranda v. Arizona*, 86 S. Ct. 1602 (1966). While in custody D made two incriminating statements concerning a murder in which he had been an accomplice; one to interrogating police officers and one, after again being given the *Miranda* warnings, to an assistant state's attorney. He was indicted by a grand jury; prior to trial he moved to suppress the two statements he had made, alleging that his arrest and detention had been illegal and therefore that the statements were inadmissible. The motion was denied and at trial evidence of both statements was admitted. The jury found D guilty of murder and sentenced him to fifteen to thirty years. On appeal the supreme court of Illinois affirmed the conviction on the basis that, although the arrest had been illegal, the subsequent giving of the *Miranda* warnings served to break the causal connection between the illegal arrest and the giving of the statements. In effect, the court held that D's act of making the statements was "sufficiently an act of free will to purge the primary taint of the unlawful invasion," (citing *Wong Sun v. United States*, 83 S. Ct. 407 (1962).

ISSUE: Does the giving of the *Miranda* warnings, by itself, break whatever causal connection may exist between an unlawful arrest and the later obtaining of incriminating statements, so as to make such statements admissible?

DECISION: No; reversed and remanded.

REASONS: In *Wong Sun* the statements and contraband taken from two of the defendants were ruled inadmissible because of the illegal action of government agents. The Court there held that the statement did not result from "an intervening independent act of a free will," and that it was not "sufficiently an act of free will to purge the primary taint of the unlawful invasion." With respect to a third defendant (Wong Sun), who was also arrested without probable cause but was properly arraigned and released on his own recognizance, the Court held that the connection between the bad arrest and his voluntary return several days later to make a confession had become so weakened as to nullify the effect of the arrest. In other words, the apt question in such a case is whether, granting an initial wrongful act by the police, the evidence objected to is a product of that illegality or by other means sufficiently distinguishable to be purged of the initial wrong.

The exclusionary rule was applied in the *Wong Sun* case primarily to protect Fourth Amendment rights, to deter lawless conduct by federal officers and to close the door of the federal courts to any use of evidence unconstitutionally obtained. The exclusionary rule is calculated to prevent, not to repair; its purpose is to compel respect for the constitutional guarantee by removing the incentive to disregard it. But despite its broad deterrent purpose, the exclusionary rule has never been interpreted to prohibit the use of illegally seized evidence in all proceedings or against all persons.

The function of the *Miranda* warnings relates to the Fifth Amendment's guarantee against coerced self-incrimination, and the exclusion of a statement made when the warnings are not given deters the taking of in-custody incriminating statements without first informing D of his rights. The *Miranda* warnings have thus far not been regarded as a means of either remedying or deterring Fourth Amendment violations. Frequently rights under the Fourth and Fifth Amendments may appear to blend together, since unreasonable searches and seizures violative of the Fourth Amendment are almost always made to compel a person to give evidence against himself in violation of the Fifth Amendment. But the exclusionary rule, when used to effectuate the Fourth Amendment, serves different interests and policies from those it serves under the Fifth Amendment. It is directed at *all* unlawful searches and seizures — not only those that produce incriminating material or testimony as fruits. On the other hand, *Miranda* warnings, and the exclusion of a confession made without them, do not alone sufficiently deter a Fourth Amendment violation.

If *Miranda* warnings, by themselves, were held to do away with the harm of an unconstitutional arrest, regardless of how wanton or purposeful the Fourth Amendment violation, the effect of the exclusionary rule would be substantially diluted. Arrests without probable cause for questioning or for "investigation" would be encouraged by the knowledge that evidence derived therefrom could be made admissible by the simple procedure of giving *Miranda* warnings. The warnings would become a "cure all" and the guarantee against unreasonable searches and seizures a mere form of words.

It is true that persons arrested illegally may decide to speak of their own will, but the *Miranda* warnings, per se and by themselves, cannot ensure that this will be the case. The question of whether a confession is the product of free will under the *Wong Sun* rule must be answered on the facts of each case. The *Miranda* warnings are only one factor to consider. The proximity in time of the arrest and confession is also a factor, as is the presence of intervening circumstances and, particularly, the purpose and flagrancy of the official misconduct. The burden of showing admissibility rests with the prosecution.

The state failed to sustain the burden of showing that the evidence was admissible under *Wong Sun*. D's first statement was made only two hours after his illegal arrest, with no intervening event of significance. The second statement was clearly the result and fruit of the first. The illegal arrest was obviously purposeful and investigatory in design and execution. It was calculated to cause surprise, fright and confusion. The Illinois courts were in error in assuming that the *Miranda* warnings, by themselves, under *Wong Sun* always purge the taint of an illegal arrest.

RULE: The link of causation between an unlawful arrest and an incriminating statement made by the arrested person shortly thereafter cannot be broken solely by the giving of the *Miranda* warnings. Other factors which must also be considered in order to determine if the statement was made with free will, or whether it was the product of the unlawful arrest, are: the amount of time which elapsed between the arrest and the statement; the presence or absence of intervening circumstances; and the purpose and flagrancy of the official misconduct.

CASE BRIEF
Dunaway v. New York, 99 S. Ct. 2248 (1979)

Majority opinion: Brennan. Concurring: White, Stevens. Dissenting: Rehnquist, joined by Burger.

FACTS: Following a lead supplied by a jail inmate, police, not having sufficient probable cause for a warrant, nevertheless picked up D and transported him to headquarters for questioning. D was not told that he was under arrest, but he would have been physically restrained had he attempted to leave. He was taken to an interrogation room and after being given the *Miranda* warnings he waived counsel and eventually made statements and drew sketches that incriminated him. At trial D moved to suppress the statements and sketches, but the motion was denied and he was convicted. The conviction was affirmed by the highest New York appellate court, the Court of Appeals. The Supreme Court of the United States granted certiorari, vacated the judgment, and remanded the case for further consideration in light of *Brown v. Illinois*, 95 S. Ct. 2254 (1975). Further factual findings were made as to whether D had been detained and as to whether the police had had probable cause. The trial court determined that D's motion to suppress should have been granted and that the controlling authority was *Brown v. Illinois*. The court based its finding on a lack of probable cause to arrest D and the failure of the *Miranda* warnings to purge the taint of D's illegal seizure.

A divided Appellate Division reversed the trial court, citing as authority *People v. Morales*, 366 N.E.2d 248 (N.Y. 1977), holding:

> * * * law enforcement officials may detain an individual upon reasonable suspicion for questioning for a reasonable and brief period of time under carefully controlled conditions which are ample to protect the individual's Fifth and Sixth Amendment rights.

The Appellate Division also held that even if D's detention was illegal, the taint of the illegal detention was sufficiently attenuated to allow the admission of his statements and sketches. The Appellate Division also emphasized that D was never threatened or abused by the police and it purported to distinguish the situation from that in *Brown v. Illinois*. The New York Court of Appeals dismissed D's application to appeal.

ISSUES: (1) May a suspect be taken into custody by the police for the purpose of interrogation when probable cause for arrest does not exist? (2) If a suspect is taken into custody for the purpose of interrogation when probable cause for arrest is lacking, are statements admissible which are made by the suspect after being given *Miranda* warnings and waiving right to counsel?

DECISION: (1) No; (2) no; reversed.

REASONS: *Mapp v. Ohio*, 81 S. Ct. 1684 (1961) applied the Fourth Amendment to the states through the Fourteenth. There can be little doubt that D was "seized" in a Fourth Amendment sense when he was taken involuntarily to the police station for questioning. The state contends that the seizure did not amount to an arrest and was permissible under the Fourth Amendment because the police had "reasonable suspicion" that D had intimate knowledge about a serious and unsolved crime. The Court rejects this argument.

Before *Terry v. Ohio*, 88 S. Ct. 1868 (1968) the requirement for probable cause for a seizure was absolute. *Terry*, for the first time, recognized an exception to the probable cause requirement. That situation involved a brief on-the-spot stop and frisk for weapons, a situation that did not fit comfortably within the traditional concept of an "arrest." In *Terry* the Court balanced the limited violation of individual privacy involved against the opposing interests in crime prevention and detection and the police officer's safety. *Terry* was therefore a departure from traditional probable cause requirements but it was a very narrow and limited holding intended primarily to permit the police to disarm dangerous suspects.

The state requests that here the balancing test, rather than the general probable cause requirement, be applied to custodial interrogations, so as to permit D's seizure on "reasonable suspicion." But *Terry* and its progeny clearly do not support such a result. In those cases the intrusions were brief and narrowly circumscribed, but in this case D was taken from a neighbor's house to a police car, transported to a police station and placed in an interrogation room. The mere fact that he was not told he was under arrest nor "booked" is not significant. It is clear he would have been physically restrained if he had attempted to leave.

Hostility to seizures based on mere suspicion was a prime motivation for the adoption of the Fourth Amendment, and decisions immediately after its adoption affirmed that "common rumor or report, suspicion, or even 'strong reason to suspect' was not adequate to support a warrant for arrest."

The standard of probable cause provides the police with a single familiar guideline when the intrusion on privacy is significant. Two important decisions since *Terry* confirm the conclusion that the treatment of D, whether or not technically characterized as an arrest, must be supported by probable cause. *Davis v. Mississippi*, 89 S. Ct. 1394 (1969) condemned the wholesale roundup of suspects for fingerprinting and interrogation when probable cause or judicial intervention did not exist, and *Brown v. Illinois*, 95 S. Ct. 2254 (1975) disapproved arrests made for "investigatory" purposes on less than probable cause.

Both *Davis* and *Brown* hold that detention for custodial interrogation — regardless of its label — intrudes so severely on interests protected by the Fourth Amendment as necessarily to trigger the traditional safeguards against illegal arrest. The police violated the Fourth and Fourteenth Amendments when, without probable cause, they seized D and transported him to the police station for interrogation.

As to the connection between the unconstitutional police conduct and the statements and sketches made by D, the tests of *Wong Sun v. United States*, 83 S. Ct. 407 (1962) and *Brown v. Illinois* must be applied. If the statements and sketches were obtained by exploitation of an illegal arrest they are inadmissible. This situation is nearly a replica of the one in *Brown;* admitted seizure without probable cause in the hope that something might turn up, followed by a confession without any intervening event of significance. To admit D's confession in such a case would be to allow law enforcement officers to violate the Fourth Amendment with impunity (seize suspects with no probable cause), safe in the knowledge that they could wash their hands in the procedural safeguards of the Fifth Amendment by administering *Miranda* warnings.

RULE: A suspect may not be seized by the police for purposes of interrogation unless his arrest may be justified by the traditional Fourth Amendment standard of probable cause, and the constitutional violation committed by such a seizure cannot be "cured" solely by the *Miranda* warning and waiver procedure prior to interrogation; statements made by the suspect under such circumstances are inadmissible.

DISSENTING: There was no "seizure" of the person in a Fourth Amendment sense; D merely voluntarily assented to a police request. But assuming arguendo that there was a seizure, the facts of this case are still different from those in *Brown;* the connection between the alleged unlawful detention and the confession was sufficiently attenuated to make the confession admissible.

In *Rawlings v. Kentucky,* 100 S. Ct. 2556 (1980) the Court applied the totality of circumstances test and held that a statement of the defendant while in illegal custody following an illegal arrest was admissible. *Miranda* warnings were given moments before he gave his incriminating statement; the detention was in the congenial atmosphere of a home; the incriminating statements were made spontaneously upon the discovery of his drugs in his girl friend's purse and the conduct of the police was not flagrant, a prophylactic exclusion of the statement was not required. The state carried its burden of showing that defendant's statements were acts of free will unaffected by any illegality in the initial detention.

Justice O'Connor in *Oregon v. Elstad,* 105 S. Ct. 1285 (1985) (briefed below) referred to the *Wong Sun* doctrine as applied in *Brown* and *Dunaway* (briefed above) as settled law requiring the exclusion of confessions obtained through custodial interrogations after an illegal arrest "unless intervening events break the causal connection between the illegal arrest and the confession so that the confession is sufficiently an act of free will as to purge the primary taint. The burden is upon the prosecution to show a sufficient break in events to undermine the inference that the confession was caused by the Fourth Amendment violation".

CASE BRIEF
Oregon v. Elstad, 105 S. Ct. 1285 (1985)

Majority opinion: O'Connor. Concurring: Burger, White, Blackmun, Powell, and Rehnquist. Dissenting: Brennan, joined by Marshall; Stevens.

FACTS: Art objects and furnishings valued at $150,000 were stolen in a burglary of the Gross family residence. D was implicated in the burglary by a witness. Police went to D's home with a warrant for his arrest and were admitted to his home by D's mother. One officer explained to her why they were there, while the other officer talked to D in another room. When asked if he knew why police were there, D said he had no idea. The officer then asked D if he knew a person by the name of Gross. D said that he did, adding that he had heard there was a robbery at the Gross house. The officer told D that he felt D was involved in it, and D replied, "Yes, I was there."

The officers then transported D to the sheriff's headquarters where, approximately one hour later, he was advised of his *Miranda* rights for the first time. D indicated he understood his rights, and having them in mind, wished to speak to the officers. There followed a complete confession of the burglary, which was later typed, reviewed, corrected and initialed by D. D conceded that no threats or promises were made, either at his home or at the sheriff's office by the police.

D was charged with first-degree burglary. He was represented at trial by retained counsel, waived a jury trial, and was tried by the circuit court judge. D moved to suppress both his oral statement and the signed confession. He argued that the oral statement, "Yes, I was there", made to police at his house, "let the cat out of the bag", and because it was made in response to in-custody interrogation without the *Miranda* requirements having been complied with, "tainted" the confession, making it "fruit of the poisonous tree". The trial judge ruled that the original statement, "Yes, I was there", was inadmissible as being obtained in violation of *Miranda*, but that the later confession obtained at the sheriff's headquarters was admissible, having been given freely, voluntarily, and knowingly, after proper warning and waiver, and not "tainted" in any way by the previous inadmissible oral statement. D was convicted of first degree burglary. The Oregon court of appeals reversed, holding D's signed confession, although voluntary, was made inadmissible by the earlier admission obtained in violation of *Miranda*.

ISSUE: Does failure by police to administer the *Miranda* warning and waiver procedure, before an initial incriminating statement is made, "taint" a subsequent confession made after D has been fully advised and has waived his *Miranda* rights?

DECISION: No. Oregon court of appeals reversed, trial court conviction reinstated.

REASONS: The Oregon court of appeals incorrectly assumed that any failure to comply with *Miranda* automatically and necessarily breeds the same consequences as police infringement of a constitutional right.

The *Miranda* decision required suppression of many statements that previously would have been admissible under traditional due process standards, by presuming that statements made in custody and without adequate warnings and waiver were protected by the Fifth Amendment. (In other words, after *Miranda*, confessions, to be admissible, not only had to be "voluntary", but also had to be obtained after prior warning and waiver.) But the Fifth Amendment is not concerned with nontestimonial evidence — nor with psychological pressures to confess emanating from sources *other than official coercion* — nor with volunteered statements.

D's "fruit of the poisonous tree" argument in this case assumes the existence of a *constitutional* violation. But the *Miranda* exclusionary rule sweeps more broadly than the Fifth Amendment itself. (The Fifth Amendment only protects against *official compulsion*.) Failure to comply with *Miranda* creates a presumption of compulsion, and requires suppression even in the absence of actual compulsion. But the *Miranda* presumption, though irrebuttable for purposes of the prosecutions' case in chief, does not require that statements and their fruits be discarded as *inherently* tainted. (Citing use for impeachment purposes in *Harris v. New York*, and use for identifying another witness in *Michigan v. Tucker*). In *Harris* and *Tucker* there was no actual compulsion or coercion which violated a constitutional right and hence no requirement to impose the *Wong Sun* "fruit of the poisonous tree" doctrine. The same reasoning applies when the alleged "fruit" of a noncoercive *Miranda* violation is neither a witness nor real evidence, but the accused's own voluntary testimony.

We have repeatedly stated that *Miranda* requirements apply only in *custodial* situations — but "custody" is a slippery concept and police cannot be expected to make no errors whatsoever. If police make errors in the application of *Miranda* procedures, they should not breed the same irremediable consequence as actual violation of the Fifth Amendment itself (coercion). Though *Miranda* requires that the unwarned admission be suppressed, the admissibility of any subsequent statement made after proper warnings and waiver should turn on whether it was knowingly and voluntarily made. The Court has never gone so far as to hold that making a confession under circumstances which prevent its use perpetually disables the confessor from making a usable one after those conditions have been removed — nor that the psychological impact of voluntary disclosure of a guilty secret qualifies as state compulsion, or compromises the voluntariness of a later informed waiver. To hold to the contrary (as the Oregon court of appeals did), would burden legitimate law enforcement activity while adding little desirable protection to the individual's right against *compulsory* self incrimination.

There is a vast difference in the consequences flowing from coercion of a confession by physical violence or other deliberate action to break a suspect's will, and the uncertain consequence of disclosure of a "guilty secret" freely given in response to an unwarned but noncoercive question.

Although D claims his waiver was not *fully informed* (because he was unaware his unwarned statement could not be used against him), we have never embraced the theory that a D's ignorance of the full consequences of his decisions does away with their voluntariness.

RULE: When, by uncoercive questioning, police obtain an incriminating response from a suspect in custody without having complied with the requirements of *Miranda*, such a statement, although inadmissible in the state's case in chief, does not prevent the suspect from later waiving his rights and giving an admissible confession after having been given the required *Miranda* warnings. It is governmental coercion, or wearing down the will of a suspect, which violates the Fifth Amendment, and to which the "fruit of the poisonous tree" doctrine applies; it does *not* apply to every noncoercive police failure to comply with *Miranda*.

DISSENT: The psychological impact of "letting the cat out of the bag" as the product of unwarned interrogation greatly *undermines* the voluntariness of any later statement. Police interrogation manuals reflect that they realize the psychological impact of the first admission of guilt. The majority opinion will probably lead to further police abuse concerning the timing of *Miranda* warnings with reference to in-custody interrogation. The suggestion of the majority that the basis of *Miranda* is in the Court's supervisory authority over interrogation practices is erroneous — it must be found in the Fifth Amendment because otherwise the Court would be powerless to enforce it against the states. Although the Court in this opinion does recognize the *irrebuttable* presumption of inadmissibility in the state's case in chief of confessions obtained in violation of *Miranda*, it does great harm in allowing the admissibility of later confessions which are *derived from* such inadmissible statements.

In *New York v. Harris*, 110 S.Ct. 1640 (1990), the issue before the Court was whether entry by police into a felony suspect's home for the purpose of arresting him, with probable cause but without a warrant, consent, or exigent circumstances, (in violation of *Payton v. New York*, 100 S.Ct. 1371 (1980)), requires suppression of all incriminating statements made by the suspect following his arrest. The Court distinguished the situation in *Harris* from that in *Brown v. Illinois*, 95 S.Ct. 2254 (1975), and *Dunaway v. New York*, 99 S.Ct. 2248 (1979) by noting that probable cause for arrest did not exist in either *Brown* or *Dunaway*, but it did exist in *Harris*. Therefore, the Court held, the *Mirandized* confession obtained while still in the suspect's home must be suppressed because of the Fourth Amendment violation, but a *Mirandized* statement made an hour later at the police station was admissible. The Court reasoned that the rule in *Payton* was designed to protect the physical integrity of the home, but not to grant criminal suspects protection from incriminating statements made outside the home when continuing custody was justified by probable cause and when *Miranda* had been followed. (*Harris* was a 5 to 4 holding. The dissenters argued that the rule in *Brown v. Illinois* should control because of the flagrant disregard by police of the arrest warrant requirement and because the majority opinion might create an incentive for police to disregard the warrant requirement in like cases, knowing that later confessions outside the home would be unaffected by the Fourth Amendment exclusionary rule.)

Sample Questions

In a few cases the courts have found that an incriminating confession obtained by the police following improper police conduct is, nevertheless, admissible if intervening events break the casual connection between the improper police conduct and the confession so that the confession is sufficiently an act of free will as to purge the primary taint. (T.) F.

Every noncoercive police failure to comply strictly with the requirements of the *Miranda* case will not result in a violation of the Fifth Amendment's protection against compulsory self-incrimination. T. F.

Once "adversary proceedings" have been initiated against an individual:
A. he has the right to legal representation when the government interrogates him, and he cannot waive this right until he confers with an attorney.
B. he has the right to legal representation when the government interrogates him, but he can voluntarily waive this right before he talks to an attorney.
C. he cannot be interrogated by the police under any circumstances.
D. his constitutional rights are null and void.
E. none of the above.

The "inevitable discovery" and the "independent source" doctrines are similar in that both can allow the admission of evidence that might otherwise be inadmissible because of police conduct. (T.) F.

If any sort of trickery or deception is used by the police in obtaining a confession, it will automatically be considered inadmissible in court. T. (F.)

The link of causation between an unlawful arrest and an incriminating statement made by the arrested person shortly thereafter can be broken by the giving of the *Miranda* warnings and obtaining a waiver of rights in just about every case. T. F.

The question of whether or not a confession will be admitted in evidence is ultimately decided by:
(A.) the judge.
B. the prosecutor.
C. the defense counsel
D. the jury.
E. the court administrator.

The procedures suggested in the *Miranda* case do not apply when there is police questioning of a person who is not in custody. (T.) F.

The courts have defined "interrogation" — in terms of the *Miranda* case — as:
A. formal police questioning of a suspect who is in custody.
B. written interrogatories only.
C. the functional equivalent of formal questioning of a suspect who is in custody, i.e., any query or conduct that the police should know is reasonably likely to elicit an incriminating response.
D. any question directed to a suspect under any circumstances.
(E.) A and C above.

§ 5.4 SIXTH AMENDMENT RIGHT TO COUNSEL IN CONFESSIONS

(A) Pre-charge questioning

The sixth amendment provides: "In all criminal prosecutions, the accused shall enjoy the right to have Assistance of Counsel for his defense." The Constitution is silent concerning the scope of this right and when it attaches. Recent decisions have held that counsel is required at those critical stages of criminal proceedings where substantial prejudice to the defendant may result from a failure to have counsel present and where counsel could help mitigate or eliminate such prejudice. *United States v. Wade.*, 87 S. Ct. 1926 (1967).

The right to counsel during the pre-indictment stage of a criminal investigation was the basis of the Court's decision in the landmark case of *Escobedo v. Illinois*, 84 S. Ct. 1758 (1964). The court held that where (1) the investigation has begun to focus on a particular suspect, (2) the suspect is taken into police custody, (3) the police interrogate to elicit incriminating statements, (4) the suspect has requested and been denied a lawyer and (5) the police have not effectively warned him of his absolute right to remain silent, the accused has been denied "the Assistance of Counsel" in violation of the Sixth Amendment, and no statement elicited by the police during the interrogation may be used against him at a criminal trial.

-------------------------------------- **Notes** --------------------------------------

Sample Questions

When two defendants have been indicted for criminal offenses and one of them, without any police involvement, decides to cooperate in the police investigation and help build a case against the other, and when the police continue their investigation:

A. nothing that the police thereafter discover can be used against the non-cooperating defendant because adversary proceedings have commenced.
B. evidence thereafter discovered against the non-cooperating defendant concerning the crimes for which he has already been indicted is inadmissible against him.
C. evidence therafter discovered against the non-cooperating defendant concerning crimes for which he has not yet been formally charged is admissible against him.
D. B and C above.
E. all evidence thereafter discovered against the non-cooperating defendant is admissible.

Police questioning of a suspect at a police station will always be held by the court to be custodial interrogation.   T.   F.

Police use a form of *Miranda* warning which stated: "Before we ask you any questions, you must understand your rights. You have the right to remain silent. Anything you say can be used against you in court. You have a right to talk to a lawyer for advice before we ask you any questions, and to have him with you during questioning. You have this right to the advice and presence of a lawyer even if you cannot afford to hire one. We have no way of giving you a lawyer, but one will be appointed for you, if you wish, if and when you go to court. If you wish to answer questions now without a lawyer present, you have the right to stop answering questions at any time. You also have the right to stop answering at any time until you've talked to a lawyer." With regard to the adequacy of the above-quoted warning, the Supreme Court, in a 5 to 4 opinion, held:

A. the warning was confusing and equivocal, and therefore inadequate.
B. in order for a *Miranda* warning to be adequate, it must use the precise language that was used in that opinion.
C. the part of the warning which was defective was the reference to a lawyer being appointed "if and when you go to court."
D. all of the above.
E. the warning "touched all of the bases required by *Miranda*" and was, therefore, an adequate warning.

The *Miranda* warnings themselves are not rights protected by the Constitution, but are instead measures to insure that the right against compulsory self-incrimination is protected.   T.   F.

A police-motorist roadside encounter in full public view, such as an officer stopping and investigating a suspected intoxicated driver, asking him a modest number of questions and submitting him to simple balancing tests, does not ordinarily involve the need for the *Miranda* warning and waiver procedure before an arrest is made.   T.   F.

(B) Post-Charge Questioning

INTERROGATION AFTER ADVERSARY PROCEEDINGS HAVE COMMENCED

The clear rule in *Massiah v. United States* (text below) is that, once adversary proceedings have commenced against an individual, he has a right to legal representation when the government interrogates him. In *Brewer v. Williams* (briefed below) the Supreme Court of the United States followed *Massiah* in holding that, where judicial proceedings had been initiated against the accused; where his retained lawyers advised both the accused and the police against interrogation; and where the police nevertheless persuaded the accused with a "Christian burial" speech to show them where the body of his victim was hidden, the accused's right to counsel was violated and the conduct of the police amounted to interrogation in violation of *Massiah*. The Court acknowledged that the right to counsel can be waived, but held it was not waived in that case. It appears that there is a high standard for waiver, judging from the facts of *Brewer*. See *Patterson v. Illinois*, discussed below, this section.

TEXT OF CASE

Massiah v. United States, 84 S. Ct. 1199 (1964)

Mr. Justice STEWART delivered the opinion of the Court.

The petitioner was indicted for violating the federal narcotics laws. He retained a lawyer, pleaded not guilty, and was released on bail. While he was free on bail a federal agent succeeded by surreptitious means in listening to incriminating statements made by him. Evidence of these statements was introduced against the petitioner at his trial over his objection. He was convicted, and the Court of Appeals affirmed. We granted certiorari to consider whether, under the circumstances here presented, the prosecution's use at the trial of evidence of the petitioner's own incriminating statements deprived him of any right secured to him under the Federal Constitution. 374 U.S. 805, 83 S. Ct. 1698, 10 L.Ed.2d 1030.

The petitioner, a merchant seaman, was in 1958 a member of the crew of the S. S. *Santa Maria*. In April of that year federal customs officials in New York received information that he was going to transport a quantity of narcotics aboard that ship from South America to the United States. As a result of this and other information, the agents searched the *Santa Maria* upon its arrival in New York and found in the afterpeak of the vessel five packages containing about three and a half pounds of cocaine. They also learned of circumstances, not here relevant, tending to connect the petitioner with the cocaine. He was arrested, promptly arraigned, and subsequently indicted for possession of narcotics aboard a United States vessel. In July a superseding indictment was returned, charging the petitioner and a man named Colson with the same substantive offense, and in separate counts charging the petitioner, Colson, and others with having conspired to possess narcotics aboard a United States vessel, and to import, conceal, and facilitate the sale of narcotics. The petitioner, who had retained a lawyer, pleaded not guilty and was released on bail, along with Colson.

A few days later, and quite without the petitioner's knowledge, Colson decided to cooperate with the government agents in their continuing investigation of the narcotics activities in which the petitioner, Colson, and others had allegedly been engaged. Colson permitted an agent named Murphy to install a Schmidt radio transmitter under the front seat of Colson's automobile, by means of which Murphy, equipped with an appropriate receiving device, could overhear from some distance away conversations carried on in Colson's car.

On the evening of November 19, 1959, Colson and the petitioner held a lengthy conversation while sitting in Colson's automobile, parked on a New York street. By prearrangement with Colson, and totally unbeknown to the petitioner, the agent Murphy sat in a car parked out of sight down the street and listened over the radio to the entire conversation. The petitioner made several incriminating statements during the course of this conversation. At the petitioner's trial these incriminating statements were brought before the jury through Murphy's testimony, despite the insistent objection of defense counsel. The jury convicted the petitioner of several related narcotics offenses, and the convictions were affirmed by the Court of Appeals.

The petitioner argues that it was an error of constitutional dimension to permit the agent Murphy at the trial to testify to the petitioner's incriminating statements which Murphy had overheard under the circumstances disclosed by this record. This argument is based upon two distinct and independent grounds. First, we are told that Murphy's use of the radio equipment violated the petitioner's rights under the Fourth Amendment, and consequently, that all evidence which Murphy thereby obtained was, under the rule of Weeks v. United States, 232 U.S. 383, 34 S. Ct. 341, 58 L.Ed. 652, inadmissible against the petitioner at the trial. Secondly, it is said that the petitioner's Fifth and Sixth Amendment rights were violated by the use in evidence against him of incriminating statements which government agents had deliberately elicited from him after he had been indicted and in the absence of his retained counsel. Because of the way we dispose of the case, we do not reach the Fourth Amendment issue.

In Spano v. New York, 360 U.S. 315, 79 S. Ct. 1202, 3 L.Ed.2d 1265, this Court reversed a state criminal conviction because a confession had been wrongly admitted into evidence against the defendant at his trial. In that case the defendant had already been indicted for first-degree murder at the time he confessed. The Court held that the defendant's conviction could not stand under the Fourteenth Amendment. While the Court's opinion relied upon the totality of the circumstances under which the confession had been obtained, four concurring Justices pointed out that the Constitution required reversal of the conviction upon the sole and specific ground that the confession had been deliberately elicited by the police after the defendant had been indicted, and therefore at a time when he was clearly entitled to a lawyer's help. It was pointed out that under our system of justice the most elemental concepts of due process of law contemplate that an indictment be followed by a trial, "in an orderly courtroom, presided over by a judge, open to the public, and protected by all the procedural safeguards of the law." 360 U.S., at 327, 79 S. Ct. at 1209, 3 L.Ed.2d 1265 (STEWART, J., concurring). It was said that a Constitution which guarantees a defendant the aid of counsel at such a trial could surely vouchsafe no less to an indicted defendant under interrogation by the police in a completely extrajudicial proceeding. Anything less, it was said, might deny a defendant "effective representation by counsel at the only stage when legal aid and advice would help him." 360 U.S., at 326, 79 S. Ct., 79 S. Ct., at 1209, 3 L.Ed.2d 1265 (DOUGLAS, J., concurring).

Ever since this Court's decision in the Spano case, the New York courts have unequivocally followed this constitutional rule. "Any secret interrogation of the defendant, from and after the finding of the indictment, without the protection afforded by the presence of counsel, contravenes the basic dictates of fairness in the conduct of criminal causes and the fundamental rights of persons charged with crime." People v. Waterman, 9 N.Y.2d 561, 565, 216 N.Y.S.2d 70, 75, 175 N.E.2d 445, 448.

This view no more than reflects a constitutional principle established as long ago as Powell v. Alabama, 287 U.S. 45, 53 S. Ct. 55, 77 L.Ed. 158, where the

Court noted that "* * * during perhaps the most critical period of the proceedings * * * that is to say, from the time of their arraignment until the beginning of their trial, when consultation, thorough-going investigation and preparation [are] vitally important, the defendants * * * [are] as much entitled to such aid [of counsel] during that period as at the trial itself." Id., 287 U.S., at 57, 53 S. Ct., at 59, 77 L.Ed. 158. And since the Spano decision the same basic constitutional principle has been broadly reaffirmed by this Court.

* * *

Here we deal not with a state court conviction, but with a federal case, where the specific guarantee of the Sixth Amendment directly applies. Johnson v. Zerbst, 304 U.S. 458, 58 S. Ct. 1019, 82 L.Ed. 1461. We hold that the petitioner was denied the basic protections of that guarantee when there was used against him at his trial evidence of his own incriminating words, which federal agents had deliberately elicited from him after he had been indicted and in the absence of his counsel. It is true that in the Spano case the defendant was interrogated in a police station, while here the damaging testimony was elicited from the defendant without his knowledge while he was free on bail. But, as Judge Hays pointed out in his dissent in the Court of Appeals, "if such a rule is to have any efficacy it must apply to indirect and surreptitious interrogations as well as those conducted in the jailhouse. In this case, Massiah was more seriously imposed upon * * * because he did not even know that he was under interrogation by a government agent." 307 F.2d at 72-73.

The Solicitor General, in his brief and oral argument, has strenuously contended that the federal law enforcement agents had the right, if not indeed the duty, to continue their investigation of the petitioner and his alleged criminal associates even though the petitioner had been indicted. He points out that the Government was continuing its investigation in order to uncover not only the source of narcotics found on the S.S. *Santa Maria*, but also their intended buyer. He says that the quantity of narcotics involved was such as to suggest that the petitioner was part of a large and well-organized ring, and indeed that the continuing investigation confirmed this suspicion, since it resulted in criminal charges against many defendants. Under these circumstances the Solicitor General concludes that the government agents were completely "justified in making use of Colson's cooperation by having Colson continue his normal associations and by surveilling them."

We may accept and, at least for present purposes, completely approve all that this argument implies, Fourth Amendment problems to one side. We do not question that in this case, as in many cases, it was entirely proper to continue an investigation of the suspected criminal activities of the defendant and his alleged confederates, even though the defendant had already been indicted. All that we hold is that the defendant's own incriminating statements, obtained by federal agents under the circumstances here disclosed, could not constitutionally be used by the prosecution as evidence against *him* at his trial.

Reversed.

[Dissenting opinion omitted.]

CASE BRIEF

Brewer v. Williams, 97 S. Ct. 1232 (1977)

Majority opinion: Stewart. Concurring: Marshall, Powell, Stevens. Dissenting: Burger, White, Blackmun, Rehnquist.

FACTS: The victim, a 10-year-old girl, was abducted by D when she left her parents go to the restroom during a wrestling match in which her brother was participating at a Y.M.C.A. in Des Moines, Iowa. D, a former mental patient who was also deeply religious, sexually abused the victim and murdered her in his room at the Y.M.C.A. Soon after the girl's disappearance, D was seen in the Y.M.C.A. lobby carrying some clothing and a large bundle wrapped in a blanket. A young boy opened the front door for D and when D put the bundle in the front seat of his car the boy "saw 2 legs in it and they were skinny and white." Before anyone could investigate, D drove away. His abandoned car was found the following day in Davenport, Iowa. A warrant was issued in Des Moines on a charge of abduction. Two days after the abduction, on the advice of M, a Des Moines lawyer whom he had called, D surrendered to the Davenport police. He was booked on the abduction charge and given the *Miranda* warnings. The Davenport police then called the Des Moines police to advise them D had surrendered. Lawyer M was at the Des Moines police station; he talked to D and told him, in the presence of the chief and Detective L, that officers would drive to Davenport and pick him up; that they would not question him or mistreat him; and that D was not to talk to the police about the missing girl before consulting with him. It was then agreed that Detective L and another officer would go to Davenport, pick up D and bring him directly back to Des Moines without questioning him.

In the meantime D was arraigned before a judge in Davenport on the arrest warrant. The judge advised D of the *Miranda* rights and committed him to jail. Before leaving the courtroom D conferred with Lawyer K, who advised him not to make any statements before consulting his lawyer back in Des Moines.

Detective L and his partner arrived in Davenport to pick up D. They met D and Lawyer K, who they understood was acting as D's laywer. Detective L repeated the *Miranda* warnings to D. Lawyer K again reminded Detective L that D was not to be questioned and that the agreement with Lawyer M, D's Des Moines lawyer, was to be carried out.

At no time during the return trip did D express a willingness to be interrogated in the absence of an attorney. Instead, he stated several times that "when we get back to Des Moines and see M, I am going to tell you the whole story."

Detective L knew that D was a former mental patient and that he was deeply religious. He soon embarked on a wide-ranging conversation with D, covering a variety of topics including religion. Then, addressing D as "Reverend," Detective L said:

> I want to give you something to think about while we're traveling down the road . . . Number one, I want you to observe the weather conditions, it's raining, it's sleeting, it's freezing, driving is very treacherous, visibility is poor, it's going to be dark early this evening. They are predicting several inches of snow for tonight, and I feel that you yourself are the only person that knows where this little girl's body is, that you yourself have only been there once, and if you get a snow on top of it you yourself may be unable to find it. And, since we will be going right past the area on the way to Des Moines, I feel that we could stop and locate the body, that the parents of this little girl should be entitled to a Christian burial for the little girl who was snatched away from them on Christmas Eve and murdered. And I feel we should stop and locate it on the way rather than waiting until morning and trying to come back out after a snow storm and possibly not being able to find it at all.

D asked Detective L why he thought the route to Des Moines would take them by the body and Detective L replied that he knew the body was in the area of Mitchellville — a town they would be passing. Then Detective L said: "I do not want you to answer me. I don't want to discuss it further. Just think about it as we're riding down the road."

After some time had passed, D asked whether the police had found the victim's shoes. Detective L said he was unsure. D directed the officers to a service station where he said he had left the shoes; but a search failed to locate them.

As they continued toward Des Moines, D asked whether the police had found the blanket, and he directed the officers to a rest area where he said he had disposed of it. Nothing was found.

They continued toward Des Moines, and as they approached Mitchellville, D said he would show the officers where the body was; he directed the officers to the body of the victim. (Detective L later testified he did not know the body was in this area, but had guessed right.)

D was indicted for first degree murder. Before trial his attorney moved to suppress all evidence relating to or resulting from anything D had said on the automobile ride from Davenport to Des Moines. The judge, noting the agreement not to question D, found that the information had been elicited during a "critical stage in the proceedings requiring the presence of counsel on his request," but the judge denied the motion, ruling that D had, under the circumstances, waived his right to have an attorney present.

D was convicted of murder and his conviction was affirmed by the Iowa supreme court by a bare majority. D then petitioned for a writ of habeas corpus in the United States District Court for the Southern District of Iowa. The district court made findings of fact and concluded as a matter of law that the evidence had been wrongly admitted at D's trial. The conclusion was based on three grounds: (1) that D had been denied his constitutional right to assistance of counsel; (2) that he had been denied constitutional protections enumerated in *Escobedo v. Illinois*, 84 S. Ct. 1758 (1964) and *Miranda v. Arizona*, 86 S. Ct. 1602 (1966); and (3) that in any event his self-incriminatory statements and actions during the automobile ride had been involuntarily made. Further, the district court ruled that there had been no waiver by D of any of his constitutional protections.

The United States Court of Appeals for the Eighth Circuit affirmed this judgment and denied a petition for rehearing en banc.

ISSUE: Under the facts and circumstances of this case, did D waive his right to assistance of counsel?

DECISION: No; judgment of court of appeals affirmed.

REASONS: The right to assistance of counsel, guaranteed by the Sixth and Fourteenth Amendments, is indispensable to the fair administration of our adversary system of criminal justice. As was stated 44 years ago in *Powell v. Alabama*, 53 S. Ct. 55 (1932):

> During perhaps the most critical period of the proceedings against these defendants, that is to say, from the time of their arraignment until the beginning of their trial, when consultation, thoroughgoing investigation and preparation were vitally important, the defendants did not have the aid of counsel in any real sense, although they were as much entitled to such aid during that period as at the trial itself.

Whatever else it may mean, the right to counsel means at least that a person is entitled to the help of a lawyer at or after the time that judicial proceedings have been initiated against him — whether by formal charge, preliminary hearing, indictment, information or arraignment.

There can be no doubt that Detective L deliberately and designedly set out to elicit information from D — as surely as — and perhaps more effectively than — if he had formally interrogated him. Detective L was fully aware that D was represented by counsel — by Lawyer K in Davenport and Lawyer M in Des Moines. Yet during the period of isolation from the lawyers, Detective L set out to elicit as much incriminating evidence as possible. Detective L conceded this when he testified at D's trial.

Detective L's "Christian burial speech" was tantamount to interrogation. The circumstances are constitutionally indistinguishable from those in *Massiah v. United States*, 84 S. Ct. 1199 (1964) (text above in this section). The clear rule of *Massiah* is that once adversary proceedings have been commenced against an individual, he has a right to legal representation when the government interrogates him.

The Iowa courts recognized that D had been denied the right to assistance of counsel but they held he had waived that right. They applied a "totality of the circumstances" test, noting that D had not expressly requested counsel, nor asserted his right or desire *not* to give information in the absence of his lawyer. But this is the wrong test. It is the *government* which bears a heavy burden to show *waiver* — *not* the defendant. It was incumbent on the state to prove "an intentional relinquishment or abandonment of a known right or privilege." Also, the courts indulge in every reasonable presumption against waiver. The record in this case falls short of sustaining the state's burden to show that D waived his right to counsel. It is true D had been informed of and appeared to understand his right to counsel. But waiver requires not merely comprehension, but relinquishment, and D's consistent reliance upon the advice of counsel in dealing with the police refutes any suggestion that he waived that right. His statements while in the police car that he would tell the whole story *after* seeing his lawyer in Des Moines were the clearest expressions by D that he desired presence of counsel before interrogation took place. D also knew of the agreement of police not to interrogate him — an agreement made with assistance of counsel on both ends of the trip — and there is no basis for concluding that he disavowed it. Detective L made no effort to remind D of his right to counsel or to determine whether he wished to waive that right before the "Christian burial speech" which was tantamount to in-custody interrogation.

Under the circumstances of this case D could have waived his Sixth and Fourteenth Amendment rights without notice to counsel; but he did not do so.

This was a senseless and brutal crime, calling for swift and energetic action by the police. Yet disinterested zeal for the public good does not assure either wisdom or right in the method it pursues. The pressures on state executive and judicial officers charged with the administration of the criminal law are great, especially when the crime is murder and the victim a small child. But it is precisely the predictability of those pressures that makes imperative a resolute loyalty to the guarantees that the Constitution extends to all.

RULE: Once adversary proceedings have been initiated against an individual, he has a right to legal representation when the government interrogates him. Should the government initiate interrogation after this time in the absence of D's counsel — or take action which is tantamount to interrogation — in the absence of a knowing, voluntary, and expressed waiver of the rights of silence and counsel by D, any incriminating evidence thereby discovered is inadmissible.

CONCURRING: Good police work is far different from catching the criminal at any price. Crime is contagious; if the government becomes a lawbreaker it breeds contempt for law, it invites every man to become a law unto himself and it invites anarchy.

There was no evidence that D knowingly and voluntarily waived his Fifth and Sixth Amendment rights.

It is difficult to decide this case dispassionately in view of its emotional aspects, but if, in the long run, we are seriously concerned about the individual's effective representation by counsel, the state cannot be permitted to dishonor its promise to this lawyer.

DISSENTING: This case involved no threat nor coercion by the police. D's disclosures were voluntary and constituted a waiver of his rights, of which he was fully aware, having been advised numerous times. A person should have the free choice to change his mind voluntarily without being required to consult a lawyer first. A balancing test should be used in applying the exclusionary rule, weighing society's need for the evidence against the need to deter police misconduct. Here, the conduct of the police was non-flagrant and there was certainly no need to suppress based on unreliability, because the body was found exactly where D said it would be found. Since suppression is not automatically required in all Fourth and Fifth Amendment cases involving police misconduct, there is no reason to require it automatically in a Sixth Amendment case. In a case such as this, where D was convicted according to due process of law and is, by the proof and by his own admission, clearly guilty, collateral attacks on the conviction (this review arose through a habeas corpus proceeding) should not be permitted. They should be permitted only when the defendant raises the kind of constitutional claim that casts some doubt on his guilt.

NOTE ON "INEVITABLE DISCOVERY" AND "INDEPENDENT SOURCE"

After the decision of *Brewer v. Williams*, 97 S. Ct. 1232 (1977) an Iowa court again tried the defendant, Williams. At this trial neither his incriminating statements nor the fact of his having led police to the body were used in evidence; however, the court did admit testimony concerning the body's location and condition on the strength of evidence that, in the normal course of events, the body would inevitably have been discovered. (A search party of some two hundred volunteers was already systematically searching the area when Williams led police to the body.) Williams was again convicted of murder and the Iowa supreme court affirmed the conviction. The federal district court denied his petition for habeas corpus, agreeing with the "inevitable discovery" theory. The court of appeals reversed, holding that an "inevitable discovery" exception to the exclusionary rule must be supported by proof, which the state had not provided, that the police had not acted in bad faith. In *Nix v. Williams*, 104 S. Ct. 2501 (1984) the Supreme Court reversed the court of appeals and reinstated Williams' second conviction. It agreed with the Iowa courts' "inevitable discovery" theory and compared it to the "independent source" doctrine (see *Wong Sun v. United States*, 83 S. Ct. 407 (1962). The Court stated that, while society has an interest in deterring police misconduct by use of the exclusionary rule, it also has a definite interest in allowing juries to hear and consider all probative evidence in a criminal case. In balancing these two interests, the court should not put the prosecution in a position which is either better or worse than it would have been in if the misconduct had not occurred. If the prosecution can prove by a preponderance of evidence that the evidence in question would inevitably have been discovered by lawful means, the "deterrence" aspect of the exclusionary rule is not an appropriate consideration. To exclude such evidence would put the prosecution in a worse position than it would have been in without the misconduct, and would fail to advance society's interest in providing the jury with important probative evidence. Thus, in invoking the "inevitable discovery" theory the state is not required to prove absence of bad faith on the part of the police, nor would the exclusion of evidence that would inevitably have been discovered add to the fairness of the trial. The fact that Williams did not waive his right to counsel, and was thus improperly questioned in violation of the Sixth Amendment, could have no bearing on the inevitable discovery of the victim's body.

The "independent source" doctrine was applied by the supreme court in a search situation in *Murray v. United States*, S. Ct. (1988), (See Sec. 4.14(a)(1)).

The police placement of informers in jail cells to obtain incriminating admissions impacts on Sixth Amendment protection if it is done after formal charges have been filed and adversary proceedings have begun. In *United States v. Henry*, 100 S. Ct. 2183 (1980) the Court held the Sixth Amendment was violated when a police informant in the jail cell with the defendant deliberately elicited statements from his cellmate. In contrast, the Court held in *Kuhlmann v. Wilson*, 106 S. Ct. 2616 (1986) that the Sixth Amendment was not violated when the informer in the cell only listened to spontaneous statements and took no action that was designed to deliberately elicit incriminating statements.

In *Maine v. Moulton*, 106 S. Ct. 477 (1985), the defendant, who had already been indicted along with a partner for theft, decided to cooperate with police and testify against his partner in return for a promise that no further charges would be brought against him. The "deal" was made at defendant's own request, after his partner had suggested that they kill a witness. Defendant's lawyer accompanied him to talk to the police. He fully confessed his involvement in the thefts and agreed to help build a case against his partner concerning other crimes. The Supreme Court held that evidence about the thefts gathered pursuant to the agreement violated the principles of *Massiah* because defendant, in effect, became an agent of the police and in his conversations with his partner in planning their defense strategy, defendant's remarks prompted incriminating statements by the partner in violation of his Sixth Amendment right to counsel. The fact that the police were investigating the partner for additional crimes that he had not yet been formally charged with did not alter the *Massiah* rule as to evidence of the thefts for which both defendants had already been indicted. But the Court also ruled that evidence so gathered concerning crimes not yet charged was admissible:

> The police have an interest in the thorough investigation of crimes for which formal charges have already been filed. They also have an interest in investigating new or additional crimes. Investigations of either type of crime may require surveillance of individuals already under indictment. Moreover, law enforcement officials investigating an individual suspected of committing one crime and formally charged with having committed another crime obviously seek to discover evidence useful at a trial of either crime. In seeking evidence pertaining to pending charges, however, the Government's investigative powers are limited by the Sixth Amendment rights of the accused. To allow the admission of evidence obtained from the accused in violation of his Sixth Amendment rights whenever the police assert an alternative, legitimate reason for their surveillance invites abuse by law enforcement personnel in the form of fabricated investigations and risks the evisceration of the Sixth Amendment right recognized in *Massiah*. On the other hand, to exclude evidence pertaining to charges as to which the Sixth Amendment right to counsel had not attached at the time the evidence was obtained, simply because other charges were pending at that time, would unnecessarily frustrate the public's interest in the investigation of criminal activities.

Once a suspect in custody has asked for the assistance of a lawyer, it is clear that the police may not initiate further interrogation of that person, under the holding of *Edwards v. Arizona*, 101 S. Ct. 1880 (1981). But the fact that a defendant has been indicted (thus clearly initiating the "accusatorial" stage of the proceeding, including the right to be represented by counsel), apparently does not automatically bar police interrogation in the absence of counsel *if the defendant has knowingly and intelligently waived his right to counsel*. This was the holding in *Patterson v. Illinois*, 108 S. Ct. 2389 (1988). In that case, as defendant was being moved from a lockup to the county jail after having been indicted for murder, he asked the officer which members of his street gang had been charged with the murder. Upon learning that a certain gang member had not been charged, defendant asked, "Why wasn't he indicted? He did everything." The officer then interrupted him, and using a standard *Miranda* form, read his rights to him aloud as defendant followed the printed form, which he then initialed and signed. Defendant then gave a lengthy statement, incriminating himself and others in the murder. Later the same day, defendant again confessed his involvement in the crime to an assistant prosecutor, after reviewing his previous warning and waiver procedure and repeating the procedure again. In upholding defendant's murder conviction, the Supreme Court distinguished this case from *Edwards* by noting that in the present case defendant *at no time asked for the assistance of a lawyer.* In deciding that his waiver of rights was both knowing and intelligent, the Court applied the familiar test of "intentional relinquishment or abandonment of a known right or privilege." The "key inquiry", the Court stated, must be: "Was the accused, who waived his Sixth Amendment rights during postindictment questioning, made sufficiently aware of his right to have counsel present during the questioning, and of the possible consequences of a decision to forgo the aid of counsel?" The Court concluded that the standard *Miranda* warnings adequately informed defendant of those rights and consequences, and it also observed that he had been unable to suggest any meaningful information that he should have, but did not, receive before his decision to waive his rights and talk to the police without a lawyer being present.

The importance of the *Patterson* case would seem to be that it clearly indicates that, in cases in which defendant does not ask to have the assistance of counsel, a careful and documented following of the *Miranda* warning and waiver procedure can be just as productive for the prosecution after a person has been formally charged as it is in pre-charge custodial interrogation.

In *Illinois v. Perkins*, 110 S. Ct. 2394 (1990), the *sole* issue before the Supreme Court was whether an undercover law enforcement officer must give *Miranda* warnings to a suspect being held in jail pending trial before asking him questions that might produce an incriminating response concerning a murder unrelated to the pending charges. The undercover officer was posing as a fellow inmate who, along with another inmate/acquaintance of D, was purporting to include D in an escape from the jail. In reversing the lower state courts' rulings that *Miranda* warnings should have been given in order for the resulting murder confession to be admissible, the Supreme Court stated:

> Conversations between suspects and undercover agents do not implicate the concerns underlying *Miranda*. The essential ingredients of a "police-dominated atmosphere" and compulsion are not present when an incarcerated person speaks freely to someone that he believes to be a fellow inmate. Coercion is determined from the persepective of the suspect.

***

As was pointed out by Justice Brennan, who concurred in the judgment, when this case is remanded back to the state courts, the D may still challenge the admissibility of the confession on other grounds, not before the Court on this appeal.

Sample Questions

A "confession" is the admission of guilt by a defendant of *all* the necessary elements of the crime charged, while an "admission" merely admits some fact which tends to connect the defendant with the alleged offense.   T.   F.

There was a time in the early English common law, when confessions were admissible even though they were the product of physical torture.   T.   F.

The first "exclusionary rule" barring the use of confessions obtained by fear or promise of reward (1783), was based on the belief that such confessions were not credible.   T.   F.

Today in the United States coerced confessions are inadmissible, (even though they may be factual), because the courts consider them to be in violation of the Constitution, and in that sense, one could say that fairness outweighs truth.   T.   F.

The general rule is that trickery used by the police to obtain a confession is considered as a part of the totality of all the circumstances which determines voluntariness, but it will not, in and of itself, render an otherwise admissible confession inadmissible.   T.   F.

The phrase "fruit of the poisonous tree" is a phrase used by the courts to indicate that generally, incriminating statements which are the product of an illegality are inadmissible except when there is a break in the causation sufficient to insulate the statement from the improper influence.   T.   F.

The practice of the police "picking someone up" solely for questioning or "holding for investigation", when there is no probable cause for arrest, or consent:
A. is unconstitutional.
B. might render inadmissible an otherwise valid confession.
C. is extremely unprofessional police practice.
D. may result in civil liability actions against the police.
E. all of the above.

An incriminating statement made to the police as a result of a mental state of anxiety and which is not the product of any police coercion, misconduct, or overreaching, is considered to be voluntary and admissible under the Constitution of the United States.   T.   F.

With regard to the content of the *Miranda* warnings, the Supreme Court of the United States has held:
A. the warnings must use the exact terminology used in the *Miranda* opinion.
B. the warnings must be read to the individual from a card prepared by a prosecutor or police legal adviser.
C. the words used to convey the warnings must be words used in the *Miranda* opinion
D. No precise formulation of words need be used as long as (1) right of silence; (2) consequence of not remaining silent; (3)right to presence of counsel during questioning; and (4) right to state-provided counsel if indigent, are adequately conveyed by the warnings.
E. none of the above are correct.

§ 5.5 FIFTH AMENDMENT SELF-INCRIMINATION ISSUES
(A) Highlights of Miranda

Miranda v. Arizona, 86 S. Ct. 1602 (1966) was actually four cases *(Miranda v. Arizona, Vignera v. New York, Westover v. United States,* and *California v. Stewart)*, all decided in one opinion. Each of these cases involved a serious crime and station-house interrogation by the police which resulted in a confession which was used to convict the defendant. In three of the cases, *Miranda, Vignera,* and *Westover,* the appellate court affirmances of conviction were reversed by a vote of 5 to 4, and in *Stewart,* the appellate court reversal of conviction was affirmed by a vote of 6 to 3.

The majority opinion may best be summarized by selected quotations:

> Our holding will be spelled out with some specificity in the pages which follow but briefly stated it is this: the prosecution may not use statements, whether exculpatory or inculpatory, stemming from custodial interrogation of the defendant unless it demonstrates the use of procedural safeguards effective to secure the privilege against self-incrimination. By custodial interrogation, we mean questioning initiated by law enforcement officers after a person has been taken into custody or otherwise deprived of his freedom of action in any significant way. As for the procedural safeguards to be employed, unless other fully effective means are devised to inform accused persons of their right of silence and to assure a continuous opportunity to exercise it, the following measures are required. Prior to any questioning, the person must be warned that he has a right to remain silent, that any statement he does make may be used as evidence against him, and that he has a right to the presence of an attorney, either retained or appointed. The defendant may waive effectuation of these rights, provided the waiver is made voluntarily, knowingly and intelligently. If, however, he indicates in any manner and at any stage of the process that he wishes to consult with an attorney before speaking there can be no questioning. Likewise, if the individual is alone and indicates in any manner that he does not wish to be interrogated, the police may not question him. The mere fact that he may have answered some questions or volunteered some statements on his own does not deprive him of the right to refrain from answering any further inquiries until he has consulted with an attorney and thereafter consents to be questioned. [86 S. Ct. at 1612.]

> An express statement that the individual is willing to make a statement and does not want an attorney followed closely by a statement could constitute a waiver. But a valid waiver will not be presumed simply from the silence of the accused after warnings are given or simply from the fact that a confession was in fact eventually obtained. [86 S. Ct. at 1628.]

> Moreover, any evidence that the accused was threatened, tricked or cajoled into a waiver will, of course, show that the defendant did not voluntarily waive his privilege. The requirement of warnings and waiver of rights is a fundamental with respect to the Fifth Amendment privilege and not simply a preliminary ritual to existing methods of interrogation. [86 S. Ct. at 1629.]

> The warnings required and the waiver necessary in accordance with our opinion today are, in the absence of a fully effective equivalent, prerequisites to the admissibility of any statement made by the defendant. No distinction can be drawn between statements which are direct confessions and statements which amount to "admissions" of part or all of an offense. [86 S. Ct. at 1629.]

> Our decision is not intended to hamper the traditional function of police officers in investigating crime. When an individual is in custody on probable

cause, the police may, of course, seek out evidence in the field to be used at trial against him. Such investigation may include inquiry of persons not under restraint. General on-the-scene questioning as to facts surrounding a crime or other general questioning of citizens in the fact-finding process is not affected by our holding. It is an act of responsible citizenship for individuals to give whatever information they may have to aid in law enforcement. In such situations the compelling atmosphere inherent in the process of in-custody interrogation is not necessarily present. [86 S. Ct. at 1629, 1630.]

In dealing with statements obtained through interrogation, we do not purport to find all confessions inadmissible. Confessions remain a proper element in law enforcement. Any statement given freely and voluntarily without compelling influences is, of course, admissible in evidence. The fundamental import of the privilege while an individual is in custody is not whether he is allowed to talk to the police without the benefit of warnings and counsel, but whether he can be interrogated. There is no requirement that police stop a person who enters a police station and states that he wishes to confess to a crime, or a person who calls the police to offer a confession or any other statement he desires to make. Volunteered statements of any kind are not barred by the Fifth Amendment and their admissibility is not affected by our holding today. [86 S. Ct. at 1630.]

To summarize, we hold that when an individual is taken into custody or otherwise deprived of his freedom by the authorities in any significant way and is subjected to questioning, the privilege against self-incrimination is jeopardized. Procedural safeguards must be employed to protect the privilege and unless other fully effective means are adopted to notify the person of his right of silence and to assure that the exercise of the right will be scrupulously honored, the following measures are required. He must be warned prior to any questioning that he has the right to remain silent, that anything he says can be used against him in a court of law, that he has the right to the presence of an attorney, and that if he cannot afford an attorney one will be appointed for him prior to any questioning if he so desires. Opportunity to exercise these rights must be afforded to him throughout the interrogation. After such warnings have been given, and such opportunity afforded him, the individual may knowingly and intelligently waive these rights and agree to answer questions or make a statement. But unless and until such warnings and waiver are demonstrated by the prosecution at trial, no evidence obtained as a result of interrogation can be used against him. [86 S. Ct. at 1630.]

------------------------------------ **Notes** --------------------------------------

(B) Applicability of Miranda

The Supreme Court of the United States, in summarizing its holding in *Miranda v. Arizona*, 86 S. Ct. 1602 (1966) indicated that the prosecution may not use statements stemming from *custodial* interrogation of the defendant unless it demonstrates the use of procedural safeguards effective to secure the privilege against self-incrimination.

The *Miranda* requirements do not apply when there is no custody, but only interrogation (*Oregon v. Mathiason*, briefed below), nor do they apply when there is custody, but no interrogation (*Bugg v. State*, text below). Only when the two elements of custody and interrogation coexist is the *Miranda* holding applicable.

"Interrogation" encompasses not only formal police inquiry but also its *functional equivalent*, i.e., any query or conduct that the police should know is reasonably likely to elicit an incriminating response. The test involves weighing several objective and subjective factors, including: (1) the nature of the police remarks, e.g., whether it was a lengthy harangue or an offhanded comment; (2) the police awareness of the accused's mental or physical stability; and (3) the intent of the police, e.g., whether they knew or should have known that their remarks would elicit an incriminating answer. *Rhode Island v. Innis*, S. Ct. 1682 (1980), briefed in this section.

CASE BRIEF

Oregon v. Mathiason, 97 S. Ct. 711 (1977)

Majority opinion: Per curiam. Dissenting: Marshall, Stevens.

FACTS: A state police officer investigating a burglary asked the lady of the house if she suspected anyone. She replied that D, a parolee and a close associate of her son, was the only one she could think of. The officer unsuccessfully tried to contact D until about 25 days after the crime, when he left his card at D's apartment with a note asking D to call him. The next day D called the officer and agreed to meet him at the state police office in about an hour and a half.

The Officer met D in the hallway, shook hands with him and invited him into an office. D was told he was not under arrest. The office door was closed and the two men sat across a desk from each other. A police radio could be heard in another room. The officer told D he wanted to talk to him about a burglary and that his truthfulness would possibly be considered by the prosecutor or judge. He said he believed D was involved in the crime and falsely told D that his fingerprints had been found at the scene.

Within five minutes of his arrival at the state police office, D admitted his guilt. The officer then advised D of his *Miranda* rights and took a taped confession.

At the conclusion of the taped confession the officer told D that he was not arresting him at this time; that he was free to return to his job and family; and that he would refer the matter to the prosecutor to determine if criminal charges would be filed. D left the office thirty minutes after he had arrived. D did not take the stand either at the trial or at the hearing on the motion to suppress; the officer gave all the testimony relevant to the issue.

D was convicted of first-degree burglary in a bench trial at which his confession was critical to the state's case. At trial D moved to suppress the confession as the fruit of in-custody questioning not preceded by the *Miranda* warnings. The trial court denied suppression, finding no custody. The Oregon court of appeals affirmed D's conviction, but the supreme court of Oregon reversed it, finding that the interrogation had taken place in a "coercive environment calling *Miranda* into play" — in a state police office behind closed doors, with the officer informing

D that he was a suspect and that evidence had been found incriminating D, who was a parolee under supervision.

ISSUE: Under the facts above was the interrogation "custodial" so as to invoke the *Miranda* requirements?

DECISION: No; reversed.

REASONS: There was no indication that D's freedom to depart was restricted in any way. He came voluntarily to the police station, where he was immediately informed that he was not under arrest. After thirty minutes he in fact did leave without hindrance. D was not in custody or otherwise deprived of his freedom of action in any significant way.

Any interview of a suspect by a policeman will have coercive aspects to it, but police officers are not required to administer *Miranda* warnings to everyone they question. The warnings are not required simply because the questioning takes place in a police station, or because the person questioned is suspected of a crime.

Miranda is effectuated only by such restrictions on freedom as to render a person "in custody."

The officer's false statement concerning the fingerprints had nothing to do with whether D was "in custody" for purposes of *Miranda*.

RULE: For purposes of the *Miranda* requirements, custodial interrogation does not consist simply of private questioning by a police officer at a police station. An officer's falsely telling the suspect that evidence of his crime has been discovered has no bearing on whether the questioning was custodial. When a suspect voluntarily goes to the police station at the request of the police for questioning; when he is not restrained from leaving; and when he in fact does leave after giving an incriminating statement, there has been no "custodial interrogation."

California v. Beheler, 103 S. Ct. 3517 (1983) again emphasized that not all interrogations occurring at police stations are necessarily "custodial" interrogations. The defendant was involved in a robbery in which one of his accomplices shot and killed the victim. Shortly afterward the defendant called the police, identifying the killer, and allowed police to search his back yard for the murder weapon. He then accompanied the police to the police station but was told that he was not under arrest. He was subjected to interrogation for about thirty minutes without being advised of, or waiving, his rights according to the *Miranda* guidelines. The defendant's statement amounted to a confession; however, he was not detained. He was arrested five days later and given the *Miranda* warnings, after which he made a second confession, which was taped. At issue was the admissibility of the statement given during the first interview. Seemingly influenced by the facts that the interview took place at the police station and that the defendant was the focus of the investigation, the California Court of Appeals ruled that, under the totality of the circumstances, defendant had been in custody during the first interview. Reversing this holding, the Supreme Court of the United States indicated that custody should not be a complicated issue: that the question was simply whether the defendant had been subjected to a formal arrest or to equivalent restraints on his freedom of movement. Here, as in *Oregon v. Mathiason*, briefed above, the Supreme Court could find no custody in that sense. It was immaterial that defendant was a prime suspect, particularly in view of the fact that it was the defendant himself who had originally contacted the police.

TEXT OF CASE

Bugg v. State, 372 N.E.2d 1156 (Ind. 1978)

PIVARNIK, Justice.

Appellant Nellie Bugg was convicted of second degree murder in the Marion Criminal Court on April 9, 1974, and sentenced to fifteen to twenty-five years imprisonment. The killing in question occurred on November 3, 1972, in the home of appellant. On that date, police officers found the appellant in her bedroom and found the victim, former husband of appellant, who was an Indianapolis police officer, dead in the bathtub. The victim's gun was in an adjoining hallway and four spent shells were found in the bathroom. The victim had two bullet wounds in the head, and one in his upper arm and upper body. Evidence indicated that the bullet wound in the upper body caused death, and that such bullet was fired by the victim's pistol. It is undisputed that appellant fired the fatal shot following an argument.

Appellant argues two errors in the proceedings of her trial below: (1) that the trial court permitted a police officer to testify as to statements made to him by appellant while appellant was incarcerated, and; (2) that there was insufficient evidence to convict the appellant for the offense of second degree murder.

* * *

Appellant's first argument is that a police officer's testimony concerning statements made by appellant to him while she was incarcerated should not have been admitted, because appellant was not properly advised of her constitutional rights required by *Miranda v. Arizona*, (1966), 384 U.S. 436, 86 S. Ct. 1602, 16 L.Ed.2d 694.

The relevant events surrounding appellant's contentions are as follows. On November 3, 1972, an Indianapolis police officer entered appellant's home and found her in one of the bedrooms and the deceased in the bathtub. At that time, appellant stated, "I shot him; there is the gun laying on the dresser drawers." Other officers arrived at the scene, and one of them advised appellant of her constitutional rights, although she was not questioned at this time. No statements made by appellant on the day of the killing are being challenged. Rather, the statements in issue were made three days later, on November 6, to Sergeant Kirkham of the Marion County Sheriff's Department. Kirkham had known appellant, Nellie Bugg, for over five years. He was neither assigned to her case, nor was he working on it. However, he had heard from a matron at the Marion County Jail that appellant was not eating, was distraught and was going into hysterics, and that there was fear that appellant would collapse. Kirkham testified that he went to see appellant as a friend, tried to calm her down and asked her if she had any problems. She then told him, "well I guess I killed Tommie." Appellant then went on and kept talking, detailing circumstances of her relationship with the deceased leading up to the day of the killing. Sergeant Kirkham never advised appellant of her *Miranda* rights.

The trial court found that appellant had been advised of her *Miranda* rights at the time of her arrest, three days earlier. * * * However, there was no testimony or evidence regarding exactly what rights had been read to her, either on direct examination of the arresting officers or on their cross-examination by appellant. The trial court then ruled that appellant's statements to Sergeant Kirkham were admissible on the basis that they were not made during a "custodial interrogation" within the meaning of *Miranda*. The objection to appellant's statements to Kirkham were not made on the basis of their general voluntariness, except that appellant stated in argument that because of her distraught condition she could not have understood her *Miranda* rights even if they had been read to her at this time. A determination of appellant's competency to make a *Miranda* waiver, however, is not necessary to support this statement's admissibility if it was not in fact made during a "custodial interrogation" and thus fell outside of the *Miranda* requirements. *Kennedy v. State* (1977), Ind., 370 N.E.2d 331.

It is settled that the procedural safeguards of *Miranda* only apply to what the United States Supreme Court has termed "custodial interrogation." * * * M. Seidman, The Law of Evidence in Indiana, pp. 99-103 (1977). This definitional prerequisite to defendant's argument based on a failure to give all or some of the *Miranda* warnings thus has two parts: first, a showing that the setting of the allegedly inadmissible confession was "custodial" within the meaning of *Miranda*, and second, a showing that what transpired between the authorities and the defendant at this place was "interrogation" within the meaning of *Miranda*. One line of our decisions deals with the first part of the requirement for giving *Miranda* warnings; the definition of "custodial." *See*, e.g., *Dillon v. State* (1971), 257 Ind. 412, 275 N.E.2d 312; *Raines v. State* (1971), 256 Ind. 404, 269 N.E.2d 378; *Owens v. State* (1971), 255 Ind. 693, 266 N.E.2d 612; *Schmidt v. State* (1970), 255 Ind. 443, 265 N.E.2d 219, *reh. denied* (1971), 256 Ind. 218, 267 N.E.2d 554. In another line of our decisions, we have found that statements of defendants were volunteered and spontaneous, and not in response to "interrogation." *Kennedy v. State* (1977), Ind., 370 N.E.2d 331; *Riddle v. State* (1976), Ind., 348 N.E.2d 635; *Lockridge v. State* (1975), 263 Ind. 678, 338 N.E.2d 275; *Jennings v. State* (1973), 262 Ind. 476, 318 N.E.2d 358; *Hewitt v. State* (1973), 261 Ind. 71, 300 N.E.2d 94; *New v. State* (1970), 254 Ind. 307, 259 N.E.2d 696.

It is obvious that this appellant was in custody at the time when she gave her oral admissions to Sergeant Kirkham. Just the same, under the circumstances presented, the trial court's ruling on the admissibility of this confession is correct without regard to the adequacy of her *Miranda* advisement. Sergeant Kirkham did not visit appellant in her jail cell for the purpose of questioning or interrogation, nor did he conduct such a procedure. Rather, he went as a friend to help calm her down, having learned that she was near collapse. He simply asked her if she was having any problems, and she began to relate a story about the crime in issue and kept talking. There was thus no "interrogation" here within the meaning of *Miranda*, and voluntary statements made any time during "custody" are admissible without *Miranda* warnings so long as there is no such questioning. *Cf. Pilcher v. Estelle* (5th Cir. 1976), 528 F.2d 623, 624, *cert. denied* (1976), 426 U.S. 953, 96 S. Ct. 3179, 49 L.Ed.2d 1192. In view of the facts presented here, neither the atmosphere of the stationhouse nor the length of appellant's custody casts any doubt upon the spontaneity and voluntariness of her statement. *Cf. New v. State* (1970), 254 Ind. 307 at 314, 259 N.E.2d 696 at 700. Appellant's statements to Sergeant Kirkham were freely, voluntarily, and spontaneously given, and there was no error in their admission at trial.

* * *

The judgment of the trial court is affirmed.
All Justices concur.

CASE BRIEF

Beckwith v. United States, 96 S. Ct. 1612 (1976)

Majority opinion: Burger. Concurring in judgment: Marshall. Dissenting: Brennan.

FACTS: Two I.R.S. agents, after considerable investigation, met with D at a private residence where he sometimes stayed; they wished to spare D the possible embarrassment of being interviewed at his place of employment. The agents presented their credentials, explaining that one of their functions was to investigate the possibility of criminal tax fraud and that they were assigned to investigate D's federal tax liability for the years 1966 through 1971. Then they read the following to D from a printed card:

> As a special agent, one of my functions is to investigate the possibility of criminal violations of the Internal Revenue laws, and related offenses.
>
> Under the Fifth Amendment to the Constitution of the United States, I cannot compel you to answer any questions or to submit any information if such answers or information might tend to incriminate you in any way. I also advise you that anything which you say and any information which you submit may be used against you in any criminal proceeding which may be undertaken. I advise you further that you may, if you wish, seek the assistance of an attorney before responding.

D acknowledged that he understood his rights and the agents interviewed him for about three hours. The agents described the conversations as "friendly" and "relaxed." Before the interview was concluded one of the agents requested that D allow them to inspect certain records. D said that the records were at his place of employment. Traveling separately, the agents met D later at his place of employment, where the senior agent advised D he was not required to furnish any books or records; D supplied the records anyway. D was convicted of tax violations and the Court of Appeals, District of Columbia Circuit affirmed the judgment. D claims the evidence used against him was obtained in violation of the *Miranda* case requirements.

ISSUE: Does *Miranda* apply to interrogation in non-custodial circumstances after a police investigation has focused on the suspect?

DECISION: No; conviction affirmed.

REASONS: D was neither arrested nor detained against his will. The narrow issue before the Court in *Miranda* was "the admissibility of statements obtained from an individual who is subjected to *custodial* police interrogation." The Court concluded that compulsion "is inherent in custodial surroundings" and, consequently, that specific safeguards were required in the case of "incommunicado interrogation of individuals in a police-dominated atmosphere, resulting in self-incriminating statements without full warnings of constitutional rights." *Miranda v. Arizona*, 86 S. Ct. 1602 (1966).

It was the compulsive aspect of custodial interrogation — not the strength or content of the government's suspicions at the time of the questioning — which led the Court to impose the *Miranda* requirements.

Although the focus of an investigation may indeed have been on D at the time of the interview, he was hardly in the custodial situation which was the basis of the *Miranda* holding. *Miranda* specifically defined "focus" for its purposes as "questioning initiated by law enforcement officers *after* a person has been taken into custody or otherwise deprived of his freedom of action in any significant way." Here the entire interview was free of coercion.

RULE: It is the inherently coercive effect of in-custody police interrogation which triggers the necessity of giving the *Miranda* warnings, and a non-custodial interview, free of coercion of any kind, will not require that the *Miranda* warnings be given simply because the interviewee is the "focus" of a criminal investigation.

CONCURRING: The Court's judgment is valid only because the quoted warning was given.

DISSENTING: The *Miranda* warnings should be given in a case like this because of psychological pressures on D.

With regard to the meaning of "interrogation" under *Miranda*, see also

Brewer v. Williams, 97 S. Ct. 1232 (1977), briefed above in §5.4, and *Rhode Island v. Innis*, briefed below in this section.

CASE BRIEF

Rhode Island v. Innis, 100 S. Ct. 1682 (1980)

Majority opinion: Stewart. Concurring: White, Burger. Dissenting: Marshall, joined by Brennan, Stevens.

FACTS: The body of a taxicab driver was found four days after his disappearance. He had been killed by a shotgun blast to the back of his head. A few days later police received a call from another taxicab driver who had been robbed by a man with a sawed-off shotgun. The victim, while at the police station for the purpose of giving a statement, noticed a picture of the robber on the bulletin board. When a photographic array was prepared, the victim picked out a picture of the same person. The police then began a search for the suspect, D, who was arrested, unarmed, the same day near the place where the taxicab driver indicated he had dropped off the robber. The arresting officer advised D of his *Miranda* rights but did not interrogate him. Other officers arrived at the scene of the arrest shortly thereafter and D was advised of his *Miranda* rights two more times. D stated that he understood these rights and that he wanted to speak with a lawyer. The officer in charge at the scene directed that D be placed in a police car with three officers and taken to the central police station, but that he was not to be interrogated or coerced in any way while en route to the central station.

While en route to the station, two of the police officers engaged in a conversation about the missing shotgun. One of the officers mentioned to the other that there was a school for handicapped children nearby and that it would be tragic if one of the children should find the shotgun and be injured or killed. The officers agreed that they should continue to search for the weapon and try to find it. D, who overheard the conversation, asked the officers to turn the car around so that he could show them where the gun was hidden. After radioing this information to their captain, the officers returned D to the scene of the arrest, where other officers were searching for the weapon. The captain again advised D of his *Miranda* rights and D stated he understood but wanted to get the gun out of the way because of the kids in the area. He then led police to a nearby field where the shotgun was hidden under rocks by the roadside.

D was indicted for kidnapping, robbery, and murder. Before trial, D moved to suppress the shotgun and statements he had made while in police custody. The trial judge ruled, after a hearing, that D had been completely and repeatedly advised of his *Miranda* rights, and that his statements and conduct were a waiver of those rights. The judge also found that it was entirely understandable that the officers should voice their concern for the safety of children in the area. Thus, the trial judge did not rule on whether the police conversation amounted to "interrogation." D was convicted by a jury on all counts. On appeal the Rhode Island supreme court, in a 5-2 decision, set aside D's conviction, relying in part on the holding in *Brewer v. Williams*, 97 S. Ct. 1232 (1977) [briefed above, §5.4].

ISSUE: Was D "interrogated" by the police officers in violation of his right under *Miranda* to remain silent until he consulted with a lawyer?

DECISION: No; judgment of Rhode Island supreme court vacated; case remanded to that court.

REASONS: D was fully informed of his *Miranda* rights; he invoked these rights when he told the police that he wanted to talk to a lawyer. It is also clear that D was in "custody" while being transported to the police station.

The starting point for defining "interrogation" is the *Miranda* opinion. While that opinion referred to "questioning," "interrogation" may have a broader meaning.

> The concern of the Court in *Miranda* was that the "interrogation environment" created by the interplay of interrogation and custody would "subjugate the individual to the will of his examiner" and thereby undermine the privilege against compulsory self-incrimination.

The *Miranda* opinion discussed police practices not involving express questioning: for example, the use of lineups in which a "coached" witness would pick D as the perpetrator, to establish his guilt as a predicate for further interrogation. Also discussed was the "reverse line-up" in which D would be identified by a coached witness as the perpetrator of a fictitious crime, with the object of inducing him to confess to the actual crime of which he was suspected in order to escape the false prosecution. The Court also discussed a variety of psychological ploys such as to show that the guilt of the subject was not morally serious or that it was the fault of society. It is clear that these techniques of persuasion, no less than express questioning, were thought, in a custodial setting, to amount to interrogation.

But not all statements obtained by the police from a person in custody are to be considered the product of interrogation. Voluntary confessions, given freely and without compelling influences, remain a proper element in law enforcement and are admissible in evidence. It is therefore clear that the special procedural safeguards outlined in *Miranda* are not required where a suspect in custody is not subjected to interrogation.

"Interrogation," as conceptualized in the *Miranda* opinion, must reflect a measure of compulsion above and beyond that inherent in custody itself.

We conclude that the *Miranda* safeguards come into play whenever a person in custody is subjected to either express questioning or its functional equivalent. That is to say, the term "interrogation" under *Miranda* refers not only to express questioning, but also to any words or actions on the part of the police (other than those normally attendant to arrest and custody) that the police should know are reasonably likely to elicit an incriminating response from the suspect. The latter portion of this definition focuses primarily upon the perceptions of the suspect, rather than on the intent of the police. This focus reflects the fact that the *Miranda* safeguards were designed to vest a suspect in custody with an added measure of protection against coercive police practices, without regard to objective proof of the underlying intent of the police. A practice that the police should know is reasonably likely to evoke an incriminating response from a suspect thus amounts to interrogation. But, since the police surely cannot be held accountable for the unforeseeable results of their words or actions, the definition of interrogation can extend only to words or actions on the part of police officers that they *should have known* were reasonably likely to elicit an incriminating response.

By this definition of "interrogation," D was not interrogated. There was no express questioning of D, but only a dialogue between two officers to which no response from D was invited. Nor can it be fairly concluded that the "functional equivalent" of questioning existed here because nothing in the record indicates the police should have known that D's conscience was peculiarly susceptible to the welfare of handicapped children. And the record does not show that D was unusually disoriented or upset at the time of his arrest.

The entire conversation between the officers appears to have been only a few offhand remarks. There was no lengthy harangue in the presence of D, nor does the record support D's contention that the officer's comments were particularly "evocative."

The Rhode Island supreme court erred in equating "subtle compulsion" with interrogation. D failed to establish that his incriminating response was the product of words or actions on the part of the police that they should have known were reasonably likely to elicit an incriminating response.

RULE: "Interrogation" exists within the meaning of the *Miranda* decision when the police subject a person in custody either to express questioning or to other words or actions (other than those normally attendant to arrest and custody) which the police should know, in light of all the circumstances, are reasonably likely to elicit an incriminating response.

DISSENTING: The officers should have known that their conversation would be likely to elicit an incriminating response; hence, the conversation was "interrogation" within the meaning of *Miranda;* the Court should have remanded the case to the trial court for a finding in light of the new definition it has established. The case will provide an incentive to police to use subtle compulsion after defendants have asked to talk to an attorney and when, under *Miranda*, no direct questioning can properly continue.

CASE BRIEF
Arizona v. Mauro, 107 S. Ct. 1931 (1987)

Majority opinion: Powell, joined by Rehnquist, White, O'Connor and Scalia.
Dissenting: Stevens, joined by Brennan, Marshall and Blackmun.

FACTS: D was in police custody for the murder of his son. After being advised of his *Miranda* rights, D said he didn't want to answer any questions until a lawyer was present. All questioning was stopped and D was placed in the police captain's office because no secure detention facility was available. At the same time, D's wife was being questioned in another room, and she insisted on talking to D. Police were at first reluctant to grant her request, but agreed on condition that an officer would be in the room with them. D's wife was brought into the room where D was being held and the officer seated himself at a desk, placing a tape recorder in plain sight on the desk. The short conversation between D and his wife was recorded, and during the conversation D told his wife not to answer questions until a lawyer was present.

At trial, D's defense was insanity. To rebut this defense, the prosecution played the taped conversation between D and his wife to show that D was sane on the day of the murder. D moved to suppress the tape on the grounds that the conversation with the officer present was tantamount to interrogation in absence of counsel. The trial court found that there was no subterfuge on behalf of the police nor any attempt to indirectly avoid *Miranda* requirements. D was convicted of murder and child abuse and sentenced to death. The Arizona supreme court reversed, holding that the police knew it was possible that D might incriminate himself in the conversation with his wife and that the procedure was equivalent to impermissible interrogation within the meaning of *Rhode Island v. Innis*, 100 S. Ct. 1682 (1980). The State of Arizona petitioned for a writ of certiorari, which was granted by the Supreme Court of the United States.

ISSUE: Was the procedure followed by the police equivalent to impermissible interrogation within the meaning of *Innis*?

DECISION: No — Reversed. (Having the effect of re-instatement of the trial court's conviction).

REASONS: (The court summarizes the Fifth Amendment protections of *Miranda*, including the rule that, once an accused has expressed a desire to deal with the police only through counsel, they are not to further interrogate him unless *he* initiates further communication with them; *Edwards v. Arizona*, 101 S. Ct. 1880 (1981)). Cases since *Miranda* have held that police activity other than express questioning can undermine the privilege against compulsory self-incrimination. Therefore, in *Innis* the Court concluded that *Miranda* safeguards were also required in situations involving the "functional equivalent" of express police questioning; that is, any words or actions on the part of the police (other than those normally attendant to arrest and custody) that they should know are reasonably likely to elicit an incriminating response from the suspect, are also within the protection of *Miranda* safeguards. Also, the primary focus is on the perceptions of the suspect, rather than on the intent of the police.

In this case the police gave D the warnings required by *Miranda* and D indicated he did not wish to be questioned without a lawyer present. D did not waive his right to have a lawyer present. Therefore the sole issue is whether the police action of allowing D's wife to talk to him only in the presence of an officer was the "functional equivalent" of police interrogation.

The record here is clear that D was not subjected to compelling influences, psychological ploys, or direct questioning by the police. It was D's wife who insisted on talking to her husband, and she was only allowed to do so after her insistence overcame initial police reluctance. The lack of a secure facility required that an officer be present for the safety and protection of D's wife. The situation was therefore not a psychological ploy created by the police for the purpose of eliciting incriminating statements. We doubt that a suspect, told by officers that his wife will be allowed to speak to him, would feel he was being coerced into incriminating himself in any way. The police were aware that there was a possibility that D might incriminate himself, but that hope on their part did not constitute the "functional equivalent" of interrogation. The purpose behind our decisions in *Miranda* and *Edwards* was to prevent police from using the coercive nature of confinement to extract confessions that would not be given without confinement. Here, the police acted reasonably and lawfully. The federal Constitution, therefore, does not bar the use of D's statements at his trial.

RULE: When a suspect in police custody has been warned of his *Miranda* rights and chooses not to answer questions without a lawyer being present, allowing the suspect's wife to talk to him, at her insistence, but only in the presence of a police officer for security purposes, does not constitute the "functional equivalent" of interrogation when there is no evidence that the police used a psychological ploy or otherwise attempted to influence D to confess.

DISSENT: The state court found as a matter of fact that the police intent was to interrogate D when they brought his wife into the room where he was being held without any advance notice to him. Therefore, this was a psychological ploy on the part of the police, and was the functional equivalent of impermissible interrogation.

CASE BRIEF

Berkemer v. McCarty, 104 S. Ct. 3138 (1984)

Majority opinion: Marshall, joined by Burger, C.J., Brennan, White, Blackmun, Powell, Rehnquist, and O'Connor. Concurring in part: Stevens.

FACTS: A trooper, observing D's car weaving in and out of traffic on a highway, stopped the car and asked D to get out. D's balance was unsteady and he had difficulty standing. (At this time the officer decided to charge D with a traffic offense, but he did not then advise him he was under arrest.) The trooper then conducted a "field sobriety test" but D could not complete it without losing his balance and falling. D was then asked if he had consumed any intoxicants and he replied — (D's speech was slurred and difficult to understand) — that he had consumed two beers and had smoked several joints of marijuana a short time before. At this point, the officer formally placed D under arrest and transported him to the county jail.

At the jail, D was given a chemical (breath) test for intoxication, which revealed no alcohol whatsoever in D's system. The trooper then resumed his interrogation of D to complete the alcohol influence report. D again answered that he had been drinking and when asked if he was under the influence of alcohol, said, "I guess, barely." After being asked if the marijuana he had smoked had been treated with any chemicals, D wrote on the report form: "No ang(el) dust or PCP in the pot. Rick McCarty." At no time during this encounter was D advised by the arresting officer or anyone else as to his *Miranda* rights.

D was charged with DWI, a misdemeanor under Ohio law punishable by a fine and/or imprisonment up to 6 months, with a minimum mandatory jail sentence of 3 days.

D moved to exclude his incriminating statements from evidence because the *Miranda* procedure had not been complied with, but the trial court denied his motion. D was convicted on a plea of no contest and sentenced to 90 days and a $300 fine, with 80 days and $100 suspended.

D appealed, and the court of appeals affirmed D's conviction, based on an Ohio case holding *Miranda* not applicable in misdemeanor cases. D's further state appeal was dismissed by the Ohio supreme court. D then filed habeas corpus in federal district court, which dismissed his petition, but a divided United States court of appeals reversed, holding *Miranda* was applicable in both felony and misdemeanor custodial interrogation, and, therefore, that some of D's statements were inadmissible. The Supreme Court granted certiorari to resolve the confusion existing in both state and federal courts.

ISSUE: Does the *Miranda* case apply in custodial interrogation situations involving misdemeanor traffic violations?

DECISION: Yes; affirmed.

REASONS: The Fifth Amendment's self-incrimination clause applies to state as well as federal proceedings. (The Court then reviews the procedural safeguards required by *Miranda*.)

The principal advantages of *Miranda* are the simplicity and clarity of its rule (*custody* and *interrogation*). Often, when police arrest suspects, they are not sure of whether they are dealing with felons or misdemeanants. Sometimes the seriousness of the offense depends on facts unknown to the arresting officer, such as whether a previous offense has been committed by the suspect, or whether the victim of an automobile accident survives or dies. Using a felony vs. misdemeanor standard for the applicability of *Miranda* would cause time-consuming and complex litigation, and would be disruptive of law enforcement because of the complex and uncertain situations which would most certainly arise.

The purposes of the *Miranda* safeguards are to ensure that police do not use coercion or trickery in obtaining confessions; to relieve the inherently compelling pressures, generated by police custody, which undermine an individual's will to resist; and, as much as possible, to free courts from having to scrutinize individual cases to determine, after the fact, whether particular confessions were voluntary. These purposes apply equally in felony and misdemeanor situations. Nor are we persuaded that across-the-board application of *Miranda* in all custodial interrogation situations will hamper law enforcement efficiency. We, therefore, hold that a person subjected to custodial interrogation is entitled to the *Miranda* safeguard regardless of the nature or severity of the offense involved.

In this case, we are obliged to also consider the issue of whether roadside questioning of a motorist detained pursuant to a routine traffic stop should be considered "custodial interrogation". We have previously acknowledged that stopping an automobile and detaining its occupants constitutes a Fourth Amendment "seizure", even though the purpose of the stop is limited and the resulting detention brief (citing *Delaware v. Prouse*, 99 S. Ct. 1391 (1979)).

But *Miranda* should be strictly enforced only in those types of situations in which pressures sufficiently impair an individual's free exercise of his privilege against self-incrimination so as to require that he be warned of his constitutional rights. Detention pursuant to a traffic stop is presumptively temporary and brief. Most such detentions last only a few minutes. The motorist usually can assume he will be obliged to spend a short time answering questions and displaying his license and registration — and that he may receive a citation — but that he will then be allowed to continue on his way. In this respect, questioning incident to an ordinary traffic stop is quite different from stationhouse questioning — (which usually involves more uncertainty and pressure). Also, the typical traffic stop is made in full view of the public and involves only one or at most two officers, so it is far less "police dominated" than the interrogation sessions giving rise to the *Miranda* rule. The usual traffic stop, therefore, more closely resembles a *"Terry"* stop, in which the officer is permitted to ask the detainee a moderate number of questions to determine identity and to conform or dispel the officer's suspicions. But the detainee is not required to respond — and unless the officer develops probable cause to arrest, the detainee must be released. We have never suggested that *Terry* stops are subject to the *Miranda* requirements and the similarity between those situations and ordinary traffic stops prompts us to hold that persons temporarily detained pursuant to such stops are not "in custody" for the purposes of *Miranda*.

(The Court then states it is unpersuaded by the argument of D that today's opinion will lead to widespread abuses by the police.) There will always be cases in which the exact moment of "custody" will be difficult to determine, but our approach today is more practical than a blanket rule that *Miranda* either does or does not apply to *all* traffic stops, which would, on one hand, inpede traffic law enforcement while doing little to protect Fifth Amendment rights, or on the other hand, enable police to circumvent *Miranda* constraints when they should apply.

(The Court then refuses to determine whether D's post-arrest statements were "harmless error", because the issue was not raised in the courts below; statements made at the roadside and later at the police station were not identical; and because of D's plea of "no contest," he has had no opportunity to try to impeach the state's evidence or present evidence of his own.)

RULE: The duty of police to follow the *Miranda* procedures turns on the coexistence of *custody* and *interrogation* and not on a felony vs. misdemeanor distinction. The ordinary traffic stop, in which a motorist is temporarily detained for purposes of identification, display of license and registration, and perhaps the issuance of a citation before release, does not constitute "custody" for the purpose of "Miranda"; but such a situation may ripen into a custodial situation if the motorist is not released, but taken from the scene by the police under formal arrest or under conditions otherwise meeting the criteria of an arrest.

CONCURRING AND DISSENTING: The only issue before the Court was whether or not *Miranda* applies in misdemeanor traffic arrests. The decision concerning admissibility of statements prior to formal arrest is not necessary to the disposition of this case. This decision violates the long-standing rule of judicial restraint.

In *Pennsylvania v. Bruder*, 109 S. Ct. 205 (1989), the Supreme Court in a *per curiam* opinion, held that the stopping of a motorist by a police officer for the purpose of checking on erratic driving, followed by a modest number of questions and a request for the motorist to perform a simple balancing test at the side of the road, did not amount to "custody" for purposes of *Miranda*. Therefore, the statements and conduct of the motorist prior to his arrest for driving while intoxicated were admissible at his trial even though the *Miranda* procedure was not followed by the officer until after the arrest was made. In this decision, the Court relied on *Berkemer v. McCarty*, 104 S. Ct. 3138 (1984).

CASE BRIEF

Pennsylvania v. Muniz,   110 S.Ct. 2638 (1990)

Majority opinion: Brennan, J. [The members of the Court were divided in their agreement with regard to the various issues presented by the case, as indicated below].

FACTS: Police officer spotted D and a passenger in a car parked on the shoulder of a highway. Checking to see if D needed assistance, the officer smelled alcoholic beverage on D's breath and observed his glazed and bloodshot eyes and flushed face. The officer directed D to remain parked until his condition improved and D said he would do so, but when the officer returned to his car, D drove off. The officer pursued D and pulled him over, and had him perform field sobriety tests, including "horizontal gaze nystagmus", "walk and turn", and "one leg stand". D performed the tests poorly and said it was because he had been drinking. The officer arrested D and transported him to a booking center, where D was advised that his actions and voice were being videotaped. D was not advised of his *Miranda* rights upon being stopped or upon his arrival at the Booking Center. An officer asked D his name, address, height, weight, eye color, date of birth, and current age. D answered each question, "stumbling" over his address and age. Then the officer asked D, "do you know what the date was of your sixth birthday?" D's reply was inaudible, and the officer repeated, "when you turned six years old, do you remember what the date was?" D replied, "No, I don't."

The officer then had D repeat the field sobriety tests, which he again performed poorly, while attempting to explain his difficulties in performing them and asking further clarification of what he was to do in performing the tests. Then D was asked to submit to a breathalyzer test and was read the Implied Consent Law, and it was explained that the consequences of refusal would be the automatic suspension of his driver's license for one year. D asked a number of questions about the law, while commenting on his state of inebriation. D ultimately refused to take the test, and at this point, for the first time, was advised of his *Miranda* rights and he signed a statement waiving his rights and admitted, during further questioning, that he had been driving while intoxicated.

Both the video and audio portions of the videotape were admitted into evidence at D's trial, plus the arresting officer's testimony concerning the roadside sobriety tests and D's incriminating remarks at that time. D was convicted of DWI. On appeal, the state appellate court ruled that the audio portion of the videotape should have been suppressed under the *Miranda* case, reversing D's conviction. The State Supreme Court denied review, and the Supreme Court of the United States granted certiorari.

ISSUE: How do the requirements of *Miranda* apply in the above-described situation?

DECISION: Lower court's judgment reversing D's conviction is vacated, and case is remanded for proceedings consistent with this opinion.

REASONS: [The several situations presented by these facts will be covered separately.]

5th Amendment Self-Incrimination Clause

The privilege does not protect a suspect from compelled production of *real* or *physical* evidence, but only from compelled production of evidence of a testimonial or communicataive nature, *Schmerber v. California*, 86 S.Ct. 1826 (1966). In *Miranda v. Arizona*, 86 S.Ct. 1602 (1966) it was reaffirmed that the privilege against compulsory self-incrimination applies not only in a courtroom setting, but also during in-custody interrogation by the police and requires protection by procedural safeguards, (the warnings and waiver). This case involves pretrial police questioning and the components of compulsion and testimonial statements. Therefore the statements of D that were both "testimonial" in nature and elicited during custodial interrogation before the *Miranda* warnings and waiver should have been suppressed. [7 Justices concur.]

Slurred Speech Evidence

The holdings in *Schmerber*, (blood sample, *United States v. Wade*, 87 S.Ct. 1926 (1967), (lineup), *Gilbert v. California*, 87 S.Ct. 1951, (1967), (handwriting sample), and *United States v. Dionisio*, 93 S.Ct. 764 (1973), (sound of voice), all distinguish between "testimonial", and "physical" evidence. Under these holding we agree that the *slurring of speech* or *lack of muscular coordination* revealed by D's responses to the initial questions are non-testimonial and therefore not protected by the Fifth Amendement privilege, and are admissible. [7 Justices concur.]

The "Sixth Birthday" Question

[The Court here discusses the historical background of the Fifth Amendment privilege (including Star Chamber practices in England), and concludes that the answer to the "sixth birthday question *was* testimonial" — a communication of facts or belief — and that it should have been suppressed]. [5 Justices concur.]

Content of Responses to the 7 "Booking" Questions

[Four Justices agree that the content of the answers to the questions about name, address, height, weight, eye color, date of birth, and current age should be admissible under a "routing booking question" exception to *Miranda* because these question are for the administrative purpose to secure the "biographical data necessary to complete booking or pretrial services". Four other Justices maintain that both the "sixth birthday" question and the 7 "booking" questions were simply *not testimonial*, but a continuation of police tests (such as nystagmus, balance, etc.), to determine the effect of alcohol on D's reactions. These four justices compare D's answers to all these questions to answers given by a person being asked to identify letters on an eye chart during an eye examination — that they do not put a person to the tests of "truth, falsity, or silence", and are therefore not the type of testimony that the Fifth Amendment applies to. It would seem than in any event, the 7 booking questions are admissible, either under a "routine booking question" exception to the *Miranda* case, or because they simply are not testimonial in character under the Fifth Amendment].

Incriminating Statements made during Sobriety Tests, and when asked to submit to Breathalyzer Examination

The officers' statements to D during the videotaped sobriety tests were instructions about how the tests were to be performed and were not likely to be perceived as words or actions calling for verbal response and therefore did not constitute "interrogation" within the meaning of the *Miranda* case. The few questions asked by the officers were to insure that D understood the instructions (and, later the Implied Consent Law, consequences, and procedure), and incriminating comments made by D during these two phases were volunteered statements, and were admissible. [7 Justices concur]

RULE: Although the *Miranda* warning and waiver procedure applies to in-custody pretrial police interrogation, it has no application to certain phases of a routine DWI processing, and, when videotaped, the entire video portion is admissible in evidence, as well as the audio portions to show, (1) slurred speech of the D; (2) content and manner of answering routine booking questions; and (3) incriminating comments volunteered by D during routine explanations of sobriety tests and implied consent requirements and procedures. Answers to questions during DWI processing prior to *Miranda* warnings and waiver which place the D between the choices of truth, falsity, and silence will be inadmissible as the product of in-custody interrogation.

Dissenting Opinion omitted.

---------------------------------------Notes---------------------------------------

(C) Volunteered statements

Spontaneous incriminating statements made by individuals before the police have an opportunity to give the warnings of *Miranda* are admissible, because they are not the product of interrogation.

CASE BRIEF
Colorado v. Connelly, 107 S. Ct. 515 (1986)

Majority Opinion: Rehnquist, joined by White, Powell, O'Connor, and Scalia.
Concurring in part: Blackmun.
Concurring in part and dissenting in part: Stevens.
Dissenting: Brennan and Marshall.

FACTS: D approached a uniformed policeman in a downtown area and without any prompting, told the officer he had murdered someone and wanted to talk about it. The policeman immediately gave D his *Miranda* warnings; D stated that he understood, but still wanted to talk about the murder. In response to questions by the officer, D denied drinking or taking drugs, but stated he had been in mental hospitals. The officer again reminded D, who appeared to fully understand the nature of his acts, that he was not obliged to say anything. A homicide detective arrived and again D received the *Miranda* warnings; the detective then asked him what was on his mind. D stated he had come all the way from Boston to Denver to confess that he had murdered a girl in November, 1982. D was taken to police headquarters and a search of records revealed that the body of an unidentified female had been found in April, 1983. Then D directed officers to the scene of the murder. During this time D acted normally.

D was held overnight. During an interview with a public defender the next morning he became visibly disoriented and confused, stating he was obeying "voices". He was sent to a hospital for evaluation and was initially found incompetent to aid in his own defense, but later was determined to be competent to stand trial. At preliminary hearings, D moved to suppress all his statements. Psychiatrists testified that D was experiencing "command hallucinations"; that he believed he was following the "voice of God"; and that his confessions were motivated by his mental condition. The trial court ruled that D's confessions must be suppressed as involuntary because they were not a product of D's intellect and free will and that his *Miranda* waiver was invalid. The Colorado supreme court affirmed, ruling that, under these facts, the absence of police coercion did not prevent a finding of involuntariness. The state petitioned for certiorari, which was granted by the Supreme Court of the United States. (Note: this is a review of a trial court ruling suppressing a confession. The case went no further; D was not tried and convicted.)

ISSUE: Can a volunteered confession to the police and a waiver of *Miranda* rights prompted by a mental condition of the confessor be ruled involuntary as a matter of Fourteenth Amendment due process when there has been no improper or coercive conduct by the police?

DECISION: No. Reversed and remanded. The confessions were admissible under the Fifth and Fourteenth Amendments.

REASONS: The Court reviews its previous decisions and holds that in all cases in which confessions were suppressed, they were deemed to be the product of coercive governmental misconduct or police overreaching. These cases have ranged from physical abuse through psychological persuasion, to police exploitation of mental problems of the confessor. But in every case there was some improper conduct of the police that was deemed to cause the confession. Some "state action" must have occurred to support a claim of violation of due process under the Fourteenth Amendment; the most outrageous behavior of a *private* party seeking to secure evidence against a defendant does not make that evidence inadmissible under the Due Process Clause. The purpose of excluding evidence seized in violation of the Constitution is to deter future violations of the Constitution by agents of the government. D's claim in this case could only be upheld if the Court were to establish a brand new constitutional right—the right of a D to confess his crime only when totally rational and properly motivated. While the states are free to adopt such a ruling under their own laws of admissibility of evidence, we hold that, under the Constitution of the United States, coercive police activity is necessary to a finding that a confession is not "voluntary" under the Due Process Clause of the Fourteenth Amendment. We also hold that a valid waiver of *Miranda* rights need only be established by a preponderance of evidence, not by "clear and convincing" evidence as held by the supreme court of Colorado, and that voluntariness of a waiver of the right against compulsory self-incrimination has always depended on the absence of police overreaching—not on "free choice" in the broader sense of considering the confessor's mental state. The record in this case does not involve any police coercion, misconduct, or overreaching. *Miranda* protects defendants against governmental coercion which leads them to surrender rights protected by the Fifth Amendment; it goes not further than that.

RULE: The voluntariness of a waiver of *Miranda* rights need only be established by a preponderance of evidence. If such a waiver and subsequent confession are prompted by a mental state of anxiety which is not in any way the product of police coercion or misconduct, the confession is admissible in evidence.

DISSENT: Due process of law and fundamental fairness require that a vital choice concerning a confession of criminal guilt, which might allow the state to deprive a person of liberty or even life, must be made with a sane mind. "Free choice" is a much broader concept than merely the absence of police overreaching.

------------------------------------- **Notes** -------------------------------------

(D) The warnings

Immediately after the decision in *Miranda v. Arizona*, 86 S. Ct. 1602 (1966) police departments were unsure of exactly what language would adquately warn a suspect of his rights—particularly his right to counsel—prior to custodial interrogation, as required by the decision. The opinion did not specify any means of providing counsel for those requesting it. Widely divergent procedures were inevitable among the numerous different police jurisdictions in which the broadly stated rule was applied. Undoubtedly some jurisdictions were able to provide counsel within 24 hours, while others could not appoint counsel until the first judicial appearance. The situation varied, not only from one state to another, but from one community to another within the same state. The problem was how to advise the indigent suspect accurately concerning right to counsel and the state's procedures for providing counsel.

One form of warning adopted by the Indiana State Police to meet this problem contained the statement:

> We have no way of furnishing you with an attorney, but one will be appointed for you, if you wish, if and when you go to court.

This statement reflected the truth in the vast majority of situations. Police stations are not manned by defense attorneys, and potential conflicts of interest and plain common sense rule against policemen securing defense lawyers for the persons they arrest. A warning which included the quoted statement was approved by the supreme court of Indiana in *Jones v. State*, 252 N.E.2d 572 (Ind. 1969) and *Rouse v. State*, 266 N.E.2d 209 (Ind. 1971). However, the United States Court of Appeals, Seventh Circuit, in *United States ex rel. Williams v. Twomey*, 467 F.2d 1248 (7th Cir. 1972) held that this warning was not clear and unequivocal, as required by *Miranda*, but instead was equivocal and ambiguous. The court said that the entire warning was at best misleading and confusing, and at worst constituted a subtle temptation to the unsophisticated indigent accused to forego the right to counsel at a critical moment.

The controversy over the *Twomey* warning came to the attention of the Supreme Court of the United States in the case of *Duckworth v. Egan*, 109 S. Ct. 2875, (1989). There, the court held that the language ending with "if and when you go to court" did *not* render an otherwise adequate *Miranda* warning invalid because it accurately described the procedure for the appointment of counsel in Indiana, and because the balance of the warning "...touched all of the bases required by Miranda."

In the case of *California v. Prysock*, 101 S. Ct. 2806 (1981), the issue was whether *Miranda* required the warnings to be a precise formulation of words taken directly from that opinion, or whether the substance and not the form determines the adequacy of the warnings. The Court held that no precise formulation of words was required, and the warnings which were found to be adequate in *Prysock* were:

> Q. Number One, you have the right to remain silent. This means you don't have to talk to me at all unless you so desire. Do you understand this?
> A. Yeh.
> Q. If you give up your right to remain silent, anything you say can and will be used as evidence against you in a court of law. Do you understand this?
> A. Yes.
> Q. You have the right to talk to a lawyer before you are questioned, have him present with you while you are being questioned, and all during the questioning. Do you understand this?
> A. Yes.
> Q. You also, being a juvenile, you have the right to have your parents present,

which they are. Do you understand this?
A. Yes.
Q. Even if they weren't here, you'd have this right. Do you understand this?
A. Yes.
Q. You all, uh, __ if, __ you have the right to have a lawyer appointed to represent you at no cost to yourself. Do you understand this?
A. Yes.

--------------------------------------- **Notes** ---------------------------------------

(E) The waiver of rights

In *North Carolina v. Butler*, 99 S. Ct. 1755 (1979) the defendant was fully warned, upon being arrested, of his rights under *Miranda v. Arizona*, 86 S. Ct. 1602 (1966); after it had been determined that he was literate, he was handed an "Advice of Rights" form, which he read. He stated that he understood his rights, but he refused to sign the waiver at the bottom of the form. He was told that he need neither speak nor sign the form, but that the agents would like to talk to him. He replied, "I will talk to you but I am not signing any form." After this exchange the defendant made incriminating statements which were later used against him at trial. (It should be noted that the defendant said nothing when advised of his right to the assistance of counsel and that at no time did he ask to talk to a lawyer or ask that the interrogation be terminated.)

Holding that *Miranda* requires an *explicit* statement of waiver, the supreme court of North Carolina observed that the defendant had refused to waive in writing his right to have a lawyer present, and also that he had not given an express oral waiver of the right. In reversing this decision, the Supreme Court of the United States stated, in part:

> This is not the first criminal case to question whether a defendant waived his constitutional rights. It is an issue with which courts must repeatedly deal. Even when the right so fundamental as that to counsel at trial is involved, the question of waiver must be determined on "the particular facts and circumstances surrounding that case, including the background, experience, and conduct of the accused." * * *
>
> We see no reason to discard that standard and replace it with an inflexible *per se* rule in a case such as this. As stated at the outset of this opinion, it appears that every court that has considered this question has now reached the same conclusion. Ten of the 11 United States Courts of Appeals and the courts of at least 17 states have held that an explicit statement of waiver is not invariably necessary to support a finding that the defendant waived the right to remain silent or the right to counsel guaranteed by the *Miranda* case. By creating an inflexible rule that no implicit waiver can ever suffice, the North Carolina Supreme Court has gone beyond the requirements of federal organic law. It follows that its judgment cannot stand, since a state court can neither add to nor subtract from the mandates of the United States Constitution. * * *

CASE BRIEF

Edwards v. Arizona, 101 S. Ct. 1880 (1981)

Majority opinion: White. Concurring: Burger, Powell, Rehnquist.

FACTS: D was arrested at his home with a warrant. He was charged with robbery, burglary, and murder. At the police station he was advised of his rights under *Miranda*. D said he understood his rights and was willing to submit to questioning. He was told that another suspect already in custody had implicated him in the crimes. He denied involvement and gave a taped statement presenting an alibi defense, claiming he was somewhere else when the crimes were committed.

D then sought to make a "deal." The police told him that they wanted a statement but had no authority to make a deal. D was allowed to call the prosecutor, but he hung up after a few moments, saying, "I want an attorney before making a deal." At that point, questioning stopped and D was taken to jail.

The next morning, when told that two other detectives wished to speak to him, D said he didn't want to talk to anyone; the jailer told D "he had" to talk to them. The officers again went through the *Miranda* procedure; D was willing to talk, but he first wanted to hear the taped statement of the accomplice that allegedly implicated him. After listening to the tape for several minutes D said he would make a statement if it was not tape recorded. The detectives told him that they could testify in court concerning whatever D said whether it was taped or not. D then said, "I'll tell you anything you want to know, but I don't want it on tape." D thereupon implicated himself in the crimes.

Before trial, D moved to suppress his confession on the grounds that his *Miranda* rights were violated when the officers came to the jail to question him after he had requested counsel. The trial court granted the motion but then reversed its ruling, and evidence concerning the confession was admitted at trial. On appeal, the Supreme Court of Arizona held that D had invoked both his right to silence and his right to counsel on the night of his arrest, but that he had waived these rights the next morning and that the confession was voluntary and admissible.

ISSUE: Do the Fifth, Sixth, and Fourteenth Amendments to the Constitution require suppression of a post-arrest confession obtained on the initiative of the police after D has invoked his right to counsel before further interrogation?

DECISION: Yes; reversed.

REASONS: Under *Miranda* a defendant in police custody has both the right to remain silent and the right to the presence of an attorney during interrogation. If a defendant indicates he wishes to remain silent, "the interrogation must cease," and if he requests counsel, "the interrogation must cease until an attorney is present."

In this case D correctly asserts that he did not validly waive his right to counsel on the morning after his arrest. The Arizona supreme court applied an erroneous standard to determine waiver when D had specifically invoked his right to counsel. Waiver of counsel must not only be voluntary but must constitute a knowing and intelligent relinquishment or abandonment of a known right or privilege.

Here the trial court found the admission of D to have been "voluntary" without separately focusing on whether D had knowingly and intelligently waived his right to counsel. The case of *Schneckloth v. Bustamonte*, 93 S. Ct. 2041 (1973) emphasized that the standard to determine voluntariness of consent or an admission on the one hand, and the standard to determine a knowing and intelligent waiver of counsel, on the other hand, are separate and discrete inquiries.

After initially being advised of *Miranda* rights, the accused may himself validly waive his rights and respond to interrogation; *North Carolina v. Butler*, 99 S. Ct. 1755 (1979). But additional safeguards are necessary when the accused asks for counsel. When an accused has invoked his right to have counsel present during custodial interrogation, a valid waiver of that right cannot be established by showing only that he responded to further police-initiated custodial interrogation, even if he has been advised of his rights. An accused, such as D here, having expressed his desire to deal with the police only through counsel, is not subject to further interrogation by the authorities until counsel has been made available to him, unless the accused himself initiates further communication, exchanges, or conversations with the police.

If the facts had been different—if D himself had initiated the second meeting with the police, nothing in the Fifth and Fourteenth Amendments would prohibit the police from merely listening to his voluntary statements, and using them against him at trial. But the police initiated the second meeting, after D had requested—but had not yet talked to—a lawyer. D also told the detention officer that he did not want to speak to anyone. Under these circumstances no waiver of counsel was demonstrated by the incriminating statement made by D at the second, police-initiated meeting; even though the statement itself was voluntary, it was inadmissible.

RULE: When a suspect in police custody has requested to have counsel present during custodial interrogation, all interrogation must stop until a lawyer is made available to D. If, before a lawyer is made available to D, the police initiate further interrogation, no waiver of counsel can be found merely from a voluntary incriminating statement made by D; even though the police have again complied with *Miranda*, such a statement will be inadmissible. However, the statement may be admissible if D, rather than the police, initiates further communication. A waiver of counsel must not only be voluntary, but it must amount to an intentional relinquishment of a known right or privilege. The determination of an intelligent waiver must depend, in each case, upon the particular facts and circumstances surrounding that case, including the background, experience, and conduct of the accused.

The Supreme Court has attempted to clarify the *Edwards* opinion on several occasions. In *Wyrick v. Fields*, 103 S. Ct. 394 (1982) the Court, in a per curiam summary opinion, ruled that the defendant, a soldier charged with rape, by initiating further communication with police had effectively waived his right to have counsel present during interrogation—*a right he had previously asserted*. The defendant had been released from custody pending trial and had consulted with both privately retained counsel and an attorney provided by the Army. After this consultation the defendant requested a polygraph examination, which was administered by the army C.I.D. Prior to the polygraph examination the defendant signed a written consent form advising him of his *Miranda* rights and his rights under the Uniform Code of Military Justice; he was also read a detailed statement concerning his right to silence, his right to counsel, civilian or military, and his right to stop answering questions at any time. He indicated that he did not want a lawyer at that time. When the polygraph test was over, the examiner indicated to the defendant that there had been some deception, and asked if he could explain why some of his answers were bothering him. Defendant then admitted sexual intercourse with the victim, but said it was with consent. He further agreed to talk the matter over with another C.I.D. agent and with local police. *Miranda* was again complied with, and the defendant gave the same statement to the local police. At issue here was whether defendant had waived counsel for the interrogation that took place immediately *after* the polygraph examination. The Supreme Court held that under the "totality of the circumstances" the defendant not only initiated further communication with the police, but by requesting a lie-detector test he also initiated further interrogation about the crime of which he was suspected. He also waived his right to have counsel present during the questioning that took place after the lie-detector test "unless the circumstances changed so seriously that his answers no longer were voluntary, or unless he no longer was making 'knowing and intelligent relinquishment or abandonment' of his rights". The Court thus ruled, in effect, that the interrogation that took place after the lie detector was turned off was a continuation of the interrogation already agreed to and that to require new warnings and waiver would be unreasonable.

In *Oregon v. Bradshaw*, 103 S. Ct. 2830 (1983) the defendant, a suspect in a traffic death, was interrogated at a police station after having been given his *Miranda* rights. He admitted supplying liquor for a party at the victim's house, but denied involvement in the fatal traffic accident. Police then placed him under arrest for supplying liquor to a minor and again advised him of his *Miranda* rights, and an officer told him of the investigator's theory of how the accident had happened: that the defendant had been driving the vehicle involved. Defendant again denied involvement and *asked for an attorney*. At this point the officer terminated the conversation. Just before or during the defendant's transfer to the county jail, he inquired of an officer, "Well, what is going to happen to me now?" The officer reminded defendant that he had requested an attorney and that he didn't have to talk with the police unless it was his own free will. Defendant said he understood and there followed a conversation about where he was being taken and what he was to be charged with. The officer suggested that the defendant might help himself by taking a polygraph examination. Defendant agreed, saying he was willing to do whatever he could to clear up the matter. The next day, after another warning of *Miranda* rights and signing of a written waiver, the defendant took the polygraph test. When it was over, the examiner told the defendant that he didn't believe he had been telling the truth. The defendant then admitted he had been driving the vehicle and had passed out from too much to drink and had run off the road, struck a tree and an embankment and overturned in a creek. Defendant's motion to suppress this statement was denied and he was convicted of manslaughter. The Supreme Court held that under these facts the defendant had initiated further conversation with the police by his question "Well, what is going to happen to me now?" (The court was careful to distinguish this type of question from others which could not be so interpreted, such as a request for a drink of water or a request to use the telephone). The defendant's statement amounted to "initiation" of conversation with the police since it "evinced a willingness and a desire for a generalized discussion about the investigation and was not merely a necessary inquiry arising out of the incidents of the custodial relationship.

Edwards v. Arizona (briefed above in this section) set forth a 'bright-line rule' that all questioning must cease after an accused requests counsel, even though the request might be ambigous. In *Smith v. Illinois*, 105 S. Ct. 490 (1984) the court held that the invocation of right to counsel and waiver thereof are entirely distinct inquiries. During the reading of the *Miranda* rights, when the officer said; "you have a right to consult with a lawyer and to have a lawyer present with you when you're being questioned. Do you understand that?" The 18 year old defendant responded, "Uh, yeah. I'd like to do that." Instead of terminating the questioning at this point, the officer proceeded to finish reading the defendant his *Miranda* rights and then said, "Do you wish to talk with me at this time without a lawyer being present?" The defendant responded with "Yeah and no, uh, I don't know what's what really." The officer said, "Well, you either have to talk with me at this time without a lawyer being present and if you do agree to talk with me without a lawyer being present you can stop me at any time you want to." The defendant responded "All right. I'll talk to you then." He then told the detectives that he knew in advance about the planned robbery but contended that he had not been a participant. After considerable probing by the detectives, the defendant confessed, "I committed it." The court held that his later responses could not be used to cast doubt upon the clarity of his initial response. In the absence of such a "bright-line" prohibition, authorities through badgering or overreaching might otherwise wear down the accused and persuade him to incriminate himself notwithstanding his earlier requests.

The Court held in *Michigan v. Jackson*, 106 S. Ct. 1404 (1987) that the assertion of right to counsel at the arraignment or initial hearing in court was an assertion of right to counsel under *Edwards v. Arizona* and police-initiated conversations with defendant thereafter would invalidate any waiver of rights. The knowledge of a request under the Sixth Amendment is imputed from one state actor (the court) to another (the police), even though there was no actual knowledge by the police of the assertion of the right to counsel in the courtroom. A similar result was reached in *Arizona v. Roberson*, briefed below.

CASE BRIEF

Minnick v. Mississippi, 111 S.Ct. 486, (1990)

Majority opinion: Kennedy, joined by White, Marshall, Blackmun, Stevens and O'Connor. Dissenting: Scalia, joined by Rehnquist.

FACTS: D was arrested with a warrant for capital murder. An FBI interrogation session ended when D asked for a lawyer, and D consulted with a lawyer 2 or 3 times. Later, while D was still in custody, a deputy sheriff initiated further interrogation of D, following proper *Miranda* procedures. D refused to sign the rights waiver form, but eventually confessed to the deputy sheriff. D's motion to suppress the confession was denied and he was tried, convicted, and sentenced to death. The state supreme court affirmed on the basis that D had been given the right to consult with a lawyer following the FBI interrogation; he had done so; and therefore, under *Edwards v. Arizona*, 101 S.Ct. 1880 (1981), the police had the right to reinitiate questioning because "counsel had been made available to D". D's petition for certiorari was granted by the Supreme Court.

ISSUE: When in-custody interrogation by police has been discontinued because of a request for counsel by the suspect, is it permissible for police to reinitiate the interrogation while D is still in custody after the suspect has consulted with his attorney?

DECISION: No; reversed and remanded.

REASONS: It would be inconsistent with the principles of both *Miranda* and *Edwards* to allow the police to reinitiate interrogation just because the suspect has conferred with a lawyer, however briefly or however extensively. The meaning of the *Edwards* requirement, that upon request for counsel interrogation must cease "until counsel has been made available to him", is that the suspect is entitled to *have counsel with him* during subsequent custodial questioning by the police.

The interpretation of the lower courts in this case would lead to uncertainty as to the *type* or *extent* of consultation needed to displace the *Edwards* requirement; it would promote a loss of respect for the underlying constitutional principle; and it would undermine the advantages of a clear guideline for the police to follow.

RULE: When a lawyer is requested, in-custody police interrogation must stop, and police may not reinitiate custodial interrogation without counsel being present, whether or not the suspect has consulted with an attorney.

DISSENT: The acts of D here amount to a *voluntary waiver* under our previous standards; majority here creates a perpetual irrebuttable presumption that police-initiated confessions under these circumstances are inadmissible; this goes too far behond the *constitutional* command to protect those *who do not know of their right to silence* or who have been *coerced* to abandon it.

--- Notes ---

Sample Questions

What is the meaning of the rule that once an in-custody suspect has requested a lawyer, police may not reinitiate questioning "until counsel has been made available to him"?

A. police may not question him unless his lawyer is with him.
B. after the suspect has spoken with his lawyer, police may question him whether his lawyer is with him or not.
C. police may again question the suspect once the court has appointed a defense lawyer.
D. police may not initiate questioning in any event.
E. B and C above.

A suspect's exercise of his right to counsel in response to *Miranda* warnings:

A. is an exercise of his Fifth Amendment privilege against compulsory self-incrimination.
B. creates a situation barring the police from initiating further interrogation of the suspect except when the suspect initiates the contact with police or when the interrogation is in the presence of the suspect's attorney.
C. does not bar other officers working on other cases from initiating interrogation of the suspect if he is thought to be involved in another case.
D. is an exercise of his Sixth Amendment right to be represented by counsel in a criminal case.
E. A and B above.

Explain in fifty words or less the basic differences in the right to counsel under the Fifth Amendment and the right to counsel under the Sixth Amendment.

If the judge appoints a lawyer to represent an indigent criminal defendant after formal charges have been filed against him, but the police have had no previous opportunity to interrogate the defendant:

A. the police may initiate contact with the defendant for the purpose of interrogating him, following all proper *Miranda* procedures, without first contacting the defendant's attorney.
B. the police must first contact the defendant's lawyer to receive permission to interrogate him.
C. the Fifth Amendment privilege against compulsory self-incrimination bars the police from initiating contact with the defendant.
D. the right to counsel stage has not yet arisen.
E. B and C above.

Explain in fifty words or less the differences between the requirement that the *Miranda* case be followed, and, the requirement that all confessions, to be admissible, must be voluntary under the totality of all the circumstances.

Explain in fifty words or less the differences between a waiver of rights and voluntary consent.

In fifty words or less give three examples of how a person may waive his *Miranda* rights.

CASE BRIEF

Arizona v. Roberson, 108 S. Ct. 2093 (1988)

Opinion: Stevens, joined by Brennan, White, Marshall, Blackmun and Scalia.
Dissenting: Kennedy, joined by Rehnquist. O'Connor not participating.

FACTS: D was arrested at the scene of a burglary. The arresting officer advised D of his *Miranda* rights, and D responded that he wanted to talk to a lawyer before answering any police questions. This request for counsel was recorded in the officer's written report.

Three days later, while still in custody for the burglary and having not yet talked to a lawyer, D was contacted by a different officer who was unaware of D's request to see a lawyer. This officer wanted to talk to D about a crime other than the one for which he was being held. After going through the *Miranda* warning and waiver procedure, D gave the officer an incriminating statement. At the trial for the second crime, the trial court suppressed the statement as being in violation of *Edwards v. Arizona*, 101 S. Ct. 1880 (1981), and the Arizona court of appeals affirmed the suppression order. The supreme court of Arizona denied a petition for review, and the Supreme Court of the United States granted certiorari to the State of Arizona.

ISSUE: Was the police-initiated interrogation by the second officer, who was unaware of D's request for counsel three days earlier, in violation of D's rights under *Edwards v. Arizona?*

DECISION: Yes. Affirmed.

REASONS: The value of the *Miranda* and *Edwards* cases is that each establishes concrete constitutional guidelines for the police and the courts. In *Miranda* we concluded that if the defendant states that he wants an attorney, the interrogation must cease until an attorney is present, and if police interrogation continues without an attorney being present, a heavy burden rests on the government to show a knowing and intelligent waiver of the privilege against self-incrimination and the right to retained or appointed counsel.

Edwards reaffirmed these principles and concluded that interrogation could resume under these conditions only if the defendant himself initiated further communications with the police. This rule also provides clear and unequivocal guidelines to law enforcement professionals. We are not persuaded that there is any value in an exception to the *Edwards* rule just because a different officer, unaware of the request for counsel, wanted to question D about a different crime.

Here, the focus is on the state of mind of D, who had expressed a desire not to answer any police questions until after having talked to an attorney, and who had not himself initiated any communications with the police. The second officer could have easily discovered D's prior request for counsel by reading the arresting officer's report.

RULE: When a defendant has requested the assistance of counsel after arrest and *Miranda* warnings, and is still in custody having not himself initiated further communications with police or talked to a lawyer, it is a violation of the guarantees of *Miranda* and *Edwards* for a different officer, even though unaware of the previous request for counsel, to initiate interrogation, even about a different crime than the one for which the defendant is being held. It is the duty of an officer, seeking to interrogate a suspect in custody, to first determine if that suspect has previously requested the assistance of counsel.

The Supreme Court found a waiver of *Miranda* rights where the defendant, a suspect in a sexual assault case, said he would not give any written statements without his lawyer present but that he had no problem in talking about the incident. He admitted his involvement in the sexual assault but refused to "put anything in writing until his attorney came". *Connecticut v. Barrett*, 107 S. Ct. 828 (1987). The Court held that the defendant's assertion of his right to counsel was limited in clear terms to making a written statement, and he unequivocally expressed his willingness to provide oral statements even though it seems clear he did not understand that an oral confession is just as admissible in evidence as a written one. The defendant's ignorance of the full consequence of his decision did not, in the courts view, vitiate its voluntariness.

CASE BRIEF
Connecticut v. Barrett, 107 S. Ct. 828 (1987)

Majority Opinion: Rehnquist, joined by White, Blackmun, Powell, O'Connor, and Scalia. Concurring in judgment: Brennan. Dissenting: Stevens and Marshall.

FACTS: D, a suspect in a serious felony case, was transported to the police station in the town where the crimes were allegedly committed. Upon arrival there, D was advised of his *Miranda* rights and he signed and dated a warning acknowledgment form. At that time, D stated he would not give the police a *written* statement, but he had "no problem" in talking about the incident. About 30 minutes later D was again advised of his *Miranda* rights prior to a period of interrogation and he signed another acknowledgment card. D stated that he understood his rights; *that he would not give a written statement unless his attorney was present*, but that he had "no problem" talking about the alleged crimes. He then orally admitted his involvement in the crime (a sexual assault).

The police then discovered that their tape recorder wasn't working, so they conducted a second interview after again (for the third time) advising D of his *Miranda* rights. D again stated he was willing to talk to them but would not put anything in writing until his attorney was present, and he repeated his previous confession. When the officers discovered that the tape recorder had again failed to work, one of the officers made notes of the content of D's confessions for use at trial.

After a suppression hearing, the trial court ruled that D's confession was admissible. The court found D had not only indicated that he understood the *Miranda* warnings, but had also stated he needed no further explanation because he understood. The court held that D had voluntarily waived his right to counsel by his conduct and it allowed testimony at trial as to the content of D's confession. D took the witness stand himself and testified that he had understood his rights as they were read to him. D was convicted and sentenced to a prison term of 9 to 18 years.

D's conviction was reversed by the Connecticut supreme court, which held that when D had refused to make a *written* statement without the presence of his attorney, this served as a request for counsel for all purposes and should have put the police on notice not to interrogate D any further unless D himself initiated the conversation. The Supreme Court of the United States granted certiorari to the State of Connecticut.

ISSUE: When a defendant in police custody, having been properly advised of his *Miranda* rights, and having acknowledged his understanding of those rights, indicates that he will not give a *written* statement unless his attorney is present, but willingly gives an incriminating oral statement to the police, has he voluntarily waived his right to counsel within the meaning of the *Miranda* case?

DECISION: Yes, supreme court of Connecticut decision reversed.

REASONS: D made clear to police that he understood his rights and was willing to talk to them. There was no evidence that D was threatened, tricked, or coaxed by the police. *Miranda* provides that a person in police custody shall have the unrestricted freedom to choose between speech and silence. To protect the D's Fifth Amendment right against compulsory self-incrimination, the *Miranda* court formulated protective rules to guide the conduct of the police. One such rule requires that once a defendant states he wants an attorney, all interrogation must stop until an attorney is present. This is a *court-originated rule, not itself required by the Fifth Amendment,* which is justified by its purpose of guarding against police coercion. But we know of no *constitutional* objective which would be served by the suppression of D's confession in this case. It is clear D wanted a lawyer present before making a *written* statement, but it is equally clear that D understood his rights and that, regardless of this knowledge, he was willing to talk to the police. The fact that the police took this opportunity to obtain an oral confession does not violate D's constitutional rights. D had the clear choice between speech and silence and he chose to speak.

Although past cases have carefully protected a defendant's ambiguous requests for counsel before giving a statement to the police, there was no ambiguity here for the court to interpret. To conclude, under the facts of this case, that D claimed his right to counsel for all purposes would require not a broad interpretation of an ambiguous statement, but a disregard of the ordinary meaning of D's statement. (That he had "no problem" in talking about the incident, and that he was willing to talk about it verbally, but didn't want to put anything in writing until his attorney came.)

We reject the argument that D's misunderstanding of the importance of a written—as opposed to a verbal—confession was so great that it requires his limited reference to right to counsel to be effective for all purposes. We have never held that defendant's illogical decision or ignorance of the full consequences of his decision will do away with its voluntariness.

RULE: If a defendant in police custody acknowledges that he understands his *Miranda* rights, having been properly advised by the police, and further states that he is willing to give a verbal statement to the police before his lawyer arrives, but will not give a written statement until his lawyer is present, the giving of a verbal statement constitutes a waiver of the right to silence and to counsel for *Miranda* purposes, and such a verbal statement is admissible.

DISSENTING: This is merely a case where a state supreme court arguably granted more protection to a citizen than is required under the federal Constitution. It is not a sufficient reason to grant certiorari to our already overcrowded docket. The facts here are similar enough to those in *Edwards v. Arizona* for that case to control and the interrogation should have been held improper and the confession inadmissible.

Another case in which the Supreme Court decided that a suspect's lack of full knowledge of certain facts did not do away with the voluntariness of his waiver of rights was *Moran v. Burbine,* briefed below. This case, which involves serious questions about police behavior and ethical conduct, has not been uniformly accepted and followed in all the states.

CASE BRIEF

Moran v. Burbine, 106 S. Ct. 1135 (1986)

Majority opinion: O'Connor, joined by Burger, White, Blackmun, Powell and Rehnquist. Dissenting: Stevens, joined by Brennan and Marshall.

FACTS: D, a burglary suspect, was arrested by Cranston, Rhode Island police and, through information from a confidential informant, was linked to a murder committed several months before in Providence. Two other suspects arrested with D, when questioned separately, also implicated D in the murder.

D was informed of his *Miranda* rights but refused to execute a written waiver. The Providence police were contacted and they came to the Cranston police headquarters, where D was held. Unknown to D, his sister, who knew he had been arrested in the burglary investigation but was not aware that he was a murder suspect, contacted the public defender's office to arrange for legal assistance for D. An assistant public defender telephoned police headquarters and stated she would act as D's counsel if police intended to put him in a lineup or question him. The police told the assistant public defender that D would not be questioned further until the next day, but did not tell her D was a murder suspect or that the Providence police had arrived to question him about the murder. Shortly thereafter, the Providence Police began to interrogate D. They complied fully with *Miranda* and obtained three signed waivers from D and also three signed statements admitting the murder. D was not aware of his sister's efforts to retain counsel for him nor that the assistant public defender had telephoned offering to serve as counsel in the burglary case. D's pretrial motion to suppress the statements was denied and he was convicted of murder. The Rhode Island supreme court affirmed the conviction. D then sought but was denied habeas corpus in federal district court, but the U.S. court of appeals reversed, holding that the police failure to inform D of the assistant public defender's call voided his waiver of his Fifth Amendment privilege against compulsory self-incrimination and his right to counsel. The State of Rhode Island petitioned for certiorari to the Supreme Court of the United States and the petition was granted.

ISSUE: Did the conduct of the police or D's lack of knowledge that an attorney was attempting to reach him make his later *Miranda* waivers ineffective?

DECISION: No, U.S. Court of Appeals ruling reversed, case remanded (upholding conviction).

REASONS: The Providence police followed the *Miranda* procedures precisely—this is clear from the record. If it is shown that a suspect's decision not to stand on his rights was uncoerced and that he knew he could remain silent and ask for a lawyer, and that he knew any statement given to the police could be used against him, his waiver of rights is valid as a matter of law. Events occurring outside the presence of and unknown to the suspect can have no bearing on his ability to understand and knowingly give up his constitutional rights. It is true that had D known of the public defender's phone call, it might have affected his decision to confess, but the Supreme Court has never ruled that the Constitution requires police to supply a suspect with a flow of information to help him decide whether to speak or stand by his rights (other than the *Miranda* warning information). There is no indication of physical or psychological pressure by the police in this case, and it appears that it was D and not the police who spontaneously started the conversation that led to the first, and most damaging confession. While the police conduct here may be objectionable as a matter of ethics, it is not relevant constitutionally to the question of waiver under *Miranda*.

The basic purpose of the *Miranda* decision was not to mold police conduct for its own sake, but to strike a balance between the inherent coerciveness of in-custody police interrogation and the public interest in effective law enforcement. Voluntary and non-coerced admissions of guilt are essential to society's compelling interest in finding, convicting, and punishing those who violate the law. Extending the reach of *Miranda* so as to require reversal of a conviction because the police misled an attorney, or because they failed to inform a suspect of an attorney's telephone call which was unsolicited by the suspect, would expand *Miranda* beyond its underlying purpose of protecting the suspect's right against compulsory self-incrimination. It is now well established that *Miranda* warnings are not themselves rights protected by the Constitution but are instead a (court-imposed) measure to protect Fifth Amendment rights. One of the principal advantages of *Miranda* is its ease and clarity of application. To extend it as suggested by D beyond its original purpose would be to muddy its otherwise relatively clear waters, to give rise to numerous other legal questions, and to upset the delicate balance *Miranda* strikes between protection of suspects' rights and effective law enforcement. But nothing we say today prevents state courts from adopting a more strict code of conduct for their employees and officials than is required under this opinion.

D also claims in this case that the misleading information given to the assistant public defender requires exclusion of his three confessions as a violation of the *Sixth Amendment*. (His claim borrows from the reasoning of *Massiah v. United States*, 84 S. Ct. 1199 (1964) and *Brewer v. Williams*, 97 S. Ct. 1232 (1977), which hold that, once the right to counsel has attached, it follows that police may not interfere with the efforts of the attorney to act as a medium between the suspect and the state—or in other words, police must "go through" retained or assigned counsel to talk to defendant once the right to counsel has attached.) But the wording of the Sixth Amendment itself and cases such as *Kirby v. Illinois*, 92 S. Ct. 1877 (1972) and *Maine v. Moulton* 106 S. Ct. 477 (1985) indicate that the right to counsel (and its accompanying right of non-interference with the attorney-client relationship) attaches when the government's role shifts from investigation to accusation (the initiation of formal charge, preliminary hearing, indictment, information or arraignment). In this case, when the assistant public defender telephoned the police station, D had not been formally charged with murder; the murder case against him was still in its investigative stage and had not yet reached the accusatory stage. Therefore, with reference to the murder, the right to counsel had not yet attached.

This concept, that the Sixth Amendment right to counsel attaches at the point of initiation of adversary judicial proceedings, was confirmed in *Moulton*, which involved an undercover investigation that yielded evidence pertaining to two different crimes. For one of the crimes, the defendant had been indicted, but for the other, he had not. As to the crime for which defendant had been indicted, the Court ruled that, after the first charging proceeding, the government may not obtain incriminating statements from an accused out of the presence of his lawyer. But it was also made clear that, as to the crime for which he had not been indicted (still in the investigative stage) the evidence obtained in the same undercover investigation would be admissible at a trial limited to those charges. Because, in *Moulton*, the defendant already had a lawyer representing him on one charge, the decision all but forecloses D's argument in this case that the phone call from the assistant public defender triggered the Sixth Amendment right to counsel, which in turn should have rendered his waiver of rights ineffective because of the conduct of the police.

D here claims, however, that the fact of custodial interrogation requires a different rule. But even though confessions obtained by the police can help to seal a defendant's fate, and the presence of a lawyer could be of great value to a suspect, the same is true as to pre-indictment lineups (as in *Kirby*) and statements elicited pertaining to an unindicted crime (as in *Moulton*). For an interrogation, no more or less than for any other "critical" pre-trial event, the possibility that the encounter may have important consequences at trial, standing alone, is insufficient to trigger the Sixth Amendment right to counsel. Until the government has committed itself to prosecute, and the adverse positions of government and defendant have solidified, the Sixth Amendment right to counsel does not attach to the point that the police conduct here complained of could be considered as a violation of that right.

Nor does the police conduct in this case so shock the sensibilities of civilized society (as it did in *Rochin v. California*) to amount to a violation of Fourteenth Amendment due process, requiring a federal intrusion into the criminal process of the states.

RULE: The right to counsel attaches at the time that a case shifts from the investigative to the accusatorial stage by means of formal charge, preliminary hearing, indictment, information, or arraignment. If a suspect in police custody is under investigation for more than one crime, this right to counsel attaches only to the criminal investigation (if any) which has proceeded through the investigative to the accusatorial stage.

If, during the investigative stage of a case, the police comply fully with the *Miranda* requirements, and it is clear that the suspect is aware of his right to remain silent and to ask for a lawyer to be present and that the police intend to use any statement he makes against him in a criminal prosecution, his waiver of these rights, if uncoerced, is valid as a matter of law. Such a waiver of rights is unaffected by events beyond the knowledge of the suspect, including an attempt, unknown to him, of a lawyer engaged by a third party, to contact him. Nor does the failure of the police to inform the suspect of the attorney's call, or misleading information given to such an attorney, (while questionable as a matter of ethics), violate the suspect's Sixth Amendment right to counsel or his right to due process of Law.

DISSENT: The Majority opinion departs from the view that ours is an accusatorial and not an inquisitorial system, and embraces incommunicado questioning by police. In doing so, the Court rejects an entire body of case law on the subject at the state level and it also rejects the American Bar Association's Standards for Criminal Justice. What happened in this case is police deception of the shabbiest kind. Well-settled principles of law lead to the conclusion that failure to inform D of his attorney's call makes his waiver of rights unvalid. The burden of proving such waiver is always on the government, and it is especially heavy in a custodial setting. *Miranda* clearly condemns threats or trickery in obtaining a waiver. Settled principles about construing waivers of constitutional rights and about the need for strict presumptions in custodial interrogations, as well as a plain reading of *Miranda* itself, overwhelmingly supports the proposition that a suspect's waiver of his right to counsel is invalid if police refuse to inform him of his lawyer's communications. The majority opinion is based on the fear that an individual will exercise his rights. As a matter of agency law, the police deception of the assistant public defender was tantamount to deception of D. What emerges from our body of case law is not that police misconduct must "shock the conscience" to violate due process, but rather the principle that due process requires fairness, integrity and honor in the operation of the criminal justice system and in the treatment of the citizen's constitutional protections.

A suspect's awareness of all the crimes about which he may be questioned is not relevant to determining the validity of his decision to waive his privilege against self-incrimination after the *Miranda* warnings are given. In *Colorado v. Spring*, 107 S. Ct. 851 (1987) federal agents from the Bureau of Alcohol, Tobacco and Firearms (ATF) had arrested the defendant for interstate transportation of stolen firearms; after giving the defendant his *Miranda* rights, they questioned him about his firearms transactions, and also asked him if he had a criminal record. He replied that he had a juvenile record for shooting his aunt. Then the agent, who was aware of a suspected murder by the suspect, asked if he had ever shot anyone else. The defendant responded, "I shot another guy once." This statement was later used against him in a murder prosecution. The Court said that the Constitution does not require that a criminal suspect know and understand every possible consequence of a waiver of the privilege against self-incrimination and the failure of the law enforcement officials to inform the defendant of the subject of the interrogation does not affect, in a constitutionally significant manner, his decision to waive his Fifth Amendment privilege.

CASE BRIEF
Colorado v. Spring, 107 S. Ct. 851 (1987)

Majority Opinion: Powell, joined by Rehnquist, White, Blackmun, Stevens, O'Connor, and Scalia. Dissenting: Marshall, joined by Brennan.

FACTS: D and another person shot and killed W while on a hunting trip in Colorado. D later became a suspect in a federal firearms case (interstate transportation of stolen firearms), through information supplied to ATF agents, who were also told of D's possible involvement in the Colorado murder. The agents set up an undercover operation to purchase firearms from D and arrested him during an undercover purchase. The agents warned D of his *Miranda* rights on two occasions prior to in-custody interrogation, and further advised him he could stop the questioning at any time or stop until an attorney could be secured for him. D indicated he understood and was willing to waive his *Miranda* rights and talk to the agents without a lawyer being present, and he signed a written waiver form.

The ATF agents at first questioned D about the firearms sale for which he had been arrested. Then they asked D about his past criminal record, and D admitted he had a juvenile record for shooting his aunt when he was 10 years old. The agents then asked him if he had ever shot anyone else, and D ducked his head and mumbled, "I shot another guy once." When asked if he had ever been to Colorado, and if he had shot W and thrown his body into a snowbank, D said no. The interrogation ended at this point.

Several weeks later, Colorado police officers visited D while he was in jail pursuant to the firearms arrest. They advised D of his *Miranda* rights and D again signed a form indicating he understood his rights and was willing to waive them. The officers told D they wanted to question him about the Colorado homicide and D stated he "wanted to get it off his chest". D then talked freely with the officers, confessing the Colorado murder without asking to terminate the interrogation or requesting counsel. D also read, edited, and signed a written summary of his confession.

Upon being charged in Colorado with murder, D moved to suppress both statements on the basis that his waiver of *Miranda* rights was invalid. He claimed that because the ATF agents did not advise him they were going to ask him about the Colorado murder, his *Miranda* waiver was ineffective and the second confession (to the Colorado officers) was the illegal product or "fruit" of the first statement. The trial court ruled against D, finding that the failure of the ATF agents to inform D that they were going to question him about the Colorado murder had no effect on the validity of his waiver of *Miranda* rights. Since D had been advised of his right of silence, his right to stop answering questions, and his right to have an attorney present, but did not exercise any of these rights after signing a waiver form indicating his understanding and waiver of these rights, the court held that the statement to the ATF agents should not be suppressed on Fifth Amendment grounds. (The trial court later ruled that D's statement that he "shot another guy once" was *irrelevant*, and for that reason the statement to the ATF agents was not admitted in the Colorado murder trial.) As to the second statement, made to the Colorado officers, the trial court ruled that it was made freely, voluntarily and intelligenty, after proper warning the waiver of *Miranda* rights, and therefore was admissible in evidence at the murder trial. D was convicted of murder.

On appeal, D pressed his argument that his confession to the Colorado officers was the illegal "fruit" of his original statement to the ATF agents, which was also inadmissible because their failure to advise him that they were going to question him about the murder had rendered his *Miranda* waiver invalid. The Colorado court of appeals agreed with D, holding that the first statement was inadmissible and that the state had failed to show that the second statement was not the illegal product or "fruit" of the first statement, and therefore, it too, was inadmissible. The courts reversed D's conviction and remanded the case for a new trial. The supreme court of Colorado affirmed. The Supreme Court of the United States granted certiorari.

ISSUE: When the police conduct an in-custody interrogation of a suspect, is the suspect's awareness of the possible subject-matter of the interrogation necessary to the validity of a waiver of *Miranda* rights?

DECISION: No, reversed.

REASONS: The interrogation by the Colorado officers was in full compliance with *Miranda*. The resulting confession cannot be the "fruit of the poisonous tree" if the tree itself (the earlier ATF interrogation) was not poisonous. Therefore, our inquiry centers on the ATF interrogation.

The *Miranda* procedural safeguards were formulated to protect the Fifth Amendment privilege against self-incrimination which is fully applicable during custodial interrogation. The Court's aim was to assure the individual's right to choose between silence and speech remains unfettered throughout the interrogation process. But the Fifth Amendment privilege may be waived if the waiver is made voluntarily, knowingly, and intelligently. In this case, D was warned of his Fifth Amendment privilege, precisely as required by *Miranda*. D indicated that he understood his rights and then proceeded to waive them by signing a waiver form. There was no element of duress or coercion. But despite this, D argues his statement was in effect compelled because he was not aware that he would be questioned about the murder. This argument strains the meaning of compulsion past the breaking point.

Giving up a right must be voluntary in the sense that it is the product of a free and deliberate choice—and not the result of intimidation, coercion or deception. Also, the waiver must be made with a full awareness both of the nature of the right being abandoned and the consequences of the decision to abandon it. The test of whether a choice is uncoerced and the consequences of the choice understood is the totality of circumstances surrounding the interrogation. Here there is no doubt that D's waiver of rights was voluntary. His complaint that the agents failed to provide him certain information before questioning has no relationship to the well-understood indicators of coercion (duration and conditions of questioning; attitude of police toward him; his physical and mental stage; or other pressures affecting his powers of resistance and self-control). There is no evidence that D's will was overborne by coercive police conduct. By the standards of *Miranda* D's waiver of his right to silence was voluntary.

As to the waiver being knowingly and intelligently made, the Constitution does not require that a criminal suspect know and understand every possible consequence of a waiver (citing *Moran v. Burbine*, 106 S. Ct. 1135 (1986). The Fifth Amendment guarantee is simple and fundamental: a defendant may not be compelled to admit his guilt by testimonial or communicative means. The *Miranda* warnings protect this privilege by ensuring that a suspect knows (1) he can refuse to talk to police; (2) that he may choose to talk to them only with his lawyer present; and (3) that he can stop talking at any time.. *The critical advice, that whatever a suspect says may be used in evidence against him, ensures that a waiver of these rights is knowingly and intelligently made.* In this case, there is no allegation of D's misunderstanding or the rights or the consequences of speaking to the police. The trial court was correct in finding a knowing and intelligent waiver under *Miranda*.

As to D's allegation that the ATF agents' failure to advise him that he would be questioned about the murder amounted to "trickery", this Court has never held that mere silence by police as to the subject matter of interrogation is "trickery" sufficient to invalidate a suspect's *Miranda* waiver, and we decline to so hold in this case. Once *Miranda* warnings are given, it is difficult to see how official silence could cause a misunderstanding of rights. One who is told he is free to refuse to answer questions is in a curious posture to later complain that his answers were compelled. In *Moran v. Burbine* we held that a valid waiver does not require a person be informed of all information "useful" in making his decision, or that police supply him with a flow of information to help him calibrate his self-interest in choosing between silence or speech. In this case as well, the additional information would have affected only the wisdom of waiver, not its voluntary and knowing nature.

There is no qualification of the broad and explicit warning required by *Miranda*.

RULE: It is not necessary that a suspect in police custody be made aware of all possible subjects of questioning in advance of interrogation in order for him to voluntarily, knowingly and intelligently waive his Fifth Amendment privilege against compulsory self-incrimination.

DISSENTING: The heavy burden required by *Miranda* for the state to establish a valid waiver of rights was not met. A suspect's decision to waive his rights is necessarily influenced by his awareness of the scope and seriousness of the matters under investigation. The psychological pressures involved in this case were coercive in nature and caused the waiver to be less than voluntary, knowing and intelligent.

-- **Notes** --

Sample Questions

If the police have a suspect in custody, and through normal noncoercive conversation they elicit an incriminating response to a question before having gone through the *Miranda* warning and waiver procedure, what effect will this probably have on the prosecution's case?

A. all charges will have to be dismissed.
B. the incriminating statement will be inadmissible, but this will not prevent compliance with *Miranda* later, and possibly obtaining an admissible statement.
C. the incriminating statement will be "fruit of the poisonous tree' and it will prevent later interrogation even though *Miranda* is fully complied with.
D. the incriminating statement obtained by the noncoercive questioning prior to the *Miranda* procedure will be admissible because it does not violate the Fifth Amendment.
E. the prosecution's case will be destroyed because of the obvious violation of the Sixth Amendment.

If two defendants are indicted, arrested, and released on bail and one of them voluntarily comes to the police, offering to turn "states evidence" to help the police make a case on the other defendant by secretly recording or broadcasting conversations with the other defendant:

A. all information so obtained by the police can be used against the non-cooperating defendant.
B. none of the information so obtained by the police can be used against the non-cooperating defendant.
C. the Sixth Amendment rights of the non-cooperating defendant are violated by this arrangement.
D. some of the information so obtained by the police (concerning criminal activity with which the non-cooperating defendant has not yet been formally charged) may be used by the police.
E. C and D are correct under federal law, (but the situation may vary under particuar state laws).

The "Christian burial speech" case, *(Brewer v. Williams)* was decided on the basis of:

A. violation of the compulsory self-incrimination clause of the Fifth Amendment.
B. violation of the Sixth Amendment right to counsel.
C. Fourth Amendment search violations.
D. the Due Process Clause of the Fifth Amendment.
E. psychological coercion under Iowa law.

Once adversary proceedings have been inititated against an individual, he has a right to legal representation when the government interrogates him.   T.   F.

When a defendant who has claimed his Fifth Amendment right against compulsory self-incrimination before a grand jury is ordered to testify by the court, only use and derivative use immunity from prosecution is required in order to satisfy the Consititution of the United States, not full transactional immunity.   T.   F.

BASIC DIFFERENCES IN RIGHT TO COUNSEL UNDER FIFTH AND SIXTH AMENDMENTS.

A person's right to counsel can be based on his claiming his right against compulsory self-incrimination (Fifth Amendment — the *Miranda* situation), or it can be based on his right to be represented by counsel at any critical stage of a criminal proceeding — which is a Sixth Amendment right.

Typically, in the *Miranda* situation, a person is in the "custody" of police, and the police wish to interrogate him while he is still in their custody, *about the offense for which he is in custody*. If such a person, having been warned of his *Miranda* rights, does not freely and voluntarily waive those rights, he may not be interrogated by the police about *any* offense until a lawyer has been made available to him, and then only in the presence of the lawyer. *Minnick v. Mississippi*, 111 S.Ct. 486 (1991).

But if the right to Counsel is based on the Sixth Amendment only, the Supreme Court has now made clear, *McNeil v. Wisconsin*, 111 S.Ct. 2204 (1991), the police may not be barred from interrogating a suspect in the absence of his lawyer — if the interrogation concerns an offense for which the suspect has not yet been formally charged.

When an accused asks to be represented by counsel (Sixth Amendment right), after the accusatory stage of the proceeding has started — such as being represented at an initial appearance on a charged offense — does this request for counsel prevent the police from initiating contact with an accused person who is in custody, to interrogate him about an *unrelated and uncharged* offense, without notifying the accused's lawyer? The answer is apparently no — but, of course, all proper *Miranda* safeguards must be followed. Not until a suspect requests counsel for the purpose of protecting his Fifth Amendment rights against compulsory self-incrimination are the police required to contact his lawyer before talking to the suspect. The Sixth Amendment right to be *represented* by counsel is "offense-specific", but the Fifth Amendment right, once claimed by a suspect, bars all police contact with the suspect, except through his lawyer.

In summary, before a person is taken into police custody, the police always have the right to ask him questions, but he has the right to refuse to answer. Once a suspect who is in custody asks for a lawyer to protect him against compulsory self-incrimination, all police questioning should cease, and the suspect should not be questioned by the police in the absence of his lawyer *about any crime* (unless the suspect himself initiates the contact with the police). *Edwards v. Arizona*, 101 S.Ct. 1880 (1981); *Arizona v. Roberson*, 108 S.Ct. 2093 (1988). But if a suspect has not asked for a lawyer for protection against self-incrimination, but has asked for a lawyer only to represent him at some stage of a criminal proceeding initiated against him, this right to counsel — Sixth Amendment — will not alone prevent police from approaching the suspect in the absence of his lawyer for purposes of interrogation *about unrelated and uncharged criminal offenses*, but it does bar police-initiated interrogation about the offense for which the suspect is currently being represented by counsel. *Michigan v. Jackson*, 106 S.Ct. 1404 (1987).

The *McNeil* holding illustrates the Supreme Court's continuing recognition of the public interest in combatting crime through proper police investigative techniques, but it is also likely to be a reminder to defense lawyers to advise their clients to claim their rights against compulsory self-incrimination whenever they are contacted by the police for questioning, even though the lawyer is fulfilling a Sixth Amendment (representative) function only.

Sample Questions

The most usual way that a criminal defendant exercises his right against compulsory self-incrimination during his own trial is:

A. by taking the witness stand as a witness in his own case and refusing to answer critical questions by "taking the 5th".
B. by not taking the witness stand at all in his own trial.
C. by refusing to attend his own trial.
D. by taking the witness stand but remaining silent in response to cross-examination by the prosecutor.
E. none of the above.

The following examples would be violations of a criminal defendant's privilege against compulsory self-incrimination:

A. extracting a confession from a suspect by use of physical torture.
B. causing a suspect to confess to a crime by using psychological coercion.
C. tricking a suspect into a confession by falsely telling him that his fingerprints were found at the scene of the crime.
D. the "Christian burial speech" used by the police officer in the case of *Brewer v. Williams,* 97 S.Ct. 1232 (1977).
E. A and B above.

The requirements specified in the *Miranda* case for police to follow in custodial interrogation sessions were set forth as a protection of the Sixth Amendment right to counsel. T F.

Two suspects are being interrogated by the police in different rooms of the police station by different officers. Both suspects are in the custody of the police and have been given their *Miranda* warnings, and have waived them. After five minutes of questioning, suspect A says, "I don't want to answer any more questions.", and suspect B says, "I want to talk to a lawyer before I answer any more questions." What should the police do in reference to each of the suspects? When can the police start to question each of them again?

John, the driver of a car involved in a property damage accident, is still at the scene of the accident when police arrive and he displays some of the symptoms of alcohol intoxication. One of the officers asks John if he will submit to a breath test for intoxication and John indicates that he will. Is the *Miranda* warning and waiver procedure a necessary step before the breath test for intoxication is administered? Why or why not?

When a witness is subpoenaed to appear to give testimony before a Grand Jury, is it necessary that the witness be advised of his *Miranda* rights and that he waive them before he is questioned?

D, a driver involved in a fatal accident has all of the usual symptoms of drunkenness at the scene of the accident but refuses to submit to a breath or blood test for the presence of alcohol. Can the prosecutor get testimony of these refusals into evidence in D's trial without violating his privilege against compulsory self-incrimination? Why or why not?

Do the *Miranda* warnings have to be worded in language specifically used in the *Miranda* opinion? If yes, what should the warnings say? If no, what is the test of their validity?

(F) Exception to Miranda Rule—When Warnings Are Not Required

In *New York v. Quarles*, 104 S. Ct. 2626 (1984) the Court created a public safety exception to *Miranda* when it held that after police officers have a suspect in custody, they may question him about the location of a gun they have reason to believe is hidden nearby. In the Court's reasoning, the danger to society in leaving a loaded revolver lying about where anyone—including the defendant's accomplices—could find it, outweighed the suspect's rights under *Miranda*. The Court concluded that the need for answers to questions in a situation posing a threat to the public safety outweighs the need for the prophylactic rule protecting the Fifth Amendment's privilege against self-incrimination. The Court expressed confidence in the judgment of police officers when it said, "We think police officers can and will distinguish almost instinctively between questions necessary to secure their own safety or the safety of the public and questions designed solely to elicit testimonial evidence from a suspect . . . . The exception which we recognize today, far from complicating the thought processes and the on-the-scene judgments of police officers, will simply free them to follow their legitimate instincts when confronting situations presenting a danger to the public safety".

CASE BRIEF
New York v. Quarles, 104 S. Ct. 2626 (1984)

Majority Opinion: Rehnquist, joined by Burger, C.J., White, Blackmun, and Powell.
Concurring in part and dissenting in part: O'Connor. Dissenting: Marshall, joined by Brennan and Stevens.

FACTS: A woman reported to police she had just been raped. She gave description of D, who she said was armed with a pistol and had just entered a nearby supermarket. Police located D in the store and captured and handcuffed him. In presence of several officers who had come to assist, but before giving the *Miranda* warnings, the arresting officer, whose search of D had revealed an empty shoulder holster, asked where the gun was. D replied, nodding toward some empty boxes, "The gun is over there." The gun was located at the place indicated, and after it was seized, D was given his *Miranda* rights; he waived them, and agreed to answer questions without an attorney being present. He then admitted the gun was his and that he had purchased it in Florida. At a suppression hearing, the New York trial court excluded the statement, "The gun is over there", the gun itself, and all other statements made by D concerning ownership and purchase of the gun because police had not complied with *Miranda* requirements before asking D about the location of the gun, even though he was clearly in custody. The appellate division affirmed; the New York Court of Appeals granted leave to appeal and affirmed, rejecting the states' position that the exigencies of the situation excused the arresting officers' delay of the *Miranda* procedure until after the gun was located. The Supreme Court granted certiorari.

ISSUE: Under these facts, should the incriminating admission of D concerning the location of the gun, which led to its discovery and the other admission, have been suppressed?

DECISION: No. Reversed.

REASONS: Under these facts, the arresting officer's concern for the public safety takes precedence over strict adherence to the literal requirements of *Miranda*. Here, we have no claim that D's statements were compelled by police conduct which overcame his will to resist; the only issue is the justification of the arresting officer's inquiry before complying with *Miranda*. We agree with the lower courts that there *was* custody in this case when the critical question was asked, but we hold that there is a "public safety" exception to the *Miranda* rule that warnings and waiver be given before a suspect's answers are admissible as evidence. We also hold that the public safety exception does not depend on the motivation of the individual officers involved. We do not believe that *Miranda* requires the rule to be applied in all its rigor to a situation in which police officers spontaneously ask questions reasonably prompted by a concern for the public safety.

In this case, in the act of apprehending a suspect, police were faced with the immediate necessity of finding a pistol which they had every reason to believe D had just removed from his empty holster and hidden in a supermarket. So long as the weapon remained concealed it obviously posed a threat to the public safety; an accomplice might use it, or a customer or employee might find it.

In such a situation, if police are required to comply fully with *Miranda* before any inquiry is made, suspects in D's position might be deterred from responding, thus prolonging the threat to the public safety.

We conclude that the need for answers to questions in a situation posing a threat to the public safety outweighs the need for the protective rule of *Miranda*. We decline to place police officers in a position of having to consider, often in a matter of seconds, whether it best serves the interests of society to ask necessary questions in disregard of *Miranda* (and thereby to render any probative evidence they uncover inadmissible), or to comply with *Miranda* and possibly destroy their ability to neutralize a dangerous situation. This public safety exception to the *Miranda* requirements will not complicate the thought processes and on-the-scene judgments of police officers, but will free them to follow their legitimate instincts when confronting situations dangerous to the public safety.

RULE: There is a limited "public safety" exception to *Miranda* requirements, in that in-custody interrogation by the police before the warning and waiver procedure is carried out will not in all cases render answers and derivative evidence discovered thereby inadmissible when the public safety interest outweighs the need to protect the self-incrimination privilege.

CONCURRING AND DISSENTING: *Miranda* should be strictly applied to render the *statements* made by D inadmissible, but the derivative evidence (the pistol), constituting real evidence, should be admissible.

DISSENTING: There was no longer any danger to the public when the question was asked. D had been captured and was in the custody of several armed police officers. This so-called "public safety" exception will forever destroy the clarity of the *Miranda* rule. The statement and all evidence derived therefrom should be suppressed, but it may be in order to remand the question of admitting the pistol as evidence to the New York Court of Appeals for consideration, in light of the "inevitable discovery" rule of *Nix v. Williams*, 104 S. Ct. 2501 (1984).

-------------------------------------- **Notes** --------------------------------------

(G) Impeachment and Miranda

The shield provided by *Miranda* cannot be perverted into a license to use perjury by way of a defense, free from the risk of confrontation with prior inconsistent utterances. *Harris v. New York*, 91 S. Ct. 2240 (1971). The accused may not take the stand and turn a constitutional "shield" into a "sword" with which to cut the truth by perjury. In *Oregon v. Hass*, 95 S. Ct. 1215 (1975), the Court said that we are, after all, always engaged in a search for truth in a criminal case so long as the search is surrounded with the safeguards provided by our Constitution.

Silence of the defendant after the defendant has been taken into custody may not be used to impeach a defendant, since this is inconsistent with the Fifth Amendment right to remain silent. *Doyle v. Ohio*, 96 S. Ct. 2240 (1976). Nonetheless, if the defendant tells the officer one story during interrogation and a different tale during trial, the prosecutor may, without running afoul of *Doyle*, highlight the obvious inconsistency by asking the accused why he did not volunteer the second account in the first place. *Anderson v. Charles*, 100 S. Ct. 2180 (1980); a suspect's silence after arrest but before *Miranda* warnings are given may sometimes be used to impeach his later testimony at trial; for example, if his defense at trial is one of self-defense, he may be asked why he failed to claim self-defense when first taken into custody. *Jenkins v. Anderson*, 100 S. Ct. 2124 (1980).

-------------------------------------- Notes --------------------------------------

Sample Questions

The test to determine "consent" — as in a search — is the absence of coercion under the totality of all the circumstances, while the test to determine a "waiver" of rights is the "intentional relinquishment or abandonment of a known right or privilege". This explains why the Supreme Court of the United States insists that warnings be given in a *Miranda* situation, but does not require warnings in a consent search situation.   T.   F.

Volunteered statements by persons in the custody of the police which are not the product of in-custody interrogation are admissible even though the *Miranda* procedure has not been complied with.   T.   F.

The *Miranda* case clearly sets out how counsel for the indigent is to be arranged.   T.   F.

Miranda requirements do not apply when there is no custody, but interrogation only.   T.   F.

All questioning that takes place in a police station is necessarily "custodial" in nature.   T.   F.

A non-custodial interview, free of coercion of any kind, will not require that the *Miranda* warnings be given simply because the interviewee is the "focus" of a criminal investigation.   T.   F.

Conversation between two police officers which takes place in the presence of a suspect who is in custody and which results in a volunteered incriminating statement by the suspect will always be considered to be "interrogation" for the purposes of *Miranda*.   T.   F.

The *Miranda* requirements have no application in misdemeanor cases, even though custody may be involved.   T.   F.

The test used to determine whether *Miranda* requirements apply is the coexistence of both "custody" and "interrogation", not whether the offense is a felony or a misdemeanor.   T.   F.

After complying fully with *Miranda* police ask a suspect if he wants to contact a lawyer or whether he will talk to them without a lawyer being present. The suspect replies that he will talk to them at that time but he will not put anything in writing until he talks to his lawyer. He then proceeds to give an oral incriminating statement. The statement will be admissible in evidence.   T.   F.

A suspect's awareness of all of the crimes about which he may be questioned is not relevant to his waiver of *Miranda* rights if the warnings have been properly given by the interrogator, and understood by the suspect.   T.   F.

If immediate concerns of the public safety outweigh the immediate need to protect a suspect's privilege against compulsory self-incrimination, the courts may find a limited "public safety" exception to the *Miranda* requirements.   T.   F.

If a suspect remains silent after receiving his *Miranda* warnings after being arrested, this silence cannot be used to impeach his testimony later at his trial.   T.   F.

(H) Self-incrimination and immunity

If a witness claims the privilege against compulsory self-incrimination and refuses to testify before a court or grand jury, he can be compelled to give testimony under the terms of an immunity statute, provided the statute protects the witness to the same extent as does the Constitution. *Kastigar v. United States*, 92 S. Ct. 1653 (1972); *Zicarelli v. New Jersey State Commission of Investigation*, 92 S. Ct. 1670 (1972).

Generally, two types of immunity are recognized in the law: transactional immunity and use and derivative use immunity.

Transactional immunity.—If A, B, and C are undergoing investigation for the murder of D, and A is called before the grand jury as a witness, he may, of course, invoke the privilege against compulsory self-incrimination at the point where his answer would lead to evidence incriminating him. The Fifth Amendment to the Constitution provides, in part: "No person shall * * * be compelled in any criminal case to be a witness against himself * * * ." The Fifth Amendment privilege has been applied against the states as a matter of Fourteenth Amendment due process. *Malloy v. Hogan*, 84 S. Ct. 1489 (1964). If the jurisdiction in which the investigation is taking place has an immunity statute requiring transactional immunity in return for A's testimony, he can be compelled to testify (probably for the purpose of obtaining evidence against B and C); in return for his testimony A will receive a guarantee that he can never be prosecuted for the "transaction" of the murder of D, even though the prosecution later develops sufficient evidence to convict him from sources wholly independent of and unrelated to his compelled testimony. Nor can he be prosecuted for any other criminal transaction revealed by his compelled testimony. Transactional immunity, therefore, gives A a "free ride" with reference to the murder of D and any other crime revealed under compulsion. He is actually in a much better position than if he had been allowed to claim the privilege and refuse to testify, because in that event he would have been subject to prosecution for the murder of D and for any other crime through the use of any admissible evidence in the prosecutor's possession.

Use and derivative use immunity.—If A, B, and C are being investigated for the murder of D, and A, being called as a witness before the grand jury, invokes the privilege against compulsory self-incrimination but is compelled to testify under a statute granting only use and derivative use immunity in return for his testimony, he can still be prosecuted for the murder of D, or any other crime, if the evidence used by the prosecution is entirely independent of and not derived from his compelled testimony. With this type of immunity A's position is the same as, but no better than, if he had been allowed to claim the privilege and not testify, and this is all that the Constitution of the United States requires. *Kastigar v. United States*, 92 S. Ct. 1653 (1972).

If a person whose testimony has been compelled under a use and derivative use immunity statute is later prosecuted for the crime to which his compelled testimony related, the government is required not merely to negate the taint of the former testimony, but to assume an affirmative duty to prove the wholly independent source of the evidence used; *Kastigar v. United States*, supra. One way that this burden could be met would be for the government to prove that the evidence used to convict was in its possession *before* the testimony was compelled.

When a witness refuses to testify after claiming the privilege against compulsory self-incrimination and after having been ordered to testify by the court under the terms of an immunity statute, he is subject to the inherent power of the court to punish him for contempt of court.

The statutory and case law of each state should be consulted to determine which type of immunity exists in any particular jurisdiction.

Sample Questions

If a police officer who is investigating a crime discovers that a prime suspect in his case has been arrested at the scene of another crime and is being held in jail pending charges of having committed that crime, and the officer goes to jail for the purpose of questioning the suspect.

A. it is the responsibility of the officer to determine whether or not the suspect has asked for a lawyer in any previous interrogation that might have taken place concerning the crime for which he is being held, before he interrogates the suspect.

B. the officer should also determine whether formal charges have been filed against the suspect for the crime for which he is being held.

C. the officer need not be concerned with either a prior request for counsel or formal charges because as long as he follows the usual *Miranda* warning and waiver procedure any statement he obtains from the suspect will be admissible.

D. if the suspect has previously asked for a lawyer, or if he has already been formally charged, these facts *may* may affect the admissibility of any statement obtained from the suspect whether or not the *Miranda* procedure is followed.

E. A is correct; C is incorrect; B and D may depend on state law.

A suspect who can read and write and who is in custody of the police is informed of his rights under the *Miranda* case and is then asked to read a form containing the same information and to sign a waiver of the rights on the bottom of that form. The reaction of the suspect is to reply, "I'll talk to you but I am not signing any form". The suspect then proceeded to make incriminating statements in the conversation with the police which followed. Was there a *waiver* or rights under the *Miranda* case?

A. there was no waiver of rights because a waiver must be explicitly executed in writng.

B. there was no waiver of rights because the suspect obviously mistakenly believed that oral statements to the police were inadmissible.

c. there was no waiver because although the waiver need not be written, it must be explicitly given, if oral.

D. there was a waiver by the decision of the suspect to go ahead and talk despite being informed orally and in writing of his right to silence and the consequences of not remaining silent.

E. B and C above.

If a suspect who is in custody has his *Miranda* rights explained to him and indicates that he understands his rights and consents to be interrogated without a lawyer being present, it is not necessary that he first be made aware of all possible subjects of the interrogation in order for him to voluntarily, knowingly, and intelligently waive his Fifth Amendment privilege against compulsory self-incrimination.   T.   F.

In circumstances in which the immediate public safety outweighs the immediate need to protect the self-incrimination privilege, the courts may find a limited "public safety exception" to the *Miranda* requirements.   T.   F.

COERCED CONFESSION — STANDARD FOR HARMLESS ERROR

In the case of *Arizona v. Fulminante*, 111 S.Ct. 1246 (1991), a five-member majority of the Supreme Court broke with precedent by holding that the erroneous admission by a trial court of a confession, later held on appellate review to have been coerced, can be "harmless error" not requiring an automatic reversal if there is enough additional evidence unaffected by the confession to prove the guilt of the defendant beyond a reasonable doubt. Prior cases had held that if a criminal conviction was based in whole or in part on a coerced confession, regardless of the amount and strength of the other evidence of guilt, an automatic reversal was required on appeal.

The standard for finding "harmless error" in the case of a constitutional violation, (such as a coerced confession), is very strict, and it must be shown that the error was harmless beyond a reasonable doubt (in other words that it did not contribute to the defendant's conviction). In the *Fulminante* case, the Court concluded that although the confession was coerced, it was *not* harmless error, and the defendant got a new trial.

The *Fulminante* case should have little effect on professional police work, as the case did not in any manner alter the usual tests for determination of admissibility of a confession (which in most cases will be *voluntariness and compliance with Miranda requirements*), but only affected the treatment of confessions found on appeal to have been coerced.

-- **Notes** --

Sample Questions

A police informant is housed in the same cell block as a suspect charged with murder. Without initiating any conversations with the suspect and without asking him any questions, the informant merely listens to what the suspect says to other inmates and reports his incriminating statements to the police. Can the police use this information against the murder suspect?

A. no, not unless the informant has given the suspect his *Miranda* warnings.
B. no, because this is an invasion of privacy by the state.
C. no, because this is a violation of the right to counsel.
D. no, because this is a violation of the privilege against compulsory self-incrimination.
E. yes.

Explain why a confession to the police may be ruled voluntary even though it is motivated by "inner voices".

Police, wishing to interrogate an in-custody suspect for the first time, follow the *Miranda* warning and waiver procedure and the suspect agrees to talk to them without a lawyer being present, but refuses to sign the waiver form. In answering police questions, the suspect incriminates himself several times, but refuses to sign or initial a typewritten copy of the questions and answers. Are the incriminating statements admissible?

A. no, there must be a written record.
B. no, because it is clear that the suspect believes that nothing he says is admissible unless it is in writing and therefore his "waiver" is not valid.
C. yes, after having been explained his *Miranda* rights, the action taken by the suspect amounts to a valid waiver.
D. no, by his actions the suspect has revealed his incompetency, and therefore nothing he does is truly voluntary.
E. none of the above are true.

Give an example of police conduct that might be held by the courts to be the "functional equivalent" of interrogation.

Police enter a supermarket to look for an armed rape suspect after having been given a detailed description of his physical appearance and clothing by the victim. Upon spotting the suspect, police seize him, but find him with an empty holster under his coat. One officer asks, "where is the gun", and the suspect indicates it is in a nearby box, where it is found. Under what theory was the question, the defendant's response, and the gun itself declared to be admissible at trial, in view of the fact that *Miranda* was not complied with before the question was asked?

A. the inevitable discovery theory.
B. the public safety exception.
C. the Carroll rule.
D. the "Terry" exception.
E. the Chadwick rule.

In *Harris v. New York*, 91 S.Ct. 643 (1971), a confession, not admissible in the prosecution's case-in-chief because it did not conform to *Miranda* requirements, was admissible for the limited purpose of impeaching the defendant's trial testimony, which was wholly inconsistent with the content of the inadmissible confession. T F.

CHAPTER 6

EYEWITNESS IDENTIFICATION AND LINEUPS

Section
6.1 Introduction
6.2 Highlights of *Wade-Gilbert*
6.3 The *Kirby* limitation on *Wade-Gilbert*
6.4 Suggestiveness
6.5 Use of photographs in identification procedures
6.6 Other developments concerning suspect identification

§ 6.1 INTRODUCTION

In the trial of crimes against the person, such as robbery, rape, battery and kidnapping, and often in other criminal trials, it is important for the victim or a witness to identify the defendant in court as the person who committed the crime. In investigating crimes, it is also helpful or even necessary to have victims or witnesses identify suspects before or shortly after arrest. This procedure has, on occasion, prevented the arrest and/or detention of innocent persons.

Four terms are commonly used to describe suspect identification procedures: the *showup*, the *lineup*, the *photographic array*, and the *in-court identification*. In a showup the police confront a suspect with the victim or a witness before or shortly after arrest, often at or near the scene of the crime or place of arrest.

A lineup is a group consisting of the suspect and other persons, similar in appearance, if possible, who are not suspects; the victim or witness is asked to indicate which of the persons, if any, committed the criminal act. A lineup is usually conducted at or near a place of confinement, such as a jail. As an alternative to a lineup, a photographic array is often used.

The most crucial identification procedure takes place in the courtroom during the trial, when the witness is under oath. In examining the witness the prosecutor might proceed as follows:

Q. Is the person who committed the acts that you have just described present here in the courtroom today?
A. Yes, he is.
Q. Will you please point him out for the court.
A. He is that man [pointing to the defendant] sitting at the table wearing a yellow shirt and blue suit.

It is obvious that such testimony would be damaging to the defendant's case. Although in-court identifications have been used in criminal trials for many years, the Supreme Court of the United States held in *United States v. Wade* (briefed in § 6.2 below) that this important evidence for the state may be challenged under certain conditions. In the companion case of *Gilbert v. California*, 87 S. Ct. 1951 (1967) the Court held that testimony of witnesses who identified the defendant in the absence of counsel must be excluded.

Sample Questions

What sort of position has the Supreme Court of the United States taken on the reliability of eyewitness identification procedures in criminal cases?
A. The Court is suspicious of the accuracy of eyewitness identification procedures because they may be infuenced by suggestiveness.
B. The Court is very comfortable with eyewitness identification procedures because they are seldom in error.
C. The Court has displayed very little concern about the reliability of eyewitness identification procedures, trusting the police to do what is fair.
D. If the witness is willing to make the identification under oath in the courtroom, its fairness or reliability cannot be questioned on appeal.
E. There is no right for the defendant to have his lawyer present at any pre-trial identification procedure.

If the prosecuting attorney, at trial, can offer evidence that the in-court identification of the defendant by the witness relates back to the time and place of the crime:
A. this evidence is of little help to the prosecution.
B. this evidence is extremely important to the prosecution.
C. he cannot lose his case for any other reason.
D. this evidence may overcome attacks by the defense on the accuracy and fairness of an intervening lineup procedure.
E. B and D above.

If a witness mistakenly identifies a person in a pretrial lineup, human nature may make it unlikely that he will change his mind later on.   T   F.

An in-court identification may be admissible despite an improper lineup if the prosecution can establish by clear and convincing evidence that the identification was based on an observation which was independent of — and unaffected by — the improper lineup.   T   F.

In the usual trial of a case involving a crime against a person, such as robbery, rape, battery, etc., what sort of effect does an in-court identification of a suspect have on the jury?
A. it has very little effect.
B. in-court identifications are not allowed in trials before juries.
C. it may depend to some degree on the appearance of certainty conveyed by the victim/witness that the person identified is the person who committed the crime.
D. it is usually very important evidence for the prosecution.
E. C and D above.

§ 6.2 HIGHLIGHTS OF WADE-GILBERT

The *Wade-Gilbert* reasoning may be summarized as follows:
1. An accused is entitled to representation by counsel at any stage of a criminal proceeding, whether formal or informal, and regardless of location, if counsel's absence might detract from the accused's fair trial.
2. The hazards of emotionalism, suggestibility, and vindictiveness, as well as the inherent untrustworthiness of the identification of strangers, make the pretrial lineup a "critical stage" in a criminal proceeding; it therefore requires the presence of counsel as an observer, so that he may better represent the defendant and, if necessary, challenge the fairness of the lineup at trial.
3. If a witness mistakenly identifies a person in a pretrial lineup, human nature makes it unlikely that he will change his mind later on.
4. While an in-court identification should relate back to the confrontation between the defendant and the witness at the commission of the crime (or to some other occasion independent of the lineup), it is possible that an improperly constituted lineup may "taint" the in-court identification, which may then become the "product" of the lineup rather than of a previous confrontation.
5. If the prosecution witness makes an in-court identification of the defendant, but the prosecution introduces no evidence of the pretrial lineup, the defense on cross-examination may challenge the validity of the lineup and its effect on the in-court identification.
6. An in-court identification is admissible despite an improper lineup, provided the prosecution can establish by clear and convincing evidence that the identification was based on observation which was independent of the improper lineup.
7. Testimony by witnesses who identified the defendant at pretrial lineup in the absence of defense counsel is subject to per se exclusion, where it is introduced to support in-court identification.
8. If the police use proper pretrial identification procedures, a witness' in-court identification of the defendant can be supported by testimony concerning the pretrial identification.

Citing *Schmerber v. California*, 86 S. Ct. 1826 (1966) the majority in *Wade* held that a pretrial lineup is not a violation of the right against compulsory self-incrimination, nor is the requirement that a lineup participant speak for the purpose of witnesses identifying the sound of his voice. In *Gilbert v. California*, 87 S. Ct. 1951 (1967) the Court held, similarly, that the obtaining of handwriting samples from a defendant prior to trial did not violate the right against compulsory self-incrimination or the right to counsel, because the obtaining of a handwriting sample for the purpose of comparison is not a "critical stage."

CASE BRIEF
United States v. Wade, 87 S. Ct. 1926 (1967)

Majority opinion: Brennan. Dissenting in part: Warren, Douglas, Fortas, Black, White, Harlan, Stewart

FACTS: A man with a small strip of tape on each side of his face entered a bank, robbed it, and drove way with an accomplice in a stolen car. D was indicted and arrested for the robbery. Fifteen days after counsel had been appointed to represent D, an FBI agent, without notice to D's lawyer, arranged for two bank employees to attend a lineup which included D and several other prisoners. Each person in the lineup wore strips of tape on his face and each repeated the words "put the money in the bag" at the direction of the agent. The bank employees identified D as the robber. At the trial these two employees, on direct examination by the state, were asked to identify D in the courtroom, which they did. On cross-examination by defense counsel, the FBI-conducted lineup was revealed. At the close of the testimony D's attorney moved for an acquittal, or in the alternative that the in-court identification be stricken, on the basis that the pretrial lineup, without notice to D's counsel, violated D's rights against compulsory self-incrimination and his right to counsel. The trial court denied the motion and D was convicted.

The court of appeals reversed and ordered a new trial in which the in-court identification was to be excluded. The court held that the Fifth Amendment right against compulsory self-incrimination had not been violated, but the Sixth Amendment right to counsel had.

ISSUE: Were D's constitutional rights violated by the holding of a postindictment pretrial lineup in the absence of D's counsel?

DECISION: Yes.

REASON: *Powell v. Alabama,* 53 S. Ct. 55 (1932) and succeeding cases require that any pretrial confrontation of the accused be scrutinized to see if the presence of counsel is necessary to preserve D's basic right to a fair trial as affected by his meaningful ability to cross-examine and have effective assistance of counsel at the trial itself.

The conduct of a pretrial lineup is not like the gathering of physical evidence. Knowledge of science and technology is sufficiently available to challenge physical evidence at trial through cross-examination. But when counsel was not present at a lineup he is less able to cross-examine as to the fairness of the lineup. The denial of the right to have counsel present at the analysis of physical evidence is not a violation of the Sixth Amendment right to counsel because such analyses are not *critical stages;* there is a minimal risk that counsel's absence might lessen the defendant's right to a fair trial.

But pretrial lineups are filled with dangers caused by the inherent untrustworthiness of the identification of strangers. The suggestive influences which are purposely or accidentally brought to bear have their effect. Also, human nature is such that a witness, once he has identified a person, is unlikely to change his mind even though the identification later proves doubtful. When lineups are conducted in privacy, secrecy creates a gap in the defense attorney's knowledge. The identity of others in the lineup is usually not known to the defendant or to his attorney. Neither witnessees nor lineup participants are likely to be alert for conditions prejudicial to the suspect, In short, the accused's inability effectively to reconstruct at trial any unfairness that occurred at the lineup may deprive him of his only meaningful opportunity to attack the credibility of the witness' courtroom identification.

Past cases of obvious unfairness include: (1) the accused being the only Oriental in the lineup; (2) the accused being the only dark-haired person in the lineup; (3) tall suspects being mixed with short persons; (4) youthful suspects being mixed with adults; (5) all but the accused being personally known by the witness; (6) gross dissimilarities between the suspect and others in the lineup; (7) only the suspect being required to wear distinctive clothing; (8) the suspect being pointed out to the witness before the lineup; (9) all persons in the lineup being asked to try on an article of clothing which fits only the suspect.

In the present case, all the other participants in the lineup were seated together except D, who was in the hallway with an FBI agent.

Other unfairnesses may occur: identification by each of several witnesses may be made in the presence of the others, causing a danger of suggestion; or the suspect may be exhibited handcuffed to a policeman.

In all of these situations the courtroom identification may very well be the fruit or product of the prior identification or lineup; thus, the pretrial lineup might actually constitute the "trial" which determines the fate of the accused.

All of these hazards make the pretrial lineup a "critical stage of the proceeding," requiring the presence of counsel. The Supreme Court must provide guidelines in this area, because neither the legislative branch nor the enforcement agencies have done so.

On the other hand, the in-court identification should not be excluded solely on the grounds of illegal pretrial lineup procedure. The government should have the opportunity to establish by clear and convincing evidence that the in-court identification was based on observations of the suspect during the crime rather than on the pretrial lineup. This would follow the test of *Wong Sun v. United States*, 83 S. Ct. 407 (1962): "whether, granting the establishment of the primary illegality, the evidence to which the instant objection is made has been come at by exploitation of that illegality or instead by means sufficiently distinguishable to be purged of the primary taint." The record here does not disclose whether the in-court identification was of independent origin.

RULE: A post-indictment, pretrial lineup at which the accused is exhibited to identifying witnesses is a critical stage of a criminal proceeding, requiring the presence of defense counsel. The conducting of such a lineup without notice to and in the absence of D's counsel violated D's Sixth Amendment right to counsel and calls into question the admissibility at trial of an in-court identification of D by witnesses who attended the lineup.

DISSENTING: The fact of the lineup was not brought out in the state's case in chief, but by the defense on cross-examination. The conviction should be affirmed on the basis of in-court identification.

The majority creates a broad constitutional rule of far-reaching effect. It is too critical and distrustful of police procedures. The rules does not bar in-court identification where there was no prior lineup and the defendant is known to be in police custody; it suggests that legislative or police safeguards could make the presence of counsel unnecessary, but it doesn't spell out such safeguards as it did in *Miranda v. Arizona*, 86 S. Ct. 1602 (1966); it seems to say that courtroom identification may be barred if counsel was not at the lineup regardless of the extent of the counsel's information about the prior confrontation. The rule may hinder effective law enforcement.

--------------------------------------- **Notes** ---------------------------------------

Sample Questions

A lineup identification procedure conducted by the police after a defendant has been formally charged with a crime:
A. is a routine police investigative procedure which does not require the notification of any person outside the police department.
B. must be conducted in the presence of the trial judge.
C. is a critical stage of a criminal proceeding requiring the presence of the defendant's lawyer as an observer.
D. can, if improperly conducted, lead to problems for the prosecutor at trial.
E. C and D above.

If, as a part of a pretrial lineup, a suspect is asked to speak certain words so the observers may hear the sound of his voice:
A. this violates the suspect's right against compulsory self-incrimination.
B. this is always improper because a lineup may involve only a visual observation of suspects and not the sound of their voices.
C. the words the suspect is asked to repeat cannot be the same words he is alleged to have said at the crime scene.
D. this procedure does not violate the suspect's right against compulsory self-incrimination.
E. this procedure violates the suspect's right against unreasonable search and seizure.

The following procedures do not violate a suspect's right against compulsory self-incrimination:
A. a pretrial lineup.
B. an involuntary blood sample taken by a professional for evidence in a drunk driving case.
C. fingerprinting for identification.
D. a handwriting sample or a recording of the sound of the suspect's voice.
E. all of the above.

If a witness or victim is acquainted with persons other than the suspect who are placed in a police lineup, this may spoil the reliability of the indentification made by the victim or the witness.   T   F.

Some of the hazards to the defendant which are involved in the usual police lineup procedures include:
A. emotionalism of the victim or witness.
B. suggestibility which may be inherent in the procedure.
C. inherent untrustworthiness which is involved in the identification of strangers.
D. vindictiveness
E. all of the above.

§ 6.3 THE KIRBY LIMITATION ON WADE-GILBERT

For some time after the *Wade-Gilbert* decisions, uncertainty existed as to the exact point, in pretrial identification procedures, at which the right to counsel attached, and particularly whether this right existed at a showup confrontation shortly after an arrest. This uncertainty (or apprehensiveness) is expressed in Justice White's dissenting opinion in *United States v. Wade*, 87 S. Ct. 1926 (1967) in which he was joined by Justices Harlan and Stewart:

> The rule applies to any lineup, to any other techniques employed to produce an identification and a fortiori to a face-to-face encounter between the witness and the suspect alone, regardless of when the identification occurs, in time or place, and whether before or after indictment or information.
>
> [R]equiring counsel at pretrial identification as an invariable rule trenches on other valid state interests. One of them is its concern with the prompt and efficient enforcement of its criminal laws. Identifications frequently take place after arrest but before indictment or information is filed. The police may have arrested a suspect on probable cause but may still have the wrong man. Both the suspect and the State have every interest in a prompt identification at that stage, the suspect in order to secure his immediate release and the State because prompt and early identification enhances accurate identification and because it must know whether it is on the right investigative track. Unavoidably, however, the absolute rule requiring the presence of counsel will cause significant delay and it may very well result in no pretrial identification at all.

Speculation as to exactly *when* the right to counsel arises in pretrial identification procedures was laid to rest by *Kirby v. Illinois*, 92 S. Ct. 1877 (1972). In *Kirby* the Supreme Court of the United States expressly refused to apply the *Wade-Gilbert* rulings to a police station showup which took place shortly after the defendant's arrest. Instead, the Court indicated that the right to have counsel present at pretrial identification procedures attaches only after the initiation of adversary judicial criminal proceedings. Recognizing that the starting point of these proceedings might differ from case to case, the Court indicated that the right to counsel could be triggered by formal charge, preliminary hearing, indictment, information, or arraignment. This holding was further clarified in *Moore v. Illinois*, 98 S. Ct. 458 (1977), in which an identification of defendant by a rape victim at preliminary hearing to determine wheither defendant was bound over to the grand jury was ruled improper in the absence of counsel.

------------------------------------- **Notes** -------------------------------------

Sample Questions

In the ordinary "showup" identification procedure conducted by the police to allow witnesses to identify (or exclude) a person as a suspect shortly after the crime and immediately after the arrest is made:
A. the arrested person's lawyer must be notified so he can be present.
B it is required in every case that at least five other persons of the same sex, race, age, and general appearance be displayed to witnesses along with the person arrested.
C. there is no requirement of notification of the suspect's attorney because this procedure occurs during the investigative, and not the accusatory stage.
D. care must still be taken to avoid unnecessary suggestiveness of the procedure.
E. C and D above.

If the court finds that an identification procedure is so suggestive that it creates a "very substatntial likelihood of misidentification", it will hold that the procedure violates:
A. the Sixth Amendment right to counsel.
B. the First Amendment right to expression.
C. due process of law.
D. the lawyer's right to represent his client.
E. equal protection of the law.

Once a witness has identified a suspect in an improperly-conducted identification procedure, there is always a possibility that the witness, when testifying during an in-court identification, may be influenced by the improperly constituted lineup rather than the encounter with the criminal at the scene of the crime.   T   F.

The case law has established that the right to counsel in a criminal case arises when?
A. the moment a crime is committed.
B. only when the trial commences.
C. at the appellate stage after the conviction of a defendant.
D. when the defendant confesses his guilt to the police.
E. after the initiation of adversary criminal proceedings.

If a victim of a violent assault is in the hospital and it is not known whether or not the victim will survive, but is conscious and capable of communicating with others:
A. a non-standard identification procedure may be a necessity.
B. cooperation with attending physicians should be sought by the police before attempting an identification procedure.
C. a procedure otherwise suggestive in nature may be necessary.
D. a photographic array of suspects may be used.
E. all of the above.

§ 6.4 SUGGESTIVENESS

The case of *Stovall v. Denno* (text below in this section) rounded out the 1967 Supreme Court decisions on pretrial identification procedures. This case involved a hospitalized victim in critical condition who was asked to identify the defendant in a one-on-one confrontation in her hospital room. The Court recognized that the confrontation was suggestive, but under the circumstances it was necessary. A new formula emerged from *Stovall* which apparently applies to all pretrial identification procedures, whether or not they are conducted with defendant's counsel present. The *Stovall* test is this: an identification procedure which is unnecessarily suggestive and conducive to irreparable misidentification may violate due process of law. Additional meaning was added to this rule by the 1972 Supreme Court decision in *Neil v. Biggers* (text below in this section).

TEXT OF CASE
Stovall v. Denno, 87 S. Ct. 1967 (1967)

Mr. Justice BRENNAN delivered the opinion of the court

This federal habeas corpus proceeding attacks collaterally a state criminal conviction for the same alleged constitutional errors in the admission of allegedly tainted identification evidence that were before us on direct review of the convictions involved in United States v. Wade, 388 U.S. 218, 87 S. Ct. 1926, 18 L.Ed.2d 1149, and Gilbert v. State of California, 388 U.S. 263, 87 S. Ct. 1951, 18 L.Ed.2d 1178. This case therefore provides a vehicle for deciding the extent to which the rules announced in *Wade* and *Gilbert*—requiring the exclusion of identification evidence which is tainted by exhibiting the accused to identifying witnesses before trial in the absence of his counsel—are to be applied retroactively. * * * A further question is whether in any event, on the facts of the particular confrontation involved in this case, petitioner was denied due process of law in violation of the Fourteenth Amendment. Cf. Davis v. State of North Carolina, 384 U.S. 737, 86 S. Ct. 1761, 16 L.Ed.2d 895.

Dr. Paul Behrendt was stabbed to death in the kitchen of his home in Garden City, Long Island, about midnight August 23, 1961. Dr. Behrendt's wife, also a physician, had followed her husband to the kitchen and jumped at the assailant. He knocked her to the floor and stabbed her 11 times. The police found a shirt on the kitchen floor and keys in a pocket which they traced to petitioner. They arrested him on the afternoon of August 24. An arraignment was promptly held but was postponed until petitioner could retain counsel.

Mrs. Behrendt was hospitalized for major surgery to save her life. The police, without affording petitioner time to retain counsel, arranged with her surgeon to permit them to bring petitioner to her hospital room about noon of August 25, the day after the surgery. Petitioner was handcuffed to one of five police officers who, with two members of the staff of the District Attorney, brought him to the hospital room. Petitioner was the only Negro in the room. Mrs. Behrendt identified him from her hospital bed after being asked by an officer whether he "was the man" and after petitioner repeated at the direction of an officer a "few words for voice identification." None of the witnesses could recall the words that were used. Mrs. Behrendt and the officers testified at the trial to her identification of the petitioner in the hospital room, and she also made an in-court identification of petitioner in the courtroom.

Petitioner was convicted and sentenced to death. The New York Court of Appeals affirmed without opinion.

* * *

We hold that *Wade* and *Gilbert* affect only those cases and all future cases which involve confrontations for identification purposes conducted in the absence of counsel after this date. The rulings of *Wade* and *Gilbert* are therefore inapplicable in the present case. We think also that on the facts of this case petitioner was not deprived of due process of law in violation of the Fourteenth Amendment. The judgment of the Court of Appeals is, therefore, affirmed.

* * *

We turn now to the question whether petitioner, although not entitled to the application of *Wade* and *Gilbert* to his case, is entitled to relief on his claim that in any event the confrontation conducted in this case was so unnecessarily suggestive and conducive to irreparable mistaken identification that he was denied due process of law. This is a recognized ground of attack upon a conviction independent of any right to counsel claim. Palmer v. Peyton, 359 F.2d 199 (4th Cir. 1966). The practice of showing suspects singly to persons for the purpose of identification, and not as part of a lineup, has been widely condemned. However, a claimed violation of due process of law in the conduct of a confrontation depends on the totality of the circumstances surrounding it, and the record in the present case reveals tha the showing of Stovall to Mrs. Behrendt in an immediate hospital confrontation was imperative. The Court of Appeals, *en banc*, state, 355 F.2d at 735,

> "Here was the only person in the world who could possibly exonerate Stovall. Her words, and only her words, 'He is not the man' could have resulted in freedom for Stovall. The hospital was not far distant from the courthouse and jail. No one knew how long Mrs. Behrendt might live. Faced with the responsibility of identifying the attacker, with the need for immediate action and with the knowledge that Mrs. Behrendt could not visit the jail, the police followed the only feasible procedure and took Stovall to the hospital room. Under these circumstances, the usual police station line-up, which Stovall now argues he should have had, was out of the question."

The judgment of the Court of Appeals is affirmed. It is so ordered.

* * *

TEXT OF CASE

Neil v. Biggers, 93 S. Ct. 375 (1972)

Mr. Justice POWELL delivered the opinion of the Court

In 1965, after a jury trial in a Tennessee court, respondent was convicted of rape and was sentenced to 20 years' imprisonment. The State's evidence consisted in part of testimony concerning a station-house identification of respondent by the victim.

* * *

We proceed, then, to consider respondent's due process claim. As the claim turns upon the facts, we must first review the relevant testimony at the jury trial and at the habeas corpus hearing regarding the rape and the identification. The victim testified at trial that on the evening of January 22, 1965, a youth with a butcher knife grabbed her in the doorway to her kitchen:

"A. [H]e grabbed me from behind and grappled—twisted me on the floor. Threw me down on the floor.
"Q. And there was no light in that kitchen?
"A. Not in the kitchen.
"Q. So you couldn't have seen him then?

"A. Yes, I could see him, when I looked up in his face.
"Q. In the dark?
"A. He was right in the doorway—it was enough light from the bedroom shining through. Yes, I could see who he was.
"Q. You could see? No light? And you could see him and know him then?
"A. Yes."

When the victim screamed, her 12-year-old daughter came out of her bedroom and also began to scream. The assailant directed the victim to "tell her [the daughter] to shut up, or I'll kill you both." She did so, and was then walked at knifepoint about two blocks along a railroad track, taken into the woods, and raped there. She testified that "the moon was shining brightly, full moon." After the rape, the assailant ran off, and she returned home, the whole incident having taken between 15 minutes and half an hour.

She then gave the police what the Federal District Court characterized as "only a very general description," describing him as "being fat and flabby with smooth skin, bushy hair and a youthful voice." Additionally, though not mentioned by the District Court, she testified at the habeas corpus hearing that she had described her assailant as being between 16 and 18 years old and between five feet ten inches and six feet tall, as weighing between 180 and 200 pounds, and as having a dark brown complexion. This testimony was substantially corroborated by that of a police officer who was testifying from his notes.

On several occasions over the course of the next seven months, she viewed suspects in her home or at the police station, some in lineups and others in showups, and was shown between 30 and 40 photographs. She told the police that a man pictured in one of the photographs had features similar to those of her assailant, but identified none of the suspects. On August 17, the police called her to the station to view respondent, who was being detained on another charge. In an effort to construct a suitable lineup, the police checked the city jail and the city juvenile home. Finding no one at either place fitting respondent's unusual physical description, they conducted a showup instead.

The showup itself consisted of two detectives walking respondent past the victim. At the victim's request, the police directed respondent to say "shut up or I'll kill you." The testimony at trial was not altogether clear as to whether the victim first identified him and then asked that he repeat the words or made her identification after he had spoken. In any event, the victim testified that she had "no doubt" about her identification. At the habeas corpus hearing, she elaborated in response to questioning.

"A. That I have no doubt, I mean that I am sure that when I—see, when I first laid eyes on him, I knew that it was the individual, because of his face—well, there was just something that I don't think I could ever forget. I believe——
"Q. You say when you first laid eyes on him, which time are you referring to?
"A. When I identified him—when I seen him in the courthouse when I was took up to view the suspect."

We must decide whether, as the courts below held, this identification and the circumstances surrounding it failed to comport with due process requirements.

We have considered on four occasions the scope of due process protection against the admission of evidence deriving from suggestive identification procedures. In Stovall v. Denno, 388 U.S. 293, 87 S. Ct. 1967, 18 L.Ed.2d 1199 (1967), the Court held that the defendant could claim that "the confrontation conducted…was so unnecessarily suggestive and conducive to irreparable mistaken identification that he was denied due process of law." *Id.* at 301-302, 87 S. Ct., at 1972. This we held, must be determined "on the totality of the circumstances." We went on to find that on the facts of the case then before us, due process was not violated, emphasizing that the critical condition of the injured witness justified a showup in her hospital room. At trial, the witness, whose view of the suspect at the time of the crime was brief, testified to the out-of-court identification, as did several police officers present in her hospital room, and also made an in-court identification.

Subsequently, in a case where the witnesses made in-court identifications arguably stemming from previous exposure to a suggestive photographic array, the Court restated the governing test:

"[W]e hold that each case must be considered on its own facts, and that convictions based on eye-witness identification at trial following a pretrial identification by photograph will be set aside on that ground only if the photographic identification procedure was so impermissibly suggestive as to give rise to a very substantial likelihood of irreparable misidentification." Simmons v. United States, 390 U.S. 377, 384, 88 S. Ct. 967, 971, 19 L.Ed.2d. 1247 (1968).

Again we found the identification procedure to be supportable, relying both on the need for prompt utilization of other ivestigative leads and on the likelihood that the photographic identifications were reliable, the witnesses having viewed the bank robbers for periods of up to five minutes under good lighting conditions at the time of the robbery.

The only case to date in which this Court has found identification procedures to be violative of due process is Foster v. California, 394 U.S. 440, 442, 89 S. Ct. 1127, 1128, 22 L.Ed.2d 402 (1969). There, the witness failed to identify Foster the first time he confronted him, despite a suggestive lineup. The police then arranged a showup, at which the witness could make only a tentative identification. Ultimately, at yet another confrontation, this time a lineup, the witness was able to muster a definite identification. We held all of the identifications inadmissible, observing that the identifications were "all but inevitable" under the circumstances. *Id.*, at 443, 89 S. Ct., at 1129.

In the most recent case of Coleman v. Alabama, 399 U.S. 1, 90 S. Ct. 1999, 26 L.Ed.2d 387 (1970), we held admissible an in-court identification by a witness who had a fleeting but "real good look" at his assailant in the headlights of a passing car. The witness testified at a pretrial suppression hearing that he identified one of the petitioners among the participants in the lineup before the police placed the participants in a formal line. Mr. Justice Brennan for four members of the Court stated that this evidence could support a finding that the in-court identification was "entirely based upon observations at the time of the assault and not at all induced by the conduct of the lineup." *Id.*, at 5-6, 90 S. Ct., at 2001.

Some general guidelines emerge from these cases as to the relationship between suggestiveness and misidentification. It is, first of all, apparent that the primary evil to be avoided is "a very substantial likelihood of irreparable misidentification." Simmons v. United States, 390 U.S., at 384, 88 S. Ct., at 971. While the phrase was coined as a standard for determining whether an in-court identification would be admissible in the wake of a suggestive out-of-court identification, with the deletion of "irreparable" it serves equally well as a standard for the admissibility of testimony concerning the out-of-court identification itself. It is the likelihood of misidentification which violates a defendant's right to due process, and it is this which was the basis of the exclusion of evidence in *Foster*. Suggestive confrontations are disapproved because they increase the likelihood of misidentification, and unnecessarily suggestive ones are condemned for the further reason that the increased chance of misidentification is gratuitous. But as *Stovall* makes clear, the admission of evidence of a showup without more does not violate due process.

What is less clear from our cases is whether, as intimated by the District Court, unnecessary suggestiveness alone requires the exclusion of evidence. While we are inclined to agree with the courts below that the police did not exhaust all possibilities in seeking persons physically comparable to respondent, we do not think that the evidence must therefore be excluded. The purpose of a strict rule barring evidence of unnecessarily suggestive confrontations would be to deter the police from using a less reliable procedure where a more reliable one may be available, and would not be based on the assumption that in every instance the admission of evidence of such a confrontation offends due process. * * * Such a rule would have no place in the present case, since both the confrontation and the trial preceded Stovall v. Denno, *supra*, when we first gave notice that the suggestiveness of confrontation procedures was anything other than a matter to be argued to the jury.

We turn, then, to the central question, whether under the "totality of the circumstances" the identification was reliable even though the confrontation procedure was suggestive. As indicated by our cases, the factors to be considered in evaluating the likelihood of misidentification include the opportunity of the witness to view the criminal at the time of the crime, the witness' degree of attention, the accuracy of the witness' prior description of the criminal, the level of certainty demonstrated by the witness at the confrontation, and the length of time between the crime and the confrontation. Applying these factors, we disagree with the District Court's conclusion.

In part, as discussed above, we think the District Court focused unduly on the relative reliability of a lineup as opposed to a showup, the issue on which expert testimony was taken at the evidentiary hearing. It must be kept in mind also that the trial was conducted before *Stovall* and that therefore the incentive was lacking for the parties to make a record at trial of facts corroborating or undermining the identification. The testimony was addressed to the jury, and the jury apparently found the identification reliable. Some of the State's testimony at the federal evidentiary hearing may well have been self-serving in that it too neatly fit the case law, but it surely does nothing to undermine the state record, which itself fully corroborated the identification.

We find that the District Court's conclusions on the critical facts are unsupported by the record and clearly erroneous. The victim spent a considerable period of time with her assailant, up to half an hour. She was with him under adequate artifical light in her house and under a full moon outdoors, and at least twice, once in the house and later in the woods, faced him directly and intimately. She was no casual observer, but rather the victim of one of the most personally humiliating of all crimes. Her description to the police, which included the assailant's approximate age, height, weight, complexion, skin texture, build, and voice, might not have satisfied Proust but was more than ordinarily thorough. She had "no doubt" that respondent was the person who raped her. In the nature of the crime, there are rarely witnesses to a rape other than the victim, who often has a limited opportunity of observation. The victim here, a practical nurse by profession, had an unusual opportunity to observe and identify her assailant. She testified at the habeas corpus hearing that there was something about his face "I don't think I could ever forget."

There was, to be sure, a lapse of seven months between the rape and the confrontation. This would be a seriously negative factor in most cases. Here, however, the testimony is undisputed that the victim made no previous identification at any of the showups, lineups, or photographic showings. Her record for reliability was thus a good one, as she had previously resisted whatever suggestiveness inheres in a showup. Weighing all the factors, we find no substantial likelihood of misidentification. The evidence was properly allowed to go to the jury.

Affirmed in part, reversed in part, and remanded.

Mr. Justice MARSHALL took no part in the consideration or decision of this case.

Mr. Justice BRENNAN, with whom Mr. Justice DOUGLAS and Mr. Justice STEWART concur, concurring in part and dissenting in part.

* * *

As the Court recognizes, a pre-*Stovall* identification obtained as a result of an unnecessarily suggestive showup may still be introduced in evidence if, under the "totality of the circumstances," the identification retains string indicia of reliability. After an extensive hearing and careful review of the state court record, however, the District Court found that, under the circumstances of this case, there existed an intolerable risk of misidentification. Moreover, in making this determination, the court specifically found that "the complaining witness did not get an opportunity to obtain a good view of the suspect during the commission of the crime," "the show-up confrontation was not conducted near the time of the alleged crime, but, rather, some seven months after its commission," and the complaining witness was unable to give "a good physical description of her assailant" to the police. The Court of Appeals, which conducted its own review of the record, upheld the District Court's findings in their entirety. 448 F.2d 91, 95 (CA 6 1971)

-------------------------------------- **Notes** --------------------------------------

§ 6.5 USE OF PHOTOGRAPHS IN IDENTIFICATION PROCEDURES

The Supreme Court of the United States stated in *Simmons v. United States*, 88 S. Ct. 967 (1968):

> [W]e hold that each case must be considered on its own facts, and that convictions based on eyewitness identification at trial following a pre-trial identification by photograph will be set aside on that ground only if the photographic identification procedure was so impermissibly suggestive as to give rise to a very substantial likelihood of irreparable mis-identification.

In the case of *United States v. Ash*, 93 S. Ct. 2568 (1973) the Supreme Court reviewed the historical role of counsel as spokesman for or advisor to the defendant, not only at trial but at other critical stages in criminal procedure. The Court compared these stages with others which are not so critical as to require the presence of counsel: fingerprinting, collecting samples of hair, clothing and blood, the prosecutor's trial preparation, and interviews with witnesses. On the basis of this comparison, the Court stated:

> We hold, then, that the Sixth Amendment does not grant the right to counsel at photographic displays conducted by the Government for the purpose of allowing a witness to attempt an identification of the offender.

The use of a single photograph in a pre-arrest identification procedure has come to the attention of the Supreme Court. In *Manson v. Brathwaite*, briefed below, the Court adopted a balancing test and held that the due process clause of the Fourteenth Amendment does not require the per se exclusion of all pretrial identification evidence which may have been suggestive and unnecessary, if the reliability of such evidence outweights the corrupting effects of the suggestive identification.

CASE BRIEF

Manson v. Brathwaite, 97 S. Ct. 2243 (1977)

Majority opinion: Blackmun. Concurring: Stevens.
Dissenting: Marshall, joined by Brennan

FACTS: G, an undercover narcotics officer, made a "buy" of heroin from a seller through an open doorway of an apartment while standing for two or three minutes within two feet of him in a hallway illuminated by natural light. A few minutes after the buy, G described the seller to another police officer as being "a colored man approximately five feet eleven inches tall, dark complexion, black hair, short Afro style, and having high cheekbones, and a heavy build." The other officer, suspecting from the description that the seller might be D, left a police photograph of D with G, who viewed it two days later and identified it as a picture of the seller. D was charged in a Connecticut court with possession and sale of heroin; at his trial, held some eight months after the crime, the photograph was received in evidence without objection and G testified that there was no doubt that the person shown in the photograph was the seller; G also made a positive in-court identification without objection. No explanation was offered by the prosecution for the failure to utilize a photographic array or to conduct a lineup. D was convicted. After the Connecticut Supreme Court affirmed the conviction, D filed a petition for habeas corpus in federal district court, alleging that the admission of the identification testimony at his state trial deprived him of due process of law in violation of the Fourteenth Amendment. The district court dismissed the petition but the court of appeals reversed, holding that evidence relating to the photograph should have been excluded, regardless of reliability, because the examination of a single photograph was unnecessary and suggestive, and that the identification was unreliable in any event.

ISSUE: Does the due process clause of the Fourteenth Amendment compel the exclusion, in a state criminal trial, of pretrial identification evidence, regardless of reliability, obtained by a police procedure that was both suggestive and unnecessary?

DECISION: No; court of appeals decision reversed.

REASONS: *Neil v. Biggers*, 93 S. Ct. 375 (1972) indicates that there is no violation of due process if the identification in question possesses sufficient reliability. But *Stovall v. Denno*, 87 S. Ct. 1967 (1967) stood for a different rule: that pretrial identification evidence should be excluded if the procedure was so unnecessarily suggestive and conducive to irreparable misidentification as to violate due process. Because the *Biggers* facts occurred before the *Stovall* opinion, the Court must decide whether the *Biggers* rule applies to post-*Stovall* confrontations. The state acknowledges that the procedure here used was suggestive (only one photograph was used) and unnecessary (there was no emergency or exigent circumstance). D. urges a per se rule of exclusion.

Since the *Biggers* decision, the courts of appeal have developed two approaches to this situation: (1) The per se approach which would exclude out-of-court identification evidence, without regard to reliability, if it was obtained through unnecessarily suggestive confrontation procedures; and (2) a more lenient approach, relying on the totality of the circumstances and permitting admission of confrontation evidence if, despite the suggestive aspect, it possesses certain features of reliability. This approach limits the societal costs imposed by a sanction that excludes relevant evidence from consideration and evaluation by the trier of fact.

D stresses the need for deterrence of improper identification practice and he feels that nothing short of per se exclusion will have a direct and immediate effect on law enforcement agents.

Several factors must be considered. *United States v. Wade*, 87 S. Ct. 1926 (1967) and its companion cases reflect the belief that the jury should not hear eyewitness testimony unless that evidence is reliable. Both approaches are responsive to this concern but the per se approach goes too far, since its application automatically, peremptorily and without consideration of alleviating factors keeps relevant and reliable evidence from the jury.

Another factor to be considered is deterrence. The totality-of-circumstances approach does have some deterrent effect, while not as much as the per se approach.

A third factor is the effect on the administration of justice. Here the per se approach has serious drawbacks: inflexible rules of exclusion may frustrate rather than promote justice. It may, on occasion, result in the guilty going free.

The due process clause of the Fourteenth Amendment requires that fairness be the standard. Reliability is the linchpin in determining admissibility of identification testimony for both pre- and post-*Stovall* confrontations. The relevant factors are set out in *Neil v. Biggers*, cited above: (1) opportunity of the witness to view the criminal at the time of the crime; (2) the witness' degree of attention; (3) the accuracy of his prior description of the criminal; (4) the level of certainty demonstrated at the confrontation; and (5) the time between the crime and the confrontation. Against these factors is to be weighd the corrupting effect of the suggestive identification itself.

Applying these criteria to the facts here, there is no substantial likelihood of irreparable misidentification. When there is some element of untrustworthiness it is for the jury to determine the weight of the identification testimony.

RULE: The due process clause of the Fourteenth Amendment does not require the per se exclusion of all pretrial identification evidence which may have been suggestive and unnecessary if the reliability of such evidence outweighs the corrupting effects of the suggestive identification.

DISSENTING: *Stovall v. Denno*, cited above, and *Simmons v. United States*, 88 S. Ct. 967 (1968) established two different due process tests for two very different situations. A per se exclusionary rule should be imposed.

CASE BRIEF

United States v. Crews, 100 S. Ct. 1244 (1980)

Majority opinion: Brennan. Concurring in part: Powell, Blackmun. Concurring in result: White, Burger, Rehnquist.

FACTS: A woman was accosted and robbed at gunpoint in the women's restroom at the Washington Monument by a young male. The robber peered at her through a 4-inch crack between the wall and the door of the stall she was occupying, asked for $10 and demanded to be let into the stall. The victim refused; the robber pointed a pistol over the top of the door, and the victim gave him the money, but he demanded more. When the victim opened the stall door to show the robber her purse was empty, he forced his way into the stall and made sexual advances. The victim pleaded with him to leave and attempted to resist. The robber eventually left after warning the victim he would shoot her if she did not wait at least 20 minutes before leaving. She complied, but immediately thereater reported the incident to the police, giving them a description of the assailant. Three days later, two other women were robbed and assaulted in the same restroom. Their descriptions of the robber closely matched the one given to police by the first victim.

Later, officers of the U.S. Park Police observed D in the vicinity of the Washington Monument concession stand and restrooms. Noting D's similarity to the victims' previous descriptions, the officers approached D, who gave them his name and said he was 16 years old. When asked why he wasn't in school, D replied he had "walked away from school." The officers, after informing D that he resembled a suspect they were looking for, allowed him to leave, and D entered the nearby restrooms. While D was inside, one of the officers talked to a tour guide who had previously reported a young man hanging around the area on the day of the first robbery. When the tour guide saw D leave the restroom, he tentatively identified him to the officers as the same young man he had reported. With this additional information, the officers again approached D and detained him. A detective arrived 10 or 15 minutes later and attempted to photograph D with a Polaroid camera, but could not get a suitable picture because of inclement weather conditions. D was then taken into custody as a "suspected truant", transported to police headquarters, and photographed. After telephoning his school and questioning him briefly, the police released him. He had been detained for no more than an hour. D was not arrested or formally charged with any offense at that time.

The next day, the police showed the victim of the first robbery an array of eight photographs, including one of D. Although the victim had previously reviewed over 100 pictures without identifying any of them, she immediately identified D's photograph as the man who had robbed her. One of the other victims also identified D. D was taken into custody, and at a court-ordered lineup he was positively identified by the same two women who had identified his photograph.

D was indicted. He filed a pre-trial motion to suppress all identification testimony, contending his detention for "truancy" was a pretext to allow the police to gather evidence of the robbery. The trial court found that D's detention for truancy was an arrest without probable cause and that the products of that arrest—the photographic array and lineup identifications—could not be introduced at trial. But the trial judge concluded that the in-court identifications by the victims related back to the crime and were based on their independent recollections and were not "tainted" by the intervening identification procedures. D was convicted of the first robbery and sentenced to four year's probation.

On appeal, the court of appeals reversed D's conviction and ordered the suppression of the first victim's in-court identification on the basis that the in-court identification was the exploitation of the Fourth Amendment violation which occurred when D was detained for truancy. In other words, but for D's unlawful arrest, the police would not have obtained the photograph that led to the identification and prosecution; therefore the in-court identification was the indirect product of the unlawful arrest. The court of appeals also found that none of the three exceptions to the exclusionary rule—"independent source", "inevitable discovery", or "attenuation"—applied in this case. The Supreme Court granted certiorari.

ISSUE: Was the victim's in-court identification of D the product of police misconduct, making it inadmissible as "fruit of the poisonous tree"?

DECISION: No. Judgment of court of appeals reversed; D's conviction reinstated.

REASONS: *Wong Sun v. United States*, 83 S. Ct. 407 (1963) requires that evidence which is either the direct or indirect product of a Fourth Amendment violation should be excluded whether the evidence is tangible, or whether it is items observed or words overheard in the course of unlawful police activity, or confessions or statements of an accused obtained during an illegal arrest and detention. But in the typical "fruit of the poisonous tree" case, the challenged evidence is acquired by the police *after* some initial Fourth Amendment violation and the question before the court is whether the chain of causation resulting from the unlawful conduct has become attenuated (weakened), or has been interrupted by an intervening circumstance so as to remove the "taint" caused by the original illegal action. Therefore in the typical case of this sort, the challenged evidence is in some sense the "product" of the illegal government activity.

Here, the "evidence" being challenged is an in-court identification. There are three distinct elements involved in an in-court identification: (1) the victim is present at trial to testify about the crime and to identify the criminal; (2) the victim possesses knowledge of and ability to testify to the prior criminal occurrence and to identify the defendant from her observations of him at the time and place of the crime; and (3) the D is also present in the courtroom so the victim can observe him and compare his appearance to her memory of the appearance of the criminal. In this case, none of these three elements is the product of a Fourth Amendment violation of D's right requiring suppression.

First, the victim's presence in the courtroom was not a product of police misconduct. She notified police immediately after the crime and fully described her assailant. This is not a case in which the victim-witness' identity was discovered or her cooperation secured as a result of a violation of D's Fourth Amendment rights. Her identity was known to the police *before* any official misconduct and so cannot be its product.

Second, the illegal arrest did not affect the witness' ability to identify D in the courtroom. Her identification related back to her observations of D at the time and place of the crime, which was a source independent from the intervening photographic lineup identifications. Her capacity to identify her assailant in court did not result from and was not biased by the unlawful police conduct occurring *after* she had observed D at the time and place of the crime. This is not to say that the intervening photographic and lineup identifications (both conceded here to be suppressible products of Fourth Amendment violation) could not under some circumstances affect the reliability of in-court identification, but the trial court in this case expressly found the in-court identification to have been made on her independent recollection.

Third, a D cannot claim immunity from prosecution simply because his appearance in court was brought about by an unlawful arrest. An illegal arrest, without more, has never been viewed as a bar to prosecution, nor a defense to a valid conviction (citing case authority). The exclusionary rule applies to evidence secured by official lawlessness. The D himself is not suppressible evidence.

D argues that his physical person is a species of evidence, but we need not decide that because the record clearly discloses the police knew his identity and had some basis to suspect his involvement in the crime *before* his illegal confinement for "truancy." The police already had the victim's description of the robber before they first encountered D. Therefore, the Fourth Amendment violation (D's later detention for "truancy", as a subterfuge to obtain his photograph), yielded nothing of *evidentiary value* that the police did not already have within their knowledge. The unlawful arrest of D served merely to link together two ingredients in his identification already in existence at the time of the arrest (the identity of the suspect and the description of the robber). The exclusionary rule does not reach backward to exclude information already obtained prior to unlawful police conduct.

(The court then distinguished this case from that of *Davis v. Mississippi*, 89 S. Ct. 1394 (1969) (a wholesale roundup of suspects without probable cause for fingerprinting purposes), and it holds that this case is more like that of *Bynum v. United States*, 262 F.2d 465 (D.C. Cir. 1958), which was cited with approval in *Davis*. In *Bynum*, fingerprints of D taken as result of unlawful arrest were matched with fingerprints found at the crime scene. A conviction resulting in part from this fingerprint match was overturned because the prints taken pursuant to the unlawful arrest should have been suppressed, but a later re-trial in which a set of D's prints already lawfully in F.B.I. files was used to match D's prints found at the crime scene resulted in a conviction which was upheld).

(A concurring opinion indicates that while all eight members of the Court concur in the result of this case [Mr. Justice Marshall did not participate in the consideration or the decision]—and while all members agree that a court's jurisdiction to try a case cannot be defeated because the D was arrested illegally, there is a difference of opinion as to whether a D's face can ever under any circumstances be considered "evidence" suppressible as the fruit of an illegal arrest).

RULE: Although testimony concerning a pre-trial photographic array and lineup identification which resulted from an unlawful arrest is suppressible at trial as "fruit of the poisonous tree", an in-court identification by the same witness in the same case is admissible if it relates back to observations made at the time and place of the crime and if it is unaffected by and independent from the identifications made as a result of the unlawful arrest. The power of a court to try a criminal case is unaffected by the unlawful arrest of the defendant, and the exclusionary rule requires only that evidence which is the product of official misconduct must be suppressed.

--------------------------------------- **Notes** ---------------------------------------

Sample Questions

A defendant is entitled to immunity from prosecution if his appearance in court is brought about by an unlawful arrest.   T.   F.

The exclusionary rule does not reach backward to exclude information already obtained lawfully by the police prior to unlawful police conduct.   T   F.

A lineup conducted by the police after the defendant has been formally charged with a crime, without notice to, and in the absence of the defendant's lawyer, violates his Sixth Amendment right to counsel and it also calls into question the admissibility at trial of an in-court identification of the defendant by a witness who attended that lineup.   T   F.

The Due Process Clause of the Fourteenth Amendment does not require in every case the exclusion of all pretrial identification which may have been to some extent suggestive and unnecessary if the reliability of such evidence outweighs the corrupting influence of the identification procedure.   T   F.

Criminal cases which rely heavily on eyewitness identification by witnesses and cases which rely heavily on confessions and admissions are viewed with greater suspicion by the Supreme Court of the United States than are criminal cases involving physical evidence. Likely reason for this are:
A. physical evidence can be scientifically examined and analyzed by both sides.
B. physical evidence is normally not subject to police coercion.
C. eyewitness identifications can be honest mistakes, or the product of suggestiveness.
D. confessions and admissions may be the result of government compulsion.
E. all of the above

Both the absence of the defendant's lawyer at a post-charge lineup, and a lineup that is "suggestive" can cause problems for the prosecution of a criminal case.   T   F.

Factors which have been used by the courts to determine the reliability of identifications of suspects made by victims include:
A. opportunity and time to observe the criminal at the scene of the crime.
B. the amount of light at the crime scene.
C. the accuracy of a previous verbal description of the criminal given to the police by the victim before the identification was made.
D. the degree of certainty displayed when the identification was finally made.
E. all of the above.

§ 6.6 OTHER DEVELOPMENTS CONCERNING SUSPECT IDENTIFICATION

In the 1972 case of *Johnson v. Louisiana*, 92 S. Ct. 1620, the defendant was arrested at his home without a warrant, as the result of an identification made from photographs by the victim of an armed robbery. The defendant claimed that the warrantless arrest in his home was unlawful (as it may very well have been under the later ruling of *Payton v. New York*, 100 S. Ct. 1371 (1980)). After his arrest he was taken before a committing magistrate, who advised him of his rights and set bail. Following this appearance, he was detained for the purpose of appearing in a lineup, at which his lawyer was present. At the lineup, he was identified by the victim of a robbery other than the one for which he had been arrested. It was for this second robbery that the defendant was prosecuted. At the trial he argued that the lineup was the "forbidden fruit" of an unlawful warrantless arrest, and therefore the identification made at the lineup by the victim of the second robbery (for which he was convicted), was not admissible evidence. The Supreme Court of the United States ruled that his challenge to the lawfulness of the warrantless arrest at his home was irrelevant because no evidence that resulted from that arrest was used against him in his trial for the second robbery. At the time of the lineup, the Court ruled, his detention had been authorized by the committing magistrate, and was not the "exploitation" of the challenged arrest, but "by means sufficiently distinguishable to be purged of the primary taint", citing *Wong Sun v. United States*, 83 S. Ct. 407 (1963).

In *Berryman v. United States*, 378 A.2d 1317 (D.C. Cir. 1977) the court held that if the defendant, on timely motion, makes a showing that eyewitness identification is materially at issue and there exists in the particular case a reasonable likelihood of mistaken identification which a lineup would tend to resolve, the court can order an out-of-court lineup, on further motion by the defendant.

A prison inmate serving a lengthy sentence was asked to appear voluntarily in a lineup and to be fingerprinted at the order of a grand jury. The inmate refused and the trial court, recognizing the futility of a contempt order, ordered reasonable physical force, including the use of restraints, to enforce the grand jury order. This was held to be within the court's power in *Appeal of Maguire*, 571 F.2d 675 (1st Cir. 1978).

The Supreme Court of Louisiana, in *State v. McGhee*, 350 So.2d 370 (La. 1977), held that the right to have counsel present at a lineup extends not only to the viewing but also to the witness' verbal or written response to the viewing. In this case the police allowed the defendants' lawyers to choose their places in the lineup and to remain in the room while witnesses viewed the suspects, but the attorneys were not allowed to be present when, following the viewing, the witnesses conferred with police in an adjacent room. In its opinion the court broke the lineup into four parts: (1) the suspect parade or assembly; (2) the witnesses' viewing of the assembly; (3) the witnesses' reaction to the viewing; and (4) the witnesses' verbal or written assertion of their reaction to the viewing. The defendants' lawyers were told that one witness had identified two of the defendants and that the other witness had identified one of the defendants; but they were not told that the latter witness had made a misidentification. To deny counsel the right to be present at the witness-response stage, the Louisiana court held, would be to undermine the purposes of *United States v. Wade*, 87 S. Ct. 1926 (1967), which are to facilitate cross-examination and to prevent improper influence and suggestiveness.

Sample Questions

The "suggestiveness" factor can be a problem in all sorts of identification procedures, including showups, lineups, and photographic arrays.   T   F.

If a photographic array is used as an identification procdure:
A. the Sixth Amendment requires that the defendant's lawyer be present to guard against suggestiveness.
B. there is no requirement that the defendant's lawyer be present.
C. the lawyer must be present but he is not entitled to see the photographs used in the identification procedure.
D. care must still be taken to void suggestiveness.
E. B and D above are both correct.

An identification photograph taken of a suspect at a time when he is being unlawfully detained by the police may result in the suppression of testimony at trial concerning an identification made by the victim which is based on that photograph.   T   F.

To guard against the harmful effects at trial of improper pre-trial identification procedures, the prosecutor should be satisfied that the victim or witness's in-court identification relates back to an observation made at the scene of the crime.   T   F.

An accused is entitled to representation by his lawyer at any stage of a criminal case, whether formal or informal, and regardless of location, if the lawyer's absence might detract from the right of the accused to a fair trial.   T   F.

One of the worst injustices that could possibly happen in the criminal justice system would be for a totally innocent person to be convicted of a crime committed by somebody else, on the basis of a mistaken identification.   T   F.

A pre-trial identification procedure can never, under any circumstances, be referred to by a witness in his testimony at trial.   T   F.

There are three distinct elements involved in an in-court identification. They are:
A. the victim or witness is present at trial to testify about the crime and to identify the criminal.
B. the victim or witness possesses knowledge of and ability to testify to the prior criminal occurrence and to identify the criminal from prior observations made at the time and place of the crime.
C. the defendant is also present in the courtroom so the victim can observe him and compare his appearance to memory of the appearance of the criminal.
D. all of the above
E. (a) the crime must have occurred within the previous two years:
(b) the crime must have occurred in the daytime; and (c) the victim or witness must have been an adult at the time the crime was committed.

A court has never ordered an unwilling person to appear in a lineup.   T   F.

CHAPTER 7

RIGHTS OF THE CONFINED AND THE CONVICTED: JAIL AND PRISON PROCEDURES

Section
7.1 Introduction
7.2 Legal Duties of Arresting Officers to the Incarcerated Suspect
7.3 Legal Rights of the Confined and the Convicted
7.4 Jail and Prison Procedures

§7.1 INTRODUCTION

Few governmental activities are subjected to more legal restrictions or require more funds than physical control over an individual, whether it is called custody, incarceration, confinement, lock-up, pre-trial detainment, jail time, commitment, or correctional detention.

All across the United States, administrators of federal and state correctional facilities and local jails have been held liable for problems in the ways citizens are confined.

Newly-appointed law enforcement officers may select work in correctional facilities as their first choice of assignments. In some cases, new officers may be required to serve tours in such institutions before receiving other assignments, such as patrolling. Veteran officers may choose duty in jails and prisons because they find they prefer it to other kinds of work they have experienced. Whatever their personal career preferences, it is important for correctional personnel and all other employees of the criminal justice system to have a basic understanding of the legal rights of inmates and the purposes and operation of the American correctional system.

The correctional responsibilities that specifically apply to local jails or lockups include the following: the orderly booking of new inmates and their eventual release; the safe-keeping of inmates' personal property; the administration of local bail procedures; and the care and custody of all pre-trial detainees who cannot make bail.

All correctional facilities, from the federal penitentiary to the local jail, share a number of additional responsibilities. These include the care and custody of all those who are confined; the prevention of inmate escapes; the maintenance of an orderly, safe, and healthy living environment; and provision for other needs of inmates, such as access to lawyers and the courts, exercise, visitation, correspondence, and religious practices. These duties and responsibilities reflect the broad objectives of the American criminal justice system: including: revenge/retribution on the part of society and the victim by punishment of the criminal; isolation of the criminal from the rest of society to prevent further offenses; deterrence of individuals from committing crimes; and hopefully, some degree of rehabilitation.

Sample Questions

The current position of the American courts concerning the rights of individuals who are convicted of criminal offenses and sentenced to serve prison terms is:
A. all constitutional rights of convicted persons have been forfeited because of the criminal conviction and the person becomes virtually a "slave of the state."
B. prisoners retain all of their consititutional rights while serving their prison sentences except those rights which come into conflict with prison regulations that are reasonably related to legitimate penological interests.
C. one of total indifference to inmate rights.
D. that courts have no constitutional power to take jurisdiction of lawsuits filed by prisoners because running prisons is wholly up to the legislative and executive branches of government.
E. A and C above.

Some of the case law that has developed as a result of prisoners filing civil rights lawsuits against state prison administrators also applies on the local jail or lockup level.   T   F.

Included in the governmental interests reasonably related to penological goals that will override individual constitutional rights of inmates are:
A. partisan political interests.
B. lack of governmental funding.
C. security.
D. orderly administration.
E. C and D above.

The Fourth Amendment right against unreasonable searches and seizures has no application in a jail or prison.   T   F.

Access to the courts is a right of a prison or jail inmate that is very carefully protected within the American judicial system.   T   F.

The writ of habeas corpus is the only legal theory upon which a prison or jail inmate may base a lawsuit.   T   F.

Prisoners have no right to the use of the mails.   T   F.

Searches conducted in prisons or jails in the interest of maintaining security might be totally unconstitutional if conducted in other settings, the guideline being what is reasonable under the circumstances.   T   F.

Racial discrimination against inmates by correctional authorities is a constitutional violation of the equal protection of the law.   T   F.

Every prisoner has a right, based in the freedom of the press, to request a TV interview for the purpose of taking his grievances to the public, and this right cannot be denied to him by the prison or jail administrator.   T   F.

If a lawsuit is filed by a jail inmate because of a jail-related problem, the arresting officer may also be named in the lawsuit because his enforcement action caused the jailing of the complainant.   T   F.

§7.2 Legal Duties of Arresting Officers to the Incarcerated Suspect

When a citizen is arrested for violating a criminal statute, incarcerating the suspect is the next task the police officer must perform.

The "custody" stage is a very challenging area from a legal standpoint; it is also a process in which the arresting officer must work closely with other professionals. Prior to making an arrest, the law enforcement officer can often have complete control of important decisions in areas such as developing informants and criminal targets, putting together probable cause, seeking arrest and search warrants, serving warrants, and conducting warrantless arrests as well as searches and seizures. Post-arrest procedures, on the other hand, present a different story.

Depending on the circumstances, the arresting officer will often have to work with third parties that the oficer does not personally know or have control over. In the confinement process, such individuals might include:

> the intake/booking officer at the local detention facility;
> jail supervisors, if the arresting officer needs to interrogate the suspect or obtain an item of evidence taken from the suspect during the booking process;
> persons responsible for the setting and processing of bail;
> hospital medical staff, if the suspect is injured;
> the prosecuting attorney's staff, to determine the legality of detention and to decide what criminal charges are to be filed;
> a local judge/magistrate, to arrange a preliminary arraignment/hearing for determining the initial legality of incarceration;
> a public defender/defense attorney, if a suspect requests that an attorney be present during any police interrogation or when a line-up is conducted after formal criminal charges have been filed; and
> news media respresentatives who desire information from the law enforcement officer concerning the circumstanes of the arrest.

From a practical standpoint, jail officers have the primary duty for the care of the incarcerated suspect, but arresting officers must realize that they too have at least a joint legal responsibility to assure that certain needs of the suspect are met, including the following:

> proper medical attention for any physical problems that the arresting officer caused during the arrest or is aware of or should have been aware of at the time of apprehension and incarceration. *City of Canton v. Harris*, 109 S. Ct. 1197 (1989);
> a reasonable opportunity to obtain legal counsel upon request, after being "mirandized" by the arresting officer but before police interrogation is conducted. *Miranda v. Arizona*, 86 S. Ct. 1602 (1966); and
> a timely preliminary arraignment/hearing before a judge. *Gerstein v. Pugh*, 95 S. Ct. 854 (1975).

In civil suits filed against jailers for jail-related problems, arresting officers are frequently made co-defendants (even though day-to-day control over the suspect is in the hands of the jail staff), under the theory that the arresting officers set in motion the chain of events which caused the jailing of the suspect. Usually the allegation is false arrest or excessive use of force causing medical problems — (which were then inadequately handled by the jail staff). Thus, it is to the benefit of arresting officers and jailers alike that there be good lines of communication between them. Arresting officers and jailers must see themselves as being on the same team, and watch out for each other's interests.

A classic example of what happens when communication breaks down is *Edwards v. Arizona*, 101 S. Ct. 1880 (1981). Investigating detectives asked a jailer's permission to see a suspect at the jail for purposes of interrogation. On his own initiative, the jail officer told the suspect (who was unwilling to be interrogated) that he *had* to see and talk with the police officers. The resulting confession was thrown out of court because of the jailer's selection of words indicating that the suspect had no choice.

Police officers should also remember that if they are called upon to make an investigation or arrest of an inmate for a crime committed while behind bars, for purposes of the new crime the inmate retains all those constitutional rights that any criminal suspect would possess.

-------------------------------------- **Notes** --

§7.3 Legal Rights of the Confined and the Convicted

While some jail standards are developed by federal or state statutes, for the most part inmates' legal rights have been formulated via court decisions interpreting the United States Constitution. The First, Fourth, Fifth, Sixth, Eighth and Fourteenth Amendments to the Constitution have provided the basis of these decisions.

These cases have established a number of important standards which every jail officer and administrator must recognize and enforce:

> Prisoners (pretrial detainees as well as convicted persons) do not forfeit all of their consititutional rights as American citizens. They retain many of them, and the government bears the burden of justifying any action which takes away or modifies such a right. *Jones v. North Carolina Prisoners' Labor Union*, 97 S. Ct. 2532 (1977); *Bell v. Wolfish*, 99 S. Ct. 1861 (1979).
>
> Lack of proper governmental funding for corrections can never justify the violation of inmates' constitutional rights. *Campbell v. McGruder*, 580 F.2d 521 (D.C. Cir. 1978).
>
> Inmates have a constitutional right to access the courts through the mail for purposes of filing a legal action. *Ex parte Hull*, 312 U.S. 546 (1941).
>
> Prisoners have a constitutional right to access attorneys through correspondence and visitation. *Johnson v. Avery*, 89 S. Ct. 747 (1969). They also have a right to access law books or a law library. *Younger v. Gilmore*, 92 S. Ct. 250 (1971); *Cruz v. Hauck*, 92 S. Ct. 313 (1971).
>
> Inmates have a constitutional right to adequate medical assistance. *Estelle v. Gamble*, 97 S. Ct. 285 (1976).
>
> Inmates have no *constitutional* right (although statutes or prison policies may permit such practices) to conjugal or other forms of contact visits. *McCray v. Sullivan*, 509 F. 2d 1332 (5th Cir. (1975)); *Block v. Rutherford*, 104 S. Ct. 3227 (1984).
>
> Members of the media have no more right of access under the First Amendment to a jail than does the general public; and prison administrators can limit or deny the media's requests to interview inmates, to make films, sound recordings, or photographs, or to gather information. *Houchins v. KQED*, 98 S. Ct. 2588 (1978).
>
> Prisoners do not have a constitutional right to conduct press conferences or to be interviewed. *Pell v. Procunier*, 94 S. Ct. 2800 (1974).
>
> Racial discrimination against inmates by correctional authorities is a violation of constitutionally guaranteed equal protection of the law. *Lee v. Washington*, 88 S. Ct. 994 (1968); *Cruz v. Beto*, 92 S. Ct. 1079 (1972).
>
> In regard to disciplinary proceedings against them, prisoners have a right to written notification and a hearing; they also have a qualified right to call witnesses (but no rights of confrontation or cross examination), as well as a right to a written statement from prison authorities setting forth evidence and reasons for disciplinary actions. *Wolff v. McDonnell*, 94 S. Ct. 2963 (1974).
>
> The totality of the environment within the correctional facility, consisting of such factors, among others, as overcrowding, sanitation, food service, conditions in isolation and segregation cells, lighting, and ventilation, can be held unconstitutional as being cruel and unusual punishment under the Eighth Amendment. *Holt v. Sarver*, 309 F. Supp. 362 (E.D. Ark 1970), *affd.* 442 F.2d 304 (8th Cir. 1971).
>
> An inmate is not constitutionally protected against searches; cell searches may be conducted at random and in the absence of the inmate; they do not have to be based on "cause". *Hudson v. Palmer*, 104 S. Ct. 3194 (1984).
>
> Inmates who are sincere members of a legitimate religious faith retain a

general right of freedom of religion under the First Amendment. *Cruz v. Beto*, 92 S. Ct. 1079 (1972).

The use of corporal punishment against inmates who break prison rules is a violation of the Eighth Amendment prohibition against cruel and unusual punishment. *Jackson v. Bishop*, 404 F. 2d 571 (8th Cir. 1968).

An issue of special concern to all associated with the task of incarceration is: when may an inmate or visitor be searched, and in what fashion? The leading case is *Bell v. Wolfish*, 99 S. Ct. 1861 (1979). While the Supreme Court has not addressed all possible questions in this area, in *Wolfish* it held that inmates, after having contacts of any kind with the outside world, may be frisked, searched by patdown or strip searched, and have their body cavities visually inspected. At the same time, the Court cautioned prison administrators that unreasonable, abusive, or malicious strip and body cavity searches would not be condoned. Physical entry into body cavities for purposes of removing suspected contraband is an unsettled issue at present; it should not even be considered unless there is specific probable cause to believe the inmate is hiding contraband within a body cavity. The issue of forced strip searching of visitors is also unsettled and should not be undertaken without specific probable cause. *(Hunter v. Auger*, 672 F.2d 668 (8th Cir. 1982). The strip searching of suspects incarcerated for minor offenses has been strongly condemned by various courts *Giles v. Ackerman*, 746 F.2d 614 (9th Cir. 1984).

--------------------------------------- **Notes** ---------------------------------------

§7.4 Jail and Prison Procedures

If a correctional staff can show that its policies and procedures are in the interest of legitimate governmental objectives, there is a good chance that they will be favorably viewed by the courts. In a prison context uppermost among these objectives is security. In examining specific cases, it is useful to consider such rights and duties as the following: the individual correctional staff member's right to defend himself and other staff members; the prison authority's right to prevent escapes, thereby protecting society; the prison authority's right to protect visitors from inmate assaults; the prison staff's obligation to protect the taxpayer's property from theft and destruction; the correctional officer's legal obligation to protect inmates from the criminal acts of other inmates; to prevent riots; and to maintain a peaceful and orderly living environment for the inmates and a safe working environment for the staff.

In 1989 the Supreme Court handed down a decision of considerable significance for correctional officials: *Thornburgh v. Abbott*, 109 S. Ct. 1874 (1989). This ruling, which drew a vehement dissent, indicates that the present majority of the Court is aware of the serious practical problems of prison administrators in dealing with the legal rights of inmates. In a class action, inmates and publishers made a First Amendment-based challenge to comprehensive Federal Bureau of Prison regulations which gave wardens the authority to withhold an incoming publication from inmates if they were "found to be detrimental to the security, good order, or discipline of the institution or if it might facilitate criminal activity."

The Court held that when prison rules relate to inmates *receiving* correspondence or published materials (from inmates and non-inmates alike), such regulations are appropriate even if they are broad. Furthermore, such regulations are constitutional if they are shown to be *reasonably related* to legitimate penological interests. In First Amendment cases prior to this decision, some lower courts had required prison officials to show a "compelling state interest" — a greater burden than "reasonableness". But the majority in *Thornburgh*, in a very telling section of the opinion, held:

> There is little doubt that the kind of censorship just described would raise grave First Amendment concerns outside the prison context. It is equally certain that "[p]rison walls do not form a barrier separating prison inmates from the protections of the Constitution," nor do they bar free citizens from exercising their own constitutional rights by reaching out to those on the "inside." We have recognized, however, that these rights must be exercised with due regard for the "inordinately difficult undertaking" that is modern prison administration.
>
> In particular, we have been sensitive to the delicate balance that prison administrators must strike between the order and security of the internal prison environment and the legitimate demands of those on the "outside" who seek to enter that environment, in person or through the written word. Many categories of nominates seek access to prisons. Access is essential to lawyers and legal assistants representing prisoner clients, to journalists seeking information about prison conditions, and to families and friends of prisoners who seek to sustain relationships with them. All these claims to prison access undoubtedly are legitimate; yet prison officials may well conclude that certain proposed interactions, though seemingly innocuous to laymen, have potentially significant implications for the order and security of the prison. Acknowledging the expertise of these officials and that the judiciary is "ill equipped" to deal with the difficult and delicate problems of prison management, this Court has afforded consider-

able deference to the determinations of prison administrators who, in the interest of security, regulate the relations between prisoners and the outside world. [citations omitted] 109 S. Ct. 1874, 1878.

--------------------------------------- **Notes** ---------------------------------------

CHAPTER 8

JUVENILE OFFENDERS AND THE POLICE

Section
8.1 Introduction
8.2 The case law
8.3 Police handling of juvenile offenders

§8.1 INTRODUCTION

That youthful offenders should not be treated as harshly under the law as adults is not a new concept. In 1769 it was written:

> Infants, under the age of discretion, ought not to be punished by any criminal prosecution whatever. What the age of discretion is, in various nations is matter of some variety. The civil law distinguished the age of minors, or those under twenty five years old, into three stages: *infantia*, from the birth till seven years of age; *pueritia*, from seven to fourteen; and *pubertas* from fourteen upwards. The period of *pueritia*, or childhood, was again subdivided into two equal parts; from seven to ten and an half was *aetas infantiae proxima*; from ten and an half to fourteen was *aetas pubertati proxima*. During the first stage of infancy, and the next half stage of childhood, *infantiae proxima*, they were not punishable for any crime. During the other half stage of childhood, approaching to puberty, from ten and an half to fourteen, they were indeed punishable, if found to be *doli capaces*, or capable of mischief; but with many mitigations, and not with the utmost rigor of the law. During the last stage (at the age of puberty, and afterwards) minors were liable to be punished, as well capitally, as otherwise. 4 Bl. Comm. 22 (1769).

As indicated above, during the time of Sir William Blackstone, persons who had reached the age of fourteen were considered to be responsible adults under the criminal law. The American Colonies, and later, the states, carried this philosophy forward, but as early as 1825 a "House of Refuge" was created in New York City as a separate correctional institution for youthful offenders. In 1867 a House of Refuge was established for juvenile offenders at Plainfield, Indiana. This pattern of activity was common in many of the states and some of these institutions became known as "reform schools". The State of Massachusetts pioneered the formation of "industrial schools" for young offenders in 1847, with emphasis being placed on teaching discipline, hard work, and learning a trade. Probation, as a substitute for imprisonment, began in Massachusetts in 1880, and gradually, the idea of treatment, supervision, and the application of the social sciences in the handling of youthful offenders began to spread. New York established separate trials, dockets, and records for juvenile cases in 1892. Similar developments were taking place in other states. Finally in 1899, the State of Illinois enacted a Juvenile Court Act, creating the first state-wide court especially for children. Created during an aura of reform, the Illinois concept spread rapidly to other states, which followed suit to create a new "jurisdiction" within the American legal system, separate and distinct from adult criminal jurisdiction and covering cases of dependency, neglect, and delinquency. Based on the idea that in England, the chancery court had exercised protective jurisdiction over all the children of the realm, the concept of juvenile jurisdiction is best described by the Latin phrase *parens patriae* - the right (and duty) of the government to take care of minors and others who do not have the capacity to care for themselves. In other words, when the parents (or family) fail in their duty to provide care, custody, control, and discipline, the government steps into the shoes of the parents through the jurisdiction of the juvenile court. Not only is juvenile jurisdiction separate and distinct from adult criminal jurisdiction, but it has its own vocabulary: *petition* replaces complaint; *summons* for warrant; *initial hearing* instead of arraignment; *finding of involvement* rather than conviction; and *disposition* in lieu of sentence. Initially, the juvenile procedure was to be informal and nonpublic, its records confidential, and children were to be detained separate from adults. A probation staff was to be appointed and youthful offenders were not to be treated as criminals nor were they to be dealt with by the criminal process. See President's Commission on Law Enforcement and Administration of Justice, *Task Force Report: Juvenile Delinquency and Youth Crime* (Washington, D.C.: U.S. Government Printing Office 1967) pp. 2-3.

Although the philosophy and spirit of the American juvenile justice system is beneficial to the youthful offender, i.e., to provide " . . . such care and guidance preferably in his own home, as will serve the emotional, mental and physical welfare of the minor and the best interests of the child; to preserve and strengthen the minor's family ties whenever possible.", these statutes also recognized that in some cases it would be necessary to provide " . . . custody, care, and discipline as nearly as possible equivalent to that which should be given by his parents." Illinois Juvenile Court Act, *Illinois Statutes*, 1899, Section 131. A necessary incident to "custody", is, of course, the deprivation of liberty, which, in the American justice system brings into play the Due Process Clause of the Fourteenth Amendment.

--------------------------------------- **Notes** ---------------------------------------

§8.2 The Case Law

It is necessary to review certain concepts and definitions that are involved in juvenile law before summarizing some of the leading cases. *First*, youthful offenders normally come into contact with the police by the commission of one or another of two types of offenses: (1) acts that are defined as crimes in the state criminal code; and (2) acts, (sometimes referred to as "status" offenses) which would not be offenses if committed by adults. Examples of some of the more common status offenses are truancy, ungovernability, violation of curfew, possession of alcoholic beverages, and running away from home. *Second*, all states have designated a particular court to handle juvenile cases. This may be a special court exercising only juvenile jurisdiction, or it may be a regular adult trial court which performs this function in addition to other judicial duties, or it may be a "family" court which deals with children, and domestic cases. The jurisdiction of these courts is normally described by the terms "exclusive original" jurisdiction, "exclusive" meaning that if the case involves a juvenile it must be initially filed in the designated juvenile court, and "original" jurisdiction meaning the power to try the case. Subject matter jurisdiction usually includes delinquency, neglect, and dependency, but sometimes excludes murder or other very serious offenses. *Third*, there is normally a procedure for transfer or "waiver" of trial jurisdiction from the juvenile to the adult felony court when the offense is very serious and a case is made out that the offender is beyond the reform or treatment capabilities of the juvenile system. *Fourth*, although the ages vary from state to state, most consider the age of 18 as adult status for purposes of criminal responsibility and under 18 as coming within the jurisdiction of the juvenile court for most purposes. See President's Commission pp. 4-5.

The subject of waiver of jurisdiction from juvenile to adult criminal court was the situation which gave rise to one of the earliest rulings of the Supreme Court of the United States on the juvenile process. In *Kent v. United States*, 86 S. Ct. 1045 (1966), a 16 year old rape and burglary suspect was implicated in the case by latent fingerprints found at the scene of the crime. The prints matched those of Kent, which were on file as a result of previous housebreakings and an attempted purse snatching committed when he was only 14. Kent was on juvenile probation in the custody of his mother. Following the procedure common at the time, the District of Columbia Juvenile Court judge handled the case very informally despite the fact that an attorney hired by Kent's mother had filed two motions with the court, one for a hearing on the matter of waiver, and the other asking for access to the social service file of his client. The juvenile judge did not rule on either motion, he held no hearing, and did not confer with Kent, his mother or his attorney. Instead, he simply entered an order transferring jurisdiction of the case to the adult criminal court, making no findings, and stating no reason for the waiver, and making no mention of the motions that had been filed on behalf of Kent. Kent was indicted, tried, and convicted for the housebreaking charges as an adult offender in the adult court. An appeal to the United States Court of Appeals resulted in the trial court's conviction being upheld, and the Supreme Court of the United States granted certiorari. In its opinion, that Court stated:

> While there can be no doubt of the original laudable purpose of juvenile courts, studies and critiques in recent years raise serious questions as to whether actual performance measures well enough against theoretical purpose to make tolerable the immunity of the process from the reach of constitutional guaranties applicable to adults. There is much evidence that some juvenile courts, including that of the District of Columbia, lack the personnel, facilities and techniques to perform adequately as representatives of the State in a *parens patriae* capacity, at least with respect to children charged with law violation. There is evidence, in fact, that there may be grounds for concern

that the child receives the worst of both worlds: that he gets neither the protections accorded to adults nor the solicitous care and regenerative treatment postulated for children.

The Supreme Court ultimately held that the waiver in Kent's case was invalid; that the waiver was a critical stage requiring a measure of due process (a hearing); that Kent was entitled to be represented by counsel at such a hearing; that the attorney was entitled to access to the social service file on request; and that if a juvenile court waives jurisdiction to an adult court, the reasons for the waiver must be stated in the record.

The *Kent* opinion noted that previously, the juvenile justice system had operated on the premise that juvenile proceedings were "civil" and not criminal in nature, and since the state was acting as *parens patriae* and not as an adversarial party, that informality was justified. The *Kent* opinion foreshadowed other rulings which were to result in a juvenile proceeding's retention of its basic benevolent purpose while assuming more and more the appearance of a criminal trial.

In 1967 the Supreme Court of the United States decided the case that was to define the course of juvenile proceedings to the present time. In the case of *In re Gault*, 87 S.Ct. 1428 (1967), building on the foundation laid in *Kent*, the Court expanded the due process rights of juvenile defendants in delinquency adjudication proceedings so as to include (1) *adequate* (meaning specific), and *timely* (meaning sufficiently in advance of hearing to allow the preparation of an answer, or defense) *notice of charges;* (2) in respect to a delinquency proceeding which may result in loss of liberty, *a notification to the child and his parents of the right to retained or appointed counsel;* (3) *warning of privilege against compulsory self-incrimination (Miranda* procedure), which, of course, may occur during the pre-hearing "investigative" stage; and (4) *sworn testimony subjected to opportunity for cross-examination* during the delinquency determination hearing. As to the further claim on behalf of Gault that he was entitled to a transcript of the proceedings, and appellate review, the Court declined to rule on these questions in view of the fact that it had never held that any state is required *by the Federal Constitution* "to provide appellate courts or a right to appellate review at all." *Note:* The *Gault* case got to the appellate stage by virtue of federal review of the state's denial of *habeas corpus;* because all states allow at least a one-stage appeal in criminal cases under their own laws, the transcript issue becomes a question of equal protection of the laws. *Mayer v. City of Chicago*, 92 S.Ct. 410 (1971).

Other important decisions involving juvenile cases include *In re Winship*. 90 S.Ct. 1068 (1970); *McKeiver v. Pennsylvania*, 91 S. Ct. 1976 (1971); *Breed v. Jones*, 95 S.Ct. 1779 (1975); and *Schall v. Martin*, 104 S. Ct. 2403 (1984).

The Court ruled in *Winship* that in a juvenile delinquency adjudication hearing in which the child was charged with an act that would be a crime if committed by an adult (theft, in that case), that due process of law requires the standard of proof to be *beyond a reasonable doubt*, rather than the lesser standard of preponderance of the evidence, which is used in civil cases. The Court thus added to the due process protections earlier outlined in *Gault*, and continued to shape the juvenile delinquency adjudication proceeding in the pattern of an adult criminal trial.

After the Gault case, much of the informality of these proceedings, which in many jurisdictions had taken place in the judge's chambers, rather than in the courtroom, had to give way to more formal procedures. The introduction of the right to counsel for the youthful offender naturally resulted in the involvement of a prosecutor for the purposes of balance. The result was more attention to legal technicalities. The state was put in the rather peculiar position of carrying out its mandated *parens patriae* responsibility, but only after clearing many of the hurdles that due process placed in its path, as if its purpose was not to treat, reform, and rehabilitate, but to punish.

The Supreme Court of the United States was not insensitive to the route that the juvenile justice case law was taking. In the case of *McKeiver v. Pennsylvania*, 91 S. Ct. 1976 (1971), the Court, after considering the possibility of negative effects on the curative purpose of the juvenile justice process that might result (further delay, formality, and similarities to the adversarial criminal trial), held that no constitutional right exists for a jury trial in a delinquency adjudication proceeding. In *McKeiver*, the Court was obviously attempting to preserve the unique purpose of the juvenile process while at the same time providing protection against arbitrary loss of individual rights. The insertion of the jury trial right as a matter of constitutional requirement would remove nearly all differences between trials of adults and children, including the non-public nature of juvenile proceedings.

In *Breed v. Jones*, 95 S. Ct. 1779 (1975), however, the Court identified yet another constitutional right of a juvenile defendant (double jeopardy), by holding that a juvenile, once adjudged as a delinquent in juvenile court, could not later be tried for the same conduct in adult criminal court.

In 1984, the Supreme Court of the United States decided the case of *Schall v. Martin*, 104 S. Ct. 2403. In this case the Court upheld the constitutionality of a New York statute which authorized pretrial detention (detention without the right of bail) for accused juvenile delinquents after a finding, upon proper notice and hearing, and supported by a statement of reasons and facts, of a "serious risk" that the child would commit an act that would constitute an adult crime before the delinquency adjudication hearing. The statute limited the period of pretrial detention to no more than 17 days, and it provided numerous safeguards against unnecessary deprivations of liberty. In this case the Court made several interesting comments:

> As an initial matter . . . we must decide whether, in the context of the juvenile system, the combined interest in protecting both the community and the juvenile himself from the consequences of future criminal conduct is sufficient to justify such detention.
>
> The "legitimate and compelling state interest" in protecting the community from crime cannot be doubted. . . . We have stressed before that crime prevention is "a weighty social objective", . . . and this interest persists undiluted in the juvenile context. The harm suffered by a victim of a crime is not dependent upon the age of the perpetrator. And the harm to society generally may even be greater in this context given the high rate of recidivism among juveniles. . . .
>
> The juvenile's countervailing interest in freedom from institutional restraints, even for the brief time involved here, is undoubtedly substantial as well. . . . But that interest must be qualified by the recognition that juveniles, unlike adults, are always in some form of custody. . . . Children, by definition, are not assumed to have the capacity to take care of themselves. They are assumed to be subject to the control of their parents, and if parental control falters, the State must play its part as *parens patriae*. (citations omitted)

Schall v. Martin clearly indicates that the Supreme Court is very much aware of the fact that juvenile offenders are capable of dangerous criminal activity and that the public safety must be considered as well as the rights of children.

Sample Questions

In the juvenile justice systems of most states:

A. children who commit acts that would be crimes if committed by adults are not initially treated by the law as criminal offenders.
B. in very serious cases children who commit acts which would be criminal offenses if committed by adults may be transferred to the jurisdiction of the adult criminal court if they are above a specified age.
C. children may come within the jurisdiction of the juvenile court by committing certain "status offenses" which would not be crimes if committed by adults, such as truancy, running away from home, and curfew violations.
D. special institutions exist for the custody, care, and treatment of child offenders who have been adjudged delinquent.
E. all of the above are true.

Under the Constitution of the United States, "custody" normally involves loss of liberty, which involves the need for "due process of law."   T   F.

Each state has its own system of juvenile courts; in some states separate juvenile or "family" courts exist, while in other states the juvenile court function is performed by courts which normally exercise jurisdiction over adults.   T   F.

The result of the cases of *Kent v. United States,* and *In re Gault,* both decided by the Supreme Court of the United States, and the cases which followed them, has been:

A. to deprive juvenile offenders of due process protections which existed in most states before those cases were decided.
B. the application of most adult due process requirements to juvenile trial proceedings, with the exception of the right to a jury trial.
C. to reduce the informality of juvenile trial proceedings.
D. to add to the informality of juvenile trial proceedings.
E. B and C above.

In the absence of special statutes, case law, or other legal guidelines within any state, the police in any state should:

A. assume that all constitutionally-based procedures that apply in adult criminal cases will also apply in juvenile cases.
B. recognize that states are free to require that police give special handling to juvenile cases.
C. take no enforcement action in juvenile cases.
D. A and B above.
E. none of the above.

A new concept of a specialized court with jurisdiction to handle cases of dependency, neglect, and juvenile delinquency was created in 1899 in the state of:

A. New York.
B. Illinois.
C. California.
D. Alaska.
E. Massachusetts.

§8.3 Police Handling of Juvenile Offenders

The case law we have summarized deals almost exclusively with juvenile court proceedings and the rights of youthful offenders during the adjudicatory stage. Because the Supreme Court of the United States has decided relatively few cases concerning the investigatory stage of a juvenile case, the guidelines for police conduct at this stage are largely a matter of state statutory and case law which should be referenced within each jurisdiction.

The *Gault* case, however, clearly indicated that the Fifth Amendment privilege against compulsory self-incrimination applies in juvenile cases. One could therefore conclude that *Miranda* procedures apply during the investigatory stage. The obvious problem with a *Miranda* situation involving a juvenile would be that of the validity of a waiver of the rights of silence and counsel. In the case of *Fare v. Michael C.*, 99 S. Ct. 2560 (1979), the Supreme Court specifically addressed that situation. The case involved a 16½ year old juvenile who had considerable past experience with the police and who was on probation to the juvenile court. In its opinion, the Court observed:

> The transcript of the interrogation reveals that the police officers conducting the interrogation took care to ensure that respondent understood his rights. They fully explained to respondent that he was being questioned in connection with a murder. They then informed him of all the rights delineated in *Miranda*, and ascertained that respondent understood those rights. There is no indication in the record that respondent failed to understand what the officers told him. Moreover, after his request to see his probation officer had been denied, and after the police officer once more had explained his rights to him, respondent clearly expressed his willingness to waive his rights and continue the interrogation.

Earlier in its opinion, the Court indicated that the test for legal sufficiency of the waiver of *Miranda* rights was the same in juvenile cases as in adult cases:

> This totality of the circumstances approach is adequate to detemine whether there has been a waiver even where interrogation of juveniles is involved. We discern no persuasive reasons why any other approach is required where the question is whether a juvenile has waived his rights, as opposed to whether an adult has done so. The totality approach permits — indeed, it mandates — inquiry into all the circumstances surrounding the interrogation. This includes evaluation of the juvenile's age, experience, education, background and intelligence, and into whether he has the capacity to understand the warnings given him, the nature of his Fifth Amendment rights, and the consequences of waiving those rights.

We must constantly remind ourselves that any state has the power, under its own constitution and laws, to create more extensive protections for persons within its jurisdiction than the protections required by the Constitution of the United States. For example, in 1972, the Supreme Court of Indiana established the following guidelines for the interrogation of juveniles in that state: (1) both the juvenile and his parents or guardian must be advised of the *Miranda* rights; and (2) the juvenile must be given a meaningful opportunity to consult with his parents, guardian, or attorney regarding the waiver of those rights before any waiver is made.

With regard to the Fourth Amendment issues of arrest, search, and seizure involving juvenile offenders, the Supreme Court of the United States has given little guidance to the police. The safest assumption is that all of the protections accorded to persons generally also apply to juveniles. But the observation of the Court in *Schall v. Martin* that ". . . juveniles, unlike adults, are always in some form of custody", and the few other cases that exist, including *New Jersey v. T.L.O.*, 105 S.Ct. 733 (1985), (summarized at Sec. 4.15(G)), may be indicators that different standards of "reasonableness " apply in school search situations, for example, which do not involve the police, and that the legitimate expectation of privacy of school children must be balanced against the need of the school authorities to maintain an environment conducive to learning.

The original intention reflected in the early statutes on juvenile procedure — to provide a caring and protective system in which treatment and reformation could take place — has been "swamped" to some extent by the rise in the rate of juvenile crime.

Although juvenile offenders should be housed separately from adult offenders while awaiting the disposition of their cases by the juvenile court, (if they cannot be released to the custody of their parents or other responsible adults), the increase in juvenile crime has overtaken the ability of many states and communities to provide these juvenile detention centers. Every police officer should acquaint himself with the approved facilities available within his jurisdiction.

A Bureau of Justice Statistics Special Report, *Survey of Youth in Custody, 1987*, reveals the following:

> Among the juveniles held in the long-term state-operated juvenile institutions surveyed, 39.3% were held for a violent offense, 45.6% for a property offense, 5.6% for a drug offense, and 7.2% for a public-order offense. Just over 2% were confined for a juvenile status offense, such as truancy, running away, or incorrigibility.
>
> Almost 43% of the juveniles had been arrested more than 5 times, with over 20% of them having been arrested more than 10 times in the past.
>
> An estimated 97% of all juveniles in custody were found to have a current or prior violent offense or to have previously been on probation or sent to a correctional institution.
>
> Nearly half (47.6%) of the juveniles reported that they were under the influence of either drugs or alcohol at the time of their current offense.
>
> Of the juveniles held for violent crime, nearly 41% used a weapon in the commission of the crime. Whether or not a weapon was used varied by the type of crime. A weapon was used in approximately 78% of homicides, 44% of robberies and assaults, and 5.3% of sexual assaults. The most frequently mentioned weapon was a gun, which was used in 19.7% of the violent crimes, 56.9% of all homicides, and 23.7% of all robberies committed by the juvenile offenders.

It is clear from the decision in *Schall v. Martin*, discussed above, that the Supreme Court is aware of the public safety implications of juvenile crime. While our justice system requires that police officers carry out their peace-keeping and law enforcement duties in a professional manner, with due regard for the rights of persons who violate the law, every officer must also be constantly mindful of his own safety, and the safety of potential victims of persons who may be children in age, but dangerous, predatory animals in deed.

--------------------------------------- **Notes** ---------------------------------------

APPENDIX A

THE CONSTITUTION OF THE UNITED STATES — SELECTED PROVISIONS

We the people of the United States, in order to form a more perfect union, establish justice, insure domestic tranquility, provide for the common defense, promote the general welfare, and secure the blessings of liberty to ourselves and our posterity, do ordain and establish this Constitution for the United States of America.

ARTICLE 1

Section 1.

1. All legislative powers herein granted shall be vested in a Congress of the United States, which shall consist of a Senate and House of Representatives.

* * *

Section 8.

1. The Congress shall have power to lay and collect taxes, duties, imposts and excises, to pay the debts and provide for the common defense and general welfare of the United States but all duties, imposts and excises shall be uniform throughout the United States;
2. To borrow money on the credit of the United States;
3. To regulate commerce with the foreign nations, and among the several States, and with the Indian tribes;
4. To establish a uniform rule of naturalization and uniform laws on the subject of bankruptcies throughout the United States;
5. To coin money, regulate the value therof, and of foreign coin, and fix the standard of weights and measures;
6. To provide for the punishment of counterfeiting the securities and current coin of the United States;
7. To establish post-offices and post-roads;
8. To promote the progress of science and useful arts, by securing for limited times to authors and inventors the exclusive right to their respective writings and discoveries;
9. To constitute tribunals inferior to the Supreme Court;
10. To define and punish piracies and felonies committed on the high seas, and offenses against the laws of nations;
11. To declare war, grant letters of marque and reprisal, and make rules concerning captures on land and water;
12. To raise and support armies, but no appropriation of money to that use shall be for a longer term than two years;
13. To provide and maintain a navy;
14. To make rules for the government and regulation of the land and naval forces;
15. To provide for calling forth the militia to execute the laws of the Union, suppress insurrections, and repel invasions;
16. To provide for organizing, arming, and disciplining the militia, and for governing such part of them as may be employed in the service of the United States, reserving to the States respectively, the appointment of the officers, and the authority of training the militia according to the discipline prescribed by Congress;

17. To exercise exclusive legislation in all cases whatsoever, over such district (not exceeding ten miles square) as may, by cession of particular States and the acceptance of Congress, become the seat of the Government of the United States, and to exercise like authority over all places purchased by the consent of the legislature of the State in which the same shall be, for the erection of forts, magazines, arsenals, dockyards, and other needful buildings; and

18. To make all laws which shall be necessary and proper for carrying into execution the foregoing powers, and all other powers vested by this constitution in the Government of the United States, or in any department or officer thereof.

Section 9.

***

2. The privilege of the writ of *habeas corpus* shall not be suspended, unless when in cases of rebellion of invasion the public safety may require it.

3. No bill of attainder or *ex post facto* law shall be passed.

***

8. No title of nobility shall be granted by the United States; and no person holding any office of profit or trust under them shall, without the consent of the Congress, accept of any present, emolument, office, or title, of any kind whatever, from any king, prince, or foreign State.

Section 10.

1. No State shall enter into any treaty, alliance, or confederation; grant letters of marque and reprisal; coin money; emit bill or credit, make anything but gold and silver coin a tender in payment of debts; pass any bill of attainder, *ex post facto* law, or law impairing the obligation of contracts, or grant any title of nobility.

***

3. No State shall without the consent of Congress, lay any duty of tonnage, keep troops or ships of war in time of peace, enter into any agreement or compact with another State, or with a foreign power, or engage in war, unless actually invaded or in such imminent danger as will not admit of delay.

ARTICLE II

Section 1.

1. The executive power shall be vested in a President of the United States of America. He shall hold his office during the term of four years and, together with the Vice-President, chosen for the same term, be elected as follows:

***

Section 2.

1. The President shall be commander-in-chief of the army and navy of the United States, and of the militia of the several States when called into actual service of the United States; he may require the opinion, in writing, of the principal officer in each of the executive departments, upon any subject relating to the duties of their respective offices, and he shall have power to grant reprieves and pardons for offenses against the United States, except in cases of

impeachment.

2. He shall have power, by and with the advice and consent of the Senate, to make treaties, provided two thirds of the Senators present concur; and he shall nominate, and, by and with the advice and consent of the Senate, shall appoint ambassadors, other public ministers and consuls, judges of the Supreme Court, and all other officers of the United States, whose appointments are not herein otherwise provided for, and which shall be established by law; but the Congress may by law vest the appointment of such inferior officers, as they think proper, in the President alone, in the courts of law, or in the heads of departments.

3. The President shall have power to fill up all vacancies that may happen during the recess of the Senate, by granting commissions which shall expire at the end of their next session.

Section 3.

1. He shall from time to time give the Congress information of the state of the Union, and recommend to their consideration such measures as he shall judge necessary and expedient; he may, on extraordinary occasions, convene both houses, or either of them, and in case of disagreement between them with respect to the time of adjournment, he may adjourn them to such time as he shall think proper; he shall receive ambassadors and other public ministers; he shall take care that the laws be faithfully executed, and shall commission all the officers of the United States.

Section 4.

1. The President, Vice-President, and all civil officers of the United States shall be removed from office on impeachment for and conviction of treason, bribery, or other high crimes and misdemeanors.

ARTICLE III

Section 1.

1. The judicial power of the United States shall be vested in one Supreme Court, and in such inferior courts as the Congress may from time to time ordain and establish. The judges, both of the supreme and inferior courts, shall hold their offices during good behavior, and shall, at stated times, receive for their services a compensation which shall not be diminished during their continuance in office.

Section 2.

1. The judicial power shall extend to all cases, in law and equity, arising under this Constitution, the laws of the United States, and treaties made, or which shall be made, under their authority; to all cases affecting ambassadors, other public ministers and consuls; to all cases of admiralty and maritime jurisdiction; to controversies to which the United States shall be a party; to controversies between two or more States; *between a State and citizens of another State;* between citizens of different States; between citizens of the same State claiming lands under grants of different States, and between a State, or the citizens thereof, and foreign States, citizens, or subjects.

2. In all cases affecting ambassadors, other public ministers and consuls, and those in which a State shall be party, the Supreme Court shall have original jurisdiction. In all the other cases before mentioned the Supreme Court shall have appellate jurisdiction, both as to law and fact, with such exceptions and under such regulations as the Congress shall make.

3. The trial of all crimes, except in cases of impeachment, shall be by jury; and such trial shall be held in the State where the said crimes shall have been committed; but when not committed within any State, the trial shall be at such place or places as the Congress may by law have directed.

Section 3.

1. Treason against the United States shall consist only in levying war against them, or in adhering to their enemies, giving them aid and comfort. No person shall be convicted of treason unless on the testimony of two witnesses to the same overt act, or on confession in open court.

2. The Congress shall have power to declare the punishment of treason, but no attainder of treason shall work corruption of blood or forfeiture except during the life of the person attained.

ARTICLE IV

Section 1.

1. Full faith and credit shall be given in each State to the public acts, records, and judicial proceedings of every other State. And the Congress maybe general laws prescribe the manner in which such acts, records, and proceedings shall be proved, and the effect thereof.

Section 2.

1. The citizens of each State shall be entitled to all privileges and immunities of citizens in the several States.

2. A person charged in any State with treason, felony, or other crime, who shall flee from justice, and be found in another State, shall, on demand of the executive authority of the State from which he fled, be delivered up, to be removed to the State having jurisdiction of the crime.

***

ARTICLE V

1. The Congress, whenever two thirds of both houses shall deem it necessary, shall propose amendments to this Constitution, or, on the application of the legislatures of two thirds of the several States, shall call a convention for proposing amendments, which in either case shall be valid to all intents and purposes as part of this Constitution, when ratified by the legislatures of three fourths of the several States, or by conventions in three fourths thereof, as the one or the other mode of ratification may be proposed by the Congress; provided that no amendment which may be made prior to the year one thousand eight hundred and eight shall in any manner affect the first and fourth clauses in the ninth section of the first article; and that no State, without its consent, shall be deprived of its equal suffrage in the Senate.

ARTICLE VI

1. All debts contracted and engagements entered into, before the adoption of this Constitution, shall be as valid against the United States under this Constitution, as under the Confederation.

2. This Constitution, and the laws of the United States which shall be made in pursuance thereof, and all treaties made, or which shall be made, under the authority of the United States, shall be the supreme law of the land; and the judges in every State shall be bound thereby, anything in the Constitution or laws of any State to the contrary notwithstanding.

3. The Senators and Representatives before mentioned, and the members of the several State legislatures, and all executive and judicial officers, both of the United States and of the several States, shall be bound by oath or affirmation to support this Constitution; but no religious test shall ever be required as a qualification to any office or public trust under the United States.

ARTICLE VII

1. The ratification of the conventions of nine States shall be sufficient for the establishment of this Constitution between the States so ratifying the same.

Done in convention by the unanimous consent of the States present, the seventeenth day of September, in the year of our Lord one thousand seven hundred and eighty-seven, and of the independence of the United States of America the twelfth. In witness whereof, we have hereunto subscribed our names.

G.º Washington — Presid. and deputy from Virginia

AMENDMENTS

The first ten amendments to the Constitution are known as the Bill of Rights and became effective on December 15, 1791.

I.

Congress shall make no law respecting an establishment of religion, or prohibiting the free exercise thereof; or abridging the freedom of speech or of the press; or the right of the people peaceably to assemble, and to petition the government for a redress of grievances.

II.

A well-regulated militia being necessary to the security of a free state, the right of the people to keep and bear arms shall not be infringed.

III.

No soldier shall, in time of peace, be quartered in any house without the consent of the owner, nor in time of war, but in manner to be prescribed by law.

IV.

The right of the people to be secure in their persons, houses, papers, and effects, against unreasonable searches and seizures, shall not be violated, and no warrants shall issue but upon probable cause, supported by oath or affirmation, and particularly describing the place to be searched and the persons or things to be seized.

V.

No person shall be held to answer for a capital or otherwise infamous crime, unless on a presentment or indictment of a grand jury, except in cases arising in the land or naval forces or in the militia when in actual service in time of war or public danger; nor shall any person be subject for the same offence to be twice put in jeopardy of life or limb; nor shall be compelled in any criminal case to be a witness against himself, nor be deprived of life, liberty, or property, without due process of law; nor shall private property be taken for public use without just compensation.

VI.

In all criminal prosecutions the accused shall enjoy the right to a speedy and public trial, by an impartial jury of the State and district wherein the crime shall have been committed, which district shall have been previously ascertained by law, and to be informed of the nature and cause of the accusation; to be confronted with the witnesses against him; to have compulsory process for obtaining witnesses in his favor, and to have the assistance of counsel for his defense.

VII.

In suits at common law, where the value in controversy shall exceed twenty dollars, the right of trial by jury shall be preserved, and no fact tried by a jury shall be otherwise re-examined in any court of the United States, than according to the rules of the common law.

VIII.

Excessive bail shall not be required, nor excessive fines imposed, nor cruel and unusual punishments inflicted.

IX.

The enumeration in the Constitution of certain rights shall not be construed to deny or disparage others retained by the people.

X.

The powers not delegated to the United States by the Constitution, nor prohibited by it to the States, are reserved to the States respectively, or to the people.

***

XIII. *(Effective December 18, 1865)*

Section 1. Neither slavery nor involuntary servitude, except as a punishment for crime whereof the party shall have been duly convicted, shall exist within the

United States or any place subject to their jurisdiction.

Section 2. Congress shall have power to enforce this article by appropriate legislation.

XIV. *(Effective July 28, 1868.)*

Section 1. All persons born or naturalized in the United States, and subject to the jurisdiction thereof, are citizens of the United States and of the State wherein they reside. No State shall make or enforce any law which shall abridge the privileges or immunities of citizens of the United States; nor shall any State deprive any person of life, liberty, or property, without due process of law; nor deny to any person within its jurisdiction the equal protection of the laws.

***

Section 5. The Congress shall have power to enforce, by approprate legislation, the provisions of this article.

XV. *(Effective March 30, 1870.)*

Section 1. The right of citizens of the United States to vote shall not be denied or abridged by the United States or by any State on account of race, color or previous condition of servitude.

Section 2. The Congress shall have power to enforce this article by appropriate legislature.

APPENDIX B

GLOSSARY

This glossary is intended for quick reference only. All students studying case law should have access to a standard law dictionary.

A

a fortiori	With all the more reason.
abandonment	Absolute relinquishment; total desertion.
abatement	The act of putting an end to; quashing.
abduct	To take away a person unlawfully.
abet	To incite, sanction, or help, especially in the commission of a crime.
abhorrent	Frightening or disgusting.
abrogate	To repeal; to make void; to annul.
abscond	To depart from the jurisdiction of the court; to hide, conceal, or absent oneself with the intent of avoiding legal process.
accessory	An active conspirator in the commission of a crime. One who aids, encourages, hires or conceals the principal in a crime.
accomplice	A person who helps another in an unlawful act; a partner in crime.
accusatorial system	A system that assumes that truth can best be discovered by a contest between opposing parties; an adversarial system.
acquit	To declare a person not guilty; to set free.
acquiesce	To "go along with"; to consent; to allow without protest.
administrative rules and regulations	Rules made by executive branch agencies, which have the force of law.
admission	A statement made by a person against his own interest.
ad hoc	For one specific purpose only.
adjudicate	To act as a judge in a dispute.
adversarial system	A system of truth determination involving opposing parties, or adversaries.
advocacy	The act of pleading another person's case and representing him.
affiant	A person who makes a sworn statement or affidavit.
affidavit	A written statement sworn to or affirmed before an officer who has authority to administer an oath or affirmation.
affirmation	A solemn declaration, not under oath, permitted to a person who has conscientious objections to taking oaths.

affirmed	Approved. (As when an appellate court upholds an opinion of a lower court.)
aggravate	To make worse or more serious.
aggregate	Separate parts gathered together.
alias	An assumed name other than a party's true name.
alibi	A defense to a crime which asserts that the accused was somewhere other than at the scene of the crime at the time of the crime.
ambivalent	Having conflicting feelings or emotions toward a person, thing, or event.
amelioration	An improvement.
amicus curiae	A person, not a party to the case, whom the court allows to volunteer information as a "friend of the court" to advise the court of what the law is.
analogy	A comparison with something similar.
appeal	The carrying of a case to a higher court in an attempt to have the decision of the lower court altered or overruled.
appellant	The party who takes an appeal from a lower to a higher court.
appellate	Relating to the jurisdiction to hear appeals or review the action of a lower court.
appellee	The party in a case against whom an appeal is taken; that is, the party who has an interest in letting the lower court decision stand.
arbitrary	Completely by personal preference; without good reason and not according to rules.
arguendo	By way of argument.
arraignment	A formal action in which the accused appears before the court, has the charge or indictment read to him, and enters a plea.
arrest (custodial)	The taking of a person into custody, that he may be held to answer for an offense.
arson	The criminal destruction, by fire or explosion, of another's property for any purpose, or of one's own property to defraud an insurer.
ascertain	To find out definitely.
asportation	The taking of an article of value from the possession of the victim into that of the thief.
assault	An attempt to commit a battery upon the person of another by one having the present ability to do so.
attempt	With the criminal intent required to commit a particular crime, engaging in conduct which constitutes a substantial step toward, but which falls short of completing the particular crime.

attenuate	To reduce in strength, value, or amount; to dilute.
attestation	The act of witnessing the signature or execution of a document and of subscribing the name of the witness in testimony of such fact.

B

bail	Money or credit deposited with the court for the temporary release of an arrested person as security to insure his later appearance for trial.
bench trial	A trial in which the right to a jury trial has been waived and the presiding judge, instead of a jury, determines the facts.
blackmail	Payment forced by a threat to make public damaging information about a person.
bona fide	In good faith.
bond	A contract under which a person or a company, as a surety, agrees to pay a sum of money conditioned on the performance or nonperformance of certain acts.
bondsman	One who has entered into a bond as a surety.
breach of the peace	A violation or disturbance of the public tranquility and order by any riotous, forcible, or unlawful proceedings.
breaking	In burglary, forcible entry or the putting aside of any such part, even a partly open door, window, or screen, intended as security against invasion.
brief	A summary of the law and facts relating to a case.
burden of proof	The necessity or duty of affirmatively proving the facts at issue in a case; the state has the burden of proof in a criminal case to prove all elements of the crime beyond a reasonable doubt.

C

capias	The general name for writs of various kinds which order an officer to arrest the person named.
capital crime.	A crime punishable by death.
capitulate	To give up.
capricious	Impulsive; without good reason.
certiorari	A writ, from a higher court to a lower court, requesting the records of a case for review.
character	Trust worthiness; a critical issue in cases where the jury must determine the credibility of a witness. Opposing counsel will attempt to "impeach" (discredit) the testimony of a witness with a reputation for untruthfulness.
chilled	Government action that makes a person afraid to publicly express his opinion. Used in connection with freedom of expression.

circumstantial evidence	Evidence introduced to prove an allegation by proving a condition, fact or event which affords a basis for a reasonable inference that the allegation is true.
civil rights	Rights guaranteed by the United States and the state constitutions, and by laws enacted pursuant thereto.
clandestine	Secret.
coercion	Force, compulsion, or pressure to act against the free will of the actor.
cogent	Compelling; convincing.
cognizant	Aware of something.
cohabit	To dwell together in the manner of husband and wife for some length of time.
collateral	Side by side, or parallel in importance; also, something pledged as assurance that an obligation will be carried out.
color of law	Misuse of power possessed by virtue of state law and made possible only because the wrongdoer is clothed with the authority of state law (in civil rights actions).
comity	Courteous cooperation; as in relationships between friendly governments.
common law	The unwritten (non-statutory) law of a country based on ancient customs and on court decisions.
commutation of sentence	A form of executive clemency in which a governor or president substitutes a lesser penalty for a greater judicially-imposed penalty.
complaint	A sworn written statement that a certain person committed a crime. Also the first paper filed by a plaintiff to start a civil lawsuit.
concurring opinion	An opinion by a member of a court which agrees with the result of the court's opinion, but partly or wholly for different reasons.
confession	An admission of guilt by a person charged with a crime.
conjecture	To guess, theorize, or speculate.
consanguinity	Blood relationship.
conspiracy	An agreement between two or more persons to commit an unlawful act or a lawful act by unlawful means. In some jurisdictions, conspiracy also requires an overt act by a party in furtherance of the agreement.
construe	To analyze or interpret.
contemporaneously	At the same time.
contempt	Any act showing disrespect for and defiance of the court, contempt of court.
contraband	Property, the possession of which is unlawful.

controlled substance	A drug or substance, the possession, sale, or use of which has been made unlawful.
corollary	Something following as a natural result of something else.
corporal	Relating to the body; e.g., corporal punishment.
corpus delicti	The body of the crime; the facts constituting a crime or establishing that a crime was committed.
corroborate	To confirm or support.
counsel	A counselor; one or more attorneys representing parties in an action.
counselor	A person giving advice about legal matters; a trial lawyer.
counterfeit	An imitation of a genuine item.
court	A group of persons, including a judge, officially assembled at a time and place appointed by law for the administration of justice.
credible	Worthy of belief; entitled to credit.
crime	An act or omission which the law prohibits or requires, and which is punishable under the law.
criminalistics	Application of scientific techniques to problems of criminal identification and apprehension; e.g., laboratory testing of physical evidence.
criminology	The scientific study of crime and criminals.
culpable	Blameworthy; censurable.
cursory	Done in a hurry, with little regard for detail.
curtilage	The inclosed space of ground and buildings immediately surrounding a dwelling house.

D

dactylography	The study of fingerprints as a means of identification.
dead letter	A law or ordinance no longer enforced, but not repealed.
deadly force	Force that creates a substantial risk of death or serious bodily injury.
declaratory judgment	A form of equitable judgment in which the court declares or makes clear the relative legal position of two parties to a legal dispute.
de facto	In fact; actual.
defendant	The party being sued or prosecuted.
de jure	By right; in accordance with the law.
delineate	To outline, sketch, or describe.
demur	In effect, to say, "so what?"; that is, to state that, even though the alleged facts are true, they don't amount to a legal wrong that would support a judgment in court.

denigrate	To belittle or "run down".
de novo	To do over from the beginning.
deposition	A written statement made by a witness, under oath, to be used as testimony in court.
devoid (of)	Completely lacking.
dictum	See "obiter dictum".
discovery	A process whereby a party to a case initiates a request with the court to ascertain the material information upon which the opposing party will base his case.
disseminate	To spread or publish widely.
dissenting opinion	The opinion of the minority of the appellate-level court which disagrees with the majority opinion.
domicile	The place where a person has his true, fixed, and permanent home, without any present intention of movng from it.
double jeopardy	A second prosecution after a previous conviction or acquittal for the same crime (excepting a second prosecution resulting from the successful appeal and reversal of a conviction).
due process	A constitutional concept which requires that laws and procedures be fair and reasonable and that governments shall not deprive persons of life, liberty, or property in an arbitrary, unfair, or unreasonable manner.
duress	Coercion or compulsion by force or threats.
dying declaration	A statement in any form of the material facts concerning the causes and circumstances of injuries received in; a fatal attack, made by the victim in the solemn belief that his own death is near at hand.

E

easement	A right or privilege that a person has another's land, such as a right-of-way.
efficacy	Effectiveness.
egregious	Extremely bad.
emancipate	To release a child from his parent's control.
en banc	The entire panel of judges of an appellate court, usually sitting in review of a decision made by a three-judge panel of the same court.
engender	To bring about or cause.
entrapment	An affirmative defense to a criminal charge, alleging that the prohibited conduct was persuaded by a law enforcement officer or his agent and that the accused was not predisposed to commit the criminal act.

equal protection	A standard of the Fourteenth Amendment to the Constitution. The government is thereby required to treat people equally, regardless of race, sex, creed, national origin, religion, or, to some extent, age.
equity	A system of rules and doctrines supplementing common and statutory law and superseding such law when it proves to be inadequate as a remedy.
estoppel	The prevention of a person from making an affirmation or denial because it is contrary to a previous affirmation or denial he has made.
et al.	And others.
et seq.	And following.
evidence	Something legally presented before a court, such as a statement of a witness, an object, a document, etc., which bears on or establishes the point in question.
exclusionary rule	A rule of law that excludes or keeps evidence from being used in a case, usually because a right of the accused has been denied or violated in the obtaining of the evidence. It may be based in the Fourth, Fifth, or Sixth Amendment rights of a defendant, or from a denial of due process of law.
exculpatory	Tending to show innocence.
execute	To complete or make valid, as to execute a deed, will, etc.; to carry out a criminal sentence.
exigent circumstances	Circumstances requiring prompt action.
exonerate	To free a person from a charge.
ex parte	In the interest of one side only; from one party.
expert witness	A person qualified by reason of special training, skill, or experience to speak authoritatively about a subject. When qualified to the satisfaction of the trial judge, the witness may give opinions and conclusions and answer hypothetical questions.
ex post facto law	A law passed or made after commission of an act, making the act a crime and creating retroactive consequences for the act. Such laws are expressly prohibited by the Constitution.
extortion	The unlawful obtaining of money or other valuable thing by compulsion, actual force, or by the force of motives applied to the will. Blackmail and "protection" rackets are forms of extortion.
extradition	The process of a state or country obtaining custody of a person, for criminal prosecution purposes, from the state or country in which the person is located.
extrajudicial	Done outside the course of regular judicial proceedings.

F

false arrest	Unlawful and unprivileged physical restraint of another's liberty.
false imprisonment	The unlawful arrest or detention of a person without a warrant, or on an illegally executed warrant, and the placing of that person in a prison, or otherwise detaining him by force and constraint.
felonious	Of, like, or constituting a felony.
felony	A serious crime, in most states punishable by imprisonment for more than one year, or, in rare cases, by death.
fence	A person who buys and sells stolen goods.
fighting words	Words spoken <u>only</u> to provoke physical violence; not protected under the First Amendment concept of freedom of speech.
forcible felony	A crime involving the threat of immediate serious bodily injury to the victim.
forensic	Characteristic of, or belonging to a court of law.
fracas	A noisy disturbance.
fraud	The intentional misrepresentation of facts for a wrongful purpose.
frisk	A quick search — also called a "pat-down search" — by a police officer, by feeling the outer portion of the suspect's clothing for the purpose of finding weapons. It is not a search for evidence, but is justified as a means of protecting the safety of the officer and others nearby.

G

good faith	Honest and sincere belief in the validity of one's authority to act, with no reason to believe otherwise.
grand jury	A panel of citizens assembled under the authority of a criminal court to investigate alleged criminal activity, and to formally charge persons against whom it finds enough evidence to justify criminal prosecution. A grand jury hearing is not a trial and it considers only evidence for the prosecution.
gravamen	The essential part of a compliant or accusation.
guardian	A person legally placed in charge of the person or the affairs of a minor or incompetent person.

H

habeas corpus	"You have the body"; the only Old English writ mentioned by name in the Constitution of the United States; it is the primary means of challenging governmental restrictions on liberty by petitioning for an immediate appearance before a court with authority to decide the lawfulness of the restriction.

habitual offender	A person who, by reason of previous convictions, qualifies for a greater penalty than is usually imposed by the court for a single commission of the crime.
hearsay evidence	Evidence based on something the witness has heard someone else say, when used for the purpose of establishing the truth of the content of the statement. It is usually inadmissible as not being reliable because the person who made the statement cannot be cross-examined in court, but there are numerous exceptions.
homicide	The killing of one human being by another. It may consist of murder or manslaughter, or it may be found to be excusable or justifiable.
hung jury	A trial jury that, after considering the evidence, is unable to reach a unanimous verdict and must be dismissed by the trial judge, who then declares a mistrial.

I

ideological	Concerned with abstract ideas.
ignominy	Disgrace or dishonor.
illicit	Not allowed by law; unlawful.
imminent	About to happen at any time.
impeach	In a trial, to discredit or challenge the credibility of a witness, as by cross-examination; also, to attempt formally to remove from office a high public officeholder.
impound	To take or hold animals or goods in legal custody.
imposition	The forcing of oneself or opinion on another without invitation.
inadmissible	Not to be admitted, allowed, granted, or received as evidence.
in articulo mortis	At the point of death.
in camera	In private or secret; not open to the public.
incarcerate	To imprison; to confine in jail.
incest	Sexual intercourse between persons too closely related by blood to legally marry.
incidental	Happening in connection with something else.
included offense	An offense, the elements of which are all a part of another, usually more serious offense.
incommunicado	Not permitted to communicate with others while in custody. Because of the basic rights of counsel and access to the courts, this practice is condemned by American law.
incompetent	Without adequate ability, knowledge, fitness, etc.; failing to meet requirements; not legally qualified. For example, a person who cannot remember an event, or who cannot describe what he does remember to a jury, is an incompetent witness.

incremental	By small amounts.
inculpatory	Incriminating.
indicia	Indications.
indictment	A charge; an accusation; specifically, a formal written accusation charging one or more persons with the commission of a crime, presented by a grand jury to the court after the grand jury has found, upon hearing the prosecutor's evidence, that there is probably a valid case to proceed to prosecution. Sometimes referred to as a "true bill".
ineluctable	Certain.
in extremis	Near the end of life; dying.
infant	A minor; a person not considered by the law to be an adult for a particular purpose.
infraction	A public offense punishable by only a civil fine, without imprisonment; commonly used in motor vehicle regulation.
inference	A logical conclusion following as an impelling probability from the circumstantial evidence which fosters it.
infiltrate	To pass through cracks or openings; to penetrate (as in the case of an undercover agent becoming a member of an illegal enterprise to gather prosecution evidence).
information	In criminal procedure, a formal written accusation filed with the court charging a person with a criminal offense. It is prepared by the prosecutor and is based on the findings used for the same purpose as an "indictment", which is prepared by a grand jury.
infra	Below; later on in the text.
inherent	Existing as a natural part of something or someone.
injunction	A legal order from a court prohibiting an act or, in the case of a mandatory injunction, requiring that an act be done.
in loco parentis	In the place of a parent.
innuendo	An indirect remark, gesture, or reference, usually implying something derogatory. In an action for libel or slander, that part of a complaint which explains the expression alleged to be libelous or slanderous.
in pari delicto	Equally guilty or at fault.
in personam	Pertaining to an action against a person as distinguished from an "in rem" action, which is against property.
inquisitorial system	A system of judicial inquiry in which the accused is forced to respond himself to questions about his guilt, and which usually does not provide the protections of a trial by jury or counsel to represent the accused.

in rem	A legal action taken against property as distinguished from an "in personam" action taken against a person.
insanity	A legal defense to a criminal charge, which pleads that the accused at the time of the alleged unlawful act was not responsible for his conduct because a mental disease or defect made it impossible for him to recognize the criminality of the act.
instruction to the jury	An explanation by the judge to the jury of the principles of law applicable to the facts brought out in evidence during the trial.
intentional	Totally conscious of the wrongfulness of the conduct engaged in.
inter alia	Among other things.
interrogatories	Written questions drawn up for a witness to answer under oath but out of court, as in the taking of a deposition of a witness.
inversely	Oppositely.
ipse dixit	He himself said it.
ipso facto	By the mere fact.

J

jeopardy	The peril or danger to life or liberty in which a person is put when he has been regularly and sufficiently charged with the commission of a crime. In a jury trial jeopardy "attaches" when the jury is impaneled and sworn; in a trial before a judge alone, when the first witness testifies.
judgment	The final sentence or decision reached by a court of competent jurisdiction in due course of legal proceedings, in which the rights of the parties have been judicially settled.
judicial notice	Acceptance by a court without proof that certain matters of common knowledge are true or in existence.
jurisdiction	The authority, right, or legal power to adjudicate a case or do a certain thing.

K

kiting	Writing checks against accounts with insufficient funds in a number of banks, with the intent to defraud.
kleptomania	An irresistible urge to steal.
knowingly	Awareness of a high probability that the conduct engaged in is unlawful.

L

latent	Not appearing on the face of a thing; hidden; in fingerprinting, discoverable prints.

libel	Any publication that is false and injurious to the reputation of another person.
lien	A claim on the property of another as security for the payment of a just debt or judgment.
litigation	The act or process of carrying on a lawsuit.
locus delicti	The place where a crime occurs.

M

magistrate	A judicial officer (judge) whose trial jurisdiction may be limited, but who may hold probable cause hearings and issue warrants.
mala in se	Wrong in and of itself; normally accepted as evil.
mala prohibita	Wrong simply because prohibited, usually by legislation.
malice	Evil and wrongful intent; a malignant state of mind, fatally bent on mischief.
mandamus	A writ, or written order, requiring that a specified thing be done, issued by a higher court to a lower court, or to a public official, etc.
manifestly	Clearly or evidently.
martial law	Temporary governmental control by military authorities over the civilian population, as in time of insurrection or invasion when civilian authority has broken down and is not in operation.
mens rea	Guilty mind; criminal intent.
military law	The branch of law concerned with the government and discipline of members of the armed forces; the Uniform Code of Military Justice.
misdemeanor	A crime less seriously punished than a felony; in many states a crime punishable by not more than a year in prison, or by a fine, or both.
mistrial	A trial made void because of an error in the proceedings or because the jury cannot reach a verdict.
mitigate	To make less severe.
modus operandi	Method of operation; a particular method of committing a crime which may help the investigator to identify the guilty person.
moot case	A case in which, because of changed conditions or circumstances, there is no longer a live issue for the court to decide.
moral turpitude	Conduct contrary to justice, honesty, modesty or good morals; present in most common law felonies and in crimes involving cheating, stealing, or lying.
motion to suppress	A legal pleading filed before trial by the defendant, seeking a ruling that specified evidence in the state's case is inadmissible because of alleged police misconduct.

moulage	A mold or form made of some plastic or plaster substance of a footprint or other object for identification purposes.

N

narcotic	A kind of controlled drug or substance.
negligence	Conduct which falls below a standard of care which would normally be exercised by a prudent person, which, if it results in harm to another, may result in civil liability in damages.
neutral and detached magistrate	A judge who is objective as to the parties and issues in a case and who is therefore constitutionally qualified to determine probable cause, issue warrants, and perform other necessary judicial acts.
nolle prosequi	A formal notice by the prosecutor that prosecution in a criminal case will be partly or entirely ended. Once a charge has been filed, requires the approval of the court.
nolo contendere	A plea by the defendant in a criminal case stating that he will not make a defense, but not amounting to an admission of guilt; a plea putting the defendant at the mercy of the court.
non compos mentis	Not of sound mind; incompetent.
non prosequitur	A judgment entered against a plaintiff who fails to appear at the court proceedings of his lawsuit or fails to prove a case.
nuisance	The use of private or public land in such a manner as to cause unreasonable interference with its normal use and enjoyment.

O

oath	A declaration, based upon an appeal to God for aid and witness, that one will speak the truth.
obiter dictum	A remark in a judicial opinion that is "by the way", and not concerning the precise issue presented to the court for decision.
obscene	Conduct not conforming to normal standards of decency; foul; immodest; lewd.
onerous	Imposing a legal obligation or burden.
opiate	A drug containing opium or its derivatives.
opprobrious	Offensive, insulting.
ordinance	A law enacted by the legislative department of a municipal government.
overt act	An act done openly, without attempt to conceal.

P

panderer	A pimp; a procurer.

paraphernalia	In drug law enforcement, those items other than the controlled substances themselves which are designed and intended to facilitate the use of drugs.
pardon	Remission of penalty by the executive (governor or president) in accordance with constitutional authority.
parole	Early, but conditional, release from a prison sentence.
parol evidence	Spoken or oral testimony of a witness.
pauper	A person so poor that he must be supported at public expense.
penal	Of, for, or constituting punishment.
per curiam	By the court; describing a court opinion of which no single justice is identified as the author.
peremptory	Absolute, barring further action, debate, or question. A peremptory challenge used in jury selection need not explain a cause for excusing the potential juror.
personal property	Any property that is movable or not attached to the land. Also referred to in the law as "personalty".
petition	A written request or plea in which specified court action is asked for.
petit jury	A trial jury, as distinguished from a grand jury.
plaintiff	A person who brings a suit into a court of law; a complainant.
plea	A statement made by or on behalf of a defendant, either answering the charges or showing why he should not be required to answer.
plurality opinion	An opinion of an appellate-level court when a majority of the judges or justices agree on a result, but do not agree on the reason for it.
police power	The constitutional power vested in legislative bodies to pass laws for the general welfare and to regulate their enforcement.
post-mortem	Happening, done, or made, after death.
power of attorney	A written statement legally authorizing one person to act on behalf of another.
precedent	A previous judicial decision which may serve as an example or rule in like or similar cases.
preliminary hearing	A hearing before a magistrate shortly after arrest, usually for the purpose of determining, among other things, if there was probable cause for the arrest. The hearing varies in scope and complexity from one jurisdiction to another.
premeditation	A degree of planning and forethought sufficient to show intent to commit an act.

preponderance of the evidence	The standard of proof required in civil cases. It simply means that, for a favorable verdict, the plaintiff must offer evidence of greater weight and more convincing than the evidence offered in opposition to it.
presentment	The notice taken or report made by a grand jury of an offense, based on the jury's own knowledge, rather than on evidence brought before it by the prosecutor. Compare with "indictment".
prima facie	On the face of it; at first sight; in evidence law, adequate proof to establish a fact or raise a presumption of fact, unless and until overcome by opposing evidence.
privileged communication	A communication that one cannot be legally compelled to divulge, such as a communication to a lawyer from his client.
probable cause	That body of facts and circumstances, from whatever source, including hearsay, that would justify a cautious and prudent person, in light of his experience, to believe that a crime was or is being committed, or that evidence is located at a certain place.
probate court	A court established to prove wills valid or invalid; to administer estates with or without wills; and to appoint guardians for minors and incompetent persons.
probation	Conditional and limited freedom in the community granted to a defendant after conviction in lieu of a sentence to prison.
probative	In the law of evidence, that which tends to prove something.
process	A judicial writ or order issued by a court, such as a warrant, summons, citation, or subpoena.
proof	The establishment of a fact by means of evidence.
proof beyond a reasonable doubt	Proof of such character that an ordinary person would be willing to rely and act upon it in the most important of his own affairs.
propensity	Tendency.
proprietary	A property interest in something.
proscription	A prohibition.
pro se	For self; pertaining to a defendant representing himself in court after waiving his right to counsel.
prostitution	The performing of sexual acts for hire.
proviso	A clause, as in a document, statute, etc., making some condition, exception, or stipulation.
provocation	Incitement to anger, emotion, or strong feeling.
proximate cause	A term originating in tort law, denoting the point in a chain of causal events at which the law will attach legal responsibility.

prurient	Tending to excite lust; lewd; lascivious.

Q

quash	To annul or set aside.
quasi	As if; in a manner of sense; seemingly.
quorum	A sufficient number of an official body necessary to conduct business; usually a majority.

R

real property	Permanent, immovable things, as land and the buildings attached thereto; realty.
reasonable doubt	Such doubt that the jurors, after they have carefully considered and compared all the evidence, cannot say they are firmly convinced of the truth of the charge.
rebut	To contradict, refute, or oppose, especially in a formal manner by argument, proof, etc.
recidivist	A repeat offender.
recklessly	Consciously and with unjustifiable disregard for the harm to others which might result.
recognizance	An obligation entered into before a court, binding a person to do a specific act such as to appear in court at a certain time to answer charges, or to keep the peace, etc.
relevant	Bearing upon or relating to the matter at hand.
remand	To send back.
reprieve	Temporary suspension by the governor or the president of the execution of a sentence.
repudiate	To refuse to acknowledge; to deny.
res gestae	Things done or words spoken along with or immediately following an event as an instinctive or spontaneous reaction; sometimes admissible as an exception to the hearsay rule.
res judicata	A matter already decided by a court of competent jurisdiction and hence not subject to further adjudication.
respondent	One who responds to a petition filed in a civil action.
restraining order	A temporary order by a court prohibiting an act while an application for an injunction against the act is pending.
reverse	To overturn the judgment of a lower court.
rigor mortis	The progressive stiffening of the body, occuring several hours after death as a result of coagulation of the muscle protein.

S

sanction	A penalty or an approval that makes the law enforceable.
scienter	Guilty knowledge.

shock sentencing	The imposition of a prison sentence which, although brief, is considered by the judge to be sufficient for punishment and deterrence.
sine qua non	Without which not; an indispensable requisite.
slander	Verbal utterance of a false statement harmful to another's reputation. If written, it is called libel.
SOP's	Standard operating procedures.
stare decisis	Let the decision stand; the rule that courts must following the precedent of previous cases except where there is a very good reason not to do so.
statute	A law passed by a legislature and set forth in an official publication.
stealth	Secrecy; slyness.
sua sponte	On one's own motion; voluntarily, without being prompted.
subpoena	A written, legal order directing a person to appear in court to testify.
substantial step	In attempt law, a considerable action; more than mere preparation but less than the completed crime.
sub rosa	Secretly; privately; confidentially.
succinctly	Briefly and to the point.
summary judgment	A judgment by the court in response to a motion of one of the parties to a civil lawsuit for a favorable judgment without a trial, because all issues and facts are clearly settled by the pleadings.
summons	An official writ ordering a person to appear in court, usually to answer a complaint filed against him.
supra	Above; cited or stated previously in the text.
surreptitious	Secret; undercover.

T

testimony	A declaration or statement made to establish a fact, under oath, by a witness in court.
tort	A wrongful act by one person against another (but not including breach of contract) for which a civil action for damages may be brought.
toxicology	The science of poisons, their recognition, effects, antidotes, etc.
transcript	An official written or typewritten copy of court proceedings, as the transcript of the record of a trial.
trespass	A wrongful interference with another's rights or property.
true bill	A bill of indictment endorsed by a grand jury upon deciding that there is sufficient evidence to justify the trial of the accused.

turpitude	Baseness; vileness; depravity.

U

ultra vires	Beyond legal power; exceeding authority.
uncontroverted	Unchallenged.
unequivocal	Clear; not ambiguous.
Uniform Code of Military Justice	The body of law governing the armed forces of the United States, adopted under the authority of Article I, Section 8 of the Constitution.
usury	The taking of interest at a rate that is excessive or unlawfully high on money loaned.
utter	To present a worthless check or instrument in payment of an obligation.

V

valid	Having legal force; properly executed and binding under law.
vehicle	A medium or method; a device for transportation.
vel non	Or not.
venire	A writ directed to the sheriff to summon persons to court to act as jurors. The term sometimes refers to the list of names of persons selected for jury duty.
venue	The place in which a case is tried: usually, the place in which the crime was committed. Change of venue is the substitution of another place of trial for the original one, to avoid a prejudiced trial.
veracity	Truth or honesty.
verdict	The formal finding of a jury on the matter submitted to it; a decision.
vicarious	Substituted; taking the place of another.
vindicate	To clear of blame.
vitiate	To invalidate or make ineffective.
volenti non fit injuria	A person consenting to be injured cannot complain of the injury.

W

waive	To forgo or relinquish voluntarily; to give up.
ward	A child or incompetent person placed by law under the care of another.
warrant	A writ or order authorizing an officer to make an arrest, search or seizure.
witness	A person who saw, or can give a firsthand account of, an event.
writ	A formal, legal document ordering or prohibiting the performance of a specific act.

APPENDIX C

Table of Cases

A

Abel v. United States, 80 S. Ct. 683 (1960), §4.13
Adams v. Williams, 92 S. Ct. 1921 (1972), §4.15(E)(3)
Agnello v. United States, 46 S. Ct. 5 (1925), §4.15(A)(1)
Aguilar v. Texas, 84 S. Ct. 1509 (1964), §§2.6(C), 4.13, 4.14 (A), 4.14(C)
Air Pollution Variance Board v. Western Alfalfa Corp., 94 S. Ct. 2114 (1974), §4.13
Alabama v. Pugh, 98 S. Ct. 3057 (1978), §2.2(A)
Alabama v. White, 110 S.Ct. 2412 (1990), §4.15(E)(5)
Alderman v. United States, 89 S. Ct. 961 (1969), §4.16(C)
Amos v. United States, 41 S. Ct. 266 (1921), §4.15(B)(1)
Anderson v. Charles, 100 S. Ct. 2180 (1980), §5.5(G)
Appeal of Maguire, 571 F.2d 675 (1st Cir. 1978), §6.6
Arizona v. Fulminante, 111 S.Ct. 1246 (1991), §5.5(H)
Arizona v. Hicks, 107 S. Ct. 1149 (1987), §§4.14(B), 4.15(D) (brief)
Arizona v. Mauro, 107 S. Ct. 1931 (1987) §5.5(B) (brief)
Arizona v. Roberson, 2108 S. Ct. 2093 (1988) §5.5(E)
Arizona v. Youngblood, 109 S. Ct. 333(1988), §2.4
Arkansas v. Sanders, 99 S. Ct. 2586 (1979), §§4.15(A)(1), 4.15(B)(3), 4.15(D)
Attreau v. Morris, 357 F.2d 871 (7th Cir. 1966), §2.2(A)

B

Barrera v. Young, 794 F.2d 1264 (7th Cir. 1986), §5.2
Beck v. Ohio, 85 S. Ct. 223 (1964), §§4.4(brief), 4.15 (A)(4)
Beckwith v. United States, 96 S. Ct. 1612 (1976), §5.5(B)(brief)
Bell v. Wolfish, 99 S. Ct. 1861 (1979), §7.3
Berger v. New York, 87 S. Ct. 1873 (1967), §4.17
Berkemer v. McCarty, 104 S. Ct. 3138 (1984) §5.5(B)(brief)
Berryman v. United States, 378 A.2d 1317 (D.C. Cir. 1977), §6.6
Bey v. State, 355, S0.2d 850 (Fla. App. 1978), §4.2
Bivens v. Six Unknown Named Agents, 91 S. Ct. 1999 (1971), §2.6(C)
Blackwood v. State, 299 N.E.2d 622 (Ind. App. 1973), §4.16(F)(1)
Block v. Rutherford, 104 S. Ct. 3227(1984), §7.3
Blum v. Stenson, 104 S. Ct. 154, (1984), §2.2(A)
Boyd v. State, 430 N.E. 2d 1146 (Ind. 1982), §5.2
Boyd v. United States, 6 S. Ct. 524 (1886), §4.15 (B)(2)
Brandenburg v. Ohio, 89 S. Ct. 1827 (1969), §3.3(brief)
Branzburg v. Hayes, 92, S. Ct. 2646 (1972), §3.4
Breed v. Jones, 95 S. Ct. 1779 (1975), §8.2
Breithaup v. Abram, 77 S. Ct. 408 (1957), §4.15(C)(2)
Brewer v. Williams, 97 S. Ct. 1232 (1977), §§4.14(D), 5.4(B)(brief), 5.5(B), 5.5(E)
Brinegar v. United States, 69 S. Ct. 1302 (1949), §4.4, 4.14(A)
Brower v. Inyo County, 109 S. Ct., 1378 (1989), §4.7 (brief)
Brown v. Illinois, 95 S. Ct. 2254 (1975), §5.3 (brief)
Brown v. Mississippi, 56 S. Ct. 461 (1936), §5.2
Brown v. United States, 93 S. Ct. 1565 (1973), §4.13
Brulay v. United States, 383 F.2d 345 (9th Cir. 1967), §§4.13
Bugg v. State, 372 N.E.2d 1156 (Ind. 1978), §5.5(B) (text)
Bumper v. North Carolina, 88 S. Ct. 1788, (1968), §4.16(C)

Burdeau v. McDowell, 41 S. Ct. 574 (1921), §4.13
Burns v. Reed, 111 S.Ct. 1934 (1991), §2.2(A)
Butz v. Economou, 98 S. Ct. 2894 (1978), §2.2(A)
Bynum v. United States, 262 F.2d 465 (D.C. Cir. 1958), §6.5
Byrd v. Brishke, 466 F.2d 6 (7th Cir. 1972), §2.2(A)

C

Cady v. Dombrowski, 93 S. Ct. 2523 (1973), §4.15(D)
California v. Acevedo, 111 S.Ct. 1982 (1991), §4.15(B)(3)(brief)
California v. Beheler, 103 S. Ct. 3517 (1983), §5.5(B)
California v. Carney, 105 S. Ct. 2066 (1985), §4.15(B)(1)
California v. Ciraolo, 106 S. Ct. 1809 (1986), §4.13
California v. Greenwood, 108 S. Ct. 1625 (1988), §§4.13, 4.16(D)
California v. Hodari D, 111 S.Ct. 1547 (1991), §4.2 (brief)
California v. Prysock, 101 S. Ct. 2806 (1981), §5.5(D)
Camara v. Municipal Court of San Francisco, 97 S. Ct. 1727 (1967), §4.15(G)
Campbell v. McGruder, 580 F.2d 521 (D.C. Cir 1978), §7.3
Carroll v. United States, 45 S. Ct. 280 (1925), §§4.6, 4.13, 41.5(A)(1), 4.15 (B)(1), (brief), 4.15 (B)(2), 4.15(B)(3), 4.15(D), 4.16(A)
Chambers v. Maroney, 90 S. Ct. 1975 (1970), §§4.15(B)(1), 4.15(B)(2) (brief), 4.15(B)(3), 4.16(A)
Chaplinsky v. New Hampshire, 62 S. Ct. 766 (1942), §3.3
Chimel v. California, 89 S. Ct. 2034 (1969), §§4.6, 4.13, 4.15(A)(1), (brief), 4.15(A)(3), 4.15(A)(4), 4.15 (B)(3), 4.15(C)(3), 4.15(D), 4.16(A)
City of Canton v. Harris, 109 S. Ct. 1197(1989), §§2.2(A),7.2
City of Houston v. Hill, 107 S. Ct. 2507, (1987), §3.3(brief)
City of Newport v. Fact Concerts, Inc., 101 S. Ct. 2748(1981), §2.2(A)
Coffey v. United States, 116 U.S 436 (1886), §4.19
Cohen v. California, 91 S. Ct. 1780 (1971), §3.3
Coleman v. Alabama, 90 S. Ct. 1999 (1970), §6.4
Colorado v. Bertine, 107 S. Ct. 738(1987), §4.15(D)(brief)
Colorado v. Connelly, 107 S. Ct. 515(1986), §5.5(C)(brief)
Colorado v. Spring, 107 S. Ct. 851 (1987), 5.5(E)(brief)
Commonwealth v. Dustin, 368 N.E.2d 1388 (Mass. 1977), §5.2
Commonwealth v. Grise, Mass Sup. Jud. Ct., 39 Crim. L. Rep. 2450 (1986), §4.9
Commonwealth v. Holmes 183 N.E.2d 279 (Mass. 1962), §4.1
Commonwealth v. Moreira, 447 N.E.2d 1221 (Mass. 1983), §4.10
Connecticut v. Barrett, 107 S. Ct. 828 (1987), §5.5(E) (brief)
Coolidge v. New Hampshire, 91 S. Ct. 2022 (1971), §§4.5,4.14(B), 4.15(C)(3), 4.15(D), 4.16(A) (brief), 4.16(B)
Cooker v. California, 87 S. Ct. 788 (1967), §4.15(D)
Cooper v. Pate, 84 S. Ct. 1733 (1964), §§2.2(A), 3.5
Craig v. State, 370 N.E. 2d 880 (1977), §5.2
Craig v. Beto, 92 S. Ct. 1079 (1974), §7.3
Cruz v. Hauck, 92 S. Ct. 313 (1971), §7.3

D

Dalton v. State, 105 N.E.2d 509 (Ind 1952), §4.16(C)
Davis v. Mississippi, 89 S. Ct. 1394 (1969), §§4.19, 5.3, 6.5
Davis v. North Carolina 86 S. Ct. 1761 (1966), §6.4
Dawson v. State, 276 A.2d 680 (Md. App. 1971), §4.14(A)(brief)
DeJonge v. Oregon, 57 S. Ct. 255 (1937) §3.5

Delaware v. Prouse, 99 S. Ct. 1391 (1979), §§4.15(D), 4.15(3), 4.15(SE)(5), 4.15(E)(6), 5.5(B)
Dillon v. State, 275 N.E. 2d 312 (1971), §5.5(B)
Dodd v. City of Norwich 827 F2d 1 (2nd Cir. 1987), §4.7
Donovan V. Dewey, 101 S. Ct. 2534 (1981), §4.15(G)
Dow Chemical v. United States, 106 S. Ct. 1819 (1986) §4.13
Doyle v. Ohio 96 S. Ct. 2240 (1976), §5.5(G)
Draper v. United States, 79 S. Ct. 329 (1959), §§4.4 (brief), 4.14(A), 4.15(A)(1)
Dunaway v. New York, 99 S. Ct. 2248 (1979), §5.3 (brief)
Durham v. State, 159 N.E. 145 (Ind. 1927), §2.2(B)
Duckworth v. Egan, 109 S. Ct. 2875 (1989), §5.5(D)

E

Eastland v. United States Servicemen's Fund, 95 S. Ct. 1813 (1975), §2.2(A)
Edwards v Arizona, 101 S. Ct. 1880 (1981), §§5.4(B), 5.5(B), 5.5(E) (brief)7.2
Empl. Div., Dept. of Hum. Res. of Oregon v. Smith, 110 S.Ct. 1595 (1990), §3.2
Escobedo v. Illinois, 84 S. Ct. 1758 (1964), §5.4(A), 5.4(B)
Estelle, v. Gamble, 97 S. Ct. 285 (1976), §7.3
Ex Parte Hull, 61 S. Ct. 640 (1941), §§3.5, 7.3

F

Fare v. Michael C., 99 S. Ct. 2560 (1979), §8.3
Fisher v. Vale, 496 F.2d. 333 (3rd Cir. 1974), §2.2(A)
Foster v. California, 89 S. Ct. 1127 (1969), §6.4
Florida v. Bostick, 111 S.Ct. 2382 (1991), §4.15(F)(1)
Florida v. Jimeno, 111 S.Ct. 1801 (1991), §4.15(F)(3)(brief)
Florida v. Meyers, 104 S. Ct. 1852 (1984), §4.15(B)(2)
Florida v. Riley, 109 S. Ct. 693 (1989), §4.13
Florida v. Rodriguez, 105 S. Ct. 308 (1984), 4.16(E)(5)
Florida v. Wells, 110 S.Ct. 1632 (1990), §4.15(D) (brief)
Foster v. California, 89 S. Ct. 1127 (1969), §6.4
Franks v. Delaware, 98 S. Ct. 2674 (1978), §§2.6(C), 4.14(D) (brief)
Frazier v. Cupp, 89 S. Ct. 1420 (1969), §5.2

G

G.M. Leasing Corp. v. United States, 97 S. Ct. 619 (1977), §4.14(B)
Gavel v. United States, 92 S. Ct. 2614 (1972), §2.2(A)
Gerstein v. Pugh, 95 S. Ct. 854 (1975), §§4.4 (brief), 7.2
Gilbert v. California, 87 S. Ct. 1951 (1967), §§6.1 through 6.4
Giles v. Ackerman, 746 7.2d 614 (9th Cir, 1984), §7.3
Gitlow v. New York, 45 S. Ct. 625 (1925), §3.4
Globe Newspaper Company v. Superior Court, 103 S. Ct. 2613 (1982), §3.4
GoBart Importing Co. v. United States, 51 S. Ct. 153 (1931), §4.15(A)(1)
Goldman v. United States, 62 S. Ct. 993 (1942), §4.17
Gouled v. United States, 41 S. Ct. 261 (1921), §§4.15(B)(1), 4.15(C)(1)
Graham v. Connor, 109 S. Ct. 1865 (1989), §4.7
Griffin v. Wisconsin, 107 S. Ct. 3164 (1987), §4.15 (G)
Gustafson v. Florida, 94 S. Ct. 488 (1973), §§4.15(A)(3) (brief), 4.15(A)(4), 4.15 (E)(2)

H

Hague v. CIO, 59 S. Ct. 954 (1935), §3.5
Harlow v. Fitzgerald, 102 S. Ct. 2727 (1982), §2.2(A)(brief)
Harris v. New York, 91 S. Ct. 2240 (1971), §5.5(G)
Harris v. United States, 67 S. Ct. 1098(1947), §§4.13, 4.15(A)(1), 4.15(D)(text)
Heckart v. City of Yakima, 708 P.2d 407 (Wash. App. 1985), §2.2(B)
Hendricks v. State, 371 N.E.2d, 1312 (Ind. 1978), §5.3
Henry v. United States, 80 5 S. Ct. 168 (1959), §4.15(B)(3)
Henzel v. United States, 296 F.2d 650 (5th Cir 1961), §4.16(C)
Hess v. Indiana, 94 S. Ct. 326 (1973), §3.3
Hester v. United States, 44 S. Ct. 445 (1924), §§4.13, 4.15(D)
Hemitt v. State, 300 N.E. 2d 94 (Ind. 1973), §5.5(B)
Hill v. California, 91 S. Ct. 1106 (1971), §§4.7, 4.14(C)
Hoffa v. United States, 87 S. Ct. 408 (1966), §4.17
Holt v. Sarver, 309 F. Supp. 362 (E.D. Ark. 1970), *affd.* 442 F.2d 304 (8th Cir. 1971), §7.3
Horton v. California, 110 S. Ct. 2301 (1990), §§4.14(B) (brief), 4.16(B)
Houchins v. KQED, 98 S. Ct. 2588 (1978), §7.3
Hudson v. Palmer, 104 S. Ct. 3194 (1984), §7.3
Hughes v. Noble, 295 F.2d. 495 (5th Cir. 1961), §2.2(A)
Hunter v. Auger, 672 F.2d 668 (8th Cir. 1982), §7.3

I

Idol v. State, 119 N.E.2d 428 (Ind. 1954), §4.16(C)
Illinois v. Gates, 103 S. Ct. 2317 (1983), §§1.1 2.6(C), 4.13, 4.14(A) (brief), 4.14(A)(2), 4.14(C), 4.15(E)(5)
Illinois v. Krull, 107 S. Ct. 1160 (1987), §2.6(C)
Illinois v. Lafayette, 103 S. Ct. 2605 (1983), §4.15(D)(brief)
Illinois v. Perkins, 110 S.Ct. 2394 (1990), §5.4(B)
Illinois v. Rodriguez, 110 S.Ct. 2793, (1990), §4.15(F)(1)
In re Gault, 87 S. Ct. 1428 (1967), §§8.2, 8.3
In re Motion for Return of Property,—F. Supp.—24 Crim. L. Rep. 2418 (S.D.N.Y. 1979), §4.16(B)
In re Winship, 90 S. Ct. 1068 (1970), §8.2

J

Jackson v. Bishop, 404 F.2d 571 (8th Cir. 1968), §7.3
Jackson v. Denno, 84 S. Ct. 1774 (1964), §5.2
Jenkins v. Anderson, 100 S. Ct. 2124 (1980), §5.5(G)
Jennings v. State, 318 N.E.2d 358 (Ind. 1973) §5.5(B)
Johnson v. Avery, 89 S. Ct. 747 (1969), §7.3
Johnson v. Glick, 481 F.2d 1028 (2d Cir. —), §4.7
Johnson, v. Louisana, 92 S. Ct. 1620 (1972), §6.6
Johnson v. United States, 68 S. Ct. 367 (1948), §4.4
Johnson v. Zerbst, 58 S. Ct. 1019 (1938), §5.4(B)
Jones v. North Carolina Prisoners' Labor Union, 97 S. Ct. 2532 (1977), §7.3
Jones v. State, 252 N.E.2d 572 (Ind. 1969), §5.5(D)
Jones v. United States 80 S. Ct. 725 (1960), §§4.14(A), 4.16(C)

K

Kastigar v. United Staes, 92 S. Ct. 1653 (1972), §5.5(H)
Katz v. United States, 88S. Ct. 507 (1967), §§4a.13, 4.16(C), 4.17 (brief), 4.18

Kennedy v. State, 370 N.E.2d 331 (Ind. 1977), §5.5(B)
Kent v. United States, 86 S. Ct. 1045 (1966), §8.2
Kentucky v. Dennison, 65 U.S. (24 How.) 717 (1861), §1.3(E)
Ker v. California, 83 S. Ct. 1623 (1963), §4.15(D)
Kirby v. Illinois 92 S. Ct. 1877 (1972), §§5.5(E), 6.3
Kuhlmann v. Wilson, 106 S. Ct. 2616 (1986), §5.4(B)

L

Lagow v. United States, 159 F.2d 245 (2d Cir. 1946), §4.16(C)
Landmark Communications, Inc. v. Virginia, 98 S. Ct. 1535 (1978), §3.4
Lawrence v. United States, 795 F.2d 1017, 39 Crim L. Rep. 2212 (D.C. Cir. 1986), §4.15(E)(5)
Leary v. United States, 383 F.2d 851 (1987), §3.2
Lee v. Washington, 88 S. Ct. 994 (1968), §7.3
Leeper v. United States, 446 F.2d 281 (10th Cir. 1971), §4.16(C)
Lester v. City of Chicago, 830 F.2d (7th Cir. 1987), §4.7
Lewis v. United States, 87 S. Ct. 424 (1966), §4.17
Lockridge v. State, 338 N.E.2d (Ind. 1975), §5.5(B)
Lopez v. United States, 83 S. Ct. 1381 (1963), §4.17
Lykken v. Vavreck, 366 F. Supp 585 (D. Minn. 1973), §2.2(A)
Lynumn v. Illinois, 83 S. Ct. 917 (1963), §5.2

M

McCray v. Sullivan, 509 F.2d, 1332 (5th Cir. 1975), §7.3
McDonald v. United States, 69 S. Ct. 191, (1948), §4.9
McKeiver v. Pennsylvania, 91 S. Ct. 1976 (1971), §8.2
McNeil v. Wisconsin, 111 S.Ct. 2204 (1991), §5.5(E)
Maine v. Moulton, 106 S. Ct. 477 (1985), §§5.4(B), 5.5(E)
Maine v. Thornton, 104 S. Ct. 1735 (1984), §4.13
Malley v. Briggs, 106 S. Ct. 1092 (1986), §4.14(A)(2)
Malloy v. Hogan, 84 S. Ct. 1489 (1964), §5.5(1H)
Mancusi v. DeForte, 88 S. Ct. 2120 (1968), §4.16(C)
Manson v. Braithwaite, 97 S. Ct. 2243, (1977), §6.5(brief)
Mapp v. Ohio, 81 S. Ct. 1684 (1961), §§1.3(G), 2.6(B)(brief), 4.14(D), 5.3
Marek v. Chesny, 105 S. Ct. 3012 (1985), §2.2(A)
Marland v. Heyse, 315 F.2d 312 (10th Cir. 1963), §2.2(A)
Marron v. United States 48 S. Ct. 74 (1927), §4.15(A)(1)
Mary Beth G. v. City of Chicago, 723 F.2d 1263 (7th Cir. 1983), §4.15(A)(4)
Maryland v. Buie, 110 S.Ct. 1093 (1990), §4.15(E)(3)
Maryland v. Garrison, 107 S. Ct. 1013 (1987), §§2.6(C), 4.5, 4.7, 4.14(C)(brief)
Maryland v. Macon, 105 S. Ct. 2778 (1985), §4.13
Massachusetts v. Sheppard, 104 S. Ct. 3424 (1984), §§1.1, 2.6(C)(brief), 4.14(A)(2)
Massachusetts v. Upton, 104 S. Ct. 2085 (1984), §4.14(C)
Massiah v. United States, 84 S. Ct. 1199 (1964), §§5.4(B) (text), 5.5(E)
Matovina v. Hult, 123 N.E.2d 893 (Ind. App. 1955), §2.2(B)
Mayer v. City of Chicago, 92 S. Ct. 410 (1971), §8.2
Meredith v. Whillock, 158 S.W. 1061 (Mo. App. 1913), §4.11
Michigan v. Chesternut, 108 S. Ct. 1975 (1988), §4.2
Michigan v. DeFillippo, 99 S. Ct. 2627 (1979), §4.11
Michigan v. Jackson, 106 S. Ct. 1404 (1987), §5.5(E)
Michigan v. Long, 103 S. Ct. 3469 (1983), §4.15(E)(3)

Michigan State Police, Petitioners, v. Sitz, 110 S.Ct. 2481 (1990), §4.15(E)(6)(brief)
Michigan v. Summers, 101 S. Ct. 2587 (1981), §4.5
Michigan v. Thomas, 102 S. Ct. 3079 (1982), §4.15(B)(2)
Michigan v. Tyler, 98 S. Ct. 1942 (1978), §4.15(C)(3)
Miller v. California, 93 S. Ct. 2607 (1973), §3.4
Miller v. United LStates, 78 S. Ct. 1190 (1950), §4.8
Mincey v. Arizona, 98 S. Ct. 2408 (1978), §4.15 (C)(3)(brief)
Minnesota v. Olson, 110 S.Ct. 1684 (1990), §4.16(C)(brief)
Minnick v. Mississippi, 111 S.Ct. 486 (1990), §5.5(E)(brief)
Miranda v. Arizona, 86 S. Ct. 1602 (1966), §§4.14(D), 4.15(A)(1), 4.15(F)(1), 5.1, 5.2, 5.3, 5.4(B), 5.5(A through G), (Text excerpts and discussion), 6.2, 7.2, 8.2, 8.3,
Monell v. Dept. of Soc. Serv. of City of New York, 98 S. Ct. 2018 (1978), §2.2(A)(brief)
Monroe v. Pape, 81 S. Ct. 473 (1961), §2.2(A)
Moore v. Illinois, 98 S. Ct. 458 (1977), §6.3
Moran v. Burbine, 106 S. Ct. 1135 (1986), §5.5(E)(brief)
Murray v. United States, 108 S. Ct. 2529 (1988), §§4.14(A)(1), 5.4(B)

N

Nardone v. United States, 58 S. Ct. 275 (1937), §4.17
Nardone v. United States, 60 S. Ct. 266 (1939) 4.17
Nebraska Press Association v. Stuart, 96 S. Ct. 2791 (1976), §3.4
Neil v. Biggers, 93 S. Ct. 375 (1972), §§6.4(text), 6.5
New v. State, 259 N.E.2d. 696 (1970), §5.5(B)
New Jersey v. T.L.O., 105 S. Ct. 733 (1985), §4.15(G), 8.3
New York v. Belton, 101 S. Ct. 2860 (1981), §§4.15(A)(1)(brief), 4.15 (A),(4), 4.15(D)
New York v. Burger, 107 S. Ct. 2636 (1987), §4.15(G)
New York v. Harris, 110 S.Ct. 1640 (1990), §5.3
New York v. P.J. Video, Inc., 106 S. Ct. 1610 (1986), §4.14(A)
New York v. Quarles, 104 S. Ct. 2626 (1984), §5.5 (F) (brief)
Nix v. Williams, 104 S. Ct. 2501 (1984), §§4.14 (A)(1), 5.4(B), 5.5(F)
Nixon v. Fitzgerald, 102 S. Ct. 2690 (1982), §2.2(A)
North Carolina v. Butler, 99 S. Ct. 1755 (1979), §5.5(E)

O

O'Connor v. Ortega, 107 S. Ct. 1492 (1987), §4.15(G)
Oliver v. United States, 104 S. Ct. 1735 (1984), §4.13
Olmstead v. United States, 48 S. Ct. 564 (1928), §4.17
On Lee v. United States, 72 S. Ct. 967 (1952), §4.17
Oregon v. Bradshaw 103 S. Ct. 2830 (1983), §5.5(E)
Oregon v. Elstad, 105 S. Ct. 1285 (1985), §5.3(brief)
Oregon v. Hass, 95 S. Ct. 1215 (1975), §5.5(G)
Oregon v. Mathiason, 97 S. Ct. 711 (1977), §(5.5)(B)(brief)
Osborne v. Ohio, 110 S.Ct. 1691 (1990), §3.4
Owen v. City of Independence, 100 S. Ct. 1398 (1980), §2.2(A)
Owens v. State, 266 N.E.2d 612 (1971), §5.5(B)

P

Palko v. Connecticut, 58 S. Ct. 149 (1937), §3.1
Palmer v. Peyton, 359 F.2d 199 (4th Cir. 1966), §6.4

Patterson v. Illinois, 108 S. Ct. 2389 (1988), §5.4(B)
Payton v. New York, 100 S. Ct. 1371 (1980), §§4.6(brief), 4.9, 4.14(B), 6.6
Pell v. Procunier, 94 S. Ct. 2800 (1974), §7.3
Pennsylvania v. Bruder, 109 S. Ct. 205 (1989), §5.5(B)
Pennsylvania v. Mimms, 98 S. Ct. 330 (1977), §4.15(E)(3)(brief)
Pennsylvania v. Muniz, 110 S.Ct. 2638, (1990), §5.5(B) (brief)
People v. Battle, 123 Cal. Rptr. 636 (Cal. App. 1975), §4.11
People v. Krivda, 486 P.2d 1262 (Cal. 1971), §4.16(D)
People v. Morales, 366 N.E.2d 248 (N.Y. 1977), §5.3
People v Russo, 239 N.Y S. 2d 374, (1963), §4.15(E)(5)
People v. Waterman, 175 N.E.2d. 445 (N.Y. 1961), §5.4(B)
People v. Woody, 394, P.2d 813, (Cal. 1964), §3.2
Perez v. United States, 91 S. Ct. 1357 (1971), §1.3(E)
Peters v. New York, 88 S. Ct. 1889 (1968), §§4.15(A)(3), 4.15(E) (1)(brief)
Pierson v. Ray, 87 S. Ct. 1213 (1987), §2.2(A)
Pilcher v. Estelle, 528 F.2d 623 (5th cir. 1976), §5.5(B)
Powell v. Alabama, 53 S. Ct. 55 (1932), §§5.4(B), 6.2
Preston v. United States, 84 S. Ct. 881 (1964), §§4.15(B)(2), 4.15(D), 4.15(E)(2)
Puerto Rico v. Branstad, 107 S. Ct. 2802 (1987), §1.3

R

Raines v. State, 269 N.E.2d 378 (1971), §5.5(B)
Rakas v. Illinois, 99 S. Ct. 421 (1978), §§4.6, 4.13, 4.16 (C)(brief)
Rawlings v. Kentucky, 100 S. Ct. 2556 (1980), §5.3
Rea v. United States, 76 S. Ct. 292 (1956), §2.6(B)
Reynolds v. United States, 98 U.S. 145 (1972), §3.2
Rhode Island v. Innis, 100 S. Ct. 1682 (1980), §5.5(B)(brief)
Richmond Newspapers, Inc. v. Virginia, 100 S. Ct. 2814 (1980), §3.4
Riddle v. State, 348 N.E.2d 635 (Ind. 1976), §5.5(B)
Riverside Co., Calif. v. McLaughlin, 111 S.Ct. 1661 (1991), §4.4
Robbins v. California, 101 S. Ct. 2841 (1981), §4.15(B)(3)
Robinson v. Jordan, 494 F.2d 793 (5th Cir. 1974), §2.2(A)
Rochin v. California, 72 S. Ct. 205 (1952), §§2.6(B), 4.15(C)(2), 5.5(E)
Roth v. United States, 77 S. Ct. 1304 (1957), §3.4
Rouse v. State, 226 N.E.2d 209 (Ind. 1971), §5.5(D)

S

Schall v. Martin, 104 S. Ct. 2403 (1984), §8.2, 8.3
Shenck v. United States, 39 S. Ct. 247 (1949), §3.3
Schmerber v. California, 86 S. Ct. 1826 (1966), §§4.15(C)(2)(brief), 4.18, 6.2
Schmidt v. State, 265 N.E.2d 219 (1970), §5.5(B)
Shneckloth v. Bustamonte, 93 S. Ct. 2041, (1973), §§4.6, 4.13, 4.15(C)(3), 4.15 (F)(1)(brief), 5.12, 5.5(E)
Screws v. United States, 65 S. Ct. 1031 (1945), §2.2(A)
See v. City of Seattle, 87 S. Ct. 1737 (1967), §4.15(G)
Segura v. United States, 104 S. Ct. 3380 (1984), §4.14(A)(1)
Sibron v. New York, 88 S. Ct. 1889 (1968), §4.15 (E)(1)(brief), 4.15(E)(2)
Silverman v. United States 81 S. Ct. 679 (1961),§4.17
Silverthorne Lumber Co. v. United States, 40 S. Ct. 182 (1920, §§4.14(A)(1), 4.15(B)(1), 4.16(C)
Simmons v. United States, 88 S. Ct. 967 (1968), §4.16(C), 6.4, 6.5
Sims v. State, 413 N.E.2d 556 (Ind. 1980), §4.16(F)(2)
Smith v. Goguen, 94 S. Ct. 1242 (1974), §3.3
Smith v. Illinois, 105 S. Ct. 490 (1984), §5.5(E)

Smith v. Maryland, 99 S. Ct. 2577 (1979), §4.17
Smith v. Wade, 103 S. Ct. 1625 (1983), 2.2(A)(brief)
Sonzinski v. United States, 57 S. Ct. 554 (1937), §1.3(E)
South Dakota v. Opperman, 96 S. Ct. 3092 (1976), §4.13, 4.15(D)(brief)
Spano v. New York, 79 S. Ct. 1202 (1959) §5.4(B)
Spence v. Washington, 94 S. Ct. 2727 (1974), §3.3(brief)
Spinelli v. United States, 89 S. Ct. 584 (1969), §§2.6(C), 4.13, 4.14(A)(brief), 4.14(C)
Stanley v. Georgia, 89 S. Ct. 1243 (1969), §3.4
State v. Blake, 468 N.E.2d 548 (Ind. App. 1984), §4.9
State v. Jamieson, 300 N.W. 809 (Minn. 1941), §4.11
State v. McGhee, 350 So.2d 370 (La. 1977), §6.6
State v. Porter, 324 N.E.2d 857 (Ind. App. 1975), §4.16)(C)
State v. Smithers, 269 N.E.2d 874 (Ind. 1971), §4.16(D)
Steagald v. United States, 101 S. Ct. 1642 (1981), §4.6(brief)
Stone v. Powell, 96 S. Ct. 3037 (1976), §2.6(C)
Stonehill v. United States, 405 F.2d 738 (9th Cir. 1968), §§4.13
Stoner v. California, 84 S. Ct. 889 (1964), §4.16(C)
Storall v. Denno, 87 S. Ct. 1967 (1967), §§6.4(text), 6.5
Stump v. Sparkman, 98 S. Ct. 1099 (1978), §2.2(A)

T

Tennessee v. Garner, 1055 S. Ct. 1694 (1985) §§4.2, 4.7(brief), 4.16(E)(4)
Terry v. Ohio, 88 S. Ct. 1868 (1968). §§4.1, 4.5, 4.13, 4.15(A)(1), 4.15(A)(3), 4.15(A)(4), 4.15(E)(1)(brief), 4.15.(E)(2) through 4.15(E)(6), 4.18, 5.3, 5.5(B)
Texas v. Brown, 103 S. Ct. 1535 (1983), 4.14(B), 4.15(D)
The King v. Warickshall, 168 Eng. Rep. 234, L. Leach Cases 263 (K.B. 1783) §5.2
Thornburgh v. Abbott, 109 S. Ct. 1874 (1989), §7.4
Tinker v. Des Moines School District, 89 S. Ct. 733 (1969), §3.3(G)
Trupiano v. United States 68 S. Ct. 1229 (1948), §4.15(A)(1)

U

United States ex rel Placek v. State of Illinois, 546 F.2d 1298 (7th Cir. 1976), §5.5(D)
United States ex rel. Williams v. Tomey, 467 F.2d 1248 (7th Cir. 1972), §5.5(D)
United States v. Ash, 93 S. Ct. 2568 (1973), §6.5
United States v. Biswell, 92 S. Ct. 1593 (1972), §4.15(G)
United States v. Buckner, 717 F.2d 297 (6th Cir. 1983), §4.6
United States v. Calandra, 94 S. Ct. 613 (1974), §2.6(C)
United States v. Chadwick, 97 S. Ct. 2476 (1977), §§4.15(A)(1), 4.15 (B)(3), 4.15(D)
United States v. Classic, 61 S. Ct. 1031 (1941), §2.2(A)
United States v. Clifford, 664 F.2d 1090 (8th Cir. 1981), §4.6
United States v. Crews, 100 S. Ct. 1244 (1980), §6.5(brief)
United States v. Dionisio, 93 S. Ct. 764 (1973), §4.18(brief)
United States v. Dunn, 107 S. Ct. 1134 (1987). §4.13
United States v. Edwards, 94 S. Ct. 1234 (1974), §4.15(D)
United States v. Eichman, 110 S.Ct. 2404, (1990), §3.3
United States v. Hamilton, 792 F.2d 837 (9th Cir. 1986), §4.15(B)(1)
United States v. Hare, 589 F.2d 1291(6th Cir. 1979), §4.16(B)
United States v. Henry, 100 S. Ct. 2183 (1980), §5.4(B)
United States v. Hensley, 105 S. Ct. 675 (1985), §4.15(E)(1)

United States v. Hill, 730 F.2d1163 (8th Cir. 1984), §4a.15(A)(3)
United States v. Jacobsen, 104 S. Ct. 1652 (1984), §4.13
United States v. Johns, 105 S. Ct. 881 (1985), §§4.15(B)(2), 4.15(B)(3)
United States v. Karo, 104 S. Ct. 3296 (1984), §4.16(C)
United States v. Kuch, 288 F. Supp. 439 (1968), §3.2
United States v. Lee, 47 S. Ct. 746 (1927), §4.15(D)
United States v. Lefkowitz, 52 S. Ct. 420 (1932), §4.15(A)(1)
United States v. Leon, 104 S. Ct. 3405 (1984), §§2.6(C)(brief), 4.14(A)(2)
United States v. Liberti, 616 F.2d 34 (2d Cir. 1980), §4.16(B)
United States v. Mazzone, 782 F.2d 757 (7th Cir. 1986), §4.15(B)(3)
United States v. Mendenhall, 100 S. Ct. 1870 (1980), §4.2
United States v. New York Telephone Co., 98 S. Ct. 364 (1977), §4.17
United States v. O'Brien, 88 S. Ct. 1673, (1968), §3.3(brief)
United States v. One Assortment of 89 Firearms, 104 S. Ct. 1099 (1984), §4.19
United States v. Place, 103 S. Ct. 2637 (1983), §4.15(E)(3)
United States v. Rabinowitz, 70 S. Ct. 430 (1950), §§4.15(A)(1), 4.16(A)
United States v. Reicherter, 647 F.2d 397 (3d Cir. 1981), §4.16(D)
United States v. Robinson,m 94 S. Ct. 467 (1973), §§4.15(A)(1),
    4.15(A)(3)(brief), 4.15(A)(4), 4.15(D), 4.15(E)(2)
United States v. Ross, 102 S. Ct. 2157 (19829(brief)§§4.15(B)(2),
    4.15(B)(3)(brief), 41.5(D)
United States v. Santana, 96 S. Ct. 2406 (1976), §§4.6(brief), 4.9
United States v. Schwimmer, 49 S. Ct. 448 (1929), §3.1
United States v. Sharpe, 105 S. Ct. 1568 (1985), §4.15(E)(3)
United States v. Sokolow, 109 S. Ct. 1581 (1989), §4.15(E)(5)(brief)
United States v. Staszcuk, 517 F.2d 53 (7th Cir. 1975), §1.3(E)
United States v. Underwood, 717 F.2d 482 (9th Cir. 1983), §4.6
United States v. United States District Court, 92 S. Ct. 2125 (1972), §4.6
United States v. Vintresca, 85 S. Ct. 741 (1965), §§2.6(C), 4.14(A), 4.14(C)
United States v. Wade, 87 S. Ct. 1926 (1967), §§5.4(A), 6.1, 6.2(brief), 6.3
    through 6.6
United States v. Watson, 96 S. Ct. 820 (1976), §4.6(brief)
United States v. White, 91 S. Ct. 1122 (1971), §4.17(brief)

W

Warden v. Hayden, 87 S. Ct. 1642 (1967), §§4.6, 4.9, 4.13, 4.14(C),
    4.15(C)(1)(brief), 4.15(C)(3), 4.16(A)
Watts v. Indiana, 69 S. Ct. 1347 (1949), §5.2
Weeks v. United States, 34 S. Ct. 341 (1914), §§2.6(A)(brief), 4.15(A)(1),
    4.15(A)(3), 4.15(B)(1), 5.4(B)
Whitney, California, 47 S. Ct. 641 (1927), §3.3
Williams v. Liberty, 461 F.2d 325 (7th Cir. 1972), §2.2(A)
Winston v. Lee, 105 S. Ct. 1611 (1985), §4.15(C)2
Wisconsin v. Yoder, 92 S. Ct. 1526 (1972), §3.2
Wolf v. Colorado, 69 S. Ct. 1359 (1949), §§2.6(B), 2.6(C)
Wolff v. McDonnell, 94 S. Ct. 2963 (1974), §7.3
Wong Sun v. United States, 83 S. Ct. 407 (1963), §§4.17, 5.3, 5.4(B), 6.2,
    6.5, 6.6
Woods v. Clusen, 794 F.2d 293 (7th Cir. 1986), §5.2
Worthington v. State, 409 N.E.2d 1261 (Ind. App. 1980), §5.1
Wrights v. McMann, 387 F.2d 519 (2nd Cir. 1967), §2.2(A)
Wyrick v. Fields, 103 S. Ct. 394 (1982), §5.5(E)

Y

Yates v. Village of Hoffman Estates, 209 S. Ct. F. Supp. 757 (N.D. Ill. 1962), §2.2(A)
Ybarra v. Illinois, 100 S. Ct. 338 (1979), §4.5
York v. Story, 324 F.2d 450 (9th Cir. 1963), §2.2(A)
Younger v. Gilmore, 92 S. Ct. 250 (1971), §7.3

Z

Zicarelli v. New Jersey State Commission of Investigation, 92 S. Ct. 1670 (1972), §5.5(H)
Zurcher v. Stanford Daily, 98 S. Ct. 1970 (1978), §3.4

APPENDIX D
CHECKLISTS

1. CHECKLIST FOR LITIGATION — WHAT TO DO IF YOU ARE SUED

When a police officer is sued in federal or state court with respect to an alleged act of civil liability, the officer should use the following information as an ongoing checklist until the action has been completed. Paying close attention to the matters listed will assist the officer in making the best defense possible to any civil cause of action.

1. Read the summons which will be attached to the complaint carefully for purposes of determining how much time you have in which to enter your appearance with or without an attorney, and to answer or otherwise plead to the complaint. Failure to file a timely answer, a motion to dismiss, or motion for continuance for purposes of filing an answer at a later date, can expose an officer to potential default judgment.

2. Note the physical location, mailing address, and telephone number for both the clerk's office and the judge's courtroom relevant to the lawsuit.

3. Determine from a department supervisor or other relevant authority, whether an attorney will be provided for your assistance as counsel in conjunction with the lawsuit. If an attorney is provided for your benefit, notify this attorney *immediately* and begin preparing an answer or other responsive pleading for purposes of avoiding a default judgment. If your employer will not provide an attorney, obtain a written letter of explanation as to why not so that if you challenge this decision, (for example, in conjunction with any disciplinary actions taken against you), you will be able to use the letter to establish your claimed right to department provided legal representation. If your department will not provide legal representation, review any collective bargaining agreement and/or written rules and regulations of your department which might address this issue.

4. If you have to hire your own attorney, check with local and surrounding police-related organizations such as the Fraternal Order of Police to see if they are willing to assist you in obtaining legal counsel. If this does not prove to be a helpful source, check to see if local or state bar associations have lawyer referral services which can be used for purposes of finding out which attorneys in your area handle civil liability cases on behalf of police officers.

5. Find out if the department has liability insurance and if so how the insurance coverage might affect legal representation and payment of any judgments that would be entered against you. If there are other governmental employees named as defendants, inquire as to whether there are potential conflicts of interest between such defendants and if one attorney or law firm will be able to ethically represent all defendants in the lawsuit. Even if the employer provides an attorney, consider the option of hiring your own attorney to assist the employer's lawyer on your behalf.

6. Determine whether there is a staff member on the department who has the responsibility to monitor department-related litigation and to act as liaison to the attorneys who represent department officers in litigation. If so, obtain the cooperation of this individual. Discover if this person maintains a separate litigation file containing copies of all pleadings filed on your behalf so that you can easily keep informed of the latest developments without having to personally meet with your attorney.

7. Review with your attorney whether the lawsuit has been timely filed with respect to any state statutory notice of tort claim requirements as well as

applicable federal or state statutes of limitations. In order to assist your attorney, make a list of all available documentation which could relate to the allegations contained in the lawsuit. In addition, make a list of all individuals connected or related to the allegations contained in the plaintiff's lawsuit and share this information with your attorney.

8. Early in the litigation process, obtain a clear understanding as to what your attorney will be doing for you as well as what your obligations and duties will be throughout the duration of the lawsuit. Determine how and when you can obtain information from your attorney. In addition, find out from your attorney the names and job titles of all other individuals who will be working on your case so that you can familiarize yourself with them. In the event you will have to testify review training materials that deal with the subject of being a good witness in a trial.

9. Do not wait for your attorney to contact you with respect to any of the above listed matters. Make it your responsibility to initiate the tasks in conjunction with these concerns. With this attitude and practice, legal mistakes will be kept to a minimum and you will be kept constantly informed of the status of your lawsuit. Furthermore, make sure that your attorney is advised of every single fact and argument in your possession which might assist you in overcoming the accusations in the lawsuit.

10. Since the litigation process is very time consuming, be patient with respect to the developments of your case and most certainly concentrate on your job duties as a police officer. Do no let the stress of the lawsuit weaken your work performance as a police officer.

11. Early in the litigation process, discuss with your attorney the advisability of filing a counterclaim against the citizen who has filed the lawsuit. In addition, if you prevail in the lawsuit filed by the citizen, discuss with your attorney whether you might be able to collect from the losing plaintiff the litigation expenses including attorney fees incurred by you in defending against the lawsuit.

12. It is critical for you to always be on time for any court-related appearance. In addition, always maintain proper demeanor and conduct whenever having contact with anyone associated with the lawsuit, both in and out of the courtroom.

13. Early in the litigation process, review department rules and procedures with supervisors in developing a thorough understanding as to what your department will be providing to you by way of litigation support. Such issues as whether you will be permitted to perform litigation-related tasks and responsibilities while on department time should be ascertained.

14. If the lawsuit relates to a pending criminal case, inquire of the prosecuting attorney as to how the progress of the criminal case might relate to your pending civil lawsuit. Check to see if there has been any discussion with respect to an agreement by the plaintiff to dismiss the civil lawsuit against you in exchange for dismissing the criminal case. These agreements will be closely reviewed by the appropriate courts.

15. If your lawsuit is to be tried before a jury, obtain from your attorney, if possible, a copy of the prospective jury list so that you can ascertain whether you have had prior dealings with any prospective jurors. Share any information with your attorney that relates to why you believe a particular prospective juror would be especially good or bad if chosen in your case.

16. At the conclusion of the trial, if the losing party initiates an appeal, investigate how this will be done and if you are the appealing party, ensure that there will be legal representation to accomplish the many short deadlines that will have to be met at the conclusion of the trial in order to perfect a proper appeal.

2. CHECKLIST FOR POLICE OFFICER WITNESSES

When you have been subpoenaed to testify in either a criminal or civil trial, your testimony is critical and should be a high priority for you. The following suggestions will assist you in meeting your objectives as a witness.

1. Verify from several different sources the exact date, time, and location for your appearance as a witness. Cross checking with independent sources will ensure that there will be no confusion as to when you will have to testify.

2. Find out from the attorney who has subpoenaed you as a witness exactly why you have been subpoenaed, what types of questions you will be asked, and how your information might relate to the issues in the case.

3. Inquire from the attorney who has subpoenaed you whether you are also being requested to bring any documents with you to the courtroom on the date of your testimony. If these documents will be provided, so inform the attorney. If they will not be provided, make sure the attorney understands the basis for refusal. Regardless, with respect to documentation, check with a department-related attorney with respect to whether the requested documentation should be provided to the attorney subpoenaing the material.

4. Prior to your appearance in the courtroom, review all of the material that you have and recall all of the events which in your opinion might relate to the case being tried. Develop a thorough recollection of these facts so that you can efficiently recall them in the courtroom when asked.

5. If there is time, review training materials that relate to public speaking skills and how to be a good witness in the courtroom. Consider getting the cooperation of your department's attorney in videotaping a practice session relating to the types of questions that might be asked of you when called upon to testify in court. With respect to being a "good witness", practice and preparation are crucial.

6. Remember the importance of being a good *listener*. It is critical for a witness to be able to respond to a specific question submitted to him during a trial or hearing. Without being a good listener, it is impossible for the witness to be completely responsive to the questions posed. Remember that your primary goals as a witness are (1) to bring facts, (2) speak the truth, (3) be neutral and objective, and (4) calmly and politely (without arguing with anyone) disseminate information for the members of the jury and /or judge.

7. Remember to speak distinctly and clearly when testifying. Develop good eye contact with the members of the jury because they decide which testimony to believe, which will determine the outcome of the trial.

8. Your visual image (body language) is important, and will be interpreted in addition to your sworn oral testimony from the witness stand. Keep this in mind even when going to or from the courtroom or when waiting to testify. Many people other than those directly associated with the trial may be observing you, including friends and family of the jurors. The judge and the jury, not being eyewitnesses to the events, must experience them through your testimony as a witness and will be influenced not only by *what* you say, but *how you say it*. A witness who portrays a positive image through both his spoken words and body language is more likely to be viewed as credible, and credibility is *the crucial factor* in the jury's task of determining the true facts from conflicting testimony.

9. Answer questions with "yes" or "no" or with appropriate short answers. On the other hand, if you need more time to answer a specific question, or if you cannot answer a question in the fashion demanded by the interrogating attorney, politely state the fact.

10. Always dress neatly. Appear in the courtroom in the same fashion that

you would be attired in when performing your duties as a police officer.

11. At the conclusion of the testimony, inquire as to whether you are being *released* as a witness. If you are going to be recalled, determine the date and time of your next appearance and determine whether there is a separation of witnesses in effect in the case which would preclude you from contacting or discussing your testimony with other persons or witnesses.

12. When you have concluded your testimony and you have been released, make a written report for your department's records as to the nature of your testimony so that your participation can be more easily recalled if a future need develops.

INDEX

References are to Sections of this Text.

A

Abandoned property and garbage, privacy interest in, §4.16(D)
Administrative remedies for police misconduct, §2.5
Affidavit for warrant
  challenge to affidavit, §4.14 (D)
  search warrant, §4.14(C)
Amendments to Constitution
  Bill of Rights, generally, §§1.1(A), 1.3(F), 2.1
  Fifth amendment, §1.3(F), Ch. 5
  First Amendment, §§1.3(F), Ch. 3
  Fourteenth Amendment, §§1.1(E), 1.3(E), 1.3(G)
  Fourth Amendment, 1.3(F), 2.6(A), to 2.7, 4.4, 4.13, 5.3
  Sixth Amendment, §5.4
American Digest, §1.2(A)(2)
American Jurisprudence, §1.2(A)(2)
American Law Report, §1.2(A)(1)
Arrest
  citizen's arrest, §4.12
  definitions, §§4.1, 4.2
  force, use of, §4.7
  forced entry, §4.8
  generally, §4.6
  incarcerated persons, police duty toward, §7.2
  knock and announce requirement, §4.8
  resistance, §4.10
  search incident to, §4.15(A)
  warrant for, §4.5
Articles of Confederation, §1.3(C)
Assembly, freedom of, §3.5
Automobiles — See Motor vehicles

B

Bill of Rights, English, §1.3(B)
Bill of Rights, United States, generally, §§1.1(A), 1.3(F), 2.1
Blackstone's Commentaries, generally, §1.3(A)
Briefing cases, instructions on, §1.2(B)
Briefs of cases in Text
  Arizona v. Hicks, §4.15(D)
  Arizona v. Mauro, §5.5(B)
  Arizona v. Roberson, §5.5(E)
  Beck v. Ohio, §4.4
  Beckwith v. United States, §5.5(B)
  Berkemer v. McCarty, §5.5(B)
  Brandenburg v. Ohio, §3.3.
  Brewer v. Williams, §5.4 (B)
  Brower v. Inyo County, §4.7
  Brown v. Illinois, §5.3
  California v. Acevedo, §4.15(B)(3)
  California v. Hodari, §4.2

Carroll v. United States, §4.15(B)(1)
Chambers v Maroney, §4.15(B)(2)
Chimel v. California, §4.15(A)
City of Houston, Texas v. Hill, §3.3
Cohen v. California, §3.3
Dawson v. State, §4.14(A)
Colorado v. Bertine, §4.15(D)
Colorado v. Connelly, §5.5(C)
Colorado v. Spring, §5.5(E)
Connecticut v. Barrett, §5.5(E)
Coolidge v. New Hampshire, §4.16(A)
Draper v. United States, §4.4
Dunaway v. New York, §5.3
Edwards v. Arizona, §5.5(E)
Florida v. Jimeno, §4.15(F)(3)
Florida v. Wells, §4.15(D)
Franks v. Delaware, §4.14(D)
Gerstein v. Pugh, §4.4
Graham v. Connor, §4.7
Gustafson v. Florida, §4.15(A)(3)
Harlow v. Fitzgerald, §2.2(A)
Horton v. California, §4.14(B)
Illinois v. Gates, §4.14(A)
Illinois v. Lafayette, §4.15(D)
Katz v. United States, §4.17
Manson v. Brathwaite, §6.5
Mapp v. Ohio, §2.6(B)
Maryland v. Garrison, §4.14(C)
Massachusetts v. Sheppard, §2.6(C)
Michigan State Police, Petitioner, v. Sitz, §4.15(E)(6)
Mincey v. Arizona, §4.15(C)(3)
Minnesota v. Olson, §4.16(C)
Minnick v. Mississippi, §5.5(E)
Monell v. Department of Social Services of the City of N.Y., §2.2(A)
Moran v. Burbine, §5.5(E)
New York v. Belton, §4.15(A)(1)
New York v. Quarles, §5.5(F)
Oregon v. Elstad, §5.3
Oregon v. Mathiason, §5.5(B)
Payton v. New York, §4.6
Pennsylvania v. Mimms, §4.15(E)(3)
Pennsylvania v. Muniz, §5.5(B)
Peters v. New York, §4.15(E)(1)
Rakas v. Illinois, §4.16(C)
Rhode Island v. Innis, §5.5(B)
Schmerber v. California, §4.15(C)(2)
Schneckloth v. Bustamonte, §4.15(F)(1)
Sibron v. New York, §4.15(E)(1)
Smith v. Wade, §2.2(A)
South Dakota v. Opperman, §4.15(D)
Spence v. Washington, §3.3
Spinelli v. United States, §4.14(A)
Steagald v. United States, §4.6
Tennessee v. Garner, §4.7
Terry v. Ohio, §4.15(E)(1)

United States v. Crews, §6.5
United States v. Dionisio, §4.18
United States v. Leon, §2.6(C)
United States v. O'Brien, §3.3
United States v. Robinson, §4.15(A)(3)
United States v. Ross, §4.15(B)(3)
United States v. Santana, §4.6
United States v. Sokolow, §4.15(E)(5)
United States v. Wade, §6.2
United States v. Watson, §4.6
United States v. White, §4.17
Warden v. Hayden, §4.15(C)(1)
Weeks v. United States, §2.6(A)
Burns Indiana Statutes Annotated, §1.2(A)(2)

C

Case law, §§1.1, 1.2
Censorship in prisons, §7.4
Child pornography, possession §3.4
Citizen's arrest, §4.12
Civil liability of police
  federal law, §2.2.(A)
  incarcerated persons, police duty toward, §7.2
  state law, §2.2.(B)
Civil liability of Prosecutors §2.2(A)
Civil Rights Act, §§2.2(A), 3.5
Civil wrongs, §§1.4, 2.2(A), 2.2(B)
Citator's §1.2(A)(2)
Clear and present danger tests, §3.3
Closed containers
  motor vehicle searches, §4.15(B)(3)
  treatment of in search incident for arrest, §§4.15(A)(1), 4.15(B)(3)
Common law, §1.2
Compelled evidence, §4.18
Confessions
  civil liability of police concerning, §2.2(A)
  coerced, standard for harmless error, §5.5(H)
  constitutional issues, §§5.3, 5.4
  following entry violating warrant requirement, §5.3
  generally, §5.1
  interrogation during adversary proceedings, §5.4(B)
  Miranda issues, §5.5(A)
  right to counsel and, §5.4(A), 5.5
  to officer posing as jail inmate, Miranda issue, §5.4(B)
  voluntariness, §§5.2, 5.5(C)
Consent searches
  exception to warrant requirement, §4.13
  forms for §§4.15(F)(1), 4.15(F)(2)
  Miranda waiver not consent, §4.15(F)(2)
  voluntariness requirement, §4.15(F)(1)
Consensual home entry, reasonable mistake §4.15(F)(1)
Constitution, history of §1.3
Constitutions, state, §1.1(E)
Continental Congress, §1.3(C)
Corpus Juris Secundum, §1.2(A)(2)

Criminal Law Reporter, §1.2(A)(1)
Criminal laws, §1.3(E)
Criminal liability of police, §2.3
Curtilage, searches within, §4.13
Custodial interrogation, §5.5
Confined persons, rights of, §§7.2, 7.3
Crimes
   common-law crimes, §1.2
   distinguished from civil wrongs, §1.4
   federal, §1.3(E)
   felony and misdemeanor distinguished, §4.3
Custody and confinement, Ch. 7

D

Decennial Digest, §1.2(A)(2)
Declaration of Independence, §§1.3(B), 2.1
Declaratory judgment, §2.4
Demonstrations, §3.5
Descriptive Word Index, §1.2(A)(2)
Digests, §1.2(A)(2)
Disciplinary actions for police misconduct, §2.5
Disclosure, §2.4
Drunken driving arrest processing, Miranda warnings, §5.5(B)
Due process of law, §1.3(G)

E

Eavesdropping, §4.17
Encyclopedias, legal, §1.2(A)(2)
Evidence
   compelled evidence, §4.18
   exclusionary rule, §2.6
Exclusionary rule
   application to state law, §2.6(B)
   criticisms, §2.6(C)
Federal rule of evidence, §2.6(A)
   good faith exception, §2.6(C)
Exigent circumstances
   close pursuit justifying warrantless search, §4.15(C)(1)
   exception to warrant requirement, §4.13
Expression, freedom of, §3.3
Eyewitness identification of suspects, Ch. 6

F

False arrest, civil liability of police officers for, §2.2(A)
Federalism, §1.3(D)
Federalist, §3.4
Felony, §4.3
Fighting words, §3.3
Federal Reporter, §1.2(A)(1)
Federal Supplement, §1.2(A)(1)
Fifth Amendment, §1.3(F), Ch. 5
First Amendment, §§1.3(F), Ch. 3
Flag desecration, §3.3

Force, use of
    civil liability of police for excessive use of, §2.2(A)
    generally, §4.7
Forced entry in making arrest, §4.8
Forfeiture of crime-related property, §4.19
Fourteenth Amendment, §§1.1(E), 1.3(E), 1.3(G)
Fourth Amendment
    applicability, guidelines, §4.13
    confession issues, §5.3
    exclusionary rule, §§2.6(A) to 2.7
    generally, §§1.1(A), 1.3(F), 4.1
    probable cause, §4.4
Fresh pursuit in making arrest
    exigent circumstances justifying warrantless entry, §4.15(C)
    generally, §4.9
    Uniform Act on Fresh Pursuit, §4.9

G

Garbage, privacy interest in, §4.16(D)
Good faith exception to exclusionary rule, §2.6(C)

H

Habeas corpus, §§2.1, 3.5
Hearsay, §4.13
Hobbes, Thomas, §2.1

I

Identification of suspects
    suggestiveness, §§6.2, 6.4
    showup, §§7.1, 6.3
    right to counsel, §§6.2, §6.3
    photographs, use of, §§6.1, 6.5
    lineup, §§6.1, 6.2, 6.6
    in-court identification, §§6.1, 6.2
    generally, §§6.1, 6.2, 6.3
Immunity, §5.5(H)
Incarcerated persons, right of, §§7.2, 7.3
Index to Legal Periodicals, §1.2(A)(3)
Informants, civil liability of police concerning, §2.2(A)
Infractions, §4.11
Injunction, §2.4
Interrogation
    Miranda issues, §5.5
    pre-charge questioning, §5.4(A)
    post-charge questioning, §5.4(B)
    right to counsel, §5.4
    volunteered statements, §5.5(C)
    waiver of rights, §5.5(E)
Intoxication, search for evidence of, §4.15(C)(2)
Inventory of impounded motor vehicle, §4.15(D)
Investigative stop, §4.15(E)
    based on anonymous tip, §4.15 (E)(3)

J

Jail and prison procedures
  censorship §7.4
  generally, §§7.1, 7.4
  incarcerated persons, rights of §7.3
Juvenile offenders
  generally, Ch. 8
  jurisdiction issues, §8.2

K

Knock and announce requirement, in making arrest, §4.8
Ku Klux Act, §2.2(A)

L

Lawyers' Edition of the U.S. Supreme Court Reports, §1.2(A)(1)
Liability of police officers, §§2.2(A), 2.2(B), 2.3, 4.14(A)(2), 7.2
Libraries, law, §1.2(A)
Lineup
  generally, §§6.1, 6.2, 6.6
  right to counsel during, §6.1, 6.2
Locke, John, §1.3(A)

M

Machiavelli, §2.1
Magna Charta, §1.3(B)
Malicious prosecution civil liability of police for, 2.2(A)
Miranda v. Arizona, §§4.15(F)(2), 5.1, 5.2, 5.5 (text excerpts and discussion)
Miranda warning,
  generally §5.5(D)
  when not required, §5.5(F)
Misdemeanor
  arrest for, §4.3
  distinguished from felony, §4.3
Motor homes, searches of, §4.15(B)(1)
Motor vehicles
  closed containers, treatment of, in motor vehicle searches, §4.15(B)(3)
  home and vehicle searches distinguished, §4.15(B)(1)
  inventory of contents of impounded vehicle, §4.15(D)
  motor homes, search of, §4.15(B)(1)
  remote searches of, §4.15(B)(2)
  standing of passengers to object to search, §4.16(C)
  warrantless searches, §4.15(B)
Municipal ordinances, §4.11
Murder scene, warrantless search of, §4.15(C)(3)

N

National Reporter System, §1.2(A)1
Negligence, civil liability of police for, §2.2(A)
North Eastern Reporter, §1.2(A)(1)

O

Obscenity, §3.4
Open fields, searches in, §4.13
Ordinance violations, §4.11
Overbreadth doctrine, §3.3

P

Petition, freedom of, §3.5
Petition of Right, §1.3(B)
Peyote, sacramental use of, §3.2
Photographs, use of, in identification, §§6.1, 6.5
Picketing, §3.5
Plain view §§4.14(B), 4.15(D), 4.16(B)
Pornography, §3.4
Press, freedom of, §3.4
Prison procedures, §§7.1, 7.4
Prisoners, rights of, Ch. 7
Privacy interest in abandoned property and garbage, §4.16(D)
Probable cause
 definition, §4.4
 search warrants, §4.14(A)
Prosecutors, civil liability, §2.2(A)
Protective sweep, §4.15(E)(3)
Public safety exception to Miranda rule, §5.5(F)
Pursuit
 Territorial jurisdiction and, §4.9
 warrant requirements and, 4.15(C)(1)

R

Religion, freedom of, §3.2
Remote searches of motor vehicles, §4.15(B)(2)
Resistance to arrest, §4.10
Right to counsel
 during questioning, §5.4
 liability of police concerning, §2.2.(A)
Right to remain silent, §5.5(G), §8.3
Roadblocks, searches and §4.15(E)(6)
Rousseau, Jean Jacques, §2.1

S

Schools and other institutions, searches in, §4.15(G)
Scope of consent search, §4.15(F)(3)
Search incident to arrest
 closed containers, treatment of, §4.15(B)(3)
 discovery of items not connected with arrest, §4.15(A)(2)
 exception to warrant requirement, §4.13
 generally, §4.15(A)(1)
 intoxication, search for evidence of §4.15(C)(2)
 justification, §4.15(A)(3)
 rules for, §4.15(A)(4)
 stop and frisk distinguished, §4.15(E)(2)
Search warrant
 affidavit for, §4.14(A), 4.14(C)
 challenge to affidavit, §4.14(D)
 discovery of items not specified in warrant, §4.14(B)
 exceptions to warrant requirement, §4.13, 4.15
 issuance of, §4.5
 murder scene search, warrant required for, §4.15(C)(3)
 probable cause, §4.14(A)
Searches and seizures
 arrest, search incident to, §4.15(A)

automobile searches, §4.15(B)
　　challenge to warrant affidavit, §4.14(A)(1), 4.14(A)(2)
　　closed containers, search of, §§4.15(A)(1), 4.15(B)(3)
　　consent searches, §4.15(F)(1)(2)(3)
　　constitutional restrictions, generally §4.13
　　crime-related property, seizure of, §4.19
　　forfeiture of crime-related property, §4.19
　　Fourth amendment restrictions, §4.13
　　home and vehicle searches distinguished, §4.15(B)(1)
　　inadvertent discovery of items not specified in warrant, §§4.14(B), 4.16(B)
　　inspections, administrative, §4.15(G)
　　intoxication, search for evidence of, §4.15(C)(2)
　　inventory of impounded motor vehicle, §4.15(D)
　　items not connected with arrest, discovery of, §4.15(A)(2)
　　items not specified in warrant, discovery of, §§4.14(B), 4.16(B)
　　jails and prisons, searches in, §7.3
　　liability of police concerning, §2.2(A)
　　murder scene search, warrant required for, §4.15(C)(3)
　　plain view, items in, §4.15(D)
　　remote searches, §4.15(B)(2)
　　roadblocks, §4.15(E)(6)
　　standing to object to search, §4.16(C)
　　stop and frisk, §4.15(E)
　　traffic stop for license and registration inspection, §4.15(E)(6)
　　workplaces and institutions, searches in, §4.15(G)
Self-incrimination
　　immunity, §5.5(H)
　　Miranda issues, §5.5
Shepard's Citations, §1.2(A)(2)
Showup, §§6.1, 6.3
Sixth Amendment, §5.4
Speech, freedom of, §3.3.
Standing to object to search, §4.16(C)
Stare decisis, §1.2
Status offenses, §8.2
Statutory law, §1.2
Stop and frisk
　　exception to warrant requirement, §4.13
　　generally, §4.15(E)(1)
　　guidelines for, §4.15(E)(4)
　　roadblocks, §4.15(E)(6)
　　search incident to arrest distinguished, §4.15(E)(2)
Sobriety checkpoints §4.15(E)(6)
Suggestiveness in identification of suspects, §§6.2, 6.4
Supreme Court Digest, §1.2(A)(2)
Supreme Court of the United States, creation of, §1.3(E)
Supreme Court Reporter, §1.2(A)(1)
Symbolic speech, §3.3.

T

Territorial jurisdiction, §4.9
Terry, v. Ohio, §§4.1, 4.15(E)(brief and discussion)
Text of case reprinted
　　Bugg v. State, §5.5(B)
　　Harris v. United States, §4.15(D)

    Massiah v. United States, §5.4(B)
    Neil v. Biggers, §6.4
    Stovall v. Denno, §6.4
Torts, §1.4
Transactional immunity, §5.5(H)
Treaty of Paris, §1.3(A)

U

Uniform Act on Fresh Pursuit, §4.9
United States Code Annotated, §1.2(A)(1)
United States Law Week, §1.2(A)(1)
United States Reports, §1.2(A)(1)

V

Void-for-vagueness doctrine, §3.3.
Voluntariness of statements
    generally, §5.2
    Miranda warnings and, §5.5(C)

W

Waiver of constitutional rights
    generally, §5.5(E)
    juveniles and, §8.2
Warrantless arrest, §4.12
Warrantless searches
    consent searches, §4.15(F)
    exigent circumstances justifying, §4.15(C)
    inspections, §4.15(G)
    search incident to arrest, §4.15(A)
    stop and frisk detentions, §4.15(E)
    when justified, §§4.13, 4.15
    workplaces and institutions, searches in, §4.15(G)
    arrest warrant, affidavit for, §4.5
    issuance of, §4.5
    liability of police officer in requesting, §4.14 (A)2
    neutral magistrate requirement, §4.16
    search warrant, §4.14
West's Annotated Indiana Code, §1.2(A)(2)
Wiretaps, §4.17
Words and phrases, §1.2(A)(2)
Workplaces, searches in, §4.15(G)